The Editor

MARIA TATAR is the John L. Loeb Professor of Germanic Languages and Literatures and Folklore and Mythology at Harvard University. She is the author of *Enchanted Hunters: The Power of Stories in Childhood, Off with Their Heads! Fairy Tales and the Culture of Childhood,* and many other books on folklore and fairy tales. She is also the editor and translator of *The Annotated Hans Christian Andersen, The Annotated Brothers Grimm, The Annotated Classic Fairy Tales, The Annotated Peter Pan,* and *The Grimm Reader.*

A NORTON CRITICAL EDITION

THE
CLASSIC FAIRY TALES

TEXTS
CRITICISM

SECOND EDITION

Edited by

MARIA TATAR
HARVARD UNIVERSITY

W · W · NORTON & COMPANY · *New York* · *London*

W. W. Norton & Company has been independent since its founding in 1923, when William Warder Norton and Mary D. Herter Norton first published lectures delivered at the People's Institute, the adult education division of New York City's Cooper Union. The firm soon expanded their program beyond the Institute, publishing books by celebrated academics from America and abroad. By midcentury, the two major pillars of Norton's publishing program—trade books and college texts—were firmly established. In the 1950s, the Norton family transferred control of the company to its employees, and today—with a staff of five hundred and hundreds of trade, college, and professional titles published each year—W. W. Norton & Company stands as the largest and oldest publishing house owned wholly by its employees.

Manufacturing by Maple Press
Book design by Antonina Krass
Production manager: Elizabeth Marotta

ISBN: 978-0-393-60297-5 (pbk.)

W. W. Norton & Company, Inc., 500 Fifth Avenue, New York, N.Y. 10110
            www.wwnorton.com
W. W. Norton & Company Ltd., 15 Carlisle Street, London W1D 3BS

7 8 9 0

For Lauren Blum and Daniel Schuker

Contents

Criticism

Introduction

"That's nothing but a fairy tale." Dismissive phrases like this one ignore just how powerfully the world of make-believe is implicated in the making of beliefs. Storytelling is anything but frivolous, juvenile, shallow, and inconsequential. If fairy tales have a high quotient of weirdness, it is because they recruit the extraordinary to help us understand the ordinary and what lies beneath it. Riddles wrapped in mysteries inside enigmas, they challenge us to make sense of nonsense.

Fairy tales may present us with counterfactuals—C. S. Lewis called them "lies breathed through silver"—but they also transmit higher truths that help us navigate reality.[1] More important, they hold forth the promise of escape to a better and more colorful Elsewhere. As Neil Gaiman puts it, what you bring back from reading fairy tales and fantasy fiction is "knowledge about the world and your predicament . . . weapons . . . armour: real things you can take back into your prison. Skills and knowledge and tools you can use to escape for real."[2]

The term *fairy tale* has not served the genre well. The sprightly supernatural creatures featured so prominently in the name rarely make an appearance in representative stories. There are no fairies in "Little Red Riding Hood," "Jack and the Beanstalk," or "Beauty and the Beast." And although there may be enchantresses and fairy godmothers in "Cinderella" and in "Rapunzel," they bear no resemblance to the woodland creatures found frequently in British and Celtic lore. It was the French, more specifically Mme d'Aulnoy, author of many literary fairy tales, who gave us the term *contes de fées*, leading us to frame the stories as if they turned on the lives of diminutive folk rather than ordinary people—men and women, girls and boys, all of whom are up against monsters of one kind or another.

1. Lewis is quoted by Wendy Berg and Mike Harris, *The Secret History of Western Religion* (Woodbury, MN: Llewellyn, 2003), p. 1.
2. Neil Gailman's essay can be found at: theguardian.com/books/2013/oct/15/neil-gaiman-future-libraries-reading-daydreaming.

There is magic in fairy tales, and the presence of enchantment is perhaps the defining feature of the genre.[3] We are not so much in the realm of fairies as in the domain of what J. R. R. Tolkien referred to as *Faërie*, that "Perilous Realm" where anything can happen. Rumpelstiltskin spins straw to gold; Hansel and Gretel discover a woodland cottage with a roof made of bread and windows of spun sugar; a skull lying on the forest floor begins to talk; a boy sails down the river in a peach. Again and again we witness transformations that create a crisis, breaking down the divide between life and death, nature and culture, animal and human, or self and other. Magic implies metamorphosis, and presto! we can see the clear link between these two defining features of the fairy tale.

Fairy tales take up deep cultural contradictions, creating what Claude Lévi-Strauss called "miniature models"—stories that dispense with extraneous details to give us primal anxieties and desires, the raw rather than the cooked, as it were. They use magic, not to falsify or delude, but rather to move us to imagine "what if?" or to wonder "why?" And that move, as both Plato and Aristotle assured us, marks the beginning of philosophy. Minimalist and miniaturized, fairy tales require us to fill in gaps, to think more and think harder about what moves the figures in them. We rarely learn what goes on in the minds of Cinderella, Jack, or Rumpelstiltskin— we just watch them in action. While fairy-tale heroes and heroines wander, we track their moves and wonder, in both senses of the term, at their adventures. It is no surprise that the term *wonder tale* has been proposed and embraced as an alternative to the misleading "fairy tale," for it captures both the animating force of fairy tales and our sense of awe before the secondary worlds they build.[4]

Fairy tales, like myths, capitalize on the kaleidoscopic with its multifaceted meanings: sparkling beauty, austere form, and visual power. Once told around the fireside or at the hearth, with adults and children sharing the storytelling space, they captured the play of light and shadow in their environment, creating special effects that yoked luminous beauty with the dark side. Imagine a time before electronic entertainments, with long nights around campsites and other sources of heat and light, and it is not much of a challenge to realize that human beings, always quick to adapt, began exchanging information, trading wisdom, and reporting gossip. "Literature," Vladimir Nabokov tells us, "was born on the day when a

---

3. As Steven Swann Jones puts it, "fairy tales depict magical or marvellous events or phenomena as a valid part of human experience." See his *The Fairy Tale: The Magic Mirror of the Imagination* (New York: Routledge, 2002), p. 9.
4. Marina Warner, *Once Upon a Time: A Short History of Fairy Tale* (Oxford: Oxford UP, 2014), p. xxii.

boy came crying wolf wolf, and there was no wolf behind him."[5] And that boy's story was no doubt compact, electrifying, and vivid. Once the conversation started about that wolf, it was easy enough, in subsequent versions, to begin adding, embellishing, exaggerating, and doing all the things that make for lively entertainments. Fairy tales are always more interesting when something is added to them. Each new telling recharges the narrative, making it crackle and hiss with cultural energy.

With the invention of printing, the rise of literacy, and the twin forces of urbanization and industrialization, fairy tales moved gradually from oral storytelling cultures into pamphlets, broadsheets, and books, with improvisational energy and antic variation shut down, not for good of course but at least slowed down. Removed from Tolkien's Cauldron of Story (where they had simmered away with successive generations adding new ingredients) as well as from Salman Rushdie's Ocean of the Streams of Story (with its swiftly moving rainbow currents), print cultures enshrined standard tale versions that made variants deviations from the norm rather than unique reinventions.[6] Those canonical versions of a story are nothing more than a fiction propping up our faith in defunct archetypes.

Giovan Francesco Straparola's *The Facetious Nights* (1551/1553), Giambattista Basile's *Pentamerone* (1634/1636), Charles Perrault's *Tales of Mother Goose* (1697), and Jacob and Wilhelm Grimm's *Children's Stories and Household Tales* (1812/1815) serve as landmarks on the path from oral storytelling traditions to print culture. These collections, like our own postmodern retellings, remind us that there is no original when it comes to fairy tales. To the contrary, these stories circulated in multiple versions, reconfigured by each teller to form a uniquely new tale with distinctly different effects, hence the advantages of referring to multiforms of a tale rather than variants. When we say the word *Cinderella*, we are referring not to a single text but to an entire array of tales with a persecuted heroine who may respond to her situation with defiance, cunning, ingenuity, self-pity, anguish, or grief. She will be called Yeh-Hsien in China, Cendrillon in Italy, Aschenputtel in Germany, and Catskin in England. Her sisters may be named One-Eye and Three-Eyes, Anastasia and Drizella, or she may have just one sister named Haloek, as is the case in an Indonesian tale. Her tasks range from tending cows to sorting peas to fetching embers for a fire.

---

5. Vladimir Nabokov, "Good Readers and Good Writers," in *Lectures on Literature*, ed. Fredson Bowers (New York: Harcourt Brace Jovanovich, 1998), p. 5.
6. Tolkien writes about the Cauldron of Story in "On Fairy-Stories," in *The Tolkien Reader* (New York: Ballantine, 1966). Rushdie refers to the "ocean of the stream of stories" in *Haroun and the Sea of Stories* (New York: Granta Books, 1990).

Although the multiforms of a tale can now be found between the covers of books and are often attributed to individual authors, editors, or compilers, the tales themselves derive largely from collective efforts. Here's how Angela Carter reminded us that no one person can claim to be an authoritative source for a fairy tale: "Who first invented meatballs? In what country? Is there a definite recipe for potato soup? Think in terms of the domestic arts. 'This is how I make potato soup.'"[7] The story of Little Red Riding Hood, for example, can be discovered the world over, yet it varies radically in texture and flavor from one culture to the next. Even in a single culture, that texture or flavor may be different enough that a listener will impatiently interrupt the telling of a tale to insist: "That's not how I heard it."

In France, Little Red Riding Hood and her grandmother are devoured by the wolf. End of story. The German version recorded by the Brothers Grimm stages a rescue scene in which a hunter intervenes to liberate the girl and her granny from the belly of the wolf. A wolf in costume invites Caterinella, an Italian Red Riding Hood, to dine on the teeth and ears of her grandmother. A Chinese girl named Goldflower manages to slay the beast that wants to devour her by throwing a spear into its mouth. The mother of an African girl rescues her daughter from a predator by placing vipers and scorpions into the sack used by the monster to stow away his victims.

Virtually every motif, trope, and image in a fairy tale, from the red riding hood of the girl in the woods to the glass slipper of the young woman at the royal ball, seems subject to change. In the British Isles, Cinderella goes by the name of Catskin, Mossycoat, or Rashin-Coatie. The challenge facing one Italian heroine is not spinning straw to gold but downing seven plates of lasagna. The father of a Norwegian Beauty pleads with his daughter to marry a white bear, while the mother in another tale runs interference for a snake. In Russia, the cannibalistic witch in the forest has a hut set on chicken legs surrounded by a fence with posts made of stacked human skulls. Rumpelstiltskin goes by many different names, among them Titelitury, Ricdin-Ricdon, Tom Tit Tot, Batzibitzili, Panzimanzi, and Whuppity Stoorie.

While there is no original or standard version of "Cinderella," "Sleeping Beauty," or "Jack and the Beanstalk," there is a basic plot structure (what folklorists refer to as a "tale type") that appears despite the rich cultural variation. "Beauty and the Beast," for example, according to the tale-type index (known as the ATU) first compiled by the Finnish folklorist Antti Aarne in 1910 and revised by

7. Angela Carter, ed., *The Virago Book of Fairy Tales* (London: Virago, 1990), p. x.

Stith Thompson and Hans-Jörg Uther, consists of the following narrative moves, presented schematically as follows:

    I. The monster as husband
   II. Disenchantment of the monster
 III. Loss of the husband
 IV. Search for the husband
  V. Recovery of the husband

Once we see the bones of the narrative known to folklorists as tale type 425C, we recognize in a flash that "Beauty and the Beast" is structurally related to "East o' the Sun and West o' the Moon," along with other stories, such as "Cupid and Psyche." The stable core offers a useful tool for comparative analysis, bringing together tales that exhibit spirited variation, with beasts that include goats, mice, hedgehogs, crocodiles, and lions, along with heroines who must cover vast tracts of land in iron shoes, sort peas from lentils in an impossibly short time, or trick a rival into letting them spend the night in a castle. Improvisational energy has always kept the fairy tale alive. Tellers walk down familiar paths but can branch off into new terrain at any moment, then wander back onto familiar territory.

Given the possibilities for creative reinvention, it seems odd that so many writers have approached fairy tales with hushed reverence. The myth of fairy tales as some kind of holy scripture was energetically propagated by Charles Dickens, who brought to what he considered the literature of childhood the same devout piety he accorded children. Like the Brothers Grimm, Dickens hailed the "simplicity," "purity," and "innocent extravagance of fairy tales," even as he praised the stories as powerful instruments of constructive socialization: "It would be hard to estimate the amount of gentleness and mercy that has made its way among us through these slight channels. Forbearance, courtesy, consideration for the poor and aged, kind treatment of animals, the love of nature, abhorrence of tyranny and brute force—many such things have been first nourished in the child's heart by this powerful aid."[8] George Cruikshank, the artist who illustrated Dickens's novels, took issue with the views of his contemporary. In the story "Hop-o'-my-Thumb," a variant of "Jack and the Beanstalk," he finds a protagonist who is an *unfeeling, artful liar, and a thief.* "Surely there is not much *'purity'* in *lying* and *thieving,* and such a display of artful falsehood and successful robbery cannot be very advantageous lessons for the juvenile mind," he added in outrage.[9]

8. Charles Dickens, "Frauds on the Fairies," in *Household Words: A Weekly Journal* (New York: McElrath & Barker, 1854), p. 97.
9. George Cruikshank, *George Cruikshank's Fairy Library* (London: Bell & Daldy, 1854), p. 38.

Even in 1944, when Allied troops were locked in combat with German soldiers, W. H. Auden decreed the Grimms' fairy tales to be "among the few indispensable, common-property books upon which Western culture can be founded." To drive home the point about fairy tales as sacred texts, he emphasized that the tales "rank next to the Bible in importance."[1] Like the devaluation of fairy tales, the overvaluation promotes a suspension of critical faculties and prevents us from taking a good, hard look at stories that are so obviously instrumental in shaping our values and aspirations. The reverence brought by some readers to fairy tales mystifies these stories, making them appear to be a source of transcendent spiritual truth and authority. That kind of mystification fosters a hands-off attitude and conceals the fact that fairy tales are constantly shape shifting, endlessly adaptable as they turn into different versions of themselves depending on the cultural surround.

In some ways it is bracing to see the fairy tale, which belongs to popular culture and draws on the vernacular, enshrined as a form of high art. Derided as "simple stories" and "children's tales," they are rarely recognized as being the plainspoken expression of complex thought. Although historical evidence points to multigenerational audiences, both male and female, as the driving force for oral storytelling cultures, inventing fairy tales has long been considered a "domestic art," at least since Plato in the *Gorgias* referred to the "old wives' tales" told by nurses to amuse and to frighten children. Virtually all of the national collections of fairy tales compiled in the nineteenth century were the work of men—dignified scholars, urban and urbane. Yet the tales themselves were ascribed to female narrators, symbolically represented as Gammer Grethel, Mother Goose, and Mother Bunch, and embodied in real life as untutored peasant women.

As early as the second century C.E., Apuleius, the North African author of *The Golden Ass*, had designated his story of Cupid and Psyche (told by a drunken and half-demented old woman) as belonging to the genre of "old wives' tales." The Italian writer Straparola claimed to have heard the stories that constituted his *Facetious Nights* "from the lips of lady storytellers," and he embedded those stories in a narrative frame featuring a circle of eloquent female narrators.[2] Giambattista Basile's *Pentamerone* also has women storytellers—quick-witted, gossipy old crones who recount "those tales that old women tell to amuse children."[3] The renowned *Tales*

---

1. W. H. Auden, "In Praise of the Brothers Grimm," *New York Times Book Review*, November 12, 1944, p. 1.
2. Giovan Francesco Straparola, *The Facetious Nights*, trans. W. G. Waters (London: Privately Printed for Members of the Society of Bibliophiles, 1901).
3. *The Pentamerone*, trans. Benedetto Croce, ed. N. M. Penzer (London: Bodley Head, 1932), p. 9.

of Mother Goose by Charles Perrault was designated by its author as a collection of old wives' tales, "told by governesses and grandmothers to little children."[4] Many of the most expansive informants consulted by the Grimms were women—family friends, servants, and acquaintances who had at their disposal a rich repertoire of folklore. The most notable among them was Dorothea Viehmann, whose rough-hewn visage became the face of the collection over the decades. Later collections too, like George Dasent's *Popular Tales from the Norse*, invoked an image of "old and feeble women" as the "depositories of these national treasures."

The association of fairy tales with the domestic arts and with old wives' tales has not done much to enhance their cultural status. "On a par with trifles," Marina Warner stresses, " 'mere old wives' tales carry connotations of error, of false counsel, ignorance, prejudice and fallacious nostrums—against heartbreak as well as headache; similarly 'fairy tale' as a derogatory term, implies fantasy, escapism, invention, the unreliable consolations of romance."[5] Fantasy, escape, recovery, and consolation—these are the quartet of terms Tolkien defined as the key positive components of fairy stories. By connecting fairy tales with the mythical rather than maternal, Tolkien succeeded, with one magical stroke, in restoring a level of dignity they apparently lacked when linked with gossips, godmothers, and grannies.

Today, our portal to fairy tales is Disney Studios, and films like *Sleeping Beauty, Beauty and the Beast,* and *The Little Mermaid* have real cultural traction because of those feature-length animated films. Disney kept the stories alive yet also created standard versions driven by market forces rather than communal energies. What was once folk culture became mass culture, moving top down rather than bottom up and mirroring values determined by a conglomerate rather than by a storytelling collective. More important, by animating fairy tales with cartoon technologies, Disney decisively moved fairy tales back to the nursery, despite advertisements trumpeting their "magic" for the young and the "young at heart." Once again, fairy tales are dismissed as childish confections meant to entertain and distract more than anything else. Disney's nostalgic appropriations form a stark contrast with many of the critically reflective adaptations in this volume. Those rescriptings bring fairy tales back and self-reflexively critique their terms by giving them new twists and turns. Yet Disney Studios also continually reinvents the fairy tale, most recently with live-action versions that mirror a growing

4. Charles Perrault, "Préface," *Contes en vers* (1694; reprint, Paris: Gallimard, 1981), p. 50.
5. Marina Warner, *From the Beast to the Blonde: On Fairy Tales and Their Tellers* (New York: Farrar, Straus & Giroux, 1994), p. 19.

understanding of the multigenerational appeal of the tales. Efforts to include characters that deviate from the flat, stereotypical wonders of *Snow White and the Seven Dwarfs* or *Cinderella* have added a form of self-conscious narrative play and subtlety not seen in the early films. As critics of arguments about the monolithic, numbing effects of the cultural industry in all its corporate manifestations have also pointed out, film viewers are anything but passive recipients. They actively engage in critique, reenactment, and recasting, often disavowing rather than embracing the terms of what they watch.

A strong case could be made that Disney's culturally conservative approach to fairy tales accounts for the resurgence of adult interest in the genre. It was the feminist critique of fairy tales (Disney versions in particular), beginning in the 1970s, which in some ways brought fairy tales back, restoring them to the canon and making them culturally relevant by pointing to the obligation to reinvent them. In what can be seen as a catalytic moment, Alison Lurie recruited fairy tales to the feminist cause,[6] while Marcia Lieberman denounced them for acculturating women to "traditional social roles." "Millions of women," she added, "must surely have formed their psycho-sexual self-concepts, and their ideas of what they could or could not accomplish, what sort of behavior could be rewarded, and the nature of reward itself, in part from their favorite fairy tales."[7]

In the very same decade that Lurie and Lieberman set the terms for later debates, Bruno Bettelheim was arguing for the revival of fairy tales and the "uses of enchantment." Drawing on psychoanalytic theories, he emphasized the importance for children of stories with a dark side, tales that enacted in symbolic form unconscious anxieties and desires. Fairy tales had the power to calm the "cauldron of seething emotions" that is the mind of the child, with its "narcissistic disappointments, oedipal dilemmas, sibling rivalries."[8] The sensational content of fairy-tale plots—there is no shortage of bloodthirsty ogres, cunning witches, flesh-eating giants, and cruel stepmothers in them—had therapeutic benefits, according to Bettelheim.

The Uses of Enchantment put fairy tales squarely back in the canon of children's literature, and at the same time the volume legitimized the academic study of fairy tales, revealing that there were multiple layers of latent meaning in the manifest content of fairy

---

6. Alison Lurie, "Fairy Tale Liberation," *New York Review of Books*, December 17, 1970, pp. 42–44.
7. Marcia K. Lieberman, "'Some Day My Prince Will Come': Female Acculturation through the Fairy Tale," *College English* 34 (1972): 383–95.
8. Bruno Bettelheim, *The Uses of Enchantment: The Meaning and Importance of Fairy Tales* (New York: Knopf, 1976), p. 6.

tales. Scholars were drawn into the orbit of the agenda Bettelheim set, studying the magic, mystery, and violence of tales in the European canon. But given the orthodox Freudian readings of fairy tales set forth in the volume, there was also much to contest and critique, setting the stage for a powerful reorientation of the field toward multiple issues ranging from the sexual politics of fairy-tale stereotypes to the cultural politics of fairy-tale adaptations.

If Disney and Bettelheim both move in the restorative mode, seeking to bring back "tales as old as time" for the young, feminist adaptations of fairy tales move along a different path, producing creative adaptations that unsettle the genre by breaking with tradition and renewing it. "Make it new" was never a piece of advice you had to give storytellers spinning yarns at communal gatherings. They were always making it new—shamelessly cutting and pasting but always improvising as well—so that their stories would tick and whirr just as smoothly as the ones told the night before. The most skillful raconteurs, then as now, were the iconoclasts. They were able to preserve the raw energy of the tales and keep them alive precisely because they were constantly trying to undo them. In the 1980s Anne Sexton took up the role of iconoclast, undermining the history and wisdom of the past encoded in fairy tales and reimagining the Grimms' fairy tales through parody and critique. Her *Transformations* takes up the excesses of fairy tales, exaggerating and inflating them until they blow up, destroying them and doing them one better at the same time.

The poems in Sexton's volume stake a claim to producing fairy tales by declaring the poet herself to be the new source of folk wisdom and of oracular authority. She positions herself as speaker, "my face in a book" (presumably the Grimms' *Children's Stories and Household Tales*), with "mouth wide, ready to tell you a story or two."[9] In a self-described appropriation of the Grimms' legacy ("I take the fairy tale and transform it into a poem of my own"), Sexton models how to create new stories that stage "very wry and cruel and sadistic and funny" psychic battles. As "middle-aged witch," Sexton presents herself as a master of the black arts, of an opaque art of illusion, and also as a disruptive force, a figure of anarchic energy that subverts conventional cultural wisdom.

Nowhere is Sexton's critique of romantic love, of the "happily ever after" of fairy tales, more searingly expressed than in the final strophe of her "Cinderella":

> Cinderella and the prince
> lived, they say, happily ever after

9. Diane Middlebrook, *Anne Sexton: A Biography* (New York: Random House, Vintage, 1992), p. 336.

> like two dolls in a museum case,
> never bothered by diapers and dust,
> never arguing over the timing of an egg,
> never telling the same story twice,
> never getting a middle-aged spread,
> their darling smiles pasted on for eternity.
> Regular Bobbsey Twins.
> That story.

Sexton's transformations reveal the gap between "that story" and reality, yet at the same time they expose the specious terms of "that story," showing just how intolerable it would be, even if true.

Sexton's smart, sassy poems entered into an impassioned dialogue with the Brothers Grimm, contesting their premises, interrogating their plots, and reinventing their conclusions. Other writers, recognizing the social energy of these tales, have followed her lead, rewriting and recasting stories written down by Perrault, the Grimms, Madame de Beaumont, Hans Christian Andersen, Alexander Afanasev, and many others. The intertextual dialogue may not always be as pronounced as is the case with Sexton's poetry. In some cases the fairy-tale inspiration will not be announced in the title, and readers will have to make their own connections, as is the case in many cinematic productions. Jane Campion's *The Piano*, for example, opens with a nod to Andersen's "Little Mermaid," then alludes repeatedly to the Grimms' "Robber Bridegroom" and Perrault's "Bluebeard."

With her collection of stories *The Bloody Chamber*, Carter joined Sexton in defamiliarizing and reworking the familiar scripts of fairy tales. Making it her business to "demythify" fairy tales, Carter aimed to mount "a critique of current relations between the sexes." She positioned herself as a "moral pornographer," a writer seeking to "penetrate to the heart of the contempt for women that distorts our culture." "Beauty and the Beast," "Little Red Riding Hood," "Bluebeard," and "Sleeping Beauty": all these stories have, according to Carter, a "violently sexual" side to them, a latent content that becomes manifest in the rescriptings of fairy tales for an adult audience.[1] Carter aims above all to demystify these sacred cultural texts, to show that we can break their magic spells and that social change is possible once we become aware of how the tales have guided our social, moral, and personal development, shaping our identity in ways we fail to process at a conscious level.

In the same era as Carter and Sexton, Margaret Atwood was writing novels and short stories that adapted and critiqued fairy tales,

---

1. Robin Ann Sheets, "Pornography, Fairy Tales, and Feminism: Angela Carter's 'The Bloody Chamber,'" *Journal of the History of Sexuality* 1 (1991): 635.

showing the degree to which the stories inform our affective life, programming our responses to romance, defining our desires, and constructing our anxieties. Like Sally, the fictional heroine of her short story "Bluebeard's Egg," Atwood questions the seemingly time-less and universal truths of our cultural stories by reflecting on their assumptions and exploring how they can be unsettled through rewrit-ing. The full self-reflexive force of critical adaptations comes to bear on this story about a woman taking a writing class in which she is given an assignment to rewrite the Grimms' "Fitcher's Bird," a vari-ant of "Bluebeard." As Jessica Tiffin notes in a study of narrative and metafiction in modern fairy tales, adaptations like Atwood's recap-ture the magic of the fairy tale as a "self-aware artifact with the power to adapt, change, and reflect the needs and concerns of its age."[2]

Not all creative adaptations take the same turn as these feminist rewritings, which set the stage for the proliferation of new fairy-tale treatments in Anglo-American cultures and beyond. In this volume I have included two authors who give us literary fairy tales that are neither restorative nor critical but something of a hybrid of the two. Both Hans Christian Andersen and Oscar Wilde were deeply familiar with oral traditions. Andersen, who grew up in impoverished circumstances, listened to fairy tales in the spinning room at the local asylum where his grandmother worked. "As a child, it was my greatest pleasure to listen to fairy tales," he wrote, "and some of those are either very little or not at all known. I have retold one of them here, and if it wins approval, I plan to retell several, and one day to publish a cycle of 'Danish Folk Tales.'"[3] Over the years, how-ever, it dawned on Andersen that he could "write" his own fairy tales rather than just reproduce the ones he remembered from childhood. His excitement about branching out into a form that would appeal to children and adults alike is captured in a letter to a friend:

> I believe that I have now found out how to write fairy tales! The first ones I wrote were, as you know, mostly old ones I had heard as a child and that I usually retold and recreated in my own fashion; those that were my very own such as "The Little Mer-maid," "The Storks," and "The Daisy," received, however, the greatest approval and that has given me inspiration. Now I tell stories of my own accord, seize an idea for adults—and then tell it for the children while still keeping in mind the fact that mother and father are listening too, and they must have a little something for thought![4]

2. Jessica Tiffin, *Marvelous Geometry: Metafiction and Narrative in Modern Fairy Tales* (Detroit: Wayne State UP, 2009), p. 234.
3. Jackie Wullschlager, *Hans Christian Andersen: The Life of a Storyteller* (New York: Knopf, 2001), p. 49.
4. Bo Grønbech, *Hans Christian Andersen* (Boston: Twayne, 1980), p. 81.

Like Andersen, Oscar Wilde, whose father had published a book on Irish superstitions in 1852 and whose mother produced a book called *Ancient Legends, Mystic Charms, and Superstitions of Ireland*, was steeped in folkloric traditions as a child as well as in his adult life. The fairy tales he wrote share much with stories from oral storytelling traditions, but, again like Andersen, he added his own creative twists, strengthened the cult of beautiful objects in the tales, and encoded them with messages about human suffering and social justice. These literary re-creations replaced what the critic André Jolles referred to as the naive morality of fairy tales ("our absolute instinctual judgment of what is good and just") with a belief in redemption through suffering as well as a heightened sense of social justice.[5] Both Andersen and Wilde inflected the tales in ways that returned them to multigenerational audiences, revealing how the compact form of the fairy tale lends itself to stories that are both intellectually engaging and consonant with cultural values of their time.

Today, "Cinderella," "Sleeping Beauty," and "Jack and the Beanstalk" keep coming back, always inflected in new ways. On screen, they trumpet their genealogy in titles like Tommy Wirkola's *Hansel & Gretel: Witch Hunters* or Tex Avery's *Red Hot Riding Hood*. But even more often they conceal their affiliations, as in Steven Spielberg's *Jurassic Park* (remember those female raptors in the kitchen, eager to make a meal of Lex and Tim?) and David Slade's *Hard Candy* (with Ellen Page sporting a red hoodie and, for a change, stalking the wolf).

Fairy tales seem to have a built-in refresh button, inviting us to adapt and repurpose them as they migrate into new scenes of storytelling and make themselves at home in new media. In the 1940s, the Bluebeard story set up shop in Hollywood, and screenwriters dropped subtle hints about their folkloric point of reference with oversize house keys, forbidden chambers, and marriages haunted by the threat of murder. The vogue was brief but intense, with George Cukor's *Gaslight* (1944), Alfred Hitchcock's *Notorious* (1946), and Fritz Lang's *Secret beyond the Door* (1947) among the most prominent examples.[6] Ever since Georges Méliès made the short film *Barbe-bleue* in 1902, we keep encountering the fairy-tale figure on screen, in works ranging from Charlie Chaplin's *Monsieur Verdoux* (1947) to Catherine Breillat's *Barbe Bleue* (2009) and Alex Garland's *Ex Machina* (2015), with its reclusive CEO of a tech company known as Blue Book.

5. *Einfache Formen: Legende, Sage, Mythe, Rätsel, Spruch, Kasus, Memorabile, Märchen, Witz* (Berlin: Walter de Gruyter, 1958).
6. For the cinematic variations, see Maria Tatar, *Secrets beyond the Door: The Story of Bluebeard and His Wives* (Princeton, NJ: Princeton UP, 2006).

The question of adaptation has been taken up productively by Cristina Bacchilega, who writes about a fairy-tale web (using a metaphor drawn from discourses about the connectedness and interdependence of fairy tales in general) and the "multimedial or transmedial proliferation of fairy-tale transformations in recent years."[7] She is concerned with how stories "mingle with, influence, anticipate, interrupt, take over, or support one another," engaging in reciprocal intertextual exchanges that cannot always be neatly identified and mapped.

This volume explores the process of adaptation—restorative, critical, and creative—and those categories that, of course, have considerable overlap with each other. The marvelous messiness of fairy-tale networks defies the systematic classification systems developed by folklorists in the past century. As such, this work can refer only in passing to the many fairy-tale motifs, tropes, and characters that fuel the imaginations of writers, poets, filmmakers, dramatists, and others. Little Red Riding Hood lurks in the shadows of many cultural productions, just as Cinderella has informed the construction of many a female protagonist. When Carrie loses a shoe in the television series *Sex and the City*, has she turned into Cinderella? When the narrator of Neil Gaiman's *The Ocean at the End of the Lane* drives down a road flanked by brambles and briar roses, is he reenacting the journey of the prince in *Sleeping Beauty*? Perhaps not, but the stories flash out at us, deepening and complicating the quests undertaken in those made-up lives.

How do we make it new today? What is the secret sauce for successful fairy-tale adaptations? Poe's "Imp of the Perverse" often steals into fairy-tale territory to animate reinventions. Snow White luxuriates in her coffin and becomes a vampiric ghoul in Neil Gaiman's "Snow, Glass, Apples"; Sleeping Beauty becomes a willing sexual slave in Anne Rice's quartet of Sleeping Beauty novels; Rumpelstiltskin is ready for a killing spree in John Katzenbach's *The Analyst*. Our adult entertainments demand fictions larger than life and twice as unnatural, and fairy tales offer up scandalous melodrama in portions that are generously extravagant, if sometimes profoundly unappetizing.

It is tempting to dismiss some of these adaptations as nothing more than guilty pleasures served up to us by a cultural industry that recognizes the power of narratives in a secular age. But fairy tales tap into something much deeper—primal questions that are not just up close and personal but also deeply implicated in our

7. Cristina Bacchilega, *Fairy Tales Transformed?: Twenty-First-Century Adaptations and the Politics of Wonder* (Detroit: Wayne State UP, 2013), p. 16.

collective aspirations. These stories are encoded with enigmas, provocative puzzles challenging us to debate their terms even if we cannot solve them. Hansel and Gretel, forced to leave home, face down a demon who embodies warmth and hospitality—offering the children comfort food and a soft bed—but she soon turns murderously hostile, fattening them up for a feast. What are we to make of this form of cruelty, masquerading as kindness? Beauty is turned over to Beast in a story that tests the limits of compassion and empathy in the face of monstrosity. How do we manage our own anxieties about alterity and the dark doubles that haunt our imaginations? Briar Rose invites riskless voyeurism in scenes that feed our desire for beauty's protection against mortality, corruption, and decay. Is Sleeping Beauty also somehow implicated in all those magazine images of fashion models who are made up to appear as lifeless as they are flawless? The constant in these stories is less character than abstract concepts, always reshuffled and reinvigorated by the values of the next generation of tellers.

"On the surface, an intelligible lie; underneath, an unintelligible truth."[8] These words, drawn from *The Unbearable Lightness of Being* (where they are applied to a painting), tell us something about the illusory surfaces in all fairy tales and about the challenging complexities of what lies beneath. The words of Milan Kundera's character remind us of why Einstein is reputed to have said, "If you want intelligent children, read them fairy tales. If you want more intelligent children, read them more fairy tales."[9] The stories possess what the philosopher Paul Ricoeur calls ontological vehemence, a bracing liveliness that challenges us to think more and to think harder.

Fairy tales deliver not only the shock of beauty, as Max Lüthi put it in a folkloric meditation on the genre, but also jolts of horror, rewiring our brains and also charging them up, challenging us to make sense of the harsh realities exposed in them. The pleasures of the genre arouse curiosity about the world around us and provide social, cultural, and intellectual capital for navigating its perils. For that reason, fairy tales have been credited with an insurrectionary and emancipatory potential that goes against the grain of conventional wisdom about fairy tales as trivial pursuits. Jack Zipes tells us that fairy tales are "informed by a human disposition to action—to transform the world and make it more adaptable to human needs, while we try to change and make ourselves fit for the

8. Milan Kundera, *The Unbearable Lightness of Being: A Novel* (New York: Harper Perennial, 2009), p. 63.
9. See en.wikiquote.org/wiki/Albert_Einstein#Disputed.

world."[1] As the philosopher Ernst Bloch put it, fairy tales hold forth the utopian promise of "something better," or a "more colorful and easier somewhere else," a place that lies over the rainbow, east o' the sun and west o' the moon, in the land of milk and honey.[2]

We are forever reinventing fairy tales, and scholarly efforts to classify, categorize, and bring order into the storytelling world can easily misfire, breaking spells in ways that destroy the spirit of stories rather than enabling critical thinking about them. Still, some part of the brain seems to light up when we discover that our Little Red Riding Hood has a distant relative in some other time and place, or that "Beauty and the Beast" has a global reach, or that Sleeping Beauty has many male counterparts in other cultures. The geographical orientation in this volume is Anglo-American and European, not for the purpose of establishing a canon but rather as a way of developing a disciplinary base. Fairy tales were not invented in Europe or Great Britain. They have flourished in every time and place since humans began telling stories to each other. Recent efforts to locate the origins of fairy tales in sixteenth-century Venice fail to take into account the fact that variants of the stories circulated in Asian and African cultures long before they were written down and became part of a print culture.

Fairy tales not only seem to be part of our DNA, they also seem to have a replicatory power of their own, operating like memes, to use Richard Dawkins's term. This volume includes units on a range of different tale types: "Little Red Riding Hood," "Beauty and the Beast," "Snow White," "Sleeping Beauty," "Cinderella," and "Bluebeard." It then turns to trickster figures, boys and girls who use their wits and courage to escape from monsters and find their way back home. Finally it concludes with literary fairy tales by Hans Christian Andersen and Oscar Wilde, stories that have become collective cultural property, on a global level in the case of Andersen. A set of critical essays forms the second part of the volume, and each of the authors offers different disciplinary approaches to fairy-tale research and introduces a range of analytic concepts that can be brought to bear on the texts included. Storytelling is a culture-building activity, as these essays reveal, one that makes the human world, but, as the tales included here are forever reminding us, they also make the world human.

Bill Willingham explains exactly why he used fairy-tale plots, characters, and tropes to construct his series of graphic novels titled Fables:

1. Jack Zipes, *The Irresistible Fairy Tale: The Cultural and Social History of a Genre* (Princeton, NJ: Princeton UP, 2013), p. 2.
2. Ernst Bloch, "The Fairy Tale Moves on Its Own in Time" in *The Utopian Function of Art and Literature: Selected Essays* (Cambridge: MIT Press, 1988).

The thing that moved me toward fairy-tale stories: One, it's a group of characters and stories that we all own. Every single person in the world owns all of these characters and stories outright. We're all born with an inheritance that we can take advantage of. I think those of us who are doing fairy-tale-based stories are the ones who are sort of cashing in on our inheritance. . . . You do not have to get anyone's permission to do a new version of *Snow White*, for example. We're social people. We get ideas from each other.[3]

This is a legacy that does not weigh us down but rather lifts us up with its beauty, poetry, and power to envision perils and possibilities. We are right to preserve it, nurture it, and watch it grow.

---

3. "Fable Master: Bill Willingham Modernized Fairy Tales before Modernizing Fairy Tales Was Cool," *Willamette Week*, April 24, 2013.

The Texts of
THE CLASSIC FAIRY TALES

NEIL GAIMAN

Instructions[†]

Touch the wooden gate in the wall you never saw before.
Say "please" before you open the latch,
go through,
walk down the path.
A red metal imp hangs from the green-painted front door,
as a knocker,
do not touch it; it will bite your fingers.
Walk through the house. Take nothing. Eat nothing.
However,
if any creature tells you that it hungers,
feed it.
If it tells you that it is dirty,
clean it.
If it cries to you that it hurts,
if you can,
ease its pain.

From the back garden you will be able to see the wild wood.
The deep well you walk past leads to Winter's realm;
there is another land at the bottom of it.
If you turn around here,
you can walk back, safely;
you will lose no face. I will think no less of you.

Once through the garden you will be in the wood.
The trees are old. Eyes peer from the undergrowth.
Beneath a twisted oak sits an old woman. She may ask for
    something;
give it to her. She
will point the way to the castle.
Inside it are three princesses.
Do not trust the youngest. Walk on.
In the clearing beyond the castle the twelve months sit
    about a fire,
warming their feet, exchanging tales.
They may do favors for you, if you are polite.
You may pick strawberries in December's frost.

† Neil Gaiman, "Instructions," in *A Wolf at the Door*, ed. Ellen Datlow and Terri Windling (New York: Simon & Schuster, 2000), pp. 405–07. Copyright © 2000 by Neil Gaiman. Reprinted by permission.

Trust the wolves, but do not tell them where you are going.
The river can be crossed by the ferry. The ferryman will take
    you.
(The answer to his question is this:
If he hands the oar to his passenger, he will be free to leave
    the boat.
Only tell him this from a safe distance.)

If an eagle gives you a feather, keep it safe.
Remember: that giants sleep too soundly; that
witches are often betrayed by their appetites;
dragons have one soft spot, somewhere, always;
hearts can be well-hidden, and you betray them with your
    tongue.

Do not be jealous of your sister.
Know that diamonds and roses
are as uncomfortable when they tumble from one's lips as
    toads and frogs:
colder, too, and sharper, and they cut.
Remember your name.
Do not lose hope—what you seek will be found.
Trust ghosts. Trust those that you have helped to help you
    in their turn.
Trust dreams. Trust your heart, and trust your story.

When you come back, return the way you came.
Favors will be returned, debts be repaid.
Do not forget your manners.
Do not look back.
Ride the wise eagle (you shall not fall)
Ride the silver fish (you will not drown)
Ride the gray wolf (hold tightly to his fur).

There is a worm at the heart of the tower; that is why it will
    not stand.

When you reach the little house, the place your journey
    started
you will recognize it, although it will seem much smaller
    than you remember.
Walk up the path, and through the garden gate you never
    saw before but once.
And then go home. Or make a home.

Or rest.

INTRODUCTION:
Little Red Riding Hood

"Little Red Riding Hood was my first love. I felt that if I could have married Little Red Riding Hood, I should have known perfect bliss."[1] When Charles Dickens made this confession, he was living in an age that knew only the innocent child in stories collected by Charles Perrault and the Brothers Grimm. In those folkloric treatments, a villainous predator squares off against a sweet, trusting child and earns a bad name for himself as a ruthless, gluttonous beast. Dickens's first love had not yet grown up to become Red Hot Riding Hood, Little Red Running Shorts, Little Red Riding Crop, or any number of other seductive sirens, attractive fashionistas, and unyielding avengers who face down the horrors of beasts in the forest.

We often think of "Little Red Riding Hood" as a story with a whiff of the archaic, but it is in fact alive and present in our own culture with near manic expressive intensity. So ubiquitous is the tale that it sometimes disappears from sight precisely because it is so familiar. The girl in red appears in story and song, on screen and on the written page, on the runway as well as on stage. A source of adult entertainment, she is also very much at home in the nursery, telling us not only about encounters between predator and prey but also about human interactions that foreground innocence and seduction.[2] Hers is a story about appetite in all shadings of the term, from primal hunger to sexual desire, both tainted by the threat of desire turning dark and deadly—desire so rapacious that it feeds on human life. We are as much in the realm of myth as of fairy tale, with stories that provide a platform for staging the consequences of desires, sinister and benign, in their most vivid and extreme form.

"Little Red Riding Hood" most likely emerged as part of a storytelling culture that took up the theme of predatory animals roaming the countryside in search of food. As Barbara Ehrenreich tells

---

1. Charles Dickens, "A Christmas Tree," in *Christmas Stories* (London: Chapman & Hall, 1898), p. 5.
2. Catherine Orenstein looks at pornographic adaptations of "Little Red Riding Hood" in her *Little Red Riding Hood Uncloaked: Sex, Morality, and the Evolution of a Fairy Tale* (New York: Basic Books, 2002).

us, "human storytelling . . . grew out of encounters with real animal predators and served as a means of fear management as well as
a means to ready the group for future encounters."[3] The earliest
versions of "Little Red Riding Hood" featured wolves on the prowl,
looking for nothing more than a tasty meal. It was only in the
course of the nineteenth century that the story bifurcated, taking
two different paths in Anglo-American and European cultures. It
migrated directly into the nursery to become a story with a disciplinary edge and all kinds of behavioral directives designed to teach
the child outside the story lessons. At the same time, in more subtle
and dispersed ways, Little Red Riding Hood entered adult culture,
where she and a metaphorical wolf dance a tango of innocence and
seduction, with a sultry Red Riding Hood perfectly capable, over
time, of playing the wolf.

The girl in red, now often positioned as a seductive innocent who
stalks a monstrous predator as much as she fears him, is no longer
a willing victim. When the heroine of the popular 1990s TV series
Buffy the Vampire Slayer dresses up as Little Red Riding Hood for
Halloween, she carries weapons in her basket. Matthew Bright's
Freeway (1996) takes us to the mean streets of southern California,
with an urban Red Riding Hood named Vanessa Lutz who sports a
red leather jacket as she tries to elude a host of predators, among
them a pedophile serial killer named Bob Wolverton. In David
Slade's *Hard Candy* (2005), a fourteen-year-old girl in a hooded red
sweatshirt, brilliantly played by a sweet-looking Ellen Page, turns
out to be not so innocent. She sets out to torture an on-line sexual
predator in ways that are nearly unimaginable. Joe Wright, the director of *Hanna* (2011), reinvents Red Riding Hood as a genetically
modified teenage assassin, who goes out for target practice dressed
in pelts. In the cabin where she lives with her father, she spends cold
Norwegian winter evenings reading the Grimms' fairy tales, pausing to reflect on "Little Red Riding Hood."

The heroine's path to predator is not as unexpected as might seem
at first blush. Fairy tales, as folklorists and historians never tire of
reminding us, have their roots in a peasant culture relatively uninhibited in its expressive energy. For centuries, agricultural laborers
and domestic workers relied on the telling of tales to shorten the
hours devoted to repetitive tasks, ranging from hoeing and harvesting to spinning and sewing. Is it surprising that, in an age without
radios, televisions, and other electronic wonders, they favored fast-
paced narratives with heavy doses of burlesque humor, melodramatic action, scatological jokes, and free-wheeling violence?

3. Barbara Ehrenreich, Foreword to *Deadly Powers: Animal Predators and the Mythic
Imagination* by Paul A. Trout (New York: Prometheus, 2011).

The French folklorist Paul Delarue published a version of "Little Red Riding Hood" that was recorded in Brittany in 1885 and part of a long-standing oral storytelling tradition that may have reached back many decades and even several centuries. "The Story of Grandmother" (p. 14), as he called the tale, recounts a girl's trip to her grandmother's house and her encounter with a wolf. But the resemblance to the Little Red Riding Hood story we know today ends there. This Gallic heroine escapes falling victim to the wolf and instead joins the ranks of trickster figures. After arriving at grandmother's house and unwittingly eating "meat" and drinking "wine" that is in fact the flesh and blood of granny, the girl removes her articles of clothing, one by one, performing a striptease before the wolf. She climbs into bed with the beast, but it soon dawns on her that she is in danger. No dimwit, she escapes by pleading with the wolf for the chance to go outdoors and relieve herself, and once released, she races back home.

Although "The Story of Grandmother" did not make it into print until nearly two centuries after Perrault wrote down his version of the story, it is presumably more faithful to oral traditions than Perrault's "Little Red Cap." After all, the folklorist who recorded it was not invested in producing a book that would end up in the nurseries of aristocratic families. Instead he worked hard to set down the words of his informant, who may have gotten some parts of the story wrong (as each teller does) but who managed to capture the spirit of narratives that were part of an adult storytelling tradition.

The heroine in "The Story of Grandmother" is, as Jack Zipes points out, "forthright, brave, and shrewd."[4] She is an expert at summoning courage and using her wits to escape danger. Perrault changed all that when he put her story between the covers of a book and eliminated vulgarities, coarse turns of phrase, and unmotivated plot elements. Gone are the references to bodily functions, the racy double entendres, and the gaps in narrative logic. As Delarue points out, Perrault removed elements that would have shocked and startled potential buyers of a volume that pictured a woman who appears to be a domestic servant, holding a spindle and seated before a fireside, with three well-dressed, attentive children surrounding her. Scenes of barbaric behavior (the girl eats granny's flesh and drinks her blood) and deep impropriety (the girl asks granny about her hairy body and big nostrils) no doubt discouraged parents from reading these "tales from times past" to their children, even when they included "morals."

Perrault worked hard to craft a tale that excised the ribald grotesqueries of the oral narrative and rescripted the events to accommodate a rational moral economy. His Little Red Riding

---

4. Jack Zipes, *The Trials and Tribulations of Little Red Riding Hood*, 2nd ed. (New York: Routledge, 1993), p. 26.

Hood has no idea that it is "dangerous to stop and listen to wolves" (p. 16). She also has a frivolous streak, stopping in the woods to have a "good time" as she gathers nuts, chases butterflies, and picks flowers. And, of course, she is not as savvy as James Thurber's "little girl," who knows that "a wolf doesn't look any more like your grandmother than the Metro-Goldwyn lion looks like Calvin Coolidge," and shoots the wolf dead with an "automatic."[5] To drive home the point that the tale is on a mission to modify behavior, the story ends with the following lesson:

> From this story one learns that children,
> Especially young girls,
> Pretty, well-bred, and genteel,
> Are wrong to listen to just anyone.
> And it's not at all strange,
> If a wolf ends up eating them.

Little Red Riding Hood's failure to fight back or to resist in any way led the psychoanalytically oriented Bruno Bettelheim to declare that the girl must be "stupid or wants to be seduced." In his view, Perrault transformed a "naïve attractive young girl, who is induced to neglect mother's warnings and enjoy herself in what she consciously believes to be innocent ways, into nothing but a fallen woman."[6] "Fallen woman" seems something of a stretch, but Little Red Riding Hood is no longer a trickster who survives through her powers of improvisation. Instead of succumbing to a rapacious beast in the woods, Little Red Riding Hood falls victim to one of those "tame wolves" who are "the most dangerous of all." It may be true that peasant cultures figured the wolf as a beast of prey, but folk raconteurs had probably already gleefully exploited the full range and play of the sexual innuendos in the story.

The Grimms' "Little Red Cap" (p. 18) erased all traces of the raw energy found in "The Story of Grandmother" and placed the action in the service of teaching lessons to the child inside and outside the story. Like many fairy tales, the Grimms' narrative begins by framing a prohibition, but this tale has difficulty moving out of the regulatory mode. Little Red Cap's mother hands her daughter cakes and wine for grandmother and proceeds to instruct her in the art of good behavior with a barrage of imperatives: "[W]hen you're out in the woods, walk properly and don't stray from the path. Otherwise you'll fall and break the glass, and then there'll be nothing for Grandmother. And when you enter her room, don't forget to say good

---

5. James Thurber, "The Little Girl and the Wolf," in *Fables for Our Time and Famous Poems Illustrated by James Thurber* (New York: Harper's, 1940), p. 3.
6. Bruno Bettelheim, *The Uses of Enchantment: The Meaning and Importance of Fairy Tales* (New York: Knopf, 1976), p. 169.

morning, and don't go peeping in all the corners of the room" (p. 18). The Grimms' efforts to encode the story with lessons could hardly be called successful. The lecture on manners embedded in the narrative is not only alien to the spirit of fairy tales—which are so plot driven that they rarely traffic in the kind of disciplinary precision on display here—but also misfires in its lack of logic. The bottle never breaks even though Red Cap strays from the path, and the straying takes place only after the wolf has already spotted his prey.

What we discover in new versions of the tale is a form of repetition compulsion on steroids. The Brothers Grimm show us a Little Red Riding Hood who has internalized the lesson she has been taught, and at the end of her story she declares: "Never again will you stray from the path and go into the woods, when mother has forbidden it" (p. 20). Pick up any one of the dozens of versions of "Little Red Riding Hood" available in child-friendly picture books today, and you will find that the girl invariably states that lesson, not only for her own benefit but also for the sake of the child outside the book. Even the versions that use humor and whimsy end up giving us the same old story, as if staying on the path would somehow have saved the girl from the predator in the woods. Never mind that the lesson itself is one that we probably don't want to transmit to children today. As Neil Gaiman writes in *The Ocean at the End of the Lane*: "Children . . . use back ways and hidden paths, adults take roads and official paths."[7] Straying from the path is actually a good thing today, yet we persist in condemning it in a story that nearly everyone hears—in one version or another—as a child.

The multiforms of "Little Red Riding Hood" are not all cautionary. But the ones we tell to children all point to a moral, resisting the notion that the tale might engage with a range of cultural binaries: the predator–prey relationship, the nature–culture divide, or the fraught tension between innocence and seduction. And the cautionary version of "Little Red Riding Hood" inevitably gives us a tableau of violence intended to drive home a lesson about the consequences of disobedience and transgression. Worse yet, the girl is faulted for her love of beauty. Bettelheim famously condemned the Grimms' Little Red Cap as beset by the "pleasure-seeking id," a girl seduced by the beauty of the flowers that line the path she takes to granny's home.[8]

The folly of trying to derive a clear moral message from "Little Red Riding Hood" in any of its versions becomes evident from Eric Berne's rendition of a Martian's reaction to the tale:

7. Neil Gaiman, *The Ocean at the End of the Lane* (New York: William Morrow, 2014), p. 111.
8. Bettelheim, *The Uses of Enchantment*, p. 171.

What kind of a mother sends a little girl into the forest where there are wolves? Why didn't her mother do it herself, or go along with LRRH? If grandmother was so helpless, why did mother leave her all by herself in a hut far away? But if LRRH had to go, how come her mother had never warned her not to stop and talk to wolves? The story makes it clear that LRRH had never been told that this was dangerous. No mother could really be that stupid, so it sounds as if her mother didn't care much what happened to LRRH, or maybe even wanted to get rid of her. No little girl is that stupid either. How could LRRH look at the wolf's eyes, ears, hands, and teeth and still think it was grandmother? Why didn't she get out of there as fast as she could?[9]

By analyzing the rhetoric of the story and showing how it subverts the very terms it establishes, Berne performs a kind of protodeconstructive analysis that challenges the notion of a straightforward moral message in "Little Red Riding Hood." For Perrault and the Brothers Grimm, the story itself never stood in the way of a message. Both their tales make the heroine responsible for the violence inflicted on her. By speaking to strangers (as Perrault has it) and by disobeying her mother and straying from the path (as the Grimms tell it), the girl in red courts her own downfall.

For every act of violence that befalls heroes and heroines of fairy tales it is easy enough to establish a cause by pointing to behavioral flaws. The aggression of the witch in "Hansel and Gretel," for example, has been read as a consequence of the children's gluttony and greed. A chain of events that might once have created burlesque, surreal effects can easily be restructured to produce a morally edifying tale. The shift from violence in the service of slapstick to violence in the service of a disciplinary regime may have added a moral backbone to fairy tales, but it rarely curbed their uninhibited displays of violence. Nineteenth-century rescriptings of "Little Red Riding Hood" are, in fact, among the most frightening, in large part because they tap into discursive practices that rely on a pedagogy of fear to regulate behavior. A verse melodrama that appeared in 1862, for example, made Little Red Riding Hood responsible for her own death and for her grandmother's demise:

> If Little Red Riding Hood had only thought
> Of these little matters as much as she ought,
> In the trap of the Wolf she would ne'er have been caught,
> Nor her Grandmother killed in so cruel a sort.[1]

9. Eric Berne, *What Do You Say after You Say Hello? The Psychology of Human Destiny* (New York: Grove, 1972), p. 43.
1. Zipes, *Trials and Tribulations*, p. 158.

Or, as Red Riding Hood's father put it in another nineteenth-century version of the tale:

> A little maid,
> Must be afraid,
> To do other than her mother told her.[2]

The story of Little Red Riding Hood seems to have lost more than it gained as it made the transition from adult oral entertainment to literary fare for children. Once a folktale full of earthy humor and high melodrama, it was transformed into a heavy-handed narrative with an adult agenda. In the process, the surreal violence of the original was converted into a frightening punishment for a relatively minor infraction. A few writers balked at the new twist given to the story and resisted blaming the girl, and, in some cases, even refused to demonize the wolf. James Thurber turned Little Red Riding Hood into a clever, resourceful heroine ("It is not so easy to fool little girls nowadays as it used to be") in his "The Little Girl and the Wolf."[3] Angela Carter ends her story "The Company of Wolves" by turning the bedroom scene into a site of reconciliation: "Sweet and sound she sleeps in granny's bed, between the paws of the tender wolf."[4]

Just as writers have felt free to tamper and tinker with "Little Red Riding Hood" (often radically revising its terms, as does Roald Dahl [p. 23]), critics have played fast and loose with the tale, displaying boundless confidence in their pronouncements about what it means. To be sure, the tale itself, by depicting a conflict between a weak, vulnerable protagonist and a large, powerful antagonist, lends itself to a certain interpretive elasticity. The girl can stand in for any innocent victim while the wolf can be any kind of predatory villain. Nazi ideologues read the story as a parable about rapacious Jews preying on innocent German purebloods; feminists read the tale as an allegory about rape; and psychoanalysts saw in it a fable about female maturation, pitting women against men who try to "play the role of a pregnant woman, having living things in [their] belly."[5]

Recent efforts to map the story of "Little Red Riding Hood" and trace its transmission reveal the importance of taking into account a story that folklorists have made the mistake of putting in a separate category. This is the tale type known as "The Wolf and the Seven Kids" (ATU 123), and it is a story about an ogre, monster, or beast that tries to break into a home, often inhabited by multiple siblings.

---

2. Ibid., p. 200.
3. James Thurber, *Fables for Our Time*, p. 3.
4. Angela Carter, *The Bloody Chamber and Other Stories* (New York: Penguin, 1979), p. 118.
5. Erich Fromm, *The Forgotten Language: An Introduction to the Understanding of Dreams, Fairy Tales and Myths* (New York: Rinehart, 1951), p. 241.

Because its cast of characters is all animal, folklorists segregated it in the category of tales featuring animal protagonists. In "The Glutton" (ATU 333), the umbrella term for "Little Red Riding Hood" stories, a single child enters a house taken over by a rapacious demon. Both "The Wolf and the Seven Kids" and "The Glutton" pit a predatory creature against vulnerable children separated temporarily from maternal protection. Can the children display courage and use their wits to survive? Or will they fall victim to the monster? Some are masterful strategists, luring villains into a tree or up onto a rooftop, then tempting them to dive back down to satisfy gluttonous ways. Others feel helpless, cower in corners, and perish.

Anthropologist Jamshid J. Tehrani has traced the evolution of the two tale types, showing how they mix and mingle, bifurcate and branch out.[6] But his phylogenetic tracking of the tale—which proposes that Asian versions blend ATU 123 with ATU 333 and that African tales are distinctly in the mode of ATU 123—fails to recognize that a sample of fifty-eight tales is insufficient to draw generalizations about global cultural differences. And his analysis captures only versions that were written down, not the multitude of tales that never made it into print. Stories about home invasion are primal and perennial. They are told in every time and place, and there is hardly anything unique about the dramatis personae and plot moves.

In a sense "The Wolf and the Seven Kids" and "The Glutton" give us foundational narratives, plots that provide an instruction manual for survival at a time when life turned on the hunter and the hunted. What is astonishing, however, is the fact that these stories, in all their global variation, feature a child as trickster or as victim, modeling tools for survival for the very young or revealing the consequences of cowardice and fear. The story lives on as a primer about predators and prey, animals and humans, life and death, survival and suffering. But its roots in the childhood of culture and its move into the culture of childhood are symptomatic of how Little Red Riding Hood is in one sense the story of stories, the rock-solid foundation on which folkloric traditions were built as cultures evolved. We could easily speak here too of how ontogeny recapitulates phylogeny, with each child moving through the various phases through which humans passed as culture emerged from nature.

This unit features two versions of "The Wolf and the Seven Kids," one from Asia and one from Africa. Some decades ago German folklorist and sinologist Wolfram Eberhard carried out fieldwork in the Kuting section of the city of Taipei in Taiwan. He had no trouble coming up, while there, with 241 versions of a story he called

---

6. Jamshid J. Tehrani, "The Phylogeny of Little Red Riding Hood," *PLoS ONE* 8.11 (2013), e78871, journals.plos.org/plosone/article?id=10.1371/journal.pone.0078871.

"Grandaunt Tiger," a colossal number that reminds us that we rarely have more than the tip of a very large iceberg when it comes to a folktale. Grandaunt Tiger is a hybrid creature, half-human, half-beast, and she preys first on a mother, then on her two "nieces," devouring one but unable to outwit the other, who is as nimble and sharp-witted as the Gallic heroine in the "Story of Grandmother." The version included here is a free translation of "The Tale of the Tiger Woman," published in 1803 in an anthology of tales. It was recorded by Huang Chengzeng at the end of the seventeenth or beginning of the eighteenth century.

"Tsélané and the Marimo" is a South African tale recorded in 1842 by two French missionaries, who, as they stated in the preface to the account of their travels, hoped to "seek out unknown tribes, to open up communication with their chiefs, to mark out plans suitable for missionary stations, to extend the influence of Christianity and civilization."[7] They also wished to give their readers some instances of the "old wives' stories with which mothers put their little ones to sleep, and inculcate betimes the first principles of Bechuana morality—that is submission to parental authority, and dread of the Marimos." The story was translated into English by anthropologist James G. Frazer, author of *The Golden Bough*, who published it in the *British Folk-Lore Journal* in 1888.

Everyone experiences the story of "Little Red Riding Hood" and "The Wolf and the Seven Kids" in different ways. To illustrate how the tales have unpredictable effects—they have, after all, been told in countless different ways—we can turn to any number of testimonials. Two, in particular, illustrate wide-ranging differences in reception, with memories that touch radically different points on an emotional spectrum, from comic to tragic. The writer Angela Carter recalled reading Perrault's "Little Red Riding Hood" as a child: "My maternal grandmother used to say, 'Lift up the latch and walk in,' when she told it [to] me when I was a child; and at the conclusion when the wolf jumps on Little Red Riding Hood and gobbles her up, my grandmother used to pretend to eat me, which made me squeak and gibber with excited pleasure."[8] Carter's grandmother, by impersonating the grandmother-devouring wolf who was also impersonating grandmothers, turns the tables by turning on her granddaughter, the girl who feasts on grandmother's flesh and blood in folk versions of the tale. Carter's account of her experience with "Little Red Riding Hood" stages the tale as one about intergenerational rivalry and love, yet it also reveals the degree to which the meaning of a tale is

7. T. Arbousset and F. Daumas, *Narrative of an Exploratory Tour to the North-East of the Colony of the Cape of Good Hope* (Cape Town: Struik, 1968), p. ix.
8. Angela Carter, ed., *The Virago Book of Fairy Tales* (London: Virago, 1990), p. 240.

generated through performance. The scene of reading or acting out a story can affect its reception far more powerfully than the morals and timeless truths inserted into versions of the tale recorded by Perrault, the Brothers Grimm, and others.

Consider Luciano Pavarotti's childhood experience with "Little Red Riding Hood" and how markedly it differs from Carter's. The renowned baritone heard the stories from his grandfather, who told "violent, mysterious tales" that "enchanted" his listeners. "My favorite one," Pavarotti declared, "was *Little Red Riding Hood*. I identified with Little Red Riding Hood. I had the same fears as she. I didn't want her to die. I dreaded her death—or what we think death is. I waited anxiously for the hunter to come."[9] Little Red Riding Hood's encounter with the wolf and her brush with death is no longer burlesque, playful, or erotically charged. Instead, it has become the site of violence, anxiety, melodrama, and mystery. The feeling of dread, coupled with a sense of enchantment, captures the fascination with matters from which children are usually shielded. Pavarotti, like Dickens, is enamored of Little Red Riding Hood, but his infatuation is driven by her ability to survive death, to emerge whole from the belly of the wolf. For centuries now, we have fallen for the girl in red, even if and perhaps precisely because she is constantly shapeshifting, reflecting our own cultural and personal anxieties and reminding us of who we are and how we came to be that way.

The Story of Grandmother[†]

There was once a woman who had made some bread. She said to her daughter: "Take this loaf of hot bread and this bottle of milk over to granny's."

The little girl left. At the crossroads she met a wolf, who asked: "Where are you going?"

"I'm taking a loaf of hot bread and a bottle of milk to granny's."

"Which path are you going to take," asked the wolf, "the path of needles or the path of pins?"[1]

"The path of needles," said the little girl.

9. Luciano Pavarotti, "Introduction," in Beni Montresor, *Little Red Riding Hood* (New York: Doubleday, 1991).

† As told by Louis and François Briffault in Nièvre, 1885. Originally published by Paul Delarue, in "Les Contes merveilleux de Perrault et la tradition populaire," *Bulletin folklorique de l'Ile-de-France* (1951): 221–22. Translated for the first edition of this Norton Critical Edition by Maria Tatar. Copyright © 1999 by Maria Tatar.

1. Yvonne Verdier ("Grand-mères, si vous saviez . . . le Petit Chaperon Rouge dans la tradition orale," *Cahiers de Littérature Orale* 4 [1978]: 17–55) reads the path of pins and the path of needles as part of a social discourse pertaining to apprenticeships for girls in sewing. In another region of France, the paths are described as the path of little stones and the path of little thorns. An Italian version refers to a path of stones and a path of roots.

"Well, then, I'll take the path of pins."

The little girl had fun picking up needles. Meanwhile, the wolf arrived at granny's, killed her, put some of her flesh in the pantry and a bottle of her blood on the shelf. The little girl got there and knocked at the door.

"Push the door," said the wolf, "it's latched with a wet straw."

"Hello, granny. I'm bringing you a loaf of hot bread and a bottle of milk."

"Put it in the pantry, my child. Take some of the meat in there along with the bottle of wine on the shelf."[2]

There was a little cat in the room who watched her eat and said: "Phooey! You're a slut if you eat the flesh and drink the blood of granny."

"Take your clothes off, my child," said the wolf, "and come into bed with me."

"Where should I put my apron?"

"Throw it into the fire, my child. You won't be needing it any longer."

When she asked the wolf where to put all her other things, her bodice, her dress, her skirt, and her stockings, each time he said: "Throw them into the fire, my child. You won't be needing them any longer."[3]

"Oh, granny, how hairy you are!"

"The better to keep me warm, my child!"

"Oh, granny, what long nails you have!"

"The better to scratch myself with, my child!"

"Oh, granny, what big shoulders you have!"

"The better to carry firewood with, my child!"

"Oh, granny, what big ears you have!"

"The better to hear you with, my child!"

"Oh, granny, what big nostrils you have!"

"The better to sniff my tobacco with, my child!"

"Oh, granny, what a big mouth you have!"

"The better to eat you with, my child!"

"Oh, granny, I need to go badly. Let me go outside!"

"Do it in the bed, my child."

"No, granny, I want to go outside."

"All right, but don't stay out long."

The wolf tied a rope made of wool to her leg and let her go outside.

When the little girl got outside, she attached the end of the rope to a plum tree in the yard. The wolf became impatient and said: "Are you making a load out there? Are you making a load?"

2. Local variations turn the flesh into tortellini in Italy and into sausage in France, while the blood is often said to be wine.
3. Many oral renditions of the tale presumably drew out the story by dwelling at length on what happens to each article of clothing.

When he realized that there was no answer, he jumped out of bed and discovered that the little girl had escaped. He followed her, but he reached her house only after she had gotten inside.

CHARLES PERRAULT

Little Red Riding Hood[†]

Once upon a time there was a village girl, the prettiest you can imagine. Her mother adored her. Her grandmother adored her even more and made a little red hood for her. The hood suited the child so much that everywhere she went she was known by the name Little Red Riding Hood.

One day, her mother baked some cakes and said to her: "I want you to go and see how your grandmother is faring, for I've heard that she's ill. Take her some cakes and this little pot of butter."

Little Red Riding Hood left right away for her grandmother's house, which was in another village. As she was walking through the woods she met old Neighbor Wolf, who wanted to eat her right there on the spot. But he didn't dare because some woodcutters were in the forest. He asked where she was going. The poor child, who did not know that it was dangerous to stop and listen to wolves, said: "I'm going to see my grandmother and am taking her some cakes and a little pot of butter sent by my mother."

"Does she live very far away?" asked the wolf.

"Oh, yes," said Little Red Riding Hood. "She lives beyond the mill that you can see over there. Hers is the first house you come to in the village."

"Well, well," said the wolf. "I think I shall go and see her too. I'll take the path over here, and you take the path over there, and we'll see who gets there first."

The wolf ran as fast as he could on the shorter path, and the little girl continued on her way along the longer path. She had a good time gathering nuts, chasing butterflies, and picking bunches of flowers that she found.

The wolf did not take long to get to Grandmother's house. He knocked: Rat-a-tat-tat.

"Who's there?"

"It's your granddaughter, Little Red Riding Hood," said the wolf, disguising his voice. "And I'm bringing you some cake and a little pot of butter sent by my mother."

---

† Charles Perrault, "Le Petit Chaperon Rouge," in *Histoires ou Contes du temps passé. Avec des Moralités* (Paris: Barbin, 1697). Translated for the first edition of this Norton Critical Edition by Maria Tatar. Copyright © 1999 by Maria Tatar.

The dear grandmother, who was in bed because she was not feeling well, called out: "Pull the bolt and the latch will open."

The wolf pulled the bolt, and the door opened wide. He threw himself on the good woman and devoured her in no time, for he had eaten nothing in the last three days. Then he closed the door and lay down on Grandmother's bed, waiting for Little Red Riding Hood, who, before long, came knocking at the door: Rat-a-tat-tat.

"Who's there?"

Little Red Riding Hood was afraid at first when she heard the gruff voice of the wolf, but thinking that her grandmother must have caught cold, she said: "It's your granddaughter, Little Red Riding Hood, and I'm bringing you some cake and a little pot of butter sent by my mother."

The wolf tried to soften his voice as he called out to her: "Pull the bolt and the latch will open."

Little Red Riding Hood pulled the bolt, and the door opened wide. When the wolf saw her come in, he hid under the covers of the bed and said: "Put the cakes and the little pot of butter on the bin and climb into bed with me."

Little Red Riding Hood took off her clothes and climbed into the bed. She was astonished to see what her grandmother looked like in her nightgown.

"Grandmother," she said, "what big arms you have!"

"The better to hug you with, my child."

"Grandmother, what big legs you have!"

"The better to run with, my child."

"Grandmother, what big ears you have!"

"The better to hear with, my child."

"Grandmother, what big eyes you have!"

"The better to see with, my child."

"Grandmother, what big teeth you have!"

"The better to eat you with!"

Upon saying these words, the wicked wolf threw himself on Little Red Riding Hood and gobbled her up.

Moral

> From this story one learns that children,
> Especially young girls,
> Pretty, well-bred, and genteel,
> Are wrong to listen to just anyone,
> And it's not at all strange,
> If a wolf ends up eating them.
> I say a wolf, but not all wolves
> Are exactly the same.
> Some are perfectly charming,

Not loud, brutal, or angry,
But tame, pleasant, and gentle,
Following young ladies
Right into their homes, into their chambers,
But watch out if you haven't learned that tame wolves
Are the most dangerous of all.

BROTHERS GRIMM

Little Red Cap[†]

Once upon a time there was a dear little girl. If you set eyes on her you could not but love her. The person who loved her most of all was her grandmother, and she could never give the child enough. Once she made her a little cap of red velvet. Since it was so becoming and since she wanted to wear it all the time, everyone called her Little Red Cap.

One day her mother said to her: "Look, Little Red Cap. Here's a piece of cake and a bottle of wine. Take them to your grandmother. She is ill and feels weak, and they will give her strength. You'd better start now before it gets too hot, and when you're out in the woods, walk properly and don't stray from the path. Otherwise you'll fall and break the glass, and then there'll be nothing for Grandmother. And when you enter her room, don't forget to say good morning, and don't go peeping in all the corners of the room."

"I'll do just as you say," Little Red Cap promised her mother.

Grandmother lived deep in the woods, half an hour's walk from the village. No sooner had Little Red Cap set foot in the forest than she met the wolf. Little Red Cap had no idea what a wicked beast he was, and so she wasn't in the least afraid of him.

"Good morning, Little Red Cap," he said.

"Thank you kindly, wolf."

"Where are you headed so early in the morning, Little Red Cap?"

"To my grandmother's."

"What's that under your apron?"

"Cake and wine. Yesterday we baked and Grandmother, who is sick and feels weak, needs something to make her feel better."

"Where does your grandmother live, Little Red Cap?"

"It's another quarter of an hour's walk into the woods. Her house is right under three large oaks. You must know the place from the hazel hedges near it," said Little Red Cap.

[†] Jacob Grimm and Wilhelm Grimm, "Rotkäppchen," in *Kinder- und Hausmärchen,* 7th ed. (Berlin: Dieterich, 1857; first published: Berlin: Realschulbuchhandlung, 1812). Translated for the first edition of this Norton Critical Edition by Maria Tatar. Copyright © 1999 by Maria Tatar.

The wolf thought to himself: "That tender young thing will make a dainty morsel. She'll be even tastier than the old woman. If you're really crafty, you'll get them both."

He walked for a while beside Little Red Cap. Then he said: "Little Red Cap, have you seen the beautiful flowers all about? Why don't you look around for a while? I don't think you've even noticed how sweetly the birds are singing. You are walking along as if you were on the way to school, and yet it's so heavenly out here in the woods."

Little Red Cap opened her eyes wide and saw how the sunbeams were dancing this way and that through the trees and how there were beautiful flowers all about. She thought to herself: "If you bring a fresh bouquet to Grandmother, she will be overjoyed. It's still so early in the morning that I'm sure to get there in plenty of time."

She left the path and ran off into the woods looking for flowers. As soon as she picked one she saw an even more beautiful one somewhere else and went after it, and so she went deeper and deeper into the woods.

The wolf went straight to Grandmother's house and knocked at the door.

"Who's there?"

"Little Red Cap, I've brought some cake and wine. Open the door."

"Just raise the latch," Grandmother called out. "I'm too weak to get out of bed."

The wolf raised the latch, and the door swung wide open. Without saying a word, he went straight to Grandmother's bed and gobbled her up. Then he put on her clothes and her nightcap, lay down in her bed, and drew the curtains.

Meanwhile, Little Red Cap had been running around looking for flowers. When she finally had so many that she couldn't carry them all, she suddenly remembered Grandmother and set off again on the path to her house. She was surprised to find the door open, and when she stepped into the house, she had such a strange feeling that she thought to herself: "Oh, my goodness, I'm usually so glad to be at Grandmother's, but today I feel so nervous."

She called out a greeting but there was no answer. Then she went to the bed and drew back the curtains. Grandmother was lying there with her nightcap pulled down over her face. She looked very strange.

"Oh, Grandmother, what big ears you have!"

"The better to hear you with."

"Oh, Grandmother, what big eyes you have!"

"The better to see you with."

"Oh, Grandmother, what big hands you have!"

"The better to grab you with!"

"Oh, Grandmother, what a big, scary mouth you have!"

"The better to eat you with!"

No sooner had the wolf spoken those words than he leaped out of bed and gobbled up poor Little Red Cap.

Once the wolf had satisfied his desires, he lay down again in bed, fell asleep, and began to snore very loudly. A huntsman happened to be passing by the house just then and thought to himself: "How the old woman is snoring! You'd better check to see what's wrong." He walked into the house and when he got to the bed he saw that the wolf was lying in it.

"I've found you at last, you old sinner," he said. "I've been after you for a while now."

He pulled out his musket and was about to take aim when he realized that the wolf might have eaten Grandmother and that she could still be saved. Instead of firing, he took out a pair of scissors and began cutting open the belly of the sleeping wolf. After making a few snips, he saw the faint outlines of a red hood. After making a few more cuts, the girl jumped out, crying: "Oh, how terrified I was! It was so dark in the wolf's belly!" And then the old grandmother found her way out alive, though she could hardly breathe. Little Red Cap quickly fetched some large stones and filled the wolf's belly with them. When he awoke, he was about to bound off, but the stones were so heavy that his legs collapsed and he fell down dead.

All three were overjoyed. The huntsman skinned the wolf and went home with the pelt. Grandmother ate the cake and drank the wine Little Red Cap had brought her and recovered her health. Little Red Cap thought to herself: "Never again will you stray from the path and go into the woods, when your mother has forbidden it."

There is also a story about another wolf who met Little Red Cap on the way to Grandmother's, as she was taking her some cakes. The wolf tried to divert her from the path, but Little Red Cap was on her guard and kept right on going. She told her grandmother that she had met the wolf and that he had greeted her. But he had looked at her in such an evil way that "If we hadn't been out in the open, he would have gobbled me right up."

"Well then," said Grandmother. "We'll just lock that door so he can't get in."

Not much later the wolf knocked at the door and called out: "Open the door, Grandmother, it's Little Red Cap. I'm bringing you some cakes."

The two kept quiet and didn't open the door. Then old Grayhead circled the house a few times and finally jumped up on the roof. He was planning on waiting until Little Red Cap went home. Then he was going to creep up after her and gobble her up in the dark. But Grandmother guessed what he had on his mind. There was a big stone trough in front of the house. She said to the child: "Here's a bucket, Little Red Cap. Yesterday I cooked some sausages. Take the water in which they were boiled and pour it into the trough."

Little Red Cap kept carrying water until that big, big trough was completely full. The smell of those sausages reached the wolf's nostrils. His neck was stretched out so long from sniffing and looking around that he lost his balance and began to slide down. He went right down the roof into the trough and was drowned. Little Red Cap walked home cheerfully, and no one did her any harm.

ITALO CALVINO

The False Grandmother[†]

A mother had to sift flour, and told her little girl to go to her grandmother's and borrow the sifter. The child packed a snack—ring-shaped cakes and bread with oil—and set out.

She came to the Jordan River.

"Jordan River, will you let me pass?"

"Yes, if you give me your ring-shaped cakes."

The Jordan River had a weakness for ring-shaped cakes, which he enjoyed twirling in his whirlpools.

The child tossed the ring-shaped cakes into the river, and the river lowered its waters and let her through.

The little girl came to the Rake Gate.

"Rake Gate, will you let me pass?"

"Yes, if you give me your bread with oil."

The Rake Gate had a weakness for bread with oil, since her hinges were rusty, and bread with oil oiled them for her.

The little girl gave the gate her bread with oil, and the gate opened and let her through.

She reached her grandmother's house, but the door was shut tight.

"Grandmother, Grandmother, come let me in."

"I'm in bed sick. Come through the window."

"I can't make it."

"Come through the cat door."

"I can't squeeze through."

"Well, wait a minute," she said, and lowered a rope, by which she pulled the little girl up through the window. The room was dark. In bed was the ogress, not the grandmother, for the ogress had gobbled up Grandmother all in one piece from head to toe, all except her teeth, which she had put on to stew in a small stew pan, and her ears, which she had put on to fry in a frying pan.

† "The False Grandmother," recorded by Antonio de Nino, 1883, in *Italian Folktales*, selected and retold by Italo Calvino, trans. George Martin (New York: Pantheon, 1980). Copyright © 1956 by Giulio Einaudi editore, s.p.a. English translation copyright © 1980 by Houghton Mifflin Harcourt. Reprinted by permission of Houghton Mifflin Harcourt Publishing Company and by Penguin Books Ltd. All rights reserved.

"Grandmother, Mamma wants the sifter."

"It's late now. I'll give it to you tomorrow. Come to bed."

"Grandmother, I'm hungry, I want my supper first."

"Eat the beans boiling in the boiler."

In the pot were the teeth. The child stirred them around and said, "Grandmother, they're too hard."

"Well, eat the fritters in the frying pan."

In the frying pan were the ears. The child felt them with the fork and said, "Grandmother, they're not crisp."

"Well, come to bed. You can eat tomorrow."

The little girl got into bed beside Grandmother. She felt one of her hands and said, "Why are your hands so hairy, Grandmother?"

"From wearing too many rings on my fingers."

She felt her chest. "Why is your chest so hairy, Grandmother?"

"From wearing too many necklaces around my neck."

She felt her hips. "Why are your hips so hairy, Grandmother?"

"Because I wore my corset too tight."

She felt her tail and reasoned that, hairy or not, Grandmother had never had a tail. That had to be the ogress and nobody else. So she said, "Grandmother, I can't go to sleep unless I first go and take care of a little business."

Grandmother replied, "Go do it in the barn below. I'll let you down through the trapdoor and then draw you back up."

She tied a rope around her and lowered her into the barn. The minute the little girl was down she untied the rope and in her place attached a nanny goat. "Are you through?" asked Grandmother.

"Just a minute." She finished tying the rope around the nanny goat. "There, I've finished. Pull me back up."

The ogress pulled and pulled, and the little girl began yelling, "Hairy ogress! Hairy ogress!" She threw open the barn and fled. The ogress kept pulling, and up came the nanny goat. She jumped out of bed and ran after the little girl.

When the child reached the Rake Gate, the ogress yelled from a distance, "Rake Gate, don't let her pass!"

But the Rake Gate replied, "Of course I'll let her pass; she gave me her bread with oil."

When the child reached the Jordan River, the ogress shouted, "Jordan River, don't you let her pass!"

But the Jordan River answered, "Of course I'll let her pass; she gave me her ring-shaped cakes."

When the ogress tried to get through, the Jordan River did not lower his waters, and the ogress was swept away in the current. From the bank the little girl made faces at her.

ROALD DAHL

Little Red Riding Hood and the Wolf[†]

As soon as Wolf began to feel
That he would like a decent meal,
He went and knocked on Grandma's door.
When Grandma opened it, she saw
The sharp white teeth, the horrid grin,   5
And Wolfie said, 'May I come in?'
Poor Grandmamma was terrified,
'He's going to eat me up!' she cried.
And she was absolutely right.
He ate her up in one big bite.   10
But Grandmamma was small and tough,
And Wolfie wailed, 'That's not enough!'
'I haven't yet begun to feel
'That I have had a decent meal!'
He ran around the kitchen yelping,   15
'I've *got* to have another helping!'
Then added with a frightful leer,
'I'm therefore going to wait right here
'Till Little Miss Red Riding Hood
'Comes home from walking in the wood.'   20
He quickly put on Grandma's clothes,
(Of course he hadn't eaten those.)
He dressed himself in coat and hat.
He put on shoes and after that
He even brushed and curled his hair,   25
Then sat himself in Grandma's chair.
In came the little girl in red.
She stopped. She stared. And then she said,

'What great big ears you have, Grandma.'
'All the better to hear you with,' the Wolf replied.   30
'What great big eyes you have, Grandma,'
   said Little Red Riding Hood.
'All the better to see you with,' the Wolf replied.

He sat there watching her and smiled.
He thought, I'm going to eat this child.   35
Compared with her old Grandmamma

She's going to taste like caviare.
Then Little Red Riding Hood said, *'But Grandma,*
what a lovely great big furry coat you have on.'
'That's wrong!' cried Wolf. 'Have you forgot
'To tell me what BIG TEETH I've got?   40
'Ah well, no matter what you say,
'I'm going to eat you anyway.'
The small girl smiles. One eyelid flickers.
She whips a pistol from her knickers.
She aims it at the creature's head   45
And *bang bang bang,* she shoots him dead.
A few weeks later, in the wood,
I came across Miss Riding Hood.
But what a change! No cloak of red,
No silly hood upon her head.   50
She said, 'Hello, and do please note
'My lovely furry WOLFSKIN COAT.'

ROALD DAHL

The Three Little Pigs[†]

The animal I really dig
Above all others is the pig.
Pigs are noble. Pigs are clever,
Pigs are courteous. However,
Now and then, to break this rule,   5
One meets a pig who is a fool.
What, for example, would you say
If strolling through the woods one day,
Right there in front of you you saw
A pig who'd built his house of STRAW?   10
The Wolf who saw it licked his lips,
And said, 'That pig has had his chips.'

'Little pig, little pig, let me come in!'
'No, no, by the hairs on my chinny-chin-chin!'
'Then I'll huff and I'll puff and I'll blow your
    house in!'   15

The little pig began to pray,
But Wolfie blew his house away.

He shouted, 'Bacon, pork and ham!
'Oh, what a lucky Wolf I am!'
And though he ate the pig quite fast,   20
He carefully kept the tail till last.
Wolf wandered on, a trifle bloated.
Surprise, surprise, for soon he noted
Another little house for pigs,
And this one had been built of TWIGS!   25

'Little pig, little pig, let me come in!'
'No, no, by the hairs of my chinny-chin-chin!'
'Then I'll huff and I'll puff and I'll blow your
    house in!'

The Wolf said, 'Okay, here we go!'
He then began to blow and blow.   30
The little pig began to squeal.
He cried, 'Oh Wolf, you've had *one* meal!
'Why can't we talk and make a deal?'
The Wolf replied, 'Not on your nelly!'
And soon the pig was in his belly.   35
'Two juicy little pigs!' Wolf cried,
'But still I am not satisfied!
'I know full well my Tummy's bulging,
'But oh, how I adore indulging.'
So creeping quietly as a mouse,   40
The Wolf approached another house,
A house which also had inside
A little piggy trying to hide.
But this one, Piggy Number Three,
Was bright and brainy as could be.   45
No straw for him, no twigs or sticks.
This pig had built his house of BRICKS.
'You'll not get *me*!' the Piggy cried.
'I'll blow you down!' the Wolf replied.
'You'll need,' Pig said, 'a lot of puff,   50
'And I don't think you've got enough.'
Wolf huffed and puffed and blew and blew.
The house stayed up as good as new.
'If I can't blow it *down*,' Wolf said,
'I'll have to blow it *up* instead.   55
'I'll come back in the dead of night
'And blow it up with dynamite!'
Pig cried, 'You brute! I might have known!'
Then, picking up the telephone,
He dialled as quickly as he could   60
The number of Red Riding Hood.

'Hello,' she said. 'Who's speaking? *Who*?'
'Oh, hello Piggy, how d'you do?'
Pig cried, 'I need your help, Miss Hood!
'Oh help me, please! D'you think you could?'   65
'I'll try, of course,' Miss Hood replied.
'What's on your mind?' . . . '*A Wolf*!' Pig cried.
'I know you've dealt with wolves before,
'And now I've got one at my door!'
'My darling Pig,' she said, 'my sweet,   70
'That's something *really* up my street.
'I've just begun to wash my hair.
'But when it's dry, I'll be right there.'
A short while later, through the wood,
Came striding brave Miss Riding Hood.   75
The Wolf stood there, his eyes ablaze
And yellowish, like mayonnaise.
His teeth were sharp, his gums were raw,
And spit was dripping from his jaw.
Once more the maiden's eyelid flickers.   80
She draws the pistol from her knickers.
Once more, she hits the vital spot,
And kills him with a single shot.
Pig, peeping through the window, stood
And yelled, 'Well done, Miss Riding Hood!'   85

Ah, Piglet, you must never trust
Young ladies from the upper crust.
For now, Miss Riding Hood, one notes,
Not only has *two* wolfskin coats,
But when she goes from place to place,   90
She has a PIGSKIN TRAVELLING CASE.

The Tale of the Tiger Woman[†]

Someone once told me a story about tigers. The district of She is
located in the Wan Mountains, and many tigers live there. One of
them was an ancient female tiger who could turn herself into a human
whenever she wanted. And when she did, she was out for blood.

In that very region, there lived a peasant with his daughter. One
day he sent his daughter out with a basket of jujuba fruit and asked

† Huang Chih-chun, Huang Chengzeng, Annette Specht, Günter Lontzen, and Jacques
Barchilon, "The Earliest Version of the Chinese 'Little Red Riding Hood': The Tale of
the Tiger-Woman," *Merveilles & Contes* 7 (1993): 513–27. Copyright © 1993 Wayne
State University Press, reprinted with the permission of Wayne State University Press.
This translation has been adapted by the editor with permission for this Norton Critical
Edition.

her to take them to his mother-in-law, who lived six miles away. The girl had a little brother, and he came along with her. The boy was about ten years old, and he held her hand all the way. Just as the sun was setting, the girl and her brother realized that they had lost their way. They met an old woman, and she asked them where they were going. "We are going to visit our grandmother." The woman, who was really a tiger, said, "Why that's me!"

The two children said, "But our mother told us that her mother has seven moles on her face. You don't look at all like her, and you have no moles at all." The woman replied, "That may be true, but this afternoon I was removing the husks from rice, and now my face is all covered with dust. Let me go wash it." She walked over to a nearby stream and gathered up seven shells. Then she popped them on her face and returned to the child. "Look here," she said. "Now you can see my moles." The two children now believed that the woman was their grandmother, and they followed her.

The three traveled through a dark forest until they reached a narrow path. There they found a dwelling that looked just like a cave. The women said, "Uncle Er has just now ordered some workers to find trees to build a separate hall. But for now we will live here in this cave."

The children followed her into the cave. The old woman was very slow as she moved around, but she was able to fix a complete supper. Once the meal was over, she told the children to go to bed. As they were climbing into bed, she asked, "Which of you is fatter? I need a bolster to prop up my chest." The brother said, "I am the heavier one." And so he became the bolster for the woman's bed. The girl slept at the other end of the bed, at her grandmother's feet. As soon as the girl stretched out in bed she felt something hairy touching her. She asked what it was. The woman replied, "It's just a worn-out sheepskin that belongs to Uncle Er. When it gets cold, I put it on to stay warm."

Around midnight, the girl began to hear the noise of someone eating, and she asked what was going on. The woman replied: "I am eating your dried jujuba fruits. It's cold out and the night is long. I'm old, and I can't go hungry." The girl said, "I'm also hungry." The woman handed her a berry, but in fact it was a human finger, cold and clammy.

The girl was terrified and leaped to her feet. "I have to go outside and find a place to go to the bathroom." The woman said, "There are many tigers out there in the forest. You might end up in a tiger's mouth. Be careful." The girl replied, "Tie a thick rope around my leg, and pull on it just in case things start to look dangerous."

The old woman thought that was a good plan. She tied a rope around the girl's leg and held on to one end of it. The girl took the other end of it and went outdoors. Then in the moonlight she noticed that what she thought was a rope was a long intestine. She quickly removed it from her leg and climbed up into a tree so that no one would find her. The woman waited for a long time. Her calls went unanswered.

She kept on calling, "Listen to me. Don't stay out there in the cold. Otherwise you will return home sick, and your mother will scold me for failing to take care of you." The old woman tugged on the cord again, and when she finally succeeded in pulling it back into the house, the girl was not at the end of it. The old woman wept and left the house to search for her. Before long she discovered the girl up in a tree. She called to her to come down but there was no answer. She decided to try to scare the girl by telling her that there were tigers in the trees. The girl answered, "I'm better off in the tree than on that mat. I know that you are really a tiger and that you ate my brother up without a second thought." The women stomped off in anger.

Before long, the sun began to rise, and a man transporting some goods passed by. The girl called out to him, "Save me from the tigers that are out here." The fellow put some clothes up in the tree and stole off with her. Later the woman returned with two tigers. She pointed up to the top of the tree and explained that a girl was up there. The tigers looked around in the tree and found the clothes. They were sure that the woman had tricked them and grew angry. Together they devoured the old woman and ran away.

Tsélané and the Marimo[†]

A man had a daughter named Tsélané. One day he set off with his family and his flocks to find fresh pastures. But his daughter refused to go with him. She said to her mother, "I'm not going. Our house is so pretty, with its white and red beads, that I can't leave."

Her mother said, "My child, since you are naughty, you will have to stay here all alone. But shut the door tight in case the Marimos[1] come and want to eat you." With that she went away. But in a few days she came back, bringing food for her daughter.

"Tsélané, my child, Tsélané, my child, take this bread, and eat it."

"I hear my mother, I can hear her. My mother speaks like an *ataga* bird, like the *tsuere* coming out of the woods."

For a long time the mother brought food to Tsélané. One day Tsélané heard a gruff voice saying, "Tsélané, my child, Tsélané, my child, take this bread and eat it." But she laughed and said, "That gruff voice is not my mother's voice. Go away, naughty Marimo." The

---

† T. Arbousset and F. Daumas, *Narrative of an Exploratory Tour to the North-East of the Colony of the Cape of Good Hope* (Cape Town: Struik, 1846), pp. 59–61. This translation has been adapted by the editor for this Norton Critical Edition.
1. A tribe of cannibals.

Marimo went away. He lit a big fire, took an iron hoe, made it red hot, and swallowed it to clear his voice. Then he came back and tried to fool Tsélané again. But he could not, for his voice was still not soft enough. So he heated another hoe, and swallowed it red-hot like the first. Then he came back and said in a still soft voice, "Tsélané, my child, Tsélané, my chee-ild, take this bread and eat it."

Tsélané thought it was her mother's voice and opened the door. The Marimo put her in his sack and walked off. Soon he felt thirsty, and, leaving his sack in the care of some little girls, he went to get some spirits in a village. The girls peeped into the sack, saw Tsélané in it, and ran to tell her mother, who happened to be nearby. The mother let her daughter out of the sack, and stuffed it with a dog, scorpions, vipers, bits of broken pots, and stones.

When the Marimo returned home with his sack, he opened it and was planning to cook and eat Tsélané. The dog and the vipers bit him, the scorpions stung him, the pot shards wounded him, and the stones bruised him. He rushed out, threw himself into a mud heap, and was changed into a tree. Bees made honey in its bark, and in the spring-time young girls came and gathered the honey for honey-cakes.

INTRODUCTION:
Beauty and the Beast

"Beauty and the Beast" may be a love story about the transformative power of compassion, but it also has an emotional ferocity that encodes messages about how we manage anxieties about monstrosity and alterity. The story ranks among the most popular of all fairy tales. It has been retold, adapted, remixed, and mashed up by countless storytellers, writers, filmmakers, philosophers, and poets. Unlike most other fairy tales, it accommodates a double trajectory, with a Beast in search of redemption, and a Beauty who learns the value of empathy. The two antithetical allegorical figures have traditionally resolved their differences in what can be seen as a heteronormative myth of romantic love, yet the story's representational energy is also channeled into the tense moral, economic, and emotional negotiations that complicate all courtship rituals.

"Animals are good to think with," as Claude Lévi-Strauss and countless other anthropologists remind us. "Beauty and the Beast" illustrates that truism supremely well, combining animal magnetism with human charms to create a symbolic story about what it means to form a partnership both passionate and principled. The odd couple featured in "Beauty and the Beast" is not so odd after all. The story is always better with the animal in it, as Yann Martel tells us in *Life of Pi*, and a curved mirror, one that distorts and takes us into the funhouse, is always more compelling—and often more true—than a purely reflective one. Nearly every culture tells "Beauty and the Beast" in one fashion or another, making the story new so that we think more and think harder about the stakes in partnerships and marriages today. There is good reason to keep renewing the terms of the tale, for it is the iconoclasts who keep the story alive, infusing it with values we hold today. The versions of "Beauty and the Beast" that follow offer an opportunity to pause and reflect on how the story has changed as it migrates across time and place.

A quick look at the tale-type index reveals that there are two versions of stories about courtships between humans and beasts: ATU 400 *The Man on a Quest for His Lost Wife* and ATU 425 *The Search for the Lost Husband*. What differentiates the one from the other? In the first, an adventurous young man must break the magic spell cast on the woman who will become his bride, while in the second, a young woman is on a mission to liberate the animal who will become her husband. In sum, we have stories about animal brides and animal grooms, yet what we call "Beauty and the Beast" insistently pairs a seductively attractive woman with a grotesquely misshapen monster. What Disney called a "tale as old as time" dominates our fairy-tale landscapes in ways that make us overlook the prominence of animal brides in our folkloric heritage.

There are two types of animal brides, with the first as the victim of abduction or seduction. These are the selkies, mermaids, seals, and swan maidens who marry mortals and become human, bearing children and keeping house until one day they are seized by a powerful sense of nostalgia. Putting their sealskins back on or donning their feathers, they abandon their families and follow the call of nature. Rooted in the idea that women have mysteriously close ties to nature, these stories reveal the dangers of what anthropologists call exogamy—marrying outside the tribe—as well as of consorting with outsiders in general. They form a sharp contrast with another set of animal brides, the many toads, birds, fish, monkeys, mice, tortoises, and dogs that seek men who can break the magic spell binding them to an animal state. Frequently they perform domestic chores, spontaneously and effortlessly carrying out prodigious tasks that demonstrate their clear superiority to the human competition.

"The Man on a Quest for His Lost Wife" is something of a misnomer, for the men who marry creatures of the earth, air, and sea often stumble upon their brides or are part of an elaborate plan orchestrated by those metamorphic women. In the Filipino "Chonguita" (p. 80), the protagonist does nothing but agree to marry a monkey, and he liberates her through an act of brutal force, hurling her against a wall. The Indian "Dog Bride" (p. 82) features a youth who witnesses a beautiful maiden shed her dog skin before bathing and resolves to marry her. In "The Enchanted Frog" (p. 77) from Spanish New Mexico, the youngest of three brothers leaves all the hard work to the frog and does nothing more than throw his amphibious bride multiple times into the sea.

One cultural variant of animal-bride stories is particularly powerful in its representation of the painful burdens of social disguise and domestic responsibilities. "The Swan Maiden" (p. 79), a tale widespread in Nordic regions, discloses the secretly oppressive nature of marriage with its attendant housekeeping and child-rearing duties. Swan maidens, domesticated by acts of violence, eventually seize the opportunity to return to a primordial natural condition. The tormented Nora of Henrik Ibsen's *Doll's House*, a figure identified again and again as a bird or creature of nature, was clearly inspired by the mythical swan maiden and her domestic tribulations. Instead of donning feathers (as swan maidens do), Nora rediscovers a diaphanous dancing dress and, after executing a frantic tarantella, takes leave of her dour husband, Torvald. The symbolic nexus connecting animal skins, costumes, and dancing is so prominent in this tale type that it points to a possible underlying link with Cinderella, Donkeyskin, and Catskin stories, showing us the dark side of what happens in a post-happily-ever-after phase.

Tales about swan maidens, selkies, seals, and mermaids may have been far more widespread than they are today. One critic has argued that the tales could once be found "in virtually every corner of the world," because in most cultures "woman *was* a symbolic outsider, was the *other*, and marriage demanded an intimate involvement in a world never quite her own."[1] Yet some animal brides lure their mortal husbands into their own worlds, hermetic spaces of timeless beauty where husbands cavort in domains of untold pleasures even as they are aware of an uncanny edge to their carefree bliss. Like Tannhäuser of medieval lore, who becomes Venus's captive in the caverns of her mountain abode, the Japanese fisherman Urashima and his many folkloric cousins dwell in a realm where they are the outsiders.

Like tales about animal brides, stories about animal grooms display an interesting bifurcation, with one set of stories going viral and mainstream, the other going dormant and, if not underground, then under the radar. The "classic" version of "Beauty and the Beast" gives us a compassionate heroine who redeems Beast with her tears. The less prominent counterpart to this tale (the best-known example of which is "East o' the Sun and West o' the Moon") features an adventurous heroine who undertakes a quest to recover a husband who has taken flight. Both sets bleach out details about the animal groom and give us a heroine enviable in the determined gusto with which she undertakes tasks. As if to compensate, illustrators and animators have turned Beast into an alluring chimera with a commanding sense of mystery and authority. In recent remediated versions, he has regained much of his nobility, status, and dignity.

The earliest known version of an animal-groom fairy tale appeared in the second century C.E. in Apuleius's *Transformations of Lucian: Otherwise Known as the Golden Ass*. The story of Cupid and Psyche is told by a "drunken and half-demented" woman to a young bride abducted by bandits on her wedding day. Perversely, the fairy tale is meant to "console" the distraught captive. While "Cupid and Psyche" shares many features with "Beauty and the Beast," as well as with "East o' the Sun and West o' the Moon," it deviates from what has

---

1. Barbara Fass Leavy, *In Search of the Swan Maiden: A Narrative on Folklore and Gender* (New York: New York UP, 1994), p. 2.

become our canonical version in a number of ways. Eros, the first "Beast," is only rumored to be a monster, and it is he who abandons Psyche, after her sisters urge her to take a look at the "enormous snake" that is her husband. More important, Psyche's story is what one critic has declared to be a "paradigm of female heroism."[2] The intrepid heroine, jilted by Cupid, never indulges in self-pity but sets off on an epic quest fraught with risks and requiring her to accomplish one task after another. Unlike her loquacious avatars in European versions of "Beauty and the Beast," Psyche is all action and no words. She undertakes a mission that not only requires the performance of feats (sorting grains, fetching a hank of golden wool, bringing Venus a jar of ice-cold water from the river Styx) but also demands that she renounce that quintessential feminine virtue known as compassion—the very trait that comes to the fore in European tales about beauties and beasts.

The animal-groom story most familiar to Anglo-American audiences was penned in 1756 by Madame de Beaumont (Jeanne-Marie Leprince de Beaumont) for her instructive *Magasin des Enfants*, designed to promote good manners in the young. Based on a baroque literary version of more than one hundred pages written in 1749 by Gabrielle-Suzanne de Villeneuve, Madame de Beaumont's child-friendly "Beauty and the Beast" (p. 39) reflects a desire to transform fairy tales from adult entertainments into parables of good behavior, vehicles for indoctrinating and enlightening children about the virtues of fine manners and good breeding, often by strategically inserting standard-issue platitudes into the narrative.

The lessons and moral imperatives encoded in Beaumont's "Beauty and the Beast" pertain almost exclusively to the tale's young women, who, in a coda, are showered with either praise or blame. As Angela Carter points out, the moral of Madame de Beaumont's tale has more to do with "being good" than with "doing well": "Beauty's happiness is founded on her abstract quality of virtue."[3] With nervous pedagogical zeal, Madame de Beaumont concludes her tale in a frenzy of plaudits and aspersions. Beauty has "preferred virtue to looks" and has "many virtues" along with a marriage "founded on virtue" (p. 49). Her two sisters, by contrast, have hearts "filled with malice and envy" (p. 49).

What exactly makes Beauty virtuous? To begin with, she seems possessed of a yen for acts of self-sacrifice. After discovering that Beast is willing to let her father go so long as one of his daughters shows up at the castle, she declares: "I feel fortunate to be able to sacrifice myself for him, since I will have the pleasure of saving my father and proving

---

2. Lee Edwards, "The Labors of Psyche: Toward a Theory of Female Heroism," *Critical Inquiry* 6 (1979): 37.
3. Angela Carter, "About the Stories," in *Sleeping Beauty and Other Favourite Fairy Tales*, ed. Angela Carter (Boston: Otter, 1991), p. 128.

my feelings of tenderness for him" (p. 43). To be sure, not all Beauties are such willing victims, valuing subordination over survival. In the Norwegian "East o' the Sun and West o' the Moon," the heroine has to be coaxed into submission with promises of wealth. She agrees to marry Beast (a white bear) because her father badgers her: "[He] kept on telling her of all the riches they would get and how well off she would be herself; and so at last she thought better of it."[4]

Marrying her daughter off to a swine does not appear to be a terrible prospect to a woman in Straparola's "Pig King" (p. 50), especially after she learns that the daughter stands to inherit a kingdom. And in words that read to us like a parody of paternal expectations, the king of Basile's "Serpent" pleads with his daughter to take a snake as her husband: "Finding myself, I know not how, bound by my promise, I beg you, if you are a dutiful daughter, to enable me to keep my word and to content yourself with the husband Heaven sends and I am forced to give you."[5]

That the desire for wealth and upward mobility motivates parents to turn their daughters over to beasts points to the possibility that these tales mirror social practices of an earlier age. Many an arranged marriage must have felt like being tethered to a monster, and the telling of stories like "Beauty and the Beast" may have furnished women with a socially acceptable channel for providing advice, comfort, and the consolations of imagination. Written at the dawn of the Enlightenment, Madame de Beaumont's tale attempted to steady the fears of young women, to reconcile them to the custom of arranged marriages, and to brace them for an alliance that required them to efface their own desires and to submit to the will of a "monster."

What many of these tales endorse in one cultural inflection after another is a strengthening of patriarchal norms, the subordination of female desire to male authority, and a glorification of filial duty and self-sacrifice. Angela Carter's "Courtship of Mr. Lyon" is unique in its effort to demystify and undo these "natural" virtues by subjecting them to grotesque exaggeration. Her heroine, who is "possessed by a sense of obligation to an unusual degree," perceives herself to be "Miss Lamb, spotless, sacrificial."[6] Untainted by any form of self-interest, she is ready, like the parade of folkloric brides preceding her, for any exercise that demands self-immolation.

Madame de Beaumont's "Beauty and the Beast" not only endorses obedience and self-denial but also doubles the significance of the

4. "East o' the Sun and West o' the Moon," in *The Blue Fairy Book*, ed. Andrew Lang (Harmondsworth: Penguin, Puffin, 1987), p. 2.
5. Giambattista Basile, "Serpent," in *The Pentamerone*, trans. Benedetto Croce, ed. N. M. Penzer (New York: Bodley Head, 1932), I:163.
6. Angela Carter, "The Courtship of Mr. Lyon," in *The Bloody Chamber and Other Stories* (Harmondsworth, UK: Penguin, 1993), p. 45.

interactions between the two characters by preaching the transformative power of empathy and the need to value essences over appearances. No matter how ugly and repulsive the beast may be, his character, mind, and soul will triumph and win the heart of a woman called, well, Beauty. That the latter message is sent in a tale with a heroine who embodies physical perfection and a seamless fit between external appearances and inner essences is an irony that seems to have been lost on the French governess. In men, external appearances and even charm count for nothing. "It is neither good looks nor great wit that makes a woman happy with her husband, but character, virtue, and kindness, and Beast has all those good qualities. I may not be in love with him, but I feel respect, friendship, and gratitude toward him" (p. 48). In an anonymous version of 1818, Beauty delivers a similar speech attesting to the way in which Beast's kindness makes his "deformity" virtually disappear.

There is an upside to what feels to us at times like thinly disguised treacle and misleading advice. Earlier folk versions of the story did not engage in the kind of messaging found in Madame de Beaumont's story. But they did indulge in tableaus of sexual assault and grotesque violence. That there are multiple alternatives to the social norms presented in "Beauty and the Beast" becomes evident not only in recent recastings of the story by Angela Carter and others but also in earlier versions that found their way into print. Consider the reckless possibilities inherent in tales about girls who marry pigs, hedgehogs, snakes, frogs, or donkeys and the ways in which folk raconteurs no doubt elaborated on courtship rituals and grew expansive about the wedding night. When the transformation from beast to man does not take place until the morning after—or many mornings later, as in Straparola's "Pig King" in the Neapolitan *Pleasant Nights*—it is not difficult to extract humor from the bedroom scenes:

> When the time had come to retire for the night, the bride went to bed and awaited her unseemly spouse. As soon as he climbed into bed, she raised the cover and told him to come lie next to her and put his head upon the pillow. . . .
>
> In the morning, the pig got up and ranged abroad to pasture, as was his wont. Not much later the queen entered the bride's chamber, expecting to find that she had met with the same fate as her sisters. But then she saw her lying in the bed, muddy as it was, looking entirely pleased and contented. And she thanked the Lord that her son had at last found a spouse that suited him.

Imagine how the grotesqueries of the Russian "Snotty goat" ("snot ran down his nose, slobber ran down his mouth")[7] and the Italian

---

7. Alexander Afanasev, "The Snotty Goat," in *Russian Fairy Tales*, trans. Norbert Guterman (New York: Pantheon, 1945), p. 201.

"Mouse with the Long Tail" ("a tail a mile long that smelled to high heaven")[8] might have enlivened long evenings devoted to household chores. That the jokes could take a crude, vulgar turn at the expense of the fabled beauties in the tales rarely curbed the impulse to improvise, embellish, and entertain. Here is a scene from "Hans My Hedgehog," a tale collected by the Brothers Grimm for the entertainment of children: Hans collects a princess as a reward and returns home with her. On the road, he pulls off her "beautiful clothes" and sticks her with his quills until she is "covered in blood." "That's what you get for trying to trick me," he tells her, "Go back home. I no longer want you."

These animal-groom stories offered more than just the opportunity for pointed wisecracks, spirited banter, and bawdy humor. The heroine of "The Snotty Goat," for example, is no self-effacing Beauty. She is described as "not a bit squeamish," willing to tolerate the vulgar habits of her betrothed yet also defiantly slapping the cheeks of anyone who tries to belittle her. Defiance is, in fact, a characteristic trait of many of the folkloric heroines who find themselves pestered by beasts. In the Grimms' "The Three Little Birds," the heroine and her two brothers encounter a large black dog that turns into a "handsome prince" after being struck in the face. The fairy-tale heroine who reacts with aversion, loathing, or anger to the beastly exterior of her prospective spouse seems no less likely to effect a magical transformation than her tenderly affectionate or compassionate counterpart.

The Grimms' "Frog King, or Iron Heinrich" (p. 55), although classified by folklorists as a tale type separate from "Beauty and the Beast," bears a distinct family resemblance to it. Like Beauty, the princess in the Grimms' tale encounters an animal suitor, but, despite her father's admonition ("You shouldn't scorn someone who helped you when you were in trouble" [p. 57]), she balks at the idea of letting the frog into her bed. Flying into a rage, she hurls the erotically ambitious frog against the wall: "Now you'll get your rest, you disgusting frog!" (p. 58).

Some variant forms of the Grimms' tale feature a princess who admits the frog to her chambers despite his revolting appearance, but most give us a princess who is perfectly capable of committing acts rivaling the cold-blooded violence of dashing a creature against a wall. Scottish and Gaelic versions of "The Frog King" show the princess beheading her suitor. A Polish variant replaces the frog with a snake and recounts in lavish detail the princess's act of tearing the creature in two. A more tame Lithuanian text requires the burning of the snake's skin before the prince is freed from his reptilian state. Acts of passion as much as acts of compassion have the power to

---

8. "The Mouse with the Long Tail," in *Italian Folktales*, trans. George Martin, comp. Italo Calvino (New York: Pantheon, 1980), p. 653.

disenchant. Although the princess in "The Frog King" is self-absorbed, ungrateful, and cruel, in the end she does as well for herself as all of the modest, obedient, and charitable Beauties that follow in the wake of Madame de Beaumont's story.

Tales about animal brides and animal grooms stand as models for plots rich in opportunities for expressing anxieties about marriage. Over the years, however, Beast has usurped the leading role. As Marina Warner points out, "the attractions of the wild, and of the wild brother in twentieth-century culture, cannot be overestimated; as the century advanced, in the cascade of deliberate revisions of the tale, Beauty stands in need of the Beast, rather than vice versa, and the Beast's beastliness is good, even adorable."[9] While eighteenth- and nineteenth-century versions of the tale celebrated the civilizing power of feminine virtue and its triumph over crude animal instincts, our own culture hails Beast's heroic defiance of civilization, with all its discontents, from the economic to the ecological.

The happy ending to Angela Carter's "Tiger's Bride" (p. 58) reverses the traditional terms of "Beauty and the Beast." Fulfilling a contract requiring her to strip before a tiger masquerading as a man, the heroine approaches her oppressor as if offering "the key to a peaceable kingdom in which his appetite need not be my extinction" (p. 74). Haunted by the "fear of devourment" (p. 74), she nonetheless has the temerity to approach Beast, and, in a flash of impressive courage, submits to a bargain that subjects her to something "harsh" and "abrasive":

> He dragged himself closer and closer to me, until I felt the harsh velvet of his head against my hand, then a tongue, abrasive as sandpaper. "He will lick the skin off me!"
> And each stroke of his tongue ripped off skin after successive skin, all the skins of a life in the world, and left behind a nascent patina of shining hairs. My earrings turned back to water and trickled down my shoulders; I shrugged the drops off my beautiful fur. (p. 74)

Beast delivers Beauty from the abject condition of being human as the artificiality of culture, symbolized by the earrings, yields to nature and returns to its primordial state.

Jon Scieszka plays fast and loose with the ground rules of folk narratives in his recasting of "The Frog King" for children, *The Frog Prince, Continued*. His story, which begins *after* the transformation into a prince, reveals "the shocking truth about life 'happily ever after.'"[1]

---

9. Marina Warner, "Go Be a Beast: Beauty and the Beast II," in *From the Beast to the Blonde: On Fairy Tales and Their Tellers* (New York: Farrar, Straus & Giroux, 1994), p. 307.
1. Jon Scieszka, *The Frog Prince, Continued* (New York: Viking, 1991).

"The princess and the prince live in such bitter marital discord that the prince flees, searching for a witch who can turn him back into a frog." Yet in the end, as in the conclusion to "The Tiger's Bride," an authentic happy end is found in a return to nature for the two partners: "The Prince kissed the Princess. They both turned into frogs. And they hopped off happily ever after."[2] Scieszka has done more than give a clever new twist to an old tale. He has effected a profound ideological shift, transforming the tale from one that celebrates the superiority of culture over nature to one that concedes nature's triumph over culture. Human beings, as it turns out, are the real beasts.

The profound shift in cultural values registered in Carter's "Tiger's Bride" and Scieszka's *Frog Prince, Continued* also finds expression in the Disney Studio version of *Beauty and the Beast*. The true villain in this cinematic tale is Gaston (Beast's rival for Belle), a man who endorses the rigid, self-destructive logic of Western civilization and sanctions ecological depredation. Disney's Beast, virile yet sensitive, remains attuned to nature and open to the notion of regeneration by cultivating his feminine side. The Disney version in this particular case gives us a Beast-centered narrative devoted almost exclusively to the development of the male figure in the story. Warner finds in Belle nothing but a cover for telling the story of Beast: "While the Disney version ostensibly tells the story of the feisty, strong-willed heroine, and carries the audience along on the wave of her dash, her impatient ambitions, her bravery, her self-awareness, and her integrity, the principal burden of the film's message concerns maleness, its various faces and masks, and, in the spirit of romance, it offers hope of regeneration from within the unregenerate male."[3]

The Hollywood dream factory has also rebelled against the literary tradition of compassionate Beauties and abject Beasts. It seems almost ironic that Disney's 1991 film is in the vanguard of that rebellion, turning Beast into a charismatic creature so winning in his animal state that Beauty seems mildly disappointed with the Fabio-lookalike who stands before her after the transformation. Dreamworks' computer-animated *Shrek* (2001) takes matters a step further when the heroine finds her Beast so attractive that she turns herself into a matching green monster. To be sure I am omitting discussion of a host of other cinematic rescriptings, from Jean Cocteau's *La Belle et la Bête* (1946) to Mike Nicholson's *Wolf* (1994) and Daniel Barnz's *Beastly* (2011). But a look at what Disney and Dreamworks are up to goes far toward clarifying the uses of enchantment and how Beast has reclaimed his animal magnetism

2. Ibid.
3. Warner, "Go Be a Beast," p. 314.

even as Beauty remains an allegorical figure that compassionately embraces otherness.

Although Disney's *Beauty and the Beast* marks a dramatic intervention in how the story has been framed, the lyrics to the most prominent song in the film emphasize the truth of the old refrain "*Plus ça change, plus c'est le même chose.*" Belle and Beast display their ballroom skills to the tune of Angela Lansbury singing "Tale as old as time / True as it can be." The song itself is "as old as rhyme" and all is "ever just the same" and "ever just as sure / as the sun will rise." And yet the kaleidoscope has been given a decisive critical turn, one that reconfigures the relationship between heroine and beast, with a young woman who stands up to Beast, even if his overpowering visual dominance shrinks her own importance.

Animal brides and animal grooms function as mediators between nature and culture. They are "impossible" hybrid creatures that help us negotiate that divide, to construct our own realities and identities through the dialectical interplay between the animal and human kingdom. Stories featuring these creatures, often as charismatic as they are monstrous, take up matters both primal and mythical as well as domestic and down to earth. As humans, we have distanced ourselves from nature, set ourselves apart as a separate breed, and yet we are perpetually drawn to the wild side, searching for an understanding of what we share with beasts even as we try to discover what makes us human.

JEANNE-MARIE LEPRINCE DE BEAUMONT

Beauty and the Beast[†]

Once upon a time there was a very wealthy merchant who lived with his six children, three boys and three girls. Since he was a man of intelligence and good sense, he spared no expense in educating his children and hiring all kinds of tutors for them. His daughters were all very beautiful, but the youngest was admired by everyone. When she was little, people used to refer to her as "the beautiful child." The name "Beauty" stuck, and, as a result, her two sisters were always very jealous. The youngest daughter was not only more beautiful than her sisters, she was also better behaved. The two older sisters were vain and proud because the family had money. They tried to act like ladies of the court and paid no attention at all to

---

† Jeanne-Marie Leprince de Beaumont, "La Belle et la Bête," in *Le Magasin des Enfants* (London: Haberkorn, 1756). Translated for the first edition of this Norton Critical Edition by Maria Tatar. Copyright © 1999 by Maria Tatar.

girls from merchant families. They chose to spend time only with
people of rank. Every day they went to balls, to the theater, to the
park, and they made fun of their younger sister, who spent most of
her time reading good books.

Since the girls were known to be very wealthy, many prominent
merchants were interested in marrying them. But the two older
sisters always insisted that they would never marry unless they found
a duke or, at the very least, a count. Beauty (as I noted, this was the
name of the youngest daughter) very politely thanked all those who
proposed to her, but she told them that she was still too young for
marriage and that she planned to keep her father company for some
years to come.

Out of the blue, the merchant lost his fortune, and he had nothing
left but a small country house quite far from town. With tears in his
eyes, he told his children that they would have to live in that house
from now on and that, by working there like peasants, they could
manage to make ends meet. The two elder daughters said that they
did not want to leave town and that they had many admirers who
would be more than happy to marry them, even though they were
no longer wealthy. But the fine young ladies were wrong. Their
admirers had lost all interest in them now that they were poor. And
since they were disliked because of their pride, people said: "Those
two girls don't deserve our sympathy. It's quite satisfying to see pride
take a fall. Let them play the ladies while tending their sheep."

At the same time, people were saying: "As for Beauty, we are very
upset by her misfortune. She's such a good girl! She speaks so kindly
to the poor. She is so sweet and sincere."

There were a number of gentlemen who would have been happy
to marry Beauty, even though she didn't have a penny. She told them
that she could not bring herself to abandon her poor father in his
distress and that she would go with him to the country in order to
comfort him and help him with his work. Poor Beauty had been
upset at first by the loss of the family fortune, but she said to herself: "No matter how much I cry, my tears won't bring our fortune
back. I must try to be happy without it."

When they arrived at the country house, the merchant and his
three sons began working the land. Beauty got up every day at four
in the morning and started cleaning the house and preparing breakfast for the family. It was hard for her at first, because she was not
used to working like a servant. At the end of two months, however,
she became stronger, and the hard work made her very healthy. After
finishing her housework, she read or sang while spinning. Her two
sisters, on the other hand, were bored to tears. They got up at ten in
the morning, took walks all day long, and talked endlessly about the
beautiful clothes they used to wear.

"Look at our sister," they said to each other. "She is so stupid and such a simpleton that she is perfectly satisfied with her miserable lot."

The good merchant did not agree with his daughters. He knew that Beauty could stand out in company in a way that her sisters could not. He admired the virtue of his daughter, above all her patience. The sisters not only made her do all the housework, they also insulted her whenever they could.

The family had lived an entire year in seclusion when the merchant received a letter informing him that a ship containing his merchandise had just arrived safely in its home port. The news made the two elder sisters giddy with excitement, for they thought they would finally be able to leave the countryside where they were so bored. When they saw that their father was ready to leave, they begged him to bring them dresses, furs, laces, and all kinds of baubles. Beauty did not ask for anything, because she thought that all the money from the merchandise would not be enough to buy everything her sisters wanted.

"Don't you want me to buy anything for you?" asked her father.

"You are so kind to think of me," Beauty answered. "Can you bring me a rose, for there are none here?"

It was not that Beauty was anxious to have a rose, but she did not want to set an example that would make her sisters look bad. Her sisters would have said that she was asking for nothing in order to make herself look good.

The good man left home, but when he arrived at the port he found that there was a lawsuit over his merchandise. After much trouble, he set off for home as impoverished as he had been on his departure. He had only thirty miles left to go and was already overjoyed at the prospect of seeing his children again when he had to cross a dense forest and got lost. There was a fierce snowstorm, and the wind was so strong that it knocked him off his horse twice. When night fell, he was sure that he was going to die of hunger or of the cold or that he would be eaten by the wolves that he could hear howling all around. All of a sudden he saw a bright light at the end of a long avenue of trees. The bright light seemed very far away. He walked in its direction and realized that it was coming from an immense castle that was completely lit up. The merchant thanked God for sending help, and he hurried toward the castle. He was surprised that no one was in the courtyard. His horse went inside a large, open stable, where he found some hay and oats. The poor animal, near death from hunger, began eating voraciously. The merchant tied the horse up in the stable and walked toward the house, where not a soul was in sight. Once he entered the great hall, however, he found a warm fire and a table laden with food, with just a single place setting. Since the rain and snow had soaked him to the bone, he went over to the fire to get dry. He thought to himself: "The master of the house, or his servants, will not be offended by the liberties I am taking. No doubt someone will be back soon."

He waited a long time. Once the clock struck eleven and there was still no one in sight, he could not resist the pangs of hunger and, trembling with fear, he took a chicken and ate it all up in two big bites. He also drank several glasses of wine and, feeling more daring, he left the great hall and crossed many large, magnificently furnished apartments. Finally he found a room with a good bed. Since it was past midnight and he was exhausted, he took it upon himself to close the door and go to bed.

When he woke up the next day, it was already ten in the morning. He was greatly surprised to find clean clothes in place of the ones that had been completely ruined by the rain. "Surely," he thought to himself, "this palace belongs to some good fairy who has taken pity on me."

He looked out the window and saw that it was no longer snowing. Before his eyes a magnificent vista of gardens and flowers unfolded. He returned to the great hall where he had dined the night before and found a small table with a cup of hot chocolate on it. "Thank you, Madame Fairy," he said out loud, "for being so kind as to remember my breakfast."

After finishing his hot chocolate, the good man left to go find his horse. Passing beneath a magnificent arbor of roses, he remembered that Beauty had asked him for a rose, and he plucked one from a branch with many flowers on it. At that very moment, he heard a loud noise and saw a beast coming toward him. It looked so dreadful that he almost fainted.

"You are very ungrateful," said the beast in a terrible voice. "I have saved your life by sheltering you in my castle, and you repay me by stealing my roses, which I love more than anything in the world. You will have to pay for your offense. I'm going to give you exactly a quarter of an hour to beg God's forgiveness."

The merchant fell to his knees and, hands clasped, pleaded with the beast: "My Liege, pardon me. I did not think I would be offending you by plucking a rose for my daughter, who asked me to bring her one or two."

"I am not called 'My Liege,'" said the monster. "My name is Beast. I don't like flattery, and I prefer that people say what they think. So don't try to move me with your compliments. But you said that you have some daughters. I am prepared to forgive you if one of your daughters consents to die in your place. Don't argue with me. Just go. If your daughters refuse to die for you, swear that you will return in three days."

The good man was not about to sacrifice one of his daughters to this hideous monster, but he thought: "At least I will have the pleasure of embracing them one last time."

He swore that he would return, and Beast told him that he could leave whenever he wished. "But I don't want you to go empty-handed," he added. "Return to the room in which you slept. There you will find a large empty chest. You can fill it up with whatever you like, and I will have it delivered to your door."

The beast withdrew, and the good man thought to himself: "If I must die, I will at least have the consolation of leaving something for my poor children to live on."

The merchant returned to the room where he had slept. He filled the great chest that Beast had described with the many gold pieces he found there. After he found his horse in the stable, he left the palace with a sadness equal to the joy he had felt on entering it. His horse instinctively took one of the forest paths, and in just a few hours, the good man arrived at his little house. His children gathered around him, but instead of responding to their caresses, the merchant burst into tears as he gazed on them. In his hand, he was holding the branch of roses he had brought for Beauty. He gave it to her and said: "Beauty, take these roses. They have cost your poor father dearly."

Then the merchant told his family about the woeful events that had befallen him. Upon hearing the tale, the two sisters uttered loud cries and said derogatory things to Beauty, who was not crying: "See what the pride of this little creature has brought down on us!" they said. "Why didn't she ask for fine clothes the way we did. No, she wanted to get all the attention. She's responsible for Father's death, and she's not even shedding a tear!"

"That would be quite pointless," Beauty replied. "Why should I shed tears about Father when he is not going to die. Since the monster is willing to accept one of his daughters, I am prepared to risk all his fury. I feel fortunate to be able to sacrifice myself for him, since I will have the pleasure of saving my father and proving my feelings of tenderness for him."

"No, sister," said her three brothers. "You won't die. We will find this monster, and we are prepared to die under his blows if we are unable to slay him."

"Don't count on that, children," said the merchant. "The beast's power is so great that I don't have the least hope of killing him. I am moved by the goodness of Beauty's heart, but I refuse to risk her life. I'm old and don't have many years left. I will only lose a few years of my life, and I don't regret losing them for your sake, my dear children."

"Rest assured, Father," said Beauty, "that you will not go to that palace without me. You can't keep me from following you. I may be young, but I am not all that attached to life, and I would rather be devoured by that monster than die of the grief which your loss would cause me."

It was no use arguing with Beauty. She was determined to go to the palace. Her sisters were delighted, for the virtues of their younger sister had filled them with a good deal of envy. The merchant was so preoccupied by the sad prospect of losing his daughter that he forgot about the chest he had filled with gold. But as soon as he repaired to his room to get some sleep, he was astonished to find it beside his bed. He decided not to tell his children that he had become rich, for his daughters would then want to return to town, and he was determined to die in the country. He did confide his secret to Beauty, who told him that several gentlemen had come during his absence and that two of them wanted to marry her sisters. Beauty begged her father to let them marry. She was so kind that she still loved her sisters with all her heart and forgave them the evil they had done her.

When Beauty left with her father, the two mean sisters rubbed their eyes with an onion in order to draw tears. But the brothers cried real tears, as did the merchant. Only Beauty did not cry at all, because she did not want to make everyone even more sad.

The horse took the road to the palace, and, when night fell, they could see that it was all lit up. The horse went by itself to the stable, and the good man went with his daughter into the hall, where there was a magnificently set table with two place settings. The merchant did not have the stomach to eat, but Beauty, forcing herself to appear calm, sat down and served her father. "You see, Father," she said while forcing a laugh, "the beast wants to fatten me up before eating me, since he paid so dearly for me."

After they had dined, they heard a loud noise, and the merchant tearfully bid adieu to his poor daughter, for he knew it was the beast. Beauty could not help but tremble at the sight of this horrible figure, but she tried as hard as she could to stay calm. The monster asked her if she had come of her own free will and, trembling, she replied that she had.

"You are very kind," said Beast, "and I am very grateful to you. As for you, my good man, get out of here by tomorrow morning and don't think of coming back here ever again. Goodbye, Beauty."

"Goodbye, Beast," she replied. Suddenly the monster vanished.

"Oh my daughter!" cried the merchant, embracing Beauty. "I am half dead with fear. Believe me, you have to let me stay," he said.

"No, Father," Beauty said firmly. "You must go tomorrow morning and leave me to the mercy of heaven. Heaven may still take pity on me."

They both went to bed thinking that they would not be able to sleep all night long, but they had hardly gotten into their beds when their eyes closed. While she was sleeping, Beauty saw a woman who said to her: "I am pleased with your kind heart, Beauty. The good deed you have done in saving your father's life will not go unrewarded."

Upon waking, Beauty recounted this dream to her father. While it comforted him a little, it did not keep him from crying out loud when he had to leave his dear daughter. After he had left, Beauty sat down in the great hall and began to cry as well. But since she was courageous, she put herself in God's hands and resolved not to bemoan her fate during the short time she had left to live. Convinced that Beast planned to eat her that very evening, she decided to walk around the grounds and to explore the castle while awaiting her fate. She could not help but admire the castle's beauty, and she was very surprised to find a door upon which was written: "Beauty's Room." She opened the door hastily and was dazzled by the radiant beauty of that room. She was especially impressed by a huge bookcase, a harpsichord, and various music books. "Someone does not want me to get bored!" she said softly. Then she realized: "If I had only one hour to live here, no one would have made such a fuss about the room." This thought lifted her spirits.

She opened the bookcase and saw a book, on the cover of which was written in gold letters: "Your wish is our command. Here you are queen and mistress."

"Alas," she sighed, "I only wish to see my poor father again and to know what he's doing now."

She had said this to herself, so you can imagine how surprised she was when she looked in a large mirror and saw her father arriving at his house with a dejected expression. Her sisters went out to meet him, and, despite the faces they made in order to look as if they were distressed, they were visibly happy to have lost their sister. A moment later, everything in the mirror vanished. Beauty could not help thinking that Beast was most obliging and that she had nothing to fear from him.

At noon, Beauty found the table set and, during her meal, she heard an excellent concert, even though she could not see a soul. That evening, as she was about to sit down at the table, she heard Beast making noises, and she could not help but tremble.

"Beauty," said the monster, "will you let me watch you dine?"

"You are my master," said Beauty, trembling.

"No, you are the only mistress here," replied Beast. "If I bother you, order me to go, and I will leave at once. Tell me, don't you find me very ugly?"

"Yes, I do," said Beauty. "I don't know how to lie. But I do think that you are very kind."

"You are right," said the monster. "But in addition to being ugly, I also lack intelligence. I know very well that I am nothing but a beast."

"You can't be a beast," replied Beauty, "if you know that you lack intelligence. A fool never knows that he is stupid."

"Go ahead and eat, Beauty," said the monster, "and try not to be bored in your house, for everything here is yours, and I would be upset if you were not happy."

"You are very kind," said Beauty. "I swear to you that I am completely pleased with your good heart. When I think of it, you no longer seem ugly to me."

"Oh, of course," Beast replied. "I have a kind heart, but I am still a monster."

"There are certainly men more monstrous than you," said Beauty. "I like you better, even with your looks, than men who hide false, corrupt, and ungrateful hearts behind charming manners."

"If I were intelligent," said Beast, "I would pay you a great compliment to thank you. But I am so stupid that all I can say is that I am very much obliged."

Beauty ate with a good appetite. She no longer dreaded the monster, but she thought that she would die of fright when he said: "Beauty, would you be my wife?"

It took her a moment to get to the point of answering. She was afraid to provoke the monster by refusing him. Trembling, she said to him: "No, Beast."

At that moment, the poor monster meant to sigh deeply, but he made such a frightful whistling sound that it echoed throughout the palace. Beauty felt better soon, however, because Beast, turning to look at her from time to time, left the room and said adieu in a sad voice. Finding herself alone, Beauty felt great compassion for poor Beast. "Alas," she said, "it is too bad he is so ugly, for he is so kind."

Beauty spent three peaceful months at the castle. Every evening, Beast paid her a visit and, while she was eating, entertained her with good plain talk, though not with what the world would call wit. Each day Beauty discovered new good qualities in the monster. Once she began seeing him every day, she became accustomed to his ugliness, and, far from fearing his arrival, she often looked at her watch to see if it was nine o'clock yet. Beast never failed to appear at that hour. There was only one thing that still bothered Beauty. The monster, before leaving, always asked her if she wanted to be his wife, and he seemed deeply wounded when she refused.

One day she said to him: "You are making me feel upset, Beast. I would like to be able to marry you, but I am far too honest to allow you to believe that that could ever happen. I will always be your friend. Try to be satisfied with that."

"I will have to," Beast replied. "I don't flatter myself, and I know that I'm horrible looking, but I love you very much. However, I am very happy that you want to stay here. Promise me that you will never leave."

Beauty blushed at these words. She had seen in her mirror that her father was sick at heart at having lost her. She had been hoping to see him again. "I can promise you that I will never leave you," she said to Beast. "But right now I am so desperate to see my father again that I would die of grief if you were to deny me this wish."

"I would rather die myself than cause you pain," said Beast. "I will send you back to your father. Stay there, and your poor beast will die of grief."

"No," Beauty said, bursting into tears, "I love you too much to be the cause of your death. I promise to return in a week. You have let me see that my sisters are married and that my brothers have left to serve in the army. Father is living all alone. Let me stay with him for just a week."

"You will be there tomorrow morning," said Beast. "But don't forget your promise. All you have to do is put your ring on the table before going to sleep when you want to return. Good-bye, Beauty."

As was his habit, Beast sighed deeply after speaking, and Beauty went to bed feeling very sad to see him so dejected. The next morning, on waking up, she was in her father's house. She pulled a cord at the side of her bed and a bell summoned a servant, who uttered a loud cry upon seeing her. The good man of the house came running when he heard the cry, and he almost died of joy when he saw his beloved daughter. They held each other tight for over a quarter of an hour. After the first wave of excitement subsided, Beauty realized that she didn't have any clothes to go out in. But the servant told her that she had just discovered in the room next door a huge trunk full of silk dresses embroidered with gold and encrusted with diamonds. Beauty thanked Beast for his thoughtfulness. She took the least ornate of the dresses and told the servant to lock up the others, for she wanted to make a present of them to her sisters. Hardly had she spoken these words when the chest disappeared. When her father told her that Beast wanted her to keep everything for herself, the dresses and the chest reappeared on the spot.

While Beauty was getting dressed, her two sisters learned about her arrival and rushed to the scene with their husbands. Both sisters were very unhappy. The older one had married a remarkably handsome gentleman, but he was so enamored of his own looks that he spent all day in front of the mirror. The other one had married a man of great wit, but he used it to infuriate everybody, first and foremost his wife. Beauty's sisters were so mortified that they felt ready to die when they saw her dressed like a princess and more beautiful than the bright day. Beauty tried in vain to shower them with attention, but nothing could restrain their jealousy, which only increased when Beauty told them how happy she was. These two envious women walked down to the garden so that they could weep freely.

They both asked themselves: "Why should this little beast enjoy more happiness than we do? Aren't we more likable than she is?"

"Dearest sister," the older one said, "I have an idea. Let's try to keep Beauty here for more than a week. Her stupid beast will get angry when he sees that she has broken her promise, and maybe he'll eat her up."

"You're right," the other one replied. "To make that work, we will have to shower her with affection and act as if we are delighted to have her here."

Having made this decision, the two nasty creatures returned to Beauty's room and showed her so much affection that she nearly wept for joy. When the week had gone by, the two sisters started tearing out their hair and performed so well that Beauty promised to stay another four or five days. At the same time she felt guilty about the grief she was causing poor Beast, whom she loved with all her heart and missed seeing. On the tenth night she spent at her father's house, she dreamed that she was in a garden of the palace when she saw Beast lying in the grass, nearly dead and reproaching her for her ingratitude. Beauty woke up with a start and began crying. "Aren't I terrible," she said, "for causing grief to someone who has done so much to please me? Is it his fault that he's ugly and lacks intelligence? He is kind. That's worth more than anything else. Why haven't I wanted to marry him? I would be more happy with him than my sisters are with their husbands. It is neither good looks nor great wit that makes a woman happy with her husband, but character, virtue, and kindness, and Beast has all those good qualities. I may not be in love with him, but I feel respect, friendship, and gratitude toward him. If I were to make him unhappy, my lack of appreciation would make me feel guilty for the rest of my life."

With these words, Beauty got up, wrote a few lines to her father to explain why she was leaving, put her ring on the table, and went back to bed. She had hardly gotten into bed when she fell sound asleep. And when she awoke in the morning, she was overjoyed to find herself in Beast's palace. She dressed up in magnificent clothes just to make him happy and spent the day feeling bored to death while waiting for the clock to strike nine. But the clock struck nine in vain. Beast was nowhere in sight.

Beauty feared that she might be responsible for his death. She ran into every room of the castle, crying out loud. She was in a state of despair. After having searched everywhere, she remembered her dream and ran into the garden, toward the canal where she had seen Beast in her sleep. She found poor Beast stretched out unconscious, and she was sure that he was dead. Feeling no revulsion at his looks, she threw herself on him and, realizing that his heart was still beating, she got some water from the canal and threw it on him. Beast opened his eyes and told Beauty: "You forgot your promise. The thought of having lost you made me decide to starve myself. But now I will die happy, for I have the pleasure of seeing you one more time."

"No, my dear Beast, you will not die," said Beauty. "You will live and become my husband. From this moment on, I give you my hand in marriage, and I swear that I belong only to you. Alas, I thought that I felt only friendship for you, but the grief I am feeling makes me realize that I can't live without you."

Scarcely had Beauty uttered these words when the castle became radiant with light. Fireworks and music alike signaled a celebration. But these attractions did not engage her attention for long. She turned back to look at her dear beast, whose perilous condition made her tremble with fear. How great was her surprise when she discovered that Beast had disappeared and that a young prince more beautiful than the day was bright was lying at her feet, thanking her for having broken a magic spell. Even though she was worried about the prince, she could not keep herself from asking about Beast. "You see him at your feet," the prince said. "An evil fairy condemned me to remain in that form until a beautiful girl would consent to marry me. She barred me from revealing my intelligence. You were the only person in the world kind enough to be touched by the goodness of my character. Even by offering you a crown, I still can't fully discharge the obligation I feel to you."

Pleasantly surprised, Beauty offered her hand to the handsome prince to help him get up. Together, they went to the castle, and Beauty nearly swooned with joy when she found her father and the entire family in the large hall. The beautiful lady who had appeared to her in a dream had transported them to the castle.

"Beauty," said the lady, who was a grand fairy, "come and receive the reward for your wise choice. You preferred virtue to looks and intelligence, and so you deserve to see those qualities united in a single person. You will become a noble queen, and I hope that sitting on a throne will not destroy your many virtues. As for you, my dear ladies," the fairy continued, speaking to Beauty's two sisters, "I know your hearts and all the malice that is in them. You will be turned into two statues, but you will keep your senses beneath the stone that envelops you. You will be transported to the door of your sister's palace, and I can think of no better punishment than being a witness to her happiness. You will not return to your former state until you recognize your faults. I fear that you may remain statues forever. You can correct pride, anger, gluttony, and laziness. But a miracle is needed to convert a heart filled with malice and envy."

The fairy waved her wand, and everyone there was transported to the great hall of the prince's realm, where the subjects were overjoyed to see him. The prince married Beauty, who lived with him for a long time in perfect happiness, for their marriage was founded on virtue.

GIOVAN FRANCESCO STRAPAROLA

The Pig King[†]

Fair ladies,[1] if we were to spend a thousand years giving thanks to our Creator for having made us in the form of humans and not of brute beasts, we could still not be grateful enough. This reflection calls to mind the story of one who was born a pig, but afterward became a comely youth. Nevertheless, to his dying day he was known to the people over whom he ruled as King Pig.

You must know, dear ladies, that Galeotto, King of Anglia, was a man highly blessed in worldly wealth, and in his wife, Ersilia, the daughter of Matthias, king of Hungary, a princess who, in virtue and beauty, outshone all the other ladies of the time. And Galeotto was a wise king, ruling his land so that no one ever complained about him. Although they had been married several years, the couple had no children and for that reason were much aggrieved. While Ersilia was walking one day in her gardens she suddenly felt weary, and, catching sight of a spot covered with fresh green grass, she walked over to it and sat down. Overcome by fatigue and soothed by the sweet singing of the birds in the green foliage, she fell asleep.

While she was sleeping, it happened that three fairies who did not think much of humans walked by. When they beheld the sleeping queen, they stopped, and, gazing upon her beauty, took counsel together how they might bless her and yet also curse her. When they agreed to a plan, the first cried out, "I command that no man shall be able to harm her, and that, the next time she lies with her husband, she will be with child and bear a son who shall not have his equal in all the world for beauty." Then the second said, "I command that no one shall ever have the power to offend her and that the prince who shall be born of her shall be gifted with every virtue under the sun." And the third said, "And I command that she shall be the wisest among women, but that the son whom she conceives shall be born in the skin of a pig, with a pig's ways and manners, and in this state he shall be constrained to remain until he shall have taken a woman to wife three times."

[†] Giovan Francesco Straparola, "The Pig King," in *The Facetious Nights of Straparola,* trans. W. G. Waters (London: Society of Bibliophiles, 1891).

1. The tales in Straparola's collection are told by a circle of ladies living in exile in Murano to pass the time during the nights of the Venetian carnival.

As soon as the three fairies had flown away, Ersilia woke up, and right away she arose and returned to the palace, taking with her the flowers she had picked. Not many days passed before she knew herself to be with child, and when the time of her delivery arrived, she gave birth to a son with members like those of a pig and not of a human being. When tidings of this prodigy came to the ears of the king, he was greatly saddened. Bearing in mind how good and wise his queen was, he often felt moved to put this offspring of hers to death and cast it into the sea so that she might be spared the shame of having given birth to him. But when he debated in his mind and considered that this son, whatever he looked like, was of his own begetting, he put aside the cruel purpose which he had been harboring, and, seized with pity and grief, he made up his mind that the son should be brought up and nurtured like a rational being and not as a brute beast. The child, therefore, being nursed with the greatest care, would often be brought to the queen, and he would put his little snout and his little hooves in his mother's lap. Moved by natural affection, she would caress him by stroking his bristly back with her hand and embracing and kissing him as if he were a human child. Then he would wiggle his tail and give other signs to show that he was aware of his mother's affection.

As he grew older, the piglet began to speak like a human being and to wander about in the city, but whenever he saw any mud or dirt he would immediately wallow in it, after the manner of pigs, and then return home covered with filth. Then, when he approached the king and queen, he would rub himself against their beautiful garments, defiling them with all manner of dirt. But because he was their own son, they endured it without complaint.

One day the pig came home covered in mud and filth, as was his wont, and he lay down on his mother's beautiful robe, and grunted, "Mother, I wish to get married." When the queen heard this, she replied, "Don't talk such foolishness. What maid would ever take you for a husband, and do you think that any noble or knight would give his daughter to someone as dirty and unsavory as you?" But the pig kept on grunting that he must have a wife of one sort or another. The queen, not knowing how to manage him in this matter, asked the king what they should do in this time of crisis: "Our son wishes to marry, but where can we find someone who would be willing to take him as a husband?" Every day the pig would return to his mother with the same demand: "I must have a wife, and I won't leave you in peace until you arrange a marriage with a certain young woman I saw today. I find her very attractive."

It happened that the young woman he had in mind was the daughter of a poor woman who had three girls, each one of them very lovely. When the queen heard this, she summoned the woman and her eldest daughter, and said, "Good mother, you are poor and burdened with children. If you will agree to what I propose, you will be rich. I have a son who is, as you see, in the form of a pig, and I would like him to marry your eldest daughter. Do not think too hard about him, but turn your attention to the king and me, and remember that your daughter will inherit this entire kingdom when the king and I are gone."

When the young girl heard what the queen had to say, she was deeply upset and blushed for shame. She then said that she had no intention of accepting the queen's proposition. But the poor mother pleaded so urgently with her to give in that at last she yielded.

When the pig came home, all covered with dirt as usual, his mother said to him, "My son, we have found for you the wife you desire." And then she had the bride brought in, who by this time had been dressed up in regal attire. She presented the young woman to the pig prince. When he saw how lovely and desirable she was, he was filled with joy. All foul and dirty as he was, he leaped up and down around her, trying with all his might to show his affection by pawing and nuzzling her. But when she saw that he was soiling her beautiful dress, she shoved him aside. The pig asked, "Why are you pushing me away? Wasn't I the one who had these garments made for you?" She answered him with disdain, "No, neither you nor any one else in this kingdom of hogs has done that for me."

When it was time to retire, the young girl said to herself, "Whatever am I going to do with this foul beast? Tonight, while he is asleep, I will kill him."

The pig prince was not far off and heard those words, but said nothing. When the two retired to their chamber he climbed into the bed, stinking and dirty as he was, and defiled the sumptuous bed with his filthy hooves and snout. He lay down next to his wife, who did not take long to fall asleep. Then he struck her with his sharp hooves and drove them into her breast until she was dead.

The next morning the queen went to visit her daughter-in-law, and to her great distress found that the pig had killed her. When the pig returned from wandering about in the city, he replied to the queen's bitter reproaches by telling her that he had only treated his wife as she was planning to treat him, and then he withdrew in a dark mood.

Not many days passed before the pig prince began to plead with the queen again, asking her to let him marry one of the other sisters. Even though the queen refused to listen to his request, he kept on insisting and threatened to destroy everything in sight if he were not allowed to remarry.

The queen learned about his threats, and she went to the king and told him everything. He said that it might be wiser to kill their ill-fated offspring before he made some real mischief in the city. But the queen still had tender maternal feelings for her child, and she loved him very dearly despite what he had done. She could not bear the thought of being separated from him. And so she summoned the poor woman to the palace again, this time with her second daughter. She talked with the child for a long time, pleading with her to marry her son. Finally, the girl agreed to take the pig prince for a husband. But her fate was no better than her sister's, for the bridegroom killed her, as he had killed his other bride, and then fled swiftly from the palace.

When he returned, as dirty as ever and smelling so foul that no one would go near him, the king and queen railed at him for having committed such an atrocity, but this time too he insisted that, had he not killed her, she would have killed him.

As before, not much time passed before the pig began to plead with his mother again to let him marry one of the sisters, the youngest this time, who was more beautiful than either of the two others. When the queen refused his request, he became more insistent than ever. He began threatening the queen's own life—in terms violent and bloodthirsty—unless the young girl was given to him as a wife. The queen, when she heard his cruel and reprehensible words, was heartbroken. She felt that she was about to go out of her mind. But putting all other considerations aside, she summoned the poor woman and her third daughter, who was named Meldina, and said the following to her, "Meldina, my child, I would be ever so pleased if you agreed to take the pig prince as your husband. Don't pay much mind to him, and just pay attention to his father and me. If you are patient and wise, you have a chance at becoming the happiest woman in the world."

Meldina turned to the queen with a grateful smile on her face and said that she was quite willing to do as the queen had asked. She thanked her humbly for seeing fit to choose her as a daughter-in-law. After all, she had nothing in the world, and it was a stroke of good fortune that a poor girl like her should become the daughter-in-law of a powerful sovereign. The queen, when she heard these kind, modest words, could not hold back tears of joy. But all the same she feared that Meldina might meet the same terrible fate as her sisters.

The new bride wore jewels and was dressed in regal fashion. She was waiting for the bridegroom. When the pig prince came in, he was dirtier and filthier than ever. What did she do but spread out the skirt of her gown and ask him to lie down by her side. The queen told her to push him away, but Meldina would not comply and said, "There are three wise maxims, gracious queen, which I remember having once heard. The first tells us that it is foolish to search for something that can't be found. The second tells us to believe only those things that bear the marks of sense and reason. The third tells us that you should hold on to and cherish any rare and precious treasures that come into your possession."

When the young woman had finished speaking, the pig prince, who had been wide awake and heard everything she said, got up and then kissed her on the face and neck and shoulders and chest with his tongue. She was not at all backward in returning his caresses, and soon he was fired with a warm love for her. When the time had come to retire for the night, the bride went to bed and awaited her unseemly spouse. As soon as he climbed into bed, she raised the cover and told him to come lie next to her and put his head upon the pillow. She covered him carefully with the blankets and drew the curtains so that he would not feel cold.

In the morning, the pig got up and ranged abroad to pasture, as was his wont. Not much later the queen entered the bride's chamber, expecting to find that she had met with the same fate as her sisters. But then she saw her lying in the bed, muddy as it was, looking entirely pleased and contented. And she thanked the Lord that her son had at last found a spouse that suited him.

A few days later, when the pig prince was talking casually with his wife, he decided to take her into his confidence. "Meldina, my beloved wife," he said, "if I can be completely sure that you can keep a secret, I will tell you one that I have, something I have kept hidden for many years. I know that you are wise and discreet and that you love me truly. And because of that I want to share my secret with you."

"Your secret is safe with me," Meldina said, "for I promise never to reveal it to anyone without your consent."

Now that he was sure of his wife's discretion and fidelity, he stood up and shook off from his body the foul and dirty skin of a pig, and stood revealed as a handsome and well-proportioned young man. That night he slept soundly in the arms of his beloved wife. But he warned her to remain silent about the miracle she had witnessed, for the time had not yet come for complete liberation from his misery.

When he left the bed, he put the dirty pig's hide on again. I leave it to your imagination to consider how great was Meldina's joy when she discovered that, instead of a pig, she now had a handsome and gallant young prince as husband. Not much later, it turned out that she was with child, and, when the time came, she gave birth to a handsome and comely boy. The joy of the king and queen was unbounded, especially when they saw that the newborn child had the form of a human being and not that of a beast.

The burden of the strange and dark secret that her husband had shared with her weighed heavily on Meldina, and one day she went to her mother-in-law and said, "Gracious queen, when I married your son I believed that I had married a beast, but now I find that you have given me the comeliest, the worthiest, and the most gallant young man ever born as my husband. You must know that when he comes into my chamber to lie by my side, he casts off his dirty hide and leaves it on the ground and changes into a graceful, handsome youth. No one could ever believe this miracle unless they saw it with their own eyes."

When the queen heard those words she was sure that her daughter-in-law must be jesting, but Meldina insisted that what she said was true. And when the queen asked to witness with her own eyes the truth of this matter, Meldina replied, "Come to my chamber tonight, just as we are falling asleep. I will keep the door open, and you will discover that what I have told you is the truth."

That same night, when the time came, and everyone else had gone to sleep, the queen had some torches lit and went, accompanied by the king, to the chamber of her son. When she walked in, she saw the pig's skin lying on the floor in the corner of the room. Then she went over to the bedside and found Meldina lying in the arms of a handsome young man. When the king and queen set eyes on the two of them, their delight was very great, and the king ordered the pig's hide to be torn to shreds before anyone left the chamber, thus lifting the curse.[2] The king and queen nearly died from the shock and joy of finding that their son had become human.

And King Galeotto, when he saw that he had so fine a son and a grandchild as well, put aside his diadem and his royal robes and passed the crown on to his son, who was made king with great pomp. Ever afterwards he was known as King Pig. To the great joy of the people in the land, the young king began his reign, and he lived long and happily with Meldina, his beloved wife.

BROTHERS GRIMM

The Frog King, or Iron Heinrich[†]

In the olden days, when wishing could help you, there lived a king whose daughters were all beautiful. But the youngest was so beautiful that even the sun, which had seen so much, was filled with wonder when it shone upon her face. There was a dark, vast forest near

2. In this version of the story, Meldina's betrayal of the pig's confidence has no consequences, but in other variants, the heroine must undertake a perilous journey or carry out "impossible" tasks to redeem herself and be reunited with her husband. The phrase *thus lifting the curse* has been added by the editor.

† Jacob Grimm and Wilhelm Grimm, "Der Froschkönig oder der eiserne Heinrich," in *Kinder- und Hausmärchen*, 7th ed. (Berlin: Dieterich, 1857; first published: Berlin: Realschulbuchhandlung, 1812). Translated for the first edition of this Norton Critical Edition by Maria Tatar. Copyright © 1999 by Maria Tatar.

the king's castle, and in that forest, beneath an old linden tree, was a well. When the weather was really hot, the king's daughter would go out into the woods and sit down at the edge of the cool well. And when she got bored, she would take out her golden ball, throw it up in the air, and catch it again. That was her favorite toy.

One day it happened that the golden ball didn't land in the princess's hands when she reached up to catch it, but fell down on the ground and rolled right into the water. The princess followed it with her eyes, but the ball had disappeared, and the well was so very deep that you couldn't see the bottom. She began to weep and wept louder and louder, unable to stop herself. While she was wailing, a voice called out to her: "What's going on, princess? Stones would be moved to pity if they could hear you."

She turned around to see where the voice was coming from and saw a frog, which had stuck its big ugly head out of the water.

"Oh, it's you, you old splasher," she said. "I'm crying because my golden ball has fallen into the well."

"Be quiet and stop crying," said the frog. "I can help you, but what will you give me if I fetch your toy?"

"Whatever you want, dear frog," she said. "My dresses, my pearls and jewels, even the golden crown I'm wearing."

The frog said: "I don't want your dresses, your pearls and jewels, or your golden crown. But if you promise to cherish me and let me be your companion and playmate, and let me sit beside you at the table and eat from your little golden plate, drink from your little cup, and sleep in your little bed, if you promise me that, I will crawl down into the well and bring back your golden ball."

"Oh, yes," she said. "I'll give you anything you want as long as you get my ball back." But to herself she thought: "What nonsense that stupid frog is talking! He's down there in the water croaking away with all the other frogs. How could anyone want him for a companion?"

Once the frog had her word, he dove down into the water head first. After a while he came paddling back up with the ball in his mouth and tossed it onto the grass. When the princess caught sight of her beautiful toy, she was overjoyed. She picked it up and ran off with it.

"Wait for me," the frog cried out. "Take me with you. I can't run the way you do."

He croaked as loudly as he could after her, but it was no use. She paid no attention, sped home, and quickly forgot about the poor frog, who crawled back down into the well.

The next day, after she had sat down for dinner with the king and all the other courtiers and was eating from her little golden plate, something came crawling up the marble staircase, splish, splash, splish, splash. When it reached the top of the stairs, it knocked at the door and called out: "Princess, youngest princess, let me in!"

She ran to the door to see who it was, and when she opened the door, the frog was waiting right there. Terrified, she slammed the door as fast as she could and went back to the table. The king could see that her heart was pounding and said: "My child, why are you afraid? Was there a giant at the door coming to get you?"

"Oh, no," she replied. "It wasn't a giant, but it was a disgusting frog."

"What does a frog want from you?"

"Oh, father dear, yesterday when I was playing at the well, my golden ball fell into the water. And because I was crying so hard, the frog fetched it for me, and because he insisted, I promised that he could be my companion. I never thought that he would be able to leave the water. Now he's outside and wants to come in to see me." Just then there was a second knock at the door, and a voice called out:

> Princess, youngest princess,
> Let me in.
> Did you forget
> Yesterday's promise
> Down by the chilly waters?
> Princess, youngest princess,
> Let me in.

Then the king said: "When you make a promise, you must keep it. Just go and let him in."

She went and opened the door. The frog hopped into the room and followed close on her heels until she reached her chair. Then he sat down and called out: "Lift me up beside you."

She hesitated, but the king ordered her to obey. Once the frog was up on the chair, he wanted to get on the table, and once he was there he said: "Push your little golden plate closer to me so that we can eat together."

She did as he said, but it was obvious that she was not happy about it. The frog enjoyed his meal, but for her almost every little morsel stuck in her throat. Finally he said: "I've had enough to eat and am tired. Carry me up to your little room and prepare your little bed with the silken covers."

The princess began to cry, and was afraid of the clammy frog. She didn't dare touch him, and now he was going to sleep in her beautiful, clean bed. The king grew angry and said: "You shouldn't scorn someone who helped you when you were in trouble."

The princess picked up the frog with two fingers, carried him up to her room, and put him in a corner. While she was lying in bed, he came crawling over and said: "I'm tired and want to sleep as much as you do. Lift me up or I'll tell your father."

Then she became really cross, picked him up, and threw him with all her might against the wall. "Now you'll get your rest, you disgusting frog!"

When he fell to the ground, he was no longer a frog but a prince with beautiful, beaming eyes. At her father's bidding, he became her dear companion and husband. He told her that a wicked witch had cast a spell on him and that she alone could release him from the well. The next day they would set out together for his kingdom. They fell asleep, and, in the morning, after the sun had woken them, a coach drove up drawn by eight white horses in golden harnesses, with white ostrich plumes on their heads. At the back of the coach stood Faithful Heinrich, the servant of the young king. Faithful Heinrich had been so saddened by the transformation of his master into a frog that he had to have three hoops placed around his heart to keep it from bursting with pain and sorrow. Now the coach was there to take the young king back to his kingdom, and Faithful Heinrich lifted the two of them in and took his place in the back again. He was overjoyed by the transformation. When they had covered some distance, the prince heard a cracking noise behind him, as if something had broken. He turned around and called out:

> "Heinrich, the coach is falling apart!"
> "No, my lord, 'tis not the coach,
> But a hoop from round my heart,
> Which was in such pain,
> While you were down in the well,
> Living there as a frog."

Two more times the prince heard the cracking noise, and he was sure that the coach was falling apart. But it was only the sounds of the hoops breaking off from Faithful Heinrich's heart, for his master had been set free and was happy.

ANGELA CARTER

The Tiger's Bride[†]

My father lost me to The Beast at cards.

There's a special madness strikes travellers from the North when they reach the lovely land where the lemon trees grow.[1] We come

† Angela Carter, "The Tiger's Bride," in *The Bloody Chamber and Other Stories* (New York: Penguin, 1993). Copyright © the Estate of Angela Carter 1995. Reprinted by permission of the Estate of Angela Carter c/o Rogers, Coleridge & White Ltd.
1. A reference to Italy, which was described in a poem by Johann Wolfgang von Goethe (1749–1832) as the "land where the lemon trees blossom."

from countries of cold weather; at home, we are at war with nature but here, ah! you think you've come to the blessed plot where the lion lies down with the lamb. Everything flowers; no harsh wind stirs the voluptuous air. The sun spills fruit for you. And the deathly, sensual lethargy of the sweet South infects the starved brain; it gasps: "Luxury! more luxury!" But then the snow comes, you cannot escape it, it followed us from Russia as if it ran behind our carriage, and in this dark, bitter city has caught up with us at last, flocking against the windowpanes to mock my father's expectations of perpetual pleasure as the veins in his forehead stand out and throb, his hands shake as he deals the Devil's picture books.

The candles dropped hot, acrid gouts of wax on my bare shoulders. I watched with the furious cynicism peculiar to women whom circumstances force mutely to witness folly, while my father, fired in his desperation by more and yet more draughts of the firewater they call "grappa," rids himself of the last scraps of my inheritance. When we left Russia, we owned black earth, blue forest with bear and wild boar, serfs, cornfields, farmyards, my beloved horses, white nights of cool summer, the fireworks of the northern lights. What a burden all those possessions must have been to him, because he laughs as if with glee as he beggars himself; he is in such a passion to donate all to The Beast.

Everyone who comes to this city must play a hand with the *grand seigneur*;[2] few come. They did not warn us at Milan, or, if they did, we did not understand them—my limping Italian, the bewildering dialect of the region. Indeed, I myself spoke up in favour of this remote, provincial place, out of fashion two hundred years, because, oh irony, it boasted no casino. I did not know that the price of a stay in its Decembral solitude was a game with Milord.

The hour was late. The chill damp of this place creeps into the stones, into your bones, into the spongy pith of the lungs; it insinuated itself with a shiver into our parlour, where Milord came to play in the privacy essential to him. Who could refuse the invitation his valet brought to our lodging? Not my profligate father, certainly; the mirror above the table gave me back his frenzy, my impassivity, the withering candles, the emptying bottles, the coloured tide of the cards as they rose and fell, the still mask that concealed all the features of The Beast but for the yellow eyes that strayed, now and then, from his unfurled hand towards myself.

"La Bestia!" said our landlady, gingerly fingering an envelope with his huge crest of a tiger rampant on it, something of fear, something of wonder in her face. And I could not ask her why they called the

---

2. French term for the lord of the manor or, in this case, the most powerful figure in the city.

master of the place "La Bestia"—was it to do with that heraldic signature?—because her tongue was so thickened by the phlegmy, bronchitic speech of the region I scarcely managed to make out a thing she said except, when she saw me: "Che bella!"[3]

Since I could toddle, always the pretty one, with my glossy, nut-brown curls, my rosy cheeks. And born on Christmas Day—her "Christmas rose," my English nurse called me. The peasants said: "The living image of her mother," crossing themselves out of respect for the dead. My mother did not blossom long; bartered for her dowry to such a feckless sprig of the Russian nobility that she soon died of his gaming, his whoring, his agonizing repentances. And The Beast gave me the rose from his own impeccable if outmoded buttonhole when he arrived, the valet brushing the snow off his black cloak. This white rose, unnatural, out of season, that now my nervous fingers ripped, petal by petal, apart as my father magnificently concluded the career he had made of catastrophe.

This is a melancholy, introspective region; a sunless, featureless landscape, the sullen river sweating fog, the shorn, hunkering willows. And a cruel city; the sombre piazza, a place uniquely suited to public executions, under the beetling shadow of that malign barn of a church. They used to hang condemned men in cages from the city walls; unkindness comes naturally to them, their eyes are set too close together, they have thin lips. Poor food, pasta soaked in oil, boiled beef with sauce of bitter herbs. A funereal hush about the place, the inhabitants huddled up against the cold so you can hardly see their faces. And they lie to you and cheat you, innkeepers, coachmen, everybody. God, how they fleeced us!

The treacherous South, where you think there is no winter but forget you take it with you.

My senses were increasingly troubled by the fuddling perfume of Milord, far too potent a reek of purplish civet at such close quarters in so small a room. He must bathe himself in scent, soak his shirts and underlinen in it; what can he smell of, that needs so much camouflage?

I never saw a man so big look so two-dimensional, in spite of the quaint elegance of The Beast, in the old-fashioned tailcoat that might, from its looks, have been bought in those distant years before he imposed seclusion on himself; he does not feel he need keep up with the times. There is a crude clumsiness about his outlines, that are on the ungainly, giant side; and he has an odd air of self-imposed restraint, as if fighting a battle with himself to remain upright when he would far rather drop down on all fours. He throws our human aspirations to the godlike sadly awry, poor fellow; only from a

---

3. "What a beauty she is!" (Italian).

distance would you think The Beast not much different from any other man, although he wears a mask with a man's face painted most beautifully on it. Oh, yes, a beautiful face; but one with too much formal symmetry of feature to be entirely human: one profile of his mask is the mirror image of the other, too perfect, uncanny. He wears a wig, too, false hair tied at the nape with a bow, a wig of the kind you see in old-fashioned portraits. A chaste silk stock stuck with a pearl hides his throat. And gloves of blond kid that are yet so huge and clumsy they do not seem to cover hands.

He is a carnival figure made of papier mâché and crêpe hair; and yet he has the Devil's knack at cards.

His masked voice echoes as from a great distance as he stoops over his hand and he has such a growling impediment in his speech that only his valet, who understands him, can interpret for him, as if his master were the clumsy doll and he the ventriloquist.

The wick slumped in the eroded wax, the candles guttered. By the time my rose had lost all its petals, my father, too, was left with nothing.

"Except the girl."

Gambling is a sickness. My father said he loved me yet he staked his daughter on a hand of cards. He fanned them out; in the mirror, I saw wild hope light up his eyes. His collar was unfastened, his rumpled hair stood up on end, he had the anguish of a man in the last stages of debauchery. The draughts came out of the old walls and bit me, I was colder than I'd ever been in Russia, when nights are coldest there.

A queen, a king, an ace. I saw them in the mirror. Oh, I know he thought he could not lose me; besides, back with me would come all he had lost, the unravelled fortunes of our family at one blow restored. And would he not win, as well, The Beast's hereditary palazzo outside the city; his immense revenues; his lands around the river; his rents, his treasure chest, his Mantegnas, his Giulio Romanos, his Cellini[4] salt-cellars, his titles . . . the very city itself.

You must not think my father valued me at less than a king's ransom; but, at *no more* than a king's ransom.

It was cold as hell in the parlour. And it seemed to me, child of the severe North, that it was not my flesh but, truly, my father's soul that was in peril.

My father, of course, believed in miracles; what gambler does not? In pursuit of just such a miracle as this, had we not travelled from the land of bears and shooting stars?

So we teetered on the brink.

---

4. Benvenuto Cellini (1500–1571), Italian sculptor and metalsmith. Andrea Mantegna (1431–1506), Italian painter and engraver. Giulio Romano (1499–1546), Italian architect and painter.

The Beast bayed; laid down all three remaining aces.

The indifferent servants now glided smoothly forward as on wheels to douse the candles one by one. To look at them you would think that nothing of any moment had occurred. They yawned a little resentfully; it was almost morning, we had kept them out of bed. The Beast's man brought his cloak. My father sat amongst these preparations for departure, staring on at the betrayal of his cards upon the table.

The Beast's man informed me crisply that he, the valet, would call for me and my bags tomorrow, at ten, and conduct me forthwith to The Beast's palazzo. Capisco?[5] So shocked was I that I scarcely did "capisco"; he repeated my orders patiently, he was a strange, thin, quick little man who walked with an irregular, jolting rhythm upon splayed feet in curious, wedge-shaped shoes.

Where my father had been red as fire, now he was white as the snow that caked the windowpane. His eyes swam; soon he would cry.

"'Like the base Indian,'"[6] he said; he loved rhetoric. "'One whose hand, / Like the base Indian, threw a pearl away / Richer than all his tribe . . .' I have lost my pearl, my pearl beyond price."[7]

At that, The Beast made a sudden, dreadful noise, halfway between a growl and a roar; the candles flared. The quick valet, the prim hypocrite, interpreted unblinking: "My master says: If you are so careless of your treasures, you should expect them to be taken from you."

He gave us the bow and smile his master could not offer us and they departed.

I watched the snow until, just before dawn, it stopped falling; a hard frost settled, next morning there was a light like iron.

The Beast's carriage, of an elegant if antique design, was black as a hearse and it was drawn by a dashing black gelding who blew smoke from his nostrils and stamped upon the packed snow with enough sprightly appearance of life to give me some hope that not all the world was locked in ice, as I was. I had always held a little towards Gulliver's opinion, that horses are better than we are,[8] and, that day, I would have been glad to depart with him to the kingdom of horses, if I'd been given the chance.

The valet sat up on the box in a natty black and gold livery, clasping, of all things, a bunch of his master's damned white roses as if

---

5. Understand? (Italian).
6. From Shakespeare's *Othello*, V.ii.346—48.
7. See Matthew 13.45—46, "Again, the kingdom of heaven is like unto a merchant man, seeking goodly pearls: Who, when he had found one pearl of great price, went and sold all that he had and bought it."
8. In part IV of Jonathan Swift's *Gulliver's Travels*, a visit to the Houyhnhnms leads Gulliver to compare horses favorably with human beings.

a gift of flowers would reconcile a woman to any humiliation. He sprang down with preternatural agility to place them ceremoniously in my reluctant hand. My tear-beslobbered father wants a rose to show that I forgive him. When I break off a stem, I prick my finger and so he gets his rose all smeared with blood.

The valet crouched at my feet to tuck the rugs about me with a strange kind of unflattering obsequiousness yet he forgot his station sufficiently to scratch busily beneath his white periwig with an over-supple index finger as he offered me what my old nurse would have called an "old-fashioned look," ironic, sly, a smidgen of disdain in it. And pity? No pity. His eyes were moist and brown, his face seamed with the innocent cunning of an ancient baby. He had an irritating habit of chattering to himself under his breath all the time as he packed up his master's winnings. I drew the curtains to conceal the sight of my father's farewell; my spite was sharp as broken glass.

Lost to The Beast! And what, I wondered, might be the exact nature of his "beastliness"? My English nurse once told me about a tiger-man she saw in London, when she was a little girl, to scare me into good behaviour, for I was a wild wee thing and she could not tame me into submission with a frown or the bribe of a spoonful of jam. If you don't stop plaguing the nursemaids, my beauty, the tiger-man will come and take you away. They'd brought him from Suma-tra, in the Indies, she said; his hinder parts were all hairy and only from the head downwards did he resemble a man.

And yet The Beast goes always masked; it cannot be his face that looks like mine.

But the tiger-man, in spite of his hairiness, could take a glass of ale in his hand like a good Christian and drink it down. Had she not seen him do so, at the sign of The George, by the steps of Upper Moor Fields when she was just as high as me and lisped and tod-dled, too. Then she would sigh for London, across the North Sea of the lapse of years. But, if this young lady was not a good little girl and did not eat her boiled beetroot, then the tiger-man would put on his big black travelling cloak lined with fur, just like your daddy's, and hire the Erl-King's galloper[9] of wind and ride through the night straight to the nursery and—

Yes, my beauty! GOBBLE YOU UP!

How I'd squeal in delighted terror, half believing her, half know-ing that she teased me. And there were things I knew that I must not tell her. In our lost farmyard, where the giggling nursemaids ini-tiated me into the mysteries of what the bull did to the cows, I heard about the waggoner's daughter. Hush, hush, don't let on to

---

9. An allusion to another poem by Goethe, "The Erl-King," in which a father tries in vain to rescue his child from the enchantments of the title figure.

your nursie we said so; the waggoner's lass, hare-lipped, squint-eyed, ugly as sin, who would have taken her? Yet, to her shame, her belly swelled amid the cruel mockery of the ostlers[1] and her son was born of a bear, they whispered. Born with a full pelt and teeth; that proved it. But, when he grew up, he was a good shepherd, although he never married, lived in a hut outside the village and could make the wind blow any way he wanted to besides being able to tell which eggs would become cocks, which hens.

The wondering peasants once brought my father a skull with horns four inches long on either side of it and would not go back to the field where their poor plough disturbed it until the priest went with them; for this skull had the jaw-bone of a *man,* had it not?

Old wives' tales, nursery fears! I knew well enough the reason for the trepidation I cosily titillated with superstitious marvels of my childhood on the day my childhood ended. For now my own skin was my sole capital in the world and today I'd make my first investment.

We had left the city far behind us and were now traversing a wide, flat dish of snow where the mutilated stumps of the willows flourished their ciliate heads athwart frozen ditches; mist diminished the horizon, brought down the sky until it seemed no more than a few inches above us. As far as eye could see, not one thing living. How starveling, how bereft the dead season of this spurious Eden in which all the fruit was blighted by cold! And my frail roses, already faded. I opened the carriage door and tossed the defunct bouquet into the rucked, frost-stiff mud of the road. Suddenly a sharp, freezing wind arose and pelted my face with a dry rice of powdered snow. The mist lifted sufficiently to reveal before me an acreage of half-derelict façades of sheer red brick, the vast man-trap, the megalomaniac citadel of his palazzo.

It was a world in itself but a dead one, a burned-out planet. I saw The Beast bought solitude, not luxury, with his money.

The little black horse trotted smartly through the figured bronze doors that stood open to the weather like those of a barn and the valet handed me out of the carriage onto the scarred tiles of the great hall itself, into the odorous warmth of a stable, sweet with hay, acrid with horse dung. An equine chorus of neighings and soft drummings of hooves broke out beneath the tall roof, where the beams were scabbed with last summer's swallows' nests; a dozen gracile muzzles lifted from their mangers and turned towards us, ears erect. The Beast had given his horses the use of the dining room. The walls were painted, aptly enough, with a fresco of horses, dogs and men in a wood where fruit and blossom grew on the bough together.

The valet tweaked politely at my sleeve. Milord is waiting.

---

1. People who care for horses, especially at inns.

Gaping doors and broken windows let the wind in everywhere. We mounted one staircase after another, our feet clopping on the marble. Through archways and open doors, I glimpsed suites of vaulted chambers opening one out of another like systems of Chinese boxes into the infinite complexity of the innards of the place. He and I and the wind were the only things stirring; and all the furniture was under dust sheets, the chandeliers bundled up in cloth, pictures taken from their hooks and propped with their faces to the walls as if their master could not bear to look at them. The palace was dismantled, as if its owner were about to move house or had never properly moved in; The Beast had chosen to live in an uninhabited place.

The valet darted me a reassuring glance from his brown, eloquent eyes, yet a glance with so much queer superciliousness in it that it did not comfort me, and went bounding ahead of me on his bandy legs, softly chattering to himself. I held my head high and followed him; but, for all my pride, my heart was heavy.

Milord has his eyrie high above the house, a small, stifling, darkened room; he keeps his shutters locked at noon. I was out of breath by the time we reached it and returned to him the silence with which he greeted me. I will not smile. He cannot smile.

In his rarely disturbed privacy, The Beast wears a garment of Ottoman design, a loose, dull purple gown with gold embroidery round the neck that falls from his shoulders to conceal his feet. The feet of the chair he sits in are handsomely clawed. He hides his hands in his ample sleeves. The artificial masterpiece of his face appals me. A small fire in a small grate. A rushing wind rattles the shutters.

The valet coughed. To him fell the delicate task of transmitting to me his master's wishes.

"My master—"

A stick fell in the grate. It made a mighty clatter in that dreadful silence; the valet started; lost his place in his speech, began again.

"My master has but one desire."

The thick, rich, wild scent with which Milord had soaked himself the previous evening hangs all about us, ascends in cursive blue from the smoke of a precious Chinese pot.

"He wishes only—"

Now, in the face of my impassivity, the valet twittered, his ironic composure gone, for the desire of a master, however trivial, may yet sound unbearably insolent in the mouth of a servant and his role of go-between clearly caused him a good deal of embarrassment. He gulped; he swallowed, at last contrived to unleash an unpunctuated flood.

"My master's sole desire is to see the pretty young lady unclothed nude without her dress and that only for the one time after which she will be returned to her father undamaged with bankers' orders for the sum which he lost to my master at cards and also a number of fine presents such as furs, jewels and horses—"

I remained standing. During this interview, my eyes were level with those inside the mask that now evaded mine as if, to his credit, he was ashamed of his own request even as his mouthpiece made it for him. Agitato, molto agitato,[2] the valet wrung his white-gloved hands.

"Desnuda[3]—"

I could scarcely believe my ears. I let out a raucous guffaw; no young lady laughs like that! my old nurse used to remonstrate. But I did. And do. At the clamour of my heartless mirth, the valet danced backwards with perturbation, palpitating his fingers as if attempting to wrench them off, expostulating, wordlessly pleading. I felt that I owed it to him to make my reply in as exquisite a Tuscan as I could master.

"You may put me in a windowless room, sir, and I promise you I will pull my skirt up to my waist, ready for you. But there must be a sheet over my face, to hide it; though the sheet must be laid over me so lightly that it will not choke me. So I shall be covered completely from the waist upwards, and no lights. There you can visit me once, sir, and only the once. After that I must be driven directly to the city and deposited in the public square, in front of the church. If you wish to give me money, then I should be pleased to receive it. But I must stress that you should give me only the same amount of money that you would give to any other woman in such circumstances. However, if you choose not to give me a present, then that is your right."

How pleased I was to see I struck The Beast to the heart! For, after a baker's dozen heartbeats, one single tear swelled, glittering, at the corner of the masked eye. A tear! A tear, I hoped, of shame. The tear trembled for a moment on an edge of painted bone, then tumbled down the painted cheek to fall, with an abrupt tinkle, on the tiled floor.

The valet, ticking and clucking to himself, hastily ushered me out of the room. A mauve cloud of his master's perfume billowed out into the chill corridor with us and dissipated itself on the spinning winds.

A cell had been prepared for me, a veritable cell, windowless, airless, lightless, in the viscera of the palace. The valet lit a lamp for me; a narrow bed, a dark cupboard with fruit and flowers carved on it bulked out of the gloom.

"I shall twist a noose out of my bed linen and hang myself with it," I said.

---

2. Agitated, very agitated (Italian).
3. Undressed (Italian).

"Oh, no," said the valet, fixing upon me wide and suddenly melancholy eyes. "Oh, no, you will not. You are a woman of honour."

And what was *he* doing in my bedroom, this jigging caricature of a man? Was he to be my warder until I submitted to The Beast's whim or he to mine? Am I in such reduced circumstances that I may not have a lady's maid? As if in reply to my unspoken demand, the valet clapped his hands.

"To assuage your loneliness, madame . . ."

A knocking and clattering behind the door of the cupboard; the door swings open and out glides a soubrette from an operetta, with glossy, nut-brown curls, rosy cheeks, blue, rolling eyes; it takes me a moment to recognize her, in her little cap, her white stockings, her frilled petticoats. She carries a looking glass in one hand and a powder puff in the other and there is a musical box where her heart should be; she tinkles as she rolls towards me on her tiny wheels.

"Nothing human lives here," said the valet.

My maid halted, bowed; from a split seam at the side of her bodice protrudes the handle of a key. She is a marvellous machine, the most delicately balanced system of cords and pulleys in the world.

"We have dispensed with servants," the valet said. "We surround ourselves, instead, for utility and pleasure, with simulacra and find it no less convenient than do most gentlemen."

This clockwork twin of mine halted before me, her bowels churning out a settecento[4] minuet, and offered me the bold carnation of her smile. Click, click—she raises her arm and busily dusts my cheeks with pink, powdered chalk that makes me cough; then thrusts towards me her little mirror.

I saw within it not my own face but that of my father, as if I had put on his face when I arrived at The Beast's palace as the discharge of his debt. What, you self-deluding fool, are you crying still? And drunk, too. He tossed back his grappa and hurled the tumbler away.

Seeing my astonished fright, the valet took the mirror away from me, breathed on it, polished it with the ham of his gloved fist, handed it back to me. Now all I saw was myself, haggard from a sleepless night, pale enough to need my maid's supply of rouge.

I heard the key turn in the heavy door and the valet's footsteps patter down the stone passage. Meanwhile, my double continued to powder the air, emitting her jangling tune but, as it turned out, she was not inexhaustible; soon she was powdering more and yet more languorously, her metal heart slowed in imitation of fatigue, her musical box ran down until the notes separated themselves out of the tune and plopped like single raindrops and, as if sleep had overtaken her, at last she moved no longer. As she succumbed to sleep,

4. Seventeenth-century (Italian).

I had no option but to do so, too. I dropped on that narrow bed as if felled.

Time passed but I do not know how much; then the valet woke me with rolls and honey. I gestured the tray away but he set it down firmly beside the lamp and took from it a little shagreen box, which he offered to me.

I turned away my head.

"Oh, my lady!" Such hurt cracked his high-pitched voice! He dextrously unfastened the gold clasp; on a bed of crimson velvet lay a single diamond earring, perfect as a tear.

I snapped the box shut and tossed it into a corner. This sudden, sharp movement must have disturbed the mechanism of the doll; she jerked her arm almost as if to reprimand me, letting out a rippling fart of gavotte.[5] Then was still again.

"Very well," said the valet, put out. And indicated it was time for me to visit my host again. He did not let me wash or comb my hair. There was so little natural light in the interior of the palace that I could not tell whether it was day or night.

You would not think The Beast had budged an inch since I last saw him; he sat in his huge chair, with his hands in his sleeves, and the heavy air never moved. I might have slept an hour, a night, or a month, but his sculptured calm, the stifling air remained just as it had been. The incense rose from the pot, still traced the same signature on the air. The same fire burned.

Take off my clothes for you, like a ballet girl? Is that all you want of me?

"The sight of a young lady's skin that no man has seen before—" stammered the valet.

I wished I'd rolled in the hay with every lad on my father's farm, to disqualify myself from this humiliating bargain. That he should want so little was the reason why I could not give it; I did not need to speak for The Beast to understand me.

A tear came from his other eye. And then he moved; he buried his cardboard carnival head with its ribboned weight of false hair in, I would say, his arms; he withdrew his, I might say, hands from his sleeves and I saw his furred pads, his excoriating claws.

The dropped tear caught upon his fur and shone. And in my room for hours I hear those paws pad back and forth outside my door.

When the valet arrived again with his silver salver, I had a pair of diamond earrings of the finest water in the world; I threw the other into the corner where the first one lay. The valet twittered with aggrieved regret but did not offer to lead me to The Beast again.

---

5. A French dance.

Instead, he smiled ingratiatingly and confided: "My master, he say: invite the young lady to go riding."

"What's this?"

He briskly mimicked the action of a gallop and, to my amazement, tunelessly croaked: "Tantivy![6] tantivy! a-hunting we will go!"

"I'll run away, I'll ride to the city."

"Oh, no," he said. "Are you not a woman of honour?"

He clapped his hands and my maidservant clicked and jangled into the imitation of life. She rolled towards the cupboard where she had come from and reached inside it to fetch out over her synthetic arm my riding habit. Of all things. My very own riding habit, that I'd left behind me in a trunk in a loft in that country house outside Petersburg that we'd lost long ago, before, even, we set out on this wild pilgrimage to the cruel South. Either the very riding habit my old nurse had sewn for me or else a copy of it perfect to the lost button on the right sleeve, the ripped hem held up with a pin. I turned the worn cloth about in my hands, looking for a clue. The wind that sprinted through the palace made the door tremble in its frame; had the north wind blown my garments across Europe to me? At home, the bear's son directed the winds at his pleasure; what democracy of magic held this palace and the fir forest in common? Or, should I be prepared to accept it as proof of the axiom my father had drummed into me: that, if you have enough money, anything is possible?

"Tantivy," suggested the now twinkling valet, evidently charmed at the pleasure mixed with my bewilderment. The clockwork maid held my jacket out to me and I allowed myself to shrug into it as if reluctantly, although I was half mad to get out into the open air, away from this deathly palace, even in such company.

The doors of the hall let the bright day in; I saw that it was morning. Our horses, saddled and bridled, beasts in bondage, were waiting for us, striking sparks from the tiles with their impatient hooves while their stablemates lolled at ease among the straw, conversing with one another in the mute speech of horses. A pigeon or two, feathers puffed to keep out the cold, strutted about, pecking at ears of corn. The little black gelding who had brought me here greeted me with a ringing neigh that resonated inside the misty roof as in a sounding box and I knew he was meant for me to ride.

I always adored horses, noblest of creatures, such wounded sensitivity in their wise eyes, such rational restraint of energy at their high-strung hindquarters. I lirruped and hurrumphed to my shining black companion and he acknowledged my greeting with a kiss on the forehead from his soft lips. There was a little shaggy pony

6. A hunting cry used when the chase is at full speed.

nuzzling away at the *trompe l'œil*[7] foliage beneath the hooves of the painted horses on the wall, into whose saddle the valet sprang with a flourish as of the circus. Then The Beast, wrapped in a black fur-lined cloak, came to heave himself aloft a grave grey mare. No natural horseman he; he clung to her mane like a shipwrecked sailor to a spar.

Cold, that morning, yet dazzling with the sharp winter sunlight that wounds the retina. There was a scurrying wind about that seemed to go with us, as if the masked, immense one who did not speak carried it inside his cloak and let it out at his pleasure, for it stirred the horses' manes but did not lift the lowland mists.

A bereft landscape in the sad browns and sepias of winter lay all about us, the marshland drearily protracting itself towards the wide river. Those decapitated willows. Now and then, the swoop of a bird, its irreconcilable cry.

A profound sense of strangeness slowly began to possess me. I knew my two companions were not, in any way, as other men, the simian retainer and the master for whom he spoke, the one with clawed forepaws who was in a plot with the witches who let the winds out of their knotted handkerchiefs up towards the Finnish border. I knew they lived according to a different logic than I had done until my father abandoned me to the wild beasts by his human carelessness. This knowledge gave me a certain fearfulness still; but, I would say, not much . . . I was a young girl, a virgin, and therefore men denied me rationality just as they denied it to all those who were not exactly like themselves, in all their unreason. If I could see not one single soul in that wilderness of desolation all around me, then the six of us—mounts and riders, both—could boast amongst us not one soul, either, since all the best religions in the world state categorically that not beasts nor women were equipped with the flimsy, insubstantial things when the good Lord opened the gates of Eden and let Eve and her familiars tumble out. Understand, then, that though I would not say I privately engaged in metaphysical speculation as we rode through the reedy approaches to the river, I certainly meditated on the nature of my own state, how I had been bought and sold, passed from hand to hand. That clockwork girl who powdered my cheeks for me; had I not been allotted only the same kind of imitative life amongst men that the doll-maker had given her?

Yet, as to the true nature of the being of this clawed magus[8] who rode his pale horse in a style that made me recall how Kublai Khan's leopards went out hunting on horseback, of that I had no notion.

7. A visual deception or a painting that gives the illusion of being real (French).
8. Magician, sorcerer.

We came to the bank of the river that was so wide we could not see across it, so still with winter that it scarcely seemed to flow. The horses lowered their heads to drink. The valet cleared his throat, about to speak; we were in a place of perfect privacy, beyond a brake of winter-bare rushes, a hedge of reeds.

"If you will not let him see you without your clothes—"

I involuntarily shook my head—

"—you must, then, prepare yourself for the sight of my master, naked."

The river broke on the pebbles with a diminishing sigh. My composure deserted me; all at once I was on the brink of panic. I did not think that I could bear the sight of him, whatever he was. The mare raised her dripping muzzle and looked at me keenly, as if urging me. This river broke again at my feet. I was far from home.

"You," said the valet, "must."

When I saw how scared he was I might refuse, I nodded.

The reed bowed down in a sudden snarl of wind that brought with it a gust of the heavy odour of his disguise. The valet held out his master's cloak to screen him from me as he removed the mask. The horses stirred.

The tiger will never lie down with the lamb; he acknowledges no pact that is not reciprocal. The lamb must learn to run with the tigers.

A great, feline, tawny shape whose pelt was barred with a savage geometry of bars the colour of burned wood. His domed, heavy head, so terrible he must hide it. How subtle the muscles, how profound the tread. The annihilating vehemence of his eyes, like twin suns.

I felt my breast ripped apart as if I suffered a marvellous wound.

The valet moved forward as if to cover up his master now the girl had acknowledged him, but I said: "No." The tiger sat still as a heraldic beast, in the pact he had made with his own ferocity to do me no harm. He was far larger than I could have imagined, from the poor, shabby things I'd seen once, in the Czar's menagerie at Petersburg, the golden fruit of their eyes dimming, withering in the far North of captivity. Nothing about him reminded me of humanity.

I therefore, shivering, now unfastened my jacket, to show him I would do him no harm. Yet I was clumsy and blushed a little, for no man had seen me naked and I was a proud girl. Pride it was, not shame, that thwarted my fingers so; and a certain trepidation lest this frail little article of human upholstery before him might not be, in itself, grand enough to satisfy his expectations of us, since those, for all I knew, might have grown infinite during the endless time he had been waiting. The wind clattered in the rushes, purled and eddied in the river.

I showed his grave silence my white skin, my red nipples, and the horses turned their heads to watch me, also, as if they, too, were

courteously curious as to the fleshly nature of women. Then The
Beast lowered his massive head; Enough! said the valet with a ges-
ture. The wind died down, all was still again.

Then they went off together, the valet on his pony, the tiger
running before him like a hound, and I walked along the river bank
for a while. I felt I was at liberty for the first time in my life. Then
the winter sun began to tarnish, a few flakes of snow drifted from
the darkening sky and, when I returned to the horses, I found The
Beast mounted again on his grey mare, cloaked and masked and
once more, to all appearances, a man, while the valet had a fine
catch of waterfowl dangling from his hand and the corpse of a young
roebuck slung behind his saddle. I climbed up on the black gelding
in silence and so we returned to the palace as the snow fell more
and more heavily, obscuring the tracks that we had left behind us.

The valet did not return me to my cell but, instead, to an elegant,
if old-fashioned boudoir with sofas of faded pink brocade, a jinn's
treasury of Oriental carpets, tintinnabulation of cut-glass chandeliers. Candles in antlered holders struck rainbows from the prismatic
hearts of my diamond earrings, that lay on my new dressing table
at which my attentive maid stood ready with her powder puff and
mirror. Intending to fix the ornaments in my ears, I took the looking glass from her hand, but it was in the midst of one of its magic
fits again and I did not see my own face in it but that of my father;
at first I thought he smiled at me. Then I saw he was smiling with
pure gratification.

He sat, I saw, in the parlour of our lodgings, at the very table where
he had lost me, but now he was busily engaged in counting out a
tremendous pile of banknotes. My father's circumstances had
changed already; well-shaven, neatly barbered, smart new clothes.
A frosted glass of sparkling wine sat convenient to his hand beside
an ice bucket. The Beast had clearly paid cash on the nail for his
glimpse of my bosom, and paid up promptly, as if it had not been
a sight I might have died of showing. Then I saw my father's trunks
were packed, ready for departure. Could he so easily leave me
here?

There was a note on the table with the money, in a fine hand. I
could read it quite clearly. "The young lady will arrive immediately."
Some harlot with whom he'd briskly negotiated a liaison on the
strength of his spoils? Not at all. For, at that moment, the valet
knocked at my door to announce that I might leave the palace at
any time hereafter, and he bore over his arm a handsome sable cloak,
my very own little gratuity, The Beast's morning gift, in which he
proposed to pack me up and send me off.

When I looked at the mirror again, my father had disappeared and
all I saw was a pale, hollow-eyed girl whom I scarcely recognized.

The valet asked politely when he should prepare the carriage, as if he did not doubt that I would leave with my booty at the first opportunity while my maid, whose face was no longer the spit of my own, continued bonnily to beam. I will dress her in my own clothes, wind her up, send her back to perform the part of my father's daughter.

"Leave me alone," I said to the valet.

He did not need to lock the door, now. I fixed the earrings in my ears. They were very heavy. Then I took off my riding habit, left it where it lay on the floor. But, when I got down to my shift, my arms dropped to my sides. I was unaccustomed to nakedness. I was so unused to my own skin that to take off all my clothes involved a kind of flaying. I thought The Beast had wanted a little thing compared with what I was prepared to give him; but it is not natural for humankind to go naked, not since first we hid our loins with fig leaves. He had demanded the abominable. I felt as much atrocious pain as if I was stripping off my own underpelt and the smiling girl stood poised in the oblivion of her balked simulation of life, watching me peel down to the cold, white meat of contract and, if she did not see me, then so much more like the market place, where the eyes that watch you take no account of your existence.

And it seemed my entire life, since I had left the North, had passed under the indifferent gaze of eyes like hers.

Then I was flinching stark, except for his irreproachable tears.

I huddled in the furs I must return to him, to keep me from the lacerating winds that raced along the corridors. I knew the way to his den without the valet to guide me.

No response to my tentative rap on his door.

Then the wind blew the valet whirling along the passage. He must have decided that, if one should go naked, then all should go naked; without his livery, he revealed himself, as I had suspected, a delicate creature, covered with silken moth-grey fur, brown fingers supple as leather, chocolate muzzle, the gentlest creature in the world. He gibbered a little to see my fine furs and jewels as if I were dressed up for the opera and, with a great deal of tender ceremony, removed the sables from my shoulders. The sables thereupon resolved themselves into a pack of black, squeaking rats that rattled immediately down the stairs on their hard little feet and were lost to sight.

The valet bowed me inside The Beast's room.

The purple dressing gown, the mask, the wig, were laid out on his chair; a glove was planted on each arm. The empty house of his appearance was ready for him but he had abandoned it. There was a reek of fur and piss; the incense pot lay broken in pieces on the floor. Half-burned sticks were scattered from the extinguished fire. A candle stuck by its own grease to the mantelpiece lit two narrow flames in the pupils of the tiger's eyes.

He was pacing backwards and forwards, backwards and forwards, the tip of his heavy tail twitching as he paced out the length and breadth of his imprisonment between the gnawed and bloody bones.

He will gobble you up.

Nursery fears made flesh and sinew; earliest and most archaic of fears, fear of devourment. The beast and his carnivorous bed of bone and I, white, shaking, raw, approaching him as if offering, in myself, the key to a peaceable kingdom in which his appetite need not be my extinction.

He went still as stone. He was far more frightened of me than I was of him.

I squatted on the wet straw and stretched out my hand. I was now within the field of force of his golden eyes. He growled at the back of his throat, lowered his head, sank on to his forepaws, snarled, showed me his red gullet, his yellow teeth. I never moved. He snuffed the air, as if to smell my fear; he could not.

Slowly, slowly he began to drag his heavy, gleaming weight across the floor towards me.

A tremendous throbbing, as of the engine that makes the earth turn, filled the little room; he had begun to purr.

The sweet thunder of this purr shook the old walls, made the shutters batter the windows until they burst apart and let in the white light of the snowy moon. Tiles came crashing down from the roof; I heard them fall into the courtyard far below. The reverberations of his purring rocked the foundations of the house, the walls began to dance. I thought: "It will all fall, everything will disintegrate."

He dragged himself closer and closer to me, until I felt the harsh velvet of his head against my hand, then a tongue, abrasive as sandpaper. "He will lick the skin off me!"

And each stroke of his tongue ripped off skin after successive skin, all the skins of a life in the world, and left behind a nascent patina of shining hairs. My earrings turned back to water and trickled down my shoulders; I shrugged the drops off my beautiful fur.

Urashima the Fisherman[†]

Young Urashima lived in Tango province, in the village of Tsutsugawa. One day in the fall of 477 (it was Emperor Yūryaku's reign), he rowed out alone on the sea to fish. After catching nothing for three

[†] From *Tango fudoki* (Account of the province of Tango), 713 C.E., in *Japanese Tales,* comp. and trans. Royall Tyler (New York: Pantheon, 1987). Copyright © 1987 by Royall Tyler. Used by permission of Pantheon Books, an imprint of the Knopf Doubleday Publishing Group, a division of Penguin Random House LLC. All rights reserved.

days and nights, he was surprised to find that he had taken a five-colored turtle. He got the turtle into the boat and lay down to sleep.

When the turtle changed into a dazzlingly lovely girl, the mystified Urashima asked her who she was.

"I saw you here, alone at sea," she answered with a smile, "and I wanted so much to talk to you! I came on the clouds and the wind."

"But where did you come from, then, on the clouds and wind?"

"I'm an Immortal and I live in the sky. Don't doubt me! Oh, be kind and speak to me tenderly!"

Urashima understood she was divine, and all his fear of her melted away.

"I'll love you as long as the sky and earth last," she promised him, "as long as there's a sun and a moon! But tell me, will you have me?"

"Your wish is mine," he answered. "How could I not love you?"

"Then lean on your oars, my darling, and take us to my Eternal Mountain!"

She told him to close his eyes. In no time they reached a large island with earth like jade. Watchtowers on it shone darkly, and palaces gleamed like gems. It was a wonder no eye had seen and no ear had ever heard tell of before.

They landed and strolled on hand in hand to a splendid mansion, where she asked him to wait; then she opened the gate and went in. Seven young girls soon came out of the gate, telling each other as they passed him that he was Turtle's husband; and eight girls who came after them told each other the same. That was how he learned her name.

He mentioned the girls when she came back out. She said the seven were the seven stars of the Pleiades, and the eight the cluster of Aldebaran. Then she led him inside.

Her father and mother greeted him warmly and invited him to sit down. They explained the difference between the human and the divine worlds, and they let him know how glad this rare meeting between the gods and a man had made them. He tasted a hundred fragrant delicacies and exchanged cups of wine with the girl's brothers and sisters. Young girls with glowing faces flocked to the happy gathering, while the gods sang their songs sweetly and clearly and danced with fluid grace. The feast was a thousand times more beautiful than any ever enjoyed by mortals in their far-off land.

Urashima never noticed the sun going down, but as twilight came on the Immortals all slipped away. He and the maiden, now alone, lay down in each other's arms and made love. They were man and wife at last.

For three years he forgot his old life and lived in paradise with the Immortals. Then one day he felt a pang of longing for the village where he had been born and the parents he had left behind. After that, he missed them more each day.

"Darling," said his wife, "you haven't looked yourself lately. Won't you tell me what's wrong?"

"They say the dying fox turns toward his lair and the lesser man longs to go home. I'd never believed it, but now I know it's true."

"Do you want to go back?"

"Here I am in the land of the gods, far from all my family and friends. I shouldn't feel this way, I know, but I can't help being homesick for them. I want so much to go back and see my mother and father!"

His wife brushed away her tears. "We gave ourselves to each other forever!" she lamented. "We promised we'd be as true as gold or the rocks of the mountains! How could a little homesickness make you want to leave me?"

They went for a walk hand in hand, sadly talking it all over. Finally they embraced, and when they separated their parting was sealed.

Urashima's parents-in-law were sad to see him go. His wife gave him a jeweled box. "Dearest," she said, "if you don't forget me and find you want to come back, then grip this box hard. But you mustn't open it, ever."

He got into his boat and they told him to close his eyes. In no time he was at Tsutsugawa, his home. The place looked entirely different. He recognized nothing there at all.

"Where's Urashima's family—Urashima the fisherman?" he asked a villager.

"Who are you?" the villager answered. "Where are you from? Why are you looking for a man who lived long ago? Yes, I've heard old people mention someone named Urashima. He went out alone on the sea and never came back. That was three hundred years ago. What do you want with him now?"

Bewildered, Urashima roamed the village for ten days without finding any sign of family or old friends. At last he stroked the box his divine lady had given him and thought of her; then, forgetting his recent promise, he opened it. Before his eyes her fragrant form, borne by the clouds and the wind, floated up and vanished into the blue sky. He understood he had disobeyed her and would never see her again. All he could do was gaze after her, then pace weeping along the shore.

When he dried his tears, he sang about her far, cloud-girdled realm. The clouds, he sang, would bring her the message of his love. Her sweet voice answered him, across the vastness of the sky, entreating him never to forget her. Then a last song burst from him as he struggled with his loss: "My love, when after a night of longing, day dawns and I stand at my open door, I hear far-off waves breaking on the shores of your paradise!"

If only he hadn't opened that jeweled box, people have said since, he could have been with her again. But the clouds hid her paradise from him and left him nothing but his grief.

The Enchanted Frog[†]

Once a poor man and woman had three sons. The first son told his parents he wanted to go and find a life for himself, the second said the same, and the youngest also said he wanted to go find himself a life. The father and mother didn't want them to go, but finally they gave them permission and a blessing, and the sons set out.

The oldest went ahead of the others and he came to a resting place by a cottonwood tree, and a frog was singing there. He liked the song and shouted from below, "Why don't you come down here so that I can marry you?"

"No, no, I can't come down," the frog replied. "You couldn't make a life with me."

Finally, after the boy had tried for a long time to get her to come down, the frog jumped and fell into the boy's cape. When the boy saw her, he said, "What do I want with a frog?" And he threw her away and went on.

Later the second brother arrived there, and when he heard the frog singing so beautifully he said, "Come down so that I can marry you."

"No, sir," the frog said. "Yesterday a boy came by here and made me come down from my chamber, and when I came down he scorned me and threw me away."

The boy said he wouldn't do that. He said he really would marry her, and he spread out his cape for her to jump down. So the frog jumped down, but when he saw it he said, "Uy, how disgusting! What do I want with a frog?" And he threw her away just as his brother had done.

So then finally the youngest brother came along and like the others he heard the enchanted frog singing in the cottonwood tree. The boy told her to come down from the cottonwood because he wanted to meet her.

"No, I can't do that," the frog told him. "Two boys have come by here and both have asked me to come down, and then they scorned me and threw me away." But the boy kept begging for her to come down until the frog said, "All right, spread out your cape for me to

† "The Enchanted Frog," as told by Alesnio Chacón, in *Cuentos de Cuanto Hay / Tales from Spanish New Mexico*, trans. Joe Hayes (Albuquerque: U of New Mexico P, 1998), pp. 103–07. Copyright © 1998 University of New Mexico Press. Reprinted by permission of the publisher.

jump down." The boy spread out the cape and the frog hopped and
fell in the cape, and the boy took her and put her in his pocket. Then
he went on down the road.

He came to the town where his two brothers were living. They
were married now and were very proud, and the youngest brother was
married too—to the frog. When they were all reunited, they wrote
to their parents to tell them they were married and to send them
presents. And wives of the older brothers also wrote; but not the
frog. The frog couldn't write. And the parents wrote back saying
they wanted to receive gifts from the wives. They told them to send
them three embroidered kerchiefs.

The youngest brother was heartsick, and when he got home to his
frog he told her what his parents had written. "Don't worry," the frog
told him. "Throw me into the sea." So he went to the sea and threw
her in, and the frog came out with a little cape made of a single cloth
embroidered with pure gold.

"Send this little cape to your parents," she told him. The sons all
sent their gifts and the parents were amazed by the gift from the
youngest son's wife—a little cape made of a single cloth embroidered
with pure gold.

But then the parents sent word to say that they wanted to meet
their sons' wives, told the sons to bring their wives for a visit. The
sons all agreed to go to visit them with their wives, but the youngest
was very worried and said to himself, "What am I going to do now?
The frog doesn't even look like a woman." But when he went home
and told the frog about it, she told him not to worry, that she would
go too.

And since the frog knew that the wives of her brothers-in-law were
spiteful, she went and started washing her hair with lye. The envious wives saw her and decided they were going to wash their hair
with lye too. They washed their hair with lye and it all fell out and
they were bald.

And then that night the frog told her husband, "Now take me and
throw me into the deepest part of the sea. Leave me there and come
for me in the morning."

The boy did that, but he was very sad because he didn't think he
would see his frog ever again. The next day he got up very early and
went to look for her at the place where he had thrown her into the
sea, and there on the bank of the sea he found a princess in an elegant carriage.

"Here I am," she told him, "I'm free from my enchantment. Now
let's go visit your parents." And they started out because the other
brothers and their wives were already on their way.

They all arrived, and the parents were pleased to see their sons
and their wives. The wives of the older two had their heads covered

so no one could see they were bald. The parents were so pleased that they gave a banquet that night.

And when they were eating, the princess pretended she was stuffing garbanzos and eggs down the front of her dress, but she was really putting in money. But the bald-headed wives really did stuff garbanzos and eggs into their dresses.

After the banquet they all went to dance, and everyone's eye was on the beautiful princess and everyone said she was the prettiest woman they had ever seen. And with each turn she took as she was dancing she scattered pesos and silver coins. But the envious wives scattered the garbanzos and eggs they had stuffed into their bosoms when they were eating.

The people ran to get the money, and the dogs ran to get the garbanzos and eggs!

The Swan Maiden†

A young peasant, in the parish of Mellby, who often amused himself with hunting, saw one day three swans flying toward him, which settled down upon the strand of a sound near by.

Approaching the place, he was astonished at seeing the three swans divest themselves of their feathery attire, which they threw into the grass, and three maidens of dazzling beauty step forth and spring into the water.

After sporting in the waves awhile they returned to the land, where they resumed their former garb and shape and flew away in the same direction from which they came.

One of them, the youngest and fairest, had, in the meantime, so smitten the young hunter that neither night nor day could he tear his thoughts from the bright image.

His mother, noticing that something was wrong with her son, and that the chase, which had formerly been his favorite pleasure, had lost its attractions, asked him finally the cause of his melancholy, whereupon he related to her what he had seen, and declared that there was no longer any happiness in this life for him if he could not possess the fair swan maiden.

"Nothing is easier," said the mother. "Go at sunset next Thursday evening to the place where you last saw her. When the three swans come, give attention to where your chosen one lays her feathery garb, take it and hasten away."

The young man listened to his mother's instructions, and, betaking himself, the following Thursday evening, to a convenient hiding

---

† "The Swan Maiden," in *Scandinavian Folk and Fairy Tales*, comp. Claire Booss (New York: Avenel, 1984). Reprinted from Herman Hofberg, *Swedish Fairy Tales*, 1895.

place near the sound, he waited, with impatience, the coming of the swans. The sun was just sinking behind the trees when the young man's ears were greeted by a whizzing in the air, and the three swans settled down upon the beach, as on their former visit.

As soon as they had laid off their swan attire they were again transformed into the most beautiful maidens, and, springing out upon the white sand, they were soon enjoying themselves in the water.

From his hiding place the young hunter had taken careful note of where his enchantress had laid her swan feathers. Stealing softly forth, he took them and returned to his place of concealment in the surrounding foliage.

Soon thereafter two of the swans were heard to fly away, but the third, in search of her clothes, discovered the young man, before whom, believing him responsible for their disappearance, she fell upon her knees and prayed that her swan attire might be returned to her. The hunter was, however, unwilling to yield the beautiful prize, and, casting a cloak around her shoulders, carried her home.

Preparations were soon made for a magnificent wedding, which took place in due form, and the young couple dwelt lovingly and contentedly together.

One Thursday evening, seven years later, the hunter related to her how he had sought and won his wife. He brought forth and showed her, also, the white swan feathers of her former days. No sooner were they placed in her hands than she was transformed once more into a swan, and instantly took flight through the open window. In breathless astonishment, the man stared wildly after his rapidly vanishing wife, and before a year and a day had passed, he was laid, with his longings and sorrows, in his allotted place in the village church-yard.

Chonguita[†]

There once lived a king who had three sons. They were called Pedro, Diego, and Juan. One day the king ordered the three young gentlemen to set out and seek their fortunes. The brothers each took a different direction, but before they separated, they agreed to meet later at a certain place in the forest.

[†] As told by Pilar Ejercito, a woman living in the province of Laguna in the Philippines. Her aunt had told her the story when she was a little girl. The tale was collected and edited by Dean S. Fansler, who published it in the *Memoirs of the American Folk-Lore Society*, 12 (1921): 244–46. Some minor stylistic emendations were made to his version by the editor of this volume.

After walking for many days, Don Juan met an old man on the road. The old man gave Don Juan some bread and told him to walk to a palace that was about a mile away. "When you enter the gate," he said, "you must divide the bread I have given you among the monkeys guarding the gate to the palace. Otherwise you won't be able to pass through the gate."

Don Juan took the bread. When he reached the palace, he did exactly as the old man had said. When he walked through the gate, he saw a big monkey. Frightened by the sight of the animal, Don Juan was about to run away when the animal called out to him and said, "Don Juan, I know that you came here to make your fortune. Right now my daughter Chonguita is willing to marry you." The archbishop of the monkeys was summoned, and Don Juan and Chonguita were married without delay.

A few days later Don Juan asked his wife for permission to go to the place where he and his brothers had agreed to meet. When Chonguita's mother heard that Don Juan was going away, she said, "If you are going away, take Chonguita with you." Don Juan was ashamed to take Chonguita because she was a monkey, but he was forced to take her, and the two set off on the road. When Don Juan met his two brothers and their beautiful wives at the appointed place, he could not get out a word. Don Diego noticed that his brother looked gloomy and asked, "What is the matter with you? Where is your wife, Don Juan?"

Don Juan sadly replied, "Here she is."

"Where?" asked Don Pedro.

"Right behind me," replied Don Juan.

When Don Pedro and Don Diego saw the monkey, they were startled. "Oh!" exclaimed Don Pedro, "What happened to you? Have you lost your mind?"

Don Juan was at a loss for words. Finally he managed to say, "Let's all go back home! Our father must be waiting for us!" With that, Don Juan turned around and began walking home. Don Pedro and Don Diego, together with their wives, followed Don Juan. Chonguita walked by her husband's side.

The king learned that his three sons had returned, and he rushed down the stairs to meet them. When he discovered that one of his sons had married a monkey, he fainted. But once he recovered his senses, he thought to himself: "This may be a stroke of bad luck, but it is God's will. I must take the news calmly and be patient." The king gave each of the couples a house to live in.

The more the king thought about it, the more disgraceful his son's marriage seemed. One day, he called his three sons together and said to them, "Tell your wives that I want each one of them to make a coat for me and to embroider it. The one who fails to finish the task in three days will be put to death." The king had issued this order with the hope that Chonguita would be put to death. He was sure she would not be able to make a coat for him. But his hopes were dashed. On the third day, the three daughters-in-law presented him with the coats they had made. The one embroidered by Chonguita was the prettiest of the three.

The king was still anxious to get rid of the monkey-wife. He ordered his daughters-in-law to embroider a cap for him in the next two days, under penalty of death if they failed. The caps were all finished right on time.

Finally he was at a loss for ideas, but he came up with the following plan. He summoned his three daughters-in-law and said, "Each of you will draw pictures on the walls of my chamber. Whoever draws the prettiest within the next three days—her husband will succeed me on the throne." At the end of the three days the pictures were finished. When the king went to inspect them, he found that Chonguita's was by far the prettiest, and so Don Juan was crowned king.

A feast was held in the palace to celebrate the new king. In the midst of the festivities, Don Juan became furious with his wife for insisting that he dance with her, and he hurled her against the wall. The hall suddenly turned dark after this brutal act took place. But then it grew bright again, and there was Chonguita, transformed into a beautiful woman.

The Dog Bride[†]

Once upon a time there lived a young man whose job it was to herd buffaloes. One day, as he was watching his animals graze, he noticed that a dog would appear every day at high noon and make its way over to a ravine with some pools of water. His curiosity was aroused, and he wondered who owned the dog and what it was doing in that ravine. He decided to start paying attention to the animal. One day when it appeared, he hid in a place where he could watch the dog. It got into the water, shed its dog skin, and out stepped a beautiful maiden. She bathed in the waters, and when she was finished, she put the skin back on and became a dog. Off she went to the village. The shepherd followed her and saw her enter a house. He asked about the owner of the house, and, once he found out his name, he went back to his work.

[†] Cecil Henry Bompas, *Folklore of the Santhal Parganas* (London: David Nutt, 1909), pp. 255–56, with some minor stylistic emendations by the editor of this volume. Santhal Pargana belongs to one of five administrative units in eastern India.

That year the shepherd's father and mother decided that it was time for him to marry. They began looking around for a suitable wife. But he announced that he had already made up his mind. He had decided to marry a dog, and he would never have a human wife.

Everyone laughed out loud when they heard what he had said. But he would not change his mind. Finally everyone began to believe that he must have the soul of a dog in him and that it was best to let him have his way. His mother and father asked whether he had any particular dog in mind for his bride. He gave them the name of the man into whose house he had tracked the dog that had bathed in the area of the ravines. The dog's master found it hilarious that anyone would want to marry his dog, but he was happy to accept a bride price from the family for her. The day was set for the wedding, and they began building a booth for the ceremony. The bridegroom's party went to the bride's house, and the wedding went off without a hitch. The bride was escorted back to her husband's house.

Every night, after her husband fell asleep, the bride would remove her dog's skin and leave the house. After her husband discovered what she was doing, he pretended the next night to go to sleep and kept an eye on her. Just as she was about to leave the room, he jumped up and grabbed her. He seized the dog skin, threw it into the fire, where it burned to ashes. The bride kept her human shape, but she was of more than human beauty. Everyone in the village found out what happened, and they congratulated the shepherd for having the wisdom to marry a dog.

Now the shepherd had a friend named Jitu, and when Jitu saw what a prize his friend had won, he decided that he could not do better than to marry a dog. His relatives did not object, and a bride was chosen. The wedding celebrations began, but when they were putting vermilion on the bride's forehead, she began to growl. Still, they dragged her to the bridegroom's home and anointed her with oil and turmeric. But when the bride's party set off for home, the dog broke loose and started running back to them. Everyone shouted at Jitu, telling him to run after his bride and bring her back. But she growled at him and then bit him so that he had to give up. Everyone laughed so hard at him that he was too ashamed to say a word. Two or three days later he hanged himself.

INTRODUCTION: Snow White

Walt Disney's *Snow White and the Seven Dwarfs* (1937) has become our cultural story about an innocent heroine, her evil stepmother, and a romantic rescue from household drudgery and maternal persecution. The film so dominates the fairy-tale landscape that it is easy to forget the many versions of it that animated storytelling in times past and still circulate in our own day. Parental cruelty and romantic love know no geographical or chronological boundaries, and the tale—both its deep structure and its standard tropes—flashes out at us in ways both predictable and unexpected. Cannibalism and necrophilia, child abandonment and sexual rivalry, beauty and monstrosity: these are the constants in the kaleidoscopic variations of Snow White stories.

Disney's story about Snow White is very different from the one we find in the canonical literary version recorded in the early nineteenth century. The Brothers Grimm called their story "Little Snow White," perhaps to emphasize the vulnerability of a young girl persecuted by her jealous stepmother. Their heroine is precociously stunning: "When she was seven years old she was as beautiful as the light of day, even more beautiful than the queen herself." Her beauty inspires huntsman, dwarfs, and prince alike to protect her from a less fair queen. Although the early versions of the Grimms' "Little Snow White" pit a biological mother against her daughter, later iterations of the tale feature a stepmother, reminding us that mortality rates for child-bearing women were exceptionally high in earlier eras and that their children were socially vulnerable and not necessarily protected by a father's second wife.

When asked why he did not stay closer to the Grimms' script, Walt Disney responded, "It's just that people now don't want fairy stories the way they were written. They were too rough. In the end, they'll probably remember the story the way we film it anyway." There is indeed much "rough" stuff in earlier cultural inflections of the tale, though one could argue that Disney, rather than lightening up the story, preserved much of the blood and gore. It may be that the Wicked Witch's plunge from a cliff in a lightning storm is less protracted than the Grimms' tableau of a woman dancing to her death in red-hot iron shoes, but the ending to the animated film feels more terrifying in its fierce pacing, with dwarfs in hot pursuit and a frenzied scramble up a cliff.

The story of Snow White varies tremendously from culture to culture in its details. Disney's princess ingests a poisoned apple, but her European counterparts fall victim to toxic combs, contaminated cakes, and, in one case, a suffocating braid. Disney's queen, who demands Snow White's heart from the huntsman who takes the girl into the woods, actually seems restrained by comparison with the Grimms' evil queen, who orders the huntsman to return with the girl's lungs and liver (she plans to eat both after boiling them in salt water). In Spain, the queen is even more bloodthirsty, asking for a bottle of blood, with the girl's toe used as a cork. In Italy, the cruel queen instructs the huntsman to return with the girl's intestines and her blood-soaked shirt. Disney's film has fetishized the coffin made of glass, but in other versions of the story it is made of gold, silver, or lead or is jewel-encrusted. While it is often displayed on a mountaintop, it can also be set adrift on a river, placed under a tree, hung from the rafters, or locked in a room gleaming with candlelight.

Nearly every critic attempting to understand the deeper meaning of "Snow White" identifies a stable core that turns on some kind of rivalry between mother and daughter. Steven Swann Jones, modifying and refining the structure of the story as outlined in the international index of tale types, breaks the story down into a sequence of nine events: birth, jealousy, expulsion, adoption, renewed jealousy, death, exhibition, resuscitation, and resolution. "The most plausible explanation for the form that the overall plot structure of 'Snow White' assumes," he declares, "is that it is a reflection of a young woman's development."[1] Jones captures the defining features of the tale, but more important the sequence he identifies reveals how the story's narrative structure is sustained by binary opposites (birth/death, expulsion/adoption, jealousy/affection). The powerful staging of mother/daughter conflicts is driven by matters primal and primary—giving birth yet also suffocating, nurturing but also withholding, caring but also competing.

Psychologists have described these conflicts as Oedipal, with mother and daughter in competition for the love and affection of an absent father. Bruno Bettelheim bases his reading of the story on the Grimms' "Snow White," which features a "good" biological mother who dies in childbirth and an "evil" queen who persecutes her seven-year-old stepdaughter. He argues that the splitting of the maternal function has a strong emotional appeal for children. The young,

---

1. Steven Swann Jones, *The New Comparative Method: Structural and Symbolic Analysis of the Allomotifs of Snow White* (Helsinki: Academia Scientiarum Fennica, 1990), p. 32.

emotionally and economically dependent on their parents, have a deep need to preserve a positive image of mother, one uncontaminated by the natural feelings of anger and hostility that arise as differences develop between mother and child. The wicked stepmother of fairy tales "permits anger at this bad 'stepmother' without endangering the goodwill of the true mother, who is viewed as a different person."[2]

The struggle between Snow White and the wicked queen so dominates the psychological landscape of this fairy tale that Sandra Gilbert and Susan Gubar have proposed renaming it "Snow White and Her Wicked Stepmother." These two critics, for whom the Grimms' tale enacts "the essential but equivocal relationship between the angel-woman and the monster-woman" of Western patriarchy, emphasize not just a generational divide but also a moral, ethical, cognitive, and aesthetic standoff.

> The central action of the tale—indeed its only real action—arises from the relationship between these two women, the one fair, young, pale, the other just as fair, but older, fiercer; the one a daughter, the other a mother; the one sweet, ignorant, passive, the other both artful and active; the one a sort of angel, the other an undeniable witch.[3]

For both Bettelheim and Gilbert and Gubar, the absent father occupies a central, if invisible, position in the domestic drama. And in fact many versions of the story show (step)mother and daughter competing for the attention of a charismatic male figure—sometimes a husband/father, but occasionally also a husband/uncle. Gilbert and Gubar find the father acoustically present if physically absent: "His, surely, is the voice of the looking glass, the patriarchal voice of judgment that rules the queen's—and every woman's self-evaluation."[4] The absence of the father is framed as an emphatic repression that reveals only the degree to which he occupies center stage.

In "The Young Slave" (p. 92) from Giambattista Basile's 1634 collection of tales published under the title *The Pentamerone*, the persecution of the heroine is explicitly motivated by an aunt's unwarranted sexual jealousy. Lisa, a Neapolitan Snow White, falls into a coma and is preserved for many years in a casket of crystal. When she awakens, she finds herself the target of frenzied envy, for her aunt believes that she has been the clandestine mistress of her husband. In the end, Lisa's uncle, who has been a model of marital

---

2. Bruno Bettelheim, *The Uses of Enchantment: The Meaning and Importance of Fairy Tales* (New York: Knopf, 1976), p. 201.
3. Sandra M. Gilbert and Susan Gubar, *The Madwoman in the Attic: The Woman Writer and the Nineteenth-Century Literary Imagination* (New Haven, CT: Yale UP, 1979), p. 16.
4. Ibid., p. 38.

fidelity, reveals a distinct preference for his niece when he drives his cruel wife out of the house. Basile's tale, one of the earliest recorded versions of "Snow White," suggests that the complex psychosexual motivations shaping the plots of fairy tales underwent a process of repression once the social venue for the stories shifted from the household and the communal hearth to the nursery.

Where Bettelheim sees a generational conflict between mother and daughter, Gilbert and Gubar see an intrapsychic drama played out between two possible developmental trajectories, one passive, docile, and compliant with patriarchal norms, the other nomadic, creative, and socially subversive. The two feminist critics invest the figure of the wicked queen with narrative energy so powerful that she becomes the story's most admirable character. For them, she is a "plotter, a plot-maker, a schemer, a witch, an artist, and impersonator, a woman of almost infinite creative energy, witty, wily, and self-absorbed as all artists traditionally are."[5] And it is the queen who foreshadows the destiny of Snow White, predicting just what will happen to the innocent, persecuted heroine as she rides off to a "happily ever after" and ascends the throne. Then she will exchange her glass coffin for an equally imprisoning looking glass, which will reflect back to her every aspect of the aging process.

Gilbert and Gubar surely took an interpretive cue from Anne Sexton's poetic transformation of the Grimms' "Snow White," in which an aging queen ("brown spots on her hand / and four whiskers over her lip") is pitted against a thirteen-year-old "lovely virgin." "Beauty is a simple passion," Sexton declares, "but, oh my friends, in the end / you will dance the fire dance in iron shoes" (p. 103). The scene that stages the queen's death juxtaposes a mobile queen, dancing to death with "her tongue flicking in and out / like a gas jet," with a frozen Snow White "rolling her china-blue doll eyes open and shut / and sometimes referring to her mirror / as women do" (p. 106). Sexton's inert Snow White is destined one day to become her mother, galvanized into action and turned into an agent of persecution by the divisive gaze in the mirror.

The mirror and the glass coffin are important as both aesthetic artifacts and psychological symbols. The looking glass can be a trope for vanity and narcissism, and for the wicked queen it is also the voice of judgment. On the one hand the mirror reflects back an image of beauty and integrity, but it is also a reminder of self-division and temporality—the image that looks back at us is subject to change. It is ephemeral and marked by mortality. Beauty may appear to mask death but its image (both in the mirror and on the face of Snow

5. Ibid., pp. 38–39.

White in her coffin) also has a sinister side, reminding us that everything is subject to decay and must die.[6]

Disney Studios has given us the culturally dominant version of
"Snow White," turning her into one of the most familiar fairy-tale
characters of all time. The Grimms' "Snow White" may not have
fared particularly well in Anglo-American cultures, but its cinematic
reincarnation as a feature-length animated film created a new portal for fairy tales. Suddenly fairy tales were turned into cartoon versions of themselves, designed to entertain children, but they were
also transformed by the new medium into powerfully present, nearly
palpable cultural narratives.

Advertisements for "Snow White" may picture the heroine and the
prince, but the seven dwarfs and the wicked queen dominate the film
visually and verbally. Snow White and the Prince, despite the use
of primary colors, are bleached-out figures, as flat and colorless as
their names. The seven dwarfs, by contrast, enliven the film with
their antics, just as the wicked queen provides surges of emotional
energy with her cruel charms. In her underground lair, surrounded
by skulls and ravens, she works with dusty tomes and a chemistry
set to concoct deadly recipes.

Disney Studios erased the Grimms' prelude, an episode that
describes the death of Snow White's biological mother in childbirth.
The only maternal figure is the stepmother in her double incarnation as beautiful, proud, and evil queen and as ugly, sinister, and
wicked witch. Notes taken at story conferences reveal that the queen
was planned as "a mixture of Lady Macbeth and the Big, Bad Wolf,"
fiercely treacherous and unforgiving.[7] Disney himself, who referred
to the transformation of the queen into an old hag as a "Jekyll and
Hyde thing," seemed unaware that there is no Jekyll component to
the figure's personality, only two Hydes.[8] Instead of the splitting of
the mother image into a good mother who dies in childbirth and an
evil queen who persecutes her stepchild, the maternal figure appears
bent on destruction in every way.

The Disney version of "Snow White" relentlessly polarizes the
notion of the feminine to produce a murderously jealous and forbid-
dingly cold woman on the one hand and an innocently sweet girl
accomplished in the art of good housekeeping on the other. Beginning with the Grimms, it is through a combination of labor and good
looks that Snow White earns a prince for herself. Here is how the
Grimms describe the housekeeping contract extended to Snow

---

6. Elisabeth Bronfen, *Over Her Dead Body: Death, Femininity, and the Aesthetic* (New
   York: Routledge, 1992), pp. 104–05.
7. Richard Holliss and Brian Sibley, *Walt Disney's "Snow White and the Seven Dwarfs"
   and the Making of the Classic Film* (New York: Simon & Schuster, 1987), p. 14.
8. Ibid., p. 14.

White by the dwarfs: "If you will keep house for us, cook, make the beds, wash, sew, knit, and keep everything neat and tidy, then you can stay with us, and we'll give you everything you need" (p. 97). But the dwarfs in the Grimms' tale are hardly in need of a housekeeper, for they appear to be models of tidiness. Everything in their cottage is "indescribably dainty and spotless" (p. 96); the table has a white cloth with tiny plates, cups, knives, forks, and spoons, and the beds are covered with sheets "as white as snow" (p. 96). Compare this description of the dwarfs' cottage with the following one taken from a book based on Disney's version of "Snow White":

> Skipping across a little bridge to the house, Snow White peeked in through one windowpane. There seemed to be no one at home, but the sink was piled high with cups and saucers and plates, which looked as though they had never been washed. Dirty little shirts and wrinkled little trousers hung over chairs, and everything was blanketed with dust.
>
> "Maybe the children who live here have no mother," said Snow White, "and need someone to take care of them. Let's clean their house and surprise them."
>
> So in she went, followed by her forest friends. Snow White found an old broom in the corner and swept the floor, while the little animals all did their best to help.
>
> Then Snow White washed all the crumpled little clothes, and set a kettle of delicious soup to bubbling on the hearth.[9]

In one post-Disney American variant of the story after another, Snow White makes it her mission to clean up after the dwarfs ("seven little boys")[1] and is represented as serving an apprenticeship in home economics ("Snow White for her part was becoming an excellent housekeeper and cook.")[2] The Disney version, made at the height of the Great Depression, has everyone whistling and singing while they work, all the while embracing the work ethic with no grumbling at all. Household drudgery becomes frolicking good fun, less work than play, since it requires no real effort, is carried out with the help of wonderfully nimble, adorable woodland creatures, and achieves dazzling results. And the dwarfs cheerfully extol the joys of spending their days underground in a diamond mine: "To dig dig dig dig dig dig dig is what we really like to do."

"We just try to make a good picture," Walt Disney once observed in connection with *Snow White and the Seven Dwarfs*. "And then the professors come along and tell us what we do."[3] The professors

9. 55 *Favorite Stories Adapted from Disney Films*. A Golden Book (n.p.: Western, 1960).
1. From *Snow White*, illus. Rex Irvine and Judie Clarke (n.p.: Superscope, 1973).
2. From *Storytime Treasury* (New York: McCall, 1969).
3. "Mouse & Man," *Time*, December 27, 1937, p. 21.

for sure, but also filmmakers who have recognized that the evil queen plays a commanding role, a source of cinematic fascination that contrasts with a figure so dull that she needs a supporting cast of seven to enliven her scenes. With a voice in which "the accents of Betty Boop are far too prominent"[4] and with a figure that has been described as a "pasty, sepulchral, sewing-pattern design scissored out of context,"[5] the Snow White character lacks the narrative charge and élan so potently present in the representation of the stepmother. Ultimately it is the stepmother's disruptive, disturbing, and divisive presence that invests the story with a degree of fascination that has facilitated its widespread circulation and that has allowed it to take hold in our culture.

In the cinematic afterlife of "Snow White," we find that productions ranging from Michael Cohn's *Snow White: A Tale of Terror* (1997) and Tarsem Singh's *Mirror Mirror* (2012) to Rupert Sanders's *Snow White and the Huntsman* (2012) and ABC's *Once Upon a Time* (2011–) continue to tell a story about generational conflict and parental cruelty, yet they also poignantly capture adult anxieties about aging and loss. Disney's brilliant compression of the aging process into a brief sequence shows us the queen drinking a magic potion. Suddenly her hair turns white, her hands become gnarled with age ("Look, my hands!"), her voice turns into a throaty cackle ("My voice!"), and finally she emerges from under her dark cloak as a hunchbacked crone. The horror of the queen's transformation from a beautiful woman into an abject old hag is still potent, especially in the film industry, where roles become scarce for actresses once they turn thirty.

Sanders's *Snow White and the Huntsman* captures deepening anxiety about aging and generational sexual rivalry in clever, self-reflexive ways, with Charlize Theron as a beautiful cougar (and established Hollywood star) threatened by a younger, sylph-like Kristin Stewart. In the world of the film, beauty is the locus of female power and is thereby fleeting in its effects (men are "enchanted" by women but "use" them until they eventually "tire" of them). Beauty becomes a source of both fascination and horror. Early on, we learn the wicked queen's backstory: she was abandoned by her first husband for a younger woman. This is meant to explain why she is so desperate to suck the life force out of local virgins, to dine on the vital organs of birds, and to reap the cosmetic effects of baths in mysterious white fluids.

The queen's quest for lasting youth is part of the story's larger exploration (in the tradition of many great myths) of how humans

4. Holliss and Sibley, *Walt Disney's "Snow White,"* p. 65.
5. V. F. Calverton, "The Snow White Fiasco," *Current History* (June 1938): 46.

relate to the natural world—whether we are of it or have mastered and moved beyond it. Efforts to remain forever young violate the natural order of generational succession and imperil life itself. The woods have always been terrifying, but never more so than in this new version of the tale, in which a despoiled Mother Nature mirrors and magnifies the wicked queen's frenzied assaults on humans. *Snow White and the Huntsman* holds a mirror up to our own vanity, narcissism, and recklessness, emphatically reminding us, as Theron proclaims shortly before her downfall, that every world gets the wicked queen it deserves.

Stewart's Snow White is nothing like the charmingly goofy princess of Disney's live-action *Enchanted* or the spunky yet vulnerable Snow White in the ABC series *Once Upon a Time*. More like a serious cousin to the spirited and radiantly youthful Snow White of Singh's campy film *Mirror Mirror*, she is ready for action. She becomes a "pure and innocent" warrior princess, an angelic savior who channels Joan of Arc and Tolkien's Aragorn as well as the four Pevensie siblings from C. S. Lewis's The Chronicles of Narnia, to save the kingdom of her late father (stabbed to death by the queen on their wedding night). Everyone is armed, and swords, scimitars, axes, snares, and shields feature as prominently in this film as they do in Tolkien's Middle Earth. Romance is edged out by the racing energy of horses speeding through dramatic landscapes and by expertly choreographed combat scenes. This is a Snow White designed to appeal to viewers of all ages, and to men and women alike.

If we are to follow the wisdom of psychologists and the self-help experts, it becomes evident that fairy tales have powerful therapeutic benefits, helping us stage our fears and desires in symbolic form and work through anxieties, both personal and cultural. But occasionally we encounter a spectacular example of what appears to illustrate the toxic effects of reading fairy tales, and one such case can be found in the life of Alan Turing, father of theoretical computer science. When Turing went to see Disney's *Snow White and the Seven Dwarfs* a year after its Hollywood debut, he fell under the spell of the scene in which the wicked queen labors in her underground hide-out, preparing the poisonous brew that will put her stepdaughter into a coma. According to his running partner Alan Garner, Turing would go over the scene in detail, describing the apple as red on one side, green on the other (the wicked queen actually starts with a green apple, which is turned red). More important, he would ritually chant the couplet: "Dip the apple in the brew / Let the Sleeping Death seep through." On June 8, 1954, Turing's landlady discovered his inert body. At the side of his bed: half an apple, and in the kitchen: a jam jar with a cyanide solution. In some ways, this is the true Turing enigma, a posthumous challenge from the man who established the foundation for artificial intelligence to those who defend the uses of enchantment as well as all the positives of reading fairy tales and watching their cinematic adaptations.

GIAMBATTISTA BASILE

The Young Slave[†]

* * *

There was once a Baron of Selvascura who had an unmarried sister. This sister used to go and play in a garden with other girls her own age. One day they found a lovely rose in full bloom, so they made a compact that whoever jumped clean over it without touching a single leaf, should win something. But although many of the girls jumped leapfrog over it, they all hit it, and not one of them jumped clean over. But when the turn came to Lilla, the Baron's sister, she stood back a little and took such a run at it that she jumped right over to the other side of the rose. Nevertheless, one leaf fell, but she was so quick and ready that she picked it up from the ground without anyone noticing and swallowed it, thereby winning the prize.

Not less than three days later, Lilla felt herself to be pregnant, and nearly died of grief, for she knew that she had done nothing compromising or dishonest, and could not understand how it was possible for her belly to have swollen. She ran at once to some fairies who were her friends, and when they heard her story, they told her not to worry, for the cause of it all was the rose-leaf she had swallowed.

When Lilla understood this, she took precautions to conceal her condition as much as possible, and when the hour of her deliverance came, she gave birth in hiding to a lovely little girl whom she named Lisa. She sent her to the fairies and they each gave her some charm, but the last one slipped and twisted her foot so badly as she was running to see the child, that in her acute pain she hurled a curse at her, to the effect that when she was seven years old, her mother, whilst combing out her hair, would leave the comb in her tresses, stuck into the head, and from this the child would perish.

At the end of seven years the disaster occurred, and the despairing mother, lamenting bitterly, encased the body in seven caskets of crystal, one within the other, and placed her in a distant room of the palace, keeping the key in her pocket. However, after some time

† Giambattista Basile, "The Young Slave," in *The Pentamerone*, trans. Benedetto Croce (London: Bodley Head, 1932). Reprinted by permission of the publisher.

her grief brought her to her grave. When she felt the end to be near, she called her brother and said to him, "My brother, I feel death's hook dragging me away inch by inch. I leave you all my belongings for you to have and dispose of as you like; but you must promise me never to open the last room in this house, and always keep the key safely in the casket." The brother, who loved her above all things, gave her his word; at the same moment she breathed, "Adieu, for the beans are ripe."

At the end of some years, this lord (who had in the meantime taken a wife) was invited to a hunting-party. He recommended the care of the house to his wife, and begged her above all not to open the room, the key of which he kept in the casket. However, as soon as he had turned his back, she began to feel suspicious, and impelled by jealousy and consumed by curiosity, which is woman's first attribute, took the key and went to open the room. There she saw the young girl, clearly visible through the crystal caskets, so she opened them one by one and found that she seemed to be asleep. Lisa had grown like any other woman, and the caskets had lengthened with her, keeping pace as she grew.

When she beheld this lovely creature, the jealous woman at once thought, "By my life, this is a fine thing! Keys at one's girdle, yet nature makes horns![1] No wonder he never let anyone open the door and see the Mahomet[2] that he worshipped inside the caskets!" Saying this, she seized the girl by the hair, dragged her out, and in so doing caused the comb to drop out, so that the sleeping Lisa awoke, calling out, "Mother, mother!"

"I'll give you mother, and father too!" cried the Baroness, who was as bitter as a slave, as angry as a bitch with a litter of pups, and as venomous as a snake. She straightway cut off the girl's hair and thrashed her with the tresses, dressed her in rags, and every day heaped blows on her head and bruises on her face, blackening her eyes and making her mouth look as if she had eaten raw pigeons.[3]

When her husband came back from his hunting-party and saw this girl being so hardly used, he asked who she was. His wife answered that she was a slave sent her by her aunt, only fit for the rope's end, and that one had to be forever beating her.

Now it happened one day, when the Baron had occasion to go to a fair, that he asked everyone in the house, including even the cats, what they would like him to buy for them, and when they had all chosen, one one thing and one another, he turned at last to the slave. But his wife flew into a rage and acted unbecomingly to a

1. The husband or wife is cuckolded.
2. The body of Mahomet was rumored to have been preserved in a coffin suspended between heaven and earth. The baron, it is implied, has been worshiping a false god.
3. Dripping with blood.

Christian, saying, "That's right, class her with all the others, this thick-lipped slave, let everyone be brought down to the same level and all use the urinal.[4] Don't pay so much attention to a worthless bitch, let her go to the devil." But the Baron who was kind and courteous insisted that the slave should also ask for something. And she said to him, "I want nothing but a doll, a knife and a pumice-stone; and if you forget them, may you never be able to cross the first river that you come to on your journey!"

The Baron bought all the other things, but forgot just those for which his niece had asked him; so when he came to a river that carried down stones and trees to the shore to lay foundations of fears and raise walls of wonder, he found it impossible to ford it. Then he remembered the spell put on him by the slave, and turned back and bought the three articles in question. When he arrived home he gave out to each one the thing for which they had asked.

When Lisa had what she wanted, she went into the kitchen, and, putting the doll in front of her, began to weep and lament and recount all the story of her troubles to that bundle of cloth just as if it had been a real person. When it did not reply, she took the knife and sharpened it on the pumice-stone and said, "Mind, if you don't answer me, I will dig this into you, and that will put an end to the game!" And the doll, swelling up like a reed when it has been blown into, answered at last, "All right, I have understood you! I'm not deaf!"

This music had already gone on for a couple of days, when the Baron, who had a little room on the other side of the kitchen, chanced to hear this song, and putting his eye to the keyhole, saw Lisa telling the doll all about her mother's jump over the rose-leaf, how she swallowed it, her own birth, the spell, the curse of the last fairy, the comb left in her hair, her death, how she was shut into the seven caskets and placed in that room, her mother's death, the key entrusted to the brother, his departure for the hunt, the jealousy of his wife, how she opened the room against her husband's commands, how she cut off her hair and treated her like a slave, and the many, many torments she had inflicted on her. And all the while she wept and said, "Answer me, dolly, or I will kill myself with this knife." And sharpening it on the pumice-stone, she would have plunged it into herself had not the Baron kicked down the door and snatched the knife out of her hand.

He made her tell him the story again at greater length, and then he embraced his niece and took her away from that house, and left her in charge of one of his relations in order that she should get

---

4. All have the same privileges (reflects a time in which using the urinal was considered a luxury).

better, for the hard usage inflicted on her by that heart of a Medea[5] had made her quite thin and pale. After several months, when she had become as beautiful as a goddess, the Baron brought her home and told everyone that she was his niece. He ordered a great banquet, and when the viands had been cleared away, he asked Lisa to tell the story of the hardships she had undergone and of the cruelty of his wife—a tale which made all the guests weep. Then he drove his wife away, sending her back to her parents, and gave his niece a handsome husband of her own choice. Thus Lisa testified that

Heaven rains favors on us when we least expect it.

BROTHERS GRIMM

Snow White[†]

Once upon a time in the middle of winter, when snow flakes were falling from the sky like feathers, a queen was sitting and sewing by a window with a black ebony frame. While she was sewing and looking out at the snow, she pricked her finger with a needle, and three drops of blood fell onto the snow. The red looked so beautiful against the white snow that she thought to herself: "If only I had a child as white as snow, as red as blood, and as black as the wood of the window frame." Soon thereafter she gave birth to a little girl, who was as white as snow, as red as blood, and as black as ebony, and she was called Snow White. The queen died after the child was born.

A year later the king married another woman. She was a beautiful lady, but proud and arrogant and could not bear being second to anyone in beauty. She had a magic mirror, and when she stood in front of it and looked at herself, she would say:

> "Mirror, mirror, on the wall,
> Who's the fairest one of all?"

The mirror would reply:

> "You, oh queen, are the fairest of all."

Then she was satisfied, for she knew that the mirror always spoke the truth.

---

5. Princess and sorceress of Colchis who helped Jason obtain the Golden Fleece and murdered her two sons when she was betrayed.

† Jacob Grimm and Wilhelm Grimm, "Schneewittchen," in *Kinder- und Hausmärchen*, 7th ed. (Berlin: Dieterich, 1857; first published: Berlin: Realschulbuchhandlung, 1812). Translated for the first edition of this Norton Critical Edition by Maria Tatar. Copyright © 1999 by Maria Tatar.

Snow White was growing up and becoming more and more beautiful. When she was seven years old, she was as beautiful as the bright day and more beautiful than the queen herself. One day the queen asked the mirror:

> "Mirror, mirror, on the wall,
> Who's the fairest one of all?"

The mirror replied:

> "My queen, you are the fairest one here,
> But Snow White is a thousand times more fair than you!"

When the Queen heard these words, she trembled and turned green with envy. From that moment on, she hated Snow White, and whenever she set eyes on her, her heart turned as cold as a stone. Envy and pride grew like weeds in her heart. Day and night, she never had a moment's peace. One day, she summoned a huntsman and said: "Take the child out into the forest. I don't want to have to lay eyes on her ever again. You must kill her and bring me her lungs and liver as proof of your deed." The huntsman obeyed and took her out into the woods, but just as he was pulling out his hunting knife and about to take aim at her innocent heart, she began weeping and pleading with him. "Alas, dear huntsman, spare my life. I promise to run into the woods and never return."

Snow White was so beautiful that the huntsman took pity on her and said: "Just run away, you poor child."

"The wild animals will devour you before long," he thought to himself. He felt as if a great weight had been lifted from his heart, for at least he did not have to kill her. Just then a young boar ran past him, and the huntsman stabbed it to death. He took out the lungs and liver and brought them to the queen as proof that he had murdered the child. The cook was told to boil them in brine, and the wicked woman ate them up, thinking that she had eaten Snow White's lungs and liver.

The poor child was left all alone in the vast forest. She was so frightened that she just stared at all the leaves on the trees and had no idea what to do next. She started running and raced over sharp stones and through thornbushes. Wild beasts darted near her at times, but they did her no harm. She ran as far as her legs could carry her. When night fell, she saw a little cottage and went inside to rest. Everything in the house was tiny, and indescribably dainty and spotless. There was a little table, with seven little plates on a white cloth. Each little plate had a little spoon, seven little knives and forks, and seven little cups. Against the wall were seven little beds in a row, each made up with sheets as white as snow. Snow White was so hungry and thirsty that she ate a few vegetables and some bread from each little plate and drank a drop of wine out of each little cup. She didn't want to take everything away from one place. Later, she was so tired that she tried out the beds, but they did not seem to be the right size. The first was too long, the second too short, but the seventh one was just right, and she stayed in it. Then she said her prayers and fell fast asleep.

After it was completely dark outside, the owners of the cottage returned. They were seven dwarfs who spent their days in the mountains mining ore and digging for minerals. They lighted their seven little lanterns, and when the cottage brightened up, they saw that someone had been there, for some things were not the way they had left them.

The first one asked: "Who's been sitting on my little chair?"

The second asked: "Who's been eating from my little plate?"

The third asked: "Who's been eating my little loaf of bread?"

The fourth asked: "Who's been eating from my little plate of vegetables?"

The fifth asked: "Who's been using my little fork?"

The sixth asked: "Who's been cutting with my little knife?"

The seventh asked: "Who's been drinking from my little cup?"

The first one turned around and saw some wrinkles on his sheets and said: "Who climbed into my little bed?"

The others came running and each shouted: "Someone's been sleeping in my bed too."

When the seventh dwarf looked in his little bed, he saw Snow White lying there, fast asleep. He shouted to the others who came running and who were so astonished that they raised their seven little lanterns to let the light shine on Snow White.

"My goodness, oh my goodness!" they exclaimed. "What a beautiful child!"

They were so delighted to see her that they decided not to wake her up and let her continue sleeping in her little bed. The seventh dwarf slept for one hour with each of his companions until the night was over.

In the morning, Snow White woke up. When she saw the dwarfs, she was frightened, but they were friendly and asked, "What's your name?"

"My name is Snow White," she replied.

"How did you get to our house?" asked the dwarfs.

Then she told them how her stepmother had tried to kill her and that the huntsman had spared her life. She had run all day long until she had arrived at their cottage.

The dwarfs told her: "If you will keep house for us, cook, make the beds, wash, sew, knit, and keep everything neat and tidy, then you can stay with us, and we'll give you everything you need."

"Yes, with pleasure," Snow White replied, and she stayed with them.

She kept house for them. In the morning, they went up to the mountains in search of minerals and gold. In the evening, they returned, and dinner had to be ready for them. Since the girl was by herself during the day, the good dwarfs gave her a strong warning:

"Beware of your stepmother. She'll know soon enough that you're here. Don't let anyone in the house."

After the queen had finished eating what she thought were Snow White's lungs and liver, she was sure that she was once again the fairest of all in the land. She went to the mirror and said:

> "Mirror, mirror, on the wall,
> Who's the fairest of them all?"

The mirror replied:

> "Here you're the fairest, dearest queen,
> But little Snow White, who plans to stay
> With the seven dwarfs far far away,
> Is now the fairest ever seen."

When the queen heard this she was horrified, for she knew that the mirror could not tell a lie. She realized that the huntsman had deceived her and that Snow White must still be alive. She thought long and hard about how she could kill Snow White. Unless she herself was the fairest in the land, she would never be able to feel anything but envy. Finally, she came up with a plan. After staining her face and dressing up as an old peddler woman, she was completely unrecognizable. She traveled beyond the seven hills to the seven dwarfs in that disguise. Then she knocked on the door and called out: "Pretty wares for a good price."

Snow White peeked out of the window and said: "Good day, old woman, what do you have for sale?"

"Nice things, pretty things," she replied. "Staylaces[1] in all kinds of colors," and she took out a silk lace woven of many colors.

"I can let this good woman in," Snow White thought to herself, and she unbolted the door and bought the pretty lace.

"Oh my child, what a sight you are. Come, let me lace you up properly."

Snow White wasn't the least bit suspicious. She stood in front of the old woman and let her put on the new lace. The old woman laced her up so quickly and so tightly that Snow White's breath was cut off, and she fell down as if dead.

"So much for being the fairest of them all," she said and hurried away.

---

1. Laces used to tighten the band of strips in a corset.

Not much later, in the evening, the seven dwarfs came home. When they saw their beloved Snow White lying on the ground, they were horrified. She didn't move in the slightest, and they were sure she was dead. They lifted her up, and when they saw that she had been laced too tightly, they cut the staylace in two. Snow White began to breathe, and little by little she came back to life. When the dwarfs heard what had happened, they said: "The old peddler woman was none other than the wicked queen. Beware, and don't let anyone in unless we're at home."

When the wicked woman returned home, she went to the mirror and asked:

> "Mirror, mirror, on the wall,
> Who's the fairest of them all?"

The mirror replied as usual:

> "Here you're the fairest, dearest queen,
> But little Snow White, who plans to stay
> With the seven dwarfs far far away,
> Is now the fairest ever seen."

The blood froze in her veins when she heard those words. She was horrified, for she knew that Snow White was still alive. "But this time," she said, "I will dream up something that will destroy you."

Using all the witchcraft in her power, she made a poisoned comb. She then changed her clothes and disguised herself as another old woman. Once again she traveled beyond the seven hills to the seven dwarfs, knocked on the door, and called out: "Pretty wares at a good price."

Snow White peeked out of the window and said: "Go away, I can't let anyone in."

"But you can at least take a look," said the old woman, and she took out the poisoned comb and held it up in the air. The child liked it so much that she was completely fooled and opened the door. When they had agreed on a price, the old woman said: "Now I'll give your hair a good combing."

Poor Snow White suspected nothing and let the woman go ahead, but no sooner had the comb touched her hair when the poison took effect, and the girl fell senseless to the ground.

"There, my beauty," said the wicked woman, "now you're finished," and she rushed away.

Fortunately, it was almost evening, and the seven dwarfs were on their way home. When they saw Snow White lying on the ground as though dead, they suspected the stepmother right away. They examined Snow White and found the poisoned comb. As soon as they pulled it out, Snow White came back to life and told them what had happened. Again they warned her to be on her guard and not to open the door to anyone.

At home, the queen stood before the mirror and said:

"Mirror, mirror, on the wall,
Who's the fairest of them all?"

The mirror answered as before:

"Here you're the fairest, dearest queen,
But little Snow White, who plans to stay
With the seven dwarfs far far away,
Is now the fairest ever seen."

When the queen heard the words of the mirror, she began trembling with rage. "Snow White must die!" she cried out. "Even if it costs me my life."

Then she went into a remote, hidden chamber where no one ever set foot and made an apple full of poison. On the outside it looked beautiful—white with red cheeks—so that if you saw it you longed for it. But anyone who took the tiniest bite would die. When the apple was finished, she stained her face, dressed up as a peasant woman, and traveled beyond the seven hills to the seven dwarfs.

She knocked at the door, and Snow White put her head out the window to say: "I can't let anyone in. The seven dwarfs won't allow it."

"That's all right," replied the peasant woman. "I'll get rid of my apples soon enough. Here, I'll give you one."

"No," said Snow White, "I'm not supposed to take anything."

"Are you afraid that it's poisoned?" asked the old woman. "Here, I'll cut the apple in two. You eat the red part, I'll eat the white."

The apple had been made so artfully that only the red part of it was poison. Snow White felt a craving for the beautiful apple, and when she saw that the peasant woman was eating it, she could no longer resist. She put her hand out the window and took the poisoned half. But no sooner had she taken a bite when she fell down on the ground dead. The queen stared at her with savage eyes and burst out laughing: "White as snow, red as blood, black as ebony! This time the dwarfs won't be able to bring you back to life!"

At home, she asked the mirror:

"Mirror, mirror, on the wall,
Who's the fairest of them all?"

And finally it replied:

"Oh queen, you are the fairest in the land."

Her envious heart was finally at peace, as much as an envious heart can be.

When the little dwarfs returned home in the evening, they found Snow White lying on the ground. Not a breath of air was coming from her lips. She was dead. They lifted her up and looked around for something that might be poisonous. They unlaced her, combed her hair, washed her with water and wine, but it was all in vain. The dear child was dead and nothing could bring her back. They placed her on a bier, and all seven of them sat down on it and mourned her. They wept for three days. They were about to bury her, but she still looked just like a living person with beautiful red cheeks.

They said: "We can't possibly lower her into the dark ground." And so they had a transparent glass coffin made that allowed Snow White to be seen from all sides. They put her in it, wrote her name on it in golden letters, and added that she was the daughter of a king. They brought the coffin up to the top of a mountain, and one of them was always there to keep vigil. Animals also came to mourn Snow White, first an owl, then a raven, and finally a dove.

Snow White lay in the coffin for a long, long time. But she did not decay and looked as if she were sleeping, for she was still white as snow, red as blood, and with hair as black as ebony.

One day the son of a king was traveling through the woods and arrived at the dwarfs' cottage. He wanted to spend the night there. On top of the mountain, he saw the coffin with beautiful Snow White lying in it, and he read what had been written in golden letters. Then he said to the dwarfs: "Let me have the coffin. I will give you whatever you want for it."

The dwarfs answered: "We wouldn't sell it for all the gold in the world."

Then he said: "Make me a present of it, for I can't live without seeing Snow White. I will honor and cherish her as if she were my beloved."

The good dwarfs took pity on him when they heard these words, and they gave him the coffin. The prince ordered his servants to carry the coffin away on their shoulders. It happened that they stumbled over a shrub, and the jolt freed the poisonous piece of apple lodged in Snow White's throat. She came to life. "Good heavens, where am I?" she cried out.

The prince was overjoyed and said: "You are with me," and he described what had happened and said: "I love you more than anything else on earth. Come with me to my father's castle. You shall be my bride." Snow White had tender feelings for him, and she departed with him. Their marriage was celebrated with great splendor.

Snow White's wicked stepmother was also invited to the wedding feast. She put on beautiful clothes, stepped up to the mirror, and said:

> "Mirror, mirror on the wall:
> Who's the fairest of them all?"

The mirror replied:

> "My queen, you may be the fairest here,
> But the young queen is a thousand times more fair."

The wicked women let loose a curse, and she became so petrified with fear that she didn't know what to do. At first she didn't want to go to the wedding feast. But she never had a moment's peace after that and had to go see the young queen. When she entered, Snow White recognized her right away. The queen was so terrified that she just stood there and couldn't budge an inch. Iron slippers had already been heated up over a fire of coals. They were brought in with tongs and set right in front of her. She had to put on the red hot iron shoes and dance in them until she dropped to the ground dead.

ANNE SEXTON

Snow White and the Seven Dwarfs[†]

No matter what life you lead
the virgin is a lovely number:
cheeks as fragile as cigarette paper,
arms and legs made of Limoges,[1]
lips like Vin Du Rhône,[2]   5
rolling her china-blue doll eyes
open and shut.
Open to say,
Good Day Mama,
and shut for the thrust   10
of the unicorn.
She is unsoiled.
She is as white as a bonefish.

Once there was a lovely virgin
called Snow White.   15
Say she was thirteen.
Her stepmother,
a beauty in her own right,

---

† Anne Sexton, "Snow White and the Seven Dwarfs," in *Transformations* (Boston: Houghton Mifflin, 1971). Copyright © 1971 by Anne Sexton, renewed 1999 by Linda G. Sexton. Reprinted by permission of Houghton Mifflin Company and by Sterling Lord Literistic, Inc. All rights reserved.
1. A type of fine porcelain.
2. Wine from the Rhône valley.

though eaten, of course, by age,
would hear of no beauty surpassing her own.   20
Beauty is a simple passion,
but, oh my friends, in the end
you will dance the fire dance in iron shoes.
The stepmother had a mirror to which she referred—

something like the weather forecast—   25
a mirror that proclaimed
the one beauty of the land.
She would ask,
Looking glass upon the wall,
who is fairest of us all?   30
And the mirror would reply,
You are fairest of us all.
Pride pumped in her like poison.

Suddenly one day the mirror replied,
Queen, you are full fair, 'tis true,   35
but Snow White is fairer than you.
Until that moment Snow White
had been no more important
than a dust mouse under the bed.
But now the queen saw brown spots on her hand   40
and four whiskers over her lip
so she condemned Snow White
to be hacked to death.
Bring me her heart, she said to the hunter,
and I will salt it and eat it.   45
The hunter, however, let his prisoner go
and brought a boar's heart back to the castle.
The queen chewed it up like a cube steak.
Now I am fairest, she said,
lapping her slim white fingers.   50

Snow White walked in the wildwood
for weeks and weeks.
At each turn there were twenty doorways
and at each stood a hungry wolf,
his tongue lolling out like a worm.   55
The birds called out lewdly,
talking like pink parrots,
and the snakes hung down in loops,
each a noose for her sweet white neck.
On the seventh week   60
she came to the seventh mountain
and there she found the dwarf house.

It was as droll as a honeymoon cottage
and completely equipped with
seven beds, seven chairs, seven forks   65
and seven chamber pots.
Snow White ate seven chicken livers
and lay down, at last, to sleep.

The dwarfs, those little hot dogs,
walked three times around Snow White,   70
the sleeping virgin. They were wise
and wattled like small czars.
Yes. It's a good omen,
they said, and will bring us luck.
They stood on tiptoes to watch   75
Snow White wake up. She told them
about the mirror and the killer-queen
and they asked her to stay and keep house.
Beware of your stepmother,
they said.   80
Soon she will know you are here.
While we are away in the mines
during the day, you must not
open the door.

Looking glass upon the wall . . .   85
The mirror told
and so the queen dressed herself in rags
and went out like a peddler to trap Snow White.
She went across seven mountains.
She came to the dwarf house   90
and Snow White opened the door
and bought a bit of lacing.
The queen fastened it tightly
around her bodice,
as tight as an Ace bandage,   95
so tight that Snow White swooned.
She lay on the floor, a plucked daisy.
When the dwarfs came home they undid the lace
and she revived miraculously.
She was as full of life as soda pop.   100
Beware of your stepmother,
they said.
She will try once more.

Looking glass upon the wall . . .
Once more the mirror told   105
and once more the queen dressed in rags

and once more Snow White opened the door.
This time she bought a poison comb,
a curved eight-inch scorpion,
and put it in her hair and swooned again.   110
The dwarfs returned and took out the comb
and she revived miraculously.
She opened her eyes as wide as Orphan Annie.
Beware, beware, they said,
but the mirror told,   115
the queen came,
Snow White, the dumb bunny,
opened the door
and she bit into a poison apple
and fell down for the final time.   120
When the dwarfs returned
they undid her bodice,
they looked for a comb,
but it did no good.
Though they washed her with wine   125
and rubbed her with butter
it was to no avail.
She lay as still as a gold piece.

The seven dwarfs could not bring themselves
to bury her in the black ground   130
so they made a glass coffin
and set it upon the seventh mountain
so that all who passed by
could peek in upon her beauty.
A prince came one June day   135
and would not budge.
He stayed so long his hair turned green
and still he would not leave.
The dwarfs took pity upon him
and gave him the glass Snow White—   140
its doll's eyes shut forever—
to keep in his far-off castle.
As the prince's men carried the coffin
they stumbled and dropped it
and the chunk of apple flew out   145
of her throat and she woke up miraculously.
And thus Snow White became the prince's bride.
The wicked queen was invited to the wedding feast
and when she arrived there were
red-hot iron shoes,   150
in the manner of red-hot roller skates,
clamped upon her feet.

First your toes will smoke
and then your heels will turn black
and you will fry upward like a frog,   155
she was told.
And so she danced until she was dead,
a subterranean figure,
her tongue flicking in and out
like a gas jet.   160
Meanwhile Snow White held court,
rolling her china-blue doll eyes open and shut
and sometimes referring to her mirror
as women do.

NEIL GAIMAN

Snow, Glass, Apples†

I do not know what manner of thing she is. None of us do. She killed
her mother in the birthing, but that's never enough to account for it.

They call me wise, but I am far from wise, for all that I foresaw
fragments of it, frozen moments caught in pools of water or in the
cold glass of my mirror. If I were wise I would not have tried to
change what I saw. If I were wise I would have killed myself before
ever I encountered her, before ever I caught him.

Wise, and a witch, or so they said, and I'd seen his face in my
dreams and in reflections for all my life: sixteen years of dreaming
of him before he reined his horse by the bridge that morning, and
asked my name. He helped me onto his high horse and we rode
together to my little cottage, my face buried in the gold of his hair.
He asked for the best of what I had; a king's right, it was.

His beard was red-bronze in the morning light, and I knew him,
not as a king, for I knew nothing of kings then, but as my love. He
took all he wanted from me, the right of kings, but he returned to
me on the following day, and on the night after that: his beard so
red, his hair so gold, his eyes the blue of a summer sky, his skin
tanned the gentle brown of ripe wheat.

His daughter was only a child: no more than five years of age when
I came to the palace. A portrait of her dead mother hung in the princess's tower room; a tall woman, hair the color of dark wood, eyes
nut-brown. She was of a different blood to her pale daughter.

The girl would not eat with us.

I do not know where in the palace she ate.

† Neil Gaiman, *Snow, Glass, Apples* (Northampton, MA: Comic Book Legal Defense Fund, 1994). Copyright © 1994 Neil Gaiman. Reprinted by permission.

I had my own chambers. My husband the king, he had his own rooms also. When he wanted me he would send for me, and I would go to him, and pleasure him, and take my pleasure with him.

One night, several months after I was brought to the palace, she came to my rooms. She was six. I was embroidering by lamplight, squinting my eyes against the lamp's smoke and fitful illumination. When I looked up, she was there.

"Princess?"

She said nothing. Her eyes were black as coal, black as her hair; her lips were redder than blood. She looked up at me and smiled. Her teeth seemed sharp, even then, in the lamplight.

"What are you doing away from your room?"

"I'm hungry," she said, like any child.

It was winter, when fresh food is a dream of warmth and sunlight; but I had strings of whole apples, cored and dried, hanging from the beams of my chamber, and I pulled an apple down for her.

"Here."

Autumn is the time of drying, of preserving, a time of picking apples, of rendering the goose fat. Winter is the time of hunger, of snow, and of death; and it is the time of the midwinter feast, when we rub the goose-fat into the skin of a whole pig, stuffed with that autumn's apples, then we roast it or spit it, and we prepare to feast upon the crackling.

She took the dried apple from me and began to chew it with her sharp yellow teeth.

"Is it good?"

She nodded. I had always been scared of the little princess, but at that moment I warmed to her and, with my fingers, gently, I stroked her cheek. She looked at me and smiled—she smiled but rarely—then she sank her teeth into the base of my thumb, the Mound of Venus, and she drew blood.

I began to shriek, from pain and from surprise; but she looked at me and I fell silent.

The little Princess fastened her mouth to my hand and licked and sucked and drank. When she was finished, she left my chamber. Beneath my gaze the cut that she had made began to close, to scab, and to heal. The next day it was an old scar: I might have cut my hand with a pocket-knife in my childhood.

I had been frozen by her, owned and dominated. That scared me, more than the blood she had fed on. After that night I locked my chamber door at dusk, barring it with an oaken pole, and I had the smith forge iron bars, which he placed across my windows.

My husband, my love, my king, sent for me less and less, and when I came to him he was dizzy, listless, confused. He could no longer make love as a man makes love; and he would not permit me to plea-sure him with my mouth: the one time I tried, he started, violently, and began to weep. I pulled my mouth away and held him tightly, until the sobbing had stopped, and he slept, like a child.

I ran my fingers across his skin as he slept. It was covered in a multitude of ancient scars. But I could recall no scars from the days of our courtship, save one, on his side, where a boar had gored him when he was a youth.

Soon he was a shadow of the man I had met and loved by the bridge. His bones showed, blue and white, beneath his skin. I was with him at the last: his hands were cold as stone, his eyes milky-blue, his hair and beard faded and lustreless and limp. He died unshriven, his skin nipped and pocked from head to toe with tiny, old scars.

He weighed near to nothing. The ground was frozen hard, and we could dig no grave for him, so we made a cairn[1] of rocks and stones above his body, as a memorial only, for there was little enough of him left to protect from the hunger of the beasts and the birds.

So I was queen.

And I was foolish, and young—eighteen summers had come and gone since first I saw daylight—and I did not do what I would do, now.

If it were today, I would have her heart cut out, true. But then I would have her head and arms and legs cut off. I would have them disembowel her. And then I would watch, in the town square, as the hangman heated the fire to white-heat with bellows, watch unblinking as he consigned each part of her to the fire. I would have archers around the square, who would shoot any bird or animal who came close to the flames, any raven or dog or hawk or rat. And I would not close my eyes until the princess was ash, and a gentle wind could scatter her like snow.

I did not do this thing, and we pay for our mistakes.

They say I was fooled; that it was not her heart. That it was the heart of an animal—a stag, perhaps, or a boar. They say that, and they are wrong.

And some say (but it is her lie, not mine) that I was given the heart, and that I ate it. Lies and half-truths fall like snow, covering the things that I remember, the things I saw. A landscape, unrecognizable after a snowfall; that is what she has made of my life.

There were scars on my love, her father's thighs, and on his ballock-pouch, and on his male member, when he died.

I did not go with them. They took her in the day, while she slept, and was at her weakest. They took her to the heart of the forest, and there they opened her blouse, and they cut out her heart, and they left her dead, in a gully, for the forest to swallow.

---

1. A heap or pile of shards or stones, used as a trail marker or to commemorate a place; here it marks a grave.

The forest is a dark place, the border to many kingdoms; no one would be foolish enough to claim jurisdiction over it. Outlaws live in the forest. Robbers live in the forest, and so do wolves. You can ride through the forest for a dozen days and never see a soul; but there are eyes upon you the entire time.

They brought me her heart. I know it was hers—no sow's heart or doe's would have continued to beat and pulse after it had been cut out, as that one did.

I took it to my chamber.

I did not eat it: I hung it from the beams above my bed, placed it on a length of twine that I strung with rowan-berries, orange-red as a robin's breast; and with bulbs of garlic.

Outside, the snow fell, covering the footprints of my huntsmen, covering her tiny body in the forest where it lay.

I had the smith remove the iron bars from my windows, and I would spend some time in my room each afternoon through the short winter days, gazing out over the forest, until darkness fell.

There were, as I have already stated, people in the forest. They would come out, some of them, for the Spring Fair: a greedy, feral, dangerous people; some were stunted—dwarfs and midgets and hunchbacks; others had the huge teeth and vacant gazes of idiots; some had fingers like flippers or crab-claws. They would creep out of the forest each year for the Spring Fair, held when the snows had melted.

As a young lass I had worked at the Fair, and they had scared me then, the forest folk. I told fortunes for the Fairgoers, scrying[2] in a pool of still water; and, later, when I was older, in a disc of polished glass, its back all silvered—a gift from a merchant whose straying horse I had seen in a pool of ink.

The stallholders at the fair were afraid of the forest folk; they would nail their wares to the bare boards of their stalls—slabs of gingerbread or leather belts were nailed with great iron nails to the wood. If their wares were not nailed, they said, the forest folk would take them, and run away, chewing on the stolen gingerbread, flailing about them with the belts.

The forest folk had money, though: a coin here, another there, sometimes stained green by time or the earth, the face on the coin unknown to even the oldest of us. Also they had things to trade, and thus the fair continued, serving the outcasts and the dwarfs, serving the robbers (if they were circumspect) who preyed on the rare travelers from lands beyond the forest, or on gypsies, or on the deer. (This was robbery in the eyes of the law. The deer were the queen's.)

---

2. Foretelling the future, using a crystal ball or some kind of reflective surface.

The years passed by slowly, and my people claimed that I ruled them with wisdom. The heart still hung above my bed, pulsing gently in the night. If there were any who mourned the child, I saw no evidence: she was a thing of terror, back then, and they believed themselves well rid of her.

Spring Fair followed Spring Fair: five of them, each sadder, poorer, shoddier than the one before. Fewer of the forest folk came out of the forest to buy. Those who did seemed subdued and listless. The stallholders stopped nailing their wares to the boards of their stalls. And by the fifth year but a handful of folk came from the forest—a fearful huddle of little hairy men, and no one else.

The Lord of the Fair, and his page, came to me when the fair was done. I had known him slightly, before I was queen.

"I do not come to you as my queen," he said.

I said nothing. I listened.

"I come to you because you are wise," he continued. "When you were a child you found a strayed foal by staring into a pool of ink; when you were a maiden you found a lost infant who had wandered far from her mother, by staring into that mirror of yours. You know secrets and you can seek out things hidden. My queen," he asked, "what is taking the forest folk? Next year there will be no Spring Fair. The travelers from other kingdoms have grown scarce and few, the folk of the forest are almost gone. Another year like the last, and we shall all starve."

I commanded my maidservant to bring me my looking-glass. It was a simple thing, a silver-backed glass disk, which I kept wrapped in a doe-skin, in a chest, in my chamber.

They brought it to me, then, and I gazed into it:

She was twelve and she was no longer a little child. Her skin was still pale, her eyes and hair coal-black, her lips as red as blood. She wore the clothes she had worn when she left the castle for the last time—the blouse, the skirt,—although they were much let-out, much mended. Over them she wore a leather cloak, and instead of boots she had leather bags, tied with thongs, over her tiny feet.

She was standing in the forest, beside a tree.

As I watched, in the eye of my mind, I saw her edge and step and flitter and pad from tree to tree, like an animal: a bat or a wolf. She was following someone.

He was a monk. He wore sackcloth, and his feet were bare, and scabbed and hard. His beard and tonsure were of a length, overgrown, unshaven.

She watched him from behind the trees. Eventually he paused for the night, and began to make a fire, laying twigs down, breaking up a robin's nest as kindling. He had a tinder-box in his robe, and he knocked the flint against the steel until the sparks caught the tinder and the fire flamed. There had been two eggs in the nest he had found, and these he ate, raw. They cannot have been much of a meal for so big a man.

He sat there in the firelight, and she came out from her hiding place. She crouched down on the other side of the fire, and stared at him. He grinned, as if it were a long time since he had seen another human, and beckoned her over to him.

She stood up and walked around the fire, and waited, an arms-length away. He pulled in his robe until he found a coin—a tiny, copper penny,—and tossed it to her. She caught it, and nodded, and went to him. He pulled at the rope around his waist, and his robe swung open. His body was as hairy as a bear's. She pushed him back onto the moss. One hand crept, spider-like, through the tangle of hair, until it closed on his manhood; the other hand traced a circle on his left nipple. He closed his eyes, and fumbled one huge hand under her skirt. She lowered her mouth to the nipple she had been teasing, her smooth skin white on the furry brown body of him.

She sank her teeth deep into his breast. His eyes opened, then they closed again, and she drank.

She straddled him, and she fed. As she did so a thin blackish liquid began to dribble from between her legs. . . .

"Do you know what is keeping the travelers from our town? What is happening to the forest people?" asked the Head of the Fair.

I covered the mirror in doe-skin, and told him that I would personally take it upon myself to make the forest safe once more.

I had to, although she terrified me. I was the queen.

A foolish woman would have gone then into the forest and tried to capture the creature; but I had been foolish once and had no wish to be so a second time.

I spent time with old books, for I could read a little. I spent time with the gypsy women (who passed through our country across the mountains to the south, rather than cross the forest to the north and the west).

I prepared myself, and obtained those things I would need, and when the first snows began to fall, then I was ready.

Naked, I was, and alone in the highest tower of the palace, a place open to the sky. The winds chilled my body; goose-pimples crept across my arms and thighs and breasts. I carried a silver basin, and a basket in which I had placed a silver knife, a silver pin, some tongs, a grey robe and three green apples.

I put them down and stood there, unclothed, on the tower, humble before the night sky and the wind. Had any man seen me standing there, I would have had his eyes; but there was no-one to spy. Clouds scudded across the sky, hiding and uncovering the waning moon.

I took the silver knife, and slashed my left arm—once, twice, three times. The blood dripped into the basin, scarlet seeming black in the moonlight.

I added the powder from the vial that hung around my neck. It was a brown dust, made of dried herbs and the skin of a particular toad, and from certain other things. It thickened the blood, while preventing it from clotting.

I took the three apples, one by one, and pricked their skins gently with my silver pin. Then I placed the apples in the silver bowl, and let them sit there while the first tiny flakes of snow of the year fell slowly onto my skin, and onto the apples, and onto the blood.

When dawn began to brighten the sky I covered myself with the grey cloak, and took the red apples from the silver bowl, one by one, lifting each into my basket with silver tongs, taking care not to touch it. There was nothing left of my blood or of the brown powder in the silver bowl, nothing save a black residue, like a verdigris, on the inside.

I buried the bowl in the earth. Then I cast a glamour on the apples (as once, years before, by a bridge, I had cast a glamour on myself), that they were, beyond any doubt, the most wonderful apples in the world; and the crimson blush of their skins was the warm color of fresh blood.

I pulled the hood of my cloak low over my face, and I took ribbons and pretty hair ornaments with me, placed them above the apples in the reed basket, and I walked alone into the forest, until I came to her dwelling: a high, sandstone cliff, laced with deep caves going back a way into the rock wall.

There were trees and boulders around the cliff-face, and I walked quietly and gently from tree to tree, without disturbing a twig or a fallen leaf. Eventually I found my place to hide, and I waited, and I watched.

After some hours a clutch of dwarfs crawled out of the cave-front—ugly, misshapen, hairy little men, the old inhabitants of this country. You saw them seldom now.

They vanished into the wood, and none of them spied me, though one of them stopped to piss against the rock I hid behind.

I waited. No more came out.

I went to the cave entrance and hallooed into it, in a cracked old voice.

The scar on my Mound of Venus throbbed and pulsed as she came towards me, out of the darkness, naked and alone.

She was thirteen years of age, my stepdaughter, and nothing marred the perfect whiteness of her skin save for the livid scar on her left breast, where her heart had been cut from her long since.

The insides of her thighs were stained with wet black filth.

She peered at me, hidden, as I was, in my cloak. She looked at me hungrily. "Ribbons, goodwife," I croaked. "Pretty ribbons for your hair. . . ."

She smiled and beckoned to me. A tug; the scar on my hand was pulling me towards her. I did what I had planned to do, but I did it more readily than I had planned: I dropped my basket, and screeched like the bloodless old peddler woman I was pretending to be, and I ran.

My grey cloak was the color of the forest, and I was fast; she did not catch me.

I made my way back to the palace.

I did not see it. Let us imagine, though, the girl returning, frustrated and hungry, to her cave, and finding my fallen basket on the ground.

What did she do?

I like to think she played first with the ribbons, twined them into her raven hair, looped them around her pale neck or her tiny waist.

And then, curious, she moved the cloth to see what else was in the basket; and she saw the red, red apples.

They smelled like fresh apples, of course; and they also smelled of blood. And she was hungry. I imagine her picking up an apple, pressing it against her cheek, feeling the cold smoothness of it against her skin.

And she opened her mouth and bit deep into it. . . .

By the time I reached my chambers, the heart that hung from the roof-beam, with the apples and hams and the dried sausages, had ceased to beat. It hung there, quietly, without motion or life, and I felt safe once more.

That winter the snows were high and deep, and were late melting. We were all hungry come the spring.

The Spring Fair was slightly improved that year. The forest folk were few, but they were there, and there were travelers from the lands beyond the forest.

I saw the little hairy men of the forest-cave buying and bargaining for pieces of glass, and lumps of crystal and of quartz-rock. They paid for the glass with silver coins—the spoils of my stepdaughter's depredations, I had no doubt. When it got about what they were buying, townsfolk rushed back to their homes, came back with their lucky crystals, and, in a few cases, with whole sheets of glass.

I thought, briefly, about having them killed, but I did not. As long as the heart hung, silent and immobile and cold, from the beam of my chamber, I was safe, and so were the folk of the forest, and, thus, eventually, the folk of the town.

My twenty-fifth year came, and my stepdaughter had eaten the poisoned fruit two winters' back, when the Prince came to my

Palace. He was tall, very tall, with cold green eyes and the swarthy skin of those from beyond the mountains.

He rode with a small retinue: large enough to defend him, small enough that another monarch—myself, for instance—would not view him as a potential threat. I was practical: I thought of the alliance of our lands, thought of the Kingdom running from the forests all the way south to the sea; I thought of my golden-haired bearded love, dead these eight years; and, in the night, I went to the Prince's room.

I am no innocent, although my late husband, who was once my king, was truly my first lover, no matter what they say.

At first the prince seemed excited. He bade me remove my shift, and made me stand in front of the opened window, far from the fire, until my skin was chilled stone-cold. Then he asked me to lie upon my back, with my hands folded across my breasts, my eyes wide open—but staring only at the beams above. He told me not to move, and to breathe as little as possible. He implored me to say nothing. He spread my legs apart. It was then that he entered me.

As he began to thrust inside me, I felt my hips raise, felt myself begin to match him, grind for grind, push for push. I moaned. I could not help myself.

His manhood slid out of me. I reached out and touched it, a tiny, slippery thing. "Please," he said, softly. "You must neither move, nor speak. Just lie there on the stones, so cold and so fair."

I tried, but he had lost whatever force it was that had made him virile; and, some short while later, I left the Prince's room, his curses and tears still resounding in my ears. He left early the next morning, with all his men, and they rode off into the forest.

I imagine his loins, now, as he rode, a knot of frustration at the base of his manhood. I imagine his pale lips pressed so tightly together. Then I imagine his little troupe riding through the forest, finally coming upon the glass-and-crystal cairn of my stepdaughter. So pale. So cold. Naked, beneath the glass, and little more than a girl, and dead.

In my fancy, I can almost feel the sudden hardness of his manhood inside his britches, envision the lust that took him then, the prayers he muttered beneath his breath in thanks for his good fortune. I imagine him negotiating with the little hairy men—offering them gold and spices for the lovely corpse under the crystal mound.

Did they take his gold willingly? Or did they look up to see his men on their horses, with their sharp swords and their spears, and realize they had no alternative? I do not know. I was not there; I was not scrying. I can only imagine . . .

Hands, pulling off the lumps of glass and quartz from her cold body. Hands, gently caressing her cold cheek, moving her cold arm, rejoicing to find the corpse still fresh and pliable.

Did he take her there, in front of them all? Or did he have her carried to a secluded nook before he mounted her?

I cannot say.

Did he shake the apple from her throat? Or did her eyes slowly open as he pounded into her cold body; did her mouth open, those red lips part, those sharp yellow teeth close on his swarthy neck, as the blood, which is the life, trickled down her throat, washing down and away the lump of apple, my own, my poison?

I imagine; I do not know.

This I do know: I was woken in the night by her heart pulsing and beating once more. Salt blood dripped onto my face from above. I sat up. My hand burned and pounded as if I had hit the base of my thumb with a rock.

There was a hammering on the door. I felt afraid, but I am a queen, and I would not show fear. I opened the door.

First his men walked in to my chamber, and stood around me, with their sharp swords, and their long spears.

Then he came in; and he spat in my face.

Finally, she walked into my chamber, as she had when I was first a queen, and she was a child of six. She had not changed. Not really.

She pulled down the twine on which her heart was hanging. She pulled off the dried rowan berries, one by one; pulled off the garlic bulb—now a dried thing, after all these years; then she took up her own, her pumping heart—a small thing, no larger than that of a nanny-goat or a she-bear—as it brimmed and pumped its blood into her hand. Her fingernails must have been as sharp as glass: she opened her breast with them, running them over the purple scar. Her chest gaped, suddenly, open and bloodless. She licked her heart, once, as the blood ran over her hands, and she pushed the heart deep into her breast.

I saw her do it. I saw her close the flesh of her breast once more. I saw the purple scar begin to fade.

Her prince looked briefly concerned, but he put his arm around her nonetheless, and they stood, side by side, and they waited.

And she stayed cold, and the bloom of death remained on her lips, and his lust was not diminished in any way.

They told me they would marry, and the kingdoms would indeed be joined. They told me that I would be with them on their wedding day.

It is starting to get hot in here.

They have told the people bad things about me; a little truth to add savor to the dish, but mixed with many lies.

I was bound and kept in a tiny stone cell beneath the palace, and I remained there through the autumn. Today they fetched me out of the cell; they stripped the rags from me, and washed the filth from me, and then they shaved my head and my loins, and they rubbed my skin with goose grease.

The snow was falling as they carried me—two men at each hand, two men at each leg—utterly exposed, and spread-eagled and cold, through the midwinter crowds; and brought me to this kiln.

My stepdaughter stood there with her prince. She watched me, in my indignity, but she said nothing.

As they thrust me inside, jeering and chaffing as they did so, I saw one snowflake land upon her white cheek, and remain there without melting.

They closed the kiln-door behind me. It is getting hotter in here, and outside they are singing and cheering and banging on the sides of the kiln.

She was not laughing, or jeering, or talking. She did not sneer at me or turn away. She looked at me, though; and for a moment I saw myself reflected in her eyes.

I will not scream. I will not give them that satisfaction. They will have my body, but my soul and my story are my own, and will die with me.

The goose-grease begins to melt and glisten upon my skin. I shall make no sound at all. I shall think no more on this.

I shall think instead of the snowflake on her cheek.

I think of her hair as black as coal, her lips as red as blood, her skin, snow-white.

INTRODUCTION:
Sleeping Beauty

Many have targeted Sleeping Beauty as the most passive and repel-
lent fairy-tale heroine of all, and they have done their best to make
her story go away. Alerting us to the perils of that tale, Madonna
Kolbenschlag urged women to "kiss Sleeping Beauty good-bye," in her
book of that title, and Jane Adams offered similar advice in *Wake
Up, Sleeping Beauty*.[1] Still, Sleeping Beauty and her German counterpart, Briar Rose, continue to turn up, in locations both unlikely
and obvious. Philosophers meditate on what they call the Sleeping
Beauty Problem in thought experiments about probability in coin
tosses. In a bid to sell perfume, Lady Gaga spent twenty-four hours,
immobile, in an installation called "Sleeping with Gaga." Psychologists from Bruno Bettelheim onward find wisdom in the story and
conclude that Sleeping Beauty's passive state symbolizes a normal
latency period for young girls. They recommend the story for therapeutic bedtime reading. Pornographers, hardcore and soft, have
found in the story a deep well of sadomasochistic possibilities. Filmmakers, artists, writers, poets, fashionistas, and musicians alike
keep responding to the call of the story, twisting and turning it,
disenchanting it and restoring its magic, always managing to keep
the fairy tale from disappearing.

Simone de Beauvoir was perhaps the first to alert us to the profound gender asymmetries in fairy tales. "Woman is the Sleeping
Beauty, Cinderella, Snow White, she who receives and submits. In
song and story the young man is seen departing adventurously in
search of a woman; he slays the dragons and giants; she is locked
in a tower, a palace, a garden, a cave, she is chained to a rock, a captive, sound asleep: she waits."[2] Women are frozen, immobile, and
comatose. The very name Sleeping Beauty invokes a double movement between a passive state ("sleeping") and a contemplative

---

1. Madonna Kolbenschlag, *Kiss Sleeping Beauty Good-Bye: Breaking the Spell of Feminine
   Myths and Models* (New York: Harper Perennial, 1990), and Jane Adams, *Wake Up,
   Sleeping Beauty* (Bloomington, IN: iUniverse, 2001).
2. Simone de Beauvoir, *The Second Sex*, trans. H. M. Parshley (London: Picador, 1988),
   p. 318.

response ("beauty") that invites a retinal reflex. Beauty may be sleeping, but *we* want to look at her to indulge in the pleasures of her visible charms. As Laura Mulvey has instructed us, that "we" is gendered male, although without precluding women's narcissistic pleasure at looking.[3] What Freud called scopophilia, or pleasure in looking at something, is natural to all humans. As curious children, we subject everything to the probing gaze, exploring what surrounds us and trying to make sense of the world. That gaze continues to operate in multiple ways in adults, most dramatically as the basis for erotic pleasure (active looking). In the visual economy of twentieth-century cinema, Mulvey argues (in views that critics—including Mulvey herself—have challenged and contested since the essay appeared), the male has become the active "bearer-of-the-look," while women have been relegated to the position of objects on display ("to-be-looked-at-ness"). These categories correspond perfectly to de Beauvoir's division between adventurous, active males and passive women, who receive, submit, await, and are "sound asleep."

Of all fairy tales, "Sleeping Beauty" is perhaps the most cinematic in its fashioning of a primal scene for visual pleasure. Curiosity and the desire to look mingle with a display that is both aesthetically and erotically charged. Our gaze is aligned with that of a prince stunned by the exquisite beauty of a woman who remains inert and puts herself on display for the enjoyment of a male viewer. It is no surprise that filmmakers from Pedro Almodóvar (*Talk to Her*, 2002) and Julia Leigh (*Sleeping Beauty*, 2011) continue to engage with the tale, taking it up covertly and also explicitly. Nor that artists ranging from Edward Burne-Jones to Maxfield Parrish have been inspired to create a rich visual culture of women, somnolent and seductive.

Although "Sleeping Beauty" so patently creates a gender divide between the comatose slumbering princess and the adventurous prince, there are also many stories in which, as in "Cupid and Psyche," the male figure sleeps and the female "marvels at the beauty she beholds." There is the entrancing Endymion, sleeping soundly after Zeus grants the wish of the moon goddess, Selene, and places him in an eternal sleep. "A thing of beauty is a joy for ever: / Its loveliness increases; it will never / Pass into nothingness," Keats wrote in his poem about the handsome youth. In Greek mythology, sleep was personified in the form of a comatose boy (Hypnos), lying next to his half-brother Death (Thanatos). And the folklore of some regions includes tales like "Fairer Than a Fairy," in which the heroine must rescue a sleeping prince. *Pretty Women* (1990) could belong to that category, with Vivian, the character played by Julia

3. Laura Mulvey, "Visual Pleasure and Narrative Cinema," *Screen* 16 (1975): 6–18.

Roberts, "rescuing" a man who has been sleepwalking his way through life, with senses deadened by corporate cultures and their single-minded focus on accumulating capital at any cost.

Sleeping Beauties from medieval times all seem to appear as a single way-station set in epics and romances with multiple adventures and feats. It was no doubt from these narratives that Giambattista Basile borrowed to tell his stand-alone tale, "Sun, Moon, and Talia," included in his lively collection known as the *Pentamerone, or The Tale of Tales* (1634–36), published in Naples.[4] Sharply different from popular versions of "Sleeping Beauty" printed today, Basile's foundational literary account tells the story of a princess destined to come to misfortune from a small flax splinter. When the splinter slides under Talia's nail, she falls into a deep sleep, disturbed only by a king who discovers her in a castle and finds himself "on fire with love." Basile coyly describes the king as gathering the "first fruits of his love." Nine months later Talia bears two children. When the king's wife gets wind of the affair, she lures the children to the castle and prepares to serve them up to her husband for dinner. A compassionate cook saves the children, and the queen ultimately suffers the punishment she planned to inflict on Talia.

With its ornate language and baroque flourishes, Basile's tale gives us a complexly layered narrative, one that moves in the mode of high drama, with a rape scene, a revenge plot, and theatrical punishments. Ending in a light-hearted manner with verse that reads to us today as perverse ("Those whom fortune favors / Find good luck even in their sleep"), the tale quickly moves out of Talia's bedroom, revealing almost nothing about her appearance: "the king beheld her charms" is followed by a harvesting of those "fruits of love." The expansive narrative, with its breathless pacing, could easily accommodate descriptive details, but it avoids them.

It is Charles Perrault who begins the process of slowing down the tale about Sleeping Beauty by displacing temporality and narrative with monumental stasis and frozen immobility. Perrault's slumbering princess inhabits a palace in which a "frightful silence" reigns, and "Death" seems to be "everywhere," with men and animals "apparently lifeless" (p. 126). Much as there is a seductive appeal to sleeping princesses, their beauty immune to decay and corruption, the attraction mingles with dread and repulsion, for the one-hundred-year sleep is surely also a proxy for death, which lurks at the borders of the castle in the corpses of the suitors entangled in the briars. Sleeping Beauty suddenly becomes the tale's main feature—iconic in mingling beauty and death, desire and dread.

---

4. Giambattista Basile, *The Tale of Tales, or Entertainment for Little Ones*, trans. Nancy Canepa (Detroit: Wayne State UP, 2007).

Still, Perrault's story does not completely dispense with action. It is filled with self-reflexive meditations on the power of stories passed on from one generation to the next. Narratives about sleeping beauties seem to have what Donald Haase refers to as "an underlying preoccupation with the creative power of language and storytelling,"[5] displaying a deep concern with words, stories, and raconteurs. Paradoxically but perhaps with some logic, a story that enshrines the pleasures of seeing and creates a figure of iconic visual delight (through words, to be sure) also extols the power of the word. The prince listens to rumors about the old castle he has discovered while hunting, a castle said to be haunted by ghosts, used as a gathering place by witches, and inhabited by a child-eating ogre. He feels himself to be "on fire" when an old peasant tells him, on the authority of his ancestors, that a beautiful princess is awaiting the arrival of a prince to awaken her from a one-hundred-year sleep.

Perrault does not hesitate to extend the time frame of the story beyond the kiss, and he includes an elaborate sequel describing the savagery of Sleeping Beauty's cannibalistic mother-in-law and her efforts to cook her grandchildren and daughter-in-law, as well as her sensational end in a vat filled with foul creatures. Sleeping Beauty stands at the center of the tale, flanked on either side by monstrous appetites that seek to possess her, either through carnal knowledge or through physical incorporation. She is the object of all desires.

Tellingly, the Grimms used the title "Dornröschen," or "Briar Rose," for their version of what Perrault called "The Sleeping Beauty in the Wood":

> Throughout the land, stories circulated about the beautiful little Briar Rose, for that was the name given to the slumbering princess. From time to time a prince would try to force his way through the hedge to get to the castle. But no one ever succeeded, because the briars clasped each other as if they were holding hands, and the young men who tried, got caught in them and couldn't pry themselves loose. They died an agonizing death.[6]

The Grimms trim, prune, and truncate, moving quickly to the pricking of the finger on the spindle and eliminating the episode with the cannibalistic mother-in-law. When it comes to awakening Briar Rose herself, the prince is all eyes after traversing the palace, with its immobilized inhabitants, and discovering a woman "so

5. Donald Haase, "Kiss and Tell: Orality, Narrative, and the Power of Words in 'Sleeping Beauty,'" *Etudes de Lettres* 289.3–4 (2011): 275–92.
6. *The Annotated Brothers Grimm: The Bicentennial Edition*, ed. Maria Tatar (New York: Norton, 2012), p. 242.

beautiful that he could not take his eyes off her" (p. 132) Time has stopped in the castle, and the narrative flow is also arrested as our productive imagination is aligned with the prince, and we construct a mental image of the magnetic Sleeping Beauty. Temporality ceases to be and, for a moment, we are in the realm of pure visuality, imagining Briar Rose.

Illustrators have clearly understood how the scene of enraptured vision in "Briar Rose" produces "iconic solidity," an effect achieved through what W. K. Wimsatt and M. Beardsley call a "sleight of words," the imitation of something "headlong and impassioned, less ordered, nearer perhaps to the subrational."[7] Through the "solidity of symbol" and "sensory verbal qualities," poetic abstractions take on the sturdiness of real-life objects and are reified and made into "enduring things." Poetry may not be able to turn language into matter but it can create a mental image invested with what Paul Ricoeur has referred to as "ontological vehemence."[8] Briar Rose, at the moment when she is discovered fast asleep and frozen in time, hovers before us almost as vividly as she does for the prince. Yet the economy of means is astonishing. Often two words are all it takes— Sleeping Beauty or Briar Rose—to ignite the imagination and to see the woods, the roses, the thorns, the drapery, the hair, and the slumbering, supine body of the princess.

The thrifty use of poetic language in fairy tales can fill us with wonder but also leave us wondering, challenging us to fill in all the descriptive and causal blanks, in short, to use our imaginations. With their witches and woods, roses and thorns, golden balls and slimy suitors, fairy tales create shimmering visuals, verbal icons— sleeping beauties, skulls decorated with flowers, homicidal birds with jewel-encrusted plumage—that oblige us to "think more" and "think harder." In short we have to interpret and backfill as well as listen and absorb.

Ever since Snow White's body was placed in a glass coffin on top of a hill for public viewing, feminist critics have suspected that her beautiful corpse, idealized and almost literally placed on a pedestal, elicits a purely aesthetic viewing of the female body, one that replaces the notion of decay and death with permanence and plenitude.[9] Seeing is privileged over touching (Perrault's prince too only gazes at his sleeping beauty), and the prince's prolonged gaze creates a reassuring moment in which aesthetic pleasure appears to displace anxieties about mortality. The beautiful corpses of Snow

---

7. W. K. Wimsatt Jr. and Monroe C. Beardsley, *The Verbal Icon: Studies in the Meaning of Poetry* (Lexington: Kentucky UP, 1967), p. 115.
8. Paul Ricoeur, *The Rule of Metaphor: Multi-Disciplinary Studies of the Creation of Meaning in Language* (Toronto: Toronto UP, 1981), p. 294.
9. See Elisabeth Bronfen, *Over Her Dead Body: Death, Femininity, and the Aesthetic* (New York: Routledge, 1992), pp. 99–107.

White and Sleeping Beauty have inspired art that ensures a double immortality, for the comatose women and the works of art representing them.

It took Angela Carter to demythologize "Sleeping Beauty" and break the magic spell that has taken us all in ever since Basile, Perrault, and the Brothers Grimm codified the fairy tale. "In a faraway land long ago": Disney's *Sleeping Beauty* begins with words that remind us of the drive to preserve the mythical power of tales from times past, to perpetuate the cult of the beautiful corpse that is the fairy tale in the form told in times past. Just as Carter's Sleeping Beauty in her story "The Lady of the House of Love" repeats "ancestral crimes," so the fairy tale enables us to lose ourselves in a mindless cycle of repetition compulsion that reproduces and reinforces social norms.[1] The house of fairy tale, like the House of Love, degenerates into ruins—"cobwebs, worm-eaten beams, crumbling plaster"—when left to its own devices, visited only by sycophantic suitors driven more by the lure of beauty than the desire to reanimate.[2] Without the right suitor, Carter's somnambulant beauty has become "a cave full of echoes," "a system of repetitions," "a closed circuit." Leading a "baleful posthumous" existence, she feeds on humans to sustain her. It is from this dark tradition that Neil Gaiman constructs his breathtakingly compelling "Snow, Glass, Apples" (p. 106).

Sleeping Beauty and Briar Rose, with their magnetic beauty and supremely passive status, remain hauntingly seductive figures in our cultural imagination, reminding us of the pleasures of beauty but also of the attractions of morbidity. They may be immobile, but they also migrate with ease into new media as counterparts to mercurial tricksters—all the warrior women who hunt, shoot, and seek revenge in today's cinematic refashioning of fairy-tale figures. That their stories have been resurrected and are constantly reimagined is a stark reminder that the emergence of a female trickster—feisty and ferocious heroines like Katniss Everdeen in *The Hunger Games* and Lisbeth Salander in The Millennium Trilogy—does not necessarily signal a seismic shift in our understanding of female agency, even if trickster tales frame new perils and possibilities for postmodern heroines.[3] Sleeping Beauty, a true hermeneutic puzzle in her many cultural incarnations, preserves the magical, mythical elements of fairy tales, even as she cries out for disenchantment.

---

1. Angela Carter, *The Bloody Chamber and Other Stories* (New York: Penguin, 1990), p. 93.
2. Katherine A. Hagopian explores how Carter's tale inverts the relationship between Cupid and Psyche, with a monstrous bride residing in a house of love rather than a "winged serpent" residing in the "house of Eros." See her "Apuleius and Gothic Narrative in Carter's 'The Lady of the House of Love,'" *Explicator* 66 (2007): 52–55.
3. Maria Tatar, "Sleeping Beauties vs. Gonzo Girls," *The New Yorker*, November 21, 2012, newyorker.com/books/page-turner/sleeping-beauties-vs-gonzo-girls.

CHARLES PERRAULT

The Sleeping Beauty in the Wood[†]

Once upon a time there lived a king and queen who were deeply distraught because they had no children. They were so troubled that words could not express their feelings of sadness. They tried all the healing waters in the world. They took vows and made pilgrimages. They did everything possible, but nothing worked. Then one day the queen discovered that she was pregnant and gave birth to a daughter. At the christening, all the fairies of the realm (seven in all) were asked to serve as godmother with the hope that each would give the child a gift. According to what was known about fairies in those days, they were able to give gifts that would endow the princess with every advantage imaginable.

After the baptism ceremony, the king invited everyone who had taken part to return to the palace, and he had a feast prepared for the fairies. Places were set for each one, with a magnificent plate and a massive gold case containing a spoon, a fork, and a knife embedded with diamonds and made of the finest gold. Just when they were all about to be seated, a fairy who was getting on in her years entered the palace. She had not been invited because she had not left the tower in which she had been living for more than fifty years. Everyone thought that she had either died or fallen under a spell.

The king ordered a place set for her, but he was unable to come up with another massive gold case because they had all been made to order for the seven other fairies. The elderly fairy considered this an insult and muttered some threats under her breath. One of the young fairies who happened to be nearby overheard her words. Worried that the older fairy might be plotting to bring the child bad luck, she hid behind a tapestry as soon as everyone rose from the table. That way she would have the last word and could repair, insofar as possible, any damage the old woman tried to inflict.

Meanwhile, the fairies could be heard presenting their gifts to the princess. The youngest declared, "She will be the most beautiful person in the world." The next fairy added, "She will have the disposition of an angel." The third decreed, "Her every movement will be marked by gracefulness." The fourth, "She will dance beyond compare." The fifth, "She will sing like a nightingale." The sixth, "She will play every instrument with consummate skill."

† Charles Perrault, "La Belle au bois dormant," in *Histoires ou Contes du temps passé. Avec des Moralités* (Paris: Barbin, 1697). Translated for this Norton Critical Edition by Maria Tatar. Copyright © 2017 by Maria Tatar.

Finally, it was the turn of the elderly fairy. Her head trembled more with malice than from old age as she decreed, "The princess will die after piercing her finger with a spindle."

The terrible pronouncement made everyone present quake with fear. No one could hold back their tears. Just then the young fairy stepped out from behind the tapestry and said in a loud voice, "Do not despair, my king and queen, for your daughter will not die. It's true that I do not have the power to undo what the other fairy has done. The princess will pierce her finger with a spindle, but she will not die. She will fall into a deep sleep that will last a hundred years. When that time is up, a king's son will appear to wake her up."

Hoping to avoid the calamity predicted by the elderly fairy, the king issued at once a public edict forbidding his subjects, under pain of death, to use a spindle or to keep any spindles in their homes.

Some fifteen or sixteen years passed. The royal couple traveled with their retinue to one of their country residences, and the princess decided to explore the rooms in it. She walked from one chamber to the next and reached a room at the top of a tower. There she entered a little garret, where an honorable old woman was at work with her distaff and spindle. This good woman had not learned about the king's prohibition on using spindles for the work of spinning.

"What are you doing there, my good woman?" asked the princess.

"I'm spinning, my lovely child," replied the old woman, who had no idea who she was.

"Oh, how pretty your work is!" the princess replied. "How do you do what you do? Let me see if I can do it as well as you."

No sooner had she touched the spindle than she pricked her hand with its point and fainted. After all, she had been reckless and a little thoughtless, but then again it had all been ordained that way. Deeply upset, the good old woman called for help, and it came from all quarters. Some people threw water on the princess's face. Others unlaced her stays and slapped her hands. Still others rubbed her temples with water from the Queen of Hungary. Nothing could revive her.

The king ran upstairs when he heard the uproar, and he remembered right away what the fairies had predicted. He wisely concluded that everything had proceeded exactly as the fairies had said. He ordered the princess carried up to the finest apartment in the palace and placed on a bed with coverlets embroidered in silver and gold. She was so beautiful that you would have thought her an angel. The swoon had not deprived her of her smooth complexion. Her cheeks were still rosy, and her lips were like coral. Her eyes were shut tight, but you could still hear the gentle sound of her breath and that showed that she was not dead. The king ordered that she be left to sleep in peace until the time came for her to wake up.

The good fairy who had saved the girl's life by decreeing that she would sleep for one hundred years lived in the Kingdom of Mataquin, twelve thousand leagues away. When the unfortunate events took place in the turret, a dwarf told the good fairy about what had happened. The dwarf owned a pair of seven-league boots—that is, a pair of boots that enabled anyone who put them on to cover seven leagues with a single stride. The fairy set out immediately, and an hour later she was seen arriving in a chariot of fire drawn by dragons. The king advanced and offered his hand to help her out of the chariot. She gave her approval to everything that he had done. But since she was a woman of great foresight, she realized that when the princess finally woke up she would feel somewhat embarrassed about finding herself all alone in that old castle. Here is what she did:

She tapped everyone in the castle with her wand—with the exception of the king and queen. Governesses, maids of honor, ladies-in-waiting, gentlemen, officers, stewards, cooks, scullions, boys, guards, porters, pages, and footmen—all were touched by her wand. She also waved her wand at all the horses in the stables, their grooms, the great mastiffs in the courtyard, and even little Pouffe, the princess's tiny dog lying on the bed beside her. As soon as she touched them with her wand, they all fell asleep, and they would not wake up again until the time came for the princess to do so. And in this way they would all be ready to wait on her if she needed them. Even the spits that were turning over the fire, with their partridges and pheasants, were enchanted, and the fire went out as well.

Everything happened almost instantly, for fairies never lose much time when they work. The king and queen kissed their precious daughter without waking her and left the castle. They issued a proclamation declaring that no one could enter the castle. Those orders were unnecessary, for in a matter of moments the park was surrounded by trees, large and small, all covered with thorny brambles. Neither man nor beast could get through. All you could see were the very tops of the castle turrets, and that only from a considerable distance. No one had any doubt that the fairy had had a hand in creating that barrier so that the princess would be spared the curiosity of strangers while she was slumbering.

A hundred years passed by, and the princess's family had been succeeded by a new family of rulers. One day the son of the king went hunting in the neighborhood and asked about the towers that he could make out above the trees in a large and dense forest. Everyone responded to the prince's inquiries with the various stories they had been told. Some said that the castle was haunted by ghosts. Others reported that all the witches in that region held their Sabbath there. The most common story told was one about an ogre who lived there and captured as many children as he could, then ate them up at his leisure. No one could follow him, for he alone was able to navigate a path through the woods. While the prince was trying to make up his mind about what to believe, an elderly peasant spoke up and said, "My Prince, it has now been over fifty years since I heard my father say that the most beautiful princess ever seen lies in that castle. He told me that she was supposed to sleep for one hundred years and that she was destined to be awakened by a chosen king's son."

The prince heard those words and felt as if he were on fire. There was no doubt in his mind that he was the one destined to undertake this wonderful adventure. Driven by love and glory, he decided instantly to find out what would happen if he set off. As soon as he approached the woods, the trees and brambles began to separate and make a path of their own accord. He was able to pass through unharmed by the thorns. He started walking toward the castle, which was at the end of a long avenue that had opened up before him. To his surprise, the trees grew back in place as soon as he passed through, and none of his attendants could follow him. But he continued to march on, for a young man in love is always courageous.

When he entered a vast courtyard, his blood froze with terror at what he saw. A frightful silence had descended on the place. Death seemed to be everywhere. All you could see were the bodies of humans and animals stretched out on the ground, apparently lifeless. But the prince soon discovered that, judging by the shiny noses and red faces of the porters, everyone was just sleeping. The goblets from which the men had been drinking still contained a few drops of wine and showed that the porters had dozed off while drinking. Passing through a courtyard paved with marble, the prince then went up a staircase. When he entered the guardroom, he saw the guards lined up, their carbines shouldered, and snoring away. He crossed several apartments filled with ladies and gentlemen, every single one asleep, some standing, some seated. Finally he entered a room that was covered entirely with gold leaf and beheld the loveliest sight he had ever looked upon. On a bed with curtains open on each side was a princess who appeared to be about fifteen or sixteen years old. Her radiant charms gave her such a luminous, otherworldly appearance that he approached her trembling, so full of admiration that he knelt down beside her. At that very moment, the spell had come to an end. The princess woke up and bestowed on him a look sweeter than a first glance would ordinarily merit.

"Is it you, my prince?" she asked. "You've kept me waiting for such a long time."

Charmed by these words, and even more by the tone in which they were uttered, the prince hardly knew how to express his joy and gratitude to her. He assured her that he loved her more than he loved himself. His words were not entirely comprehensible, but the princess liked him all the more for that. The less eloquence, the more love, as they say. He was much more flustered than she was, and that makes complete sense, for the princess had had plenty of time to think up what she would say to him. There is reason to believe (though history makes no mention of it) that the good fairy had seen to it that the princess's dreams were all charming and pleasant during her long sleep. The two talked for many hours without expressing half of what they wanted to tell each other.

In the meantime, everyone at the palace had woken up exactly when the princess did. They all remembered their duties at the court. Since they were not madly in love, they were all famished. The lady-in-waiting, as hungry as everyone else, grew impatient and announced in a loud voice to the princess that dinner was ready. The prince helped the princess get up from the bed. She was fully dressed, and her clothes were magnificent. But the prince was careful to avoid telling her that she was wearing a dress that looked like his grandmother's, complete with ruffs. Still she looked beautiful in what she was wearing.

The prince and the princess walked into a room with mirrors on all sides, and there the stewards served them supper. The violins and oboes played old-fashioned but lovely pieces of music. And after supper the chaplain lost no time and married them in the royal chapel. The maid of honor discreetly drew the curtains around the bed.

The two did not sleep much. The princess did not need much sleep to begin with, and the prince left at sunrise to return to his city, where his father was anxiously awaiting news of his whereabouts. The prince told his father that he had lost his way in the forest while hunting and that he had spent the night in the hut of a charcoal-burner, who had given him some black bread and cheese for supper.

The prince's father was a trusting soul and believed his son, but his mother was not fully convinced. She noticed that he went hunting now nearly every day and that he always made up some story as an excuse for staying away for a couple of days. She was sure that he was keeping a mistress. In fact, he had been living with the princess for over two years and had two children with her. The first was a girl name Aurora, and the second a son called Day, because he was even more beautiful than his sister.

The queen began telling her son that he should settle down, and she was hoping she could persuade him to tell her the truth. But the prince did not trust her with his secret. Although he loved her, he was also afraid of her, for she belonged to the race of ogres. The king had married her only for her money. There were rumors that she possessed all the desires of an ogress. Whenever she saw little children, she found it hard to restrain herself from pouncing on them. And for that reason, the prince did not breathe a word about his adventures.

Two years later the king died, and the prince became his heir. He made a public declaration about his marriage and went with pomp and circumstance to fetch his wife. With her two children at her side, the queen made a magnificent entrance.

Not much later, the king went to war with a neighbor named Emperor Cantalabutte. He told his mother the queen to govern in his absence and to take care of his wife and children. Since he was more than likely to be at war for the entire summer, the queen mother sent her daughter-in-law with her children to a country house in the forest. She was hoping to gratify her horrible urges more easily now that he was away. A few days later, she followed them there, and one evening she said to the steward: "I would like to have little Aurora for dinner tomorrow night."

"Ah, madam!" the steward exclaimed.

"I'm giving you an order," said the queen, and she spoke those words like an ogre longing to eat fresh meat. "I want her served up with a *sauce Robert*."

The poor man saw that there was no use in arguing with an ogress. He pulled out his knife and made his way to little Aurora's room. She was about four years old at the time. She skipped over to him, threw her arms around him with a giggle, and asked him for some sweets. He burst into tears, and the knife fell from his hands. He decided to go downstairs into the kitchen court, where he slaughtered a lamb and served it up in such a delicious sauce that his mistress assured him that she had never eaten anything like it. In the meantime he carried off little Aurora and gave her to his wife, who hid her in their lodgings at the far end of the kitchen court.

A week later, the wicked queen said to the steward, "Now I would like to have little Day for supper."

Determined to fool her as he had done before, he did not reply. He went to look for little Day, who was just three years old, and found him with a tiny sword in his hand, fencing with a large monkey. He took the boy over to his wife, who hid him in the same place where his sister was kept. Then he cooked a tender little goat instead of little Day, and the ogress found the meal delicious.

Everything was going well until one evening the wicked queen said to the steward, "Now I would like to have the queen for supper, with the same sauce you used for the children."

This time the poor steward was in despair and felt sure he would not be able to fool her again. The young queen was now twenty years old, not counting the one hundred years she had slept. Her skin was a little tough, but it was fair and beautiful. Where in the world was he going to find an animal that was as tough as she was?

He decided that the only way to save his own life was to cut the queen's throat, and he went up to the royal apartment with that plan. He worked up his courage and entered the young queen's chambers, dagger in hand. But since he did not want to take her by surprise, he decided to tell her that he was carrying out the orders of the queen mother.

"Do what you have to do!" she said, making her neck as long as possible. "Carry out the orders given to you. Then I will finally be reunited with my children, my poor children, that I loved so much."

The young queen was sure that they had died after being carried away with no explanation.

"No, no, madam!" the poor steward replied, deeply moved. "You shall not die, and you will see your children again. You can find them in my house, where they have been hiding. And I will fool the queen one more time by serving her a young hind in your stead."

He took her straight to his own quarters, where there was a tearful reunion, and he then cooked up a hind that the queen ate for supper with just as much gusto as if it had been the young queen. Her cruel urges had been appeased, and she planned to tell the king, when he returned, that some ferocious wolves had devoured his wife and two children.

One evening, while she was prowling about as usual around the courtyards and poultry yards of the castle to inhale the scent of fresh meat, she overheard little Day crying because his mother was about to give him a slap for being naughty. She could also hear little Aurora begging forgiveness for her brother. The ogress recognized the voices of the queen and her children and was in a rage about being duped. She gave orders in a way that made everyone tremble with fear. "Bring a large copper vat into the middle of the courtyard early tomorrow morning."

Once the vat was there the next day, she had it filled up with toads, vipers, adders, and serpents. She was planning to fling the queen, her children, the steward, his wife, and their maidservant into it.

"Bring them to me with their hands tied behind their backs," she commanded.

As they stood before her, the executioners began preparing to throw them into the copper vat. Just then the king, who had not been expected back until later, rode into the courtyard. He had come posthaste. Greatly astonished, he demanded to know the meaning of the horrible spectacle, but no one dared say a word. The ogress, enraged at the sight of the king, flung herself headfirst into the vat and was devoured by the repulsive reptiles she had ordered put in there. The king could not help but feel sorry for her, because she was his mother, after all. But he soon found consolation with his beautiful wife and their two children.

Moral

> Waiting so long,
> For a man refined and strong,
> Is not at all unusual.
> But it is rare to wait a hundred years.
> Indeed no woman today   5
> Is that patient for a mate.
>
> Our tale was meant to show
> That when marriage is deferred,
> It is no less happy than the ones you know.
> Nothing's lost after a century or so.   10
> And yet, for lovers whose passion
> Cannot be controlled and who run off,
> Who has the heart to denounce them
> Or to teach them a moral lesson?

BROTHERS GRIMM

Briar Rose[†]

Long, long ago there lived a king and a queen. Day after day they said to each other: "Oh, if only we could have a child!" but nothing ever happened. One day, while the queen was bathing, a frog crawled out of the water, crept ashore, and said to her: "Your wish shall be fulfilled. Before a year goes by, you will give birth to a daughter."

The frog's prediction came true, and the queen gave birth to a girl who was so beautiful that the king was beside himself with joy and arranged a great feast. He invited relatives, friends, and acquaintances, and he also sent for the Wise Women of the kingdom, for he wanted to be sure that they would be kindly disposed toward his child. There were thirteen Wise Women in all, but since the king had only twelve golden plates for them to dine on, one of the women had to stay home.

The feast was celebrated with great splendor, and when it drew to a close, the Wise Women bestowed their magic gifts on the girl. One

† Jacob Grimm and Wilhelm Grimm, "Dornröschen," in *Kinder- und Hausmärchen*, 7th ed. (Berlin: Dieterich, 1857; first published: Berlin: Realschulbuchhandlung, 1812). Translated for this Norton Critical Edition by Maria Tatar. Copyright © 2017 by Maria Tatar.

conferred virtue on her, a second gave her beauty, a third wealth, and on it went until the girl had everything in the world you could ever want. Just as the eleventh woman was presenting her gift, the thirteenth in the group appeared out of nowhere. She had not been invited, and now she wanted her revenge. Without so much as a greeting or even a glance at anyone there, she cried out in a loud voice: "When the daughter of the king turns fifteen, she will prick her finger on a spindle and fall down dead." And without another word, she turned her back on those assembled and left the hall.

Everyone was horrified, but just in the nick of time the twelfth of the Wise Women stepped forward. She had not yet made her wish. Although she could not lift the evil spell, she could temper it, and so she said: "The princess will not die, but she will fall into a deep sleep that will last for a hundred years." The king, who was intent on preventing any harm from coming to his child, sent out an order that every spindle in the entire kingdom was to be burned to ashes.

As for the girl, all the wishes made by the Wise Women came true, for she was so beautiful, kind, charming, and sensible that everyone who set eyes on her could not help but love her. On the very day that the princess turned fifteen, the king and the queen happened to be away from home, and the girl was left all alone. She wandered around in the castle, poking her head into one room after another, and eventually she came to the foot of an old tower. After climbing up a narrow, winding staircase in the tower, she ended up in front of a little door with a rusty old key in its lock. As she turned the key, the door burst open to reveal a tiny little room, in which an old woman was sitting with her spindle, busily spinning flax.

"Good afternoon, granny," said the princess. "What are you doing here?"

"I'm spinning flax," the old woman replied, and she nodded to the girl.

"What is that thing bobbing about so oddly?" asked the girl, and she put her hand on the spindle, for she too wanted to spin. The magic spell began to take effect at once, for she had pricked her finger on the spindle.

The instant she felt the prick on her finger, she slumped down on the bed that was in the room and fell into a deep sleep. The sleep spread through the entire palace. The king and the queen, who had just returned home and were entering the hall, fell asleep too, and their attendants along with them. The horses fell asleep in the stables, the dogs in the courtyard, the doves on the roof, the flies on the walls, and, yes indeed, even the fire flickering in the hearth died down and dozed off, and the roast stopped sizzling, and the cook, who was about to pull the hair of the kitchen boy because he had done something stupid, let go and fell asleep. The wind also died down so that not a leaf was stirring on the trees outside the castle.

Soon a hedge of briars began to grow all around the castle. Every year it grew higher until one day it surrounded the entire place. It had grown so thick that you could not even see the banner on the turret of the castle. Throughout the land, stories circulated about the beautiful Briar Rose, for that was the name given to the slumbering princess. From time to time a prince would try to force his way through the hedge to get to the castle. But no one ever succeeded, because the briars clasped each other as if they were holding hands, and the young men who tried, got caught in them and couldn't pry themselves loose. They died an agonizing death.

After many, many years had passed, another prince appeared in the land. He heard an old man talking about a briar hedge that was said to conceal a castle where a wondrously beautiful princess named Briar Rose had been sleeping for a hundred years, and with her the king, the queen, and the entire court. The old man had learned from his grandfather that many other princes had tried to make their way through the briar hedge, but they had gotten caught on the briars and perished in horrible ways. The young man said: "I am not afraid. I am going to find that castle so that I can see the beautiful Briar Rose." The kind old man did his best to discourage the prince, but he refused to listen.

It so happened that the period of one hundred years had just ended, and the day on which Briar Rose was to awaken had arrived. When the prince approached the briar hedge, he found nothing but big, beautiful flowers. They opened to make a path for him and to let him pass unharmed; then they closed behind him to form a hedge.

In the courtyard the horses and the spotted hounds were lying in the same place fast asleep, and the doves were roosting with their little heads tucked under their wings. The prince made his way into the castle and saw how the flies were fast asleep on the walls. The cook was still in the kitchen, with his hand up in the air as if he were about to grab the kitchen boy, and the maid was still sitting at a table with a black hen that she was about to pluck.

The prince walked along a little farther, over to the great hall, where he saw the entire court fast asleep, with the king and the queen sleeping right next to their thrones. He continued on his way, and everything was so quiet that he could hear his own breath. Finally he reached the tower, and he opened up the door to the little room in which Briar Rose was sleeping. There she lay, so beautiful that he could not take his eyes off her, and he bent down to kiss her.

No sooner had the prince touched Briar Rose's lips than she woke up, opened her eyes, and smiled sweetly at him. They went down the stairs together. The king, the queen, and the entire court were now all awake too, and they were all staring at each other in amazement. The horses in the courtyard stood up and shook themselves. The hounds jumped to their feet and wagged their tails. The doves pulled their heads out from under their wings, looked around, and flew off into the fields. The flies began crawling on the walls. The fire in the kitchen flickered, flared up, and began cooking the food again. The roast started to sizzle. The cook slapped the boy so hard that he let out a screech. The maid finished plucking the hen.

The wedding of Briar Rose and the prince was celebrated in great splendor, and the two lived out their days in happiness.

GABRIEL GARCIA MÁRQUEZ

Sleeping Beauty and the Airplane[†]

She was beautiful and lithe, with soft skin the color of bread and eyes like green almonds, and she had straight black hair that reached to her shoulders, and an aura of antiquity that could just as well have been Indonesian as Andean. She was dressed with subtle taste: a lynx jacket, a raw silk blouse with very delicate flowers, natural linen trousers, and shoes with a narrow stripe the color of bougainvillea. "This is the most beautiful woman I've ever seen," I thought when I saw her pass by with the stealthy stride of a lioness while I waited in the check-in line at Charles de Gaulle Airport in Paris for the plane to New York. She was a supernatural apparition who existed only for a moment and disappeared into the crowd in the terminal.

It was nine in the morning. It had been snowing all night, and traffic was heavier than usual in the city streets, and even slower on the highway, where trailer trucks were lined up on the shoulder and automobiles steamed in the snow. Inside the airport terminal, however, it was still spring.

I stood behind an old Dutch woman who spent almost an hour arguing about the weight of her eleven suitcases. I was beginning to feel bored when I saw the momentary apparition who left me breathless, and so I never knew how the dispute ended. Then the ticket clerk brought me down from the clouds with a reproach for my distraction. By way of an excuse, I asked her if she believed in love at first sight. "Of course," she said. "The other kinds are impossible." She kept her eyes fixed on the computer screen and asked whether I preferred a seat in smoking or nonsmoking.

† From Gabriel Garcia Márquez, *Strange Pilgrims: Twelve Stories,* trans. Edith Grossman (London: Cape, 1993). © 1992 Gabriel García Márquez y Herederos del Gabriel García Márquez.

"It doesn't matter," I said with intentional malice, "as long as I'm not beside the eleven suitcases."

She expressed her appreciation with a commercial smile but did not look away from the glowing screen.

"Choose a number," she told me: "Three, four, or seven."

"Four."

Her smile flashed in triumph.

"In the fifteen years I've worked here," she said, "you're the first person who hasn't chosen seven."

She wrote the seat number on my boarding pass and returned it with the rest of my papers, looking at me for the first time with grape-colored eyes that were a consolation until I could see Beauty again. Only then did she inform me that the airport had just been closed and all flights delayed.

"For how long?"

"That's up to God," she said with her smile. "The radio said this morning it would be the biggest snowstorm of the year."

She was wrong: it was the biggest of the century. But in the first-class waiting room, spring was so real that there were live roses in the vases and even the canned music seemed as sublime and tranquilizing as its creators had intended. All at once it occurred to me that this was a suitable shelter for Beauty, and I looked for her in the other waiting areas, staggered by my own boldness. But most of the people were men from real life who read newspapers in English while their wives thought about someone else as they looked through the panoramic windows at the planes dead in the snow, the glacial factories, the vast fields of Roissy devastated by fierce lions. By noon there was no place to sit, and the heat had become so unbearable that I escaped for a breath of air.

Outside I saw an overwhelming sight. All kinds of people had crowded into the waiting rooms and were camped in the stifling corridors and even on the stairways, stretched out on the floor with their animals, their children, and their travel gear. Communication with the city had also been interrupted, and the palace of transparent plastic resembled an immense space capsule stranded in the storm. I could not help thinking that Beauty too must be somewhere in the middle of those tamed hordes, and the fantasy inspired me with new courage to wait.

By lunchtime we had realized that we were ship-wrecked. The lines were interminable outside the seven restaurants, the cafeterias, the packed bars, and in less than three hours they all had to be closed because there was nothing left to eat or drink. The children, who for a moment seemed to be all the children in the world, started to cry at the same time, and a herd smell began to rise from the crowd. It was a time for instinct. In all that scrambling, the only thing I could find to eat were the last two cups of vanilla ice cream in a children's shop. The waiters were putting chairs on tables as the patrons left, while I ate very slowly at the counter, seeing myself in the mirror with the last little cardboard cup and the last little cardboard spoon, and thinking about Beauty.

The flight to New York, scheduled for eleven in the morning, left at eight that night. By the time I managed to board, the other first-class passengers were already in their seats, and a flight attendant led me to mine. My heart stopped. In the seat next to mine, beside the window, Beauty was taking possession of her space with the mastery of an expert traveler. "If I ever wrote this, nobody would believe me," I thought. And I just managed to stammer an indecisive greeting that she did not hear.

She settled in as if she were going to live there for many years, putting each thing in its proper place and order, until her seat was arranged like the ideal house, where everything was within reach. In the meantime, a steward brought us our welcoming champagne. I took a glass to offer to her, but thought better of it just in time. For she wanted only a glass of water, and she asked the steward, first in incomprehensible French and then in an English only somewhat more fluent, not to wake her for any reason during the flight. Her warm, serious voice was tinged with Oriental sadness.

When he brought the water, she placed a cosmetics case with copper corners, like a grandmother's trunk, on her lap, and took two golden pills from a box that contained others of various colors. She did everything in a methodical, solemn way, as if nothing unforeseen had happened to her since her birth. At last she pulled down the shade on the window, lowered the back of her seat as far as it would go, covered herself to the waist with a blanket without taking off her shoes, put on a sleeping mask, turned her back to me, and then slept without a single pause, without a sigh, without the slightest change in position, for the eight eternal hours and twelve extra minutes of the flight to New York.

It was an ardent journey. I have always believed that there is nothing more beautiful in nature than a beautiful woman, and it was impossible for me to escape even for a moment from the spell of that storybook creature who slept at my side. The steward disappeared as soon as we took off and was replaced by a Cartesian attendant who tried to awaken Beauty to hand her a toiletry case and a set of earphones for listening to music. I repeated the instructions she had given the steward, but the attendant insisted on hearing from Beauty's own lips that she did not want supper either. The steward had to

confirm her instructions, and even so he reproached me because
Beauty had not hung the little cardboard "Do Not Disturb" sign
around her neck.

I ate a solitary supper, telling myself in silence everything I would
have told her if she had been awake. Her sleep was so steady that at
one point I had the distressing thought that the pills she had taken
were not for sleeping but for dying. With each drink I raised my glass
and toasted her.

"To your health, Beauty."

When supper was over the lights were dimmed and a movie was
shown to no one, and the two of us were alone in the darkness of
the world. The biggest storm of the century had ended, and the
Atlantic night was immense and limpid, and the plane seemed
motionless among the stars. Then I contemplated her, inch by inch,
for several hours, and the only sign of life I could detect were the
shadows of the dreams that passed along her forehead like clouds
over water. Around her neck she wore a chain so fine it was almost
invisible against her golden skin, her perfect ears were unpierced,
her nails were rosy with good health, and on her left hand was a
plain band. Since she looked no older than twenty, I consoled myself
with the idea that it was not a wedding ring but the sign of an ephemeral engagement. "To know you are sleeping, certain, secure, faithful channel of renunciation, pure line, so close to my manacled
arms," I thought on the foaming crest of champagne, repeating the
masterful sonnet by Gerardo Diego.[1] Then I lowered the back of my
seat to the level of hers, and we lay together, closer than if we had
been in a marriage bed. The climate of her breathing was the same
as that of her voice, and her skin exhaled a delicate breath that could
only be the scent of her beauty. It seemed incredible: The previous
spring I had read a beautiful novel by Yasunari Kawabata[2] about the
ancient bourgeois of Kyoto who paid enormous sums to spend the
night watching the most beautiful girls in the city, naked and
drugged, while they agonized with love in the same bed. They could
not wake them, or touch them, and they did not even try, because
the essence of their pleasure was to see them sleeping. That night,
as I watched over Beauty's sleep, I not only understood that senile
refinement but lived it to the full.

"Who would have thought," I said to myself, my vanity exacerbated
by champagne, "that I'd become an ancient Japanese at this late
date."

1. Gerardo Diego Cendoya (1896–1987) was a Spanish poet.
2. Yasunari Kawabata (1899–1972) was a Japanese novelist who wrote a work called *The
Sleeping Beauty.*

I think I slept several hours, conquered by champagne and the mute explosions of the movie, and when I awoke my head was splitting. I went to the bathroom. Two seats behind mine the old woman with the eleven suitcases lay in an awkward sprawl, like a forgotten corpse on a battlefield. Her reading glasses, on a chain of colored beads, were on the floor in the middle of the aisle, and for a moment I enjoyed the malicious pleasure of not picking them up.

After I got rid of the excesses of champagne, I caught sight of myself, contemptible and ugly, in the mirror, and was amazed that the devastation of love could be so terrible. The plane lost altitude without warning, then managed to straighten out and continue full speed ahead. The "Return to Your Seat" sign went on. I hurried out with the hope that God's turbulence might awaken Beauty and she would have to take refuge in my arms to escape her terror. In my haste I almost stepped on the Dutchwoman's glasses and would have been happy if I had. But I retraced my steps, picked them up, and put them on her lap in sudden gratitude for her not having chosen seat number four before I did.

Beauty's sleep was invincible. When the plane stabilized, I had to resist the temptation to shake her on some pretext, because all I wanted in the last hour of the flight was to see her awake, even if she were furious, so that I could recover my freedom, and perhaps my youth. But I couldn't do it. "Damn it," I said to myself with great scorn. "Why wasn't I born a Taurus!"

She awoke by herself at the moment the landing lights went on, and she was as beautiful and refreshed as if she had slept in a rose garden. That was when I realized that, like old married couples, people who sit next to each other on airplanes do not say good morning to each other when they wake up. Nor did she. She took off her mask, opened her radiant eyes, straightened the back of the seat, moved the blanket aside, shook her hair that fell into place of its own weight, put the cosmetics case back on her knees, and applied rapid, unnecessary makeup, which took just enough time so that she did not look at me until the plane door opened. Then she put on her lynx jacket, almost stepped over me with a conventional excuse in pure Latin American Spanish, left without even saying good-bye or at least thanking me for all I had done to make our night together a happy one, and disappeared into the sun of today in the Amazon jungle of New York.

138

WILFRED OWEN

The Sleeping Beauty[†]

Sojourning through a southern realm in youth,
I came upon a house by happy chance
Where bode a marvellous Beauty. There, romance
Flew faerily until I lit on truth—
For lo! the fair Child slumbered. Though, forsooth,   5
She lay not blanketed in drowsy trance,
But leapt alert of limb and keen of glance,
From sun to shower; from gaiety to ruth;
Yet breathed her loveliness asleep in her:
For, when I kissed, her eyelids knew no stir.   10
So back I drew tiptoe from that Princess,
Because it was too soon, and not my part,
To start voluptuous pulses in her heart,
And kiss her to the world of Consciousness.

† From Wilfred Owen, *The Complete Poems and Fragments,* ed. Jon Stallworthy (New York: Norton, 1984). First published in 1914.

INTRODUCTION: Cinderella

Who does not love a Cinderella story? Or for that matter a Cinderella team or a Cinderella ending? Our quintessential story about a rise from rags to riches has also become a cultural meme for capturing dramatic turnarounds, hard-won victories that are earned by a deserving underdog. The tropes that accompany versions of the story—missing shoes or cruel stepsisters—have migrated into many different narratives, flashing out at us as reminders of a fairy-tale drama that mingles persecution at home and class differences with romance that takes the form of love at first sight.

The version of "Cinderella" best known in Anglo-American and European cultures comes from Charles Perrault, who published his "Cendrillon" in 1697. Disney's 1950 feature-length animated *Cinderella* opens to the image of a book with a voice-over that gives us the beginning of Perrault's tale about a beleaguered heroine, an evil stepmother and her daughters, a fairy godmother, a pumpkin, glass slippers, and a midnight spell. Since Disney, the story's staying power has derived from its depiction of maternal cruelty and sibling rivalry as well as its staging of the power of radiant beauty. Both Cinderella and the Prince are transformed, with one rising phoenix-like from the ashes and the other determined to find his soul mate via a sole mate.

The double transformation that fuels the narrative energy of "Cinderella" leads to a happily ever after in virtually every version of her story. But the heroine's stepsisters rarely fare well. Who can forget the final scene of the Grimms' "Cinderella," which graphically describes the fate of those ill-tempered, disagreeable pretenders to the throne?

> When the couple went to church, the elder sister was on the right, the younger on the left side: the doves pecked one eye from each one. Later, when they left the church, the elder sister was on the left, the younger on the right. The doves pecked the other eye from each one. (p. 153)

For their "wickedness and malice" (p. 153) the sisters are punished with blindness for the rest of their lives. This ending, along with the details of the mutilation of their feet, is often cited as evidence of the brutal, violent turn taken by German fairy tales. Yet the Grimms' punishment for the stepsisters is relatively mild when compared to what befalls their counterparts in other cultures. An Indonesian Cinderella forces her stepsister into a cauldron of boiling water, then has the body cut up, pickled, and sent to the girl's mother as "salt meat" for her next meal. A Filipino variant shows the stepmother and her daughters "pulled to pieces by wild horses." And a Japanese stepsister is dragged around in a basket, tumbles over the edge of a deep ditch, and falls to her death.[1]

Many versions of "Cinderella," however, end on a conciliatory note. Charles Perrault offers what is perhaps the fullest elaboration of a reconciliation between the heroine and her stepsisters, who throw themselves at Cinderella's feet and beg her forgiveness. This Cinderella, who is as good as she is beautiful, not only pardons the sisters but also invites them to join her in the palace and loses no time in marrying them to two high-ranking court officials. An Armenian Cinderella falls at the feet of her wicked sisters as they are leaving church, weeps copious tears with them, and bears them no grudge.[2] And finally, a recent American version marketed through elementary schools stages a crudely sentimental reconciliation scene, presumably designed to appeal to the educators and parents buying the book:

> [The sisters] begged Cinderella to forgive them for being so
>   mean to her.
> Cinderella told them they were forgiven.
> "I am sure you will never be mean to me again," she said.
> "Oh, never," said the older sister.
> "Never, ever," said the younger sister.[3]

Cinderella has been reinvented by so many different cultures that it is hardly surprising to find that she is sometimes cruel and vindictive, at other times compassionate and kind. Even within a single cultural zone, she can appear genteel and self-effacing in one story, clever and enterprising in another, coy and manipulative in a third.[4] Still, Jane Yolen may have a point when she asserts that the shrewd, resourceful heroine of folktales from earlier centuries has been supplanted by a "passive princess" waiting for Prince Charming to rescue her. Disney's Cinderella, as we shall see, is a shrinking violet by comparison with some of her folkloric ancestors, who refuse to

1. Neil Philip, *The Cinderella Story: The Origins and Variations of the Story Known as 'Cinderella'* (London: Penguin, 1989), pp. 21–31, 113–21, 32–35.
2. Ibid., pp. 46–51.
3. Jane Yolen, "America's Cinderella," *Children's Literature in Education* 8 (1977): 21–29.
4. Ruth B. Bottigheimer, "Fairy Tales and Children's Literature: A Feminist Perspective," in *Teaching Children's Literature: Issues, Pedagogy, Resources*, ed. Glen Edward Sadler (New York: Modern Language Association of America, 1992), pp. 101–08.

stay at home suffering in silence and who become adept at engineering their own rescues.

Just how spirited and resourceful was Cinderella in her earliest incarnations? Answering that question requires surveying a vast array of tales featuring heroines known not only as Cinderella, Cendrillon, Ash Girl, and Cenerentola, but also as Rashin Coatie, Mossy Coat, Catskin, Katie Woodencloak, and Donkeyskin. The Aarne-Thompson-Uther index of tale types identifies two distinct Cinderella tales: ATU 510A ("Cinderella") and ATU 510B ("The Dress of Gold, of Silver, and of Stars," also known as "Cap o' Rushes," etc.). The two narratives encoded in the tale-type indexes seem virtually unrelated at first glance. The plots of "Cinderella" stories are driven by the anxious jealousy of biological mothers and stepmothers who subject the heroine to one ordeal of domestic drudgery after another; the plots of "Catskin" tales are fueled by the erotic passion of fathers, whose unseemly behavior drives their daughters from home.

In tales depicting the social persecution of a girl by her stepmother, the central focus comes to rest on the unbearable family situation produced by a father's remarriage. But while the father's responsibility for creating turmoil by choosing an inappropriate marriage partner recedes into the background or is suppressed over time (even as the father himself is virtually eliminated as a character), the foul deeds of his wife come to occupy center stage. We see her throwing her stepdaughter into a river, instructing a hunter to kill her and recover her lungs and liver for dinner, sending her into a snowstorm wearing nothing but a shift, depriving her of food, and making her life wretched in every way.

In tales depicting erotic persecution of a daughter by her father, stepmothers and their daughters tend to vanish from the central arena of action. Yet the father's desire for his daughter in the second tale type furnishes a powerful motive for a stepmother's jealous rages and unnatural deeds in the first tale type. Psychoanalytic criticism has read "Cinderella" and "Catskin" as enactments of Oedipal desires, with each tale suppressing one component (love for the father or hatred of the mother) of the Oedipal plot. Many "Catskin" narratives, among them Perrault's "Donkeyskin" (p. 154) and the Grimms' "Thousandfurs," mount two phases of action: in the first the heroine is persecuted by her father, in the second she turns into a Cinderella figure, obliged to spend her days in domestic servitude under the supervision of a despotic cook or a queen.

Yet there is an even more compelling case for arguing that the tales captured the hard facts of everyday life, staging domestic arrangements that led to the physical and sexual abuse of girls, with cruel parents and stepparents who exploit rather than protect the young. Our headlines today reveal that the dark side of fairy tales like "Cinderella" and "Donkeyskin" still come true today. They are a stark reminder that domestic violence does not belong exclusively to the "long ago and far away."

While wicked stepmothers figure prominently in fairy tales disseminated in our culture, fathers who persecute their daughters by showing them too much affection are virtually unknown. "Cinderella," "Snow White," and "Hansel and Gretel" are the tales from Perrault and from the Grimms that continue to thrive even on foreign soil, while stories such as "Donkeyskin" and "Thousandfurs" have either failed to take root or have been modified beyond recognition, with the result that fathers have a surprisingly limited role in fairy tales transmitted today.

It is important to bear in mind that the passive or absent father was, even a century ago, not the rule in fairy tales. As Marian Cox's nineteenth-century study of 345 variants of "Cinderella" makes clear, at least two widespread and pervasive versions of the tale attributed the heroine's social degradation either to what Cox describes in characteristic Victorian language as an "unnatural father" or to a father who attempts to extract from his daughter a statement about her filial devotion.[5] Of the 226 tales belonging unambiguously to one of the three categories labeled by Cox as (1) ill-treated heroine (with mothers, stepmothers, and their progeny as victimizers), (2) unnatural father, and (3) King Lear judgment, 130 belong to the first class, 77 to the second, and 19 to the third. Thus in the tales examined by Cox, the versions that cast (step)mothers in the role of villain only slightly outnumber those that ascribe Cinderella's misfortune to an importunate father. Cinderella and her cousins were, therefore, once almost as likely to flee the household because of their father's perverse erotic attachment to them or because of his insistence on a verbal declaration of love, as they were to be banished to the hearth and degraded to domestic servitude by an ill-tempered stepmother.

That our own culture would suppress the theme of paternal erotic pursuit and indulge freely in elaborate variations on the theme of maternal tyranny is perhaps not surprising on a number of counts. Since tales such as Perrault's "Donkeyskin" and the Grimms' "Thousandfurs" make for troubling reading matter for adults, it hardly seems advisable to put them between the covers of books for children. But Marina Warner has argued that there is something more at stake in this evolutionary turn in the Cinderella story:

> When interest in psychological realism is at work in the mind of the receiver of traditional folklore, the proposed marriage of a father to his daughter becomes too hard to accept. But it is only

5. Marian Roalfe Cox, *Cinderella: Three Hundred and Forty-Five Variants of Cinderella, Catskin, and Cap o' Rushes,* ed. Andrew Lang (London: David Nutt, 1893).

too hard to accept precisely because it belongs to a different order of reality/fantasy from the donkeyskin disguise or the gold excrement or the other magical motifs: because it is not impossible, because it could actually happen, and is known to have done so. It is when fairy tales coincide with experience that they begin to suffer from censoring, rather than the other way around.[6]

The censorship to which Warner refers seems to have led to dramatic editorial interventions very early on, perhaps as the tale made its way from an oral culture to a literary tradition. In Straparola's seventeenth-century "Catskin" tale, the king is described as a "wicked father" with "evil designs," "execrable lust," and a "wicked and treacherous passion." Yet it is his wife who decrees that the object of his lust and passion be their daughter Doralice. On her deathbed, the queen beseeches her husband Tebaldo never to take anyone as wife whose finger does not perfectly fit her own wedding ring. Faithful husband that he is, Tebaldo makes it a condition "that any damsel who might be offered to him in marriage should first try on her finger his wife's ring, to see whether it fitted." When the king fails to find a woman whose finger fits the ring, he turns to his daughter and discovers that the fit is perfect. As Tebaldo tells his daughter, he is obliged to marry her for it is the only way "I shall satisfy my own desire without violating the promise I made to your mother."[7]

While some readers will not be persuaded by Tebaldo's logic and by the narrator's efforts to exonerate the king, many others have clearly bought right into the rhetoric of self-justification set forth in other Catskin tales. Consider one critic's gloss on the family dynamics in Perrault's "Donkeyskin": "The dying queen had a vengeful streak: she made her husband . . . swear not to remarry unless he found a woman superior to her in beauty and goodness. Entrapped, the king eventually discovers that only his lovely daughter can fill the bill."[8] Another critic finds that "Rashie-Coat's degradation is consequent upon her dying mother's unfortunate imprudence."[9] Again and again, mothers are the real villains, extracting promises that end by victimizing both father and daughter. Everywhere we look, the tendency to defame women and to magnify maternal evil emerges. Even when a tale turns on a father's incestuous desires, the mother becomes more than complicit: she has stirred up the trouble in the first place by setting the conditions for her husband's remarriage.

6. Marina Warner, "The Silence of the Fathers: Donkeyskin II," in *From the Beast to the Blonde: On Fairy Tales and Their Tellers* (New York: Farrar, Straus & Giroux, 1994), p. 349.
7. Giovan Francesco Straparola, *The Facetious Nights of Straparola,* trans. W. G. Waters (London: Society of Bibliophiles, 1901), p. 82.
8. Philip Lewis, *Seeing through the Mother Goose Tales: Visual Turns in the Writings of Charles Perrault* (Stanford, CA: Stanford UP, 1996), p. 155.
9. W. R. S. Ralston, "Cinderella," in *Cinderella: A Casebook,* ed. Alan Dundes (Madison: U of Wisconsin P, 1981), p. 41.

The ring episode in Straparola's "Catskin" does suggest one hith-
erto neglected point of contact between "Cinderella" tales and
"Catskin" stories. Finding the perfect fit between fingers and rings
and between feet and shoes becomes a task set to both fathers and
princes, who now and then collaborate with each other (as in the
Grimms' "Cinderella"), who sometimes work in succession (as in
Perrault's "Donkeyskin"), and who are occasionally concurrent
rivals, as in an Indian tale titled "The Father Who Wanted to Marry
His Daughter."[1] What these stories demonstrate, perhaps more
forcefully than anything else, is the way in which the path to happy
heterosexual unions depends on a successful transfer of filial love
and devotion from a father to a "prince," on a move from a false "perfect fit" to a true "perfect fit."

While Catskin tales raise the charged issue of incestuous desire
and place the heroine in jeopardy, they also furnish a rare stage for
creative action. Unlike Cinderella, who endures humiliation at home
and becomes the beneficiary of lavish gifts, the heroine of Catskin
tales is mobile, active, and resourceful. She begins with a strong
assertion of will, resistant to the paternal desires that would claim
her. Fleeing the household, she moves out into an alien world that
requires her to be inventive, energetic, and enterprising if she is to
reestablish herself, to reclaim her royal rank, and to marry the
prince. To be sure, her resourcefulness is confined largely to sarto-
rial and culinary arts, but these were, after all, the two areas in
which women traditionally could distinguish themselves. The
Grimms' Thousandfurs dazzles with her dress, and she successfully
uses her cuisine to lure the prince. Donkeyskin's powers of attraction are also explicitly linked to her wardrobe and her baking skills.

That these stories are disappearing from the folkloric arena is perhaps not surprising. The theme of incest alone would account for
the steady erosion of interest in anthologizing the tale. But in addition, the story's critique of paternal authority and its endorsement
of filial disobedience turn it into an unlikely candidate for bedtime
reading. What are we to make of a story that positions a father as
the agent of transgressive sexuality and the daughter as the enforcer
of cultural law and order? Perrault, who felt that fairy tales ought to
transmit lessons to children about virtue and vice, was so mystified
by "Donkeyskin" that he appended a comment that is absurdly irrelevant to the terms of the text: "The story of Donkeyskin may be hard
to believe, but as long as there are children, mothers, and grandmothers in this world, it will be fondly remembered by all" (p. 162).
What is far harder to believe than the story itself is the idea that
this particular tale could generate "fond" memories.

1. A. K. Ramanujan, ed., Folktales from India (New York: Pantheon, 1991), pp. 186–89.

In staging the attempted violation of a sacred taboo, Catskin stories celebrate daughters as agents of resistance, yet also enshrine them as maintaining the sanctity of cultural codes. Giambattista Basile captured exactly what made this story unacceptable to later generations when he spelled out its moral:

> The wise man spoke well when he said that one cannot obey commands of gall with obedience sweet as sugar. Man must give only well-measured commands if he expects well-weighed obedience, and resistance springs from wrongful orders, as happened in the case of the King of Roccaspra, who, by asking for what was unseemly from his daughter, caused her to run away at the peril of her life and honor.[2]

While there are virtually no male counterparts to Catskin (mother/son incest seems to resist representation in folktales), male Cinderellas abound in the folklore of many cultures. Aarne and Thompson felt obliged to accommodate these male Cinderellas in their index of tale types by setting up a separate category of Cinderella tales identified by the rubric AT 511 ("One-Eye, Two-Eyes, and Three-Eyes" for female Cinderellas) and AT 511A ("The Little Red Ox" for male Cinderellas). The distinction is little more than theoretical, for in practice, tales such as "The Little Red Ox" (a story in which the protagonist's mother returns in the form of a donor-ox) seem to feature girls almost as often as boys. These tales neutralize the persecutions of a wicked stepmother with the sustenance, nurturing, and rescue provided by an animal that is clearly identified with the dead mother. The Indian "Story of the Black Cow" (p. 169) belongs to a tale type that has virtually disappeared from our folkloristic repertoire but once enjoyed the kind of popularity that "Cinderella" has attained today. That male Cinderellas have vanished from our own cultural horizon challenges us to understand exactly what it was that once allowed both girls and boys to participate in the developmental trajectory outlined in the tale.

Rhodopis[†]

They tell the fabulous story that, when [Rhodopis] was bathing, an eagle snatched one of her sandals from her maid and carried it to

---

2. Giambattista Basile, "The She-Bear," in *The Pentamerone of Giambattista Basile*, trans. Benedetto Croce, ed. N. M. Penzer (London: Bodley Head, 1932), p. 170.
† The story of Rhodopis was told in the 1st century B.C.E. by the Greek historian Strabo in his work *Geography*. Reprinted from *Geography*, trans. Horace Leonard Jones, Loeb Classical Library Volume 267 (Cambridge: Harvard UP, 1928; reprint 1935, 1949), IV:391. Loeb Classical Library® is a registered trademark of the President and Fellows of Harvard College.

Memphis; and while the king was administering justice in the open
air, the eagle, when it arrived above his head, flung the sandal into
his lap; and the king, stirred both by the beautiful shape of the sandal and by the strangeness of the occurrence, sent men in all directions into the country in quest of the woman who wore the sandal;
and when she was found in the city of Naucratis, she was brought
up to Memphis, became the wife of the king, and when she died was
honoured with the above-mentioned tomb.

Yeh-hsien[†]

Among the people of the south there is a tradition that before the
Ch'in and Han dynasties there was a cave-master called Wu. The
aborigines called the place the Wu cave. He married two wives.
One wife died. She had a daughter called Yeh-hsien, who from
childhood was intelligent and good at making pottery on the wheel.
Her father loved her. After some years the father died, and she was
ill-treated by her step-mother, who always made her collect firewood in dangerous places and draw water from deep pools. She
once got a fish about two inches long, with red fins and golden eyes.
She put it into a bowl of water. It grew bigger every day, and after
she had changed the bowl several times she could find no bowl big
enough for it, so she threw it into the back pond. Whatever food
was left over from meals she put into the water to feed it. When she
came to the pond, the fish always exposed its head and pillowed it
on the bank; but when anyone else came, it did not come out. The
step-mother knew about this, but when she watched for it, it did not
once appear. So she tricked the girl, saying, "Haven't you worked
hard! I am going to give you a new dress." She then made the girl
change out of her tattered clothing. Afterwards she sent her to get
water from another spring and reckoning that it was several hundred leagues, the step-mother at her leisure put on her daughter's
clothes, hid a sharp blade up her sleeve, and went to the pond. She
called to the fish. The fish at once put its head out, and she chopped
it off and killed it. The fish was now more than ten feet long. She
served it up and it tasted twice as good as an ordinary fish. She hid
the bones under the dung-hill. Next day, when the girl came to the
pond, no fish appeared. She howled with grief in the open countryside, and suddenly there appeared a man with his hair loose over
his shoulders and coarse clothes. He came down from the sky. He

† "The Chinese Cinderella Story," *Folk-Lore*, vol. 58 (London: The Folklore Society,
    1947), pp. 226–38. Narrated by Li Shih-yüan and recorded by Tuan Ch'eng-shih (c. 850
    C.E.); translated by Arthur Waley (1947). Reprinted by permission of the Folklore Soci-
    ety. www.folklore-society.com.

consoled her saying, "Don't howl! Your step-mother has killed the fish and its bones are under the dung. You go back, take the fish's bones and hide them in your room. Whatever you want, you have only to pray to them for it. It is bound to be granted." The girl followed his advice, and was able to provide herself with gold, pearls, dresses and food whenever she wanted them.

When the time came for the cave-festival, the step-mother went, leaving the girl to keep watch over the fruit-trees in the garden. She waited till the step-mother was some way off, and then went herself, wearing a cloak of stuff spun from kingfisher feathers and shoes of gold. Her step-sister recognized her and said to the step-mother, "That's very like my sister." The step-mother suspected the same thing. The girl was aware of this and went away in such a hurry that she lost one shoe. It was picked up by one of the people of the cave. When the step-mother got home, she found the girl asleep, with her arms round one of the trees in the garden, and thought no more about it.

This cave was near to an island in the sea. On this island was a kingdom called T'o-han. Its soldiers had subdued twenty or thirty other islands and it had a coast-line of several thousand leagues. The caveman sold the shoe in T'o-han, and the ruler of T'o-han got it. He told those about him to put it on; but it was an inch too small even for the one among them that had the smallest foot. He ordered all the women in his kingdom to try it on; but there was not one that it fitted. It was light as down and made no noise even when treading on stone. The king of T'o-han thought the cave-man had got it unlawfully. He put him in prison and tortured him, but did not end by finding out where it had come from. So he threw it down at the wayside. Then they went everywhere through all the people's houses and arrested them. If there was a woman's shoe, they arrested them and told the king of T'o-han. He thought it strange, searched the inner-rooms and found Yeh-hsien. He made her put on the shoe, and it was true.

Yeh-hsien then came forward, wearing her cloak spun from halcyon feathers and her shoes. She was as beautiful as a heavenly being. She now began to render service to the king, and he took the fish-bones and Yeh-hsien, and brought them back to his country.

The step-mother and step-sister were shortly afterwards struck by flying stones, and died. The cave people were sorry for them and buried them in a stone-pit, which was called the Tomb of the Distressed Women. The men of the cave made mating-offerings there; any girl they prayed for there, they got. The king of T'o-han, when he got back to his kingdom made Yeh-hsien his chief wife. The first year the king was very greedy and by his prayers to the fish-bones got treasures and jade without limit. Next year, there was no response, so the king buried the fish-bones on the sea-shore. He covered them with a hundred bushels of pearls and bordered them with gold. Later there was a mutiny of some soldiers who had been conscripted and their general opened (the hiding-place) in order to make better provision for his army. One night they (the bones) were washed away by the tide.

BROTHERS GRIMM

Cinderella[†]

The wife of a rich man fell ill. When she realized that the end was near, she called her only daughter to her bedside and said: "Dear child, if you are good and say your prayers, our dear Lord will always be with you, and I shall look down on you from heaven and always be with you." Then she shut her eyes and passed away.

Every day the girl went to the grave of her mother and wept. She was always good and said her prayers. When winter came, the snow covered the grave with a white blanket, and when the sun had taken it off again in the spring, the rich man remarried.

His new wife brought with her two daughters, whose features were beautiful and white, but whose hearts were foul and black. This meant the beginning of a hard time for the poor stepchild. "Why should this silly goose be allowed to sit in the parlor with us?" the girls said. "If you want to eat bread, you'll have to earn it. Out with the kitchen maid!"

They took away her beautiful clothes, dressed her in an old gray smock, and gave her some wooden shoes. "Just look at the proud princess in her finery!" they shouted and laughed, taking her out to the kitchen. From morning until night she had to work hard. Every day, she got up before daybreak to carry water, start the fire, cook, and wash. On top of that the two sisters did everything imaginable to make her life miserable. They ridiculed her and threw peas and lentils into the ashes so that she would have to get down and pick them out. In the evening, when she was completely exhausted from work, she didn't have a bed but had to lie down next to the hearth in ashes. She always looked so dusty and dirty that people started to call her Cinderella.

One day, the father was going to the fair and he asked his two stepdaughters what they wanted from there. "Beautiful dresses," said one.

† Jacob Grimm and Wilhelm Grimm, "Aschenputtel," in *Kinder- und Hausmärchen*, 7th ed. (Berlin: Dieterich, 1857; first published: Berlin: Realschulbuchhandlung, 1812). Translated for the first edition of this Norton Critical Edition by Maria Tatar. Copyright © 1999 by Maria Tatar.

"Pearls and jewels," said the other.

"But you, Cinderella," he asked, "what do you want?"

"Father," she said, "break off the first branch that brushes against your hat on the way home and bring it to me."

And so he bought beautiful dresses, pearls, and jewels for the two stepsisters. On the way home, when he was riding through a thicket of green bushes, a hazel branch brushed against him and knocked his hat off. When he arrived home, he gave his stepdaughters what they had asked for, and to Cinderella he gave the branch from the hazel bush. Cinderella thanked him, went to her mother's grave, and planted a hazel sprig on it. She cried so hard that her tears fell to the ground and watered it. It grew and became a beautiful tree. Three times a day Cinderella went and sat under it, and wept and prayed. Each time a little white bird would also fly to the tree, and if she made a wish, the little bird would toss down what she had asked for.

It happened that one day the king announced a festival that was to last for three days and to which all the beautiful young ladies of the land were invited from whom his son might choose a bride. When the two stepsisters heard that they too had received invitations to attend, they were in high spirits. They called Cinderella and said: "Comb our hair, brush our shoes, and fasten our buckles. We're going to the wedding at the king's palace."

Cinderella did as she was told, but she wept, for she too would have liked to go to the ball, and she begged her stepmother to let her go.

"Cinderella," she said, "How can you go to a wedding when you're covered with dust and dirt? How can you want to go to a ball when you have neither a dress nor shoes?"

Cinderella kept pleading with her, and so she finally said: "Here, I've dumped a bowlful of lentils into the ashes. If you can pick out the lentils in the next two hours, then you may go."

The girl went out the back door into the garden and called out: "O tame little doves, little turtledoves, and all you little birds in the sky, come and help me put

the good ones into the little pot,
the bad ones into your little crop."

Two little white doves came flying in through the kitchen window, followed by little turtledoves. And finally all the birds in the sky came swooping and fluttering and settled down in the ashes. The little doves nodded their heads and began to peck, peck, peck, peck, and then the others began to peck, peck, peck, peck and put all the good lentils into the bowl. Barely an hour had passed when they were finished and flew back out the window.

The girl brought the bowl to her stepmother and was overjoyed because she was sure that she would now be able to go to the wedding. But the stepmother said: "No, Cinderella, you have nothing to wear, and you don't know how to dance. Everybody would just laugh at you."

When Cinderella began to cry, the stepmother said: "If you can pick out two bowlfuls of lentils from the ashes in the next hour, then you can go."

But she thought to herself: "She'll never be able to do it."

After she had dumped the two bowlfuls of lentils into the ashes, the girl went out the back door into the garden and called out: "O tame little doves, little turtledoves, and all you little birds in the sky, come and help me put

> the good ones into the little pot,
> the bad ones into your little crop."

Two little white doves came flying in through the kitchen window, followed by little turtledoves. And finally all the birds in the sky came swooping and fluttering and settled down in the ashes. The little doves nodded their heads and began to peck, peck, peck, peck, and then the others began to peck, peck, peck, peck and put all the good lentils into the bowl. Barely a half hour had passed when they were finished and flew back out the window.

The girl brought the bowls back to her stepmother and was overjoyed because she was sure that she would now be able to go to the wedding. But her stepmother said: "It's no use. You can't come along since you have nothing to wear and don't know how to dance. We would be so embarrassed." Turning her back on Cinderella, she hurried off with her two proud daughters.

Now that no one was at home any longer, Cinderella went to her mother's grave under the hazel tree and called:

> "Shake your branches, little tree,
> Toss gold and silver down on me."

The bird tossed down a dress of gold and silver, with slippers embroidered with silk and silver. She slipped the dress on hastily and left for the wedding. Her sisters and her stepmother had no idea who she was. She looked so beautiful in the dress of gold that they thought she must be the daughter of a foreign king. They never imagined it could be Cinderella for they were sure that she was at home, sitting in the dirt and picking lentils out of the ashes.

The prince approached Cinderella, took her by the hand, and danced with her. He had no intention of dancing with anyone else and never let go of her hand. Whenever anyone else asked her to dance, he would say: "She is my partner."

Cinderella danced until it turned dark, then she wanted to go home. The prince said: "I will go with you and be your escort," for he wanted to find out about the beautiful girl's family. But she managed to slip away from him and bounded into a dovecote. The prince waited until Cinderella's father arrived and told him that the strange girl had bounded into the dovecote. The old man thought: "Could it be Cinderella?" He sent for an ax and pick and broke into the dovecote, but no one was inside it. And when they went back to the house, there was Cinderella, lying in the ashes in her filthy clothes with a dim little oil lamp burning on the mantel. Cinderella had jumped down from the back of the dovecote and had run over to the little hazel tree, where she slipped out of her beautiful dress and put it on the grave. The bird took the dress back, and Cinderella slipped into her gray smock and settled back into the ashes in the kitchen.

The next day, when the festivities started up again and the parents had left with the stepsisters, Cinderella went to the hazel tree and said:

> "Shake your branches, little tree,
> Toss gold and silver down on me."

The bird tossed down a dress that was even more splendid than the previous one. And when she appeared at the wedding in this dress, everyone was dazzled by her beauty. The prince, who had been waiting for her to arrive, took her by the hand and danced with her alone. Whenever anyone came and asked her to dance, he would say: "She is my partner."

At night she wanted to leave, and the prince followed her, hoping to see which house she would enter. But she bounded away and disappeared into the garden behind the house, where there was a beautiful, tall tree from whose branches hung magnificent pears. She climbed up through the branches as nimbly as a squirrel, and the prince had no idea where she was. He waited until her father got there and said to him: "The strange girl has escaped, but I believe that she climbed up into the pear tree."

The father thought: "Could it be Cinderella?" and he sent for an ax and chopped down the tree. But no one was in it. When they went into the kitchen, Cinderella was, as usual, lying in the ashes, for she had jumped down on the other side of the tree, taken the beautiful dress to the bird on the hazel tree, and slipped on her little gray smock again.

On the third day, when the parents and sisters had left, Cinderella went to her mother's grave and said to the little tree:

> "Shake your branches, little tree,
> Toss gold and silver down on me."

The bird tossed down a dress more splendid and radiant than anything she had ever had, and the slippers were covered in gold. When she arrived at the wedding in that dress, everyone was speechless with amazement. The prince danced with her alone, and if someone asked her to dance, he would say: "She is my partner."

At night, Cinderella wanted to leave, and the prince wanted to escort her, but she slipped away so quickly that he was unable to follow her. The prince had planned a trick. The entire staircase had been coated with pitch, and as the girl went running down the stairs, her left slipper got stuck. The prince lifted it up: it was a dainty little shoe covered with gold.

The next morning he went with it to his father and said to him: "No one else will be my bride but the woman whose foot fits this golden shoe." The two sisters were overjoyed, for they both had beautiful feet. The elder went with her mother into a room to try it on. But the shoe was too small for her, and she couldn't get her big toe into it. Her mother handed her a knife and said: "Cut the toe off. Once you're queen, you won't need to go on foot any more."

The girl sliced off her toe, forced her foot into the shoe, gritted her teeth, and went out to meet the prince. He lifted her up on his horse as his bride, and rode away with her. But they had to pass by the grave, where two little doves were perched in the little hazel tree, calling out:

> "Roo coo coo, roo coo coo,
> blood's in the shoe:
> the shoe's too tight,
> the real bride's waiting another night."

When he looked down at her foot, he saw blood spurting from it and turned his horse around. He brought the false bride back home, and said that since she was not the true bride, her sister should try the shoe on. The sister went into her room and succeeded in getting her toes into the shoe, but her heel was too big. Her mother handed her a knife and said: "Cut off part of your heel. Once you're queen, you won't need to go on foot any more."

The girl sliced off a piece of her heel, forced her foot into the shoe, gritted her teeth, and went out to meet the prince. He lifted her up on his horse as his bride, and rode away with her. When they passed by the little hazel tree, two little doves were perched there, calling out:

> "Roo coo coo, roo coo coo,
> blood's in the shoe:
> the shoe's too tight,
> the real bride's waiting another night."

When he looked down at her foot, he saw blood spurting from it and staining her white stockings completely red. Then he turned his horse around and brought the false bride back home. "She's not the true bride either," he said. "Don't you have another daughter?"

"No," said the man, "there's only puny little Cinderella, my dead wife's daughter, but she can't possibly be the bride."

The prince asked that she be sent for, but the mother said: "Oh no, she's much too dirty to be seen."

The prince insisted, and Cinderella was summoned. First she washed her hands and face completely clean, then she went and curtsied before the prince, who handed her the golden shoe. She sat down on a stool, took her foot out of the heavy wooden shoe, and put it into the slipper. It fit perfectly. And when she stood up and the prince looked her straight in the face, he recognized the beautiful girl with whom he had danced and exclaimed: "She is the true bride." The stepmother and the two sisters were horrified and turned pale with rage. But the prince lifted Cinderella up on his horse and rode away with her. When they passed by the little hazel tree, the two little white doves called out:

> "Roo coo coo, roo coo coo,
> no blood in the shoe:
> the shoe's not tight,
> the real bride's here tonight."

After they had called out these words, the doves both came flying down and perched on Cinderella's shoulders, one on the right, the other on the left, and there they stayed.

On the day of the wedding to the prince, the two false sisters came and tried to be charming and share in Cinderella's good fortune. When the couple went to church, the elder sister was on the right, the younger on the left side: the doves pecked one eye from each one. Later, when they left the church, the elder sister was on the left, the younger on the right. The doves pecked the other eye from each one. And so they were punished for their wickedness and malice with blindness for the rest of their lives.

Cinderella[†]

Po' little Cinderella was livin' with her auntie. De woman had two daughter of her own. An' she live in de fire-heart'. Wouldn' let her

---

† *Folk-Lore of the Sea Islands, South Carolina,* ed. Elsie Clews Parsons (New York: American Folklore Society, 1923), pp. 120–21. Told by James Murray and his wife, Pinky Murray, who were living on Hilton Head Island; this version of "Cinderella" is remarkably like the Grimms' tale in its unedited form, complete with hacked off heels and toes. Gullah, the dialect used to tell this story, was spoken on the once-isolated Sea Islands, which stretch out along the coast of South Carolina. Failing to recognize the triumph of slaves creating a distinct idiom of their own, one native informant told Elsie Clews Parsons, who collected this tale: "Dere is not'in' de matter wid us but bad grammar."

sleep in no bed no' not'in'. An' ev'y night her an' de two girls dress up des' as fine as dey could be, go out to de dance, big feas', havin' all kind of fun. Po' little Cinderella had to stay home in de ashes, nakin', an' havin' not'in' to eat. Ev'y time dey come home, dey huff up po' little Cinderella. Say she an't do what they leave her to do. De two girls d'ess up in robe in diamon's all ower, an' was goin' to de dance, goin' t'rough de woods. So de king an' de queen give a dance. An' de king inwited dem out. An' he had a gol' slippers (I think he was number two). An' dese fancy girls had wanted dem. An' de king said who de slipper fitted would be his wife dat night. De dove come an' bring some clothes fo' Cinderella. Den Cinderella gone out to de dance, an' dey didn' know her, dress so much. Dey was wonderin' what strange woman dat is. Den de king tryin' on de shoe on dey all feet. Some cut off deir toe, tryin' to make de shoe fit dem. Some trim deir heels off, tryin' to make de shoe fit dem. After all, de shoes couldn' fit none of dem dat been dere. Den po' little Cinderella she come right on up in dat time, an' she grab de shoes. An' fit her right on de feet. Den she become de queen, married to de king, an' ride in de firs' chariot.

CHARLES PERRAULT

Donkeyskin[†]

Once upon a time there lived a king who was the most powerful ruler on earth. Gentle in peace and terrifying in war, he had no rivals. While his neighbors feared him, his subjects were perfectly content. Under his protection, civic virtues and the fine arts flourished everywhere. His better half, his faithful companion, was so charming and so beautiful, with a disposition so sweet and generous, that he was prouder about being her husband than about being king. From their pure, tender marriage, which was full of affection and pleasure, was born a girl with so many virtues that they easily compensated for the lack of additional progeny.

Everything in the king's palatial, luxurious castle was magnificent. It was teeming with vast numbers of courtiers and servants. In the stables were steeds large and small, of every description, covered with handsome trappings, embroidery, and braids of gold. But what surprised everyone on entering was that the most visible place in the castle was occupied by Master Donkey, who displayed his two

† From Charles Perrault, *Griselidis, Nouvelle, avec le conte de Peau d'Ane et celui des Souhaits ridicules* (Paris: Coignard, 1694). Translated for the first edition of this Norton Critical Edition by Maria Tatar. Copyright © 1999 Maria Tatar.

immense ears for everyone to see. This incongruity may surprise you, but once you become aware of the superlative virtues of this creature, you too will agree that he was well worth his keep. Nature had formed him in such a way that instead of dropping dung he excreted all kinds of beautiful gold coins that were gathered from his golden litter every morning when he awoke.

Heaven sometimes tires of letting people enjoy happiness and always mingles the good with the bad just like rain with good weather. Out of the blue, a nasty illness attacked the queen and ended her days of joy. Help was summoned from all quarters, but neither erudite physicians nor the charlatans who appeared were able to arrest the fire started by the fever and fueled by it.

In her dying hour, the queen said to her husband the king: "Before I die I want to make one request of you. If you wish to remarry when I am no more. . . ."

"Oh," said the king, "your fears are unnecessary. I'd never in my life think of it. Rest assured of that."

"I believe you," answered the queen. "Your ardent love proves it to me. But just to be absolutely certain, I want you to swear that you will pledge your love and marry only if you meet a woman more beautiful, more accomplished, and more wise than I am." Confidence in her own qualities convinced the queen that the promise, cunningly extracted, was as good as an oath never to marry. His eyes bathed in tears, the king swore to do everything the queen desired. And the queen died in his arms. Never did a king make such a display of his emotions. To hear him sobbing both day and night one would have thought that his grief could not endure and that he was mourning his deceased wife like a man eager to put an end to the affair quickly.

And indeed, that was the case. After a few months, he wanted to go ahead and choose a new wife. But this was not an easy matter. He had to keep the promise that the new wife would be more charming and attractive than the one who had just been buried. Neither the court with its many beauties, nor the country, nor the city, nor the neighboring kingdoms where they were making the rounds could provide such a woman. Only his own daughter was more beautiful, and she even possessed certain charms that his dead wife never had. The king noticed it himself and, burning with a desire that drove him mad, he took it into his head that she ought to marry him. He even found a sophist who agreed that a case could be made for the marriage. But the young princess, saddened by this kind of love, mourned and wept night and day.

With a heart grieving with a thousand sorrows, the princess went to find her godmother, who lived some distance in a remote grotto made of pearls and lavishly adorned with coral. She was an extraordinary fairy, unrivaled in her art. There is no need to tell you what a fairy was in those radiant days, for I am sure that your loved ones told you about them when you were very young.

"I know what has brought you here," the fairy godmother said, looking at the princess. "I understand the deep sadness in your heart. But with me by your side, there is no need to worry. Nothing can harm you so long as you follow my advice. It is true that your father wants to marry you, and it would be a fatal mistake to pay attention to his mad demand. But there is a way of refusing him without defying him. Tell him that before you are willing to give your heart to him, he must satisfy your desires and give you a dress the color of the seasons. No matter how rich and powerful he is and no matter how much he is favored by the heavens, he will never be able to fulfill your request."

Trembling with fear, the young princess went right away to her amorous father, who instantly ordered the most renowned tailors in the land to make a dress the color of the sky without delay. If not, they could rest assured that he would have them all hanged.

It was not yet dawn the next day when the desired dress was brought in. The most beautiful blue of the firmament, even when it is encircled with large clouds of gold, is not a deeper azure. Transfixed with joy and with sorrow, the child did not know what to say or how to get around the agreement. The godmother said to her in a low voice: "Ask for a dress more brilliant and less commonplace, one the color of the moon. He will never be able to give it to you."

No sooner had the princess placed the request when the king said to his embroiderer: "I want a dress more splendid than the star of the night, and I want it ready without fail in four days."

The elegant dress was ready on the designated day, just as the king had decreed. When the night unfurls its veils in the skies, the moon, whose brilliant voyage makes the stars turn pale, was no more majestic than this dress. The princess admired the wonderful dress and was about to give her consent when, inspired by her godmother, she said to the amorous king: "I can't be satisfied until I have a dress the color of the sun, but even more radiant."

The king, who loved the princess with a passion beyond compare, summoned a wealthy jeweler and ordered him to make a superb garment of gold and diamonds. He told him that if he failed to carry out the work in satisfactory fashion, he would have him tortured to death.

The king did not have to go to that trouble, for the industrious worker brought him the precious work before the week was over. It was so beautiful, vibrant, and radiant that the blond lover of Clymene,[1] who drives his chariot of gold along the arch of the heavens, was not dazzled by a more brilliant light.

---

1. Reference to Apollo, the Greek god of light and of the sun.

These gifts so confused the child that she did not know what to say to her father, the king. Her godmother took her by the hand and whispered in her ear: "You don't have to stay on this lovely path. Are these gifts that you have received really so marvelous when he has a donkey that, as you know, continually fills his coffers with gold coins? Ask him for the skin of that extraordinary animal. Unless I'm badly mistaken, you won't get it from him, since it is the sole source of his wealth."

This fairy was very learned, and yet she was unaware that passionate love, provided that it has a chance, takes no notice of money or gold. The skin was gallantly bestowed on the child as soon as she asked for it. When the skin was brought to her, she was filled with horror and complained bitterly about her fate. Her godmother arrived and explained that as long as she did the right thing, she would not have to be afraid. She should let the king believe that she was completely prepared to take her wedding vows with him, but at the same time she must disguise herself and flee all alone to a distant country to avoid an evil destiny so certain and so near.

"Here's a large trunk," she added. "We'll put all your clothes, your mirror, your toilet articles, your diamonds and your rubies into it. I will also give you my wand. If you hold it in your hand, the trunk will remain hidden beneath the ground and follow wherever you go. And if you ever want to open it, as soon as my wand touches the ground, it will appear right before your eyes. The hide of the donkey will be the perfect disguise to make you unrecognizable. Conceal yourself carefully under that skin. It is so hideous that no one will ever believe it covers anything beautiful."

The princess put on her disguise and left the wise fairy while the dew was still in the air. The king, who was just then preparing for his joyous wedding feast, learned with horror of the dark turn of events. Every house, road, and avenue was searched forthwith, but it was all in vain. No one could imagine what had become of her. A deep and dark sadness spread throughout the land. No more weddings, no more feasts, no more tarts, no more sugared almonds. Most of the ladies of the court were completely disappointed that they were unable to dine, but the priest felt the greatest sorrow, for he not only missed a meal but, what's worse, nothing was put on the offering plate.

In the meantime, the child continued her journey, her face dirtied with mud. She put out a hand to anyone who passed by her, trying to find a place to work. But these vulgar and unfortunate people saw someone so disagreeable and unkempt that they were not inclined to pay attention to her, let alone to take in a creature so dirty.

And so she journeyed farther and farther, and farther still, until she arrived at a farm where the farmer's wife needed a scullery maid

who would be energetic enough to wash the dish rags and to clean
the trough for the pigs. She was put into a back corner of the kitchen,
where the valets, those insolent scoundrels, ridiculed, attacked, and
mocked her all the time. They played tricks on her whenever they
could, tormenting her at every turn. She became the butt of all their
jokes, and they jeered at her day and night.

On Sundays she was able to get a little more rest than usual. Having done her chores early in the morning, she went to her room and
closed the door. She cleaned herself, then opened her chest, carefully set up a dressing table for herself, with her little jars on top.
Cheerful and pleased with herself, she stood before a large mirror
and first put on the dress of the moon, then the one from which the
fire of the sun burst forth, and finally the beautiful blue dress, which
all the blue of the heavens could not match. Her only regret was that
there was not enough room on the floor to spread out their long
trains. She loved to see herself looking youthful, in ruby and white,
a hundred times more elegant than anyone else. This sweet pleasure kept her going from one Sunday to the next.

I forgot to mention that on that large farm owned by a powerful
and regal king there was an aviary. There, chickens from Barbary,
rails, guinea fowls, cormorants, goslings raised on musk, ducks, and
thousands of other types of exotic birds, each different from the
next, could fill with envy the hearts of ten whole courts.

After hunting, the king's son frequently went over to that charming place to rest for a while and to raise a glass with the nobles of
the court. Even the handsome Cephalus[2] could not compete with
him, with his regal air, his martial bearing, which could fill the most
proud battalions with fear. Donkeyskin watched him with tenderness from a distance. She had the confidence to know that, beneath
the dirt and rags covering her, she preserved the heart of a princess.

"What a grand manner he has, even though he is dressed casually. How agreeable he is," she said to herself. "And how happy must
be the beauty who has won his heart! If he honored me with the
most modest dress, I would feel myself graced far more than by all
the dresses I have here."

One day the young prince was wandering aimlessly from one
courtyard to another and came upon an obscure path where Donkeyskin had her humble abode. By chance, he put an eye to the keyhole. Since it was a holiday that day, she had dressed up in elegant
clothes, and her magnificent dress, which was made of fine gold and
of large diamonds, rivaled the sun in its pure brightness. The prince
looked at her and was at the mercy of his desires. He almost lost his

2. A hunter of Greek mythology who was carried away for his beauty by the goddess of the
dawn.

breath while he was gazing at her, so taken was he with her. No matter what her dress was like, the beauty of her face, her lovely profile, her warm, ivory skin, her fine features, and her fresh youthfulness moved him a hundred times more. But most of all, his heart was captured by a wise and modest reserve that bore witness to the beauty of her soul.

Three times he was about to push her door open; but each time his arm was arrested by the admiration he felt for this seemingly divine creature. He returned to the palace, where, day and night, he sighed pensively. He didn't want to attend the balls, even though it was the season of Carnival. He hated the idea of hunting or of going to the theater. His appetite was gone, and everything seemed to pain him. A deep, lethal melancholy was at the root of his ailment.

He made inquiries about the remarkable nymph who was living in one of the lower courtyards at the end of a squalid alley where you couldn't see a thing, even in broad daylight.

"It's Donkeyskin," he was told. "There's nothing beautiful about her, and she is not at all a nymph. She is called Donkeyskin because of the skin that she wears on her back. She's the ideal remedy for someone in love. Simply put, only wolves are uglier than she is." They spoke in vain, for he never believed them. The traces left by love were so powerfully inscribed in his memory that they could never be erased.

Meanwhile, his mother the queen, whose only child he was, wept in her anguish. She urged him to tell her what was wrong, but it was no use. He moaned, he wept, he sighed, but he didn't say a thing except that he wanted Donkeyskin to make him a cake with her own hands. The mother had no idea what her son meant.

"Good heavens, madam," everyone said. "Donkeyskin is nothing but a black drab, uglier and dirtier than the most filthy scullion."

"It doesn't matter," the queen said. "We must satisfy his wish, and that's all that counts." His mother loved him so much that she would have given him gold, if he wanted to eat that.

Donkeyskin took some flour that she had ground to make her dough as fine as possible and mixed it with salt, butter, and fresh eggs. Then she locked herself up in her room to make the cake as carefully as she could. First she washed her hands, her arms and her face. Then she put on a silver smock in honor of the work she was about to undertake and laced it up.

It is said that she worked a little too hastily and that one of her precious rings accidentally fell from her finger into the dough. But those thought to be knowledgeable about the outcome to this story claim that she put it in there with a purpose. As for me, quite frankly, I believe it, for I am sure that when the prince stopped at her door and saw her through the keyhole, she knew exactly what was happening. In these matters, women are so discerning and their eyes are so sharp that you can't look at them for a moment without their knowing it. I have no doubts, and I give you my word that she was confident that her young admirer would accept the ring with gratitude.

No one had ever kneaded a morsel so dainty, and the prince thought that the cake tasted so good that if he had been just a little more famished, he would have swallowed the ring along with the cake. When he saw the wonderful emerald and the narrow band of gold which revealed the shape of a finger, he was so moved that he felt incredible joy in his heart. He put it by his bedside right away. But his ailment became more serious, and the doctors observed how he was wasting away from day to day. Wise with experience, they used their great scientific erudition to conclude that he was lovesick.

People may say bad things about marriage, but it is an excellent remedy for lovesickness. The prince, it was decided, was to marry. He took some time to think about it, then said: "I'll be happy to get married provided that it is to the person whose finger fits this ring."

The queen and the king were greatly surprised by this strange demand, but their son was ailing so badly that they did not dare say no. And so a search was undertaken to find the woman who would be elevated to a high rank by the ring, no matter what her background. There was not a woman around who was not prepared to present her finger, and not a one around who was willing to give up the right to try the ring.

Since a rumor had been spreading that you had to have a very slender finger to aspire to marry the prince, every charlatan around, in order to make his reputation, claimed to possess the secret of making fingers small. One woman, following a strange whim, scraped her finger as if it were a radish. Another cut off a small piece of it. A third squeezed it so that it would become smaller. A fourth used a certain kind of liquid to make the skin fall off so that her finger would be smaller. There was not a single trick left unused by women trying to make their fingers fit the ring.

The selection began with young princesses, marquesses, and duchesses, but no matter how delicate their fingers were, they were always too large to get into the ring. Countesses, baronesses, and all manner of nobility presented their hands one at a time, but they presented them in vain. Next came the working girls, whose fingers, pretty and slender (for there are many who are well-proportioned), seemed almost to fit the ring. But each time the ring, which rejected everyone with equal disdain, was either too small or too large.

Finally they had to summon servants, scullery maids, chambermaids, and peasant girls, in short, all the riffraff whose reddened and blackened hands aspired, no less than the delicate hands, to a happy fate. Many girls arrived with big, thick fingers which fit the ring of the prince about as well as a rope trying to get through the eye of a needle.

They all believed that it was over, for there was really no one left but poor Donkeyskin in the corner of the kitchen. But who could believe that the heavens had destined her to rule!

The prince said: "Why not? Let her come here."

Everyone began laughing and shouted out loud: "You mean to say that you are going to let that dirty little fright come in here?"

But when she drew a little hand as white as ivory and colored by a touch of crimson from under the black skin and when the destined ring fit her little finger with unmatched precision, the court was in a state of astonishment and shock.

Everyone wanted to take her to the king right away, but she insisted that she wanted some time to change her clothes before appearing before her lord and master. If truth be told, everyone was about to burst out laughing because of those clothes. She arrived at the king's chambers and crossed the rooms in her ceremonial clothes whose radiant beauty had never before been seen. Her lovely blond hair glittered with diamonds that emitted a bright light with their many rays. Her blue eyes, large and soft, were filled with a proud majesty, but never inflicted pain and gave only pleasure when they looked at you. Her waist was so small and fine that you could encircle it with two hands. Even showing their charms and their divine grace, the women of the court and all their ornaments lost any kind of appeal by comparison.

With all the rejoicing and commotion of those assembled, the good king was beside himself when he saw the charms of his daughter-in-law. The queen was taken with her as well. And the prince, her ardent lover, found his heart filled with a hundred pleasures and succumbed to the sway of his passion.

Preparations were made right away for the wedding. The monarch invited all the kings from the surrounding countries, who, radiant in their diverse finery, left their lands to attend the great event. You could see those from the East mounted on huge elephants; and from distant shores came the Moors, who were so black and ugly that they frightened little children. Guests arrived from every corner of the world and descended on the court in great numbers.

No prince or potentate arrived there with as much splendor as the father of the bride, who, though he had once been in love with her, had since purified the fires that had inflamed his heart. He had purged himself of all lawless desires and all that was left in his heart of that wicked flame had been transformed into paternal devotion. When he saw her, he said: "May the heavens be blessed for allowing me to see you again, dearest child." With tears of joy in his eyes, he rushed over to embrace her tenderly. Everyone was deeply moved by his happiness, and the future husband of the bride was delighted to learn that he was going to be the son-in-law of such a powerful king. Just then the godmother arrived to tell the whole story, and through her narrative she succeeded in covering Donkeyskin with glory.

It is not difficult to see that the moral to this story teaches children that it is better to expose yourself to harsh adversity than to neglect your duty. Virtue may sometimes seem ill-fated, but it is always crowned with success. Even the most powerful logic is no defense against frenzied love and ardent ecstasy, especially when a lover is prepared to squander his rich treasures. Finally this story shows that pure water and brown bread are enough nourishment for young women, so long as they have beautiful clothes, and that there is no woman on earth who does not believe that she is beautiful and who does not see herself as getting the golden apple if she were to be mixed in with the three beauties of that famous contest.[3]

The story of Donkeyskin may be hard to believe, but as long as there are children, mothers, and grandmothers in this world, it will be fondly remembered by all.

The Three Gowns[†]

A gentleman and his wife had a daughter named Rosa. The wife had a ring she always wore, and one day she said to her husband, "Take this ring, for I am dying, and whoever can fit it to her finger is the one you must marry."

The mother died, and within a few days word went out that the wearer of the dead woman's ring would have the rich widower for a husband. Eligible ladies from all over came to try on the ring. For some it was too big. For others, too small. And all this took many days.

With one thing and another the ring got lost, and it was missing for oh, about a year. In the meantime the gentleman's daughter had reached the age of marrying. And one day dear little Rosa was sweeping and found the ring. When she tried it on, it fit her exactly.

3. Reference to the golden apple thrown by Eris down among the assembled gods. Inscribed "For the fairest," it became the prize of beauty in a contest among Hera, Athena, and Aphrodite.
† *Latin American Folktales: Stories from Hispanic and Indian Traditions*, ed. John Bierhorst (New York: Pantheon Books, 2002), pp. 67–71. Copyright © 2002 by John Bierhorst. Used by permission of Pantheon Books, an imprint of the Knopf Doubleday Publishing Group, a division of Penguin Random House LLC. All rights reserved.

Her father, who was just returning from a sea voyage, noticed at once that his daughter was wearing the ring. He was enchanted. "You'll have to marry me," he said, "because your mother said so."

The daughter cried out, "Oh, Papa! How can I marry my own father?"

"Never mind. You'll do it and that's that."

"Very well, father. But before I marry you, you'll have to bring me a gown the color of all the stars in the sky."

"Why not!" And off he went to find such a gown.

After two or three days he came home carrying the outfit, and poor Rosa was more upset than ever.

"Very well, Papa, but I must have a gown the color of all the fish in the sea."

He rushed off at once. Three days later, when she saw him coming back with the gown, she started to cry. "Oh, Papa, I can't get married with only two gowns. I'd have to have three. Bring me one more, and it had better be the color of all the flowers on earth."

As she required, so he provided. The very next day, there it was, a gown the color of all the flowers on earth. And without pausing to rest he went into town to make arrangements for the wedding.

The moment he was out of sight she tied her clothes together, along with a magic wand she happened to have, and off she ran with the whole bundle, deep into the forest.

After living in the wild for a few days she came upon a young lioness and managed to kill it. She took its skin and put it on. Mind you, whatever she did she always asked the little wand for assistance.

Nearby in a certain kingdom, there was a prince who had gone into the forest to do some shooting. Spotting a dove, he took a pop at it and it started off. The dove flitted from snag to snag with the prince hurrying behind. He stumbled on. Suddenly he caught sight of a lion cub. He said to himself, "I'll bring this back as a pet for my mother." He caught it easily and took it home. "Mama!" he cried. "Look what I've brought. A young lioness to keep you company."

The queen took the little lioness into her arms, then tied it to a leg of the stove. She put down a dish of food for it.

The following Saturday the young prince, Juanito, for that was his name, was hosting a ball, and when the hour arrived he tidied himself up. In no time he was on his way. When he'd gone and it began to get dark, the lioness, who spoke only to the queen, said, "I'd love to go to the ball."

"You must realize," said the queen, "that if Juanito found a lion in the ballroom he'd have it shot."

"Why worry? He wouldn't dream of shooting me."

"Then go."

On the way to the ball she asked the wand to give her a horse saddled in gold. She put on her gown the color of all the stars, mounted the horse, and rode off.

When she arrived at the ball, every guest came to the door to see this princess decked out in silver and gold. Juanito had come with his intended, but in his excitement he completely forgot she was there and began to dance with the princess. He was so infatuated that he made her a promise, which she did not reject, and when dawn came he gave her a gold band inscribed with his name. In exchange she gave him a gold band of her own. Then she jumped on her horse and sped away, slipping into the lion's skin as soon as she was out of view.

Later that morning Juanito came bursting into the palace, telling his mother all about a certain princess he had seen. He chattered on, with the lioness murmuring,

> *I might imply,*
> *I might deny,*
> *I might imply*
> *That it was I.*

The queen picked up the poker from in front of the stove and gave her a whack to shut her up. Juanito continued, "Mama, I must announce another ball for next Saturday."

He did just that, planning a ball even grander than the one he had held the week before. When the day came, and he'd sped away, the lioness said to the old mother, "How about it? Untie me!"

"God forbid that you shouldn't go!"

"I'm on my way."

As soon as she was out the door she instructed the wand, "As pretty as you made me last Saturday, make me prettier tonight. Make the horse nicer, too." Then she put on her gown the color of all the fish in the sea and rode off.

When she arrived at the dance, there were cries of excitement. And Juanito? He was enraptured. But at the crack of dawn she told him again, just as she'd told him the week before, "It's late. I must leave at once." Quick as a wink he gave her a little gold chain, and she gave him some token or other, mounted her horse, and vanished. They all ran to catch up with her but found no trace of her anywhere. And there was Juanito, panting with lovesickness.

Before she got back to the palace she changed into the lion's skin. When Juanito arrived, all he could say was, "Oh, Mama, I'm dying. That princess was more beautiful than ever," while the lioness, from her spot next to the stove, chimed in,

I might imply,
I might deny,
I might imply
That it was I.

The queen gave her a tap with the coal shovel, and Juanito went on, "But don't worry. There's going to be another dance next Saturday."

As delightful as the first two balls had been, the third, he hoped, would surpass them both. And when the day came he refused to eat. He went early to the ballroom to wait for the princess. When he had gone, just at the stroke of six, the little lioness asked her mistress for permission to follow him, and the dotty old queen threw up her hands and said, "Go ahead, get yourself killed!"

Once on the road, she changed into her gown the color of all the flowers on earth. Her horse was bridled in silver and gold, and as radiant as she had seemed the other two times, she was even more radiant now. Juanito rushed toward her and locked his arm in hers. He swept her into the ballroom. They began to dance. Just to be safe, he doubled the guard at the door so she couldn't escape. But nothing could stand in her way. When he'd given her a jeweled ring, and she'd handed him a gift in exchange, she suddenly disappeared.

The guards ran after her, but already she was far in the distance. Poor Juanito suffered a fainting spell.

Once more she pulled on the snug little lion's skin. Later, when Juanito returned to the palace, he went straight to bed, so badly smitten that even a swallow of water wouldn't go down his throat. His mother was beside herself; Juanito was her only child.

And this went on for a week, then another week. At last the little lioness asked her mistress if she thought the prince might like a few tarts. The prince was asked. He said no, he couldn't eat a thing. But shouldn't she make them anyway, just on a chance? No, no, said the queen. Goodness! If he knew that a lioness had made them, why would he touch them?

The lioness said, "Why would he know?"

So the little lioness made three tarts. In one she put the gold band, in another the gold chain, and in the third the jeweled ring. If the prince wouldn't eat them, at least he could cut them open.

The queen brought the tarts to his room, and when he opened the first, there was the gold band. In the second, the gold chain. And in the third, the jeweled ring. The breath of life returned to his body. "Mama, who made these tarts?"

Already the lioness had changed into her gown the color of all the stars in the sky, and when she came into the prince's room he said to his mama, "This is the princess I told you about."

He recovered immediately. There were royal feasts and dances. They called in a priest, who performed the wedding. Then Juanito became king. Rosa was queen. And they went right on living with Juanito's mama.

JOSEPH JACOBS

Catskin†

Well, there was once a gentleman who had fine lands and houses, and he very much wanted to have a son to be heir to them. So when his wife brought him a daughter, bonny as bonny could be, he cared nought for her, and said, "Let me never see her face."

So she grew up a bonny girl, though her father never set eyes on her till she was fifteen years old and was ready to be married. But her father said, "Let her marry the first that comes for her." And when this was known, who should be first but a nasty rough old man. So she didn't know what to do, and went to the hen-wife and asked her advice. The hen-wife said, "Say you will not take him unless they give you a coat of silver cloth." Well, they gave her a coat of silver cloth, but she wouldn't take him for all that, but went again to the hen-wife, who said, "Say you will not take him unless they give you a coat of beaten gold." Well, they gave her a coat of beaten gold, but still she would not take him, but went to the hen-wife, who said, "Say you will not take him unless they give you a coat made of the feathers of all the birds of the air." So they sent a man with a great heap of peas; and the man cried to all the birds of the air, "Each bird take a pea, and put down a feather." So each bird took a pea and put down one of its feathers: and they took all the feathers and made a coat of them and gave it to her; but still she would not, but asked the hen-wife once again, who said, "Say they must first make you a coat of catskin." So they made her a coat of catskin; and she put it on, and tied up her other coats, and ran away into the woods.

So she went along and went along and went along, till she came to the end of the wood, and saw a fine castle. So there she hid her fine dresses, and went up to the castle gates, and asked for work. The lady of the castle saw her, and told her, "I'm sorry I have no better place, but if you like you may be our scullion." So down she went into the kitchen, and they called her Catskin, because of her dress. But the cook was very cruel to her and led her a sad life.

Well, it happened soon after that the young lord of the castle was coming home, and there was to be a grand ball in honour of the

† Joseph Jacobs, "Catskin," in *English Fairy Tales* (London: David Nutt, 1890).

occasion. And when they were speaking about it among the servants, "Dear me, Mrs. Cook," said Catskin, "how much I should like to go."

"What! you dirty impudent slut," said the cook, "you go among all the fine lords and ladies with your filthy catskin? A fine figure you'd cut!" and with that she took a basin of water and dashed it into Catskin's face. But she only briskly shook her ears, and said nothing.

When the day of the ball arrived Catskin slipped out of the house and went to the edge of the forest, where she had hidden her dresses. So she bathed herself in a crystal waterfall, and then put on her coat of silver cloth, and hastened away to the ball. As soon as she entered all were overcome by her beauty and grace, while the young lord at once lost his heart to her. He asked her to be his partner for the first dance, and he would dance with none other the livelong night.

When it came to parting-time, the young lord said, "Pray tell me, fair maid, where you live." But Catskin curtsied and said:

> "Kind sir, if the truth I must tell,
> At the sign of the 'Basin of Water' I dwell."

Then she flew from the castle and donned her catskin robe again, and slipped into the scullery again, unbeknown to the cook.

The young lord went the very next day to his mother, the lady of the castle, and declared he would wed none other but the lady of the silver dress, and would never rest till he had found her. So another ball was soon arranged for, in hope that the beautiful maid would appear again. So Catskin said to the cook, "Oh, how I should like to go!" Whereupon the cook screamed out in a rage, "What, you, you dirty impudent slut! You would cut a fine figure among all the fine lords and ladies." And with that she up with a ladle and broke it across Catskin's back. But she only shook her ears, and ran off to the forest, where she first of all bathed, and then put on her coat of beaten gold, and off she went to the ballroom.

As soon as she entered all eyes were upon her; and the young lord soon recognized her as the lady of the "Basin of Water," and claimed her hand for the first dance, and did not leave her till the last. When that came, he again asked her where she lived. But all that she would say was:

> "Kind sir, if the truth I must tell,
> At the sign of the 'Broken Ladle' I dwell."

and with that she curtsied, and flew from the ball, off with her golden robe, on with her catskin, and into the scullery without the cook's knowing.

Next day when the young lord could not find where was the sign of the "Basin of Water," or of the "Broken Ladle," he begged his mother to have another grand ball, so that he might meet the beautiful maid once more.

All happened as before. Catskin told the cook how much she would like to go to the ball, the cook called her "a dirty slut," and broke the skimmer across her head. But she only shook her ears, and went off to the forest, where she first bathed in the crystal spring, and then donned her coat of feathers, and so off to the ballroom.

When she entered everyone was surprised at so beautiful a face and form dressed in so rich and rare a dress; but the young lord soon recognized his beautiful sweetheart, and would dance with none but her the whole evening. When the ball came to an end, he pressed her to tell him where she lived, but all she would answer was:

> "Kind sir, if the truth I must tell,
> At the sign of the 'Broken Skimmer' I dwell;"

and with that she curtsied, and was off to the forest. But this time the young lord followed her, and watched her change her fine dress of feathers for her catskin dress, and then he knew her for his own scullery-maid.

Next day he went to his mother, the lady of the castle, and told her that he wished to marry the scullery-maid, Catskin. "Never," said the lady, and rushed from the room. Well, the young lord was so grieved at that, that he took to his bed and was very ill. The doctor tried to cure him, but he would not take any medicine unless from the hands of Catskin. So the doctor went to the lady of the castle, and told her her son would die if she did not consent to his marriage with Catskin. So she had to give way, and summoned Catskin to her. But she put on her coat of beaten gold, and went to the lady, who soon was glad to wed her son to so beautiful a maid.

Well, so they were married, and after a time a dear little son came to them, and grew up a bonny lad; and one day, when he was four years old, a beggar woman came to the door, so Lady Catskin gave some money to the little lord and told him to go and give it to the beggar woman. So he went and gave it, but put it into the hand of the woman's child, who leant forward and kissed the little lord. Now the wicked old cook—why hadn't she been sent away?—was looking on, so she said, "Only see how beggars' brats take to one another." This insult went to Catskin's heart, so she went to her husband, the young lord, and told him all about her father, and begged he would go and find out what had become of her parents. So they set out in the lord's grand coach, and travelled through the forest till they came to Catskin's father's house, and put up at an inn near, where Catskin stopped, while her husband went to see if her father would own her.

Now her father had never had any other child, and his wife had died; he was all alone in the world and sat moping and miserable.

When the young lord came in he hardly looked up, till he saw a chair close up to him, and asked him: "Pray, sir, had you not once a young daughter whom you would never see or own?"

The old gentleman said: "It is true; I am a hardened sinner. But I would give all my worldly goods if I could but see her once before I die." Then the young lord told him what had happened to Catskin, and took him to the inn, and brought his father-in-law to his own castle, where they lived happy ever afterwards.

The Story of the Black Cow[†]

There was a certain Brahmin whose wife died leaving him one little son. For some time the two lived happily together, but at last the Brahmin married for a second time, and the woman, who had a daughter of her own, was very unkind to her little stepson.

Each day the two children went out together to attend to the cattle, and at night they returned home to eat their food. But the cakes made by the Brahmin's wife for her stepson were of ashes, with just a little flour mixed in to give them the appearance of food, that the Brahmin might not notice; and the child ate in silence, for he was afraid to complain, yet, when he was alone in the forest he wept from hunger, and a black cow, one of the herd, saw this, and asked him what was the matter.

The boy told her everything, and presently she beat her hoofs upon the ground. As she did so, sweets of all kinds appeared, which the child ate greedily, and shared with his little sister, warning her the while not to mention at home what the black cow had done, lest the stepmother should be angry.

The stepmother meanwhile wondered to see how well the boy looked, and she resolved to keep watch, for she suspected that he drank the milk while tending her cows; so she told her little daughter to keep a good look-out on all his doings, and to let her know. At last the girl confessed that they ate sweets every day, and the black cow provided the feast.

That day when the Brahmin came home his wife begged him to sell the black cow, and said she would neither sleep nor eat until this was done.

The poor boy was sad indeed when he heard this, and went at once to his favourite, where, throwing himself on the black cow's neck, he wept bitterly.

† From *Simla Village Tales, or Folk Tales from the Himalayas*, ed. Alice Elizabeth Dracott (London: Murray, 1906).

"Do not weep, my child, but get up on my back, and I will carry you to a place of safety where we can still be together."

So they escaped to a forest, and there lived in peace and security for many days.

Now, in the forest was a hole, which led to the home of the Great Snake, which, together with a bull, holds up the universe. Into this hole the black cow poured five seers[1] of milk daily to feed the snake. This pleased the snake so much that he said one day: "I must go up into the world and see for myself the creature who is so good to me and who sends me such good milk to drink."

When he came he saw the black cow grazing with the boy beside her.

The cow asked no favours for herself, but when the snake asked what she would like, she said she would like her son, as she called the Brahmin's son, to be clothed in gold from head to foot, and that all his body might shine as gold.

This wish the snake readily granted, but both cow and boy afterwards regretted their request, for they feared robbers.

One day as the boy had his bath by the river, and combed his long locks of pure gold, some of his golden hair fell into the water, and was swallowed by a fish. This fish was caught by a fisherman, and taken for sale to the King's Palace. When they cut it open all present admired the lovely golden hair, and when the Princess saw it, she said she would never be happy again until she met the owner. The fisherman was asked where he caught the fish, and people were dispatched in all directions in boats to search both far and wide.

At last a man in one of the boats espied in the distance a beautiful shining object taking a bath by the river-side. Little by little the boat came closer and closer, until it was alongside; then the man called out and asked the bather to come a little nearer. At first the Brahmin's son would not listen, but after a time he came up to the boat, when, to his surprise, he was at once seized, tied up, and carried away.

Arrived at the King's Palace he met the Princess, who was very beautiful; and when he saw her he forgot everything else, and thought only of her.

After a short time they were married, and spent many happy days together; but some one chanced to offer them a sweetmeat made of curds, such as the black cow often gave her boy, and in a frenzy of remorse, the Brahmin's son remembered his faithful friend and hastened to the place in the distant forest where he had last seen her. Arrived there he found only a few bones of dead cattle strewn about.

1. A unit of measurement used in many parts of Asia before the twentieth century.

He was heart-broken at the sight, and gathered all the bones together into a funeral pyre, upon which he declared he would lay down his own life; but just as he was about to do this who should appear but his old friend, the black cow.

They were overjoyed to see each other, and she told him she had only kept the bones there to test his affection; but now that she was satisfied that he had not forgotten her, the meeting was full of happiness and joy, so they held a great feast for many days and then went their separate ways as before.

LIN LAN

[Cinderella]†

There were once two sisters. The elder was very beautiful, and everyone called her Beauty. But the younger had a face covered with pock marks, so that everyone called her Pock Face. She was the daughter of the second wife, and was so spoiled that she was a very unpleasant girl. Beauty's real mother had died when Beauty was very young. After her death she turned into a yellow cow and lived in the garden. Beauty adored the yellow cow, but it had a miserable existence because the stepmother treated it so badly.

One day the stepmother took the ugly daughter to the theater and left Beauty at home. Beauty wanted to accompany them, but the stepmother said, "I will take you tomorrow if you straighten the hemp in my room."

Beauty went off and sat down in front of the stack of hemp, but after a long time she had only divided half of it. Bursting into tears, she took it off to the yellow cow, who swallowed the whole mass and then spat it out again all neatly arranged piece by piece. Beauty dried her tears, and gave the hemp to her mother on her return home. "Mother, here is the hemp. I can go to the theater tomorrow, can't I?"

When the next day came, her stepmother again refused to take her, saying, "You can go when you have separated the sesame seeds from the beans."

The poor girl had to divide them seed by seed, until the exhausting task made her eyes ache. Again she went to the yellow cow, who said to her, "You stupid girl! You must separate them with a fan." Now she understood, and the sesame and beans were soon divided. When she brought the seeds all nicely separated, her stepmother knew that she could no longer prevent her going to the theater.

† Lin Lan, "San-ko yüan-wang (Three Wishes)" (Shanghai, 1933), in *Folktales of China*, trans. Wolfram Eberhard and Desmond Parsons (Chicago: U of Chicago P, 1965). Copyright © 1965. Reprinted by permission of the University of Chicago Press.

However, she asked her, "How can a servant girl be so clever? Who helped you?"

Beauty had to admit that the yellow cow had advised her, which made the stepmother very angry. Therefore, without saying a word, she killed and ate the cow. Beauty had loved the cow so dearly that she could not eat its flesh. Instead, she put the bones in an earthenware pot and hid them in her bedroom.

Day after day, the stepmother would still not take Beauty to the theater. One evening, when the stepmother had gone to the theater with Pock Face, Beauty was so cross that she smashed everything in the house, including the earthenware pot containing the cow's bones. Whereupon there was a loud crackling sound, and a white horse, a new dress, and a pair of embroidered shoes came out. The sudden appearance of these things gave Beauty a terrible start, but she soon saw that they were real objects. Quickly pulling on the new dress and the shoes, she jumped on the horse and rode out of the gate.

While she was riding along, one of her shoes slipped off and fell into the ditch. She wanted to dismount and pick it up, but could not do so; at the same time she did not want to leave it lying there.

She was in a real quandary, when a fishmonger appeared. "Brother fishmonger, please pick up my shoe," she said to him. He answered with a grin, "With great pleasure, if you will marry me." "Who could marry you?" she said crossly. "Fishmongers always stink." Seeing that he had no chance, the fishmonger went on his way.

Next, a clerk from a rice shop went by, and she said to him, "Brother rice broker, please give me my shoe." "Certainly, if you will marry me," said the young man. "Marry a rice broker! Their bodies are all covered with dust."

The rice broker departed, and soon an oil merchant came by, whom she also asked to pick up her shoe. "I will pick it up if you consent to marry me," he replied. "Who could want to marry you?" Beauty said with a sigh. "Oil merchants are always so greasy."

Shortly a scholar came by, whom she also asked to pick up her shoe. The scholar turned to look at her, and then said, "I will do so at once if you promise to marry me." The scholar was very handsome, and so she nodded her head in agreement. He picked up the shoe and put it on her foot. Then he took her back to his house and made her his wife.

Three days later, Beauty went with her husband to pay the necessary respects to her parents. Her stepmother and sister had quite changed their manner, and treated them both in the most friendly and attentive fashion. In the evening they wanted to keep Beauty at home, and she, thinking they meant it kindly, agreed to stay and to follow her husband in a few days.

The next morning her sister took her by the hand and said to her with a laugh, "Sister, come and look into the well. We will see which of us is the more beautiful." Suspecting nothing, Beauty went to the well and leaned over to look down. At this moment her sister gave her a shove and pushed her into the well; then she quickly covered the well with a basket. Poor Beauty lost consciousness and was drowned.

After ten days the scholar began to wonder why his wife had still not returned. He sent a messenger to inquire, and the stepmother sent back a message that his wife was suffering from a bad attack of smallpox and would not be well enough to return for some time. The scholar believed this, and every day he sent salted eggs and other sickbed delicacies, all of which found their way into the stomach of the ugly sister.

After two months the stepmother was irritated by the continual messages from the scholar, and decided to deceive him by sending back her own daughter as his wife. The scholar was horrified when he saw Pock Face, and said, "Goodness! How changed you are! Surely you are not Beauty. My wife was never such a monster. Good Heavens!" Pock Face replied seriously, "If I am not Beauty, who do you think I am then? You know perfectly well I was very ill with smallpox, and now you want to disown me. I shall die! I shall die!" She began to howl. The tender-hearted scholar could not bear to see her weeping, and although he still had some doubts he begged her forgiveness and tried to console her. Gradually she stopped weeping.

Beauty, however, had been transformed into a sparrow, and she used to come and call out when Pock Face was combing her hair, "Comb once, peep; comb twice, peep; comb thrice, up to the spine of Pock Face." The wicked wife answered, "Comb once, comb twice, comb thrice, to the spine of Beauty." The scholar was very mystified by this conversation, and he said to the sparrow, "Why do you sing like that? Are you by any chance my wife? If you are, call three times, and I will put you in a golden cage and keep you as a pet." The sparrow called out three times, and the scholar brought a golden cage to keep it in.

The ugly sister was very angry when she saw that her husband was keeping the sparrow, and so she secretly killed it and threw it into the garden. It was at once transformed into a bamboo with many shoots. When Pock Face ate the bamboo shoots, an ulcer formed on her tongue, but the scholar found them excellent. The wicked woman became suspicious again, and had the bamboo cut down and made into a bed. When she lay on it, innumerable needles pricked her, but the scholar found it extremely comfortable. Again she became very cross and threw the bed away.

Next door to the scholar lived an old woman who sold money bags. One day on her way home she saw the bed and thought to herself, "No one has died here; why have they thrown the bed away? I shall take it." She took the bed into her house and had a very comfortable night.

The next day she saw that the food in the kitchen was already cooked. She ate it up, but naturally she felt a little nervous, not having any idea who could have prepared it. For several days she found she could have dinner the moment she came home. Finally, being no longer able to contain her anxiety, she came back early one afternoon and went into the kitchen, where she saw a dark shadow washing rice. She ran up quickly and clasped the shadow round the waist. "Who are you?" she asked, "and why do you cook food for me?" The shadow replied, "I will tell you everything. I am the wife of your neighbor the scholar and am called Beauty. My sister threw me into the well; I was drowned, but my soul was not destroyed. Please give me a rice pot as head, a stick as hand, a dish cloth as entrails, and firehooks as feet, and then I can assume my former shape again."

The old woman gave her what she asked for, and in a moment a beautiful girl appeared. The old woman was delighted at seeing such a charming girl, and she questioned her very closely about who she was and what had happened to her. She told the old woman everything, and then said, "Old woman, I have a bag which you must offer for sale outside the scholar's house. If he comes out, you must sell it to him." And she gave her an embroidered bag.

The next day the old woman stood outside the scholar's house and shouted that she had a bag for sale. Maddened by the noise, he came out to ask what kind of bags she sold, and she showed him Beauty's embroidered bag. "Where did you get this bag?" he asked. "I once gave it to my wife." The old woman then told the whole story to the scholar, who was overjoyed to hear that his wife was still alive. He arranged everything with the old woman, put a red cloth on the ground, and brought Beauty back to his house.

When Pock Face saw her sister return, she gave her no peace. She began to grumble and say that the woman was only pretending to be Beauty, and that actually she was a spirit. She wanted to have a trial to see which was the genuine wife. Beauty, of course, knew that she herself was the real bride. She said, "Good. We will have a test." Pock Face suggested that they should walk on eggs, and whoever broke the shells would be the loser. Although Pock Face broke all the eggs, and Beauty none, Pock Face refused to admit her loss and insisted on another trial.

This time they were to walk up a ladder made of knives. Beauty went up and down first without receiving the tiniest scratch, but before Pock Face had gone two steps her feet were cut to the bone.

Although she had lost again, she insisted on another test—that of jumping into a caldron of hot oil. She hoped that Beauty, who would have to jump first, would be burned. Beauty, however, was quite unharmed by the boiling oil, but the wicked sister jumped into it and did not come up again.

Beauty put the roasted bones of the wicked sister into a box and sent them over to her stepmother by a stuttering old servant woman, who was told to say, "Your daughter's flesh." But the stepmother loved carp and understood "carp flesh" instead of "your daughter's flesh." She thought her daughter had sent her over some carp, and opened the box in a state of great excitement; but when she saw the charred bones of her daughter lying inside, she let out a piercing scream and fell down dead.

The Princess in the Suit of Leather[†]

Neither here nor elsewhere lived a king who had a wife whom he loved with all his heart and a daughter who was the light of his eyes. The princess had hardly reached womanhood when the queen fell ill and died. For one whole year the king kept vigil, sitting with bowed head beside her tomb. Then he summoned the matchmakers, elderly women wise in the ways of living, and said, "I wish to marry again. Here is my poor queen's anklet. Find me the girl, rich or poor, humble or well-born, whose foot this anklet will fit. For I promised the queen as she lay dying that I would marry that girl and no other."

The matchmakers traveled up and down the kingdom looking for the king's new bride. But search and search as they would, they could not find a single girl around whose ankle the jewel would close. The queen had been such that there was no woman like her. Then one old woman said, "We have entered the house of every maiden in the land except the house of the king's own daughter. Let us go to the palace."

When they slipped the anklet onto the princess's foot, it suited as if it had been made to her measure. Out of the seraglio went the women at a run, straight into the king's presence, and said, "We have visited every maiden in your kingdom, but none was able to squeeze her foot into the late queen's anklet. None, that is, except the princess your daughter. She wears it as easily as if it were her own." A wrinkled matron spoke up. "Why not marry the princess? Why give her to a stranger and deprive yourself?" The words were

† This Egyptian folktale appears in *Arab Folktales,* trans. and ed. Inea Bushnaq (New York: Pantheon, 1986). Copyright © 1986 by Inea Bushnaq Books. Used by permission of Pantheon Books, an imprint of Knopf Doubleday Publishing Group, a division of Penguin Random House LLC. All rights reserved.

hardly spoken when the king summoned the *qadi*[1] to pen the papers for the marriage. To the princess he made no mention of his plan.

Now there was a bustle in the palace as the jewelers, the clothiers, and the furnishers came to outfit the bride. The princess was pleased to know that she was to be wed. But who her husband was she had no inkling. As late as the "night of the entering," when the groom first sees the bride, she remained in ignorance even though the servants with their whispers were busy around her, combing and pinning and making her beautiful. At last the minister's daughter, who had come to admire her in her finery, said, "Why are you frowning? Were not women created for marriage with men? And is there any man whose standing is higher than the king's?"

"What is the meaning of such talk?" cried the princess. "I won't tell you," said the girl, "unless you give me your golden bangle to keep." The princess pulled off the bracelet, and the girl explained how everything had come about so that the bridegroom was no other than the princess's own father.

The princess turned whiter than the cloth on her head and trembled like one who is sick with the forty-day fever. She rose to her feet and sent away all who were with her. Then, knowing only that she must escape, she ran onto the terrace and leaped over the palace wall, landing in a tanner's yard which lay below. She pressed a handful of gold into the tanner's palm and said, "Can you make me a suit of leather to hide me from head to heels, showing nothing but my eyes? I want it by tomorrow's dawn."

The poor man was overjoyed to earn the coins. He set to work with his wife and children. Cutting and stitching through the night they had the suit ready, before it was light enough to know a white thread from a dark. Wait a little! and here comes our lady, the princess. She put on the suit—such a strange spectacle that anyone looking at her would think he was seeing nothing but a pile of hides. In this disguise she left the tanner and lay down beside the city gate, waiting for the day.

Now to return to my lord the king. When he entered the bridal chamber and found the princess gone, he sent his army into the city to search for her. Time and again a soldier would stumble upon the princess lying at the gate and ask, "Have you seen the king's daughter?" And she would reply,

> My name is Juleidah for my coat of skins,
> My eyes are weak, my sight is dim,
> My ears are deaf, I cannot hear.
> I care for no one far or near.

1. Judge of an Islamic court of justice.

When it was day and the city gate was unbarred, she shuffled out until she was beyond the walls. Then she turned her face away from her father's city and fled.

Walking and running, one foot lifting her and one foot setting her down, there was a day when, with the setting of the sun, the princess came to another city. Too weary to travel a step farther, she fell to the ground. Now her resting place was in the shadow of the wall of the women's quarters, the harem of the sultan's palace. A slave girl, leaning from the window to toss out the crumbs from the royal table, noticed the heap of skins on the ground and thought nothing of it. But when she saw two bright eyes staring out at her from the middle of the hides, she sprang back in terror and said to the queen, "My lady, there is something monstrous crouching under our window. I have seen it, and it looks like nothing less than an Afreet!"[2] "Bring it up for me to see and judge," said the queen.

The slave girl went down shivering with fear, not knowing which was the easier thing to face, the monster outside or her mistress's rage should she fail to do her bidding. But the princess in her suit made no sound when the slave girl tugged at a corner of the leather. The girl took courage and dragged her all the way into the presence of the sultan's wife.

Never had such an astonishing creature been seen in that country. Lifting both palms in amazement, the queen asked her servant, "What is it?" and then turned to the monster and asked, "Who are you?" When the heap of skins answered—

> My name is Juleidah for my coat of skins,
> My eyes are weak, my sight is dim,
> My ears are deaf, I cannot hear.
> I care for no one far or near.

—how the queen laughed at the quaint reply! "Go bring food and drink for our guest," she said, holding her side. "We shall keep her to amuse us." When Juleidah had eaten, the queen said, "Tell us what you can do, so that we may put you to work about the palace." "Anything you ask me to do, I am ready to try," said Juleidah. Then the queen called, "Mistress cook! Take this broken-winged soul into your kitchen. Maybe for her sake God will reward us with His blessings."

So now our fine princess was a kitchen skivvy, feeding the fires and raking out the ashes. And whenever the queen lacked company and felt bored, she called Juleidah and laughed at her prattle.

One day the *wazir*[3] sent word that all the sultan's harem was invited to a night's entertainment in his house. All day long there

---

2. A cunning demon or spirit from the Djinn world.
3. Minister or chief courtier.

was a stir of excitement in the women's quarters. As the queen prepared to set out in the evening, she stopped by Juleidah and said, "Won't you come with us tonight? All the servants and slaves are invited. Aren't you afraid to stay alone?" But Juleidah only repeated her refrain,

> My ears are deaf, I cannot hear.
> I care for no one far or near.

One of the serving girls sniffed and said, "What is there to make her afraid? She is blind and deaf and wouldn't notice an Afreet even if he were to jump on top of her in the dark!" So they left.

In the women's reception hall of the *wazir*'s house there was dining and feasting and music and much merriment. Suddenly at the height of the talk and enjoyment, such a one entered that they all stopped in the middle of the word they were speaking. Tall as a cypress, with a face like a rose and the silks and jewels of a king's bride, she seemed to fill the room with light. Who was it? Juleidah, who had shaken off her coat of leather as soon as the sultan's harem had gone. She had followed them to the *wazir*'s, and now the ladies who had been so merry began to quarrel, each wanting to sit beside the newcomer.

When dawn was near, Juleidah took a handful of gold sequins from the fold of her sash and scattered them on the floor. The ladies scrambled to pick up the bright treasure. And while they were occupied, Juleidah left the hall. Quickly, quickly she raced back to the palace kitchen and put on the coat of leather. Soon the others returned. Seeing the heap of hides on the kitchen floor, the queen poked it with the toe of her red slipper and said, "Truly, I wish you had been with us to admire the lady who was at the entertainment." But Juleidah only mumbled, "My eyes are weak, I cannot see . . ." and they all went to their own beds to sleep.

When the queen woke up next day, the sun was high in the sky. As was his habit, the sultan's son came in to kiss his mother's hands and bid her good morning. But she could talk only of the visitor at the *wazir*'s feast. "O my son," she sighed, "it was a woman with such a face and such a neck and such a form that all who saw her said, 'She is the daughter of neither a king nor a sultan, but of someone greater yet!'" On and on the queen poured out her praises of the woman, until the prince's heart was on fire. Finally his mother concluded, "I wish I had asked her father's name so that I could engage her to be your bride." And the sultan's son replied, "When you return tonight to continue your entertainment, I shall stand outside the *wazir*'s door and wait until she leaves. I'll ask her then about her father and her station."

At sunset the women dressed themselves once more. With the folds of their robes smelling of orange blossom and incense and their bracelets chinking on their arms, they passed by Juleidah lying on the kitchen floor and said, "Will you come with us tonight?" But Juleidah only turned her back on them. Then as soon as they were safely gone, she threw off her suit of leather and hurried after them.

In the *wazir's* hall the guests pressed close around Juleidah, wanting to see her and ask where she came from. But to all their questions she gave no answer, whether yes or no, although she sat with them until the dawning of the day. Then she threw a fistful of pearls on the marble tiles, and while the women pushed one another to catch them, she slipped away as easily as a hair is pulled out of the dough.

Now who was standing at the door? The prince, of course. He had been waiting for this moment. Blocking her path, he grasped her arm and asked who her father was and from what land she came. But the princess had to be back in her kitchen or her secret would be known. So she fought to get away, and in the scuffle, she pulled the prince's ring clean off his hand. "At least tell me where you come from!" he shouted after her as she ran. "By Allah, tell me where!" And she replied, "I live in a land of paddles and ladles." Then she fled into the palace and hid in her coat of hides.

In came the others, talking and laughing. The prince told his mother what had taken place and announced that he intended to make a journey. "I must go to the land of the paddles and ladles," he said. "Be patient, my son," said the queen. "Give me time to prepare your provisions." Eager as he was, the prince agreed to delay his departure for two days—"But not one hour more!"

Now the kitchen became the busiest corner of the palace. The grinding and the sieving, the kneading and the baking began and Juleidah stood watching. "Away with you," cried the cook, "this is no work for you!" "I want to serve the prince our master like the rest!" said Juleidah. Willing and not willing to let her help, the cook gave her a piece of dough to shape. Juleidah began to make a cake, and when no one was watching, she pushed the prince's ring inside it. And when the food was packed Juleidah placed her own little cake on top of the rest.

Early on the third morning the rations were strapped into the saddlebags, and the prince set off with his servants and his men. He rode without slackening until the sun grew hot. Then he said, "Let us rest the horses while we ourselves eat a mouthful." A servant, seeing Juleidah's tiny loaf lying on top of all the rest, flung it to one side. "Why did you throw that one away?" asked the prince. "It was the work of the creature Juleidah; I saw her make it," said the servant. "It is as misshapen as she is." The prince felt pity for the strange half-wit and asked the servant to bring back her cake. When he tore open the loaf, look, his own ring was inside! The ring he lost the night of the *wazir's* entertainment. Understanding now where lay the land of ladles and paddles, the prince gave orders to turn back.

When the king and queen had greeted him, the prince said, "Mother, send me my supper with Juleidah." "She can barely see or even hear," said the queen. "How can she bring your supper to you?" "I shall not eat unless Juleidah brings the food," said the prince. So when the time came, the cooks arranged the dishes on a tray and helped Juleidah lift it onto her head. Up the stairs she went, but before she reached the prince's room she tipped the dishes and sent them crashing to the floor. "I told you she cannot see," the queen said to her son. "And I will only eat what Juleidah brings," said the prince.

The cooks prepared a second meal, and when they had balanced the loaded tray upon Juleidah's head, they sent two slave girls to hold her by either hand and guide her to the prince's door. "Go," said the prince to the two slaves, "and you, Juleidah, come." Juleidah began to say,

> My eyes are weak, my sight is dim,
> I'm called Juleidah for my coat of skins,
> My ears are deaf, I cannot hear.
> I care for no one far or near.

But the prince told her, "Come and fill my cup." As she approached, he drew the dagger that hung at his side and slashed her leather coat from collar to hem. It fell into a heap upon the floor—and there stood the maiden his mother had described, one who could say to the moon, "Set that I may shine in your stead."

Hiding Juleidah in a corner of the room, the prince sent for the queen. Our mistress cried out when she saw the pile of skins upon the floor. "Why, my son, did you bring her death upon your neck? The poor thing deserved your pity more than your punishment!" "Come in, Mother," said the prince, "Come and look at our Juleidah before you mourn her." And he led his mother to where our fine princess sat revealed, her fairness filling the room like a ray of light. The queen threw herself upon the girl and kissed her on this side and on that, and bade her sit with the prince and eat. Then she summoned the *qadi* to write the paper that would bind our lord the prince to the fair princess, after which they lived together in the sweetest bliss.

Now we make our way back to the king, Juleidah's father. When he entered the bridal chamber to unveil his own daughter's face and found her gone, and when he had searched the city in vain for her, he called his minister and his servants and dressed himself for travel. From country to country he journeyed, entering one city and leaving the next, taking with him in chains the old woman who had first suggested to him that he marry his own daughter. At last he reached the city where Juleidah was living with her husband the prince.

Now the princess was sitting in her window when they entered the gate, and she knew them as soon as she saw them. Straightway she sent to her husband urging him to invite the strangers. Our lord went to meet them and succeeded in detaining them only after much pressing, for they were impatient to continue their quest. They dined in the prince's guest hall, then thanked their host and took leave with the words, "The proverb says: 'Have your fill to eat, but then up, onto your feet!'"—while he delayed them further with the proverb, "Where you break your bread, there spread out your bed!"

In the end the prince's kindness forced the tired strangers to lie in his house as guests for the night. "But why did you single out these strangers?" the prince asked Juleidah. "Lend me your robes and head-cloth and let me go to them," she said. "Soon you will know my reasons."

Thus disguised, Juleidah sat with her guests. When the coffee cups had been filled and emptied, she said, "Let us tell stories to pass the time. Will you speak first, or shall I?" "Leave us to our sorrows, my son," said the king her father. "We have not the spirit to tell tales." "I'll entertain you, then, and distract your mind," said Juleidah. "There once was a king," she began, and went on to tell the history of her own adventures from the beginning to the end. Every now and then the old woman would interrupt and say, "Can you find no better story than this, my son?" But Juleidah kept right on, and when she had finished she said, "I am your daughter the princess, upon whom all these troubles fell through the words of this old sinner and daughter of shame!"

In the morning they flung the old woman over a tall cliff into the wadi.[4] Then the king gave half his kingdom to his daughter and the prince, and they lived in happiness and contentment until death, the parter of the truest lovers, divided them.

---

4. Riverbed or ravine.

INTRODUCTION: Bluebeard

"Bluebeard" is the stuff of nightmares: raised scimitars, forbidden chambers, corpses hanging from hooks, bloody basins, and dismembered bodies. The tale made its literary debut in Charles Perrault's seventeenth-century *Tales of Mother Goose,* a collection that took the lead in transforming the oral narratives from adult storytelling cultures into bedtime reading for children. Over the years it has served as a master-narrative about the perils of marriage and continues to haunt cinematic culture in particular, sometimes explicitly, as in Catherine Breillat's *Bluebeard* (2009), sometimes covertly, as in Alex Garland's *Ex Machina* (2015). Like many of the fairy tales in Perrault's collection, "Bluebeard" has a happy ending: the heroine marries "a very worthy man, who banished the memory of the miserable days she had spent with Bluebeard" (p. 192). Yet most readers—even those willing to suspend disbelief about the pleasures of the next marriage—will find themselves unable to erase the graphic impressions left by the "miserable time" of the first marriage. In the narrative economy of Perrault's text, the verbal energy is invested almost exclusively in exposing Bluebeard's wife to horrors of extraordinary vividness and power.

Just who was Bluebeard and how did he come by his bad name? As Anatole France reminds us in his story "The Seven Wives of Bluebeard," Perrault composed "the first biography of this *seigneur*" and established his reputation as "an accomplished villain" and "the most perfect model of cruelty that ever trod the earth."[1] Cultural historians have been quick to claim that Perrault's "Bluebeard" is based on fact, that it broadcasts the misdeeds of various noblemen, among them Cunmar of Brittany and Gilles de Rais. But neither Cunmar the Accursed, who decapitated his pregnant wife, Triphine, nor Gilles de Rais, the marshal of France who was hanged in 1440 for murdering hundreds of children, present themselves as compelling models for Bluebeard. This French aristocrat remains a construction of collective fantasy, a figure firmly anchored in the realm of folklore.

---

1. Anatole France, "The Seven Wives of Bluebeard," in *Spells of Enchantment: The Wondrous Fairy Tales of Western Culture*, ed. Jack Zipes (New York: Viking, 1991), p. 567.

Perrault's "Bluebeard" recounts the story of an aristocratic gentle-man (known in Italy as "Silver Nose," in England as "Mr. Fox") and his marriage to a young woman whose desire for opulence conquers her feelings of revulsion for blue beards. The French tale contains what folklorists have identified as the three distinctive features of Bluebeard narratives: a forbidden chamber, an agent of prohibition who also metes out punishments, and a figure who violates the pro-hibition. From Perrault's time onward, the tale has been framed as a story about transgressive desire, as a text that enunciates the dire consequences of curiosity and disobedience.

Perrault presents Bluebeard's wife as a figure who suffers from an excess of desire for knowledge of what lies beyond the door. Blue-beard's wife enters the forbidden chamber and sees a pool of clot-ted blood in which are reflected the bodies of her husband's wives, hanging from the wall. Horrified, she drops the key (in some ver-sions it is an egg, a straw, or a rose) into the pool of blood and is unable to remove the telltale stain from the key. But Bluebeard's wife, both in Perrault's rendition and in its many cultural inflections, is a canny survivor. Her husband may try to behead her for her act of disobedience, but she succeeds in delaying the execution long enough that her brothers, summoned by Sister Anne, arrive in time to rescue her and to cut Bluebeard down with their swords.

"Bluebeard" stands virtually alone among fairy tales in its depic-tion of marriage as an institution haunted by the threat of murder. While canonical fairy tales like "Cinderella," "Snow White," and "Beauty and the Beast" begin with unhappy situations at home, cen-ter on a romantic quest, and end in visions of marital bliss, "Blue-beard" stories show us women leaving the safety of home and entering the risky domains of their husband's castles. In these tales, mothers, sisters, and brothers mobilize to rescue the heroine rather than to do her in. Family solidarity triumphs over stranger danger.

While "Bluebeard" may not necessarily be an appropriate story for children, it remains a powerful text challenging the myth of roman-tic love encapsulated in the "happily ever after" of fairy tales and presenting a message with a social logic compelling for Perrault's day and age. Anxious fantasies about sex and marriage would hardly be surprising in seventeenth- and eighteenth-century Europe, where women married at a relatively young age, where the mortality rate for women in childbirth was high, and where a move away from home might rightly be charged with fears about isolation, violence, abuse, and marital estrangement. While it is tempting to promote stories that stage the joys of heterosexual romantic unions and to banish grisly stories about murderous husbands (especially once the venue for the tales shifted to the nursery), it is important to preserve our cultural memory of this particular story and to understand exactly what is at stake in it. "Bluebeard" may not appear with great frequency between the covers of twentieth-century anthologies of fairy tales, but it is a story whose cultural resilience becomes quickly evident when we enter the arena of contemporary literary and cinematic production for adults.

Folklore often trades in the sensational—breaking taboos, enacting the forbidden, staging hidden desires, and exploring pathologies with uninhibited investigative energy. In many ways, the story of a wife's transgressive curiosity about her husband's violent past could be seen as a self-reflexive meditation on how fairy tales feed our undiminished appetite for horror. "Bluebeard" is also without doubt the most stunning piece of evidence that folktales can be seen as the legitimate precursors of cinematic horror, another genre notorious for trading on collective fears and fantasies. Stories like "Bluebeard" prefigure the gothic plots of modern horror and construct desires and fears that remain remarkably intact (despite cultural variations) as we move from one century to the next and as we cross from one popular form of entertainment to another. In "Bluebeard," as in cinematic horror, we have not only a killer who is propelled by psychotic rage but also the abject victims of his serial murders, along with a "final girl" (Bluebeard's wife), who either saves herself or arranges her own rescue. The "terrible place" of horror, a dark, tomb-like site that harbors grisly evidence of the killer's derangement, manifests itself as Bluebeard's forbidden chamber.[2]

It is not only in cinematic horror from the 1970s onward that the Bluebeard story manifests its cultural staying power. In what one critic has tellingly called "paranoid woman's films," we also find the Bluebeard syndrome at work in all its melodramatic theatricality.[3] These films, which were made in the wake of Hitchcock's *Rebecca* (1940) and include such classic thrillers as Robert Stevenson's *Jane Eyre* (1944), George Cukor's *Gaslight* (1944), and Fritz Lang's *Secret beyond the Door* (1948), all feature a heroine who is beset by fears that her husband is planning to murder her. Driven by hermeneutic desire, these women investigators search for the key to understanding the cryptic behavior of their sinister husbands, always by penetrating the mysteries of a chamber in the house where they have taken up residence. In Hitchcock's *Rebecca*, the boathouse and Rebecca's bedroom are forbidden or uncanny spaces for the character played by Joan Fontaine; in *Jane Eyre* the title character must unlock the secret of the tower room in which

2. Carol J. Clover draws up an inventory of generic properties of the horror film in *Men, Women, and Chainsaws: Gender in the Modern Horror Film* (Princeton, NJ: Princeton UP, 1992), pp. 26–44.
3. Mary Ann Doane, "Paranoia and the Specular," in *The Desire to Desire: The Woman's Film of the 1940s* (Bloomington: Indiana UP, 1987), pp. 123–54.

Bertha Mason is housed; in *Gaslight* it is the attic, along with the husband's locked desk, that are taboo; and in *Secret beyond the Door*, the heroine is barred from entering room 7, a replica of her own bedroom built to provide her husband with the scene of his next crime.

In much the same way that cinema criticism has been obsessed with the "paranoia" of a wife rather than by the very real threat posed by a husband who seems to be restaging the Bluebeard story, folklorists have shown surprising interpretive confidence in reading Perrault's "Bluebeard" as a story about a woman's marital disobedience or sexual infidelity rather than about her husband's murderous violence. "Bloody key as sign of disobedience"—this is the motif that folklorists consistently read as the defining moment in the tale. The bloodstained key points to a double transgression, one that is at once moral and sexual. For one critic, it becomes a sign of "marital infidelity";[4] for another it marks the heroine's "irreversible loss of her virginity";[5] for a third, it stands as a sign of "defloration."[6] If we recall that the bloody chamber in Bluebeard's castle is strewn with the corpses of previous wives, this reading of the bloodstained key as a marker of sexual infidelity becomes willfully wrongheaded in its effort to vilify Bluebeard's wife.

Illustrators, commentators, and retellers alike seem to have fallen in line with Perrault's stated view in his moral to the story that "Bluebeard" is about the evils of female curiosity. Walter Crane's illustration of Bluebeard's wife on her way to the forbidden chamber shows her descending the stairs, framed by a tapestry of Eve giving in to temptation in the Garden of Eden. "Succumbing to temptation" is the "sin of the fall, the sin of Eve," one representative critical voice asserts. A nineteenth-century Scottish version of the tale summarizes in its title what appears to be the collective critical wisdom on this tale: "The Story of Bluebeard, or, the effects of female curiosity."[7]

Bluebeard's wife may have an inquiring mind, but her curiosity is clearly intellectual rather than sexual. It turns her into an energetic investigator, determined to acquire knowledge of the secrets hidden behind the door of the castle's forbidden chamber. Perrault's story, by underscoring the heroine's kinship with certain literary, biblical, and mythical figures (most notably Psyche, Eve, and Pandora), gives us a tale that willfully undermines a robust folkloric tradition in

---

4. Bruno Bettelheim, *The Uses of Enchantment: The Meaning and Importance of Fairy Tales* (New York: Knopf, 1976), p. 302.
5. Carl-Heinz Mallett, *Kopf ab! Gewalt im Märchen* (Hamburg: Rasch & Röhring, 1985), p. 201.
6. Alan Dundes, "Projection in Folklore: A Plea for Psychoanalytic Semiotics," in *Interpreting Folklore* (Bloomington: Indiana UP, 1980), p. 46.
7. These critical voices are cited in Maria Tatar, *The Hard Facts of the Grimms' Fairy Tales* (Princeton, NJ: Princeton UP, 1987), pp. 157–64.

which the heroine is a resourceful agent of her own salvation. Rather than celebrating the courage and wisdom of Bluebeard's wife in discovering the dreadful truth about her husband's murderous deeds, Perrault and other tellers of the tale often cast aspersions on her for engaging in an unruly act of insubordination.

The French folklorist Paul Delarue has mapped out the evolution of "Bluebeard," documenting the liberties taken by Perrault in transforming an oral folktale into a literary text.[8] The folk heroines of "Bluebeard" delay their executions by insisting on donning bridal clothes for the event (thus buttressing the folkloric connection between marriage and death), and they prolong the possibility of rescue by recounting each and every item of clothing. Perrault's heroine, by contrast, who asks her husband for "a little time to say my prayers" (p. 191), becomes a model of repentent piety. Unlike many folk heroines, who become agents of their own rescue by dispatching fleet-footed pet dogs or talking birds to their families with urgent calls for help, Perrault's heroine sends her sister up to the castle tower to watch for the brothers who were to visit her that very day. Most important, folk versions of the tale do not fault the heroine for her curiosity. To the contrary, when the young women stand before the forbidden chamber, they feel duty-bound to open its door. "I have to know what is in there," one young woman reflects just before turning the key. The pangs of conscience that beset Perrault's heroine are absent.

Once we move from the classic, canonical versions of the tale, we discover heroines who are often described as courageous: curiosity and valor enable them to come to the rescue of their sisters by reconstituting them physically (putting their dismembered parts back together again) and by providing them with safe passage home. Calculated to maximize melodramatic effects, many of the less-well-known stories side with the heroine, who becomes the agent of her own rescue. In versions of the story told by Jamaican storytellers, African Americans in the U.S. South, or Pueblo Indians, the wives of Bluebeard figures engineer a breathtaking escape that ends with a triumphant return home.

While the story of Bluebeard has been read by countless contemporary commentators as turning on the issue of sexual fidelity, what really seems to be at issue, if one considers the folkloric evidence, is the heroine's discovery of her husband's misdeeds, her craft in delaying the execution of his murderous plans, and her ability to engineer her own rescue. In its bold proclamation about the perils of some marriages, "Bluebeard" endorses, above all, allegiance to family and celebrates a return to the safety and security of home, a

---

8. Paul Delarue, "Barbe-Bleue," in *Le Conte populaire français* (Paris: Editions Erasme, 1976), I:182–99.

regressive move back to the household of the heroine's childhood. Bluebeard's wife becomes a double of the British Jack, liquidating the ogre and climbing back down the beanstalk to live happily ever after at home.

When we consider the form in which "Bluebeard" circulated in an oral culture, it quickly becomes evident that the story must be closely related to two tales recorded by the brothers Grimm. The first of these, "Fitcher's Bird" (p. 193), shows us the youngest of three sisters using her "cunning" to escape the snares set by a clever sorcerer and to rescue her two sisters. The heroine of "The Robber Bridegroom" (p. 196) also engineers a rescue, mobilizing her wits and her narrative skills to escape from the thieves with whom her betrothed consorts. Oddly enough, however, these two variants of the "Bluebeard" story seem to have fallen into a cultural black hole, while tales like Perrault's "Bluebeard" have been preserved and rewritten as cautionary tales warning women about the hazards of disobedience and curiosity. It is telling that an author like Margaret Atwood turned to "Fitcher's Bird" and "The Robber Bridegroom" for narrative inspiration and that a visual artist like Cindy Sherman created a picture book of the Grimms' "Fitcher's Bird." This new cultural investment in old tales about bad marriages clearly has something to do with the discovery that older versions of "Bluebeard" stressed the resourcefulness of the heroine and with the revelation that Perrault's "Bluebeard" was not the sole source of narrative authority for this particular marriage tale.

Margaret Atwood, who grew up reading the Grimms, recognized that fairy tales were not at all as culturally repressive as some feminist critics had made them out to be.

> The unexpurgated *Grimm's Fairy Tales* contain a number of fairy tales in which women are not only the central characters but win by using their own intelligence. Some people feel fairy tales are bad for women. This is true if the only ones they're referring to are those tarted-up French versions of "Cinderella" and "Bluebeard," in which the female protagonist gets rescued by her brothers. But in many of them, women rather than men have the magic powers.[9]

Atwood, who weaves fairy-tale motifs throughout her narratives with almost unprecedented creative energy, also produced a new version of "Bluebeard," one that has embedded in it the Grimms' story "Fitcher's Bird." "Bluebeard's Egg," unlike any fairy tale, is told from the protagonist's point of view: it charts Sally's drive to solve "the

---

9. Sharon R. Wilson, *Margaret Atwood's Fairy-Tale Sexual Politics* (Jackson: UP of Mississippi, 1993), pp. 11–12.

puzzle . . . Ed" (p. 219) and reveals that Ed Bear (who may not sport a beard on his face but surely has one encrypted in his nickname) is not as transparent as Sally once assumed. His inner life becomes a kind of secret chamber, a space that Sally is unable to penetrate. But Atwood challenges our interpretive faculties by refusing to write a text that offers unproblematic parallels with "Bluebeard." In the profusion of references to other fairy tales (Ed is a "third son" [p. 206], a "brainless beast" [p. 206], and a "Sleeping Beauty" waiting to be wakened by Sally, who is both a princess and a false bride), Atwood makes it clear that she taps multiple cultural stories for this work. And by transforming the forbidden chamber of Blue-beard's castle into everything from Ed's enigmatic mind and his "new facility" (p. 214) to the anatomical cavities of the human heart and the keyhole desk before which Ed betrays his sexual infidelity, Atwood unsettles the traditional story of "Bluebeard" and chal-lenges us to understand the complexities of what she calls "power politics." Ed cannot be reduced to Bluebeard, and Sally is more than his investigative wife. In focalizing the story through Sally and showing how her effort to come to terms with the Grimms' "Fitch-er's Bird" leads her to powerful revelations about her own life, Atwood suggests that engagement with our cultural stories can open our eyes to realities that—however disruptive, painful, and disturbing—are not without a liberating potential. Hence the story ends on an ambiguous note, with a sense of anxiety but also with the possibility of hope about what will hatch from the "almost puls-ing" (p. 227) egg of Sally's dream vision.

There is always another side to every story, and Edna St. Vincent Millay's "Bluebeard" poem reminds us of the perils of wanting to know too much when it comes to romance. A sharp stick against snooping, prying, nosiness, and spying, it reminds us that sometimes there is nothing to suspicions aroused, sometimes there is "no trea-sure hid, / The sought-for truth, no heads of women slain" (p. 228). Curiosity kills not only the cat but also a love that might have endured.

CHARLES PERRAULT

Bluebeard†

There once lived a man who had fine houses, both in the city and in the country, dinner services of gold and silver, chairs covered

---

† Charles Perrault, "Le Barbe bleue," in *Histoires ou Contes du temps passé. Avec des Moralités* (Paris: Barbin, 1697). Translated for the first edition of this Norton Critical Edition by Maria Tatar. Copyright © 1999 Maria Tatar.

with tapestries, and coaches covered with gold. But this man had the misfortune of having a blue beard, which made him look so ugly and frightful that women and girls alike fled at the sight of him.

One of his neighbors, a respectable lady, had two daughters who were perfect beauties. He asked for the hand of one, but left it up to the mother to choose which one. Neither of the two girls wanted to marry him, and the offer went back and forth between them, since they could not bring themselves to marry a man with a blue beard. What added even more to their sense of disgust was that he had already married several women, and no one knew what had become of them.

In order to cultivate their acquaintance, Bluebeard threw a party for the two girls with their mother, three or four of their closest friends, and a few young men from the neighborhood in one of his country houses. It lasted an entire week. Every day there were parties of pleasure, hunting, fishing, dancing, and dining. The guests never even slept, but cavorted and caroused all night long. Everything went so well that the younger of the two sisters began to think that the beard of the master of the house was not so blue after all and that he was in fact a fine fellow. As soon as they returned to town, the marriage was celebrated.

After a month had passed, Bluebeard told his wife that he had to travel to take care of some urgent business in the provinces and that he would be away for at least six weeks. He urged her to enjoy herself while he was away, to invite her close friends and to take them out to the country if she wished. Above all, she was to stay in good spirits.

"Here," he said, "are the keys to my two large store rooms. Here are the ones for the gold and silver china that is too good for everyday use. Here are the ones for my strongboxes, where my gold and silver are kept. Here are the ones for the caskets where my jewels are stored. And finally, this is the passkey to all the rooms in my mansion. As for this particular key, it is the key to the small room at the end of the long passage on the lower floor. Open anything you want. Go anywhere you wish. But I absolutely forbid you to enter that little room, and if you so much as open it a crack, there will be no limit to my anger."

She promised to follow the orders he had just given exactly. After kissing his wife, Bluebeard got into the carriage and embarked on his journey.

Friends and neighbors of the young bride did not wait for an invitation before coming to call, so great was their impatience to see the splendors of the house. They had not dared to call while the husband was there, because of his blue beard, which frightened them. In no time they were darting through the rooms, the closets, and the wardrobes, each of which was more splendid and sumptuous than the next. Then they went upstairs to the storerooms, where they could not find words to describe the number and beauty of the tapestries, beds, sofas, cabinets, stands, and tables. There were looking glasses, in which you could see yourself from head to toe, some of which had frames of glass, others of silver or gilded lacquer, but all of which were more splendid and magnificent than anyone there had ever seen. They kept on expressing praise even as they felt envy for the good fortune of their friend who, however, was unable to take any pleasure at all from the sight of these riches because she was so anxious to get into that room on the lower floor. So tormented was she by her curiosity that, without stopping to think about how rude it was to leave her friends, she raced down a little staircase so fast that more than once she thought she was going to break her neck. When she reached the door to the room, she stopped to think for a moment about how her husband had forbidden her to enter, and she reflected on the harm that might come her way for being disobedient. But the temptation was so great that she was unable to resist it. She took the little key and, trembling, opened the door.

At first she saw nothing, for the windows were closed. After a few moments, she began to realize that the floor was covered with clotted blood and that the blood reflected the bodies of several dead women hung up on the walls (these were all the women Bluebeard had married and then murdered one after another).

She thought she would die of fright, and the key to the room, which she was about to pull out of the lock, dropped from her hand. When she regained her senses, she picked up the key, closed the door, and went back to her room to compose herself. But she didn't succeed, for her nerves were too frayed. Having noticed that the key to the room was stained with blood, she wiped it two or three times, but the blood would not come off at all. She tried to wash it off and even to scrub it with sand and grit. The bloodstain would not come off because the key was enchanted and nothing could clean it completely. When you cleaned the stain from one side, it just returned on the other.

That very night, Bluebeard returned unexpectedly from his journey and reported that, on the road, he had received letters informing him that the business upon which he had set forth had just been settled to his satisfaction. His wife did everything that she could to make it appear that she was thrilled with his speedy return. The next day, he asked to have the keys back, and she returned them, but with a hand trembling so much that he knew at once what had happened.

"How is it," he asked, "that the key to the little room isn't with the others?"

"I must have left it upstairs on my dressing table," she replied.

"Don't forget to bring it to me soon," Bluebeard told her.

After making one excuse after another, she had to bring him the key. Bluebeard examined it and said to his wife: "Why is there blood on this key?"

"I have no idea," answered the poor woman, paler than death.

"You have no idea," Bluebeard replied. "But I have an idea. You tried to enter that little room. Well, madam, now that you have opened it, you can go right in and take your place beside the ladies whom you saw there."

She threw herself at her husband's feet, weeping and begging his pardon, with all the signs of genuine regret for disobeying him. She looked so beautiful and was so distressed that she would have melted a heart of stone, but Bluebeard had a heart harder than any rock.

"You must die, madam," he declared, "and it will be right away."

"Since I must die," she replied, gazing at him with eyes full of tears, "give me a little time to say my prayers."

"I will give you a quarter of an hour," Bluebeard said, "but not a moment more."

When she was alone, she called her sister and said to her: "Sister Anne"—for that was her name—"I implore you to go up to the top of the tower to see if my brothers are on the way here. They told me that they were coming to visit today. If you catch sight of them, signal them to hurry."

Sister Anne went up to the top of the tower, and the poor distressed girl cried out to her from time to time: "Anne, Sister Anne, do you see anyone coming?"

Sister Anne replied: "I see nothing but the sun shining and the green grass growing."

In the meantime, Bluebeard took an enormous cutlass in hand and cried out at the top of his voice to his wife: "Come down at once or I'll go up there!"

"Just a moment more, I beg you," his wife replied and at the same time she called out softly: "Anne, Sister Anne, do you see anyone coming?"

And Sister Anne replied: "I see nothing but the sun shining and the green grass growing."

"Come down at once," Bluebeard called, "or I'll go up there!"

"I'm coming," his wife replied, and then she called: "Anne, Sister Anne, do you see anyone coming?"

"I can see a great cloud of dust coming this way," replied Sister Anne.

"Is it my brothers?"

"No, oh no, sister, it's just a flock of sheep."

"Are you coming down?" Bluebeard roared.

"Just one moment more," his wife replied, and then she called: "Anne, Sister Anne, do you see anyone coming?"

"I see two horsemen coming this way, but they're still far away," she replied. "Thank God," she shouted a moment later, "it must be our brothers. I'll signal to them to hurry up."

Bluebeard began shouting so loudly that the entire house shook. His poor wife came downstairs, in tears and with disheveled hair. She threw herself at his feet.

"That won't do you any good," said Bluebeard. "Prepare to die." Then, taking her by the hair with one hand and raising his cutlass with the other, he was about to chop off her head. The poor woman turned to him and implored him with a gaze that had death written on it. She begged for one last moment to prepare herself for death. "No, no," he said, "prepare to meet your maker." And lifting his arm . . .

Just at that moment there was such a loud pounding at the gate that Bluebeard stopped short. The gate was opened, and two horsemen, swords in hand, dashed in and made straight for Bluebeard. He realized that they were the brothers of his wife: the one a dragoon and the other a musketeer. He fled instantly in an effort to escape. But the two brothers were so hot in pursuit that they trapped him before he could get to the stairs. They plunged their swords through his body and left him for dead. Bluebeard's wife was as close to death as her husband and barely had the strength to rise and embrace her brothers.

It turned out that Bluebeard had left no heirs, and so his wife took possession of the entire estate. She devoted a portion of it to arranging a marriage between her sister Anne and a young gentleman with whom she had been in love for a long time. Another portion of it was used to buy commissions for her two brothers. She used the rest to marry herself to a very worthy man, who banished the memory of the miserable days she had spent with Bluebeard.

Moral

Curiosity, in spite of its many charms,
Can bring with it serious regrets;
You can see a thousand examples of it every day.
Women succumb, but it's a fleeting pleasure;
As soon as you satisfy it, it ceases to be.
And it always proves very, very costly.

Another Moral

If you just take a sensible point of view,
And study this grim little story,

You will understand that this tale
Is one that took place many years ago.
No longer are husbands so terrible,
Demanding the impossible,
Acting unhappy and jealous.
With their wives they toe the line;
And whatever color their beards might be,
It's not hard to tell which of the pair is master.

BROTHERS GRIMM

Fitcher's Bird[†]

There was once a sorcerer who would disguise himself as a poor man, then go begging from door to door in order to capture pretty girls. No one knew what he did with them, for they were never seen again.

One day he appeared at the door of a man who had three beautiful daughters. He looked like a poor, weak beggar and had a basket on his back, as if to collect alms. He asked for something to eat, and when the eldest girl went to the door and was about to hand him a piece of bread, he just touched her and she jumped into his basket. Then he made long legs and rushed off to get her to his house, which was in the middle of a dark forest.

Everything in the house was splendid. He gave the girl everything she wanted, and said: "My darling, I'm sure you'll be happy here with me, for you'll have everything your heart desires." After a few days went by, he said: "I have to take a journey and must leave you alone for a short while. Here are the keys for the house. You can go anywhere you want and look around at everything, but don't go into the room that this little key opens. I forbid it under penalty of death."

He also gave her an egg and said: "Carry it with you wherever you go, because if it gets lost, something terrible will happen." She took the keys and the egg and promised to do exactly what he had said. After he left, she went over the house from top to bottom, taking a good look at everything. The rooms glittered with silver and gold, and it seemed to her that she had never before seen such magnificence. Finally she came to the forbidden door and planned to walk right by it, but curiosity got the better of her. She examined the key, and it was just like the others. When she put it in the lock and just turned it a little bit, the door sprang open.

† Jacob Grimm and Wilhelm Grimm, "Fitchers Vogel," in *Kinder- und Hausmärchen*, 7th ed. (Berlin: Dieterich, 1857; first published: Berlin: Realschulbuchhandlung, 1812). Translated for the first edition of this Norton Critical Edition by Maria Tatar. Copyright © 1999 by Maria Tatar.

But what did she see when she entered! In the middle of the room was a large, bloody basin filled with dead people who had been chopped to pieces. Next to the basin was a block of wood with a gleaming ax on it. She was so horrified that she dropped the egg she was holding into the basin. She took it right out and wiped off the blood, but to no avail, for the stain immediately returned. She wiped it and scraped at it, but it just wouldn't come off.

Not much later the man returned from his journey, and the first things he demanded were the keys and the egg. She gave them to him, but she was trembling, and when he saw the red stains, he knew she had been in the bloody chamber. "You entered the chamber against my wishes," he said. "Now you will go back in against yours. Your life is over."

He threw her down, dragged her in by the hair, chopped her head off on the block, and hacked her into pieces so that her blood flowed all over the floor. Then he tossed her into the basin with the others.

"Now I'll go and get the second one," said the sorcerer, and he went back to the house dressed as a poor man begging for alms. When the second daughter brought him a piece of bread, he caught her as he had the first just by touching her. He carried her off, and she fared no better than her sister. Her curiosity got the better of her: she opened the door to the bloody chamber, looked inside it, and when he returned she had to pay with her life.

The man went to fetch the third daughter, but she was clever and cunning. After handing over the keys and egg, he went away, and she put the egg in a safe place. She explored the house and entered the forbidden chamber. And what did she see! There in the basin were her two sisters, cruelly murdered and chopped to pieces. But she set to work gathering all their body parts and put them in their proper places: heads, torsos, arms, legs. When everything was in place, the pieces began to move and joined themselves together. The two girls opened their eyes and came back to life. Overjoyed, they kissed and hugged each other.

On his return, the man asked at once for the keys and egg. When he could not find a trace of blood on the egg, he declared: "You have passed the test, and you shall be my bride." He no longer had any power over her and had to do her bidding. "Very well," she replied. "But first you must take a basketful of gold to my father and mother, and you must carry it on your own back. In the meantime, I'll make the wedding arrangements."

She ran to her sisters, whom she had hidden in a little room and said: "Now is the time when I can save you. That brute will be the one who carries you home. But as soon as you get home, send help for me."

She put both girls into a basket and covered them with gold until they could not be seen. Then she summoned the sorcerer and said:

"Pick up the basket and go. But don't you dare stop to rest along the way. I'll be looking out of my little window, keeping an eye on you."

The sorcerer lifted the basket onto his shoulders and set off with it. But it weighed so much that sweat began to pour down his face. He sat down to rest for a moment, but right away one of the girls cried out from the basket: "I'm looking out my little window, and I see that you're resting. Get a move on." He thought his bride was calling to him, and he went on his way. A second time he wanted to sit down, but again the voice called out: "I'm looking out my little window and I see that you're resting. Get a move on." Whenever he stopped, the voice called out and he had to move along until finally, gasping for breath and groaning, he carried the basket with the gold and the two girls in it into their parent's house.

Back at home the bride was preparing the wedding celebration to which she had invited all the sorcerer's friends. She took a skull with grinning teeth, crowned it with jewels and a garland of flowers, carried it upstairs and set it down at an attic window, facing out. When everything was ready, she crawled into a barrel of honey, cut open a featherbed and rolled in the feathers until she looked like a strange bird that not a soul would recognize. She left the house and on her way met some wedding guests, who asked:

> "Oh, Fitcher's feathered bird, where are you from?"
> "From feathered Fitze Fitcher's house I've come."
> "And the young bride there, what has she done?"
> "She's swept the house all the way through,
> And from the attic window, she's looking right at you."

She met the bridegroom, who was walking back home very slowly. He too asked:

> "Oh, Fitcher's feathered bird, where are you from?"
> "From feathered Fitze Fitcher's house I've come."
> "And my young bride there, what has she done?"
> "She's swept the house all the way through,
> And from the attic window, she's looking right at you."

The bridegroom looked up and saw the decorated skull. He thought it was his bride, nodded, and waved to her. But when he got to the house with his guests, the brothers and relatives who had been sent to rescue the bride were already there. They locked the doors to the house so that no one could escape. Then they set fire to it so that the sorcerer and his crew burned to death.

BROTHERS GRIMM

The Robber Bridegroom[†]

There was once a miller who had a beautiful daughter, and when she was grown, he wanted to make sure that she was provided for and well married. He thought: "If the right kind of suitor comes along and asks for her hand, I shall give her to him."

Not much later a suitor turned up who seemed to be rich, and since the miller could find nothing wrong with him, he promised him his daughter. But the girl didn't care for him as a girl should care for her betrothed, and she didn't trust him. Whenever she looked at him or thought of him, her heart filled with dread.

One day he said to her: "You're engaged to me, and yet you've never once visited me."

The girl replied: "I don't know where you live."

The bridegroom answered: "My house is out in the dark forest."

The girl made excuses and claimed that she couldn't find the way there. But the bridegroom said: "Next Sunday you have to come to my place. I've already invited the guests, and I'll put ashes on the path so that you can find your way through the woods."

When Sunday came and the girl was supposed to leave, she became dreadfully frightened without knowing why, and she filled both her pockets with peas and lentils to mark the way. At the entrance to the woods she found the trail of ashes and followed it, but at every step she threw some peas on the ground, first to the right and then to the left. She walked almost the entire day until she got to the middle of the forest, where it was the gloomiest. There she saw a house standing by itself, but she didn't like the look of it because it seemed dark and spooky. She walked in. It was deadly silent, and no one was around. Suddenly a voice cried out:

"Turn back, turn back, my pretty young bride,
In a house of murderers you've arrived."

The girl looked up and saw that the voice was coming from a bird in a cage hanging on the wall. Once again it cried out:

"Turn back, turn back, my pretty young bride,
In a house of murderers you've arrived."

† Jacob Grimm and Wilhelm Grimm, "Der Räuberbräutigam," In Kinder- und Haus-märchen, 7th ed. (Berlin: Dieterich, 1857; first published: Berlin: Realschulbuchhand-lung, 1812). Translated for the first edition of this Norton Critical Edition by Maria Tatar. Copyright © 1999 by Maria Tatar.

The beautiful bride went all over the house from one room to the next, but it was completely empty and not a soul could be found in it. Finally she went down to the cellar, where she found a woman as old as the hills, her head bobbing up and down.

"Can you tell me if my betrothed lives here?" asked the girl.

"Oh, you poor child!" said the old woman. "How did you get here? This is a den of murderers. You think you're a bride about to be married, but the only wedding you'll celebrate is one with death. Look over here! I had to heat up this big pot of water for them. When you get into their hands, they'll show no mercy and chop you into pieces, cook you, and eat you, for they are cannibals. You're lost unless I take pity on you and try to save you."

The old woman hid her behind a big barrel, where no one could see her. "Be still as a mouse," she said. "Don't stir and don't move or it'll be the end of you. At night, when the robbers are sleeping, we'll escape. I've been waiting for this moment for a long time."

No sooner had she spoken than the ungodly crew returned home, dragging another maiden in with them. They were drunk and paid no attention to her screams and sobs. They gave her wine to drink, three glasses full, one white, one red, one yellow, and soon her heart burst in two. They tore off her fine clothes, put her on a table, chopped her beautiful body into pieces, and sprinkled them with salt.

The poor girl was trembling and shaking from her hiding place behind the barrel, for she now understood what the robbers had in store for her. One of them caught sight of a gold ring on the little finger of the murdered girl, and when he couldn't pull it off right away, he took an ax and chopped the finger off. The finger went flying through the air up over the barrel and landed right in the girl's lap. The robber took a candle and wanted to go looking for it but couldn't find it. Another of the robbers asked: "Have you looked over there behind that big barrel?" Just then the old woman called out: "Come and eat! You can look again tomorrow. The finger isn't going to go running off."

"The old woman's right," the robbers said, and they put an end to their search and sat down to eat. The old woman put a few drops of a sleeping potion into their wine, and soon they retired to the cellar where they were snoring away in their sleep.

When the bride heard them snoring, she came out from behind the barrel and made her way over the sleeping bodies arranged in rows on the ground. She was terrified that she might wake one of them up, but God guided her footsteps. The old woman went up the stairs with her, opened the door, and they ran as fast as they could from the den of murderers. The wind had scattered the ashes, but the peas and lentils had sprouted and showed the way in the moonlight. The two walked all night long. In the morning they reached the mill, and the girl told her father about everything that had happened.

When the day of the wedding celebration arrived, the groom appeared, as did all the friends and relatives invited by the miller. When they sat down for dinner, each person was asked to tell a story. The bride sat quietly and didn't utter a word. Finally the bridegroom said to his bride: "Don't you have anything to say, my love? You have to tell us something."

"Very well," she replied, "I will tell you about a dream I had. I was walking alone through the woods and came across a house. Not a soul was living in it, but on the wall there was a cage, and in it was a bird that cried out:

'Turn back, turn back, my pretty young bride,
In a house of murderers you've arrived.'

"Then it repeated those words. My dear, I must have been dreaming all this. Then I walked from room to room and each was completely empty. Everything was so spooky. Finally I went down to the cellar, and there I saw a woman as old as the hills, her head bobbing up and down. I asked her: 'Does my betrothed live here?' She replied: 'Oh, you poor child, you have stumbled into a den of murderers. Your betrothed lives here, but he is planning to chop you up and kill you, and then he'll cook you and eat you up.' My dear, I must have been dreaming all this. The old woman hid me behind a big barrel, and no sooner was I hidden than the robbers returned home, dragging a maiden with them. They gave her three kinds of wine to drink, white, red, yellow, and her heart burst in two. My dear, I must have been dreaming all this. Then they tore off her fine clothes, chopped her beautiful body into pieces, and sprinkled it with salt. My dear, I must have been dreaming all this. One of the robbers caught sight of a gold ring on her finger and since it was hard to pull off, he took an ax and chopped it off. The finger flew through the air up behind the big barrel and landed in my lap. And here is the finger with the ring."

With these words, she pulled it out and showed it to everyone there.

The robber, who had turned white as a ghost while she was telling the story, jumped up and tried to escape, but the guests seized him and turned him over to the authorities. He and his band were executed for their dreadful deeds.

JOSEPH JACOBS

Mr. Fox[†]

Lady Mary was young, and Lady Mary was fair. She had two brothers, and more lovers than she could count. But of them all, the bravest and most gallant was a Mr. Fox, whom she met when she was down at her father's country house. No one knew who Mr. Fox was; but he was certainly brave, and surely rich, and of all her lovers Lady Mary cared for him alone. At last it was agreed upon between them that they should be married. Lady Mary asked Mr. Fox where they should live, and he described to her his castle, and where it was; but, strange to say, did not ask her or her brothers to come and see it.

So one day, near the wedding day, when her brothers were out, and Mr. Fox was away for a day or two on business, as he said, Lady Mary set out for Mr. Fox's castle. And after many searchings, she came at last to it, and a fine strong house it was, with high walls and a deep moat. And when she came up to the gateway she saw written on it:

Be bold, be bold.[1]

But as the gate was open, she went through it, and found no one there. So she went up to the doorway, and over it she found written:

Be bold, be bold, but not too bold.

Still she went on, till she came into the hall, and went up the broad stairs till she came to a door in the gallery, over which was written:

Be bold, be bold, but not too bold,
Lest that your heart's blood should run cold.

But Lady Mary was a brave one, she was, and she opened the door, and what do you think she saw? Why, bodies and skeletons of beautiful young ladies all stained with blood. So Lady Mary thought it was high time to get out of that horrid place, and she closed the door, went through the gallery, and was just going down the stairs, and out of the hall, when who should she see through the window but Mr. Fox dragging a beautiful young lady along from the gateway to the door. Lady Mary rushed downstairs, and hid herself behind a cask, just in time, as Mr. Fox came in with the poor young lady, who seemed to have fainted. Just as he got near Lady Mary, Mr. Fox saw a diamond ring glittering on the finger of the young lady he was dragging, and

† Joseph Jacobs, "Mr. Fox," in *English Fairy Tales* (London: David Nutt, 1890).
1. The admonition "Be bold" appears also in Edmund Spenser's *Faerie Queen* (1590): "How over that same Door was likewise writ, / *Be bold, Be bold*, and every where *Be bold*" (Book III, Canto XI, stanza 54).

he tried to pull it off. But it was tightly fixed, and would not come off, so Mr. Fox cursed and swore, and drew his sword, raised it, and brought it down upon the hand of the poor lady. The sword cut off the hand, which jumped up into the air, and fell of all places in the world into Lady Mary's lap. Mr. Fox looked about a bit, but did not think of looking behind the cask, so at last he went on dragging the young lady up the stairs into the Bloody Chamber.

As soon as she heard him pass through the gallery, Lady Mary crept out of the door, down through the gateway, and ran home as fast as she could.

Now it happened that the very next day the marriage contract of Lady Mary and Mr. Fox was to be signed, and there was a splendid breakfast before that. And when Mr. Fox was seated at table opposite Lady Mary, he looked at her. "How pale you are this morning, my dear." "Yes," said she, "I had a bad night's rest last night. I had horrible dreams." "Dreams go by contraries," said Mr. Fox; "but tell us your dream, and your sweet voice will make the time pass till the happy hour comes."

"I dreamed," said Lady Mary, "that I went yestermorn to your castle, and I found it in the woods, with high walls, and a deep moat, and over the gateway was written:

> Be bold, be bold."

"But it is not so, nor it was not so,"[2] said Mr. Fox.
"And when I came to the doorway, over it was written:

> Be bold, be bold, but not too bold."

"It is not so, nor it was not so," said Mr. Fox.
"And then I went upstairs, and came to a gallery, at the end of which was a door, on which was written:

> Be bold, be bold, but not too bold,
> Lest that your heart's blood should run cold."

"It is not so, nor it was not so," said Mr. Fox.
"And then—and then I opened the door, and the room was filled with bodies and skeletons of poor dead women, all stained with their blood."

"It is not so, nor it was not so. And God forbid it should be so," said Mr. Fox.

"I then dreamed that I rushed down the gallery, and just as I was going down the stairs I saw you, Mr. Fox, coming up to the hall door, dragging after you a poor young lady, rich and beautiful."

---

2. Cf. Shakespeare, *Much Ado about Nothing* (I.i.146): "Like the old tale, my Lord, 'It is not so, nor t'was not so, but, indeed, God forbid it should be so!'"

"It is not so, nor it was not so. And God forbid it should be so," said Mr. Fox.

"I rushed downstairs, just in time to hide myself behind a cask, when you, Mr. Fox, came in dragging the young lady by the arm. And, as you passed me, Mr. Fox, I thought I saw you try and get off her diamond ring, and when you could not, Mr. Fox, it seemed to me in my dream, that you out with your sword and hacked off the poor lady's hand to get the ring."

"It is not so, nor it was not so. And God forbid it should be so," said Mr. Fox, and was going to say something else as he rose from his seat, when Lady Mary cried out:

"But it is so, and it was so. Here's hand and ring I have to show," and pulled out the lady's hand from her dress, and pointed it straight at Mr. Fox.

At once her brothers and her friends drew their swords and cut Mr. Fox into a thousand pieces.

Mr. Bluebeard[†]

There was a man named Mr. Bluebeard. He got his wife in his house, an' he general catch people an' lock up into a room, an' he never let him wife see that room.

One day he went out to a dinner an' forgot his key on the door. An' his wife open the door an' find many dead people in the room. Those that were not dead said: "Thanky, Missis; Thanky Missis."

An' as soon as the live ones get away, an' she was to lock the door, the key drop in blood. She take it up an' wash it an' put it in the lock. It drop back into the blood.

An' Mr. Bluebeard was an old-witch an' know what was going on at home. An' as he sat at dinner, he called out to get his horse ready at once. An' they said to him: "Do, Mr. Bluebeard, have something to eat before you go."

"No! Get my horse ready."

So they bring it to him. Now he doesn't ride a four-footed beast, he ride a t'ree-foot horse.[1]

An' he get on his horse an' start off itty-itty-hap,[2] itty-itty-hap, until he get home.

---

† *Jamaican Song and Story: Annancy Stories, Digging Sings, Ring Tunes, and Dancing Tunes*, ed. Walter Jekyll (London: David Nutt, 1907), pp. 35–37.
1. The three-legged horse is thought to be a kind of phantom beast that rides only at night in the moonlight and can gallop faster than any other horse. It can kill people by breathing on them.
2. Onomatopoeic phrase meant to capture the gait of the three-legged horse.

Now Mrs. Bluebeard two brother was a hunter-man in the wood. One of them was old-witch, an' he said: "Brother, brother, something home wrong with me sister."

"Get 'way you little foolish fellah," said the biggest one.

But the other say again: "Brother, brother, something wrong at home. Just get me a white cup and a white saucer, and fill it with water, and put it in the sun, an' you will soon see what to do with the water."

Directly the water turn blood.

An' the eldest said: "Brother, it is truth, make we go."

An' Mrs. Bluebeard was afraid, because he knew Mr. Bluebeard was coming fe kill him.[3] An' he was calling continually to the cook, Miss Anne: "Sister Anne, Sister Anne, Ah! You see anyone coming? Sister Anne, Sister Anne, Ah! You see anyone coming?"

An' Sister Anne answer: "Oh no, I see no one is coming but the dust that makes the grass so green."

An' as she sing done they hear Mr. Bluebeard coming, itty-itty-hap, itty-itty-hap.

Him jump straight off a him t'ree-foot beast an' go in a the house, and catch Mrs. Bluebeard by one of him plait-hair an' hold him by it, an' said: "This is the last day of you."

An' Mrs. Bluebeard said: "Do, Mr. Bluebeard, allow me to say my last prayer."

But Mr. Bluebeard still hold him by the hair while he sing: "Sister Anne, Sister Anne, Ah! You see anyone coming? Sister Anne, Sister Anne, Ah! You see anyone coming?"

Sister Anne answer this time: "Oh—yes! I see someone is coming, and the dust that makes the grass so green."

Then Mr. Bluebeard took his sword was to cut off him neck, an' his two brother appear, an' the eldest one going to shot after Mr. Bluebeard, an' he was afraid an' begin to run away. But the young one wasn't going to let him go so, an' him shot PUM and kill him 'tiff dead.

Jack Mantora me no choose none.[4]

---

3. In the dialect used for the story, "he knew" is equivalent to "she knew" and "to kill him" means "to kill her."
4. In some Jamaican tales Jack Mantora (possibly the gatekeeper to heaven) appears as a listener, and the narrator closes with this phrase, which has been read to mean either "Don't blame me for the tale I've just told" or "I didn't have you in mind when I chose this tale."

The Forbidden Room[†]

Once upon a time there was a man had one daughter. Every man come to marry her, she said, "No." So a man came, all over was gold. And she married him. He had a horse name Sixty-Miles, for every time he jump it was sixty miles. So they went. The more he goes, his gold was dropping. Mary Bell wanted to know why his gold was dropping. He said, "That is all right." They reached home soon. He gave her a big bunch of keys and take her around to all the room in the house. "You can open all the room except one room; for if you open it, I will kill you." She start to wonder why her husband didn't want her to open it. So one day she open it. It was great surprise. She saw heads of woman hanging up. She also saw a cast of blood. Her key dropped in the blood, and she couldn't get it off. So she began to mourn. The Devil daughter told her not to cry. She took three needles and gave it to her. "He is coming; but when you first drop one, there will be a large forest, and so on." She went and get Sixty-Miles, and she went. Now the Devil came from the wood. He had a rooster. He told his master, "Massa, massa, your pretty girl gone home this morning 'fore day. Massa, massa, your pretty girl gone home this morning 'fore day." The Devil look about the house for his wife, he didn't see her. So he went to get Sixty-Miles, and he couldn't find it. So he get Fifty-Miles. Start after her. He spy her far down the road. He said, "Mary Bell, O Mary Bell! what harm I done you?"

> You done me no harm, but you done me good. Bang-a-lang!
> Hero, don't let your foot touch, bang-a-lang!
> Hero, don't let your foot touch!

The Devil catch at her. She drop a needle, and it became a large forest. He said, "Mary Bell, O Mary Bell! how shall I get through?"—"Well," said she, "go back home, get your axe and cut it out." And he did. He saw her again, and catch at her. She drop another needle, and a large brick wall stood in the way. He said, "Mary Bell, how shall I get through?"—"Go get your shovel and axe, and dig and pick your way." He done just the same way. And he get through all right. He spy her again. He said, "Mary Bell, what harm I done you?"

> You done me no harm, but you done me good. Bang-a-lang!
> Hero, don't let your foot touch.

[†] *Folk-Lore of the Sea Islands, South Carolina*, ed. Elsie Clews Parsons (New York: American Folklore Society, 1923), pp. 47–49. The tale was told to Parsons by Julius Jenkins, a pupil in Edding's Point School on the island of St. Helena off the coast of South Carolina.

He catch at her. She step into her father's house. The Devil get so mad, he carry half of the man's house.

> I step on a t'in', the t'in' bend.
> My story is end.

Mast-Truan[†]

Once upon a time a chief of Acoma had a lovely daughter. One day a handsome stranger stole her and took her away to his home, which was in the heart of the Snow Mountain (Mt. San Mateo). He was none other than Mast-Truan, one of the Storm-Gods. Bringing his captive home, the powerful stranger gave her the finest clothing and treated her very nicely. But most of the time he had to be away from home, attending to the storms, and she became very lonesome, for there was no one to keep her company, but Mast-Truan's wrinkled old mother.

One day when she could stand the loneliness no longer, she decided to take a walk through the enormous house and look at the rooms which she had not seen. Opening a door she came into a very large room toward the east; and there were a lot of women crying and shivering with cold, for they had nothing to wear. Going through this room she came to another, which was full of gaunt, starving women, and here and there one lay dead upon the floor; and in the next room were scores of bleached and ghastly skeletons. And this was what Mast-Truan did with his wives when he was tired of them. The girl saw her fate, and, returning to her room, sat down and wept—but there was no escape, for Mast-Truan's old hag of a mother forever guarded the outer door.

When Mast-Truan came home again, his wife said, "It is now long that I have not seen my father. Let me go home for a little while."

"Well," said he, "here is some corn which must be shelled. When you have shelled it and ground it, I will let you out"; and he showed her four great rooms piled from floor to ceiling with ears of corn. It was more than one could shell in a year; and when her husband went out, she sat down again to cry and bemoan her fate.

Just then a queer little old woman appeared before her, with a kindly smile. It was a cumúshquio.[1]

"What is the matter, my daughter?" asked the old fairy, gently, "and why do you weep?"

The captive told her all, and the fairy said, "Do not fear, daughter, for I will help you, and we will have all the corn shelled and ground in four days."

† Charles F. Lummis, *Pueblo Indian Folk-Stories* (New York: Century, 1910), pp. 203–05.
1. Fairy woman.

So they fell to work. For two days the girl kept shelling; and though she could not see the old fairy at all, she could always hear at her side the click of the ears together. Then for two days she kept grinding on her metate,[2] apparently alone, but hearing the constant grind of another metate close beside her. At the end of the fourth day the last kernel had been scrubbed into blue meal, and she was very happy. Then the old fairy-woman appeared again, bringing a large basket and a rope. She opened the doors to all the rooms where the poor women were prisoners, and bade them all get into the basket one by one. Mast-Truan had taken away the ladder from the house when he left, that no one might be able to get out; but with her basket and rope the good old fairy-woman let them all down to the ground, and told them to hurry home—which they did as fast as ever their poor, starved legs could carry them. Then the fairy-woman and the girl escaped, and made their way to Acoma. So there was a Moon again—and that it was the Moon, we may be very sure; since this same girl became the mother of the Hero Twins, who were assuredly Children of the Moon.

MARGARET ATWOOD

Bluebeard's Egg[†]

Sally stands at the kitchen window, waiting for the sauce she's reducing to come to a simmer, looking out. Past the garage the lot sweeps downwards, into the ravine; it's a wilderness there, of bushes and branches and what Sally thinks of as vines. It was her idea to have a kind of terrace, built of old railroad ties, with wild flowers growing between them, but Edward says he likes it the way it is. There's a playhouse down at the bottom, near the fence; from here she can just see the roof. It has nothing to do with Edward's kids, in their earlier incarnations, before Sally's time; it's more ancient than that, and falling apart. Sally would like it cleared away. She thinks drunks sleep in it, the men who live under the bridges down there, who occasionally wander over the fence (which is broken down, from where they step on it) and up the hill, to emerge squinting like moles into the light of Sally's well-kept back lawn.

Off to the left is Ed, in his windbreaker; it's officially spring, Sally's blue scylla is in flower, but it's chilly for this time of year. Ed's

---

2. A stone used for grinding maize.
† Margaret Atwood, "Bluebeard's Egg," in *Bluebeard's Egg and Other Stories*. (Toronto: McClelland & Stewart, 1983). Copyright © 1983, 1986 by O. W. Toad Ltd. Reprinted by permission of Houghton Mifflin Harcourt Publishing Company, of Penguin Random House UK, and of McClelland & Stewart, a division of Penguin Random House Canada Limited.

windbreaker is an old one he won't throw out; it still says WILDCATS, relic of some team he was on in high school, an era so prehistoric Sally can barely imagine it; though picturing Ed at high school is not all that difficult. Girls would have had crushes on him, he would have been unconscious of it; things like that don't change. He's puttering around the rock garden now; some of the rocks stick out too far and are in danger of grazing the side of Sally's Peugeot, on its way to the garage, and he's moving them around. He likes doing things like that, puttering, humming to himself. He won't wear work gloves, though she keeps telling him he could squash his fingers.

Watching his bent back with its frayed, poignant lettering, Sally dissolves; which is not infrequent with her. *My darling Edward*, she thinks. *Edward Bear,*[1] *of little brain. How I love you.* At times like this she feels very protective of him.

Sally knows for a fact that dumb blondes were loved, not because they were blondes, but because they were dumb. It was their helplessness and confusion that were so sexually attractive, once; not their hair. It wasn't false, the rush of tenderness men must have felt for such women. Sally understands it.

For it must be admitted: Sally is in love with Ed because of his stupidity, his monumental and almost energetic stupidity: energetic, because Ed's stupidity is not passive. He's no mere blockhead;[2] you'd have to be working at it to be that stupid. Does it make Sally feel smug, or smarter than he is, or even smarter than she really is herself? No; on the contrary, it makes her humble. It fills her with wonder that the world can contain such marvels as Ed's colossal and endearing thickness. He is just so *stupid.* Every time he gives her another piece of evidence, another tile that she can glue into place in the vast mosaic of his stupidity she's continually piecing together, she wants to hug him, and often does; and he is so stupid he can never figure out what for.

Because Ed is so stupid he doesn't even know he's stupid. He's a child of luck, a third son who, armed with nothing but a certain feebleminded amiability, manages to make it through the forest with all its witches and traps and pitfalls and ends up with the princess, who is Sally, of course. It helps that he's handsome.

On good days she sees his stupidity as innocence, lamblike, shining with the light of (for instance) green daisied meadows in the sun. (When Sally starts thinking this way about Ed, in terms of the calendar art from the service-station washrooms of her childhood, dredging up images of a boy with curly golden hair, his arm thrown around the neck of an Irish setter—a notorious brainless beast, she

---

1. Christopher Robin's formal name for Winnie-the-Pooh.
2. Reference to blockheads and numbskulls in folklore.

reminds herself—she knows she is sliding over the edge, into a ghastly kind of sentimentality, and that she must stop at once, or Ed will vanish, to be replaced by a stuffed facsimile, useful for little else but an umbrella stand. Ed is a real person, with a lot more to him than these simplistic renditions allow for; which sometimes worries her.) On bad days though, she sees his stupidity as willfulness, a stubborn determination to shut things out. His obtuseness is a wall, within which he can go about his business, humming to himself, while Sally, locked outside, must hack her way through the brambles[3] with hardly so much as a transparent raincoat between them and her skin.

Why did she choose him (or, to be precise, as she tries to be with herself and sometimes is even out loud, *hunt him down*), when it's clear to everyone she had other options? To Marylynn, who is her best though most recent friend, she's explained it by saying she was spoiled when young by reading too many Agatha Christie murder mysteries, of the kind in which the clever and witty heroine passes over the equally clever and witty first-lead male, who's helped solve the crime, in order to marry the second-lead male, the stupid one, the one who would have been arrested and condemned and executed if it hadn't been for her cleverness. Maybe this is how she sees Ed: if it weren't for her, his blundering too-many-thumbs kindness would get him into all sorts of quagmires, all sorts of sink-holes he'd never be able to get himself out of, and then he'd be done for.

"Sink-hole" and "quagmire" are not flattering ways of speaking about other women, but this is what is at the back of Sally's mind; specifically, Ed's two previous wives. Sally didn't exactly extricate him from their clutches. She's never even met the first one, who moved to the west coast fourteen years ago and sends Christmas cards, and the second one was middle-aged and already in the act of severing herself from Ed before Sally came along. (For Sally, "middle-aged" means anyone five years older than she is. It has always meant this. She applies it only to women, however. She doesn't think of Ed as middle-aged, although the gap between them is considerably more than five years.)

Ed doesn't know what happened with these marriages, what went wrong. His protestations of ignorance, his refusal to discuss the finer points, is frustrating to Sally, because she would like to hear the whole story. But it's also cause for anxiety: if he doesn't know what happened with the other two, maybe the same thing could be happening with her and he doesn't know about that, either. Stupidity like Ed's can be a health hazard, for other people. What if he wakes up one day and decides that she isn't the true bride[4] after all, but the

3. An allusion to "Briar Rose" or "Sleeping Beauty."
4. A reference to fairy tales that pit a false bride against the heroine, or true bride.

false one? Then she will be put into a barrel stuck full of nails[5] and rolled downhill, endlessly, while he is sitting in yet another bridal bed, drinking champagne. She remembers the brand name, because she bought it herself. Champagne isn't the sort of finishing touch that would occur to Ed, though he enjoyed it enough at the time.

But outwardly Sally makes a joke of all this. "He doesn't know," she says to Marylynn, laughing a little, and they shake their heads. If it were them, they'd know, all right. Marylynn is in fact divorced, and she can list every single thing that went wrong, item by item. After doing this, she adds that her divorce was one of the best things that ever happened to her. "I was just a nothing before," she says. "It made me pull myself together."

Sally, looking across the kitchen table at Marylynn, has to agree that she is far from being a nothing now. She started out re-doing people's closets, and has worked that up into her own interior-design firm. She does the houses of the newly rich, those who lack ancestral furniture and the confidence to be shabby, and who wish their interiors to reflect a personal taste they do not in reality possess.

"What they want are mausoleums," Marylynn says, "or hotels," and she cheerfully supplies them. "Right down to the ash-trays. Imagine having someone else pick out your ash-trays for you."

By saying this, Marylynn lets Sally know that she's not including her in that category, though Sally did in fact hire her, at the very first, to help with a few details around the house. It was Marylynn who redesigned the wall of closets in the master bedroom and who found Sally's massive Chinese mahogany table, which cost her another seven hundred dollars to have stripped. But it turned out to be perfect, as Marylynn said it would. Now she's dug up a nineteenth-century keyhole desk, which both she and Sally know will be exactly right for the bay-windowed alcove off the living room. "Why do you need it?" Ed said in his puzzled way. "I thought you worked in your study." Sally admitted this, but said they could keep the telephone bills in it, which appeared to satisfy him. She knows exactly what she needs it for: she needs it to sit at, in something flowing, backlit by the morning sunlight, gracefully dashing off notes. She saw a 1940's advertisement for coffee like this once; and the husband was standing behind the chair, leaning over, with a worshipful expression on his face.

Marylynn is the kind of friend Sally does not have to explain any of this to, because it's assumed between them. Her intelligence is the kind Sally respects.

Marylynn is tall and elegant, and makes anything she is wearing seem fashionable. Her hair is prematurely grey and she leaves it

5. A punishment frequently meted out to fairy-tale villains.

that way. She goes in for loose blouses in cream-coloured silk, and eccentric scarves gathered from interesting shops and odd corners of the world, thrown carelessly around her neck and over one shoulder. (Sally has tried this toss in the mirror, but it doesn't work.) Marylynn has a large collection of unusual shoes; she says they're unusual because her feet are so big, but Sally knows better. Sally, who used to think of herself as pretty enough and now thinks of herself as doing quite well for her age, envies Marylynn her bone structure, which will serve her well when the inevitable happens.

Whenever Marylynn is coming to dinner, as she is today—she's bringing the desk, too—Sally takes especial care with her clothes and makeup. Marylynn, she knows, is her real audience for such things, since no changes she effects in herself seem to affect Ed one way or the other, or even to register with him. "You look fine to me" is all he says, no matter how she really looks. (But does she want him to see her more clearly, or not? Most likely not. If he did he would notice the incipient wrinkles, the small pouches of flesh that are not quite there yet, the network forming beneath her eyes. It's better as it is.)

Sally has repeated this remark of Ed's to Marylynn, adding that he said it the day the Jacuzzi overflowed because the smoke alarm went off, because an English muffin she was heating to eat in the bathtub got stuck in the toaster, and she had to spend an hour putting down newspaper and mopping up, and only had half an hour to dress for a dinner they were going to. "Really I looked like the wrath of God," said Sally. These days she finds herself repeating to Marylynn many of the things Ed says: the stupid things. Marylynn is the only one of Sally's friends she has confided in to this extent.

"Ed is cute as a button," Marylynn said. "In fact, he's just like a button: he's so bright and shiny. If he were mine, I'd get him bronzed and keep him on the mantelpiece."

Marylynn is even better than Sally at concocting formulations for Ed's particular brand of stupidity, which can irritate Sally: coming from herself, this sort of comment appears to her indulgent and loving, but from Marylynn it borders on the patronizing. So then she sticks up for Ed, who is by no means stupid about everything. When you narrow it down, there's only one area of life he's hopeless about. The rest of the time he's intelligent enough, some even say brilliant: otherwise, how could he be so successful?

Ed is a heart man, one of the best, and the irony of this is not lost on Sally: who could possibly know less about the workings of hearts, real hearts, the kind symbolized by red satin surrounded by lace and topped by pink bows, than Ed? Hearts with arrows in them. At the

same time, the fact that he's a heart man is a large part of his allure.
Women corner him on sofas, trap him in bay-windows at cocktail
parties, mutter to him in confidential voices at dinner parties. They
behave this way right in front of Sally, under her very nose, as if she's
invisible, and Ed lets them do it. This would never happen if he were
in banking or construction.

As it is, everywhere he goes he is beset by sirens. They want him
to fix their hearts. Each of them seems to have a little something
wrong—a murmur, a whisper. Or they faint a lot and want him to
tell them why. This is always what the conversations are about,
according to Ed, and Sally believes it. Once she'd wanted it herself,
that mirage. What had she invented for him, in the beginning? A
heavy heart, that beat too hard after meals. And he'd been so sweet,
looking at her with those stunned brown eyes of his, as if her heart
were the genuine topic, listening to her gravely as if he'd never heard
any of this twaddle before, advising her to drink less coffee. And
she'd felt such triumph, to have carried off her imposture, pried out
of him that miniscule token of concern.

Thinking back on this incident makes her uneasy, now that she's
seen her own performance repeated so many times, including the
hand placed lightly on the heart, to call attention of course to the
breasts. Some of these women have been within inches of getting
Ed to put his head down on their chests, right there in Sally's living room. Watching all this out of the corners of her eyes while
serving the liqueurs, Sally feels the Aztec rise within her. *Trouble
with your heart? Get it removed*, she thinks. *Then you'll have no
more problems.*

Sometimes Sally worries that she's a nothing, the way Marylynn
was before she got a divorce and a job. But Sally isn't a nothing;
therefore, she doesn't need a divorce to stop being one. And she's
always had a job of some sort; in fact she has one now. Luckily Ed
has no objection; he doesn't have much of an objection to anything
she does.

Her job is supposed to be full-time, but in effect it's part-time,
because Sally can take a lot of the work away and do it at home, and,
as she says, with one arm tied behind her back. When Sally is being
ornery, when she's playing the dull wife of a fascinating heart man—
she does this with people she can't be bothered with—she says she
works in a bank, nothing important. Then she watches their eyes
dismiss her. When, on the other hand, she's trying to impress, she
says she's in P.R. In reality she runs the in-house organ for a trust
company, a medium-sized one. This is a thin magazine, nicely
printed, which is supposed to make the employees feel that some of
the boys are doing worthwhile things out there and are human

beings as well. It's still the boys, though the few women in anything resembling key positions are wheeled out regularly, bloused and suited and smiling brightly, with what they hope will come across as confidence rather than aggression.

This is the latest in a string of such jobs Sally has held over the years: comfortable enough jobs that engage only half of her cogs and wheels, and that end up leading nowhere. Technically she's second-in-command: over her is a man who wasn't working out in manage-ment, but who couldn't be fired because his wife was related to the chairman of the board. He goes out for long alcoholic lunches and plays a lot of golf, and Sally runs the show. This man gets the offi-cial credit for everything Sally does right, but the senior executives in the company take Sally aside when no one is looking and tell her what a great gal she is and what a whiz she is at holding up her end.

The real pay-off for Sally, though, is that her boss provides her with an endless supply of anecdotes. She dines out on stories about his dimwittedness and pomposity, his lobotomized suggestions about what the two of them should cook up for the magazine; *the organ*, as she says he always calls it. "He says we need some fresh blood to perk up the organ," Sally says, and the heart men grin at her. "He actually said that?" Talking like this about her boss would be reckless—you never know what might get back to him, with the world as small as it is—if Sally were afraid of losing her job, but she isn't. There's an unspoken agreement between her and this man: they both know that if she goes, he goes, because who else would put up with him? Sally might angle for his job, if she were stupid enough to disregard his family connections, if she coveted the trappings of power. But she's just fine where she is. Jokingly, she says she's reached her level of incompetence. She says she suffers from fear of success.

Her boss is white-haired, slender, and tanned, and looks like an English gin ad. Despite his vapidity he's outwardly distinguished, she allows him that. In truth she pampers him outrageously, indulges him, covers up for him at every turn, though she stops short of behav-ing like a secretary: she doesn't bring him coffee. They both have a secretary who does that anyway. The one time he made a pass at her, when he came in from lunch visibly reeling, Sally was kind about it.

Occasionally, though not often, Sally has to travel in connection with her job. She's sent off to places like Edmonton, where they have a branch. She interviews the boys at the middle and senior levels; they have lunch, and the boys talk about ups and downs in oil or the slump in the real-estate market. Then she gets taken on tours of shopping plazas under construction. It's always windy, and grit blows into her face. She comes back to home base and writes a piece on the youthfulness and vitality of the West.

She teases Ed, while she packs, saying she's going off for a ren-
dezvous with a dashing financier or two. Ed isn't threatened; he tells
her to enjoy herself, and she hugs him and tells him how much she
will miss him. He's so dumb it doesn't occur to him she might not
be joking. In point of fact, it would have been quite possible for Sally
to have had an affair, or at least a one- or two-night stand, on several of these occasions: she knows when those chalk lines are being
drawn, when she's being dared to step over them. But she isn't interested in having an affair with anyone but Ed.

She doesn't eat much on the planes; she doesn't like the food. But
on the return trip, she invariably saves the pre-packaged parts of the
meal, the cheese in its plastic wrap, the miniature chocolate bar,
the bag of pretzels. She ferrets them away in her purse. She thinks
of them as supplies, that she may need if she gets stuck in a strange
airport, if they have to change course because of snow or fog, for
instance. All kinds of things could happen, although they never have.
When she gets home she takes the things from her purse and throws
them out.

Outside the window Ed straightens up and wipes his earth-smeared
hands down the sides of his pants. He begins to turn, and Sally
moves back from the window so he won't see that she's watching. She
doesn't like it to be too obvious. She shifts her attention to the sauce:
it's in the second stage of a *sauce suprême*, which will make all the
difference to the chicken. When Sally was learning this sauce, her
cooking instructor quoted one of the great chefs, to the effect that
the chicken was merely a canvas. He meant as in painting, but Sally,
in an undertone to the woman next to her, turned it around. "Mine's
canvas anyway, sauce or no sauce," or words to that effect.

Gourmet cooking was the third night course Sally has taken. At the
moment she's on her fifth, which is called *Forms of Narrative Fiction*.
It's half reading and half writing assignments—the instructor doesn't
believe you can understand an art form without at least trying it
yourself—and Sally purports to be enjoying it. She tells her friends
she takes night courses to keep her brain from atrophying, and her
friends find this amusing: whatever else may become of Sally's brain,
they say, they don't see atrophying as an option. Sally knows better,
but in any case there's always room for improvement. She may have
begun taking the courses in the belief that this would make her more
interesting to Ed, but she soon gave up on that idea: she appears to be
neither more nor less interesting to Ed now than she was before.

Most of the food for tonight is already made. Sally tries to be well
organized: the overflowing Jacuzzi was an aberration. The cold water-
cress soup with walnuts is chilling in the refrigerator, the chocolate
mousse ditto. Ed, being Ed, prefers meatloaf to sweetbreads with pine

nuts, butterscotch pudding made from a package to chestnut purée topped with whipped cream. (Sally burnt her fingers peeling the chestnuts. She couldn't do it the easy way and buy it tinned.) Sally says Ed's preference for this type of food comes from being pre-programmed by hospital cafeterias when he was younger: show him a burned sausage and a scoop of instant mashed potatoes and he salivates. So it's only for company that she can unfurl her *boeuf en daube* and her salmon *en papillote*,[6] spread them forth to be savoured and praised.

What she likes best about these dinners though is setting the table, deciding who will sit where and, when she's feeling mischievous, even what they are likely to say. Then she can sit and listen to them say it. Occasionally she prompts a little.

Tonight will not be very challenging, since it's only the heart men and their wives, and Marylynn, whom Sally hopes will dilute them. The heart men are forbidden to talk shop at Sally's dinner table, but they do it anyway. "Not what you really want to listen to while you're eating," says Sally. "All those tubes and valves." Privately she thinks they're a conceited lot, all except Ed. She can't resist needling them from time to time.

"I mean," she said to one of the leading surgeons, "basically it's just an exalted form of dress-making, don't you think?"

"Come again?" said the surgeon, smiling. The heart men think Sally is one hell of a tease.

"It's really just cutting and sewing, isn't it?" Sally murmured. The surgeon laughed.

"There's more to it than that," Ed said, unexpectedly, solemnly.

"What more, Ed?" said the surgeon. "You could say there's a lot of embroidery, but that's in the billing." He chuckled at himself.

Sally held her breath. She could hear Ed's verbal thought processes lurching into gear. He was delectable.

"Good judgement," Ed said. His earnestness hit the table like a wet fish. The surgeon hastily downed his wine.

Sally smiled. This was supposed to be a reprimand to her, she knew, for not taking things seriously enough. *Oh, come on, Ed,* she could say. But she knows also, most of the time, when to keep her trap shut. She should have a light-up JOKE sign on her forehead, so Ed would be able to tell the difference.

The heart men do well. Most of them appear to be doing better than Ed, but that's only because they have, on the whole, more expensive tastes and fewer wives. Sally can calculate these things and she figures Ed is about par.

6. Baked in paper. *"Boeuf en daube"*: braised beef.

These days there's much talk about advanced technologies, which Sally tries to keep up on, since they interest Ed. A few years ago the heart men got themselves a new facility. Ed was so revved up that he told Sally about it, which was unusual for him. A week later Sally said she would drop by the hospital at the end of the day and pick Ed up and take him out for dinner; she didn't feel like cooking, she said. Really she wanted to check out the facility; she likes to check out anything that causes the line on Ed's excitement chart to move above level.

At first Ed said he was tired, that when the day came to an end he didn't want to prolong it. But Sally wheedled and was respectful, and finally Ed took her to see his new gizmo. It was in a cramped, darkened room with an examining table in it. The thing itself looked like a television screen hooked up to some complicated hardware. Ed said that they could wire a patient up and bounce sound waves off the heart and pick up the echoes, and they would get a picture on the screen, an actual picture, of the heart in motion. It was a thousand times better than an electrocardiogram, he said: they could see the faults, the thickenings and cloggings, much more clearly.

"Colour?" said Sally.

"Black and white," said Ed.

Then Sally was possessed by a desire to see her own heart, in motion, in black and white, on the screen. At the dentist's she always wants to see the X-rays of her teeth, too, solid and glittering in her cloudy head. "Do it," she said, "I want to see how it works," and though this was the kind of thing Ed would ordinarily evade or tell her she was being silly about, he didn't need much persuading. He was fascinated by the thing himself, and he wanted to show it off.

He checked to make sure there was nobody real booked for the room. Then he told Sally to slip out of her clothes, the top half, brassière and all. He gave her a paper gown and turned his back modestly while she slipped it on, as if he didn't see her body every night of the week. He attached electrodes to her, the ankles and one wrist, and turned a switch and fiddled with the dials. Really a technician was supposed to do this, he told her, but he knew how to run the machine himself. He was good with small appliances.

Sally lay prone on the table, feeling strangely naked. "What do I do?" she said.

"Just lie there," said Ed. He came over to her and tore a hole in the paper gown, above her left breast. Then he started running a probe over her skin. It was wet and slippery and cold, and felt like the roller on a roll-on deodorant.

"There," he said, and Sally turned her head. On the screen was a large grey object, like a giant fig, paler in the middle, a dark line running down the centre. The sides moved in and out; two wings fluttered in it, like an uncertain moth's.

"That's it?" said Sally dubiously. Her heart looked so insubstantial, like a bag of gelatin, something that would melt, fade, disintegrate, if you squeezed it even a little.

Ed moved the probe, and they looked at the heart from the bottom, then the top. Then he stopped the frame, then changed it from a positive to a negative image. Sally began to shiver.

"That's wonderful," she said. He seemed so distant, absorbed in his machine, taking the measure of her heart, which was beating over there all by itself, detached from her, exposed and under his control.

Ed unwired her and she put on her clothes again, neutrally, as if he were actually a doctor. Nevertheless this transaction, this whole room, was sexual in a way she didn't quite understand; it was clearly a dangerous place. It was like a massage parlour, only for women. Put a batch of women in there with Ed and they would never want to come out. They'd want to stay in there while he ran his probe over their wet skins and pointed out to them the defects of their beating hearts.

"Thank you," said Sally.

Sally hears the back door open and close. She feels Ed approaching, coming through the passages of the house towards her, like a small wind or a ball of static electricity. The hair stands up on her arms. Sometimes he makes her so happy she thinks she's about to burst; other times she thinks she's about to burst anyway.

He comes into the kitchen, and she pretends not to notice. He puts his arms around her from behind, kisses her on the neck. She leans back, pressing herself into him. What they should do now is go into the bedroom (or even the living room, even the den) and make love, but it wouldn't occur to Ed to make love in the middle of the day. Sally often comes across articles in magazines about how to improve your sex life, which leave her feeling disappointed, or reminiscent: Ed is not Sally's first and only man. But she knows she shouldn't expect too much of Ed. If Ed were more experimental, more interested in variety, he would be a different kind of man altogether: slyer, more devious, more observant, harder to deal with.

As it is, Ed makes love in the same way, time after time, each movement following the others in an exact order. But it seems to satisfy him. Of course it satisfies him: you can always tell when men are satisfied. It's Sally who lies awake, afterwards, watching the pictures unroll across her closed eyes.

Sally steps away from Ed, smiles at him. "How did you make out with the women today?" she says.

"What women?" says Ed absently, going towards the sink. He knows what women.

"The ones out there, hiding in the forsythia," says Sally. "I counted at least ten. They were just waiting for a chance."

She teases him frequently about these troops of women, which follow him around everywhere, which are invisible to Ed but which she can see as plain as day.

"I bet they hang around outside the front door of the hospital," she will say, "just waiting till you come out. I bet they hide in the linen closets and jump out at you from behind, and then pretend to be lost so you'll take them by the short cut. It's the white coat that does it. None of those women can resist the white coats. They've been conditioned by Young Doctor Kildare."[7]

"Don't be silly," says Ed today, with equanimity. Is he blushing, is he embarrassed? Sally examines his face closely, like a geologist with an aerial photograph, looking for telltale signs of mineral treasure: markings, bumps, hollows. Everything about Ed means something, though it's difficult at times to say what.

Now he's washing his hands at the sink, to get the earth off. In a minute he'll wipe them on the dishtowel instead of using the hand towel the way he's supposed to. Is that complacency, in the back turned to her? Maybe there really are these hordes of women, even though she's made them up. Maybe they really do behave that way. His shoulders are slightly drawn up: is he shutting her out?

"I know what they want," she goes on. "They want to get into that little dark room of yours and climb up onto your table. They think you're delicious. They'll gobble you up. They'll chew you into tiny pieces. There won't be anything left of you at all, only a stethoscope and a couple of shoelaces."

Once Ed would have laughed at this, but today he doesn't. Maybe she's said it, or something like it, a few times too often. He smiles though, wipes his hands on the dishtowel, peers into the fridge. He likes to snack.

"There's some cold roast beef," Sally says, baffled.

Sally takes the sauce off the stove and sets it aside for later: she'll do the last steps just before serving. It's only two-thirty. Ed has disappeared into the cellar, where Sally knows he will be safe for a while. She goes into her study, which used to be one of the kids' bedrooms, and sits down at her desk. The room has never been completely redecorated: there's still a bed in it, and a dressing table with a blue flowered flounce Sally helped pick out, long before the kids went off to university: "flew the coop," as Ed puts it.

7. A physician in a television series of the 1960s.

Sally doesn't comment on the expression, though she would like to say that it wasn't the first coop they flew. Her house isn't even the real coop, since neither of the kids is hers. She'd hoped for a baby of her own when she married Ed, but she didn't want to force the issue. Ed didn't object to the idea, exactly, but he was neutral about it, and Sally got the feeling he'd had enough babies already. Anyway, the other two wives had babies, and look what happened to them. Since their actual fates have always been vague to Sally, she's free to imagine all kinds of things, from drug addiction to madness. Whatever it was resulted in Sally having to bring up their kids, at least from puberty onwards. The way it was presented by the first wife was that it was Ed's turn now. The second wife was more oblique: she said that the child wanted to spend some time with her father. Sally was left out of both these equations, as if the house wasn't a place she lived in, not really, so she couldn't be expected to have any opinion.

Considering everything, she hasn't done badly. She likes the kids and tries to be a friend to them, since she can hardly pretend to be a mother. She describes the three of them as having an easy relationship. Ed wasn't around much for the kids, but it's him they want approval from, not Sally; it's him they respect. Sally is more like a confederate, helping them get what they want from Ed.

When the kids were younger, Sally used to play Monopoly with them, up at the summer place in Muskoka Ed owned then but has since sold. Ed would play too, on his vacations and on the weekends when he could make it up. These games would all proceed along the same lines. Sally would have an initial run of luck and would buy up everything she had a chance at. She didn't care whether it was classy real estate, like Boardwalk or Park Place, or those dingy little houses on the other side of the tracks; she would even buy train stations, which the kids would pass over, preferring to save their cash reserves for better investments. Ed, on the other hand, would plod along, getting a little here, a little there. Then, when Sally was feeling flush, she would blow her money on next-to-useless luxuries such as the electric light company; and when the kids started to lose, as they invariably did, Sally would lend them money at cheap rates or trade them things of her own, at a loss. Why not? She could afford it.

Ed meanwhile would be hedging his bets, building up blocks of property, sticking houses and hotels on them. He preferred the middle range, respectable streets but not flashy. Sally would land on his spaces and have to shell out hard cash. Ed never offered deals, and never accepted them. He played a lone game, and won more often than not. Then Sally would feel thwarted. She would say she guessed she lacked the killer instinct; or she would say that for herself she didn't care, because after all it was only a game, but he ought to allow the kids to win, once in a while. Ed couldn't grasp the concept of allowing other people to win. He said it would be condescending towards the children, and anyway you couldn't arrange to have a dice game turn out the way you wanted it to, since it was partly a matter of chance. If it was chance, Sally would think, why were the games so similar to one another? At the end, there would be Ed, counting up his paper cash, sorting it out into piles of bills of varying denominations, and Sally, her vast holdings dwindled to a few shoddy blocks on Baltic Avenue, doomed to foreclosure: extravagant, generous, bankrupt.

On these nights, after the kids were asleep, Sally would have two or three more rye-and-gingers than were good for her. Ed would go to bed early—winning made him satisfied and drowsy—and Sally would ramble about the house or read the endings of murder mysteries she had already read once before, and finally she would slip into bed and wake Ed up and stroke him into arousal, seeking comfort.

Sally has almost forgotten these games. Right now the kids are receding, fading like old ink; Ed on the contrary looms larger and larger, the outlines around him darkening. He's constantly developing, like a Polaroid print, new colours emerging, but the result remains the same: Ed is a surface, one she has trouble getting beneath.

"Explore your inner world," said Sally's instructor in *Forms of Narrative Fiction,* a middle-aged woman of scant fame who goes in for astrology and the Tarot pack and writes short stories, which are not published in any of the magazines Sally reads. "Then there's your outer one," Sally said afterwards, to her friends. "For instance, she should really get something done about her hair." She made this trivial and mean remark because she's fed up with her inner world; she doesn't need to explore it. In her inner world is Ed, like a doll within a Russian wooden doll, and in Ed is Ed's inner world, which she can't get at.

She takes a crack at it anyway: Ed's inner world is a forest, which looks something like the bottom part of their ravine lot, but without the fence. He wanders around in there, among the trees, not heading in any special direction. Every once in a while he comes upon a strange-looking plant, a sickly plant choked with weeds and briars. Ed kneels, clears a space around it, does some pruning, a little skillful snipping and cutting, props it up. The plant revives, flushes with health, sends out a grateful red blossom. Ed continues on his way. Or it may be a conked-out squirrel, which he restores with a drop from his flask of magic elixir. At set intervals an angel appears, bringing him food. It's always meatloaf. That's fine with Ed, who hardly notices what he eats, but the angel is getting tired of being an angel. Now Sally begins thinking about the angel: why are its wings frayed and dingy grey around the edges, why is it looking so withered and frantic? This is where all Sally's attempts to explore Ed's inner world end up.

She knows she thinks about Ed too much. She knows she should stop. She knows she shouldn't ask, "Do you still love me?" in the plaintive tone that sets even her own teeth on edge. All it achieves is that Ed shakes his head, as if not understanding why she would ask this, and pats her hand. "Sally, Sally," he says, and everything proceeds as usual; except for the dread that seeps into things, the most ordinary things, such as rearranging the chairs and changing the burnt-out light-bulbs. But what is it she's afraid of? She has what they call everything: Ed, their wonderful house on a ravine lot, something she's always wanted. (But the hill is jungly, and the house is made of ice. It's held together only by Sally, who sits in the middle of it, working on a puzzle.[8] The puzzle is Ed. If she should ever solve it, if she should ever fit the last cold splinter into place, the house will melt and flow away down the hill, and then . . .) It's a bad habit, fooling around with her head this way. It does no good. She knows that if she could quit she'd be happier. She ought to be able to: she's given up smoking.

She needs to concentrate her attention on other things. This is the real reason for the night courses, which she picks almost at random, to coincide with the evenings Ed isn't in. He has meetings, he's on the boards of charities, he has trouble saying no. She runs the courses past herself, mediaeval history, cooking, anthropology, hoping her mind will snag on something; she's even taken a course in geology, which was fascinating, she told her friends, all that magma. That's just it: everything is fascinating, but nothing enters her. She's always a star pupil, she does well on the exams and impresses the teachers, for which she despises them. She is familiar with her brightness, her techniques; she's surprised other people are still taken in by them.

Forms of Narrative Fiction started out the same way. Sally was full of good ideas, brimming with helpful suggestions. The workshop part of it was anyway just like a committee meeting, and Sally knew how to run those, from behind, without seeming to run them: she'd done it lots of times at work. Bertha, the instructor, told Sally she had a vivid imagination and a lot of untapped creative energy. "No wonder she never gets anywhere, with a name like Bertha," Sally said, while having coffee afterwards with two of the other night-coursers. "It goes with her outfits, though." (Bertha sports the macramé look, with health-food sandals and bulky-knit sweaters and hand-weave skirts that don't do a thing for her square figure, and too many Mexican rings on her hands, which she

8. Atwood is alluding here to "The Snow Queen" by Hans Christian Andersen.

doesn't wash often enough.) Bertha goes in for assignments, which she calls learning by doing. Sally likes assignments: she likes things that can be completed and then discarded, and for which she gets marks.

The first thing Bertha assigned was The Epic. They read *The Odyssey* (selected passages, in translation, with a plot summary of the rest); then they poked around in James Joyce's *Ulysses*, to see how Joyce had adapted the epic form to the modern-day novel. Bertha had them keep a Toronto notebook, in which they had to pick out various spots around town as the ports of call in *The Odyssey*, and say why they had chosen them. The notebooks were read out loud in class, and it was a scream to see who had chosen what for Hades. (The Mount Pleasant Cemetery, McDonald's, where, if you eat the forbidden food, you never get back to the land of the living, the University Club with its dead ancestral souls, and so forth.) Sally's was the hospital, of course; she had no difficulty with the trench filled with blood, and she put the ghosts in wheelchairs.

After that they did The Ballad, and read gruesome accounts of murders and betrayed love. Bertha played them tapes of wheezy old men singing traditionally, in the Doric mode, and assigned a newspaper scrapbook, in which you had to clip and paste up-to-the-minute equivalents. The *Sun* was the best newspaper for these. The fiction that turned out to go with this kind of plot was the kind Sally liked anyway, and she had no difficulty concocting a five-page murder mystery, complete with revenge.

But now they are on Folk Tales and the Oral Tradition, and Sally is having trouble. This time, Bertha wouldn't let them read anything. Instead she read to them, in a voice, Sally said, that was like a gravel truck and was not conducive to reverie. Since it was the Oral Tradition, they weren't even allowed to take notes; Bertha said the original hearers of these stories couldn't read, so the stories were memorized. "To recreate the atmosphere," said Bertha, "I should turn out the lights. These stories were always told at night." "To make them creepier?" someone offered. "No," said Bertha. "In the days, they worked." She didn't do that, though she did make them sit in a circle.

"You should have seen us," Sally said afterwards to Ed, "sitting in a circle, listening to fairy stories. It was just like kindergarten. Some of them even had their mouths open. I kept expecting her to say, 'If you need to go, put up your hand.'" She was meaning to be funny, to amuse Ed with this account of Bertha's eccentricity and the foolish appearance of the students, most of them middle-aged, sitting in a circle as if they had never grown up at all. She was also intending to belittle the course, just slightly. She always did this with her night courses, so Ed wouldn't get the idea there was anything in her life that was even remotely as important as he was. But Ed didn't seem to need this amusement or this belittlement. He took her information earnestly, gravely, as if Bertha's behaviour was, after all, only the procedure of a specialist. No one knew better than he did that the procedures of specialists often looked bizarre or incomprehensible to onlookers. "She probably has her reasons," was all he would say.

The first stories Bertha read them, for warm-ups ("No memorizing for *her*," said Sally), were about princes who got amnesia and forgot about their true loves and married girls their mothers had picked out for them. Then they had to be rescued, with the aid of magic. The stories didn't say what happened to the women the princes had already married, though Sally wondered about it. Then Bertha read them another story, and this time they were supposed to remember the features that stood out for them and write a five-page transposition, set in the present and cast in the realistic mode. ("In other words," said Bertha, "no real magic.") They couldn't use the Universal Narrator, however: they had done that in their Ballad assignment. This time they had to choose a point of view. It could be the point of view of anyone or anything in the story, but they were limited to one only. The story she was about to read, she said, was a variant of the Bluebeard motif, much earlier than Perrault's sentimental rewriting of it. In Perrault, said Bertha, the girl has to be rescued by her brothers; but in the earlier version things were quite otherwise.[9]

This is what Bertha read, as far as Sally can remember:

There were once three young sisters. One day a beggar with a large basket on his back came to the door and asked for some bread. The eldest sister brought him some, but no sooner had she touched him than she was compelled to jump into his basket, for the beggar was really a wizard in disguise. ("So much for United Appeal," Sally murmured. "She should have said, 'I gave at the office.'") The wizard carried her away to his house in the forest, which was large and richly furnished. "Here you will be happy with me, my darling," said the wizard, "for you will have everything your heart could desire."

This lasted for a few days. Then the wizard gave the girl an egg and a bunch of keys. "I must go away on a journey," he said, "and I am leaving the house in your charge. Preserve this egg for me, and carry it about with you everywhere; for a great misfortune will follow from its loss. The keys open every room in the house. You may go into each of them and enjoy what you find there, but do not go into the small room at the top of the house, on pain of death." The girl promised, and the wizard disappeared.

9. What follows is an abbreviated version of the Grimms' "Fitcher's Bird" (see p. 193).

At first the girl contented herself with exploring the rooms, which contained many treasures. But finally her curiosity would not let her alone. She sought out the smallest key, and, with beating heart, opened the little door at the top of the house. Inside it was a large basin full of blood, within which were the bodies of many women, which had been cut to pieces; nearby were a chopping block and an axe. In her horror, she let go of the egg which fell into the basin of blood. In vain did she try to wipe away the stain: every time she succeeded in removing it, back it would come.

The wizard returned, and in a stern voice asked for the egg and the keys. When he saw the egg, he knew at once she had disobeyed him and gone into the forbidden room. "Since you have gone into the room against my will," he said, "you shall go back into it against your own." Despite her pleas he threw her down, dragged her by the hair into the little room, hacked her into pieces and threw her body into the basin with the others.

Then he went for the second girl, who fared no better than her sister. But the third was clever and wily. As soon as the wizard had gone, she set the egg on a shelf, out of harm's way, and then went immediately and opened the forbidden door. Imagine her distress when she saw the cut-up bodies of her two beloved sisters; but she set the parts in order, and they joined together and her sisters stood up and moved, and were living and well. They embraced each other, and the third sister hid the other two in a cupboard.

When the wizard returned he at once asked for the egg. This time it was spotless. "You have passed the test," he said to the third sister. "You shall be my bride." ("And second prize," said Sally, to herself this time, "is *two* weeks in Niagara Falls.") The wizard no longer had any power over her, and had to do whatever she asked. There was more, about how the wizard met his come-uppance and was burned to death, but Sally already knew which features stood out for her.

At first she thought the most important thing in the story was the forbidden room. What would she put in the forbidden room, in her present-day realistic version? Certainly not chopped-up women. It wasn't that they were too unrealistic, but they were certainly too sick, as well as being too obvious. She wanted to do something more clever. She thought it might be a good idea to have the curious woman open the door and find nothing there at all, but after mulling it over she set this notion aside. It would leave her with the problem of why the wizard would have a forbidden room in which he kept nothing.

That was the way she was thinking right after she got the assignment, which was a full two weeks ago. So far she's written nothing. The great temptation is to cast herself in the role of the cunning heroine, but again it's too predictable. And Ed certainly isn't the wizard; he's nowhere near sinister enough. If Ed were the wizard, the room would contain a forest, some ailing plants and feeble squirrels, and Ed himself, fixing them up; but then, if it were Ed the room wouldn't even be locked, and there would be no story.

Now, as she sits at her desk, fiddling with her felt-tip pen, it comes to Sally that the intriguing thing about the story, the thing she should fasten on, is the egg. Why an egg? From the night course in Comparative Folklore she took four years ago, she remembers that the egg can be a fertility symbol, or a necessary object in African spells, or something the world hatched out of. Maybe in this story it's a symbol of virginity, and that is why the wizard requires it unbloodied. Women with dirty eggs get murdered, those with clean ones get married.

But this isn't useful either. The concept is so outmoded. Sally doesn't see how she can transpose it into real life without making it ridiculous, unless she sets the story in, for instance, an immigrant Portuguese family, and what would she know about that?

Sally opens the drawer of her desk and hunts around in it for her nail file. As she's doing this, she gets the brilliant idea of writing the story from the point of view of the egg. Other people will do the other things: the clever girl, the wizard, the two blundering sisters, who weren't smart enough to lie, and who will have problems afterwards, because of the thin red lines running all over their bodies, from where their parts joined together. But no one will think of the egg. How does it feel, to be the innocent and passive cause of so much misfortune?

(Ed isn't the Bluebeard: Ed is the egg. Ed Egg, blank and pristine and lovely. Stupid, too. Boiled, probably. Sally smiles fondly.)

But how can there be a story from the egg's point of view, if the egg is so closed and unaware? Sally ponders this, doodling on her pad of lined paper. Then she resumes the search for her nail file. Already it's time to begin getting ready for her dinner party. She can sleep on the problem of the egg and finish the assignment tomorrow, which is Sunday. It's due on Monday, but Sally's mother used to say she was a whiz at getting things done at the last minute.

After painting her nails with *Nuit Magique*,[1] Sally takes a bath, eating her habitual toasted English muffin while she lies in the tub. She begins to dress, dawdling; she has plenty of time. She hears Ed coming up out of the cellar; then she hears him in the bathroom, which he has entered from the hall door. Sally goes in through the other door, still in her slip. Ed is standing at the sink with his shirt off, shaving. On the weekends he leaves it until necessary, or until Sally tells him he's too scratchy.

---

1. Magic Night (French).

Sally slides her hands around his waist, nuzzling against his naked back. He has very smooth skin, for a man. Sally smiles to herself: she can't stop thinking of him as an egg.

"Mmm," says Ed. It could be appreciation, or the answer to a question Sally hasn't asked and he hasn't heard, or just an acknowledgement that she's there.

"Don't you ever wonder what I think about?" Sally says. She's said this more than once, in bed or at the dinner table, after dessert. She stands behind him, watching the swaths the razor cuts in the white of his face, looking at her own face reflected in the mirror, just the eyes visible above his naked shoulder. Ed, lathered, is Assyrian, sterner than usual; or a frost-covered Arctic explorer; or demi-human, a white-bearded forest mutant. He scrapes away at himself, methodically destroying the illusion.

"But I already know what you think about," says Ed.

"How?" Sally says, taken aback.

"You're always telling me," Ed says, with what might be resignation or sadness; or maybe this is only a simple statement of fact.

Sally is relieved. If that's all he's going on, she's safe.

Marylynn arrives half an hour early, her pearl-coloured Porsche leading two men in a delivery truck up the driveway. The men install the keyhole desk, while Marylynn supervises: it looks, in the alcove, exactly as Marylynn has said it would, and Sally is delighted. She sits at it to write the cheque. Then she and Marylynn go into the kitchen, where Sally is finishing up her sauce, and Sally pours them each a Kir. She's glad Marylynn is here: it will keep her from dithering, as she tends to do just before people arrive. Though it's only the heart men, she's still a bit nervous. Ed is more likely to notice when things are wrong than when they're exactly right.

Marylynn sits at the kitchen table, one arm draped over the chairback, her chin on the other hand; she's in soft grey which makes her hair look silver, and Sally feels once again how banal it is to have ordinary dark hair like her own, however well-cut, however shiny. It's the confidence she envies, the negligence. Marylynn doesn't seem to be trying at all, ever.

"Guess what Ed said today?" Sally says.

Marylynn leans further forward. "What?" she says, with the eagerness of one joining in a familiar game.

"He said, 'Some of these femininists go too far,'" Sally reports. "'*Femininists.*' Isn't that sweet?"

Marylynn holds the pause too long, and Sally has a sudden awful thought: maybe Marylynn thinks she's showing off, about Ed. Marylynn has always said she's not ready for another marriage yet; still,

Sally should watch herself, not rub her nose in it. But then Marylynn laughs indulgently, and Sally, relieved, joins in.

"Ed is unbelievable," says Marylynn. "You should pin his mittens to his sleeves when he goes out in the morning."

"He shouldn't be let out alone," says Sally.

"You should get him a seeing-eye dog," says Marylynn, "to bark at women."

"Why?" says Sally, still laughing but alert now, the cold beginning at the ends of her fingers. Maybe Marylynn knows something she doesn't; maybe the house is beginning to crumble, after all.

"Because he can't see them coming," says Marylynn. "That's what you're always telling me."

She sips her Kir; Sally stirs the sauce. "I bet he thinks I'm a feminist," says Marylynn.

"You?" says Sally. "Never." She would like to add that Ed has given no indication of thinking anything at all about Marylynn, but she doesn't. She doesn't want to take the risk of hurting her feelings.

The wives of the heart men admire Sally's sauce; the heart men talk shop, all except Walter Morly, who is good at by-passes. He's sitting beside Marylynn, and paying far too much attention to her for Sally's comfort. Mrs. Morly is at the other end of the table, not saying much of anything, which Marylynn appears not to notice. She keeps on talking to Walter about St. Lucia, where they've both been.

So after dinner, when Sally has herded them all into the living room for coffee and liqueurs, she takes Marylynn by the elbow. "Ed hasn't seen our desk yet," she says, "not up close. Take him away and give him your lecture on nineteenth-century antiques. Show him all the pigeon-holes. Ed loves pigeon-holes." Ed appears not to get this.

Marylynn knows exactly what Sally is up to. "Don't worry," she says, "I won't rape Dr. Morly; the poor creature would never survive the shock," but she allows herself to be shunted off to the side with Ed.

Sally moves from guest to guest, smiling, making sure everything is in order. Although she never looks directly, she's always conscious of Ed's presence in the room, any room; she perceives him as a shadow, a shape seen dimly at the edge of her field of vision, recognizable by the outline. She likes to know where he is, that's all. Some people are on their second cup of coffee. She walks towards the alcove: they must have finished with the desk by now.

But they haven't, they're still in there. Marylynn is bending forward, one hand on the veneer. Ed is standing too close to her, and as Sally comes up behind them she sees his left arm, held close to his side, the back of it pressed against Marylynn, her shimmering upper thigh, her ass to be exact. Marylynn does not move away.

It's a split second, and then Ed sees Sally and the hand is gone; there it is, on top of the desk, reaching for a liqueur glass.

"Marylynn needs more Tia Maria," he says. "I just told her that people who drink a little now and again live longer." His voice is even, his face is as level as ever, a flat plain with no signposts.

Marylynn laughs. "I once had a dentist who I swear drilled tiny holes in my teeth, so he could fix them later," she says.

Sally sees Ed's hand outstretched towards her, holding the empty glass. She takes it, smiling, and turns away. There's a roaring sound at the back of her head; blackness appears around the edges of the picture she is seeing, like a television screen going dead. She walks into the kitchen and puts her cheek against the refrigerator and her arms around it, as far as they will go. She remains that way, hugging it; it hums steadily, with a sound like comfort. After a while she lets go of it and touches her hair, and walks back into the living room with the filled glass.

Marylynn is over by the french doors, talking with Walter Morly. Ed is standing by himself, in front of the fireplace, one arm on the mantelpiece, his left hand out of sight in his pocket.

Sally goes to Marylynn, hands her the glass. "Is that enough?" she says.

Marylynn is unchanged. "Thanks, Sally," she says, and goes on listening to Walter, who has dragged out his usual piece of mischief: some day, when they've perfected it, he says, all hearts will be plastic, and this will be a vast improvement on the current model. It's an obscure form of flirtation. Marylynn winks at Sally, to show that she knows he's tedious. Sally, after a pause, winks back.

She looks over at Ed, who is staring off into space, like a robot which has been parked and switched off. Now she isn't sure whether she really saw what she thought she saw. Even if she did, what does it mean? Maybe it's just that Ed, in a wayward intoxicated moment, put his hand on the nearest buttock, and Marylynn refrained from a shriek or a flinch out of good breeding or the desire not to offend him. Things like this have happened to Sally.

Or it could mean something more sinister: a familiarity between them, an understanding. If this is it, Sally has been wrong about Ed, for years, forever. Her version of Ed is not something she's perceived but something that's been perpetrated on her, by Ed himself, for reasons of his own. Possibly Ed is not stupid. Possibly he's enormously clever. She thinks of moment after moment when this cleverness, this cunning, would have shown itself if it were there, but didn't. She has watched him so carefully. She remembers playing Pick Up Sticks, with the kids, Ed's kids, years ago: how if you moved one stick in the tangle, even slightly, everything else moved also.

She won't say anything to him. She can't say anything: she can't afford to be wrong, or to be right either. She goes back into the kitchen and begins to scrape the plates. This is unlike her—usually she sticks right with the party until it's over—and after a while Ed wanders out. He stands silently, watching her. Sally concentrates on the scraping: dollops of *sauce suprême* slide into the plastic bag, shreds of lettuce, rice, congealed and lumpy. What is left of her afternoon.

"What are you doing out here?" Ed asks at last.

"Scraping the plates," Sally says, cheerful, neutral. "I just thought I'd get a head start on tidying up."

"Leave it," says Ed. "The woman can do that in the morning." That's how he refers to Mrs. Rudge, although she's been with them for three years now: *the woman*. And Mrs. Bird before her, as though they are interchangeable. This has never bothered Sally before. "Go on out there and have a good time."

Sally puts down the spatula, wipes her hands on the hand towel, puts her arms around him, holds on tighter than she should. Ed pats her shoulder. "What's up?" he says; then, "Sally, Sally." If she looks up, she will see him shaking his head a little, as if he doesn't know what to do about her. She doesn't look up.

Ed has gone to bed. Sally roams the house, fidgeting with the debris left by the party. She collects empty glasses, picks up peanuts from the rug. After a while she realizes that she's down on her knees, looking under a chair, and she's forgotten what for. She goes upstairs, creams off her make-up, does her teeth, undresses in the darkened bedroom and slides into bed beside Ed, who is breathing deeply as if asleep. *As if.*

Sally lies in bed with her eyes closed. What she sees is her own heart, in black and white, beating with that insubstantial moth-like flutter, a ghostly heart, torn out of her and floating in space, an animated valentine with no colour. It will go on and on forever; she has no control over it. But now she's seeing the egg, which is not small and cold and white and inert but larger than a real egg and golden pink, resting in a nest of brambles, glowing softly as though there's something red and hot inside it. It's almost pulsing; Sally is afraid of it. As she looks it darkens: rose-red, crimson. This is something the story left out, Sally thinks: the egg is alive, and one day it will hatch. But what will come out of it?

EDNA ST. VINCENT MILLAY

Bluebeard[†]

This door you might not open, and you did;
So enter now, and see for what slight thing
You are betrayed. . . . Here is no treasure hid,
No cauldron, no clear crystal mirroring
The sought-for truth, no heads of women slain   5
For greed like yours, no writhings of distress,
But only what you see. . . . Look yet again—
An empty room, cobwebbed and comfortless.
Yet this alone out of my life I kept
Unto myself, lest any know me quite;   10
And you did so profane me when you crept
Unto the threshold of this room to-night
That I must never more behold your face.
This now is yours. I seek another place.

† From Edna St. Vincent Millay, *Renascence and Other Poems* (New York: Mitchell Kennerley, 1917), p. 73.

INTRODUCTION: Tricksters

In real life, every unhappy family may be unhappy in its own way, but in fairy tales unhappy families are all very much alike. Children square off against evil stepmothers and contend with cowardly fathers. Lacking any promise at all, they are called blockheads and dummies and must prove their mettle by leaving home, conquering monsters, and looting their homes. The child protagonists of fairy tales do battle with dark forces, but, more important, they begin as victims of hostile powers at home.

It may well be that the harsh social realities of a past era, when life was nasty, brutish, and short, account for some of the cruelty found in fairy tales. But fantasy, more than fact, seems to serve as the basis for that vast class of stories in which the central figure is a victimized innocent—abandoned by parents in the woods, sent out on the road with little more than a crust of bread or a few pennies, or subjected to constant humiliation at home.

Magic tales concerned with harsh family conflicts typically take place in a domain where the supernatural is accepted as part and parcel of everyday reality. The appearance of witches, gnomes, or ogres may arouse fear, dread, or curiosity, but it never evokes the slightest degree of astonishment. Fairy-tale characters rarely marvel at the marvelous, and instead embark on adventures taking them from the drab world of everyday reality—a place of suffering, deficiency, and lack—to a shining new reality. They are the underdogs who turn the tables on their oppressors and establish, out of the least promising materials imaginable, a new social order characterized by measured abundance and amiable good will.

Food—its presence and its absence—shapes the world of fairy tales in profound ways, particularly when the protagonists are young, vulnerable, and dependent on parental protections. It is not at all uncommon for a peasant hero, faced with three wishes, to ask first for a plate of meat and potatoes or to be so distracted by hunger that he yearns out loud for a sausage while contemplating the limitless possibilities before him. "What shall I command?" asks the hero of a Greek tale when told he can have anything he wants. Without a moment's hesitation, he responds by asking for "Food to eat!"[1] Wish-fulfillment in fairy tales often has more to do with the stomach than with the heart. As Robert Darnton has pointed out in his study of the fairy tale's origins in an adult peasant culture, "To eat one's fill, eat until the exhaustion of the appetite (*manger à sa faim*), was the principal pleasure that the peasants dangled before their imaginations, and one that they rarely realized in their lives."[2] The same could be said about small children. While many folktales take us into the rugged and often brutal world of peasant life, where survival depends on getting your next meal, fairy tales with child protagonists often take us squarely into the household, where everyone seems to be anxious, not only about what's for dinner but more important about who's for dinner. The peasants of folktales may have to worry about famines, but children in fairy tales live perpetually under the double threat of starvation and cannibalism.

"I've got to kill you so that I can have something to eat!" a woman cries out in desperation to her two daughters in the Grimms' story "The Children of Famine." Happily, this tale cannot be found between the covers of most standard editions of the Grimms' *Nursery and Household Tales*, but that it was ever included at all is telling, for it makes clear that the threat of being devoured was not seen as arising from supernatural monsters alone. The sheer number of cannibalistic fiends in fairy tales is impressive. Giants, ogres, stepmothers, cooks, witches, and mothers-in-law all seem driven by a voracious appetite for human fare, for the flesh and blood (in some cases the liver and lungs will do) of the weak and vulnerable. The victims, both potential and real, are often children: a boy is chopped up and cooked into a stew eagerly devoured by his father ("The Juniper Tree"), siblings are served up to their grandmother in a sauce Robert (Perrault's "Sleeping Beauty in the Wood"), and a child is fattened up for a feast of human flesh ("Hansel and Gretel").

Like many fairy tales, the Grimms' "Hansel and Gretel" is set in a time of famine. While the parents in Perrault's "Little Thumbling" take their children into the woods because they cannot bear to see them starve to death, the stepmother of Hansel and Gretel is driven to abandon the children by brutish self-interest. She urges her husband to lead the children deep into the forest and is glad to be "rid of them" (p. 236), for their needs jeopardize her own survival. A look at the version of "Hansel and Gretel" first recorded by the Grimms reveals that the children's cruel stepmother was in fact

1. "The Grateful Animals and the Talisman," in *Modern Greek Folktales*, comp. and trans. R. M. Dawkins (Oxford: Clarendon, 1953), p. 42.
2. Robert Darnton, "Peasants Tell Tales: The Meaning of Mother Goose," in *The Great Cat Massacre and Other Episodes in French Cultural History* (New York: Random House, Vintage, 1985), p. 34.

a creation of Wilhelm Grimm's fantasy. The tale, as the brothers first heard it, featured a biological mother who conspires with her husband to abandon the children. To be sure, Wilhelm Grimm may have made the change in order to align the tale with the realities of nineteenth-century family life, but more likely, he transformed the mother into a stepmother simply because he could not bear to pass on stories about mothers so intent on surviving a famine that they are willing to sacrifice their own children.

The villainous stepmother in "Hansel and Gretel" reemerges in the woods as a monster equipped with powers far more formidable than those she exercised at home. In the woods, the children are no longer pitted against a hostile, human adversary, but locked in combat with a superhuman opponent armed with daunting powers. Just what is at stake in the conflict between children and witch?

Few fairy tales take us as deeply into the woods as "Hansel and Gretel." Its forests are compounded of dread and desire, offering a double thrill as the children face down the seductive terrors of the witch's house. The children's efforts to keep themselves alive, in the midst of a struggle for survival, have not earned them immunity to criticism. Bruno Bettelheim famously described them as victims of anxious fantasies: "Hansel and Gretel are convinced that their parents plan to starve them to death!" Regression and denial, he asserted, are the two strategies the children use to solve their problems. Carried away by their "oral craving" and "cannibalistic inclinations," they give in to "untamed id impulses, as symbolized by their uncontrolled voraciousness."[3] Moving seamlessly from manifest content to latent meaning, Bettelheim reads the tale as a Freudian allegory about children who project all their unruly desires and fears on innocent adults. The cruel stepmother at home and the cannibalistic witch in the woods are nothing more than phantoms of the children's imaginations and projections of their own desires.[4]

The two children facing down the witch can, however, also be seen as models of heroic behavior, learning, step by step, how to survive and find a way out of the woods. Linked with the classic trickster figures of folklore and mythology, they are driven by hunger and loss to improvise, to use deceit, and to discover a range of strategies

3. Bruno Bettelheim, *The Uses of Enchantment: The Meaning and Importance of Fairy Tales* (New York: Knopf, 1976), p. 162.
4. Anne Leblans argues that the children are "starved" and "cannot resist the temptation to eat from the gingerbread house. . . . What would be more natural than that she would do to them what they do to her?" She too sees the children as succumbing to projection in order to free themselves from dependency on the mother. She draws a number of interesting parallels between the children's destruction of the witch and the Grimms' own disavowal of the feminine oral storytelling tradition from which they culled the tales in their collection. See "Anthropology and the German Enlightenment: Perspectives on Humanity," *Bucknell Review* 38 (1995): 76–100.

for survival. Hansel and Gretel may not appear to be capable of managing the weight-bearing duties of the mythical trickster, but in the
swift narrative strokes used to draw their characters, it is not difficult
to identify trickster's uncanny ability to develop creative intelligence
in times of famine. More important, like trickster figures, Hansel
and Gretel enact the paradox that spying, eavesdropping, mimick-
ing, telling lies, and challenging property boundaries can not only
enable survival but also move them along the path toward acquir-
ing adult agency. If Hansel takes the lead in the first part of the
story, Gretel comes out from behind to join him in the use of cunning to defeat the witch. Hansel substitutes a bone for his finger,
and Gretel cleverly asks the witch to model how to climb into the
oven. Later, Gretel chants words that summon a duck to help the
two return home. The children's strategies for survival begin with
precocious listening; shade into duplicity; and end with a deadly
ruse, a clever theft, and the use of art and poetry.

That ill will and evil are so often personified as adult female figures in fairy tales raises some weighty questions that challenge the
notion of fairy tales as therapeutic reading for children. However
satisfying the tales may seem from a child's point of view, however
much they may map developmental paths endorsed by orthodox
Freudians, they still perpetuate strangely inappropriate notions
about what it means to live happily ever after. In this tight micro-
drama of a dysfunctional family, Hansel and Gretel may save themselves by using their wits and learning how to do things with words,
but they do so only after eradicating the witch in the woods and
eliminating the stepmother at home.

In "The Juniper Tree," a tale that can be seen as presenting the
male counterpart to the female developmental trajectory mapped out
in "Snow White," the stepmother is also a troublemaker *par excellence*, stirring things up and unsettling the family in an unspeak-
ably radical fashion. At the end of the Grimms' version of the tale,
she gets into real trouble for her wicked ways: "*bam!* the bird dropped
the millstone on her head and crushed her to death" (p. 252). As in
"Hansel and Gretel," happily ever after comes in the form of a new
family constellation: the children are reunited with their father in a
household without a maternal presence.

With its lurid descriptions of decapitation and cannibalism, "The
Juniper Tree" (also known as "My Mother Slew Me; My Father Ate
Me" [ATU 720]) is probably the most shocking of all fairy tales. In
most versions, the central character is a boy, yet occasionally, as in
the British story "The Rose-Tree" (collected by Joseph Jacobs), a girl
undergoes the transformation into a bird. The scenes of the boy's
beheading by the mother and consumption by the father have not

prevented P. L. Travers from referring to the tale as "beautiful,"[5] nor have they deterred J. R. R. Tolkien from describing it as a story of "beauty and horror" with an "exquisite and tragic beginning."[6] The "beauty" of the story probably turns less on its aesthetic appeal than on its engagement with cultural anxieties that fascinate us in their evocation of sheer dread. In the stepmother, we have a figure who represents maternal power run mad, an incarnation of a natural force so cruel and inexorable that it heightens our own sense of weakness and helplessness. In the Grimms' version, the boy is transformed back to human form and reunited with his father and sister to live in a motherless household. But in some versions, as in the Scottish "Pippety Pew," the boy remains a bird while "the goodman and his daughter lived happy and died happy."[7] In a version of the story that migrated to the U.S. South and was collected by a professor of romance languages at Tulane University, the mother of twenty-five children decides to get through hard times by cooking up her children, one by one, so that her husband will not starve. His enraged reaction leads to the same desire for revenge enacted in European fairy tales.

Fathers and father figures do not always fare as well as they do in "Hansel and Gretel," "The Juniper Tree," and "The Rose-Tree." Who can forget the downfall of the ogres in British folklore who "eat little children" and the defeat of the giants who hunt down diminutive boys in French folklore? Many of the underdogs who battle monsters belong to a genealogy that includes David slaying Goliath and Odysseus defeating the Cyclops. Using brains because they lack brawn, these diminutive heroes outsmart their antagonists and triumphantly return home to their impoverished parent(s) with treasure in the form of magical artifacts, gold, and jewels.

Little Thumbling, in the tale of that title, is one of seven boys abandoned in a shockingly matter-of-fact fashion by parents who have too many mouths to feed. A "sickly" child, he is seen as stupid and blamed for anything that goes wrong. Thumbling may not speak a word, but he listens "carefully" to everything and learns quickly. From the ogre's wife, who fools her husband into thinking that the scent of fresh meat is nothing more than the smell of a roasting calf, Thumbling learns how to deceive through substitution. Replacing the crowns worn by the ogre's daughters with the caps worn by his brothers, he engineers the murder of the girls and the rescue of the boys. This is a fairy tale that self-reflexively celebrates the power of

---

5. P. L. Travers, "The Black Sheep," in *What the Bee Knows: Reflections on Myth, Symbol, and Story* (Wellingborough, Northamptonshire: Aquarian, 1989), p. 232.
6. J. R. R. Tolkien, "On Fairy-Stories," in *The Tolkien Reader* (New York: Balantine, 1966), p. 31.
7. Norah Montgomerie and William Montgomerie, comps., "Pippety Pew," in *The Well at the World's End: Folk Tales of Scotland* (London: Bodley Head, 1956), p. 209.

lying and stealing (what are fairy tales, after all, but lies that per-petually infringe on intellectual property rights?) and ends with the triumph of a trickster figure who continues his stealth operations as spy to the king and courier to the wealthy.

Jack of Beanstalk fame has higher aspirations than his French counterpart. The beanstalk, like the biblical Jacob's ladder, the Bud-dhist bo-tree, and the mythological yggdrasil, reminds us of the human longing to ascend to the heavens and discover the beauty, both spiritual and material, hidden away in the heights. Jack's theft of a bag of gold, a hen that lays golden eggs, and a harp that plays by itself (in some versions Jack supports himself by taking the harp on the road) reveals his kinship to trickster figures, all of whom are ruthless in their drive to secure wealth as a badge of their success.

The adventures of Jack were first recorded by Benjamin Tabart in 1807 as *The History of Jack and the Bean-Stalk*. Tabart no doubt relied on oral versions in circulation at the time, though he claimed to base his tale on an "original manuscript." What is particularly striking about Tabart's Jack is his evolution from an "indolent, care-less, and extravagant" boy into a son who is both "dutiful and obe-dient." Instead of marrying a princess and ascending to a throne, Jack lives with his mother "a great many years and continued to be always happy."

Tabart's Jack becomes an exemplary character, a role model for children listening to his story. He is not at all a master thief who makes off with the giant's possessions but a dispossessed boy who is recovering what by rights belonged to him. From a fairy, Jack learns that his father was swindled and murdered by the giant and that he was destined to avenge his father's death. A powerful moral overlay turns what was once probably a tale of high adventure and shrewd maneuvering into a morally edifying story.

When Joseph Jacobs began compiling stories for his anthology *English Fairy Tales*, he dismissed Tabart's *History of Jack and the Bean-Stalk* as "very poor" and reconstructed the version he recalled from childhood. Drawing on the memory of a tale told by his child-hood nursemaid in Australia around 1860, Jacobs produced a story that is relatively free of the moralizing impulse that permeates Tab-art's story. The British folklorist Katherine Briggs has referred to Jacobs's version as "original," but it is in fact simply one of many efforts to recapture the spirit of the oral versions in widespread cir-culation during the nineteenth century.

"Hansel and Gretel" and "The Juniper Tree" give us high melodrama—abandonment, treachery, betrayal, and joyous reunions. "Tom Thumb," by contrast, offers comic relief in the form of spunky adventurers who use their wits to turn the tables on adversaries with daunting powers. Interestingly, stories about spirited adventurers who conquer ogres and giants seem to be no match for the seductive sentimentality of "Hansel and Gretel" or the tragic power of "The Juniper Tree." What George Cruikshank had to say about "Puss in Boots" goes far in explaining why child tricksters have not enjoyed the success of other fairy-tale characters: "As it stood, the tale was a succession of successful falsehoods—a clever lesson in lying!—a system of imposture rewarded by the greatest worldly advantage!—a useful lesson, truly, to be impressed upon the minds of children!"[8] It is not surprising that adults are more likely to prefer the sufferings of the "God-fearing" siblings in "Hansel and Gretel" to the irreverent antics of Molly Whuppie or Tom Thumb.

Unlike Jack and Tom Thumb, who take possession of a giant's treasures by using their wits, Vasilisa, the Russian peasant bride, gets her reward by carrying out household chores—sweeping the yard, clearing a hut, cooking dinner, washing linen, and sorting grains. She becomes a consummate spinner and seamstress, winning the heart of a tsar with her beautiful fabrics and handicraft.

The story of Vasilisa reflects the cultural values of an earlier age, of a time in which excellence in the household crafts was treasured as highly as beauty. But Vasilisa is more than spinner and seamstress. She also nurtures the doll given to her by her mother, understanding that she must sacrifice some of her own needs in order to benefit from her advice and help. As a figure who brings light (in the form of fire) back to her home, Vasilisa becomes a cultural heroine who restores order and creates the conditions for a real home. In the end she works hard to promote a happy ending that includes not only herself and the tsar but also her father and the woman who sheltered her.

The Japanese fairy tale "Momotaro, the Peach Boy" gives us an all-action hero, a boy who stands as a model of unalloyed courage and redemptive passion. Momotaro, a figure recruited for Japanese propaganda during World War II, floats down the river and makes his home with a childless couple. Once grown up, he wins over allies with gifts of food and travels on to an island inhabited by devils, ogres, or monsters (depending on the version). In a finale reminiscent of Maurice Sendak's *Where the Wild Things Are*, Momotaro triumphantly returns home after conquering rapacious monsters. The demons haunting Momotaro's world are, for once, not all in the family.

---

8. George Cruikshank, *Puss in Boots* (London: Arnold, 1864), p. 1.

BROTHERS GRIMM

Hansel and Gretel[†]

At the edge of a great forest, there once lived a poor woodcutter with his wife and two children. The little boy was called Hansel, and the girl's name was Gretel. There was never much to eat in the house, and once, during a time of famine, the woodcutter could no longer put bread on the table. At night, he would lie in bed worrying, tossing and turning in his distress. One day he said to his wife with a sigh: "What will become of us? How can we provide for our poor children when we don't even have enough for ourselves?"

"Listen to me," his wife replied. "Tomorrow at daybreak we'll take the children out into the darkest part of the woods. We'll make a fire there and give them each a piece of bread. Then we'll go about our work and leave them alone. They'll never find their way home, and then we'll be rid of them."

"No," her husband replied. "I can't do it. I don't have the heart to leave the children all alone in the woods and let wild beasts come and tear them to pieces."

"You fool," she said. "Then all four of us will end up starving to death. You might as well start sawing the boards for our coffins."

She didn't give her husband a moment's peace until he agreed to the plan. "But still, I feel sorry for the poor children," he said.

The two children hadn't been able to sleep either, because they were so hungry, and they heard every word their stepmother had said to their father. Gretel wept bitter tears and said to Hansel: "Well, now we're lost."

"Be quiet, Gretel," said Hansel, "and stop worrying. I'll figure out something."

As soon as the old folks had fallen asleep, he climbed out of bed, put on his little jacket, opened the lower half of the door, and slipped out. The moon was shining brightly, and the white pebbles in front of the house glittered like silver coins. Hansel stooped down and put as many as would fit into his jacket pocket. Then he went back and said to Gretel: "Don't worry, dear little sister. Sleep peacefully. God will not forsake us." And he went back to bed.

At daybreak, just before sunrise, the wife came and woke the two children. "Get up, you lazybones, we're going to go into the forest to fetch some wood."

[†] Jacob Grimm and Wilhelm Grimm, "Hänsel und Gretel," in *Kinder- und Hausmärchen*, 7th ed. (Berlin: Dieterich, 1857; first published: Berlin: Realschulbuchhandlung, 1812). Translated for the first edition of this Norton Critical Edition by Maria Tatar. Copyright © 1999 by Maria Tatar.

The wife gave each child a crust of bread and said: "Here's something for lunch. But don't eat it before then, because you're not getting anything else."

Gretel put the bread under her apron because Hansel had the pebbles in his pocket. Then they all set out together on the path into the forest. After a little while, Hansel stopped to look back at the house. He kept looking back. His father said: "Hansel, why are you always stopping and staring? Watch out, and don't forget what your legs are for."

"Oh, Father," said Hansel. "I'm looking at my white kitten, which is sitting up on the roof saying good-bye to me."

The woman said: "You fool, that's not your kitten. Those are the rays of the sun, shining on the chimney."

But Hansel had not been looking at the kitten. He had been taking the shiny pebbles from his pocket and dropping them on the ground.

When they arrived in the middle of the forest, the father said: "Go gather some wood, children. I'll build a fire so that you won't get cold."

Hansel and Gretel gathered brushwood until they had a little pile of it. The brushwood was lit, and when the flames were high enough, the woman said: "Now lie down by the fire, children, and get some rest. We're going into the forest to chop some wood. When we're done, we'll return and take you back home."

Hansel and Gretel sat by the fire. At noon they ate their crusts of bread. Since they could hear the sounds of an ax, they were sure that their father was nearby. But it wasn't an ax that they heard, it was a branch their father had fastened to a dead tree, and the wind was banging it back and forth. They sat and waited for so long that finally their eyes closed from exhaustion, and they fell fast asleep. When they awoke, it was pitch dark. Gretel began to cry and said: "How will we ever get out of the woods!"

Hansel comforted her: "Just wait until the moon appears. Then we will find our way back."

When the full moon appeared, Hansel took his sister by the hand and followed the pebbles, which were shimmering like newly minted coins. They marked the way back home. The two walked all night long and arrived at their father's house at daybreak. They knocked at the door, and when the woman opened the door and saw that it was Hansel and Gretel, she said: "You wicked children! Why did you sleep so long in the woods? We were sure you were never going to come back."

But the father was overjoyed, because he was upset at how he had abandoned the children in the woods.

Not long after that, every square inch of the country was stricken by famine. One night the children heard what the mother was saying to their father while they were in bed: "We've eaten everything up again. All that's left is half a loaf of bread, and then we are done for. The children have to go. This time we'll take them deeper into the forest so that they won't be able find their way back home. Otherwise there's no hope for us."

The husband's heart was heavy, and he thought: "It would be better if you shared the last crumb of bread with your children." But the woman refused to pay attention to anything he said. She fussed and fumed. In for a penny, in for a pound, and since he had given in the first time, he had to give in a second time.

The children were still awake and overheard the entire conversation. While their parents were sleeping, Hansel got up and wanted to go out to pick up some pebbles as he had the last time, but the woman had locked the door, and Hansel couldn't get out. He comforted his sister and said: "Don't cry, Gretel. Just sleep peacefully. The Lord will protect us."

Early the next morning the woman came and woke the children up. They each got a crust of bread, this time even smaller than last time. On the way into the woods, Hansel crushed the bread in his pocket and stopped from time to time to scatter crumbs on the ground.

"Hansel, why do you keep stopping and staring?" the father asked. "Keep going!"

"I'm looking at my little dove, the one sitting on the roof and trying to bid me farewell," Hansel replied.

"Fool," said the woman. "That isn't your little dove. Those are the rays of the morning sun shining up on the chimney."

After a while, Hansel had scattered all the crumbs on the path.

The woman took the children even deeper into the woods, where they had never been before in their lives. Once again a large fire was built, and the mother said: "Don't move from there, children. If you feel tired, you can sleep for a while. We're going to go into the forest to chop some wood. In the evening, when we're done, we'll come to get you."

At noon Gretel shared her bread with Hansel, who had scattered bits of his piece on the path. Then they fell asleep. The evening went by, but no one came to get the poor children. They awoke when it was pitch dark, and Hansel comforted his sister by saying: "Just wait, Gretel, until the moon appears. Than we will be able to see the crumbs of bread I scattered. They will mark the way home for us."

When the moon appeared, they set off, but they couldn't find the crumbs because the many thousands of birds flying through the forest and over the fields had eaten them. Hansel said to Gretel: "We'll find our way back," but they didn't find it. They walked all night long and then another day from early in the morning until late at night.

But they still couldn't find their way out of the woods, and they grew hungrier and hungrier, for they had nothing to eat but the few berries they found on the ground. After a while, they were so tired that their legs could no longer carry them, and they lay down under a tree and fell asleep.

It was now the third morning after they had left their father's house. They started walking again, but they just ended up moving deeper and deeper into the woods. If help did not come their way soon, they were sure to perish. At noon they saw a beautiful bird, white as snow, perched on a branch. It sang so beautifully that they stopped to listen. When the bird had finished its song, it flapped its wings and flew on ahead of them. They followed it until they came to a little house, and the bird perched on its roof. As they approached the house, they realized it was built of bread and had a roof made of cake as well as transparent windows made of sugar.

"Let's see what it tastes like," said Hansel. "May the Lord bless our meal. I'll try a piece of the roof, Gretel, and you can try the window. That's sure to taste sweet." Hansel reached up and broke off a small piece of the roof to see what it tasted like. Gretel went over to the windowpane and nibbled on it. Suddenly a gentle voice called from inside:

> "Nibble, nibble, little mouse?
> Who's that nibbling at my house?"

The children replied:

> "The wind so mild,
> The heavenly child."

and they continued eating, without getting distracted. Hansel, who liked the taste of the roof, tore off a big chunk, and Gretel knocked out an entire windowpane and sat down on the ground to taste it. Suddenly the door opened, and a woman, old as the hills, hobbled out, leaning on a crutch. Hansel and Gretel were so terrified that they dropped everything they were holding. The old woman said, with her head shaking: "Well, dear children, how in the world did you get here? Come right inside and stay with me. No harm will come to you here."

She took them by the hand and led them into her little house. They were served a wonderful meal of milk and pancakes with sugar, apples, and nuts. Later, two beautiful little beds were made up for them with white sheets. Hansel and Gretel lay down in them and felt as if they were in heaven.

The old woman had only pretended to be so friendly. She was really a wicked witch, who lay in wait for children. She had built the little house of bread just to lure them inside. As soon as a child was in her power, she killed it, cooked it, and ate it. That was a real feast day for her. Witches have red eyes and can't see very far, but they have a keen sense of smell, like animals, and they can always tell when a human being is around. When Hansel and Gretel got near her, she laughed fiendishly and sneered: "They're mine! This time they won't get away from me!" Early in the morning, before the children were awake, she climbed out of bed and looked at the two of them resting so sweetly, with their big red cheeks. She muttered to herself: "They will make a tasty morsel."

Then she grabbed Hansel with her scrawny hand, took him to a small shed, and locked the door, which had bars on it. He could shout as loud as he wanted, it did him no good. Then she went over to Gretel, shook her until she woke up, and cried out: "Get up, lazybones, fetch some water and cook your brother something good. He's staying outside in a shed, waiting to be fattened up. When he's put on enough weight, I'll eat him."

Gretel began to cry bitter tears, but it did no good. She had to do what the wicked witch demanded. The finest food was cooked for poor Hansel, and Gretel got nothing but crab shells. Every morning the old woman would slink over to the little shed and shout: "Hansel, hold out your finger so that I can tell if you're plump enough."

Hansel would stick a little bone out, and the old woman, who had poor eyesight, thought that it was Hansel's finger and wondered why he wasn't putting on weight. When four weeks had passed and Hansel was still as scrawny as ever, she lost her patience and decided not to wait any longer. "Hey there, Gretel," she called out to the girl, "go get some water and be quick about it. I don't care whether Hansel's plump or scrawny. He's going to be slaughtered tomorrow, and then I'll cook him."

"Oh," the poor little sister wailed, and how the tears flowed down her cheeks! "Dear God, help us," she cried out. "If only the wild animals in the forest had eaten us, at least then we would have died together."

"Spare me your tears!" the old woman said. "Nothing can help you now."

Early in the morning Gretel had to go fill the kettle with water and light the fire. "First we'll do some baking," the old woman said. "I've already heated up the oven and kneaded the dough."

She pushed poor Gretel over to the oven, from which flames were leaping. "Crawl in," said the witch, "and see if it's hot enough to slide the bread in."

The witch was planning to shut the door as soon as Gretel climbed into the oven. Then she was going to bake her and eat her up too. But Gretel saw what was on her mind and said: "I don't know how to get in there. How do I do it?"

"Silly goose," said the old woman. "The opening is big enough. Just look. Even I can get in," and she scrambled over to the oven and stuck her head in it. Gretel gave her a big push that sent her sprawling. Then she shut the iron door and bolted it. Phew! the witch began screeching dreadfully. But Gretel ran away and the godless witch burned miserably to death.

Gretel ran straight to Hansel, opened the little shed and cried out: "Hansel, we're free! The old witch is dead."

Hansel hopped out as soon as the door opened, like a bird leaving its cage. How thrilled they were: they hugged and kissed, and jumped up and down for joy! Since there was nothing more to fear, they went straight back to the witch's house. In every corner there were chests filled with pearls and jewels. "These are even better than pebbles," said Hansel, and he put as much as he could into his pockets.

Gretel said, "I'll take something home too," and she filled up her little apron.

"Let's get going now," said Hansel. "We have to make our way out of this witch's forest."

After walking for a few hours, they reached a large body of water. "We can't get across," said Hansel. "There's not a bridge in sight."

"There aren't any ships around," Gretel said, "but here comes a white duck. It will help us cross, if I ask it." She called out:

> "Help us, help us, little duck
> Hansel and Gretel are out of luck.
> There's no bridge, not far or wide,
> Help us, give us both a ride."

The duck came paddling over. Hansel got on it and told his sister to sit down next to him. "No," said Gretel, "that would be too heavy a load for the little duck. It can take us over one at a time."

That's just what the good little creature did. When they were safely on the other side and had marched on for some time, the woods became more and more familiar. Finally they could see their father's house from afar. They began running, and then they raced into their father's house, throwing their arms around him. The man had not had a happy hour since the day that he had abandoned the children in the forest. His wife had died. Gretel emptied her apron, and the pearls and jewels rolled all over the floor. Hansel reached into his pockets and pulled out one handful of jewels after another. Their worries were over, and they lived together in perfect happiness.

My fairy tale is done. See the mouse run. Whoever catches it can make a great big fur hat out of it.

Fulano de Tal and His Children[†]

Once in a town somewhere there was a married couple. They had a boy and a girl. The girl was nine years old and the boy was five. That married couple lived very happily. They got along with each other very well. But the woman had an illness and died and the man was left with the two children, the girl and the boy. Well, the children went to school and the father took good care of them. He fed them, he took care of their needs, he sent them to school, he combed their hair.

Well one day the children's teacher fell in love with their father and gave caramels to the children. She gave them good things. The girl said, "Father, look, you have to marry our teacher. She gives us bread and honey." But their father replied, "Oh my daughter, some day she'll give you bread and bile. Bad things." Every day the children said, "Father, you have to marry our teacher. She gives us bread and honey." He said, "Oh my children, some day you will suffer bread and bile." Well, they insisted so much that the father fell in love with the teacher and they were married.

On the second night, when the father and the teacher were having supper after the boy and girl were in bed, the teacher said to her husband, "Look, I'm going to tell you that those children have to disappear from the house. You have to take them to the forest." The children were in bed and heard everything. The girl, who was a little smarter, went about the house and found a little sack of flour. She put a little bit of the flour into her pockets. The father got them up at three in the morning. "Father, where are you taking us?" the girl asked. "Look daughter, we're going to a wedding and I'm going to take you to be with your aunt for a few days," replied the father. Well, that's how he tricked them. The girl, who was the smarter because she was nine years old going on ten, took the flour. They went down the road, and the girl left a little trail of flour whenever she felt like it. The father came to a great big forest where he left the boy and the girl. He said, "Look daughter, stay here. I'm going to prepare a load of firewood. I'll come back and you'll go with me. We'll look for your aunt." Then the father left, and the girl picked up the trail of flour. Plam, plam, plam, plam.

They came home and hid in a little corner of the kitchen. The teacher and their father were eating supper. A little of their supper was left over and the teacher said, "Look here, if your little children

† "Fulano de Tal and His Children," as told by Julio Lopez in James M. Taggart, "'Hansel and Gretel' in Spain and Mexico," *The Journal of American Folklore* 99.394 (Oct.–Dec. 1986): 440–41. Reprinted by permission of the American Folklore Society.

were here, they could eat this." The father declared, "We can go call them." But the teacher protested, "No, no, no, don't call them." The children said to each other, "We're here and they don't want to give us any supper." They came out of their hiding place and said, "You won't give any to us!" They were dying of hunger and they ate what was left over.

Well they went to bed and the teacher said again, "Look, today they came home. Tomorrow you have to take them to another forest much thicker than the last one. Don't let them come back. I don't want to see them in this house." Then the girl, who was smart, went into the house and found a sack of figs. She filled her little pockets with figs and dropped them along the road. "Father where are you taking us? Once you told us our mother would give us bread and bile," said the little girl. "No daughter, no. Yes, your mother loves you a lot. Your mother adores you. Let's go to town. We're going to a wedding," replied the father. "Well fine," agreed the girl. The father took them to a much thicker forest and told them, "You stay here. I'm going to talk to your aunt so we can all be there. You'll see." He went down the road and headed home. The girl picked up the trail of figs, and the children went home again. They hid in the same place in the kitchen. The father and stepmother were having supper and a little was left over again. The woman said to the man, "Look here, if your little children were here, they could eat this. Well you should fetch them. You can give it to them." The girl said to the boy, "Here we are and they do not want to give us any supper." They came out again and ate it. When they were in bed, the woman said, "Look, this is the last time. If you bring the children home again, you will be the first one I'll poison and kill. Make sure you take them far away from here. Don't let them return again."

Of course the poor little girl went about the house because the girl always listened to what the woman said. She didn't find anything besides a sack of wheat. She put the wheat into her pockets and spread it to leave signs for finding the way home again. But the birds ate the wheat and left the road clean behind them. The children went into the forest and their father told them the same things as before. He told them to stay put and he tried to trick them by saying he was going on the same errand. But he didn't fool the girl. The children followed him after he left, but they lost the trail. They couldn't find their way home because the birds had eaten the wheat.

Now they were lost. They walked from one place to the next in the forest. They walked and they walked and spotted a light from a house in the distance. "Father must be looking for us. That light, let's see what it is," one of the children said. They were dying of hunger when they got to the house. The outside walls were entirely of caramels and other good things to eat. Sweet things. It was a house of candy. They followed along the walls eating the candy and a witch came out. "Who is licking my wall?" she asked. She saw the two children and said, "Oh but what are you doing here children?" "Eating," they said. "Come in, come inside," she told them. She had the girl sweep, wash and help clean the house. She put the boy, who was thin, into a room so small that he almost didn't fit inside. She gave him chickens to fatten him up. Every day a chicken, every day a chicken, every day a chicken.

The day came when the old woman said, "This boy doesn't get fat. He isn't getting fat at all. Well tomorrow I'm going to tell him to show me his hand. Let's see what is going on." When she took him something to eat, she said, "Boy, show me your hand." But he showed her a chicken's claw instead. "Oh, how thin you are!" the old woman exclaimed. "With all you eat, you're so thin!" She went upstairs saying, "Well no matter what, I'm going to bake him in the oven tomorrow." The sister went down and told her brother, "Look, tomorrow you're going to be baked in the oven." The boy was nice and fat by this time. The sister continued, "Look, the old woman is going to light the oven. When she calls the two of us to go to the oven and tells you to blow, tell her you don't know how. Tell her to blow first. She'll insist that she doesn't know how, but you tell her that you don't know how either."

The old woman lit the oven, removed the boy, and said, "Oh, what a tasty morsel. How you fooled me." When she arrived at the door of the oven she said, "Blow son, blow. Blow son, blow." "No lady, I don't know how to blow. You blow so I can see how you do it," replied the boy. The old woman had to blow because the boy told her that he didn't know how. The children grabbed her and put her into the oven and they closed the oven door. Instead of baking the boy, they baked the old woman. That entire caramel house turned into gold.

The children went home and didn't recognize their parents. They asked, "Are you Fulano de Tal?" "Yes," replied the father. "Did you have a boy and girl whom you took to the forest?" they asked. And the woman, the stepmother, said, "Quiet! quiet girl! I'm going to chase you far away from my house!" She said that because she didn't like what the girl might say. "Quiet, quiet girl, get away from my house. Don't let me see you." And the father said, "Yes, tell it all. Tell me how I'll know if you're my daughter and the boy is my son." The girl explained to him who they were. The father embraced her and, as for the woman, well he snatched a tool and cut off her head and hung her head above his bed. He slapped her head three times when he went to bed and three more times when he got up.

BROTHERS GRIMM

The Juniper Tree[†]

A long time ago, as many as two thousand years ago, there lived a
rich man with a beautiful and devout wife. They loved each other
dearly, but they had no children, even though they longed for them.
Day and night the wife prayed for a child, but still they had no
children.

Now in front of the house there was a garden, and in the garden
there grew a juniper tree. Once, in the wintertime, the wife was
peeling an apple under the tree, and while she was peeling it, she
cut her finger. Blood dripped on the snow. "Ah," said the woman,
and she sighed deeply. "If only I had a child as red as blood and as
white as snow!" Having said that, she began to feel better, for she
had a feeling that something would come of it. Then she went back
in the house.

A month went by, and the snow melted. Two months passed, and
everything was green. Three months went by, and the flowers grew
and blossomed. Four months passed, and all the trees in the woods
grew tall, with their green branches intertwining. The woods
resounded with the melodies of birds, and blossoms began to fall
from the trees. And so the fifth month went by. And when the woman
stood under the juniper tree, her heart leaped for joy because it
smelled so sweet. She fell to her knees and was beside herself with
joy. When the sixth month had passed, the fruit grew large and firm,
and she became quite still. In the seventh month she picked the juniper berries and gorged on them until she became melancholy and
ill. After the eighth month went by, she called her husband and said
to him with tears in her eyes: "If I die, bury me under the juniper
tree." After that she felt better and was happy until the end of the
ninth month. Then she bore a child as white as snow and as red as
blood. When she saw the child she was so happy that she died.

Her husband buried her under the juniper tree, and he wept day
after day. After a while he began to feel better, but he still was in
tears from time to time. Eventually he stopped and then he took a
second wife.

The man had a daughter with his second wife. The child from the
first marriage was a little boy, as red as blood and as white as snow.
Whenever the woman looked at her daughter, she felt love for her,

[†] Jacob Grimm and Wilhelm Grimm, "Von dem Machandelboom," in *Kinder- und Hausmärchen*, 7th ed. (Berlin: Dieterich, 1857; first published: Berlin: Realschulbuchhandlung, 1812). Translated for the first edition of this Norton Critical Edition by Maria
Tatar. Copyright © 1999 by Maria Tatar.

but when her eyes landed on the little boy, she was sick at heart. It seemed that, no matter where he went, he was somehow in the way. The woman kept thinking about how she needed to get her hands on the entire family fortune for her daughter. The devil seized hold of her so that she began to hate the little boy, and she slapped him around and pinched him here and cuffed him there. The poor child lived in terror, and when he came home from school, he had no peace whatsoever.

One day the woman went to the pantry. Her little daughter followed her and said: "Mother, give me an apple."

"All right, my child," said the woman, and she gave her a beautiful apple from a chest that had a big heavy lid with a sharp iron lock on it.

"Mother," said the little girl, "can't Brother have one too?"

The woman was irritated by these words, but she just said: "Yes, he can have one when he comes back from school."

When she looked out the window and saw the boy coming home, it was as if the devil had taken hold of her, and she snatched the apple out of her daughter's hand and said: "You can't have one before your brother." Then she tossed the apple into the chest and shut it.

The little boy walked in the door, and the devil got her to speak sweetly to him and say: "My son, would you like an apple?" But she gave him a look full of hate.

"Mother," said the little boy, "how dreadful you look! Yes, give me an apple."

Then she felt as if she had to keep leading him on. "Come over here," she said, and she lifted the lid. "Now pick out an apple."

And when the little boy bent down, the devil prompted her, and *bam*! She slammed the lid down so hard that the boy's head flew off and fell into the chest with the apples. Then she was overcome with fear and thought: "How am I going to fix this?" She went to her room and took a white kerchief from her dresser drawer. She put the boy's head back on his neck and tied the scarf around it so that you couldn't see anything was wrong. Then she sat him down on a chair in front of the door and put an apple in his hand.

Later on Little Marlene came into the kitchen to see her mother, who was standing by the fire, stirring a pot of hot water round and round. "Mother," said Little Marlene, "Brother is sitting by the door, and he looks so pale. He has an apple in his hand, and when I asked him to give me the apple, he didn't answer. It was very scary."

"Go back to him," the mother said, "and if he doesn't answer, slap his face."

And so Little Marlene went back to him and said: "Brother, give me the apple."

But he wouldn't answer. So she gave him a slap, and his head went flying off. Little Marlene was so terrified that she began sobbing. Then she ran to her mother and said: "Mother, I've knocked my brother's head off!" And she cried so hard that she couldn't stop.

"Little Marlene," said her mother, "what a dreadful thing you've done! But don't breathe a word to anyone, for there's nothing we can do. We'll cook him up in a stew."

And so the mother took the little boy and chopped him up. Then she put the pieces into a pot and cooked him up in a stew. Little Marlene stood nearby and wept so hard that the stew didn't need salt because of all her tears.

When the father came home, he sat down at the table and said: "Where's my son?"

The mother brought in a huge dish of stew, and Little Marlene wept so hard that she couldn't stop.

"Where's my son?" the father asked again.

"Oh," said the mother, "he went off to the country to visit his mother's great uncle. He plans to stay there a while."

"What's he going to do there? He didn't even say good-bye to me."

"Well, he really wanted to go, and he asked if he could stay for six weeks. They'll take good care of him."

"Oh, that makes me so sad," said the husband. "It's not right. He should have stayed and said his farewells."

Then he began eating and said: "Little Marlene, why are you crying? Your brother will be back soon." Then he said: "Oh, wife, this stew tastes so good! Give me some more."

The more he ate the more he wanted. "Give me some more," he said. "No one else may have any. Somehow I feel as if it's all mine."

He kept eating, and he tossed the bones under the table until he had finished it all. Meanwhile, Little Marlene went to her dresser and took out her best silk kerchief. She picked up all the bones from beneath the table, tied them up in her silk kerchief, and carried them outside. Then she wept bitter tears. She laid the bones out on the green grass under the juniper tree. Once she had put them down, she suddenly felt much better and stopped crying. The juniper tree began stirring. Its branches parted and joined back together again as though it were clapping its hands for joy. A mist arose from the tree, and in the middle of the mist burned a flame, and from the flame a beautiful bird emerged and began singing gloriously. It soared up in the air, and then it vanished. The tree was as it had been before, but the kerchief with the bones was gone. Little Marlene felt just as happy and relieved as if her brother were still alive. She returned home filled with joy and sat down at the table to eat.

Meanwhile the bird flew away, landed on a perch at a goldsmith's house, and began singing:

"My mother, she slew me,
My father, he ate me,
My sister, Little Marlene,
Gathered up my bones,
Tied them up in silk,
And put them under the juniper tree.
Tweet, tweet, what a fine bird I am!"

The goldsmith was sitting in his shop, making a chain of gold. He heard the bird singing on his roof and found its song very beautiful. He stood up and, when he walked across the threshold, one of his slippers came off. Still, he kept right on going out into the middle of the street, wearing one sock and one slipper. He also had on his apron, and in one hand he had the gold chain, in the other his pliers. The sun was shining brightly on the street. He stopped to look at the bird and said: "Bird, you sing so beautifully. Sing me that song again."

"No," said the bird. "I never sing the second time for nothing. Give me that golden chain, and I'll sing for you again."

"Here," said the goldsmith. "Here's the golden chain. Now sing the song again."

The bird came flying down. Taking the golden chain in its right claw, it landed on a perch in front of the goldsmith and began singing:

"My mother, she slew me,
My father, he ate me,
My sister, Little Marlene,
Gathered up my bones,
Tied them up in silk,
And put them under the juniper tree.
Tweet, tweet, what a fine bird I am!"

Then the bird flew off to a shoemaker's house, perched on the roof, and sang:

"My mother, she slew me,
My father, he ate me,
My sister, Little Marlene,
Gathered up my bones,
Tied them up in silk,
And put them under the juniper tree.
Tweet, tweet, what a fine bird I am!"

When the shoemaker heard the song, he ran out the door in his shirtsleeves and looked up at the roof. He had to put his hand over his eyes to keep the sun from blinding him. "Bird," he said, "you sing so beautifully." Then he called into the house: "Wife, come out here for a moment. There's a bird up there. See it? How beautifully it sings!"

He called his daughter and her children, along with apprentices, a hired hand, and a maid. They all came running out into the street to look at the bird and see how beautiful it was. It had red and green feathers, and around its neck was a band of pure gold, and the eyes in its head sparkled like stars.

"Bird," said the shoemaker, "sing that song again."

"No," said the bird, "I never sing the second time for nothing. You have to give me something."

"Wife," said the man, "go up to the attic. On the top shelf you'll find a pair of red shoes. Get them for me."

His wife went and fetched the shoes.

"Here," said the man. "Now sing that song again."

The bird came flying down. Taking the shoes in its left claw, it flew back up on the roof and sang:

> "My mother, she slew me,
> My father, he ate me,
> My sister, Little Marlene,
> Gathered up my bones,
> Tied them up in silk,
> And put them under the juniper tree.
> Tweet, tweet, what a fine bird I am!"

When the bird had finished the song, it flew away. It had the chain in its right claw and the shoes in its left, and it flew far away to a mill. The mill went "clickety-clack, clickety-clack, clickety-clack." Inside the mill sat twenty of the miller's men, hewing a stone, "hick hack hick hack hick hack." And the mill kept going "clickety-clack, clickety-clack, clickety-clack." And so the bird went and perched on a linden tree outside the mill and sang:

> "My mother, she slew me,"

and one of the men stopped working,

> "My father, he ate me,"

and two more stopped working and listened,

> "My sister, Little Marlene,"

then four men stopped working,

> "Gathered up my bones,
> Tied them up in silk,"

now only eight kept hewing,

> "And put them under . . ."

now only five,

> ". . . the juniper tree."

now only one.

> "Tweet, tweet, what a fine bird I am!"

The last one stopped to listen to the final words. "Bird," he said, "you sing so beautifully! Let me hear the whole thing too. Sing that song again."

"I never sing the second time for nothing. If you give me the millstone, I'll sing the song again."

"If it belonged to me alone," he said, "I would give it to you."

"If the bird sings again," the others said, "it can have the millstone."

Then the bird swooped down, and the miller's men, all twenty of them, set the beam to and raised up the stone. "Heave-ho-hup, heave-ho-hup, heave-ho-hup." And the bird stuck its neck through the hole, put the stone on as if it were a collar, flew back to the tree, and sang:

> "My mother, she slew me,
> My father, he ate me,
> My sister, Little Marlene,
> Gathered up my bones,
> Tied them up in silk,
> And put them under the juniper tree.
> Tweet, tweet, what a fine bird I am!"

When the bird had finished its song, it spread its wings. In its right claw was the chain, in its left the shoes, and round its neck was the millstone. Then it flew away, far away to the house of its father.

The father, mother, and Little Marlene were sitting at the table in the parlor, and the father said: "How happy I feel! My heart feels so easy."

"Not me," said the mother. "I feel frightened. It feels like a big storm is brewing."

Meanwhile, Little Marlene just sat there weeping. The bird flew up into the air and, when it landed on the roof, the father said: "How happy I'm feeling. And outside the sun is shining so brightly! I feel as if I'm about to see an old friend again."

"I don't," said the woman. "I'm so frightened that my teeth are chattering, and I feel as if fire is running through my veins."

She tore at her bodice to loosen it, while little Marlene sat there weeping. The girl held her apron up to her eyes and wept so hard that it was completely soaked with tears. The bird swooped down to the juniper tree, perched on a branch, and sang:

"My mother, she slew me . . ."

The mother stopped up her ears and closed her eyes, for she didn't want to see or hear anything. But the roaring in her ears was like the wildest of storms, and her eyes burned and flashed like lightning.

"My father, he ate me . . ."

"Oh, Mother," said the man, "there's a beautiful bird out there, and it's singing so gloriously. The sun is shining so warmly, and the air smells like cinnamon."

"My sister, Little Marlene . . ."

Little Marlene put her head in her lap and just kept crying and crying. But the husband said: "I'm going outside. I have to see this bird close up."

"Oh, don't go," said the wife. "It feels as if the whole house is shaking and about to go up in flames!"

But the husband went out and looked at the bird.

"Gathered up my bones,
Tied them up in silk,
And put them under the juniper tree.
Tweet, tweet, what a fine bird I am!"

After finishing its song, the bird dropped the golden chain, and it fell right around the man's neck, fitting him perfectly. He went inside and said: "Just see what a fine bird is out there! It gave me this beautiful golden chain, as beautiful as it is."

But the woman was so terrified that she fell down flat on the floor, and the cap she was wearing flew off her head. And the bird sang once again:

"My mother, she slew me . . ."

"Oh, if only I were a thousand feet under the ground so that I wouldn't have to hear this!"

"My father, he ate me . . ."

Then the woman fell down again as if dead.

"My sister, Little Marlene . . ."

"Oh," said Little Marlene, "I want to go outside and see if the bird will give me something too." And she went out.

"Gathered up my bones,
Tied them up in silk,"

And the bird tossed her the shoes.

"And put them under the juniper tree.
Tweet, tweet, what a fine bird I am!"

Little Marlene felt lighthearted and happy. She put on the new
red shoes and came dancing and skipping into the house.

"Oh," she said, "I was so sad when I went out, and now I feel so
cheerful. What a fine bird is out there. It gave me a pair of red shoes."

The woman jumped to her feet and her hair stood straight on end
like tongues of flame. "I have a feeling that the world is coming to
an end. Maybe I'd feel better if I went outside."

As she went out the door, *bam*! the bird dropped the millstone on
her head and crushed her to death. The father and Little Marlene
heard the crash and went outside. Smoke, flames, and fire were rising up from the spot, and when they vanished, little brother was
standing there. He took his father and Little Marlene by the hand,
and the three of them were overjoyed. Then they went into the house,
sat down at the table, and dined.

JOSEPH JACOBS

The Rose-Tree[†]

There was once upon a time a good man who had two children: a
girl by a first wife, and a boy by the second. The girl was as white as
milk, and her lips were like cherries. Her hair was like golden silk,
and it hung to the ground. Her brother loved her dearly, but her
wicked stepmother hated her. "Child," said the stepmother one day,
"go to the grocer's shop and buy me a pound of candles." She gave
her the money; and the little girl went, bought the candles, and
started on her return. There was a stile to cross. She put down the
candles whilst she got over the stile. Up came a dog and ran off with
the candles.

She went back to the grocer's, and she got a second bunch. She
came to the stile, set down the candles, and proceeded to climb over.
Up came the dog and ran off with the candles.

She went again to the grocer's, and she got a third bunch; and just
the same happened. Then she came to her stepmother crying, for
she had spent all the money and had lost three bunches of candles.

The stepmother was angry, but she pretended not to mind the loss.
She said to the child: "Come, lay your head on my lap that I may
comb your hair." So the little one laid her head in the woman's lap,
who proceeded to comb the yellow silken hair. And when she

---

† Joseph Jacobs, "The Rose-Tree," in *English Fairy Tales* (London: David Nutt, 1890).

combed, the hair fell over her knees, and rolled right down to the ground.

Then the stepmother hated her more for the beauty of her hair; so she said to her, "I cannot part your hair on my knee, fetch a billet of wood." So she fetched it. Then said the stepmother, "I cannot part your hair with a comb, fetch me an axe." So she fetched it.

"Now," said the wicked woman, "lay your head down on the billet whilst I part your hair."

Well! she laid down her little golden head without fear; and whist! down came the axe, and it was off. So the mother wiped the axe and laughed.

Then she took the heart and liver of the little girl, and she stewed them and brought them into the house for supper. The husband tasted them and shook his head. He said they tasted very strangely. She gave some to the little boy, but he would not eat. She tried to force him, but he refused, and ran out into the garden, and took up his little sister, and put her in a box, and buried the box under a rose-tree; and every day he went to the tree and wept, till his tears ran down on the box.

One day the rose-tree flowered. It was spring, and there among the flowers was a white bird; and it sang, and sang, and sang like an angel out of heaven. Away it flew, and it went to a cobbler's shop, and perched itself on a tree hard by; and thus it sang:

> "My wicked mother slew me,
> My dear father ate me,
> My little brother whom I love
> Sits below, and I sing above
>   Stick, stock, stone dead."

"Sing again that beautiful song," said the shoemaker. "If you will first give me those little red shoes you are making." The cobbler gave the shoes, and the bird sang the song; then flew to a tree in front of the watchmaker's, and sang:

> "My wicked mother slew me
> My dear father ate me,
> My little brother whom I love
> Sits below, and I sing above
>   Stick, stock, stone dead."

"Oh, the beautiful song! sing it again, sweet bird," said the watchmaker. "If you will give me first that gold watch and chain in your hand." The jeweler gave the watch and chain. The bird took it in one foot, the shoes in the other, and, after having repeated the song, flew away to where three millers were picking a millstone. The bird perched on a tree and sang:

"My wicked mother slew me,
My dear father ate me,
My little brother whom I love
Sits below, and I sing above
    Stick!"

Then one of the men put down his tool and looked up from his work,

"Stock!"

Then the second miller's man laid aside his tool and looked up,

"Stone!"

Then the third miller's man laid down his tool and looked up,

"Dead!"

Then all three cried out with one voice: "Oh, what a beautiful song! Sing it, sweet bird, again." "If you will put the millstone round my neck," said the bird. The men did what the bird wanted and away to the tree it flew with the millstone round its neck, the red shoes in one foot, and the gold watch and chain in the other. It sang the song and then flew home. It rattled the millstone against the eaves of the house, and the stepmother said: "It thunders." Then the little boy ran out to see the thunder, and down dropped the red shoes at his feet. It rattled the millstone against the eaves of the house once more, and the stepmother said again: "It thunders." Then the father ran out and down fell the chain about his neck.

In ran father and son, laughing and saying, "See, what fine things the thunder has brought us!" Then the bird rattled the millstone against the eaves of the house a third time; and the stepmother said: "It thunders again; perhaps the thunder has brought something for me," and she ran out; but the moment she stepped outside the door, down fell the millstone on her head; and so she died.

The Singing Bones†

Once upon a time there lived a man and a woman who had twenty-five children. They were very poor; the man was good, the woman was bad. Every day when the husband returned from his work the wife served his dinner, but always meat without bones.

"How is it that this meat has no bones?"

---

† *Louisiana Folktales: Lupin, Bouki, and Other Creole Stories in French Dialect and English Translation*, ed. Alcée Fortier (1895; Lafayette: U of Louisiana at Lafayette P, 2011), p. 61.

"Because bones are heavy, and meat is cheaper without bones. They give more for the money."

The husband ate, and said nothing.

"How is it you don't eat meat?"

"You forget that I have no teeth. How do you expect me to eat meat without teeth?"

"That is true," said the husband, and he said nothing more, because he was afraid to grieve his wife, who was as wicked as she was ugly.

When you have twenty-five children you cannot think of them all the time, and you do not notice if one or two are missing. One day, after his dinner, the husband asked for his children. When they were by him he counted them, and found only fifteen. He asked his wife where were the ten others. She answered that they were at their grandmother's, and every day she would send one more for them to get a change of air. That was true, every day there was one that was missing.

One day the husband was at the threshold of his house, in front of a large stone which was there. He was thinking of his children, and he wanted to go and get them at their grandmother's when he heard voices that were saying:

> Our mother killed us,
> Our father ate us.
> We are not in a coffin,
> We are not in the cemetery.

At first he did not understand what that meant, but he raised the stone, and saw a great quantity of bones, which began to sing again. He then understood that it was the bones of his children, whom his wife had killed, and whom he had eaten. Then he was so angry that he killed his wife, buried his children's bones in the cemetery, and stayed alone at his house. From that time he never ate meat, because he believed it would always be his children that he would eat.

CHARLES PERRAULT

Little Thumbling[†]

Once upon a time there lived a woodcutter and his wife who had seven children, all boys. The oldest was ten years old, and the youngest was only seven. Everyone was astonished that the

---

† Charles Perrault, "Le Petit Poucet," in *Histoires ou Contes du temps passé. Avec des Moralités* (Paris: Barbin, 1697). Translated for the first edition of this Norton Critical Edition by Maria Tatar. Copyright © 1999 by Maria Tatar.

woodcutter had had so many children in so short a time, but his wife didn't waste any time, and she never had fewer than two at a time.

These people were very poor. Having seven children was a great burden, because not one of them was able to earn his own living. To their great distress, the youngest was very sickly and did not speak a word. They mistook for stupidity what was in reality the sign of a kind and generous nature.

This youngest boy was very small. At birth he was hardly larger than a thumb, and as a result he was called "Little Thumbling." The poor child was the underdog in the family, and he took the blame for anything that went wrong. All the same, he was the wisest and shrewdest of the brothers, and though he may have spoken little, he listened carefully to everything.

There came a year of misfortune, when hunger was so widespread that these poor people resolved to get rid of their children. One evening, after the children had gone to bed, the woodcutter was sitting by the fire with his wife. His heart was heavy with sorrow when he said to her: "It must be obvious to you that we can no longer feed our children. I can't bear to watch them die of hunger before my very eyes, and I've made up my mind to take them out into the woods tomorrow and to leave them there. It won't be difficult to leave them behind, for collecting firewood will distract them, and we can disappear without their noticing it."

"Oh," cried the woodcutter's wife, "do you mean to say that you have the stomach to abandon your own children?" Her husband tried in vain to remind her of their terrible poverty, but she would not give her consent. She was poor, but she was still their mother. In the end, however, when she thought about how distressing it would be to watch them die of hunger, she agreed to the plan and, weeping, went off to bed.

Little Thumbling heard everything that was said. While lying in bed, he realized that serious things were being discussed, and he got up quietly and slipped under his father's stool in order to listen without being seen. He went back to bed, but didn't sleep a wink for the rest of the night, for he was thinking about what to do. In the morning, he got up very early and went to the bank of the river. There he filled his pockets with little white pebbles and returned home.

The family set out for the woods, and Little Thumbling did not say a word to his brothers about what he had learned. They entered a forest so dense that at ten paces they could not see each other. The woodcutter began his work, and the children started collecting twigs for firewood. The father and mother, seeing them busy at their work, stole gradually away, and then suddenly dashed off along a little side path.

When the children realized that they were all alone, they began to weep and sob with all their might. Little Thumbling let them cry, since he felt sure that he would be able to get them back home. On the way, he had dropped the little white pebbles that he had been carrying in his pocket.

"Don't be afraid, brothers," he said to them. "Mother and Father have left us here, but I will take you back home again. Just follow me."

They fell in behind him, and he took them straight home by the same path they had taken into the forest. At first they were afraid to go into the house. Instead, they leaned against the door to hear what their father and mother were saying. Now the woodcutter and his wife had no sooner reached home than the lord of the manor sent them a sum of ten crowns that he had owed them for a long time and that they had despaired of ever getting. This gave them a new lease on life, for the poor creatures had been dying of hunger.

The woodcutter sent his wife off to the butcher at once, and since it had been such a long time since they had eaten anything, she bought three times more meat than was needed for two people to dine. When they sat down at the table, the woodcutter's wife said: "Alas! where are our poor children now! They could get a good meal from our leftovers. Mind you, William, it was you who wanted to abandon them. I said over and over again that we would regret it. What are they doing now in the forest? God in heaven, the wolves may already have eaten them! What a monster you are for having abandoned your children."

The woodcutter finally lost his patience, for she had repeated more than twenty times that he would regret it and also that she had told him so. He threatened to beat her if she did not hold her tongue. It was not that the woodcutter was any less distressed than his wife, but she drove him crazy, and he was of the same opinion as many other people, who like women to say the right thing, but are troubled when they are always right. The woodcutter's wife burst into tears: "Alas, where are my children now, my poor children?"

She said it so loudly that the children, who were at the door, heard her words and began to cry out at once: "Here we are! Here we are!"

She rushed to open the door for them, and, as she kissed them, she said: "How happy I am to see you again, dear children! You must be very tired and very hungry. And you, little Pierrot, how muddy you are! Come and let me wash you!"

Pierrot was the oldest son, whom she loved more than all the others because he was something of a redhead, and she herself had reddish hair.

They sat down at the table and ate with an appetite that gave pleasure to their father and mother. They all talked at once as they told of how frightened they had been in the forest.

The good people were overjoyed to have their children back with them again, but the pleasure lasted only as long as the ten crowns. When the money was spent, they lapsed back into their previous despair. Once again they decided to abandon the children, and to make sure they would not fail this time, they took them much farther away than the first time. But they were not able to talk about it quietly enough to escape being heard by Little Thumbling, who made up his mind to get out of this difficulty just as he had on the previous occasion. Although he rose early in the morning to go and collect his little stones, this time he could not carry out his plan because he found the door to the house had a double lock on it.

He could not think what to do until the woodcutter's wife gave them each a piece of bread for breakfast. Then it occurred to him to use the bread instead of the stones, by scattering crumbs along the path they were taking. He tucked his piece tightly into his pocket.

The father and mother took the children into the deepest and darkest part of the forest, and as soon as they arrived there, they slipped off on a side path and abandoned them. This did not cause Little Thumbling much distress, for he was sure that he would be able to find the way back by following the bread crumbs he had scattered on the path. But to his dismay he could not find a single crumb. Birds had come along and eaten them all up.

They were in real trouble now, for with every step they went further astray and plunged deeper and deeper into the forest. Night fell, and a strong wind began to blow, making them feel anxious and scared. Everywhere they seemed to hear the howling of wolves that were coming toward them to eat them up. They hardly dared to talk with each other or even to turn their heads. Then it began raining so heavily that they were soaked to the bone. At every step they tripped and fell into the mud, getting up again all covered with mud and not knowing what to do with their hands.

Little Thumbling climbed to the top of a tree to take a look around. Surveying the area, he could see a little light that looked like a candle far away on the other side of the forest. He climbed down the tree and was disappointed to find that, once back on the ground, he couldn't see the light any more. After walking some distance in the direction of the light, however, he caught a glimpse of it, as they were about to leave the forest. At last they reached the house where the light was burning, not without a good deal of anxiety, for they lost sight of it every time they had to go down into a hollow. They knocked at the door, and a good woman opened the door. She asked them what they wanted.

Little Thumbling explained that they were poor children who had lost their way in the forest and who had come begging for a night's lodging. Noticing what lovely children they were, the woman began to weep: "Alas, my poor children! Don't you realize where you are? Haven't you heard that this house belongs to an ogre who eats little children?"

"Alas, Madam!" answered Little Thumbling, who was trembling as visibly as his brothers. "What shall we do? If you don't take us in, the wolves in the forest will surely devour us this very night. Since that's the case, we might as well be eaten by your husband. If you plead for us, maybe he will take pity on us."

The ogre's wife, who thought she might be able to hide them from her husband until the next morning, let them come in and warm themselves by a roaring fire, where a whole sheep was cooking on the spit for the ogre's supper. Just as the boys were beginning to get warm, they heard three or four loud knocks at the door. The ogre had returned. His wife hid the boys quickly under the bed and went to open the door.

The ogre asked right away whether supper was ready and whether the wine had been drawn. Then he sat down to eat dinner. Blood was still dripping from the sheep, but it seemed all the better for that. He sniffed to the right, then to the left, insisting that he could smell fresh meat. His wife said: "You must be smelling the calf that I just dressed."

"I'll tell you again that I smell fresh meat," the ogre responded, looking at his wife suspiciously, "and there's something going on here that I don't get."

At that he got up from the table and went straight to the bed. "Aha!" he said. "So that's how you deceive me, you cursed woman! I don't know what's stopping me from eating you too! It's lucky for you that you're an old beast! I'm expecting three ogre friends for a visit in the next few days, and this excellent game will come in handy to entertain them!"

He pulled the children out from under the bed, one after another. The poor things fell to their knees, begging for mercy, but they were dealing with the cruelest of all ogres. Far from feeling pity for them, he was already devouring them with his eyes. He told his wife that if she cooked them up with a tasty sauce, they would make dainty morsels. He went to get a big knife, which he sharpened on a long stone in his left hand as he began walking toward the poor children. He had already grabbed one of them when his wife said to him: "Why are you doing this now? Can't it wait until tomorrow?"

"Hold your tongue," replied the ogre. "They will be all the more tender."

"But you already have plenty of meat on your plate," his wife countered. "There's a calf, two sheep, and half a pig."

"You're right," said the ogre. "Give them a good supper to eat so they won't lose any weight and put them to bed."

The good woman was overjoyed and brought them a tasty supper, but the boys were so terrified that they couldn't eat a thing. As for the ogre, he went back to his drinking, thrilled at the prospect of having such a treat to regale his friends. He drank a dozen glasses more than usual, and had to go to bed early, for the wine had gone to his head.

Now the ogre had seven daughters who were still just little children. These ogresses all had the loveliest complexions, because, like their father, they ate fresh meat. But they had little grey eyes, which were completely round, crooked noses, and very large mouths, with long and dreadfully sharp teeth, set far apart. They were not yet terribly vicious, but they showed great promise, for already they were in the habit of killing little children to suck their blood.

They had gone to bed early, and all seven were in one large bed, each wearing a crown of gold upon her head. In that same room was another bed of the same size. The ogre's wife had put the seven boys into it. Then she lay down next to her husband and went to sleep.

Little Thumbling was afraid that the ogre might suddenly regret not having cut the throats of the boys that evening. Having noticed that the ogre's daughters all had golden crowns upon their heads, he got up in the middle of the night and gently put his own cap and those of his brothers on their heads, after having removed the crowns of gold and put them on his own and on his brothers' heads. In this way, the ogre would take them for his daughters and his daughters for the boys whom he wanted to eat.

Everything worked just as Little Thumbling had predicted. The ogre, waking up at midnight, regretted having postponed until tomorrow what he could have done that night. He leaped headlong out of bed and grabbed a knife, saying: "Now then, let's see how the little rascals are faring. I won't make the same mistake twice!"

He stole his way up to the room where his daughters were sleeping and walked over to the bed with the seven little boys, who were all asleep except for Little Thumbling. When the ogre's hand moved from the heads of each of his brothers to his own head, Thumbling was paralyzed with fear.

"Well, well," said the ogre, when he felt the golden crowns. "I almost made a mess of this job! It's obvious that I had a little too much to drink last night!"

He went straight to the bed where his daughters were sleeping, and after feeling the boys' little caps, he cried: "Aha, here are the little rascals. Now let's get down to work!"

At that, without a moment's hesitation, he cut the throats of his seven daughters. Completely satisfied with his work, he got back into bed and lay down next to his wife.

As soon as Little Thumbling heard the ogre snoring, he woke his brothers up and told them to get dressed fast and to follow him. They crawled quietly down to the garden and jumped over the walls. They ran almost all night, trembling with fear and having no idea where they were going.

When the ogre woke up, he said to his wife: "Go upstairs and dress those little rascals who were here last night."

The wife was surprised by her husband's good will, never once suspecting the manner in which he was ordering her to have them dressed. She thought that he was telling her to go and put on their clothes. When she got upstairs, she was horrified to find her seven daughters with their throats cut, bathed in blood. She fainted instantly (the first resort of almost all women in similar circumstances). The ogre, fearing that his wife was taking too long to carry out his orders, went upstairs to help her. He was no less horrified than his wife at the terrible spectacle that met his eyes.

"What have I done?" he shouted. "I will make those wretches pay, and it will be now."

He threw a jugful of water in his wife's face, and after reviving her, said: "Fetch me my seven-league boots so that I can catch those boys."

He got right down to it and, after having run far and wide in all directions, he came to the road the poor children were traveling. They were not more than a hundred steps from their father's house when they saw the ogre striding from one mountain to the next, and stepping across rivers as though they were nothing but little brooks. Little Thumbling, who noticed a cave in some rocks close to where they were, hid his six brothers there and squeezed inside, always keeping an eye on the ogre's movements.

Now the ogre was feeling exhausted after having traveled so far in vain (for seven-league boots are very fatiguing to their owner), and he wanted to rest for a while. By chance, he happened to sit down on the very rock beneath which the boys were concealed. Since he could go no farther, he fell asleep after a while and began snoring so dreadfully that the poor children were no less frightened than when he had put his long knife to their throats. Little Thumbling was not as alarmed, and he told his brothers to race at once to the house while the ogre was still sleeping so soundly. They were not to worry about him. The brothers took his advice and got home fast.

Little Thumbling went over to the ogre and gently pulled off his boots and put them on his own feet. The boots were very roomy and very long, but since they were enchanted, they had the power to become larger or smaller according to the feet wearing them. As a result they fit his feet and his ankles as if they had been made just for him. He went straight to the ogre's house, where he found the ogre's wife weeping over her murdered daughters.

"Your husband," said Little Thumbling, "is in great danger, for he has been captured by a band of thieves who have sworn to kill him if he does not hand over all his gold and silver. Just as they were putting a dagger to his throat, he caught sight of me and begged me to come to you and to alert you to the plight he is in. He said that you should give me everything he has of value, without holding back anything, otherwise he'll be slain without mercy. Since time is of the essence, he wanted me to take his seven-league boots, to make haste, and also to show you that I am no impostor."

The ogre's wife was terribly frightened and immediately gave Thumbling everything she had, for the ogre had always been a very good husband, even though he ate little children. Loaded down with the ogre's entire wealth, Little Thumbling returned to his father's house, where he was welcomed with open arms.

Many people do not agree about this last adventure and claim that Little Thumbling never stole money from the ogre, just the seven-league boots about which he had no qualms, since they had been used to chase little children. These people insist that they are in a position to know, having been wined and dined at the woodcutter's cottage. They claim that when Little Thumbling put on the ogre's boots, he went to the court, where he knew there was great anxiety about the army and about the outcome of a battle being fought two hundred leagues away. They say that Little Thumbling went to look for the king and told him that if he was interested he could get news of the army before the day was out. The king promised him a large sum of money if he were to succeed.

Little Thumbling brought news that very night, and this first errand having made his reputation, he could then earn as much as he wanted. The king paid him handsomely to carry orders to the army, but countless ladies gave him any price he named to get news of their lovers, and this became his best source of income. Some wives entrusted him with letters to their husbands, but they paid him so badly, and this activity brought him in so little, that he didn't even bother to keep track of what he made from it.

After working as courier for some time and amassing a small fortune, Little Thumbling returned to his father's house, where everyone was overjoyed to see him again. He saw to it that the entire family lived comfortably, buying newly created positions for his father and brothers. In this way he got them all established at the same time that he managed to do perfectly well for himself at the court.

Moral

You never worry about having too many children
When they are handsome, well bred, strong,
And when they shine.
But if one is sickly or mute,
He is despised, scorned, ridiculed.
But sometimes it is the little runt
Who makes the family's happiness.

ALEXANDER AFANASEV

Vasilisa the Fair[†]

Once upon a time there lived a merchant in a faraway kingdom. Although he had been married twelve years, he had only one child, and she was called Vasilisa the Fair. When Vasilisa was eight years old, her mother fell ill. She called her daughter to her side, took a doll out from under her coverlet, and gave it to the girl, saying: "Listen, Vasilisushka. Pay attention to my last words, and remember what I say. I'm dying, and all I can leave you is my maternal blessing with this doll. Keep the doll with you wherever you go, but don't show her to anyone. If you get into trouble, just give her some food and ask her advice. After she has eaten, she will tell you what to do." The mother kissed her daughter farewell and died.

Following his wife's death, the merchant mourned her in proper fashion and then began to think about remarrying. He was a handsome man and had no difficulty finding a bride, but he liked a certain widow best. This widow had two daughters of her own, who were almost the same age as Vasilisa, and the merchant thought she would make a good housekeeper and mother. And so he married her, but he was wrong, for she did not turn out to be a good mother for his Vasilisa.

Vasilisa was the fairest girl in the entire village, and her stepmother and stepsisters were jealous of her beauty. They tormented her by giving her all kinds of work to do, hoping that she would grow bony from toil and weatherbeaten from exposure to the wind and the sun. And indeed, her life was miserable. But she bore it all without complaint and became lovelier with every passing day, while the stepmother and her daughters, who sat around all day doing nothing, grew thin and ugly as a result of spitefulness.

† Originally published in *Narodnye russkie skazki* (Russian Fairy Tales; Moscow: A. Semena, 1855–63). Translated by Maria Tatar for *The Annotated Classic Fairy Tales* (New York: Norton, 2002), pp. 172–85. Copyright © 2002 by Maria Tatar. Used by permission of W. W. Norton & Company.

How did all this come about? Things would have been different without the doll. Without her aid the girl could never have managed all the work. Some days Vasilisa did not eat anything at all. She would wait until everyone was in bed in the evening and then lock herself in the room where she slept. Giving her doll a tasty morsel, she would say: "Eat this, little doll, and listen to my troubles. I live in my father's house, but I'm deprived of joy. That stepmother of mine is going to be the death of me. Tell me how I should live and what I should do." First the doll would eat, and then she gave Vasilisa advice and comforted her in her woe. And in the morning she would take care of all the chores, while Vasilisa rested in the shade and picked flowers. The doll weeded the flowerbeds, watered the cabbages, went to the well, and fired the stove. The doll even showed Vasilisa an herb that would protect her against sunburn. Thanks to the doll, Vasilisa's life was easy.

The years passed, and Vasilisa grew up, reaching the age of marriage. All the young men in the village wanted to marry her, and they never so much as cast a glance at the stepmother's daughters. The stepmother grew to hate Vasilisa more than ever. To all the suitors she declared: "I will not give the youngest in marriage before the elder ones." Then she vented her anger on Vasilisa with cruel blows.

One day Vasilisa's father had to go on a long journey in order to trade in distant lands. The stepmother moved to another house near the edge of a deep forest. In the glade of that forest was a hut, and in the hut lived Baba Yaga. She never allowed anyone to come near her and ate human beings just as if they were chickens. The merchant's wife hated Vasilisa so much that, at the new house, she would send her stepdaughter into the woods for one thing or another. But Vasilisa always returned home safe and sound. Her doll showed her the way and kept her well clear of Baba Yaga's hut.

One evening in autumn the stepmother gave each of the girls a task. She told the oldest to make lace, the second to knit stockings, and Vasilisa was supposed to spin. Then she snuffed out all the candles in the house except for the one in the room where the girls were working. For a while the girls carried out their tasks quietly. Then the candle began to smoke. One of the stepsisters took a pair of scissors and pretended to trim the wick, but instead, following her mother's orders, she snuffed it out, as if by accident.

"What on earth should we do now?" said the stepsisters. "There's no light in the house, and we haven't even come close to finishing our tasks. Someone must run to Baba Yaga to get some fire."

"I'm not going," said the girl who was making lace. "I can see by the light of my pins."

"I'm not going," said the girl who was knitting stockings. "I can see by the light of my knitting needles."

"That means you have to go," they both shouted to their stepsister. "Get going! Go and see your friend Baba Yaga!" And they pushed Vasilisa out of the room.

Vasilisa went into her own little room, laid out the supper she had prepared for her doll, and said: "There, dolly, eat and help me in my need. They want me to go to Baba Yaga for fire, and she will eat me up." The doll ate her supper. Her eyes glowed like two candles. "Don't be afraid, Vasilisushka," she said. "Go where they send you. Only be sure to take me with you. If I'm in your pocket, Baba Yaga can't hurt you."

Vasilisa got ready to go, put the doll in her pocket, and crossed herself before setting out for the deep forest. She trembled with fear as she walked through the woods. Suddenly a horseman galloped past her. His face was white, he was dressed in white, and he was riding a white horse with white reins and stirrups. After that it began to grow light.

Vasilisa walked deeper into the forest, and a second horseman galloped past her. His face was red, he was dressed in red, and he was riding a red horse. Then the sun began to rise.

Vasilisa walked all night and all day long. Late on the second evening she arrived in the clearing where Baba Yaga's hut was standing. The fence around it was made of human bones. Skulls with empty eye sockets stared down from the posts. The gate was made from the bones of human legs; the bolts were made from human hands; and the lock was a jaw with sharp teeth. Vasilisa was terrified and stood rooted to the spot. Suddenly another horseman galloped past her. His face was black, he was dressed in black, and he was riding a black horse. He galloped up to Baba Yaga's door and vanished, as though the earth had swallowed him up. Then it was night. But it wasn't dark for long. The eyes on all the skulls on the fence began to gleam, and the clearing grew bright as day. Vasilisa shuddered with fright. She wanted to run away, but didn't know which way to turn.

A dreadful noise sounded in the woods. The trees creaked and groaned. The dead leaves rustled and crunched. Baba Yaga appeared, flying in a mortar, prodding it with her pestle, and sweeping her traces with a broom. She rode up to the gate, stopped, and sniffed the air around her. "Foo, Foo! This place smells of a Russian girl! Who's there?"

Vasilisa went up to the old witch and, trembling with fear, bowed down low and said: "It is I, Granny. My stepsisters sent me to get some light."

"Very well," said Baba Yaga. "I know your sisters all right. But before I give you fire you must stay and work for me. If you don't, I'll have you for dinner!" Then she turned to the gate and shouted:

"Slide back, my strong bolts! Open up, my wide gates!" The gates opened, and Baba Yaga rode in with a shrill whistle. Vasilisa followed her, and then everything closed up again.

Baba Yaga went into the hut, stretched herself out on a bench, and said to Vasilisa: "I'm hungry. Bring me whatever's in the oven!" Vasilisa lit a taper from the skulls on the fence and began serving Baba Yaga the food from the oven. There was enough to feed ten people. She brought kvass, mead, beer, and wine from the cellar. The old woman ate and drank everything put before her, leaving for Vasilisa only a little bowl of cabbage soup, a crust of bread, and a scrap of pork.

Baba Yaga got ready for bed and said: "Tomorrow, after I leave, see to it that you sweep the yard, clean the hut, cook supper, wash the linen, and go to the corn bin and sort out a bushel of wheat. And if you haven't finished by the time I get back, I'll eat you up!" After giving the orders, Baba Yaga began snoring. Vasilisa took her doll out of her pocket and placed Baba Yaga's leftovers before it. Then she burst out crying and said: "There, doll, have some food and help me out! Baba Yaga has given me impossible tasks and has threatened to eat me up if I don't take care of everything. Help me." The doll replied: "Don't be afraid, Vasilisa the Fair! Eat your supper, say your prayers, and go to sleep. Mornings are wiser than evenings."

Vasilisa got up early. Baba Yaga was already up and about. When Vasilisa looked out the window, she saw that the lights in the skulls' eyes were fading. Then the white horseman galloped by, and it was daybreak. Baba Yaga went out into the yard and gave a whistle. Her mortar, pestle, and broom appeared. The red horseman flashed by, and the sun rose. Baba Yaga sat down in her mortar, prodded it on with her pestle, and swept over her traces with the broom.

Vasilisa was alone, and she looked around Baba Yaga's hut. She had never seen so many things to do in her life and couldn't figure out where to begin. But lo and behold, all the work was done. The doll was picking out the last bits of chaff from the wheat. "You've saved me!" Vasilisa said to her doll. "If it weren't for you, I would have been gobbled up tonight."

"All you have to do now is prepare supper," said the doll as it climbed back into her pocket. "Cook it with God's blessing, and then get some rest so that you'll stay strong."

Toward evening Vasilisa set the table and waited for Baba Yaga. It grew dark, and when the black horseman galloped by, it was night. The only light came from the skulls on the fence. The trees creaked and groaned; the dry leaves crackled and crunched. Baba Yaga was on her way. Vasilisa went out to meet her. "Is everything done?" asked Baba Yaga. "See for yourself, Granny," Vasilisa replied.

Baba Yaga went all around the hut. She was annoyed that there was nothing to complain about, and said: "Well done." Then she shouted: "My faithful servants, my dear friends, grind the wheat!" Three pairs of hands appeared. They took the wheat and whisked it away. Baba Yaga ate her fill, made ready to sleep, and again gave Vasilisa her tasks. "Tomorrow," she ordered, "do just what you did today. Then take the poppy seeds out of the bin and get rid of the dust, speck by speck. Someone threw dust into the bins just to annoy me." Baba Yaga turned over and began to snore.

Vasilisa began to feed her doll. The doll ate everything in front of her, and repeated just what she had said the day before: "Pray to God and go to sleep. Mornings are wiser than evenings. Everything will get done, Vasilisushka."

The next morning Baba Yaga rode off again in her mortar. With the help of her doll, Vasilisa finished the housework in no time at all. The old witch returned in the evening, looked everything over, and cried out: "My faithful servants, my dear friends, press the oil from these poppy seeds." Three pairs of hands appeared, took the bin of poppy seeds, and whisked it away. Baba Yaga sat down to dine. Vasilisa stood silently next to her while she ate. "Why don't you talk to me?" Baba Yaga asked. "You stand there as though you were mute."

"I did not dare speak," said Vasilisa, "but if you'll give me permission, there is something I'd like to ask."

"Ask away!" said Baba Yaga. "But be careful. Not every question has a good answer. If you know too much, you will soon grow old."

"Oh, Granny, I only want to ask you about some things I saw on the way here. When I was on my way over here, a horseman with a white face, riding a white horse, and dressed in white overtook me. Who was he?"

"That was the bright day," Baba Yaga replied.

"Then another horseman overtook me. He had a red face, was riding a red horse, and was dressed in red. Who was he?"

"He is my red sun," Baba Yaga replied.

"Then who was the black horseman I met at your gate, Granny?"

"He is my dark night. The three of them are my faithful servants."

Vasilisa remembered the three pairs of hands, but kept her mouth shut. "Don't you want to ask about anything else?" Baba Yaga said.

"No, Granny, that's enough. You were the one who said that the more you know, the sooner you grow old."

"You are wise," Baba Yaga said, "to ask only about things you saw outside my house, not inside it. I don't like to have my dirty linen aired in public, and if people get too curious, I eat them up. And now I have a question for you. How did you get all that work done so fast?"

"I was helped by my mother's blessing," said Vasilisa.

"Oh, so that's how you did it!" Baba Yaga shrieked. "Get out of here, blessed daughter! I don't want any blessed ones in my house." She dragged Vasilisa out of the room and pushed her out through the gate. Then she took one of the skulls with blazing eyes from the fence, stuck it on the end of a stick, and gave it to the girl, saying: "Here's fire for your stepsisters. Take it. That's what you came here for, isn't it?"

Vasilisa ran home, using the fire from the skull to light the path. At dawn the fire went out, and by evening she reached the house. As she was approaching the gate, she was about to throw the skull away, thinking that her stepsisters surely already had fire, when she heard a muffled voice coming from the skull: "Don't throw me away. Take me to your stepmother." She looked at the stepmother's house and, seeing that there was no light in the window, decided to enter with her skull. For the first time the stepmother and stepsisters received her kindly. They told her that since she had left, they had had no fire at all in the house. They had been unable to produce a flame themselves. They had tried to bring one back from the neighbors, but it went out as soon as they crossed the threshold.

"Perhaps your fire will last," said the stepmother. Vasilisa carried the skull in. Its eyes began to stare at the stepmother and two sisters. It burned them. They tried to hide, but the eyes followed them wherever they went. By morning they had turned into three heaps of ashes on the floor. Only Vasilisa remained untouched by the fire.

Vasilisa buried the skull in the garden, locked up the house, and went to the nearest town. An old woman without children gave her shelter, and there she lived, waiting for her father's return. One day she said to the woman, "I am weary of sitting here with nothing to do, Granny. Buy me the best flax you can find. Then at least I'll get some spinning done."

The old woman bought some of the best flax around, and Vasilisa set to work. She spun as fast as lightning, and her threads were even and fine as hair. She spun a great deal of yarn. It was time to start weaving it, but there were no combs fine enough for Vasilisa's yarn, and no one was willing to make one. Vasilisa asked her doll for help. The doll said: "Bring me an old comb, an old shuttle, and a horse's mane. I will make a loom for you." Vasilisa did as the doll said, went to sleep, and found a wonderful loom waiting for her the next morning.

By the end of the winter the linen was woven. It was so fine that you could pass it through the eye of a needle. In the spring, the linen was bleached, and Vasilisa said to the old woman: "Granny, sell this linen and keep the money for yourself."

The old woman looked at the cloth and gasped. "No, my child! No one can wear linen like this except the tsar. I shall take it to the palace."

The old woman went to the tsar's palace and began walking back and forth beneath the windows. The tsar saw her and asked: "What do you want, Granny?"

"Your Majesty," she answered, "I have brought some rare merchandise. I don't want to show it to anyone but you."

The tsar ordered the old lady to appear before him, and when he saw the linen, he gazed at it in amazement. "What do you want for it?" he asked.

"I can't put a price on it, Little Father Tsar! It's a gift." The tsar thanked her and loaded her down with presents.

The tsar ordered shirts made from the linen. He had them cut, but no one could find a seamstress who was willing to sew them. Finally, he summoned the old woman and said: "You were able to spin and weave this linen. You must be able to sew it into shirts for me."

"I was not the one who spun and wove this linen, Your Majesty," said the old woman. "This is the work of a girl to whom I gave shelter."

"Well then, let her sew the shirts," the tsar ordered.

The old woman returned home and told Vasilisa everything. "I knew all along that I would have to do this work," Vasilisa told her. Vasilisa locked herself in her room and began sewing. She worked without stopping and soon a dozen shirts were ready.

The old woman took the shirts to the tsar. Vasilisa washed up, combed her hair, dressed in her finest clothes, and sat down by the window to see what would happen. She saw one of the tsar's servants enter the courtyard. The messenger came into the room and said: "His Majesty wishes to meet the seamstress who made his shirts and wants to reward her with his own hands."

Vasilisa appeared before the tsar. When the tsar saw Vasilisa the Fair, he fell head over heels in love with her. "No, my beauty," he said. "I shall never part from you. You will be my wife."

The tsar took Vasilisa by her white hands and sat her down next to him. The wedding was celebrated at once. Soon afterward Vasilisa's father returned. He was overjoyed with her good fortune and went to live in his daughter's house. Vasilisa took the old woman into her home as well and carried the doll in her pocket until the day she died.

Momotaro, or the Peach Boy[†]

If you'll believe me there was a time when the fairies were none so shy as they are now. That was the time when beasts talked to men, when there were spells and enchantments and magic every day, when there was great store of hidden treasure to be dug up, and adventures for the asking.

At that time, you must know, an old man and an old woman lived alone by themselves. They were good and they were poor and they had no children at all.

One fine day, "What are you doing this morning, good man?" says the old woman.

"Oh," says the old man, "I'm off to the mountains with my bill-hook to gather sticks for our fire. And what are you doing, good wife?"

"Oh," says the old woman, "I'm off to the stream to wash clothes. It's my washing day," she adds.

So the old man went to the mountains and the old woman went to the stream.

Now, while she was washing the clothes, what should she see but a fine ripe peach that came floating down the stream! The peach was big enough, and rosy red on both sides.

"I'm in luck this morning," said the dame, and she pulled the peach to shore with a split bamboo stick.

By-and-by, when her good man came home from the hills, she set the peach before him. "Eat, good man," she said. "This is a lucky peach I found in the stream and brought home for you."

But the old man never got a taste of the peach. And why did he not?

All of a sudden the peach burst in two and there was no stone to it, but a fine boy baby where the stone should have been.

"Mercy me!" says the old woman.

"Mercy me!" says the old man.

The boy baby first ate up one half of the peach and then he ate up the other half. When he had done this he was finer and stronger than ever.

"Momotaro! Momotaro!" cries the old man. "The eldest son of the peach."

"Truth it is indeed," says the old woman. "He was born in a peach."

Both of them took such good care of Momotaro that soon he was the stoutest and bravest boy of all that country-side. He was a

† "Momotaro, or the Peach Boy" as told by Yei Theodora Ozaki in *Japanese Fairy Tales by Lafcadio Hearn and Others* (New York: Boni and Liveright, 1918), pp. 154–60.

credit to them, you may believe. The neighbors nodded their heads and they said, "Momotaro is the fine young man!"

"Mother," says Momotaro one day to the old woman, "make me a good store of *kimi-dango*" (which is the way that they call millet dumplings in those parts).

"What for do you want *kimi-dango*?" says his mother.

"Why," says Momotaro, "I'm going on a journey, or as you may say, an adventure, and I shall be needing the *kimi-dango* on the way."

"Where are you going, Momotaro?" says his mother.

"I'm off to the Ogres' Island," says Momotaro, "to get their treasure, and I should be obliged if you'd let me have the *kimi-dango* as soon as may be," he says.

So they made him the *kimi-dango*, and he put them in a wallet, and he tied the wallet to his girdle and off he set.

"*Sayonara*, and good luck to you, Momotaro!" cried the old man and the old woman.

"*Sayonara! Sayonara!*" cried Momotaro.

He hadn't gone far when he fell in with a monkey.

"Kia! Kia!" says the monkey. "Where are you off to, Momotaro?"

Says Momotaro, "I'm off to the Ogres' Island for an adventure."

"What have you got in the wallet hanging at your girdle?"

"Now you're asking me something," says Momotaro. "Sure, I've some of the best millet dumplings in all Japan."

"Give me one," says the monkey, "and I will go with you."

So Momotaro gave a millet dumpling to the monkey, and the two of them jogged on together. They hadn't gone far when they fell in with a pheasant.

"Ken! Ken!" said the pheasant. "Where are you off to, Momotaro?"

Says Momotaro, "I'm off to the Ogres' Island for an adventure."

"What have you got in your wallet, Momotaro?"

"I've got some of the best millet dumplings in all Japan."

"Give me one," says the pheasant, "and I will go with you."

So Momotaro gave a millet dumpling to the pheasant, and the three of them jogged on together.

They hadn't gone far when they fell in with a dog.

"Bow! Wow! Wow!" says the dog. "Where are you off to, Momotaro?"

Says Momotaro, "I'm off to the Ogres' Island."

"What have you got in your wallet, Momotaro?"

"I've got some of the best millet dumplings in all Japan."

"Give me one," says the dog, "and I will go with you."

So Momotaro gave a millet dumpling to the dog, and the four of them jogged on together. By-and-by they came to the Ogres' Island.

"Now, brothers," says Momotaro, "listen to my plan. The pheasant must fly over the castle gate and peck the Ogres. The monkey must climb over the castle wall and pinch the Ogres. The dog and I will break the bolts and bars. He will bite the Ogres, and I will fight the Ogres."

Then there was the great battle.

The pheasant flew over the castle gate: "Ken! Ken! Ken!"

Momotaro broke the bolts and bars, and the dog leapt into the castle courtyard. "Bow! Wow! Wow!"

The brave companions fought till sundown and overcame the Ogres. Those that were left alive they took prisoners and bound with cords—a wicked lot they were.

"Now, brothers," says Momotaro, "bring out the Ogres' treasure." So they did.

The treasure was worth having, indeed. There were magic jewels there, and caps and coats to make you invisible. There was gold and silver, and jade and coral, and amber and tortoise-shell and mother-of-pearl.

"Here's riches for all," says Momotaro. "Choose, brothers, and take your fill."

"Kia! Kia!" says the monkey. "Thanks, my Lord Momotaro."

"Ken! Ken!" says the pheasant. "Thanks, my Lord Momotaro."

"Bow! Wow! Wow!" says the dog. "Thanks, my dear Lord Momotaro."

JOSEPH JACOBS

Jack and the Beanstalk[†]

There was once upon a time a poor widow who had an only son named Jack, and a cow named Milky-white. And all they had to live on was the milk the cow gave every morning, which they carried to the market and sold. But one morning Milky-white gave no milk, and they didn't know what to do.

"What shall we do, what shall we do?" said the widow, wringing her hands.

"Cheer up, mother, I'll go and get work somewhere," said Jack.

"We've tried that before, and nobody would take you," said his mother; "we must sell Milky-white and with the money start shop, or something."

"All right, mother," says Jack; "it's market-day today, and I'll soon sell Milky-white, and then we'll see what we can do."

---

† Joseph Jacobs, "Jack and the Beanstalk," *English Fairy Tales*, 3rd ed. (London: David Nutt in the Strand, 1898).

So he took the cow's halter in his hand, and off he started. He hadn't gone far when he met a funny-looking old man, who said to him: "Good morning, Jack."

"Good morning to you," said Jack, and wondered how he knew his name.

"Well, Jack, and where are you off to?" said the man.

"I'm going to market to sell our cow here."

"Oh, you look the proper sort of chap to sell cows," said the man; "I wonder if you know how many beans make five."

"Two in each hand and one in your mouth," says Jack, as sharp as a needle.

"Right you are," says the man, "and here they are, the very beans themselves," he went on, pulling out of his pocket a number of strange-looking beans. "As you are so sharp," says he, "I don't mind doing a swap with you—your cow for these beans."

"Go along," says Jack; "wouldn't you like it?"

"Ah! you don't know what these beans are," said the man; "if you plant them overnight, by morning they grow right up to the sky."

"Really?" said Jack; "you don't say so."

"Yes, that is so, and if it doesn't turn out to be true you can have your cow back."

"Right," says Jack, and hands him over Milky-white's halter and pockets the beans.

Back goes Jack home, and as he hadn't gone very far it wasn't dusk by the time he got to his door.

"Back already, Jack?" said his mother; "I see you haven't got Milky-white, so you've sold her. How much did you get for her?"

"You'll never guess, mother," says Jack.

"No, you don't say so. Good boy! Five pounds, ten, fifteen, no, it can't be twenty."

"I told you you couldn't guess. What do you say to these beans; they're magical, plant them overnight and—"

"What!" says Jack's mother, "have you been such a fool, such a dolt, such an idiot, as to give away my Milky-white, the best milker in the parish, and prime beef to boot, for a set of paltry beans? Take that! Take that! Take that! And as for your precious beans here they go out of the window. And now off with you to bed. Not a sup shall you drink, and not a bit shall you swallow this very night."

So Jack went upstairs to his little room in the attic, and sad and sorry he was, to be sure, as much for his mother's sake, as for the loss of his supper.

At last he dropped off to sleep.

When he woke up, the room looked so funny. The sun was shining into part of it, and yet all the rest was quite dark and shady. So Jack jumped up and dressed himself and went to the window. And what do you think he saw? Why, the beans his mother had thrown out of the window into the garden had sprung up into a big beanstalk which went up and up and up till it reached the sky. So the man spoke truth after all.

The beanstalk grew up quite close past Jack's window, so all he had to do was to open it and give a jump on to the beanstalk which ran up just like a big ladder. So Jack climbed, and he climbed and he climbed and he climbed and he climbed and he climbed and he climbed till at last he reached the sky. And when he got there he found a long broad road going as straight as a dart. So he walked along and he walked along and he walked along till he came to a great big tall house, and on the doorstep there was a great big tall woman.

"Good morning, mum," says Jack, quite polite-like. "Could you be so kind as to give me some breakfast?" For he hadn't had anything to eat, you know, the night before and was as hungry as a hunter.

"It's breakfast you want, is it?" says the great big tall woman, "it's breakfast you'll be if you don't move off from here. My man is an ogre and there's nothing he likes better than boys broiled on toast. You'd better be moving on or he'll soon be coming."

"Oh! please, mum, do give me something to eat, mum. I've had nothing to eat since yesterday morning, really and truly, mum," says Jack. "I may as well be broiled as die of hunger."

Well, the ogre's wife was not half so bad after all. So she took Jack into the kitchen, and gave him a hunk of bread and cheese and a jug of milk. But Jack hadn't half finished these when thump! thump! thump! the whole house began to tremble with the noise of someone coming.

"Goodness gracious me! It's my old man," said the ogre's wife, "what on earth shall I do? Come along quick and jump in here." And she bundled Jack into the oven just as the ogre came in.

He was a big one, to be sure. At his belt he had three calves strung up by the heels, and he unhooked them and threw them down on the table and said: 'Here, wife, broil me a couple of these for breakfast. Ah! what's this I smell?

> "Fee-fi-fo-fum,
> I smell the blood of an Englishman,
> Be he alive, or be he dead
> I'll have his bones to grind my bread."

"Nonsense, dear," said his wife, "you're dreaming. Or perhaps you smell the scraps of that little boy you liked so much for yesterday's dinner. Here, you go and have a wash and tidy up, and by the time you come back your breakfast'll be ready for you."

So off the ogre went, and Jack was just going to jump out of the oven and run away when the woman told him not. "Wait till he's asleep," says she; "he always has a doze after breakfast."

Well, the ogre had his breakfast, and after that he goes to a big chest and takes out of it a couple of bags of gold, and down he sits and counts till at last his head began to nod and he began to snore till the whole house shook again.

Then Jack crept out on tiptoe from his oven, and as he was passing the ogre he took one of the bags of gold under his arm, and off he pelters till he came to the beanstalk, and then he threw down the bag of gold, which, of course, fell into his mother's garden, and then he climbed down and climbed down till at last he got home and told his mother and showed her the gold and said: "Well, mother, wasn't I right about the beans? They are really magical, you see."

So they lived on the bag of gold for some time, but at last they came to the end of it, and Jack made up his mind to try his luck once more at the top of the beanstalk. So one fine morning he rose up early, and got on to the beanstalk, and he climbed and he climbed and he climbed and he climbed and he climbed and he climbed till at last he came out on to the road again and up to the great big tall house he had been to before. There, sure enough, was the great big tall woman a-standing on the doorstep.

"Good morning, mum," says Jack, as bold as brass, "could you be so good as to give me something to eat?"

"Go away, my boy," said the big tall woman, "or else my man will eat you up for breakfast. But aren't you the youngster who came here once before? Do you know, that very day my man missed one of his bags of gold."

"That's strange, mum," said Jack, "I dare say I could tell you something about that, but I'm so hungry I can't speak till I've had something to eat."

Well, the big tall woman was so curious that she took him in and gave him something to eat. But he had scarcely begun munching it as slowly as he could when thump! thump! they heard the giant's footstep, and his wife hid Jack away in the oven.

All happened as it did before. In came the ogre as he did before, said: "Fe-fi-fo-fum," and had his breakfast of three broiled oxen. Then he said: "Wife, bring me the hen that lays the golden eggs." So she brought it, and the ogre said: "Lay," and it laid an egg all of gold. And then the ogre began to nod his head, and to snore till the house shook.

Then Jack crept out of the oven on tiptoe and caught hold of the golden hen, and was off before you could say "Jack Robinson." But this time the hen gave a cackle which woke the ogre, and just as Jack got out of the house he heard him calling: "Wife, wife, what have you done with my golden hen?"

And the wife said: "Why, my dear?"

But that was all Jack heard, for he rushed off to the beanstalk and climbed down like a house on fire. And when he got home he showed his mother the wonderful hen, and said "Lay" to it; and it laid a golden egg every time he said "Lay."

Well, Jack was not content, and it wasn't very long before he determined to have another try at his luck up there at the top of the beanstalk. So one fine morning, he rose up early, and got on to the beanstalk, and he climbed and he climbed and he climbed and he climbed till he got to the top. But this time he knew better than to go straight to the ogre's house. And when he got near it, he waited behind a bush till he saw the ogre's wife come out with a pail to get some water, and then he crept into the house and got into the copper. He hadn't been there long when he heard thump! thump! thump! as before, and in came the ogre and his wife.

"Fee-fi-fo-fum, I smell the blood of an Englishman," cried out the ogre. "I smell him, wife, I smell him."

"Do you, my dearie?" says the ogre's wife. "Then, if it's that little rogue that stole your gold and the hen that laid the golden eggs he's sure to have got into the oven." And they both rushed to the oven. But Jack wasn't there, luckily, and the ogre's wife said: "There you are again with your fee-fi-fo-fum. Why, of course, it's the boy you caught last night that I've just broiled for your breakfast. How forgetful I am, and how careless you are not to know the difference between live and dead after all these years."

So the ogre sat down to the breakfast and ate it, but every now and then he would mutter: "Well, I could have sworn—" and he'd get up and search the larder and the cupboards and everything, only, luckily, he didn't think of the copper.

After breakfast was over, the ogre called out: "Wife, wife, bring me my golden harp." So she brought it and put it on the table before him. Then he said: "Sing!" and the golden harp sang most beautifully. And it went on singing till the ogre fell asleep, and commenced to snore like thunder.

Then Jack lifted up the copper-lid very quietly and got down like a mouse and crept on hands and knees till he came to the table, when up he crawled, caught hold of the golden harp and dashed with it towards the door. But the harp called out quite loud: "Master! Master!" and the ogre woke up just in time to see Jack running off with his harp.

Jack ran as fast as he could, and the ogre came rushing after, and would soon have caught him only Jack had a start and dodged him a bit and knew where he was going. When he got to the beanstalk the ogre was not more than twenty yards away when suddenly he saw Jack disappear like, and when he came to the end of the road he saw Jack underneath climbing down for dear life. Well, the ogre didn't like trusting himself to such a ladder, and he stood and waited, so Jack got another start. But just then the harp cried out: "Master! Master!" and the ogre swung himself down on to the beanstalk, which shook with his weight. Down climbs Jack, and after him climbed the ogre. By this time Jack had climbed down and climbed down and climbed down till he was very nearly home. So he called out: "Mother! Mother! bring me an axe, bring me an axe." And his mother came rushing out with the axe in her hand, but when she came to the beanstalk she stood stock still with fright, for there she saw the ogre with his legs just through the clouds.

But Jack jumped down and got hold of the axe and gave a chop at the beanstalk which cut it half in two. The ogre felt the beanstalk shake and quiver, so he stopped to see what was the matter. Then Jack gave another chop with the axe, and the beanstalk was cut in two and began to topple over. Then the ogre fell down and broke his crown, and the beanstalk came toppling after.

Then Jack showed his mother his golden harp, and what with showing that and selling the golden eggs, Jack and his mother became very rich, and he married a great princess, and they lived happy ever after.

INTRODUCTION:
Hans Christian Andersen

"He was a perfect wizard," August Strindberg declared in a tribute to the author whose stories had captivated him as a child.[1] Strindberg has never been alone in his enthusiasm for Hans Christian Andersen. According to UNESCO, the United Nations Educational, Scientific, and Cultural Organization, Andersen ranks among the ten most widely translated authors in the world, along with William Shakespeare and Karl Marx. His stories have become collective cultural property, operating almost like malleable folk tales rather than fixed literary texts. Children in Beijing, Calcutta, Beirut, and Montreal have wept over "The Little Match Girl," admired the child in "The Emperor's New Clothes," and identified with the abject baby swan in "The Ugly Duckling."

Walt Disney Studios has done much to sustain and extend the global reach of Andersen's fairy tales, first with its animated film *The Little Mermaid* (1989), then with *Frozen* (2013), inspired by Andersen's "Snow Queen." That Andersen is not just for the young becomes quickly apparent from the many adult adaptations of the tales, from Kathryn Davis's *The Girl Who Trod on a Loaf* through Sandra Gilbert's "The Last Poems about the Snow Queen" to Joyce Carol Oates's "You, Little Match Girl." These contemporary writers, along with Henry James, Hermann Hesse, W. H. Auden, and Thomas Mann, grew up with Andersen's stories and then grew into them, admiring their imaginative force and allowing it to seep into their own art.

We remember Andersen for the beauty of his images—for the shiny red shoes that captivate Karen, the golden slipper hung around the neck of the melodious nightingale, and the chunks of ice dancing for joy in the palace of the Snow Queen. In "The Little Mermaid," the sun looks like a "purple flower with light streaming from its calyx" (p. 284); the eleven brothers in "The Wild Swans" write on "golden tablets with pencils of diamond"; and the soldier in "The

1. Maria Tatar, *The Annotated Hans Christian Andersen* (New York: Norton, 2007), p. xv.

Tinderbox" enters a hall where "hundreds of lamps" are shining. The bright wonders and vivid marvels in Andersen's stories go far toward explaining what drew artists like Arthur Rackham, Edmund Dulac, and Kay Nielsen to illustrate the fairy tales.

Andersen's paper cuttings, sketches, and collages remind us that he was supremely dedicated to the visual, a painter as much as a poet. He was committed to everything that glitters, dazzles, and shines, yet he was also deeply concerned with what lies beneath appearances. Surface and depth were equally important. We not only witness the suffering of the Little Mermaid and the Little Match Girl, we also get inside the skin of the two characters, empathizing with them and experiencing their feelings vicariously. Andersen uses beautiful objects to enliven his stories, enabling us to visualize other worlds, but also moves from surfaces to interiority so that we not only see what his characters see but also feel what they feel. His moving pictures harness aesthetic effects to animate narrated worlds as well as the real-life reader outside the text.

If Andersen's magic lies in his ability to combine beautiful surfaces with emotional power surges, critics have been reluctant to dwell on it. Instead they focus on autobiographical features, showing how the tales mirror their maker. In *Hans Christian Andersen: The Life of a Storyteller*, Jackie Wullschlager begins by declaring that her subject is a "compulsive autobiographer" and proceeds to document in superbly comprehensive ways how the art charts the stations of its author's troubled soul. In the fairy tales, we discover, the truest self-portraits are etched in generous and fulsome detail. "He is the triumphant Ugly Duckling," she declares, "and the loyal Little Mermaid, the steadfast Tin Soldier and the king-loving Nightingale, the demonic Shadow, the depressive fir tree, the forlorn Little Matchgirl."[2] Here is another authority on the Danish writer: "Andersen never stopped telling his own story. . . . Sometimes he tells it in an idealized form, sometimes with self-revelatory candor. In tale after tale . . . he is the hero who triumphs over poverty, persecution, and plain stupidity, and who sometimes, in a reversal of the facts, marries the princess . . . or scorns her."[3]

In some ways, these critics are staging a familiar argument, one that legitimizes the study of Andersen's fairy tales by seeing in them a prism of adult fears and desires. After all, if the tales are just "simplistic narratives for children," they are hardly worthy of adult attention. *More Than Just Fairy Tales*, the title of a recent volume of essays on Andersen's stories, is symptomatic. Academic anxiety

---

2. Jackie Wullschlager, *Hans Christian Andersen: The Life of a Storyteller* (New York: Knopf, 2000), p. 3.
3. Reginald Spink, *Hans Christian Andersen: The Man and His Work*, 3rd ed. (Copenhagen: Høst, 1981), p. 10.

about analyzing fairy tales runs high, less because they belong to the regime of popular culture than because they were so long consigned to the nursery.[4]

Andersen's fairy tales promote a cult of classical beauty, with all its seductive power to lure us into the world of surfaces, but they add a sinister edge, as a reminder of the perils of aesthetic enchantments. They also add a cult of grotesque suffering to their narrative circuits, one equally compelling in its evocation of the emotionally gratifying satisfactions of witnessing pain and empathizing with its victims—feeling bad in order to feel good. The double face of beauty is brilliantly represented in the invisible cloth woven by the two swindlers in "The Emperor's New Clothes." That fabric captivates, making us do the imaginative work of seeing something beautiful even when it has no material reality and is constructed from mere words. The cloth is "*magnifique*" (p. 316), "light as spider webs" (p. 317), and "exquisite" (pp. 315, 316). Here we are in the realm of a self-reflexive allegory about how verbal art is both captivatingly beautiful illusion and ludicrous fraud. Stories take us in so long as we are willing collaborators and co-conspirators, but it is also easy to mock them as mirages with no grounding in reality.

Andersen's "The Nightingale" takes us almost seamlessly from aesthetics and the pleasure principle to a poetics of pain by building a contrast between the songs of two very different birds. Both nightingales in the story are enchanting, but the real nightingale, as opposed to the jewel-encrusted mechanical one, sings with a voice "so lovely" (p. 321) that tears roll down the emperor's cheeks. Beauty moves the emperor to tears, and the scene of his emotional release enables us to see a possible link between unalloyed, organic beauty and the healing power of suffering. The nightingale's song restores the emperor's health, but in tales like "The Red Shoes," the protagonist's love of beauty is shadowed by sadistic punishments that lead to suffering that is anything but transcendent. The magic of the beautiful new shoes made for Karen turns against her, taking possession of her feet, compelling her to dance endlessly in a frenzied spectacle that ends with the amputation of her feet. For Andersen, beauty has transformative energy, but its link with vanity arouses profound fears about excesses both evil and dangerous. And it can easily tip into the unsightly and grotesque.

Andersen, committed to success on the stage more than anything else, took up fairy tales as a sideline. He inserted himself into a tradition that famously staged spectacular punishments, nearly always reserved for ogres and other evildoers. The witch from "Hansel and

---

4. Julie K. Allen, *More Than Just Fairy Tales: New Approaches to the Stories of Hans Christian Andersen* (San Diego: Cognella, 2014).

Gretel" perishes in the oven; the evil stepmother in "Snow White" dances to her death in red-hot iron shoes; and like a latter-day David, Jack slides down the beanstalk and vanquishes a giant. Andersen's stories rarely indulge in enacting revenge fantasies or deserved punishments. Instead we have scenes of suffering, tableaux designed to evoke compassion and stir pity rather than to enunciate triumphant programs for survival.

Take the Little Match Girl, a character whose story begins as follows: "It was bitterly cold." Already we are plunged into a world of painful sensation. "Poor mite, she was the picture of misery as she trudged along, hungry and shivering with cold." We swiftly move into the girl's head, feeling the sharpness of her pain: "She knew that her father would beat her, and besides, it was almost as cold at home as it was here." Suddenly we move from a gaze that takes in externals to a place inside the girl's head. "Ah! Maybe a lighted match," she thinks, "would do some good." All that follows is focalized through the little match seller, and as readers, we see what she sees, feel what she feels. "No one could imagine what beautiful things she had seen," Andersen writes at the end of her story. That may be true for those who find her corpse on the cold sidewalk, but certainly not for those who read about her New Year's Eve visions.

In "The Little Mermaid," Andersen moves us almost immediately into the consciousness of the youngest of the Sea-King's daughters. She is the one who loves to hear about the human world, who longs to rise to the surface, and who cannot take her eyes off the young prince and his ship. And we witness her suffering when she loses her voice and feels as if her heart is breaking "for grief." When she drinks the potion of the Sea Witch, we feel the "sharp pain" that courses through her body as well as the force of the "double-edged sword" slicing through her and the "sharp knives" on which she walks. This tale, like "The Little Match Girl," shows how a curious transvaluation takes places as Andersen struggles with the cruelty of those who enjoy a cult of beauty and pleasure (the bon vivants celebrating New Year's Eve at home in "The Little Match Girl" and the royals feasting and dancing in the prince's palace in "The Little Mermaid") while others suffer in silence. The two "pictures of misery" draw our notice more powerfully than the warmth and light of interior scenes. We gaze and empathize more than we admire and wonder.

Our own culture's answer to Andersen's spiritually triumphant mermaid appears in the adventurous, rebellious, curious, and "upwardly mobile"[5] Ariel created by Disney Studios. As one shrewd

5. Laura Sells, "'Where Do the Mermaids Stand?' Voice and Body in *The Little Mermaid*," in *From Mouse to Mermaid: The Politics of Film, Gender and Culture*, ed. Elizabeth Bell, Lynda Haas, and Laura Sells (Bloomington: Indiana UP, 1995), p. 179.

critic of *The Little Mermaid* observes, the Disney film establishes a powerful hierarchical relationship dividing the blithe Caribbean-equivalent sea creatures from the humans above who engage in labor and transform nature into culture. Ariel's longing for this realm, which manifests itself in the commodity fetishism of her enthusiastic collecting of booty from shipwrecks, is fulfilled through Ursula, a grotesque Medusa-like octopus who, like Andersen's Sea Witch, represents the monstrosity of feminine power. Ariel may regain her voice when she is assimilated to the human world in the end, but Disney conveniently leaves us in the dark about the cost, allowing the couple's final embrace to erase Ariel's rebelliousness, her troubled relationship with the feminine, and the painful self-mutilation involved in her transformation. As Patrick D. Murphy points out, "the escapist character of the film" is especially evident in its avoidance of the problem that will inevitably arise when "Ariel's former friend Flounder shows up on the dinner table one evening."[6]

Maurice Sendak, renowned for creating vibrantly spirited and scrappy child characters, was disturbed by the "disquieting passivity" in Andersen's books for children. "At his worst," Sendak comments on Andersen, "he dreadfully sentimentalizes children; they rarely have the spunk, shrewdness, and character with which he endows inanimate objects."[7] The Little Mermaid, the Little Match Girl, and Karen of "The Red Shoes" he found particularly "irritating," surely in part for the simple reason that the stories of all these creatures end with their deaths. "His heroines always wind up going to the bosom of God (if they're good), or else they're praying or being saved from Hell by someone else's prayers," the illustrator Trina Schart Hyman observed in recollecting her childhood reading of Andersen.[8]

Andersen's fairy tales may still begin with "What if?" and move us to ask "What's next?" but they are also unusual in inspiring us to ask "Why?" Causation is no longer random and arbitrary, but psychologically motivated and realistically portrayed. In both "The Little Match Girl" and "The Little Mermaid," beauty co-exists with suffering in ways that create a new aesthetic, one that turns from a cult of beautiful objects to a commitment to widening the gaze to include scenes that inspire compassion as much as wonder. We may enter the tales through the gates of Beauty but we linger in the

6. Patrick D. Murphy, "'The Whole Wide World Was Scrubbed Clean': The Androcentric Animation of Denatured Disney," in *From Mouse to Mermaid*, p. 133.
7. Maurice Sendak, "Hans Christian Andersen," in *Caldecott & Co.: Notes on Books & Pictures* (New York: Farrar, Straus & Giroux, Michael di Capua Books, 1988), pp. 33–34.
8. Trina Schart Hyman, "'Cut It Down, and You Will Find Something at the Roots,'" in *The Reception of Grimms' Fairy Tales: Responses, Reactions, Revisions,* ed. Donald Haase (Detroit: Wayne State UP, 1993), p. 294.

precincts of the unsightly and grotesque, in places that lead us to look in horror rather than to gaze in pleasure. As compensation we exit these narratives with a renewed sense of compassion and connection but, more important, with a more capacious sense of what beauty and its grim opposite can do.

The Little Mermaid[†]

Far out at sea, the water is as blue as the petals of the prettiest cornflowers and as clear as the purest glass. But it's very deep out there, so deep that even the longest anchor line can't touch bottom. You would have to pile up countless church steeples, one on top of the other, to get from the bottom of the sea all the way up to the surface. The sea people live down there.

Now you mustn't think for a moment that there is nothing but bare, white sand down there. Oh, no! The most wondrous trees and plants grow at the bottom of the sea, with stalks and leaves so supple that they stir with life at the slightest ripple in the water. The fish everywhere, large and small, dart between the branches, just the way birds fly through the trees up here. At the very deepest spot of all stands the castle of the Sea King. Its walls are coral, and the tall, arched windows are made of the clearest amber. The roof is formed of shells that open and close with the current. It's a beautiful sight, for each shell has a dazzling pearl, any one of which would make a splendid jewel in a queen's crown.

The Sea King had been a widower for many years, and his aged mother kept house for him. She was a wise lady, but also very proud of her noble birth. And that's why she wore twelve oysters on her tail, while everyone else of high rank had to settle for six. In every other way she deserved great praise, for she was deeply devoted to her granddaughters, the little sea princesses. They were six beautiful children, but the youngest was the fairest of them all. Her skin was as clear and soft as a rose petal. Her eyes were as blue as the deepest sea. But like all the others, she had no feet, and her body ended in a fish tail.

All day long the sea princesses played in the great halls of the castle, where real flowers were growing right out of the walls. When the large amber windows were open, fish swam right in, just as swallows fly into our homes when we open the windows. The fish glided up to the princesses, ate out of their hands, and let themselves be caressed.

† From *The Annotated Hans Christian Andersen*, trans. Maria Tatar (New York: Norton, 2008), pp. 120, 124–25, 127–29, 131–36, 138–45, 147–53, 155. Copyright © 2008 by Maria Tatar. Used by permission of W. W. Norton & Company.

Outside the castle there was an enormous garden with trees that were deep blue and fiery red. Their fruit glittered like gold, and their blossoms looked like flames of fire, with leaves and stalks constantly aflutter. The soil itself was the finest sand, but blue like a sulphur flame. A wondrous blue glow permeated everything in sight. Standing down there, you really had no idea that you were at the bottom of the sea, and you might as well have been high up in the air with nothing but sky above you and below. When the sea was perfectly calm, you could catch sight of the sun, which looked like a purple flower with light streaming from its calyx.

Each little princess had her own plot in the garden, where she could dig and plant as she pleased. One arranged her flower bed in the shape of a whale; another thought it nicer to make hers look like a little mermaid; but the youngest made hers perfectly round like the sun, and she wanted nothing but flowers that shone just as red as it was. She was a curious child, quiet and thoughtful. While her sisters decorated their gardens with the wondrous objects they had gathered from sunken ships, she wanted only one thing apart from the rose-red flowers that were like the sun high above: a beautiful marble statue. The statue was of a handsome boy, chiseled from pure white stone, and it had landed on the bottom of the sea after a shipwreck. Next to it, the little princess had planted a crimson weeping willow that grew splendidly, draping its fresh foliage over the statue and touching the blue, sandy ocean bottom. It cast a violet shadow that, like its branches, was in constant motion. The roots and crown of the tree seemed always at play with each other, as if trying to kiss.

Nothing made the princess happier than learning about the human world up above. She made her grandmother tell her everything she knew about ships and towns, people and animals. She found it strangely beautiful that flowers up on the land had a fragrance—at the bottom of the sea they had none—and also that the trees in the forest were green and that the fish flying in the trees up there sang so clearly and beautifully that it was delightful to listen to them. Grandmother called the little birds *fish*, because otherwise the little sea princesses, never having seen a bird, would have no idea what she was talking about.

"When you turn fifteen," Grandmother told them, "you'll be allowed to swim up to the surface of the sea to sit on the rocks in the moonlight and watch the tall ships that pass by. You will also have the chance to see both forests and towns." In the coming year, one of the sisters was going to turn fifteen, but the others—well, they were each born a year apart, and the youngest of them had to wait five whole years before she could venture up from the depths to see how things look up here. But each promised to tell the others what she had seen and what she had liked the most on that first visit. Their grandmother had not told them nearly enough, and there was so much that they still wanted to know.

No one longed to go up more than the youngest sister, the one who was so silent and thoughtful, and who also had the longest wait. Many a night she would stand at the open window and gaze up through the dark blue waters, where the fish were fluttering their fins and tails. She could see the moon and the stars, even though their light shone rather pale. Through the water they looked much bigger than they do to our eyes. If a black cloud passed beneath the stars, she knew that it was either a whale swimming overhead or a ship filled with many passengers. The people on board never imagined that a pretty little mermaid was waiting below, stretching her white arms up toward the keel of the ship.

As soon as the eldest princess turned fifteen, she was allowed to swim up to the surface.

When she returned, she had hundreds of things to report. The loveliest moment, she said, was lying on a sandbar close to the shore in the moonlight while the sea was calm. From there, you could see a city—its lights were twinkling like a hundred stars. You could hear the sounds of music and the commotion of carriages and people. You could see all the church towers and spires and hear their bells ringing. And because she could not get close to all those wonderful things, she longed for them all the more.

Oh, how the youngest sister drank it all in! And later that evening, while she stood at the open window gazing up through the dark blue waters, she thought of the big city with all its hustle and bustle, and she even fancied that she could hear the church bells ringing down to her.

The following year, the second sister was allowed to rise up through the water and swim wherever she liked. She reached the surface just as the sun was setting, and that, she said, was the loveliest sight of all. The whole sky was covered in gold, she declared, and the clouds—well, she just couldn't describe how beautiful they were, with their crimson and violet hues, as they sailed over her head. Even more rapidly than the clouds, a flock of wild swans flew like a long white veil across the water toward the setting sun. The second sister swam off in that direction, but the sun sank, and its rosy glow was swallowed up by the sea and the clouds.

Another year passed, and the third sister swam up to the surface. She was the most daring of them all, and she swam upstream into a wide river that flowed into the sea. She could see beautiful green hills covered with grapevines; castles and manors peeked out from magnificent woods; she could hear birds singing; and the sun was so hot that she often had to dive underwater to cool off her burning face. In a small cove she came upon a whole troop of human children, jumping around, quite naked, in the water. She wanted to play with them, but they were terrified and fled. Then a little black animal appeared. It was a dog, but she had never seen one before. The animal barked so ferociously at her that she became frightened and headed for the open sea. But she would never forget the magnificent woods, the green hills, and the darling children, who could swim even though they lacked tails.

The fourth sister was not nearly as daring. She stayed far out in the wild ocean and declared that it was the loveliest place of all. You could see for miles and miles around, and the sky overhead was like a big glass bell. She had seen ships, but at a distance so great that they looked like seagulls. Dolphins were sporting in the waves, and enormous whales spouted water so powerfully from their nostrils that they seemed to be surrounded by a hundred fountains.

And now it was the fifth sister's turn. Since her birthday was in the winter, she saw things the others had not seen on their first outings. The sea had turned quite green, and there were large icebergs floating in it. Each one looked like a pearl, she said, and still they were larger than the church steeples built by humans. They appeared in the most fantastic shapes and glittered just like diamonds. She sat down on one of the largest, and all the ships seemed terrified, giving her a wide berth and sailing rapidly past. She stayed put, with the wind blowing through her long hair. Later that evening the sky became overcast. Thunder rolled and lightning flashed, and the dark waves lifted great chunks of ice high into the air, making them gleam when bolts of red lightning struck. The sails were taken in on all the ships, but amid the general horror and alarm, the mermaid remained serene on her drifting iceberg, watching blue lightning bolts zigzag down toward the glittering sea.

When any one of the sisters reached the surface for the first time, she would be delighted by the many new and beautiful things up there. But as the princesses grew older and were allowed to go up as often as they liked, they began to lose interest. They longed to return home, and, after a month had passed, they declared that it was really much nicer down below. It was such a comfort to be at home.

Many an evening, the five sisters would link arms to form a row and rise up out of the water. They had lovely voices, more beautiful than the sound of any human voice. If a storm was raging and they expected a shipwreck, the sisters would swim in front of the vessels and sing seductively about the delights found in the depths of the sea. They told the sailors not to be afraid to go down there, but the sailors never understood the words they sang. They thought they were hearing the howling of the storm. Nor did they ever see the beauty promised by the mermaids, because when their ships finally sank, the sailors drowned, and, by the time they reached the palace of the Sea King, they were dead.

When the sisters floated up, arm in arm, through the water in the evening, the youngest among them would be left behind, all alone, gazing after them. She would have cried, but mermaids cannot shed tears, and so they suffer even more than we do.

"Oh, if only I were fifteen years old," she would say. "I know that I would come to love the world up there and all the people who live in it."

Finally she turned fifteen.

"Well now, soon we'll have you off our hands," said the old dowager queen, her grandmother. "Come here, and let me dress you up like your sisters," and she put a wreath of white lilies in her hair. Each flower petal was half a pearl, and the old woman clamped eight big oysters onto the princess's tail to show her high rank.

"Ow! That really hurts," said the little mermaid.

"Yes, beauty has its price," the grandmother replied.

Oh, how the mermaid would have loved to shake off all that finery and remove that heavy wreath! The red flowers in her garden would have suited her so much better, but she did not dare make any changes. "Farewell," she said, as she rose up through the water as swiftly and brightly as a bubble moves up to the surface.

The sun had just set when her head rose up through the waves, but the clouds were still gleaming like roses and gold. Up in the pale pink sky the evening star was shining bright and clear. The air was mild and fresh, and the sea was perfectly calm. A tall three-masted ship was drifting in the water, with only one sail hoisted because there was not so much as a breeze. The sailors could be seen taking it easy on the rigging and in the masts. There was music and singing on board, and when it grew dark, hundreds of colored lanterns were lit. They made it look like the flags of all nations were fluttering in the wind.

The little mermaid swam right up to the porthole of the cabin, and, every time a wave lifted her, she could see a throng of elegantly dressed people through the clear glass. Among them was a young prince, the handsomest person there, with big dark eyes. He could not have been more than sixteen. It was his birthday, and that's why the festivities were taking place. When the young prince came out on the deck, where the sailors were dancing, more than a hundred rockets were shot into the air. They lit up the sky, making it look like daytime, and the little mermaid was so startled that she dove back down into the water. But she quickly popped her head back out again. It looked just as if all the stars up in heaven were falling down on her. Never before had she seen such fireworks. Huge suns were spinning around; magnificent fire fish went swooping through the blue air, and the entire display was reflected in the clear, calm waters below. The ship itself was so brightly illuminated that you could see even the smallest piece of rope—not to mention all the people there. How handsome the young prince looked! He shook hands with everyone, laughing and smiling as music filled the lovely night air.

It was growing late, but the little mermaid could not tear herself away from the ship or from the handsome prince. The colored lanterns had long been extinguished; the rockets were no longer being fired into the air; and the cannon volleys had stopped. Now you could hear the sea churning and groaning deep down below. Still the mermaid stayed on the surface, bobbing up and down so that she could look into the cabin. The ship began gathering speed as one sail after another caught the wind. The waves rose higher; heavy clouds darkened the sky; and lightning flashed in the distance. A dreadful storm was brewing, and so the crew took in the sails, while the great ship rocked and scudded through the raging sea. The waves rose higher and higher until they were like huge black mountains, threatening to bring down the mast. The ship dove like a swan between the waves and then rose again on their lofty, foaming crests. The little mermaid thought it must be fun to sail so fast, but the crew didn't think so. The vessel groaned and creaked; the stout planks burst under the heavy pounding of the sea against the ship; and the mast snapped in two as if it were a reed. The ship rolled onto its side as water came rushing into the hold.

The little mermaid suddenly realized that the ship was in real danger. She herself had to watch out for the beams and bits of wreckage drifting in the water. For an instant it was so dark that she couldn't see a thing, but then a flash of lightning lit everything up so that she could make out everyone on board. Now it was every man for himself. She was searching for the young prince and, just as the ship broke apart, she saw him disappear into the depths of the sea. At first she was overjoyed, for she believed that he would now live in her part of the world. But then she remembered that human beings could not survive underwater and that only as a dead man could he come down to her father's palace. No, no, he mustn't die! And so she darted in among the drifting beams and planks, oblivious to the danger of being crushed. She dove deep down and came right back up again among the waves, and at last she found the young prince, who barely had the strength to keep afloat in the stormy waters. His limbs were failing him; his beautiful eyes were shut; and he would surely have drowned if the little mermaid had not come to his rescue. She held his head above water and let the waves carry the two of them along.

By morning the storm had died down, and there was not a trace left of the ship. The sun, red and glowing, rose up out of the water and seemed to bring color back into the prince's cheeks. But his eyes remained closed. The mermaid kissed his fine, high brow and smoothed back his wet hair. She thought that he looked just like the marble statue in her little garden. She kissed him again and made a wish that he might live.

Soon the mermaid saw land before her—lofty blue mountains topped with glittering white snow that made them look like nestling swans. Near the coast were lovely green forests, and close by was some kind of building, whether church or cloister she could not say. Lemon and orange trees were growing in the garden, and you could see tall palm trees by the gate. The sea formed a small bay at this point, and the water in it was quite calm, though very deep all the way up to the dunes, where fine white sand had washed ashore. The mermaid swam over there with the handsome prince, laid him down in the warm sunshine, and made a pillow for his head with the sand.

Bells began ringing in the large white building, and a group of young girls came walking through the garden. The little mermaid swam farther out from the shore, hiding behind some large boulders that rose out of the water. She covered her hair and chest with sea foam so that no one could see her. Then she watched to see who would come to help the poor prince.

It was not long before a young girl came by. She had a frightened look on her face, but only for a moment, and she quickly ran away to get help. The mermaid watched as the prince came back to life and began to smile at everyone around him. But there was no smile for her, because of course he had no idea that she had rescued him. After he was taken into the large building, she was overcome with sorrow and dove back into the water to return to her father's palace.

The little mermaid had always been silent and thoughtful, but now she was even more so. Her sisters asked what she had seen during her first visit up above, but she did not say a word.

Many a morning and many an evening she swam up to the spot where she had left the prince. She saw the fruits in the garden ripen and watched as they were picked. She saw the snow melt on the peaks. But she never saw the prince, and so she always returned home, filled with even greater sorrow than before. Her one consolation was sitting in her little garden, with her arms wrapped around the beautiful marble statue that looked so like the prince. She gave up tending her flowers, and they grew into a kind of wilderness out over the paths, winding their long stalks and leaves around the branches of the trees until everything became quite gloomy.

Finally she could bear it no longer and told one of her sisters everything. The others learned about it soon enough, but no one else knew about it, except for a few other mermaids who didn't breathe a word to anyone (apart from their closest friends). One of them knew who the prince was. She too had seen the festival held on board and knew where the prince came from as well as where his kingdom lay.

"Come, little sister!" the other princesses said. And with their arms on each other's shoulders, they rose in one long row to the surface, right in front of where the prince's castle stood.

The castle had been built with a gleaming, pale yellow stone, and it had grand marble staircases, one of which led straight down to the sea. Magnificent gilded domes rose above the rooftops, and between the pillars that surrounded the entire building stood lifelike marble statues. Through the clear glass of the tall windows you could see grand rooms decorated with sumptuous silk curtains and tapestries. The walls were covered with huge paintings that were a pleasure to behold. In the center of the largest room was a fountain that sprayed sparkling jets high up to the glass dome of the ceiling. The sun shone through it down on the water and on the beautiful plants growing in the large pool.

Now that the little mermaid knew where the prince lived, she spent many an evening and many a night at that spot. She swam much closer to the shore than any of the others dared. She even went up the narrow channel to reach the fine marble balcony that threw its long shadow across the water. Here she would sit and gaze at the young prince, who believed that he was completely alone in the bright moonlight.

Often in the evening, the little mermaid saw him go out to sea in his splendid vessel, with flags hoisted, to the strains of music. She peeked out from among the green rushes, and, when the wind caught her long silvery-white veil and people saw it, they just fancied it was a swan, spreading its wings.

On many nights, when the fishermen were out at sea with their torches, she heard them praising the young prince, and that made her all the more happy about saving his life on the day he was drifting half dead on the waves. And she remembered how she had cradled his head on her chest and how lovingly she had kissed him. But he knew nothing about any of this and never even dreamed she existed.

The little mermaid grew more and more fond of human beings and longed deeply for their company. Their world seemed far vaster than her own. They could fly across the ocean in ships and climb the steep mountains high above the clouds. And the lands they possessed, their woods and their fields, stretched far beyond where she could see. There was so much she would have liked to know, and her sisters weren't able to answer all her questions. And so she went to visit her old grandmother, who knew all about the world above, which she quite rightly called the lands above the sea.

"If human beings don't drown," asked the little mermaid, "can they go on living forever? Don't they die, as we do down here in the sea?"

"Of course they do," the old woman replied. "They too must die, and their lifetime is even shorter than ours. We sometimes live for three hundred years, but when we cease to exist, we turn into foam on the sea. We don't even have a grave down here among our loved ones. We lack an immortal soul, and we shall never have another life. We're like the green rushes. Once they've been cut, they stop growing. But human beings have a soul that lives on forever, even after their bodies have turned to dust. It rises up through the pure air until it reaches the shining stars. Just as we rise up from the sea to behold the lands of humans, they rise up to beautiful, unknown regions that we shall never see."

"Why weren't we given an immortal soul?" the little mermaid asked mournfully. "I would give all three hundred years of my life in return for becoming human for just one day and having a share in that heavenly world."

"You mustn't waste your time worrying about these things," the grandmother told her. "We're really much happier and also better off than the human beings who live up there."

"So then I'm doomed to die and to drift like foam on the sea, never to hear the music of the waves or see the lovely flowers and the red sun. Is there nothing I can do to gain an immortal soul?"

"No," said the old woman. "Only if a human loved you so much that you meant more to him than his father and mother. If he were to love you with all his heart and soul and had the priest place his right hand in yours with the promise of remaining faithful and true here and in all eternity—then his soul would glide into your body and you too would share in human happiness. He would give you a soul and still keep his own. But that will never happen! Your fish tail, which we find so beautiful, looks hideous to people on earth. They don't know any better. To be beautiful up there, you have to have those two clumsy pillars that they call legs."

The little mermaid sighed and looked mournfully at her fish tail.

"Let's celebrate," said the old woman. "Let's dance and be joyful for the three hundred years we have to live—that's really quite time enough. After that we have plenty of time to rest in our graves. Tonight there will be a royal ball."

That event was more splendid than anything we ever see on earth. The walls and ceiling of the great ballroom were made of thick, transparent crystal. Hundreds of colossal seashells, rose-red and grass-green, were lined up on all sides, each burning with a blue flame. They lit up the entire room and, by shining through the walls, also lit up the sea. Countless fish, large and small, could be seen swimming toward the crystal walls. The scales on some of them glowed with a purple-red brilliance; others appeared to be silver and gold. Down the middle of the ballroom flowed a wide rippling current, and in it mermen and mermaids were dancing to their own sweet songs. No human beings have voices so beautiful. The little mermaid sang more sweetly than anyone else, and everyone applauded her. For a moment there was joy in her heart, because she knew that her voice was more beautiful than any other on land or in the sea. But then her thoughts turned to the world above. She was unable to forget the handsome prince or her deep sorrow that she did not possess the same immortal soul humans possess. And so she slipped out of her father's palace, and, while everyone inside was singing and making merry, she sat in her own little garden, feeling sad.

Suddenly the little mermaid heard the sound of a hunting horn echoing down through the water, and she thought: "Ah, there he is, sailing up above—the one I love more than my father or my mother, the one who is always in my thoughts and in whose hands I would gladly place my happiness. I would risk anything to win him and to gain an immortal soul. While my sisters are dancing away in Father's castle, I'll go visit the Sea Witch. I've always been terrified of her, but maybe she can give me some advice and help me out."

The little mermaid left her garden and set out for the place where the Sea Witch lived, on the far side of the roaring maelstroms. She had never been over there before. There were no flowers growing there and no sea grass at all. Nothing was there but the bare, gray, sandy bottom of the sea, stretching right up to the maelstroms, where the water went swirling around like roaring mill wheels and pulled everything it got hold of down into the depths. She had to pass through the middle of those churning whirlpools in order to reach the domain of the Sea Witch. For a long stretch, there was no other path than one that took her over hot, bubbling mud—the witch called it her swamp.

The witch's house lay behind the swamp in the middle of a strange forest. All the trees and bushes were sea polyps, half animal and half plant. They looked like hundred-headed serpents growing out of the ground. Their branches looked like long slimy arms, with fingers like slithering worms. Joint by joint from the root up to the very tip, they were constantly on the move, and they wound themselves tight around anything they could grab hold of from the sea, and then they would not let go.

The little mermaid was terrified and paused at the edge of the wood. Her heart was pounding with fear, and she came close to turning back. But then she remembered the prince and the human soul, and her courage returned. She tied her long flowing hair tightly around her head so that the polyps wouldn't be able to grab hold of it. Then she folded her arms across her chest and darted forward like a fish shooting through the water, right in among the hideous polyps that reached out to snatch her with their nimble arms and fingers. She noticed how each of the sea polyps had caught something and was holding it fast with a hundred little arms that were like hoops of iron. The white skeletons of humans who had perished at sea and sunk down into the deep waters became visible in the arms of the polyps. Ship rudders and chests were held in their grip, along with the skeletons of land animals and—most horrifying of all—a small mermaid, whom they had caught and throttled.

She finally reached a great slimy clearing in the woods, where big fat water snakes were romping in the mire and showing off their hideous, whitish-yellow bellies. In the middle of the clearing stood a house, built with the bones of shipwrecked human folk. There sat the Sea Witch, letting a toad feed from her mouth, exactly the way you can feed a canary with a lump of sugar. She called the hideous water snakes her little chickadees and let them cavort all over her big spongy chest.

"I know exactly what you want," the Sea Witch said. "How stupid of you! But I'm going to grant your wish, and it will bring you misfortune, my lovely princess. You're hoping to get rid of that fish tail and replace it with two stumps to walk on like a human being. You're sure that the young prince will then fall in love with you, and then you can win him along with an immortal soul."

And with that the witch let out such a loud, repulsive laugh that the toad and the water snakes tumbled to the ground and went sprawling. "You've come here just in time," said the witch. "Tomorrow, once the sun is up, I wouldn't be able to help you for another year. I shall prepare a potion for you. You will have to swim to land with it before sunrise, sit down on the shore, and swallow it. Your tail will then split in two and shrink into what human beings call pretty legs. But it will hurt. It will feel like a sharp sword passing through you. Everyone who sees you will say that you are the loveliest human child they have ever encountered. You will keep your graceful movements—no dancer will ever glide so lightly—but every step you take will make you feel as if you were treading on a sharp knife, enough to make your feet bleed. If you are willing to endure all that, I think I can help you."

"Yes," said the little mermaid, but her voice trembled. And she turned her thoughts to the prince and the prize of an immortal soul.

"Think about it carefully," said the witch. "Once you take on the form of a human, you can never again be a mermaid. You'll never be able to swim back through the water to your sisters or to your father's palace. The only way you can acquire an immortal soul is to win the prince's love and make him willing to forget his father and mother for your sake. He must cling to you always in his thoughts and let the priest join your hands to become man and wife. If the prince marries someone else, the morning after the wedding your heart will break, and you will become foam on the waves."

"I'm ready," said the little mermaid, and she turned pale as death.

"But first you will have to pay me," said the witch. "And it's not a small thing that I'm demanding. You have a voice more beautiful than anyone else's down here at the bottom of the sea. You may be planning to charm the prince with it, but you are going to have to give it to me. I want the dearest thing you possess in exchange for my precious potion. You see, I have to add my own blood to make sure that the drink will be as sharp as a double-edged sword."

"But if you take my voice away," said the little mermaid, "what will I have left?"

"Your lovely figure," said the witch, "your graceful movements, and your expressive eyes. With all that you can easily enchant a human heart. Well, where's your courage? Stick out your little tongue and let me cut it off in payment. Then you shall have your powerful potion."

"So be it," said the little mermaid, and the witch placed her cauldron on the fire to brew the magic potion.

"Cleanliness above everything else," she said, as she scoured the cauldron with the water snakes, which she had tied into a large knot. Then she made a cut in her chest and let her black blood ooze out. The steam from the cauldron created strange shapes, terrifying to behold. The witch kept tossing fresh things into the cauldron, and when the brew began to boil, it sounded like a crocodile weeping. At last the magic potion was ready, and it looked just like clear water.

"There you go!" said the witch as she cut out the little mermaid's tongue. Now she was mute and could neither speak nor sing.

"If the polyps try to grab you on your way out through the woods," said the witch, "just throw a single drop of this potion on them, and their arms and fingers will burst into a thousand pieces." But the little mermaid didn't need to do that. The polyps shrank back in terror when they caught sight of the luminous potion glowing in her hand like a glittering star. And so she passed quickly through the woods, the marsh, and the roaring whirlpools.

The little mermaid could now see her father's palace. The lights in the ballroom were out, and everyone was probably fast asleep by now. But she did not dare to go take a look, for she could not speak and was about to leave them forever. Her heart was aching with sorrow. She stole into the garden, took a flower from the beds of each of her sisters, blew a thousand kisses toward the palace, and then swam up through the dark blue waters.

The sun had not yet risen when she caught sight of the prince's palace and made her way up the beautiful marble steps. The moon was shining clear and bright. The little mermaid drank the bitter, fiery potion, and it felt to her as if a double-edged sword was passing through her delicate body. She fainted and fell down as if dead.

When the sun came shining across the sea, it woke her up. She could feel a sharp pain, but right there in front of her stood the handsome young prince. He stared at her so intently with his coal-black eyes that she cast down her own and saw that her fish tail was gone. She had as charming a pair of white legs as any young girl could want. But she was quite naked, and so she wrapped herself in her long, flowing hair. The prince asked who she was and how she had found her way there, and she could only gaze back at him tenderly and sadly with her deep blue eyes, for of course she could not speak. Then he took her by the hand and escorted her into the palace. Every step she took, as the witch had predicted, made her feel as if she were treading on sharp knives and piercing needles, but she willingly endured it. Hand in hand with the prince, she moved as lightly as a bubble. He and everyone else marveled at the beauty of her graceful movements.

She was given costly dresses of silk and muslin after she arrived. She was the most beautiful creature in the palace, but she was mute and could not speak or sing. Enchanting slave girls dressed in silk and gold came out and danced before the prince and his royal parents. One sang more beautifully than all the others, and the prince clapped his hands and smiled at her. The little mermaid felt sad, for she knew that she herself had once sung far more beautifully. And she thought, "Oh, if only he knew that I gave my voice away forever in order to be with him."

The slave girls performed a graceful, swaying dance to the most sublime music. And the little mermaid raised her beautiful white arms, lifting herself up on the tips of her toes, and floating across the floor, dancing as no one had ever danced before. She looked more and more lovely with every step, and her eyes spoke more deeply to the heart than the songs of the slave girls.

Everyone was enraptured, especially the prince, who called her his little foundling. She kept on dancing, even though it felt like she was treading on sharp knives every time her foot touched the ground. The prince insisted that she must never leave him, and she was allowed to sleep outside his door on a velvet cushion.

The prince had a page's costume made for her so that she could ride on horseback with him. They galloped through fragrant woods, where green boughs brushed her shoulders and little birds sang among the fresh, new leaves. She climbed with the prince to the tops of high mountains and, although her delicate feet began to bleed and everyone could see the blood, she just laughed and followed the prince until they could look down and see clouds fluttering in the air like flocks of birds on their way to distant lands.

At night, back in the prince's palace, when everyone in the household was fast asleep, the little mermaid would go over to the marble steps and cool her burning feet by standing in the icy seawater. And then she would think about those who were living down there in the deep.

One night her sisters rose up and sang mournfully as they floated arm in arm on the water. She beckoned to them, and they recognized her and told her how unhappy she had made them all. From then on, they started visiting her every night, and one night she even saw, far off in the distance, her old grandmother, who had not been up to the surface for many years, and she also saw the old Sea King, wearing his crown on his head. They both stretched their arms out toward her, but they did not dare to venture as close to the shore as her sisters.

With each passing day, the prince grew fonder of the little mermaid. He loved her as one loves a dear, sweet child, and it never even occurred to him to make her his queen. And yet she had to become his wife or else she would never receive an immortal soul. On his wedding morning, she would dissolve into foam on the sea.

"Do you care for me more than anyone else?" the little mermaid's eyes seemed to ask when he took her in his arms and kissed her lovely brow.

"Yes, you are more precious to me than anyone else," said the prince, "for you have the kindest heart of anyone I know. And you are more devoted to me than anyone else. You remind me of a young girl I once met, but shall probably never see again. I was in a shipwreck, and the waves cast me ashore near a holy temple, where several young girls were performing their duties. The youngest of them found me on the beach and saved my life. I saw her just twice. She is the only one in the world whom I could ever love. But you look so much like her that you have almost driven her image out of my mind. She belongs to the holy temple, and my good fortune has sent you to me. We will never part!"

"Ah, little does he know that it was I who saved his life," thought the little mermaid. "I carried him across the sea to the temple in the woods, and I waited in the foam for someone to come and help. I saw the beautiful girl that he loves better than he loves me." And the mermaid sighed deeply, for she did not know how to shed tears.

"He says the girl belongs to the holy temple and that she will therefore never return to the world. They will never again meet. I will stay by his side and can see him every day. I will take care of him and love him and devote my life to him."

Not long after that, there was talk that the prince was going to marry and that his wife would be the beautiful daughter of a neighboring king. And that's why he was rigging out a splendid ship. They said that he was going to pay a visit to the lands of a neighboring kingdom, but in fact he was going to visit the neighboring king's daughter. He was taking a large entourage with him. The little mermaid shook her head and laughed. She knew the prince's thoughts far better than anyone else.

"I shall have to go," he told her. "I must visit this beautiful princess—my parents insist. But they would never force me to bring her back here as my wife. I could never love her. She's not at all like the beautiful girl in the temple, whom you resemble. When I have to choose a bride someday, it is much more likely to be you, my quiet little orphan child with your expressive eyes." And he kissed the mermaid's red lips, played with her long hair, and laid his head on her heart so that she began to dream of human happiness and an immortal soul.

"You are not at all afraid of the sea, are you, my dear quiet child?" he asked, when they stood on board the splendid ship that was carrying them to the neighboring kingdom. He told her about powerful storms and calm waters, about the strange fish in the deep, and what divers had seen down there. She smiled at his tales, for she knew better than any one else about the wonders at the bottom of the sea.

In the moonlit night when everyone was asleep but the helmsman at his wheel, the little mermaid stood by the railing of the ship and gazed down through the clear water. She thought she could see her father's palace, and there at the top of it was her old grandmother, a silver crown on her head as she stared up through the turbulent currents at the keel of the vessel. Then her sisters rose up to the surface and looked at her with eyes filled with sorrow, wringing their white hands. She beckoned to them and smiled and would have liked to tell them that she was happy and that all was going well for her. But the cabin boy came up just then, and the sisters dove back down, and the boy thought that the whiteness he had seen was nothing but foam on the water.

The next morning the ship sailed into the harbor of the neighboring king's magnificent capital. All the church bells were ringing, and trumpeters blew a fanfare from the towers. Soldiers saluted with flying colors and flashing bayonets. Every day brought a new festival.

Balls and banquets followed one another, but the princess had not yet appeared. It was reported that she had been raised and educated in a holy temple, where she was learning all the royal virtues. At last she appeared.

The little mermaid was eager for a glimpse of her beauty, and she had to admit that she had never seen a more enchanting person. Her delicate skin glowed with health, and her warm blue eyes shone with deep sincerity from behind her long, dark lashes.

"It's you," said the prince. "You're the one who rescued me when I was lying half dead on the beach." And he reached out and drew his blushing bride toward him. "Oh, I'm really overjoyed," he said to the little mermaid. "The best thing imaginable—more than I ever dared hope for—has been given to me. My happiness is sure to give you pleasure, for you are fonder of me than anyone else." The little mermaid kissed his hand, and she could feel her heart breaking. The day of the wedding would mean her death, and she would turn into foam on the ocean waves.

All the church bells were ringing when the heralds rode through the streets to proclaim the betrothal. Perfumed oils were burning in precious silver lamps on every altar. The priests were swinging the censers, while the bride and bridegroom joined hands to receive the blessing of the bishop. Dressed in silk and gold, the little mermaid was holding the bride's train, but her ears could not take in the festive music, and her eyes never saw the holy rites. All she could think about was her last night on earth and about everything in this world that she had lost.

That same evening, bride and bridegroom went aboard the ship. Cannons roared, flags were waving, and in the center of the ship a sumptuous tent of purple and gold had been raised. It was strewn with luxurious cushions, for the bridal couple was to sleep there during the calm, cool night. The sails swelled in the breeze, and the ship glided lightly and smoothly across the clear seas.

When it grew dark, colored lanterns were lit, and the sailors danced merrily on deck. The little mermaid could not help but think of that first time she had come up from the sea and gazed on just such a scene of splendor and joy. And now she joined in the dance, swerving and swooping as lightly as a swallow does to avoid pursuit. Cries of admiration greeted her from all sides. Never before had she danced so elegantly. It was as if sharp knives were cutting into her delicate feet, but she didn't notice, for the pain in her heart was far keener. She knew that this was the last night she would ever see the prince, the man for whom she had forsaken her family and her home, given up her beautiful voice, and suffered hours of agony without his suspecting a thing. This was the last evening that she would

breathe the same air that he did or gaze into the deep sea and up at
the starry sky. An eternal night, without thoughts or dreams, awaited
her, since she did not have a soul and would never win one. All was
joy and merriment on board until long past midnight. She laughed
and danced with the others although the thought of death was
in her heart. The prince kissed his lovely bride, while she played
with his dark hair, and arm in arm they retired to the magnificent
tent.

The ship was now hushed and quiet. Only the helmsman was
standing there at his wheel. The little mermaid was leaning on the
railing with her white arms and looking to the east for a sign of the
rosy dawn. She knew that the first ray of sunlight would mean her
death. Suddenly she saw her sisters rising up from the sea. They were
as pale as she, but their beautiful long hair was no longer blowing
in the wind—it had been cut off.

"We gave our hair to the witch," they said, "so that she would help
save you from the death that awaits you tonight. She gave us a
knife—take a look! See how sharp it is? Before sunrise you must
plunge it into the prince's heart. Then, when his warm blood spatters
on your feet, they will grow back together to form a fish tail, and you
will be a mermaid again. You can come back down to us in the
water and live out your three hundred years before being changed
into dead, salty sea foam. Hurry up! One of you will die before the
sun rises. Our old grandmother has been so grief-stricken that her
white hair started falling out, just the way ours fell to the witch's
scissors. Kill the prince and come back to us! Hurry—look at the red
streaks in the sky. In a few minutes the sun will rise, and then you
will die." And with a strange, deep sigh, they sank down beneath the
waves.

The little mermaid drew back the purple curtain of the tent, and
she saw the lovely bride sleeping with her head on the prince's
chest. She bent down and kissed his handsome brow, then looked
at the sky where the rosy dawn was growing brighter and brighter.
She gazed at the sharp knife in her hand and fixed her eyes again
on the prince, who was whispering the name of his bride in his
dreams. She was the only one in his thoughts. The little mermaid's
hand began to tremble as she took the knife—then she flung it far
out over the waves. The water turned red where it fell, and it looked
as if blood was oozing up, drop by drop, through the water. With one
last glance at the prince from eyes half-dimmed, she threw herself
from the ship into the sea and felt her body dissolve into foam.

And now the sun came rising up from the sea. Its warm and gentle rays fell on the deadly cold sea foam, but the little mermaid did
not feel as if she were dying. She saw the bright sun and realized

that there were hundreds of lovely transparent creatures hovering over her. Looking right through them, she could see the white sails of the ship and rosy clouds up in the sky. Their voices were melodious, but so ethereal that human ears could not hear them, just as mortal eyes could not behold them. They soared through the air on their own lightness, with no need for wings. The little mermaid realized that she had a body like theirs and that she was rising higher and higher out of the foam.

"Where am I?" she asked, and her voice sounded like that of the other beings, more ethereal than any earthly music.

"Among the daughters of the air," they replied. "Mermaids do not have an immortal soul, and they can never have one without gaining the love of a human being. Eternal life depends on a power outside them. The daughters of the air do not have immortal souls either, but through good deeds they can earn one for themselves. We can fly to the hot countries, where sultry, pestilential air takes people's lives. We bring cool breezes. We carry the fragrance of flowers through the air and send relief and healing. Once we have struggled to do all the good we can in three hundred years, immortal souls are bestowed on us, and we enjoy the eternal happiness humans find. You, my dear little mermaid, have struggled with all your heart to do what we do. You have suffered and endured and now you have been transported to the world of the spirits of the air. Through good deeds, you too can earn an immortal soul in three hundred years."

The little mermaid lifted her transparent arms toward God's sun, and for the first time she could feel tears coming to her eyes.

Over by the ship, there were sounds of life, with people bustling about. The mermaid could tell that the prince and his beautiful bride were searching for her. With deep sorrow, they were staring out at the pearl-colored foam, as if they knew that she had thrown herself into the waves. Unseen, the mermaid kissed the bride's forehead, smiled at the prince, and then, with the other children of the air, rose up into the pink clouds that were sailing across the skies.

"In three hundred years we will soar like this into the heavenly kingdom."

"And we may arrive there even sooner," one of her companions whispered. "Invisible to human eyes, we float into homes where there are children. For every day we find a good child who makes his parents happy and deserves their love, God shortens our time of trial. Children never know when we are going to fly into their rooms, and if we smile with joy when we see the child, then a year is taken away from the three hundred. But a mean or naughty child makes us shed tears of sorrow, and each of those tears adds another day to our time of trial."

The Little Match Girl[†]

It was bitterly cold. Snow was falling, and before long it would be dark. It was the last day of the year: New Year's Eve. In the cold darkness, a poor little girl, with nothing on her head and with bare feet, was walking down the street. Yes, it's true, she had been wearing slippers when she left home. But what good could they do? They were great big slippers that had belonged to her mother—that's how big they were! The little girl had lost them while scurrying across the road to avoid two carriages rushing by at a terrifying speed. One slipper was nowhere to be found, and a boy had run off with the other, declaring that he would use it as a cradle when he had children of his own someday.

The little girl walked along on her tiny, bare feet, which were red and blue from the cold. She was carrying matches in an old apron, and she had a bundle in her hand as well. No one had bought anything from her all day long, and she had not received so much as a penny. Poor mite, she was the picture of misery as she trudged along, hungry and shivering with cold. Snowflakes fell on her long, fair hair, which settled into beautiful curls at the nape of her neck. But you can be sure that she wasn't worrying about how she looked. Lights were shining in every window, and the tempting aroma of roast goose drifted out into the streets. You see, it was New Year's Eve, and the little girl was thinking about that.

Over in a little nook between two houses, one of which jutted out into the street more than the other, she sat down and curled up, with her legs tucked beneath her. But even there she just grew colder and colder. She didn't dare return home, for she had not sold any of her matches and had not earned a single penny. She knew that her father would beat her, and besides, it was almost as cold at home as it was here. They had only the roof to protect them, and the wind howled right through it, even though the worst cracks had been stopped up with straw and rags.

The girl's little hands were almost numb from the cold. Ah! Maybe a lighted match would do some good. If only she dared pull one from the bunch and strike it against the wall, just to warm her fingers. She pulled one out—scratch!—how it sputtered, how it flamed! Such a bright warm light—it felt just like a little lamp when she cupped her hand around it. Yes, what a strange light it was! The little girl imagined that she was sitting in front of a big iron stove, with shiny brass knobs and brass feet. The fire was burning so cheerfully, and

† From *The Annotated Hans Christian Andersen*, trans. Maria Tatar (New York: Norton, 2008), pp. 216–17, 219, 222. Copyright © 2008 by Maria Tatar. Used by permission of W. W. Norton & Company.

it warmed her up! But—oh no! The little girl was just stretching out her toes to warm them up too, when—out went the flame. The stove vanished, and there she sat with the end of a burned match in her hand.

She struck another match. It flared up, and when the light shone on the wall, it began to turn transparent, like a piece of gauze. She could see right into a dining room, where a table was covered with a snowy white cloth and fine china. The air was filled with the delicious scent of roast goose stuffed with apples and prunes. And what was even more amazing, the goose jumped right off the dish and waddled across the floor, with a carving knife and a fork still in its back. It marched right up to the poor little girl. But then the match went out, and there was nothing left to see but the cold, solid wall.

She lit another match. Now she was sitting beneath the most beautiful Christmas tree. It was even taller and more splendidly decorated than the one she had seen last Christmas through the glass doors of a house belonging to a wealthy merchant. Thousands of candles were burning on the green branches, and colorful pictures, just like the ones she had seen in shop windows, looked down at her. The little girl stretched both hands up in the air—and the match went out. The Christmas candles all rose higher and higher into the air, and she saw them turn into bright stars. One of them turned into a shooting star, leaving behind it a streak of sparkling fire.

"Someone is dying," the little girl thought, for her grandmother, the only person who had ever been kind to her and who was no longer alive, had once said that a falling star means that a soul is rising up to God.

She struck another match against the wall. Light shone all around her, and right there in the midst of it was her old grandmother, looking so bright and sparkling, so kind and blessed.

"Oh, Grandma," the little girl cried out. "Please take me with you! I know you will be gone when the match burns out—just like the warm stove, the lovely roast goose, and the big beautiful Christmas tree." And she quickly lit the entire bundle of matches, because she wanted to hold on tight to her grandmother. The matches burned with such intensity that it was suddenly brighter than broad daylight. Grandma had never looked so tall and beautiful. She gathered up the little girl in her arms and together they flew in brightness and joy higher and higher above the earth to where it is no longer cold, and there is neither hunger nor fear. They were now with God!

In the cold dawn, the little girl was still huddled between the two houses, with rosy cheeks and a smile on her lips. She had frozen to death on the last night of the old year. The New Year dawned on the frozen body of the little girl, who was still holding matches in her hand, one bundle used up. "She was trying to get warm," people said. No one could imagine what beautiful things she had seen and in what glory she had gone with her old grandmother into the joy of the New Year.

The Girl Who Trod on the Loaf †

You have probably heard about the tribulations of the girl who trod on a loaf of bread to keep from soiling her shoes. The story has been written down and put into print as well.

She was a poor child, but proud and vain. And people said that she had a bad streak. As a very small child, she enjoyed catching flies, pulling off their wings, and turning them into creeping things. She would take a May bug and a beetle, stick each of them on a pin, then place a green leaf or bit of paper up against their feet. The poor creatures would cling to it, twisting and turning, trying to get off the pin.

"Now the May bug is reading," little Inger would say. "Look how it's turning over the leaves!"

As she grew older, she became worse rather than better. But she was very pretty, and that was probably her misfortune, for otherwise she would have been punished more often than she was.

"It'll take some desperate remedies to cure your stubborn ways," her mother told her. "When you were little, you used to stomp all over my aprons. Now that you're older, I'm worried that you will stomp all over my heart."

And, sure enough, that's what she did.

One day she went out to work for gentry living in the countryside. They treated her as kindly as if she were their own child and dressed her in the same way. She looked very beautiful now and became more vain than ever.

After she had been with the family for about a year, her mistress said to her: "Isn't it time to go back and visit your parents, Inger dear?"

So she did, but she only went because she wanted to show off and let them see how refined she had become. When she reached the village, she caught sight of a group of girls gossiping with some young fellows near a pond. Her mother was there too, pausing to rest on a rock, with a bundle of firewood she had gathered in the forest. Inger

† From *The Annotated Hans Christian Andersen,* trans. Maria Tatar (New York: Norton, 2008), pp. 316, 318–29. Copyright © 2008 by Maria Tatar. Used by permission of W. W. Norton & Company.

was ashamed that she, who was dressed so smartly, should have a mother who went about in rags collecting sticks. She wasn't in the least sorry to turn back. But she was annoyed.

Another six months went by.

"You really should go home sometime soon to visit your old parents, Inger dear," her mistress said. "Here, you can take this big loaf of white bread to them. They'll be happy to see you again."

Inger put on her best clothes and wore a pair of fine new shoes. She picked up the hem of her skirt and walked very carefully so that her shoes would stay nice and clean. No one can blame her for that! But when she reached the place where her path crossed over marshy ground, with a stretch of puddles and mud before her, she flung the loaf down on the ground as a stepping-stone so that she could make her way across with dry shoes. Just as she put one foot down on the bread and lifted the other, the loaf began to sink, carrying her down deeper and deeper until she disappeared altogether and there was nothing to see but a black, bubbling swamp!

That's the story.

What became of her? She went down to the Marsh Woman, who brews underground. The Marsh Woman is aunt to the elf maidens, who are known everywhere, for people sing songs about them and paint pictures of them. But nobody knows much about the Marsh Woman, except that when the meadows begin steaming in the summer, it means that the old woman is brewing things below. Inger sank down into her brewery, and that's not a place you can stay for very long. A cesspool is a place of luxury compared with the Marsh Woman's brewery. Every vat reeks so horribly that you would faint, and they are all packed closely together. Even if you could find a space wide enough to squeeze through, you wouldn't be able to get by because of all the slimy toads and the fat snakes tangled up in there. That's where Inger landed. The whole nasty, creepy mess was so icy cold that her every limb began to shiver, and she grew stiffer and stiffer. The loaf was still sticking to her feet, dragging her down, just as amber attracts bits of straw.

The Marsh Woman was at home, for the brewery was being visited that day by the devil and his great-grandmother, an extremely venomous old creature whose hands are never idle. She always has some needlework with her, and she had it with her this time too. Her pincushion was with her that day so that she could give people pins and needles in their legs and make them get up and run around. And she was busy embroidering lies and crocheting rash words that might have fallen harmlessly to the ground had she not woven them into mischief and slander. How cleverly that old great-granny could sew, embroider, and weave!

When the devil's great-grandmother saw Inger, she put on her spectacles and took a good look at her. "That girl has talent," she declared. "I'd like to take her back with me as a souvenir. She'd make a perfect statue for my great-grandson's entrance hall." And she got her!

That's how little Inger ended up in hell. People can't always go straight down there, but if they have a little talent, they can get there in a roundabout way.

The antechamber there seemed endless. It made you dizzy to look straight ahead and dizzy to look back. A crowd of anxious, miserable souls were waiting for the gates of mercy to be flung open. They would have to wait for a long time! Huge, hideous, fat spiders were spinning webs that would last a thousand years around the feet of those waiting, and the webs were like foot screws or manacles that clamped down as strongly as copper chains on the feet. On top of all that, there was a deep sense of despair in every soul, a feeling of anxiety that was itself a torment. Among the crowd was a miser who had lost the key to his money box and now remembered that he had left it in the lock. But wait—it would take far too long to describe all the pain and torment suffered in that place. Inger began to feel the torture of standing still, just like a statue. It was as if she were riveted to the ground by the loaf of bread.

"This is what comes from trying to keep your shoes clean," she said to herself. "Look at how they're all staring at me." Yes, it's true, they were all staring at her, with evil passions gleaming in their eyes. They spoke without a sound coming from their mouths, and it was horrifying to look at them!

"It must be a pleasure to look at me," Inger thought. "I have a pretty face and nice clothes." And then she turned her eyes, for her neck was too stiff to move. Goodness, how dirty she had become in the Marsh Woman's brewery! She hadn't thought of that. Her dress was covered with one great streak of slime; a snake had wound itself into her hair and was dangling down her neck; and from each fold in her dress an ugly toad was peeping out, making a croaking noise that sounded like the bark of a wheezy lapdog. It was most disagreeable. "Still," she consoled herself, "the others down here look no less dreadful."

Worst of all was the terrible hunger Inger felt. If she could just stoop down and break off a bit of the loaf on which she was standing! Impossible—for her back had stiffened, her arms and hands had stiffened, and her entire body was like a statue made of stone. All she could do was roll her eyes, roll them right around so that she could see what was behind her, and that was truly a ghastly sight. Flies began to land on her, and they crawled back and forth across her eyes. She blinked, but the flies wouldn't go away. They couldn't fly away because their wings had been pulled off, and they had become creeping insects. That made Inger's torment even worse, and, as for the pangs of hunger, it began to feel to her as if her innards were eating themselves up. She began to feel so empty inside, so terribly empty.

"If this goes on much longer, I won't be able to bear it," she said, but she had to bear it, and everything just became worse than ever.

Suddenly a hot tear fell on her forehead. It trickled down her face and chest, right down to the loaf of bread. Then another tear fell, and many more followed. Who could be weeping for little Inger? Didn't she have a mother up there on earth? The tears of grief shed by a mother for her wayward child can always reach her, but they only burn and make the torture all the greater. And now this unbearable hunger—and the impossibility of getting even a mouthful from the loaf she had trod underfoot! She was beginning to have the feeling that everything inside her must have eaten itself up. She was like a thin, hollow reed that absorbs every sound it hears. She could hear everything said about her on earth above, and what she heard was harsh and spiteful. Her mother may have been weeping and feeling deep sorrow, but still she said: "Pride goes before a fall. That's what led to your ruin, Inger. You have created so much sorrow for your mother!"

Inger's mother and everyone else up above were all aware of her sin and how she had trod upon the loaf, sunk down, and disappeared. They had learned about it from the cowherd, who had seen it for himself from the crest of a hill.

"You have brought me so much grief, Inger," her mother said. "Yes, I always knew it would happen."

"I wish I had never been born!" Inger thought. "I would have been so much better off. Mother's tears can do me no good now."

Inger heard her master and mistress speaking, those good people who had been like parents to her. "She was always a sinful child," they said. "She had no respect for the gifts of our Lord, but trampled them underfoot. It will be hard for her to squeeze through the gates of mercy."

"They should have done a better job raising me," Inger thought. "They should have cured me of my bad ways, if I had any."

Inger heard that a ballad had been written about her—"The proud young girl who stepped on a loaf to keep her shoes clean." It was being sung from one end of the country to the other.

"Why should I have to suffer and be punished so severely for such a little thing?" Inger thought. "Why aren't others punished for their sins as well? There would be so many people to punish. Oh, I am in such pain!"

Inger's heart became even harder than her shell-like form. "Nothing will ever improve while I'm in this company! And I don't want to get better. Look at them all glaring at me!"

Her heart grew even harder and was filled with hatred for all humans.

"I dare say that they will have something to talk about now. Oh, I am in such pain!"

And she could hear people telling her story to children as a warning, and the little ones called her Wicked Inger. "She was so horrid," they said, "so nasty that she deserved to be punished."

The children had nothing but harsh words for her.

One day, when hunger and resentment were gnawing deeply away in her hollow body, she heard her name spoken. Her story was being told to an innocent child, a small girl who burst into tears when she heard about proud Inger and her love of finery.

"Won't she ever come back up again?" the girl asked. And she was told: "She will never return."

"What if she asks for forgiveness and promises never to do it again?"

"But she won't ask to be forgiven," they replied.

"Oh, how I wish that she would!" the little girl said in great distress. "I'll give up my doll's house if they let her return. It's so horrible for poor Inger!"

These words went straight to Inger's heart and seemed to do her good. It was the first time anyone had said "Poor Inger" without adding anything about her faults. An innocent little child had wept and prayed for her. She was so moved that she would have liked to weep as well, but the tears would not flow, and that too was torture.

The years passed by up there, but down below nothing changed. Inger heard fewer words from above and there was less talk about her. Then one day she heard a deep sigh: "Inger, Inger, what sorrow you have brought me! I always said you would!" Those were her mother's dying words.

Sometimes she heard her name mentioned by her former mistress, who always spoke in the mildest way: "I wonder if I shall ever see you again, Inger. There's no knowing where I'll end up." But Inger knew well enough that her honest mistress would never end up in the place where she was.

A long time passed, slowly and bitterly. Then Inger heard her name spoken once again, and she saw above her what looked like two bright stars shining down on her. They were two gentle eyes that were about to close on earth. So many years had passed since the time when a small girl had cried inconsolably for "Poor Inger" that the child was by now an old woman, and the good Lord was about to call her to himself. In that final hour, when all the thoughts and deeds of a lifetime pass before you, the woman recalled clearly how, as a small child, she had wept bitter tears when hearing the sad story of Inger. That moment and the sense of sorrow following it were so vivid in the old woman's mind at the hour of her death that she cried out these heartfelt words: "Dear Lord, have I not too, like poor Inger, sometimes thoughtlessly trampled underfoot your blessings and counted them without value? Have I not also been guilty of pride and vanity in my inmost heart? And yet you, in your mercy, did not let me sink but held me up. Do not forsake me in this final hour!"

The old woman's eyes closed, and the eyes of her soul were opened to what had been hidden. And because Inger had been so profoundly present in her final thoughts, the old woman was actually able to see her and to understand how deeply she had sunk. At the dreadful sight of her, the saintly soul burst into tears. She stood like a child in the kingdom of heaven and wept for poor Inger. Her tears and prayers rang like an echo down into the hollow, empty shell that held an imprisoned, tormented soul. Inger was overwhelmed by all the unexpected love from above. To think that one of God's angels would be weeping for her! How did she deserve this act of kindness? The tormented soul thought back on every deed she had performed during her life on earth and was convulsed with sobs, weeping in ways that the old Inger could never have wept. Inger was filled with sorrow for herself, and she felt certain the gates of mercy would never open for her. She was beginning to realize this with the deepest humility, when, suddenly, a brilliant ray flashed down into the bottomless pit, one more powerful than the sunbeams that melt the snowmen that boys build outdoors. And at the touch of this ray—faster than a snowflake turns into water when it lands on a child's warm lips—Inger's stiffened, stony figure vanished. A tiny bird soared like forked lightning up toward the world of humans.

The bird seemed timid and afraid of everything around it, as if ashamed and wanting to avoid the sight of all living creatures. It hastened to find shelter and discovered it in the dark hole of a crumbling wall. It cowered there, and trembled all over, without uttering a sound, for it had no voice. It stayed there for a long time before it dared to peer out and take in the beauty all around. And, yes indeed, it was beautiful. The air was so fresh, the breeze gentle, and the moon was shining brightly. Among the fragrant trees and flowers, the bird was perched in a cozy spot, its feathers clean and dainty. How much love and splendor there was in all created things! The bird was eager to express in song the thoughts bursting from its heart, but it could not. It wanted to sing like the nightingale or the cuckoo in the springtime. Our Lord, who can hear even the voiceless hymn of the worm, understood the hymn of praise that swelled up in chords of thought, like the psalms that resonated in David's heart before they took shape in words and music.

For days and weeks, these mute songs grew stronger. Someday they would surely find a voice, perhaps with the first stroke of a wing performing a good deed. Was the time not ripe?

The holy feast of Christmas was nigh. A farmer had put a pole up near the wall and had tied an unthreshed bundle of oats to it, so that creatures of the air might also have a merry Christmas and a cheerful meal in this season of the Savior.

The sun rose that Christmas morning and shone down brightly upon the sheaf of oats and all the twittering birds gathered around it. A faint "tweet, tweet" sounded from the wall. The swelling thoughts had finally turned into sound, and the feeble chirp turned into a hymn of joy. The idea of a good deed had awakened, and the bird flew out from its hiding place. In heaven they knew exactly what kind of bird it was.

Winter began in earnest; the ponds were frozen over with thick ice; and the birds and wild creatures were short of food. The tiny bird flew along country roads, and, there, in the tracks of sledges, it managed to find a grain of corn here and there, or in the best places, a few crumbs of bread. It would eat but a single grain of corn and then alert the other famished birds so that they too could find food. It also flew into the towns, inspecting the ground, and wherever a kindly hand had scattered breadcrumbs from the window for birds, it would take just a single crumb and give the rest away.

By the end of the winter the bird had collected and given away so many crumbs that they equaled in weight the loaf upon which little Inger had trod to keep her fine shoes from being soiled. And when it had found and given away the last crumb, the bird's gray wings turned white and spread out.

"Look, there's a tern flying across the lake," the children cried out when they saw the white bird. First it dipped down into the water, then it rose into the bright sunshine. The bird's wings glittered so brightly in the air that it was impossible to see where it was flying. They say that it flew straight into the sun.

The Red Shoes[†]

There was once a little girl who was delicate and pretty but so poor that she had to go barefoot all summer long. In the winter, she had to wear big wooden clogs that chafed against her ankles until they turned red. It was just dreadful.

[†] From *The Annotated Hans Christian Andersen*, trans. Maria Tatar (New York: Norton, 2008), pp. 252, 254, 256–62. Copyright © 2008 by Maria Tatar. Used by permission of W. W. Norton & Company.

Old Mother Shoemaker lived right in the middle of the village. She took some old strips of red cloth and did her best to turn them into a little pair of shoes. They may have been crudely made, but she meant well, and the girl was to have them. The little girl's name was Karen.

On the day that her mother was buried, Karen was given the red shoes and wore them for the very first time. It's true that they were not the proper shoes for mourning, but they were all she had, and so she put them on her bare feet, walking behind the plain coffin made of straw.

Just then a grand old carriage passed by, and inside it sat a grand old woman. She looked at the little girl and took pity on her. And she said to the pastor: "How about giving the little girl to me? I will treat her kindly."

Karen thought that all this had happened because she had been wearing the red shoes, but the old woman declared that the shoes were hideous, and she had them burned. Karen was then dressed in proper new clothing. She had to learn to read and sew, and people said that she was pretty. But the mirror told her: "You are more than pretty—you're beautiful!"

One day the queen came traveling through the country with her little daughter, who was a princess. People were swarming around the castle, and Karen was there too. The little princess was dressed in fine white clothing and stood at the window for all to admire. She wasn't wearing a train, and she didn't have a golden crown on her head, but she was wearing splendid red shoes made of fine leather. Of course they were much nicer than the ones Old Mother Shoemaker had made for little Karen. There's nothing in the world like a pair of red shoes!

When Karen was old enough to be confirmed, she was given new clothes, and she was to have new shoes as well. A prosperous shoemaker in town measured her little feet. The shop was right in his house, and the parlor had big glass cases, with stylish shoes and shiny boots on display. Everything in them looked attractive, but since the old woman could not see well, the display gave her no pleasure. Among the many shoes was a pair of red ones that looked just like the shoes worn by the princess. They were beautiful! The shoemaker told Karen that he had made them for the daughter of a count, but that the fit had not been right.

"They must be made of patent leather," the old woman said. "See how they shine!"

"Yes, they are shiny!" Karen said. And since the shoes fit, the old woman bought them, but she had no idea they were red. If she had known, she would never have let Karen wear them to be confirmed, but that is exactly what Karen did.

Everyone looked at Karen's feet when she walked down the aisle in the church toward the doorway for the choir. Even the old paintings on the crypts—the portraits of pastors and their wives wearing stiff collars and long black gowns—seemed to have their eyes fixed on her red shoes. That was all Karen could think about, even when the pastor placed his hand on her head and spoke of the holy baptism, the covenant with God, and the fact that she should now be a good Christian. The organ played solemnly, the children sang sweetly, and the old choir leader sang too, but, still, Karen could think only about her red shoes.

By the afternoon, the old woman had heard from everyone in the parish about the red shoes. She told Karen that wearing red shoes to church was dreadful and not the least bit proper. From that day on, whenever Karen went to church, she was to wear black shoes, even if they were worn out.

The following Sunday Karen was supposed to go to communion. She looked at her black shoes, and she looked at the red ones. And then she looked at the red ones again and put them on.

It was a beautiful, sunny day. Karen and the old woman took the path through the cornfields, where it was rather dusty.

At the church door they met an old soldier, who was leaning on a crutch. He had a long, odd-looking beard that was more red than white—in fact it was red. He made a deep bow, and then he asked the old woman if he could polish her shoes. Karen stretched out her little foot as well. "Just look at those beautiful dancing shoes," the soldier said. "May they stay on tight when you dance," and he tapped the soles of the shoes.

The old woman gave the soldier a penny and then went into the church with Karen.

Everyone in the church stared at Karen's red shoes, and all the portraits stared at them too. And when Karen knelt down at the altar and put the chalice to her lips, all she could think of were her red shoes, which seemed to be floating in the chalice. She forgot to sing the hymn, and she also forgot to recite the Lord's Prayer.

Everyone was leaving the church, and the old woman climbed into the carriage. As Karen was lifting her foot to follow her in, the old soldier standing nearby said: "Take a look at those beautiful dancing shoes!" Karen could not help herself—she just had to take a few dance steps. But once she started, her feet could not stop. It was as if the shoes had taken control. She danced around the corner of the church—she could not stop herself. The coachman had to chase after her, grab hold of her, and lift her into the carriage. But even in there her feet kept on dancing, and she gave the kind old woman a few terrible kicks. Finally they managed to get the shoes off, and her legs began to calm down.

Once they were home, the shoes were put into a cupboard, but Karen could not help going over to look at them.

Not much later, the old woman was taken ill, and it was said that she would not live long. She needed someone to take care of her and nurse her, and who better to do it than Karen?

But in town there was to be a grand ball, and Karen had been invited. She looked at the old woman, who didn't, after all, have much longer to live. Then she looked at the red shoes, for there was no harm in that. She put them on, for there was no harm in that either. Then she left for the ball and began dancing.

When Karen turned to the right, the shoes turned left. When she wanted to dance up the ballroom floor, the shoes danced down the floor. They danced down the stairs, into the street, and out through the town gate. Dance she did, and dance she must, right out into the dark forest.

Something was shining brightly above the trees, and Karen thought it must be the moon, because it resembled a face, but it turned out to be the old soldier with the red beard. He nodded and said: "Take a look at those beautiful dancing shoes!"

Karen was horrified and tried to take the shoes off, but they wouldn't come off. She tore off her stockings, but the shoes had grown onto her feet. And dance she did, for dance she must, over hill and dale, rain or shine, night and day. Nighttime was the most terrible time of all.

Karen danced into the open churchyard, but the dead did not join in her dance. They had better things to do than dance. She wanted to sit down on a pauper's grave, where bitter tansy weed grows, but there was no rest or peace for her there. When she danced toward the open church door, she realized that it was guarded by an angel in long white robes, with wings that reached from his shoulders down to the ground. His expression was stern and solemn, and in his hand he held a broad, gleaming sword.

"Dance you shall!" he said to her. "Dance in your red shoes until you turn pale and cold, and your skin shrivels up like a mummy. Dance you shall from door to door, and wherever you find children who are proud and vain, you will knock on the door so that they will hear you and fear you! Dance you shall! Dance!"

"Have mercy!" Karen shouted. But she did not hear the angel's reply, for the shoes were already carrying her through the gate, along highways and byways, and she had to keep on dancing.

One morning, she danced past a door she knew well. Inside you could hear a hymn, and then a coffin covered with flowers was carried out. Karen knew that the old woman must have died. Now she was all alone in the world and cursed by the angel of God.

Dance she did and dance she must, dance through the dark night. Her shoes took her through thickets with briars that scratched her until she bled. She danced across the heath until she reached a lonely little house. She knew that this was the home of the executioner, and she tapped on the window with her finger and said: "Come outside! Come outside! I can't come in because I'm dancing!"

The executioner said: "You don't know who I am, do you? I chop off the heads of evil people, and I can feel that my ax is getting impatient."

"Don't chop my head off!" Karen cried. "If you do, I won't be able to repent. But go ahead and chop the red shoes off my feet."

Karen confessed her sins, and the executioner chopped off the feet in those red shoes. And the shoes danced across the fields and into the deep forest, with the feet still in them.

The executioner made wooden feet and crutches for her. He taught her a hymn that was sung by sinners. Then she kissed the hand that had wielded the ax, and off she went across the heath.

"I have suffered long enough because of those red shoes," she said. "It's time to go to church and let everyone see me." She hobbled over as fast as she could to the church door, and, when she got there, the red shoes were dancing in front of her. Horrified, she turned back.

All week long she was miserable and wept many bitter tears. When Sunday came, she said: "I have suffered and struggled long enough. I have a feeling that I am just as good as many of the people sitting in church and holding their heads high." She set out confidently, but when she reached the gate she saw the red shoes dancing in front of her. She turned away horrified and, this time, repented her sins with all her heart.

Karen went over to the parsonage and asked if she might be taken into service there. She promised to work hard and to do everything asked of her. Wages were of no interest to her. All she needed was a roof over her head and the chance to stay with good people. The parson's wife took pity on her and hired her. Karen was thoughtful and hardworking. In the evening, she would sit quietly and listen to the parson as he read from the Bible. The children were all fond of her, but whenever they talked about dressing up in frills and finery and looking as beautiful as a queen, she would shake her head.

The next Sunday they all went to church and asked if she wanted to join them. Tears came to her eyes as she looked with sorrow over at her crutches. The others went to hear the word of God while she retreated to her lonely little room, just big enough to hold a bed and a chair. She sat down with her hymnal and was reading it devoutly when the wind carried the sounds of the organ from the church to her. She raised her tear-stained face upward and said: "Help me, O Lord!"

The sun began to shine brightly, and an angel in white robes—the one that she had seen at night in the church doorway—appeared before her. Where he had once held a sword with a sharp blade he now had a beautiful green branch covered with roses. He touched the ceiling with the branch, and it rose high up into the air. A golden star was shining on the spot he had touched. Then he touched the walls, and they moved outward and away. Karen looked at the organ and heard it playing. She saw the portraits of the pastors and their wives. The congregation was seated in carved pews and singing from hymnals.

The church itself had come to the poor girl in her tiny crowded room, or perhaps she had gone to the church. She was sitting in a pew with others from the parsonage. When they finished the hymn, they looked up, nodded in her direction, and said: "It was right for you to come, Karen."

"I'm here by the grace of God," she replied.

The organ swelled, and the children in the choir lifted their voices in soft and beautiful sounds. Bright, warm sunshine flooded through the window into the church pew where Karen was seated. Her heart was so filled with sunshine, and with peace and joy, that it burst. Her soul flew on the rays of the sun up to God, and no one there asked her about the red shoes.

The Emperor's New Clothes[†]

Many years ago there lived an Emperor who cared so much about beautiful new clothes that he spent all his money on dressing stylishly. He took no interest at all in his soldiers, nor did he care to attend the theater or go out for a drive, unless of course it gave him a chance to show off his new clothes. He had a different outfit for every hour of the day and, just as you usually say that kings are sitting in council, it was always said of him: "The Emperor is in his dressing room right now."

In the big city where the Emperor lived, there were many distractions. Strangers came and went all the time, and one day two swindlers appeared. They claimed to be weavers and said that they knew how to weave the loveliest cloth you could imagine. Not only were the colors and designs they created unusually beautiful, but the clothes made from their fabrics also had the amazing ability of becoming invisible to those who were unfit for their posts or just hopelessly stupid.

† From *The Annotated Hans Christian Andersen*, ed. Maria Tatar (New York: Norton, 2008), pp. 5–6, 8–10, 13. Copyright © 2008 by Maria Tatar. Used by permission of W. W. Norton & Company.

"Those must be lovely clothes!" thought the Emperor. "If I wore something like that, I could tell which men in my kingdom were unfit for their posts, and I would also be able to tell the smart ones from the stupid ones. Yes, I must have some of that fabric woven for me at once." And he paid the swindlers a large sum of money so that they could get started at once.

The swindlers assembled a couple of looms and pretended to be working, but there was nothing at all on their looms. Straightaway they demanded the finest silk and the purest gold thread, which they promptly stowed away in their own bags. Then they worked far into the night on their empty looms.

"Well, now, I wonder how the weavers are getting on with their work," the Emperor thought. But he was beginning to feel some anxiety about the fact that anyone who was stupid or unfit for his post would not be able to see what was being woven. Not that he had any fears about himself—he felt quite confident on that score—but all the same it might be better to send someone else out first, to see how things were progressing. Everyone in town had heard about the cloth's mysterious power, and they were all eager to discover the incompetence or stupidity of their neighbors.

"I will send my honest old minister to the weavers," the Emperor thought. "He's the best person to inspect the cloth, for he has plenty of good sense, and no one is better qualified for his post than he is."

So off went the good-natured old minister to the workshop where the two swindlers were laboring with all their might at the empty looms. "God save us!" thought the minister, and his eyes nearly popped out of his head. "Why, I can't see thing!" But he was careful not to say that out loud.

The two swindlers invited him to take a closer look—didn't he find the pattern beautiful and the colors lovely? They gestured at the empty frames, but no matter how widely he opened his eyes, he couldn't see a thing, for there was nothing there. "Good Lord!" he thought. "Is it possible that I'm an idiot? I never once suspected it, and I mustn't let on that it is a possibility. Can it be that I'm unfit for my post? No, it will never do for me to admit that I can't see the cloth."

"Well, why aren't you saying anything about it?" asked one of the swindlers, who was pretending to be weaving.

"Oh, it's enchanting! Quite exquisite!" the old minister said, peering over his spectacles. "That pattern and those colors! I shall tell the Emperor right away how much I like it."

"Ah, we are so glad that you like it," the weavers replied, and they described the colors and extraordinary patterns in detail. The old minister listened attentively so that he would be able to repeat their description to the Emperor when he returned home—which he duly did.

The swindlers demanded more money, more silk, and more gold thread, which they insisted they needed to keep weaving. They stuffed it all in their own pockets—not a thread was put on the loom—while they went on weaving at the empty frames as before.

After a while, the Emperor sent a second respected official to see how the weaving was progressing and to find out when the cloth would be ready. What had happened to the first minister also happened to him. He looked as hard as he could, but since there was nothing there but an empty loom, he couldn't see a thing.

"There, isn't this a beautiful piece of cloth!" the swindlers declared, as they described the lovely design that didn't exist at all.

"I'm not stupid," thought the man. "This can only mean that I'm not fit for my position. That would be ridiculous, so I'd better not let on." And so he praised the cloth he could not see and declared that he was delighted with its beautiful hues and lovely patterns. "Yes, it's quite exquisite," he said to the Emperor.

The splendid fabric soon became the talk of the town.

And now the Emperor wanted to see the cloth for himself while it was still on the loom. Accompanied by a select group of people, including the two stately old officials who had already been there, he went to visit the crafty swindlers, who were weaving for all they were worth without using a bit of yarn or thread.

"Look, isn't it *magnifique*?" the two venerable officials exclaimed. "If Your Majesty will but take a look. What a design! What colors!" And they pointed at the empty loom, feeling sure that all the others could see the cloth.

"What on earth!" thought the Emperor. "I can't see a thing! This is appalling! Am I stupid? Am I unfit to be Emperor? This is the most horrible thing I can imagine happening to me!"

"Oh, it's very beautiful!" the Emperor said. "It has our most gracious approval." And he gave a satisfied nod as he inspected the empty loom. He wasn't about to say that he couldn't see a thing. The courtiers who had come with him strained their eyes, but they couldn't see any more than the others. Still, they all said exactly what the Emperor had said: "Oh, it's very beautiful!" They advised him to wear his splendid new clothes for the first time in the grand parade that was about to take place. "It's *magnifique*!" "Exquisite!" "Superb!"—that's what you heard over and over again. Everyone was really pleased with the weaving. The Emperor knighted each of the two swindlers and gave them medals to wear in their buttonholes, along with the title Imperial Weaver.

On the eve of the parade, the rogues sat up all night with more than sixteen candles burning. Everyone could see how busy they were finishing the Emperor's new clothes. They pretended to remove the cloth from the loom; they cut the air with big scissors; and they sewed with needles that had no thread. Then at last they announced: "There! The Emperor's clothes are ready at last!"

The Emperor, with his most distinguished courtiers, went in person to the weavers, who each stretched out an arm as if holding something up and said: "Just look at these trousers! Here is the jacket! This is the cloak." And so on. "They are all as light as spiderwebs. You can hardly tell you are wearing anything—that's the virtue of this delicate cloth."

"Yes, indeed," the courtiers declared. But they were unable to see a thing, for there was absolutely nothing there.

"Now, would it please His Imperial Majesty to remove his clothes?" asked the swindlers. "Then we can fit you with the new ones, over there in front of the long mirror."

And so the Emperor took off the clothes he was wearing, and the swindlers pretended to hand him each of the new garments they claimed to have made, and they held him at the waist as if they were attaching something . . . it was his train. And the Emperor twisted and turned in front of the mirror.

"Goodness! How splendid His Majesty looks in the new clothes. What a perfect fit!" they all exclaimed. "What patterns! What colors! What priceless attire!"

The master of ceremonies came in with an announcement. "The canopy for the parade is ready and waiting for Your Majesty."

"I am quite ready," said the Emperor. "The clothes suit me well, don't they!" And he turned around one last time in front of the mirror, trying to look as if he were examining his fine new clothing.

The chamberlains who were supposed to carry the train groped around on the floor as if they were picking it up. As they walked, they held out their hands, not daring to let on that they couldn't see anything.

The Emperor marched in the parade under the lovely canopy, and everyone in the streets and at the windows said: "Goodness! The Emperor's new clothes are the finest he has ever worn. What a lovely train on his coat! What a perfect fit!" People were not willing to let on that there was nothing at all to see, because that would have meant they were either unfit for their posts or very stupid. Never had the Emperor's clothes made such a great impression.

"But he isn't wearing anything at all!" a little child declared.

"Goodness gracious! Did you hear the voice of that innocent child!" cried the father. And the child's remark was whispered from one person to the next.

"Yes, he isn't wearing anything at all!" the crowd shouted at last. And the Emperor cringed, for he was beginning to suspect that everyone was right. But then he realized: "I must go through with it now, parade and all." And he drew himself up even more proudly than before, while his chamberlains walked behind him carrying the train that was not there at all.

The Nightingale[†]

In China, as you may know, the Emperor is Chinese, and everyone there is also Chinese. This story took place many years ago, but that's exactly why you should listen to it, before it's forgotten.

The Emperor's palace was the most magnificent in the world. It was made entirely of fine porcelain, so costly and delicate that you had to be careful when you touched it. In the garden you could find the most wondrous flowers. The most splendid among the flowers were trimmed with little silver bells that jingled, and you couldn't walk by without noticing them. Yes, everything was arranged quite artfully in the Emperor's garden, which stretched so far back that even the gardener could not say where it ended. If you kept on walking, you reached the loveliest forest with tall trees and deep lakes. The forest stretched all the way out to the deep, blue sea. Tall ships sailed right under the branches of the trees. In those branches lived a nightingale whose song was so enchanting that even a poor fisherman, who had many chores before him, would pause when taking his nets in at night to listen. "My God! That's really beautiful," he would say. But then he would return to his chores and forget all about the bird's song. The next evening, when the fisherman was back at work, the bird would start singing again, and he would say the same thing: "My God! That's really beautiful."

Travelers came from all over the world to visit the Emperor's city and to admire his palace and gardens. If they happened to hear the nightingale singing, they would all agree: "That's just the best of all."

When the travelers returned home, they would describe what they had seen, and learned men wrote many books about the city, the palace, and the garden. They never forgot the nightingale—in fact they praised the bird above all other things. Those who could write poetry composed the loveliest poems about the nightingale that lived in the forest by the deep sea.

The books themselves traveled around the world, and some of them found their way to the Emperor of China. One day, he was sitting on his golden throne, reading one book after another, nodding his head in delight over the splendid descriptions of his city, palace, and garden. "The nightingale is the best of all!" the books declared.

† From *The Annotated Hans Christian Andersen*, ed. Maria Tatar (New York: Norton, 2008), pp. 80, 82–83, 85–86, 88, 90, 92–93, 95–97. Copyright © 2008 by Maria Tatar. Used by permission of W. W. Norton & Company.

"What on earth!" the Emperor exclaimed. "A nightingale! I don't know a thing about it! Is it possible that a bird like that exists in my empire, let alone in my own garden? And to think that I had to read about it in a book."

The Emperor summoned the Chamberlain, who was so refined that when anyone of a lower rank had the audacity to address him or to ask a question, his only reply was "Puh!" which really means nothing at all.

"Apparently there is a truly extraordinary bird around here called a nightingale," said the Emperor. "They say it's better than anything else in all my domains. Why hasn't anyone said a word to me about it?"

"I've never heard anyone say a word about it," the Chamberlain said. "And no one has ever presented the bird at the imperial court."

"I want it to appear here tonight to sing for me," the Emperor said. "The rest of the world knows more about what's in my kingdom than I do!"

"I've never heard anyone say a word about it," the Chamberlain said again. "But I shall look for it, and I will find it."

But where could the nightingale be? The Chamberlain sped up and down the stairs, through rooms and corridors, but nobody he met had ever heard of the nightingale. And so the Chamberlain raced back to the Emperor and told him that the bird must have been in a fable invented by those who write books. "Your Imperial Majesty should not believe what people write today. It's all made up and about what can be called black magic."

"But the book I was reading was sent to me by the mighty Emperor of Japan," the Emperor said. "So it really must be true. I am determined to hear this nightingale. It must be here by this evening. I've granted it my high imperial favor. If it doesn't show up by then, I'll have every courtier punched in the stomach right after supper."

"Tsing-pe!" the Chamberlain shouted, and once again he sped up and down the stairs, through all the rooms and corridors. And half the court ran along with him, for no one wanted to be punched in the stomach. Everyone was asking questions about the mysterious nightingale, which was so famous all over the world but unknown at home.

They finally found a poor little girl in the kitchen, who said: "Good Lord! The nightingale? Of course I know all about it. Yes, indeed, it can really sing! Every evening they let me take home a few scraps from the table to my poor, sick mother. She lives down by the sea. When I start back, I am so tired that I have to stop to rest in the woods. That's when I hear the nightingale sing. It brings tears to my eyes. It's just as if my mother were giving me a kiss."

"Little kitchen maid," the Chamberlain said. "I'll arrange a lifetime post for you in the kitchen and give you permission to watch the Emperor dine if you can take us to the nightingale. It is supposed to give a command performance at court tonight."

And so they all set off for the forest, to the place where the nightingale was said to sing. Half of the court followed. On the way into the forest a cow began mooing.

"Aha!" said the royal squires. "That must be it. What remarkable power for such a tiny creature. We're sure that we've heard that song once before."

"No, those are cows lowing," the little kitchen girl said. "We still have a long way to go."

Then the frogs began croaking in the marshes.

"How lovely!" the imperial Chinese chaplain declared. "It sounds just like little church bells."

"No, those are just frogs," said the little kitchen maid. "But I have a feeling we will hear the nightingale soon."

Then the nightingale began to sing.

"There it is," said the little kitchen maid. "Just listen. And now you can see it!" And she pointed to a little gray bird perched on a branch.

"Can it be?" exclaimed the Chamberlain. "That's not at all how I imagined the bird to be. How plain it looks! It must have lost all its color from seeing all the distinguished persons gathered around."

"Little nightingale," the kitchen maid called out in a loud voice. "Our gracious Emperor so wants you to sing for him."

"With the greatest pleasure," the nightingale replied, and it sang to everyone's delight.

"It sounds just like crystal bells," the Lord Chamberlain said. "And just look at the bird's little throat—you can tell it's singing with all its might. It's astonishing that we have never heard it before. It will be a great success at court."

"Shall I sing again for the Emperor?" the nightingale asked, for it believed that the Emperor was present.

"My splendid little nightingale," the Lord Chamberlain said. "I have the great honor of inviting you to court this evening, and there you will enchant his Imperial Grace with your charming voice."

"My song sounds best outdoors," the nightingale replied, but it was glad to return with them when it learned of the Emperor's wishes.

The palace had been cleaned and polished with great care. The walls and floors, made of porcelain, were gleaming from the light of thousands of golden lamps. The loveliest flowers, trimmed with little bells, had been placed in the corridors. The commotion from all the comings and goings made the bells start ringing, and you could scarcely hear yourself think.

In the middle of the great hall in which the Emperor was seated, a golden perch had been set up, and it was for the nightingale. The entire court had assembled there. The little kitchen maid had been given permission to stand behind the door, for she now held the title of Real Kitchen Maid. People were dressed in their finery, and, when the Emperor graciously nodded, everyone fixed their eyes on the little gray bird.

The nightingale's voice was so lovely that tears began to fill the Emperor's eyes and roll down his cheeks. The bird sang even more beautifully, and the music went straight to his heart. The Emperor was so delighted that he ordered his own golden slipper to be hung around the nightingale's neck. But the nightingale graciously declined it and declared that it had received reward enough.

"I have seen tears in the eyes of the Emperor," it said. "For me that is the greatest treasure. The tears of an Emperor have a wondrous power. God knows that I have received my reward." And it sang once again with a sweet, sublime voice.

"We've never seen such lovable flirtatiousness," the ladies all declared. And they put water in their mouths so they would twitter whenever they talked. They were hoping that they too could be nightingales. Even the footmen and chambermaids declared that they were satisfied, which is saying a lot, for they are the hardest to please. Yes, indeed, the nightingale was a complete success!

The nightingale was supposed to stay at the palace and have its own cage, as well as the freedom to go on outings twice a day, and once at nighttime. Twelve servants stood in attendance, each one holding tight to a silk ribbon attached to the bird's leg. There was no pleasure at all in outings like that.

The whole town was talking about the remarkable bird. If two people happened to meet, the first just said "Night!" and the other would respond with "Gale!" and then they would both just sigh, with no need for words. What's more, eleven grocers named their children "Nightingale," although not a single one of them was able to carry a tune.

One day a big package arrived for the Emperor. The word "Nightingale" had been written on it.

"It must be a new book about our famous bird," the Emperor said. But it was not a book. Inside the box was a work of art, a mechanical nightingale that was supposed to look just like the real one except that it was covered with diamonds, rubies, and sapphires. When it was wound up, the mechanical bird sang one of the melodies of the real bird, all the while beating time with its gleaming tail of gold and silver. Around its neck hung a little ribbon, and on it were the words: "The Emperor of Japan's nightingale is a paltry thing compared with the one owned by the Emperor of China."

"Isn't it lovely!" they all said, and the person who had delivered the contraption was immediately given the title Supreme Imperial Nightingale Transporter.

"Let's have them sing together. What a duet that will be!"

And so the two birds sang a duet, but it didn't work, because the real nightingale had her own style, while the mechanical bird ran on cylinders. "You can't blame it for that," the Music Master said. "It keeps perfect time, entirely in line with my theories." And so the mechanical bird sang on its own. It pleased them all just as much as the real bird, and on top of that it was far prettier to look at, for it sparkled just the way that bracelets and brooches do.

The mechanical bird sang the same tune thirty-three times without tiring out. Everyone would have been happy to hear it again, but the Emperor thought that the real nightingale should also take a turn. But where had it gone? No one had noticed that it had flown out the window, back to the green forests.

"Well, what kind of behavior is that?" the Emperor exclaimed. And the courtiers all sneered at the nightingale, declaring it to be a most ungrateful creature. "Fortunately, the best bird of all is still with us," they said. And the mechanical bird started singing the same tune, now for the thirty-fourth time. But no one knew it by heart yet, because it was a terribly difficult piece. The Imperial Music Master lavished great praise on the mechanical bird. Yes, he assured them, this contraption was far better than any real nightingale, not only because of how it looked on the outside with its many beautiful diamonds but also because of its inner qualities.

"Ladies and gentlemen—and above all Your Imperial Majesty: You never know what will happen when it comes to a real nightingale. But with a mechanical bird everything is completely under control. It will sound a certain way, and no other way. You can explain it; you can open it up and take it apart; you can see how the mechanical wheels operate, how they whirl around, and how one interlocks with the other."

"My sentiments precisely," they all said. And the Music Master was given permission to put the bird on display for all to see on the following Sunday. They too should hear it sing, the Emperor declared. And hear it they did, with so much pleasure that it was as if they had all become tipsy from drinking tea, in the Chinese fashion. Everyone said "Oh!" and held up a finger—the one you lick the pot with—and then nodded. But the poor fisherman, the one who had heard the real nightingale sing, said: "That sounds nice enough, and it's very close to the real thing. Something's missing, but I'm not sure what it is."

The real nightingale was banished from the realm.

The mechanical bird took up its place on a silk cushion near the Emperor's bed. It was surrounded by the many gifts people had given it—gold and precious stones. It had also risen in office to become Supreme Imperial Nightstand Singer. In rank it was number one to the left, for the Emperor believed the left side of the body was nobler. After all, that's where the heart is, even the Emperor's.

The Music Master wrote twenty-five volumes about the mechanical bird—books so learned, long-winded, and full of obscure Chinese words that everyone claimed to have read them and understood them, because otherwise people would have said they were stupid and they would have been punched in the stomach.

A year went by in this way, and the Emperor, his court, and all the people in China knew every little twitter of the mechanical bird's song by heart, and that was exactly why they liked it so much more than anything else. They could sing its song on their own, and they did. Boys and girls in the streets sang: "Zi-zi-zi! Click, click, click," and the Emperor sang along with them. Oh, yes, it was that lovely!

But one evening, when the mechanical bird was singing with all its might and the Emperor was lying in bed listening, something inside the bird went "boing!" Something else burst and went "whirr!" Gears began spinning wildly, and then the music stopped.

The Emperor jumped right out of bed and sent for the royal physician. But what could he do? They summoned a watchmaker, who deliberated and investigated, then finally patched up the bird after a fashion. The watchmaker warned that the bird had to be kept from overdoing things, for the cogs inside it were badly worn and, if they were replaced, the music would not sound right. That was really dreadful! No one dared to let the bird sing more than once a year, and even that was almost too much. But before long the Music Master gave a little speech full of big words and claimed that the bird was just as good as new. And so it *was* just as good as new.

Five years went by, and the entire country was in deep mourning, for everyone was really fond of their ruler, and he was ill—so ill that he would probably not survive. A new Emperor had already been chosen. People were standing outside in the streets, waiting to ask the Chamberlain how the Emperor was faring.

"Puh!" he said and shook his head.

The Emperor was lying in a huge, magnificent bed, and he looked cold and pale. All the courtiers were sure that he was already gone, and they were hurrying to get out of the palace to pay homage to the new Emperor. The footmen darted around, spreading the news, and the chambermaids were holding a big party and drinking coffee. Mats had been put down in all the rooms and passageways to muffle the sound of footsteps, and that's why it was so quiet, ever so quiet. But the Emperor was not yet dead. He lay stiff and pale in his magnificent bed with its long velvet curtains and heavy golden tassels. High above him was an open window, and the moon was shining in through it on the Emperor and his mechanical bird.

The poor Emperor could barely breathe. He felt as if something was sitting on his chest. When he opened his eyes, he realized that it was Death, and he was wearing the Emperor's crown on his head, holding the Emperor's golden sword in one hand, and carrying the Emperor's splendid banner in the other. Eerie-looking faces peered out between the folds of the great velvet curtains. Some looked perfectly dreadful, others were gentle and sweet. They were the Emperor's deeds, good and bad, and they had come back to haunt him now that Death was seated on his heart.

"Do you remember this?" they whispered one after the other. "Do you remember that?" And they told him so many things that he began to break out into a cold sweat.

"I never knew that!" the Emperor exclaimed. "Music, music! Sound the great drum of China," he cried, "so that I won't have to listen to everything they are saying."

But they would not stop, and Death nodded, like a Chinaman, at every word that was uttered.

"Music, music!" the Emperor shouted. "My blessed little golden bird! Sing for me, sing! I've given you gold and precious jewels. I've even put my golden slipper around your neck. Sing for me, please sing!"

But the bird remained silent. No one was there to wind it up, and without help, it couldn't sing. Death kept on looking at the Emperor with his great hollow sockets, and everything was quiet—so dreadfully quiet.

Suddenly the loveliest song could be heard from just outside the window. It was the little nightingale—the living one—perched on a branch outdoors. It had learned of the Emperor's distress and had come from afar to sing and offer comfort and hope. While it was singing, the phantoms all around began to grow more and more pale, and the blood in the Emperor's enfeebled body began to flow more and more quickly. Death itself was listening, and said, "Keep singing, little nightingale! Keep singing!"

"Yes, I will, if you give me the imperial golden sword! And if you give me the splendid banner! And if you give me the Emperor's crown!"

Death returned each of the treasures in exchange for a song. The nightingale kept on singing. It sang about silent churchyards where white roses grow, where elder trees make the air sweet, and where the grass is always green, watered by the tears of those left behind. Death began to long for his own garden and drifted out the window in a cold, gray mist.

"Thank you, thank you, you divine little bird!" the Emperor exclaimed. "Now I recognize you. I banished you once from my realm. And even then you sang until all those evil faces disappeared from around my bedside. You drove Death from my heart. How can I ever repay you?"

"You have already given me my reward," the nightingale said. "I brought tears to your eyes when I first sang for you, and I will never forget that about you. Those are the jewels that warm the hearts of singers. But go to sleep now and grow hale and hearty while I sing to you." The bird continued singing until the Emperor fell into a sweet slumber—a gentle and refreshing sleep.

The sun was shining through the windows when the Emperor awoke, restored and healthy. Not one of his servants had yet returned, for they all believed that he was dead. The nightingale was still there, singing.

"You must stay with me forever," the Emperor said. "You only have to sing when you wish, and, as for that mechanical bird, I'll smash it into a thousand pieces."

"Don't do that," the nightingale said. "It has done the very best it could—and you really should keep it. I can't live inside the palace, but let me come for a visit whenever I wish. In the evening, I'll alight on the branch by your window and bring you pleasure and wisdom with my song. I will sing about those who are happy and those who suffer. I'll sing about the good and evil that remains hidden from you. A little songbird gets around—to the poor fishermen, to the rooftops of farmers, to everyone who is far away from you and your court. I love your heart more than I love your crown, but there is something sacred about your crown. I'll come to sing for you, but you must promise me one thing."

"Anything!" the Emperor replied, standing there in the imperial robes that he himself had donned and holding his heavy golden sword against his heart.

"Just one thing," the nightingale asked. "You must not let anyone know that you have a little bird that tells you everything, for things will go better that way."

Then the nightingale flew away.

The servants came in to attend their dead Emperor. Yes—there they stood. And the Emperor said to them, "Good morning!"

INTRODUCTION: Oscar Wilde

Oscar Wilde and fairy tales? Putting the two into the same sentence has a jarring effect, especially considering that Wilde once declared that it was his "first duty" in life to be "as artificial as possible."[1] The Brothers Grimm told us long ago that simplicity, artlessness, and spontaneity are the chief features of fairy tales, stories that are home-spun rather than ornate, sophisticated, and complex. And yet fairy tales, with their stylized openings, predictable plots, repetitive tropes, and ritualized endings, are, in the realm of prose, artfully constructed with a starkly simple yet ornamental beauty. And so it comes as no surprise that Oscar Wilde wrote so many of them.

Oscar Wilde's claim to fame was, in any case, never based on a fool-ish consistency, and this teller of tales found in fairy tales a congenial vehicle for displaying the flip slide to his natural talent for inventive satire and coruscating wit. Admirers of Wilde's urbane and sophisti-cated prose have anxiously tried to explain the interest in writing fairy tales as the symptom of a developmental defect, of his sexual orienta-tion, or of some odd identity confusion. One critic claims that Wilde was drawn to fairy tales because he was "emotionally undeveloped";[2] a second attributes his decision to embrace the genre to "homosexual tendencies";[3] and a third traces the engagement with fairy tales to "sexual ambivalence."[4] A feature described as literary "degeneration" was identified in Wilde's fairy tales and explicitly linked to his sexual orientation: "Something had happened to Wilde. He met Mr. Robert Baldwin Ross. The effect of this unfortunate encounter is to be seen in Wilde's work. . . . *The Happy Prince* appeared in 1888; and was fol-lowed up in the year 1891, when Wilde made his second unfortunate friendship, with Lord Alfred Douglas, by *The House of Pomegran-ates.* . . . There is nothing here for exultation."[5]

That Wilde's fairy tales are considered aesthetically and ethically suspect (one critic found their style "fleshy" and unsuitable for chil-dren) seems peculiar in light of their emphatic articulation of moral

1. Alvin Redman, ed., *The Epigrams of Oscar Wilde* (London: Alvin Redman, 1952), p. 116.
2. Hesketh Pearson, *The Life of Oscar Wilde* (London: Methuen, 1946), p. 141.
3. Leon Lémonnier, *Oscar Wilde* (Paris: Didier, 1938), p. 122.
4. Robert Merle, *Oscar Wilde* (Paris: Editions, 1948), p. 261.
5. St. John Ervine, *Oscar Wilde: A Present Time Appraisal* (New York: William Morrow, 1952), p. 167.

truths.[6] The same author who recited with glee such dandyish maxims as "To love oneself is the beginning of a life-long romance" embedded in his fairy tales stinging critiques of boorish self-absorption, willful selfishness, and brazen greed. Wilde clearly modeled his stories more on Andersen's literary tales, with their ostentatious moral orientation and displays of pious self-denial, than on the Irish folklore that his mother collected. The kinship between Wilde's tales and Andersen's stories did not escape contemporary reviewers, who found Wilde to be writing "somewhat after the manner of Hans Andersen," whose works had been available in English translation since 1846.[7] That Wilde deeply respected the Danish writer becomes evident from "The Fisherman and His Soul" (clearly inspired by "The Little Mermaid") and by the unmistakable tribute to "The Little Match Girl" in one of the many visions of human misery in "The Happy Prince."

In a note to his friend G. H. Kersely, Wilde commented on the implied audience for his collection. The tales, he insisted, were "an attempt to mirror modern life in a form remote from reality." In other words they would be set in another time and place even as they remained relevant to contemporary concerns. Conceding that the stories were meant "partly for children," Wilde in the same breath declared the tales to be "slight and fanciful, and written, not for children, but for childlike people from eighteen to eighty!"[8]

Why would Wilde exclude children from his implied audience, as he ultimately does in setting a lower limit of eighteen years for the stories? Wilde, like Andersen, may have begun some of his fairy tales with the phrase "Once upon a time," but he never ended them with "happily ever after." In fact, almost every story culminates in gloom and exhaustion, often with an obligatory scene of death, dismantling, or destruction. The statue of the "Happy Prince" is razed. After his conversion, the Selfish Giant is found "lying dead . . . all covered with white blossoms" (p. 334). The self-sacrificing little Hans in "The Devoted Friend" is found drowned, floating in a ditch. "The Fisherman and His Soul" ends with the death of both mermaid and fisherman. The dwarf enamored of a princess in "The Birthday of the Infanta" dies of a broken heart. Even the eponymous hero of the "Remarkable Rocket" expires, without a trace of the glory to which he aspires.

No fairy tale by Wilde is more expansive in its description of the mortal agony of death throes than "The Nightingale and the Rose."

6. Review of A *House of Pomegranates* by Oscar Wilde, *Pall Mall Gazette*, as quoted in Maria Edelson, "The Language of Allegory in Oscar Wilde's Tales," in *Anglo-Irish and Irish Literature*, ed. Birgit Bramsbäck and Martin Croghan (Stockholm: Almqvist and Wiksell and Bromsbäck, 1985), p. 167.
7. Norbert Kohl, *Oscar Wilde: The Works of a Conformist Rebel*, trans. David Henry Wilson (Cambridge: Cambridge UP, 1989), p. 58.
8. *The Letters of Oscar Wilde*, ed. Rupert Hart-Davis (London: Rupert Hart-Davis, 1962), p. 219.

Hoping to produce a red rose of unsurpassed beauty for a lovelorn student, a nightingale sings all night, with her breast pressed against the thorn of a rosebush:

> So the Nightingale pressed closer against the thorn, and the thorn touched her heart, and a fierce pang of pain shot through her. Bitter, bitter was the pain, and wilder and wilder grew her song, for she sang of the Love that is perfected by Death, of the Love that dies not in the tomb. (p. 345)

The songbird's bid for love marked by transcendent beauty becomes a form of sacrificial suffering, missing its mark (for the student and his beloved have no emotional depth whatsoever) but leading to the expression of her own peerless longing for spiritual release. Beauty, if not salvation, emerges from passionate self-sacrifice, which often takes the form of mortification of the flesh.

In "The Happy Prince," the statue also engages in a form of self-consuming sacrifice, distributing its excessive ornamentation to relieve suffering. The commemorative artwork in that story is "gilded all over with thin leaves of fine gold" and decorated with sapphires and a "large red ruby." Much admired by the city's residents, the figure creates a "golden bedroom" for a swallow, a migratory bird that has responded to the tears flowing out of the prince's eyes and delays its travel plans: "His face was so beautiful in the moonlight that the little Swallow was filled with pity." Why is the statue in tears? The Prince, who repudiates the life of self-indulgent pleasures he once lived, is suddenly in a position to see "all the ugliness and all the misery" of the city.

In this story there is a double movement at work. First we have a bird, the Swallow that beholds beauty and becomes the agent of justice, redeploying the wealth used for the statue built to honor the prince: "In he hopped, and laid the great ruby on the table beside the woman's thimble. Then he flew gently round the bed, fanning the boy's forehead with his wings." The feverish boy, a victim of poverty, begins to heal and sinks into a "delicious slumber." Then there is the prince, the statue that beholds what Susan Sontag describes as "repulsive attractions."[9] Staring at misery may be driven by voyeuristic impulses and other "unworthy desires," but those impulses can be redeemed and take an ethical direction when followed by sympathetic identification and political action. The prince sees, feels, and acts in ways that transform his gaze, both panoramic and telescopic, from what might have been an ethical violation into a redemptive act of healing. Paradoxically, he comes to life only in death, through the statue erected to honor him.

9. Susan Sontag, *Regarding the Pain of Others* (New York: Farrar, Straus, & Giroux, 2003), p. 96.

Why would Oscar Wilde, the writer for whom beauty is the "wonder of wonders," have been moved to disavow the pleasures of the Happy Prince's lived experience? How is it that an itch for compassion not only trumps beauty but also corrodes it and chips away at it? By the end of Wilde's story, the Happy Prince has been melted down and reduced to nothing but a "leaden heart."

"There is no Mystery so great as Misery," the Happy Prince confides to a swallow. "You tell me of marvellous things," he avows, "but more marvellous than anything is the suffering of men and of women" (p. 340). That there is something sacred about anguish, grief, and distress is not an argument one expects to hear in a fairy tale. Even more surprising, especially from the hand of an artist who has been seen as an apostle of art and artifice, is the celebration of the unsightly, bizarre, and grotesque in a genre traditionally directed at children. In "The Birthday of the Infanta," what is conventionally beautiful becomes rank and fetid: "The pomegranates split and cracked with the heat, and showed their bleeding hearts." The grotesque has the power to vanquish beauty, as becomes evident when the dwarf in that story discovers his mirror image:

> Of all the rooms this was the brightest and the most beautiful. The walls were covered with a pink-flowered Lucca damask, patterned with birds and dotted with dainty blossoms of silver; the furniture was of massive silver, festooned with florid wreaths, and swinging Cupids; in front of the two large fireplaces stood great screens broidered with parrots and peacocks, and the floor, which was of sea-green onyx, seemed to stretch far away into the distance. Nor was he alone. Standing under the shadow of the doorway, at the extreme end of the room, he saw a little figure watching him. . . .
>
> It was a monster, the most grotesque monster he had ever beheld. Not properly shaped as all other people were, but hunchbacked, and crooked-limbed, with a huge lolling head and mane of black hair.[1]

The elaborate description of the interior decorations is not merely a foil to the dwarf's hideous appearance; it also frames him, turning him into an icon of abject despair, foregrounded by his startling ugliness. The monster in the mirror is as riveting to the reader as it is to the dwarf, and the enthralling spectacle of the misshapen body becomes a powerful magnet of narrative interest.

Hans Christian Andersen might have seen in the dwarf's shocked discovery of his exterior appearance a moment of redemptive suffering, but Wilde deflates such expectations in the coda to his

---

1. Oscar Wilde, "The Birthday of the Infanta," in *Complete Short Fiction*, ed. Ian Small (New York: Penguin, 1994), pp. 97, 112.

stories. When the Spanish Infanta learns that the dwarf's heart has broken in two, she curls her lip "in pretty disdain" and declares: "For the future let those who come to play with me have no hearts."[2] Just as the dwarf's deformed body becomes the dominant figure in the decorative background of the palace's "brightest and most beautiful" room,[3] so too the Infanta's sneering remark takes center stage, effacing the tragic pathos of the truth that dawns on the dwarf as he looks in the mirror. Wilde may find suffering marvelous and charged with mystery, but he also is not always willing to endow it with transcendent meaning.

The promise of redemption typically rings hollow in Wilde's tales. The nightingale may be Christ-like in her martyrdom, but she suffers in vain, unable to transform the cynical selfishness of the student and his beloved. In "The Happy Prince," both the statue and the swallow annihilate themselves in an effort to do good works and end by demonstrating how charity consumes itself. In a sense, they could be seen as staging Wilde's maxim that "no good deed goes unpunished."

Wilde, unlike Andersen, does not seem to find salvation, Christian or otherwise, in suffering. In "The Soul of Man under Socialism," the Irish author made it clear that pain was not "the ultimate mode of perfection," as it appears to be for Andersen's Little Match Girl. Pain, he asserted in that essay, is "provisional and a protest":

> It has reference to wrong, unhealthy, unjust surroundings. When the wrong, and the disease, and the injustice are removed, it will have no further place. It will have done its work. . . .
>
> Nor will man miss it. *For what man has sought for is, indeed, neither pain nor pleasure, but simply Life.* Man has sought to live intensely, fully, perfectly. When he can do so without exercising restraint on others, or suffering it ever, and his activities are all pleasurable to him, he will be saner, healthier, more civilized, more himself. Pleasure is Nature's test, her sign of approval.[4]

If Wilde himself really believed that "the people who do most harm are the people who try to do the most good," then the efforts of the Happy Prince, the Selfish Giant, and the prodigal nightingale to alleviate misery and heartache are in vain. That the world is more likely to be improved by resisting the impulse to demonstrate charity and compassion may have been a lesson preached in "The Soul of Man under Socialism," but it did not carry over perfectly into Wilde's literary practice, where altruistic impulses remain stubbornly admirable even if they do not improve matters in the grand scheme of things. The cult of beauty may be impossible to destroy

2. Ibid., p. 114.
3. Ibid., p. 112.
4. Oscar Wilde, "The Soul of Man Under Socialism," in *The Artist as Critic: Critical Writings of Oscar Wilde*, ed. Richard Ellmann (New York: Vintage, 1968), pp. 288–89.

but it begins to crumble in Wilde's work under the pressure of economic realities in which abject misery becomes a moving picture with its own compelling aesthetic power.

Attractions both beautiful and repulsive have the power to move readers, though each with its own emotional vector, one moving in the direction of animation and generosity, the other in the mode of empathy and action. Wilde's fairy tales shuttle between these two competing aesthetic regimes, with each regime taking an ethical turn in ways far more subtle and compelling than the "morals" often attached to fairy tales. The turn is as intellectual as it is ethical, for it leads us to think more about the stakes in fairy tales and to think harder about their impact on our own minds.

The Selfish Giant[†]

Every afternoon, as they were coming from school, the children used to go and play in the Giant's garden.

It was a large lovely garden, with soft green grass. Here and there over the grass stood beautiful flowers like stars, and there were twelve peach-trees that in the spring-time broke out into delicate blossoms of pink and pearl, and in the autumn bore rich fruit. The birds sat on the trees and sang so sweetly that the children used to stop their games in order to listen to them. "How happy we are here!" they cried to each other.

One day the Giant came back. He had been to visit his friend the Cornish ogre, and had stayed with him for seven years. After the seven years were over he had said all that he had to say, for his conversation was limited, and he determined to return to his own castle. When he arrived he saw the children playing in the garden.

"What are you doing here?" he cried in a very gruff voice, and the children ran away.

"My own garden is my own garden," said the Giant; "any one can understand that, and I will allow nobody to play in it but myself." So he built a high wall all round it, and put up a notice-board.

> TRESPASSERS
> WILL BE
> PROSECUTED

He was a very selfish Giant.

[†] *Oscar Wilde: Complete Short Fiction*, ed. Ian Small (London: Penguin Books, 1994), pp. 19–23.

The poor children had now nowhere to play. They tried to play
on the road, but the road was very dusty and full of hard stones, and
they did not like it. They used to wander round the high wall when
their lessons were over, and talk about the beautiful garden inside.

"How happy we were there," they said to each other.

Then the Spring came, and all over the country there were little
blossoms and little birds. Only in the garden of the Selfish Giant it
was still Winter. The birds did not care to sing in it as there were no
children, and the trees forgot to blossom. Once a beautiful flower
put its head out from the grass, but when it saw the notice-board it
was so sorry for the children that it slipped back into the ground
again, and went off to sleep. The only people who were pleased were
the Snow and the Frost. "Spring has forgotten this garden," they
cried, "so we will live here all the year round." The Snow covered
up the grass with her great white cloak, and the Frost painted all
the trees silver. Then they invited the North Wind to stay with them,
and he came. He was wrapped in furs, and he roared all day about the
garden, and blew the chimney-pots down. "This is a delightful spot,"
he said, "we must ask the Hail on a visit." So the Hail came. Every day
for three hours he rattled on the roof of the castle till he broke most
of the slates, and then he ran round and round the garden as fast as
he could go. He was dressed in grey, and his breath was like ice.

"I cannot understand why the Spring is so late in coming," said
the Selfish Giant, as he sat at the window and looked out at his cold
white garden; "I hope there will be a change in the weather."

But the Spring never came, nor the Summer. The Autumn gave
golden fruit to every garden, but to the Giant's garden she gave none.
"He is too selfish," she said. So it was always Winter there, and the
North Wind, and the Hail, and the Frost, and the Snow danced
about through the trees.

One morning the Giant was lying awake in bed when he heard
some lovely music. It sounded so sweet to his ears that he thought it
must be the King's musicians passing by. It was really only a little lin-
net singing outside his window, but it was so long since he had heard
a bird sing in his garden that it seemed to him to be the most beautiful music in the world. Then the Hail stopped dancing over his head,
and the North Wind ceased roaring, and a delicious perfume came
to him through the open casement. "I believe the Spring has come at
last," said the Giant; and he jumped out of bed and looked out.

What did he see?

He saw a most wonderful sight. Through a little hole in the wall
the children had crept in, and they were sitting in the branches of
the trees. In every tree that he could see there was a little child.
And the trees were so glad to have the children back again that they
had covered themselves with blossoms, and were waving their

arms gently above the children's heads. The birds were flying about and twittering with delight, and the flowers were looking up through the green grass and laughing. It was a lovely scene, only in one corner it was still Winter. It was the farthest corner of the garden, and in it was standing a little boy. He was so small that he could not reach up to the branches of the tree, and he was wandering all round it, crying bitterly. The poor tree was still quite covered with frost and snow, and the North Wind was blowing and roaring above it. "Climb up! little boy," said the Tree, and it bent its branches down as low as it could; but the boy was too tiny.

And the Giant's heart melted as he looked out. "How selfish I have been!" he said; "now I know why the Spring would not come here. I will put that poor little boy on the top of the tree, and then I will knock down the wall, and my garden shall be the children's playground for ever and ever." He was really very sorry for what he had done.

So he crept downstairs and opened the front door quite softly, and went out into the garden. But when the children saw him they were so frightened that they all ran away, and the garden became Winter again. Only the little boy did not run, for his eyes were so full of tears that he did not see the Giant coming. And the Giant stole up behind him and took him gently in his hand, and put him up into the tree. And the tree broke at once into blossom, and the birds came and sang on it, and the little boy stretched out his two arms and flung them round the Giant's neck, and kissed him. And the other children, when they saw that the Giant was not wicked any longer, came running back, and with them came the Spring. "It is your garden now, little children," said the Giant, and he took a great axe and knocked down the wall. And when the people were going to market at twelve o'clock they found the Giant playing with the children in the most beautiful garden they had ever seen.

All day long they played, and in the evening they came to the Giant to bid him good-bye.

"But where is your little companion?" he said: "the boy I put into the tree." The Giant loved him the best because he had kissed him.

"We don't know," answered the children; "he has gone away."

"You must tell him to be sure and come here tomorrow," said the Giant. But the children said that they did not know where he lived, and had never seen him before; and the Giant felt very sad.

Every afternoon, when school was over, the children came and played with the Giant. But the little boy whom the Giant loved was never seen again. The Giant was very kind to all the children, yet he longed for his first little friend, and often spoke of him. "How I would like to see him!" he used to say.

Years went over, and the Giant grew very old and feeble. He could not play about any more, so he sat in a huge armchair, and watched the children at their games, and admired his garden. "I have many beautiful flowers," he said; "but the children are the most beautiful flowers of all."

One winter morning he looked out of his window as he was dressing. He did not hate the Winter now, for he knew that it was merely the Spring asleep, and that the flowers were resting.

Suddenly he rubbed his eyes in wonder, and looked and looked. It certainly was a marvellous sight. In the farthest corner of the garden was a tree quite covered with lovely white blossoms. Its branches were all golden, and silver fruit hung down from them, and underneath it stood the little boy he had loved.

Downstairs ran the Giant in great joy, and out into the garden. He hastened across the grass, and came near to the child. And when he came quite close his face grew red with anger, and he said, "Who hath dared to wound thee?" For on the palms of the child's hands were the prints of two nails, and the prints of two nails were on the little feet.

"Who hath dared to wound thee?" cried the Giant; "tell me, that I may take my big sword and slay him."

"Nay!" answered the child; "but these are the wounds of Love."

"Who art thou?" said the Giant, and a strange awe fell on him, and he knelt before the little child.

And the child smiled on the Giant, and said to him, "You let me play once in your garden, today you shall come with me to my garden, which is Paradise."

And when the children ran in that afternoon, they found the Giant lying dead under the tree, all covered with white blossoms.

The Happy Prince[†]

High above the city, on a tall column, stood the statue of the Happy Prince. He was gilded all over with thin leaves of fine gold, for eyes he had two bright sapphires, and a large red ruby glowed on his sword-hilt.

He was very much admired indeed. "He is as beautiful as a weathercock," remarked one of the Town Councillors who wished to gain a reputation for having artistic tastes; "only not quite so useful," he added, fearing lest people should think him unpractical, which he really was not.

"Why can't you be like the Happy Prince?" asked a sensible mother of her little boy who was crying for the moon. "The Happy Prince never dreams of crying for anything."

† *Oscar Wilde: Complete Short Fiction*, ed. Ian Small (London: Penguin Books, 1994), pp. 3–11.

"I am glad there is some one in the world who is quite happy," muttered a disappointed man as he gazed at the wonderful statue.

"He looks just like an angel," said the Charity Children[1] as they came out of the cathedral in their bright scarlet cloaks, and their clean white pinafores.

"How do you know?" said the Mathematical Master, "you have never seen one."

"Ah! but we have, in our dreams," answered the children; and the Mathematical Master frowned and looked very severe, for he did not approve of children dreaming.

One night there flew over the city a little Swallow. His friends had gone away to Egypt six weeks before, but he had stayed behind, for he was in love with the most beautiful Reed. He had met her early in the spring as he was flying down the river after a big yellow moth, and had been so attracted by her slender waist that he had stopped to talk to her.

"Shall I love you?" said the Swallow, who liked to come to the point at once, and the Reed made him a low bow. So he flew round and round her, touching the water with his wings, and making silver ripples. This was his courtship, and it lasted all through the summer.

"It is a ridiculous attachment," twittered the other Swallows, "she has no money, and far too many relations"; and indeed the river was quite full of Reeds. Then, when the autumn came, they all flew away.

After they had gone he felt lonely, and began to tire of his lady-love. "She has no conversation," he said, "and I am afraid that she is a coquette, for she is always flirting with the wind." And certainly, whenever the wind blew, the Reed made the most graceful curtsies. "I admit that she is domestic," he continued, "but I love travelling, and my wife, consequently, should love travelling also."

"Will you come away with me?" he said finally to her; but the Reed shook her head, she was so attached to her home.

"You have been trifling with me," he cried, "I am off to the Pyramids. Good-bye!" and he flew away.

All day long he flew, and at night-time he arrived at the city. "Where shall I put up?" he said; "I hope the town has made preparations."

Then he saw the statue on the tall column. "I will put up there," he cried; "it is a fine position with plenty of fresh air." So he alighted just between the feet of the Happy Prince.

"I have a golden bedroom," he said softly to himself as he looked round, and he prepared to go to sleep; but just as he was putting his head under his wing a large drop of water fell on him. "What a curious thing!" he cried, "there is not a single cloud in the sky, the stars are quite clear and bright, and yet it is raining. The climate in the

---

1. Pupils in institutions known as Charity Schools, which are funded by public endowments.

north of Europe is really dreadful. The Reed used to like the rain, but that was merely her selfishness."

Then another drop fell.

"What is the use of a statue if it cannot keep the rain off?" he said; "I must look for a good chimney-pot," and he determined to fly away.

But before he had opened his wings, a third drop fell, and he looked up, and saw—Ah! what did he see?

The eyes of the Happy Prince were filled with tears, and tears were running down his golden cheeks. His face was so beautiful in the moonlight that the little Swallow was filled with pity.

"Who are you?" he said.

"I am the Happy Prince."

"Why are you weeping then?" asked the Swallow; "you have quite drenched me."

"When I was alive and had a human heart," answered the statue, "I did not know what tears were, for I lived in the Palace of Sans-Souci[2] where sorrow is not allowed to enter. In the daytime I played with my companions in the garden, and in the evening I led the dance in the Great Hall. Round the garden ran a very lofty wall, but I never cared to ask what lay beyond it, everything about me was so beautiful. My courtiers called me the Happy Prince, and happy indeed I was, if pleasure be happiness. So I lived, and so I died. And now that I am dead they have set me up here so high that I can see all the ugliness and all the misery of my city, and though my heart is made of lead yet I cannot choose but weep."

"What, is he not solid gold?" said the Swallow to himself. He was too polite to make any personal remarks out loud.

"Far away," continued the statue in a low musical voice, "far away in a little street there is a poor house. One of the windows is open, and through it I can see a woman seated at a table. Her face is thin and worn, and she has coarse, red hands, all pricked by the needle, for she is a seamstress. She is embroidering passion-flowers on a satin gown for the loveliest of the Queen's maids-of-honour to wear at the next Courtball. In a bed in the corner of the room her little boy is lying ill. He has a fever, and is asking for oranges. His mother has nothing to give him but river water, so he is crying. Swallow, Swallow, little Swallow, will you not bring her the ruby out of my sword-hilt? My feet are fastened to this pedestal and I cannot move."

"I am waited for in Egypt," said the Swallow. "My friends are flying up and down the Nile, and talking to the large lotus-flowers. Soon they will go to sleep in the tomb of the great King. The King is there himself in his painted coffin. He is wrapped in yellow linen, and embalmed with spices. Round his neck is a chain of pale green jade, and his hands are like withered leaves."

2. Without care (French); also the name of Frederick the Great's palace in Potsdam.

"Swallow, Swallow, little Swallow," said the Prince, "will you not stay with me for one night, and be my messenger? The boy is so thirsty, and the mother so sad."

"I don't think I like boys," answered the Swallow. "Last summer, when I was staying on the river, there were two rude boys, the miller's sons, who were always throwing stones at me. They never hit me, of course; we swallows fly far too well for that, and besides, I come of a family famous for its agility; but still, it was a mark of disrespect."

But the Happy Prince looked so sad that the little Swallow was sorry. "It is very cold here," he said; "but I will stay with you for one night, and be your messenger."

"Thank you, little Swallow," said the Prince.

So the Swallow picked out the great ruby from the Prince's sword, and flew away with it in his beak over the roofs of the town.

He passed by the cathedral tower, where the white marble angels were sculptured. He passed by the palace and heard the sound of dancing. A beautiful girl came out on the balcony with her lover. "How wonderful the stars are," he said to her, "and how wonderful is the power of love!" "I hope my dress will be ready in time for the Stateball," she answered; "I have ordered passion-flowers to be embroidered on it; but the seamstresses are so lazy."

He passed over the river, and saw the lanterns hanging to the masts of the ships. He passed over the Ghetto, and saw the old Jews bargaining with each other, and weighing out money in copper scales. At last he came to the poor house and looked in. The boy was tossing feverishly on his bed, and the mother had fallen asleep, she was so tired. In he hopped, and laid the great ruby on the table beside the woman's thimble. Then he flew gently round the bed, fanning the boy's forehead with his wings. "How cool I feel," said the boy, "I must be getting better"; and he sank into a delicious slumber.

Then the Swallow flew back to the Happy Prince, and told him what he had done. "It is curious," he remarked, "but I feel quite warm now, although it is so cold."

"That is because you have done a good action," said the Prince. And the little Swallow began to think, and then he fell asleep. Thinking always made him sleepy.

When day broke he flew down to the river and had a bath. "What a remarkable phenomenon," said the Professor of Ornithology as he was passing over the bridge. "A swallow in winter!" And he wrote a long letter about it to the local newspaper. Every one quoted it, it was full of so many words that they could not understand.

"To-night I go to Egypt," said the Swallow, and he was in high spirits at the prospect. He visited all the public monuments, and sat a long time on top of the church steeple. Wherever he went the Sparrows chirruped, and said to each other, "What a distinguished stranger!" so he enjoyed himself very much.

When the moon rose he flew back to the Happy Prince. "Have you any commissions for Egypt?" he cried; "I am just starting."

"Swallow, Swallow, little Swallow," said the Prince, "will you not stay with me one night longer?"

"I am waited for in Egypt," answered the Swallow. "To-morrow my friends will fly up to the Second Cataract.[3] The river-horse couches there among the bulrushes, and on a great granite throne sits the God Memnon.[4] All night long he watches the stars, and when the morning star shines he utters one cry of joy, and then he is silent. At noon the yellow lions come down to the water's edge to drink. They have eyes like green beryls,[5] and their roar is louder than the roar of the cataract."

"Swallow, Swallow, little Swallow," said the Prince, "far away across the city I see a young man in a garret. He is leaning over a desk covered with papers, and in a tumbler by his side there is a bunch of withered violets. His hair is brown and crisp, and his lips are red as a pomegranate, and he has large and dreamy eyes. He is trying to finish a play for the Director of the Theatre, but he is too cold to write any more. There is no fire in the grate, and hunger has made him faint."

"I will wait with you one night longer," said the Swallow, who really had a good heart. "Shall I take him another ruby?"

"Alas! I have no ruby now," said the Prince; "my eyes are all that I have left. They are made of rare sapphires, which were brought out of India a thousand years ago. Pluck out one of them and take it to him. He will sell it to the jeweller, and buy food and firewood, and finish his play."

"Dear Prince," said the Swallow, "I cannot do that"; and he began to weep.

"Swallow, Swallow, little Swallow," said the Prince, "do as I command you."

So the Swallow plucked out the Prince's eye, and flew away to the student's garret. It was easy enough to get in, as there was a hole in the roof. Through this he darted, and came into the room. The young man had his head buried in his hands, so he did not hear the flutter of the bird's wings, and when he looked up he found the beautiful sapphire lying on the withered violets.

"I am beginning to be appreciated," he cried; "this is from some great admirer. Now I can finish my play," and he looked quite happy.

The next day the Swallow flew down to the harbour. He sat on the mast of a large vessel and watched the sailors hauling big chests

---

3. This reference and other details of the journey (including the stay at the Temple of Baalbec) are taken from a poem by Théophile Gautier, "Ce que disent les hirondelles" (What the swallows say).
4. Reference to the statue of Memnon at Thebes, which is said to emit music when struck by the sun's rays.
5. Transparent pale green stones.

out of the hold with ropes. "Heave a-hoy!" they shouted as each chest came up. "I am going to Egypt!" cried the Swallow, but nobody minded, and when the moon rose he flew back to the Happy Prince.

"I am come to bid you good-bye," he cried.

"Swallow, Swallow, little Swallow," said the Prince, "will you not stay with me one night longer?"

"It is winter," answered the Swallow, "and the chill snow will soon be here. In Egypt the sun is warm on the green palm-trees, and the crocodiles lie in the mud and look lazily about them. My companions are building a nest in the Temple of Baalbec, and the pink and white doves are watching them, and cooing to each other. Dear Prince, I must leave you, but I will never forget you, and next spring I will bring you back two beautiful jewels in place of those you have given away. The ruby shall be redder than a red rose, and the sapphire shall be as blue as the great sea."

"In the square below," said the Happy Prince, "there stands a little match-girl. She has let her matches fall in the gutter, and they are all spoiled. Her father will beat her if she does not bring home some money, and she is crying. She has no shoes or stockings, and her little head is bare. Pluck out my other eye, and give it to her, and her father will not beat her."

"I will stay with you one night longer," said the Swallow, "but I cannot pluck out your eye. You would be quite blind then."

"Swallow, Swallow, little Swallow," said the Prince, "do as I command you."

So he plucked out the Prince's other eye, and darted down with it. He swooped past the match-girl, and slipped the jewel into the palm of her hand. "What a lovely bit of glass," cried the little girl; and she ran home, laughing.

Then the Swallow came back to the Prince. "You are blind now," he said, "so I will stay with you always."

"No, little Swallow," said the poor Prince, "you must go away to Egypt."

"I will stay with you always," said the Swallow, and he slept at the Prince's feet.

All the next day he sat on the Prince's shoulder, and told him stories of what he had seen in strange lands. He told him of the red ibises, who stand in long rows on the banks of the Nile, and catch gold fish in their beaks; of the Sphinx, who is as old as the world itself, and lives in the desert, and knows everything; of the merchants, who walk slowly by the side of their camels, and carry amber beads in their hands; of the King of the Mountains of the Moon,[6] who is as black as ebony, and worships a large crystal; of the great green snake that sleeps in a palm-tree, and has twenty priests to

6. A range in Uganda.

feed it with honey-cakes; and of the pygmies who sail over a big lake on large flat leaves, and are always at war with the butterflies.

"Dear little Swallow," said the Prince, "you tell me of marvellous things, but more marvellous than anything is the suffering of men and of women. There is no Mystery so great as Misery. Fly over my city, little Swallow, and tell me what you see there."

So the Swallow flew over the great city, and saw the rich making merry in their beautiful houses, while the beggars were sitting at the gates. He flew into dark lanes, and saw the white faces of starving children looking out listlessly at the black streets. Under the archway of a bridge two little boys were lying in one another's arms to try and keep themselves warm. "How hungry we are!" they said. "You must not lie here," shouted the Watchman, and they wandered out into the rain.

Then he flew back and told the Prince what he had seen.

"I am covered with fine gold," said the Prince, "you must take it off, leaf by leaf, and give it to my poor; the living always think that gold can make them happy."

Leaf after leaf of the fine gold the Swallow picked off, till the Happy Prince looked quite dull and grey. Leaf after leaf of the fine gold he brought to the poor, and the children's faces grew rosier, and they laughed and played games in the street. "We have bread now!" they cried.

Then the snow came, and after the snow came the frost. The streets looked as if they were made of silver, they were so bright and glistening; long icicles like crystal daggers hung down from the eaves of the houses, everybody went about in furs, and the little boys wore scarlet caps and skated on the ice.

The poor little Swallow grew colder and colder, but he would not leave the Prince, he loved him too well. He picked up crumbs outside the baker's door when the baker was not looking, and tried to keep himself warm by flapping his wings.

But at last he knew that he was going to die. He had just strength to fly up to the Prince's shoulder once more. "Good-bye, dear Prince!" he murmured, "will you let me kiss your hand?"

"I am glad that you are going to Egypt at last, little Swallow," said the Prince, "you have stayed too long here; but you must kiss me on the lips, for I love you."

"It is not to Egypt that I am going," said the Swallow. "I am going to the House of Death. Death is the brother of Sleep, is he not?"

And he kissed the Happy Prince on the lips, and fell down dead at his feet.

At that moment a curious crack sounded inside the statue, as if something had broken. The fact is that the leaden heart had snapped right in two. It certainly was a dreadfully hard frost.

Early the next morning the Mayor was walking in the square below in company with the Town Councillors. As they passed the column he looked up at the statue: "Dear me! how shabby the Happy Prince looks!" he said.

"How shabby indeed!" cried the Town Councillors, who always agreed with the Mayor, and they went up to look at it.

"The ruby has fallen out of his sword, his eyes are gone, and he is golden no longer," said the Mayor; "in fact, he is little better than a beggar!"

"Little better than a beggar," said the Town Councillors.

"And here is actually a dead bird at his feet!" continued the Mayor. "We must really issue a proclamation that birds are not to be allowed to die here." And the Town Clerk made a note of the suggestion.

So they pulled down the statue of the Happy Prince. "As he is no longer beautiful he is no longer useful,"[7] said the Art Professor at the University.

Then they melted the statue in a furnace, and the Mayor held a meeting of the Corporation to decide what was to be done with the metal. "We must have another statue, of course," he said, "and it shall be a statue of myself."

"Of myself," said each of the Town Councillors, and they quarrelled. When I last heard of them they were quarrelling still.

"What a strange thing!" said the overseer of the workmen at the foundry. "This broken lead heart will not melt in the furnace. We must throw it away." So they threw it on a dust-heap where the dead Swallow was also lying.

"Bring me the two most precious things in the city," said God to one of His Angels; and the Angel brought Him the leaden heart and the dead bird.

"You have rightly chosen," said God, "for in my garden of Paradise this little bird shall sing for evermore, and in my city of gold the Happy Prince shall praise me."

The Nightingale and the Rose[†]

"She said that she would dance with me if I brought her red roses," cried the young Student; "but in all my garden there is no red rose."

From her nest in the holm-oak tree the Nightingale heard him, and she looked out through the leaves, and wondered.

"No red rose in all my garden!" he cried, and his beautiful eyes filled with tears. "Ah, on what little things does happiness depend! I have

---

7. Note Wilde's aphorism "All art is quite useless."

† *Oscar Wilde: Complete Short Fiction*, ed. Ian Small (London: Penguin Books, 1994), pp. 12–18.

read all that the wise men have written, and all the secrets of philosophy are mine, yet for want of a red rose is my life made wretched."

"Here at last is a true lover," said the Nightingale. "Night after night have I sung of him, though I knew him not: night after night have I told his story to the stars, and now I see him. His hair is dark as the hyacinth-blossom, and his lips are red as the rose of his desire; but passion has made his face like pale ivory, and sorrow has set her seal upon his brow."

"The Prince gives a ball to-morrow night," murmured the young Student, "and my love will be of the company. If I bring her a red rose she will dance with me till dawn. If I bring her a red rose, I shall hold her in my arms, and she will lean her head upon my shoulder, and her hand will be clasped in mine. But there is no red rose in my garden, so I shall sit lonely, and she will pass me by. She will have no heed of me, and my heart will break."

"Here indeed is the true lover," said the Nightingale. "What I sing of, he suffers: what is joy to me, to him is pain. Surely Love is a wonderful thing. It is more precious than emeralds, and dearer than fine opals. Pearls and pomegranates cannot buy it, nor is it set forth in the market-place. It may not be purchased of the merchants, nor can it be weighed out in the balance for gold."

"The musicians will sit in their gallery," said the young Student, "and play upon their stringed instruments, and my love will dance to the sound of the harp and the violin. She will dance so lightly that her feet will not touch the floor, and the courtiers in their gay dresses will throng round her. But with me she will not dance, for I have no red rose to give her"; and he flung himself down on the grass, and buried his face in his hands, and wept.

"Why is he weeping?" asked a little Green Lizard, as he ran past him with his tail in the air.

"Why, indeed?" said a Butterfly, who was fluttering about after a sunbeam.

"Why, indeed?" whispered a Daisy to his neighbour, in a soft, low voice.

"He is weeping for a red rose," said the Nightingale.

"For a red rose!" they cried; "how very ridiculous!" and the little Lizard, who was something of a cynic, laughed outright.

But the Nightingale understood the secret of the Student's sorrow, and she sat silent in the oak-tree, and thought about the mystery of Love.

Suddenly she spread her brown wings for flight, and soared into the air. She passed through the grove like a shadow, and like a shadow she sailed across the garden.

In the centre of the grass-plot was standing a beautiful Rose-tree, and when she saw it, she flew over to it, and lit upon a spray.

"Give me a red rose," she cried, "and I will sing you my sweetest song."

But the Tree shook its head.

"My roses are white," it answered; "as white as the foam of the sea, and whiter than the snow upon the mountain. But go to my brother who grows round the old sun-dial, and perhaps he will give you what you want."

So the Nightingale flew over to the Rose-tree that was growing round the old sun-dial.

"Give me a red rose," she cried, "and I will sing you my sweetest song."

But the Tree shook its head.

"My roses are yellow," it answered; "as yellow as the hair of the mermaiden who sits upon an amber throne, and yellower than the daffodil that blooms in the meadow before the mower comes with his scythe. But go to my brother who grows beneath the Student's window, and perhaps he will give you what you want."

So the Nightingale flew over to the Rose-tree that was growing beneath the Student's window.

"Give me a red rose," she cried, "and I will sing you my sweetest song."

But the Tree shook its head.

"My roses are red," it answered, "as red as the feet of the dove, and redder than the great fans of coral that wave and wave in the ocean-cavern. But the winter has chilled my veins, and the frost has nipped my buds, and the storm has broken my branches, and I shall have no roses at all this year."

"One red rose is all I want," cried the Nightingale, "only one red rose! Is there no way by which I can get it?"

"There is a way," answered the Tree; "but it is so terrible that I dare not tell it to you."

"Tell it to me," said the Nightingale, "I am not afraid."

"If you want a red rose," said the Tree, "you must build it out of music by moonlight, and stain it with your own heart's-blood. You must sing to me with your breast against a thorn. All night long you must sing to me, and the thorn must pierce your heart, and your life-blood must flow into my veins, and become mine."

"Death is a great price to pay for a red rose," cried the Nightingale, "and Life is very dear to all. It is pleasant to sit in the green wood, and to watch the Sun in his chariot of gold, and the Moon in her chariot of pearl. Sweet is the scent of the hawthorn, and sweet are the bluebells that hide in the valley, and the heather that blows on the hill. Yet Love is better than Life, and what is the heart of a bird compared to the heart of a man?"

So she spread her brown wings for flight, and soared into the air. She swept over the garden like a shadow, and like a shadow she sailed through the grove.

The young Student was still lying on the grass, where she had left him, and the tears were not yet dry in his beautiful eyes.

"Be happy," cried the Nightingale, "be happy; you shall have your red rose. I will build it out of music by moonlight, and stain it with my own heart's-blood. All that I ask of you in return is that you will be a true lover, for Love is wiser than Philosophy, though she is wise, and mightier than Power, though he is mighty. Flame-coloured are his wings, and coloured like flame is his body. His lips are sweet as honey, and his breath is like frankincense."

The Student looked up from the grass, and listened, but he could not understand what the Nightingale was saying to him, for he only knew the things that are written down in books.

But the Oak-tree understood, and felt sad, for he was very fond of the little Nightingale who had built her nest in his branches.

"Sing me one last song," he whispered; "I shall feel very lonely when you are gone."

So the Nightingale sang to the Oak-tree, and her voice was like water bubbling from a silver jar.

When she had finished her song the Student got up, and pulled a note-book and a lead-pencil out of his pocket.

"She has form," he said to himself, as he walked away through the grove—"that cannot be denied to her; but has she got feeling? I am afraid not. In fact, she is like most artists; she is all style, without any sincerity. She would not sacrifice herself for others. She thinks merely of music, and everybody knows that the arts are selfish. Still, it must be admitted that she has some beautiful notes in her voice. What a pity it is that they do not mean anything, or do any practical good." And he went into his room, and lay down on his little pallet-bed, and began to think of his love; and, after a time, he fell asleep.

And when the Moon shone in the heavens the Nightingale flew to the Rose-tree, and set her breast against the thorn. All night long she sang with her breast against the thorn, and the cold crystal Moon leaned down and listened. All night long she sang, and the thorn went deeper and deeper into her breast, and her life-blood ebbed away from her.

She sang first of the birth of love in the heart of a boy and a girl. And on the topmost spray of the Rose-tree there blossomed a marvellous rose, petal following petal, as song followed song. Pale was it, at first, as the mist that hangs over the river—pale as the feet of the morning, and silver as the wings of the dawn. As the shadow of a rose in a mirror of silver, as the shadow of a rose in a water-pool, so was the rose that blossomed on the topmost spray of the Tree.

But the Tree cried to the Nightingale to press closer against the thorn. "Press closer, little Nightingale," cried the Tree, "or the Day will come before the rose is finished."

So the Nightingale pressed closer against the thorn, and louder and louder grew her song, for she sang of the birth of passion in the soul of a man and a maid.

And a delicate flush of pink came into the leaves of the rose, like the flush in the face of the bridegroom when he kisses the lips of the bride. But the thorn had not yet reached her heart, so the rose's heart remained white, for only a Nightingale's heart's-blood can crimson the heart of a rose.

And the Tree cried to the Nightingale to press closer against the thorn. "Press closer, little Nightingale," cried the Tree, "or the Day will come before the rose is finished."

So the Nightingale pressed closer against the thorn, and the thorn touched her heart, and a fierce pang of pain shot through her. Bitter, bitter was the pain, and wilder and wilder grew her song, for she sang of the Love that is perfected by Death, of the Love that dies not in the tomb.

And the marvellous rose became crimson, like the rose of the eastern sky. Crimson was the girdle of petals, and crimson as a ruby was the heart.

But the Nightingale's voice grew fainter, and her little wings began to beat, and a film came over her eyes. Fainter and fainter grew her song, and she felt something choking her in her throat.

Then she gave one last burst of music. The white Moon heard it, and she forgot the dawn, and lingered on in the sky. The red rose heard it, and it trembled all over with ecstasy, and opened its petals to the cold morning air. Echo[1] bore it to her purple cavern in the hills, and woke the sleeping shepherds from their dreams. It floated through the reeds of the river, and they carried its message to the sea.

"Look, look!" cried the Tree, "the rose is finished now"; but the Nightingale made no answer, for she was lying dead in the long grass, with the thorn in her heart.

And at noon the Student opened his window and looked out.

"Why, what a wonderful piece of luck!" he cried; "here is a red rose! I have never seen any rose like it in all my life. It is so beautiful that I am sure it has a long Latin name"; and he leaned down and plucked it.

Then he put on his hat, and ran up to the Professor's house with the rose in his hand.

The daughter of the Professor was sitting in the doorway winding blue silk on a reel, and her little dog was lying at her feet.

"You said that you would dance with me if I brought you a red rose," cried the Student. "Here is the reddest rose in all the world.

---

1. In classical mythology, a mountain nymph who repeats the last words uttered by others.

You will wear it to-night next your heart, and as we dance together it will tell you how I love you."

But the girl frowned.

"I am afraid it will not go with my dress," she answered; "and, besides, the Chamberlain's nephew has sent me some real jewels, and everybody knows that jewels cost far more than flowers."

"Well, upon my word, you are very ungrateful," said the Student angrily; and he threw the rose into the street, where it fell into the gutter, and a cart-wheel went over it.

"Ungrateful!" said the girl. "I tell you what, you are very rude; and, after all, who are you? Only a Student. Why, I don't believe you have even got silver buckles to your shoes as the Chamberlain's nephew has"; and she got up from her chair and went into the house.

"What a silly thing Love is," said the Student as he walked away. "It is not half as useful as Logic, for it does not prove anything, and it is always telling one of things that are not going to happen, and making one believe things that are not true. In fact, it is quite unpractical, and, as in this age to be practical is everything, I shall go back to Philosophy and study Metaphysics."

So he returned to his room and pulled out a great dusty book, and began to read.

CRITICISM

ERNST BLOCH

The Fairy Tale Moves on Its Own in Time[†]

Certainly good dreams can go too far. On the other hand, do not the simple fairy-tale dreams remain too far behind? Of course, the fairy-tale world, especially as a magical one, no longer belongs to the present. How can it mirror our wish-projections against a background that has long since disappeared? Or, to put it a better way: How can the fairy tale mirror our wish-projections other than in a totally obsolete way? Real kings no longer even exist. The atavistic and simultaneously feudal-transcendental world from which the fairy tale stems and to which it seems to be tied has most certainly vanished. However, the mirror of the fairy tale has not become opaque, and the manner of wish-fulfillment that peers forth from it is not entirely without a home. It all adds up to this: the fairy tale narrates a wish-fulfilment that is not bound by its own time and the apparel of its contents. In contrast to the legend, which is always tied to a particular locale, the fairy tale remains unbound. Not only does the fairy tale remain as fresh as longing and love, but the demonically evil, which is abundant in the fairy tale, is still seen at work here in the present, and the happiness of 'once upon a time,' which is even more abundant, still affects our visions of the future.

The young protagonist who sets out to find happiness is still around, strong as ever. And the dreamer, too, whose imagination is caught up with the girl of his dreams and with the distant secure home. One can also find the demons of old times who return in the present as economic ogres. The politics of the leading 200 families is fate. Thus, right in America, a country without feudal or transcendental tradition, Walt Disney's fairy-tale films revive elements of the old fairy tale without making them incomprehensible to the viewers. Quite the contrary. The favourably disposed viewers think about a great deal. They think about almost everything in their lives. They, too, want to fly. They, too, want to escape the ogre. They, too, want to transcend the clouds and have a place in the sun. Naturally, the fairy-tale world of America is more of a dreamed-up social life with the kings and saints of big business life. Yet, even if it is deceiving, the connection emanates partly from the fairy tale. The dream of the little employee or even—with different contents— of the average businessman is that of the sudden, the miraculous

† Ernst Bloch, *The Utopian Function of Art and Literature*, trans. Jack Zipes and Frank Mecklenburg (Cambridge and London: MIT Press, 1988), pp. 163–66. Originally published 1930. © 1987 Massachusetts Institute of Technology, by permission of The MIT Press and Suhrkamp AG, Berlin.

rise from the anonymous masses to visible happiness. The lightning
of gold radiates upon them in a fairy-tale-like way. The sun shines
upon them from commanding heights. The name of the fairy-tale
world is publicity (even if it is only for a day). The fairy-tale princess
is Greta Garbo. Certainly, these are petty bourgeois wishes with
very untrimmed, often adulterated fairy-tale material. However,
this material has remained. And where does one ever really get out
of the bourgeois style of living? Yet, there is a certain surrealistic
charm in presenting old, fairy-tale materials in modern disguise
(or, also, in divesting them of their apparel). It is precisely the
unbound character of the fairy tale that has floated through the
times that allows for such developments, such new incarnations in
the present, incarnations that not only occur in the form of economic ogres or film stars.

However, if one turns from here, that is, from the old story that
remains eternally new, to the really new and newest history, to the
fantastic changes of technology, then it is not surprising to see even
here a place for forming fairy tales, i.e., for technological-magical
utopias.

Jules Verne's *Journey around the World in Eighty Days* has by now
become significantly shortened in reality, but *The Journey to the
Middle of the Earth* and *The Journey to the Moon* and other creative
narrations of a technological capacity or not-yet-capacity are still
pure formations of fairy tales. What is significant about such kinds
of 'modern fairy tales' is that it is reason itself that leads to the wish
projections of the old fairy tale and serves them. Again what proves
itself is a harmony with courage and cunning, as that earliest kind
of enlightenment which already characterizes *Hansel and Gretel*:
consider yourself as born free and entitled to be totally happy, dare
to make use of your power of reasoning, look upon the outcome of
things as friendly. These are the genuine maxims of fairy tales, and
fortunately for us they appear not only in the past but in the now.
Unfortunately we must equally contend with the smoke of witches
and the blows of ogres habitually faced by the fairy-tale hero in the
now. The fairy-tale hero is called upon to overcome our miserable
situation, regretfully just in mere fairy tales. However, this takes
place in such tales in which the unsubjugated often seems to be
meant—tiny, colorful, yet unmistaken in aim.

ERNST BLOCH

From Better Castles in the Sky at the Country Fair and Circus, in Fairy Tales and Colportage[†]

> Little duck, little duck,
> Hansel and Gretel need some luck.
> No way to go, no bridge in sight.
> Take us across on your back so white.
> *Hansel and Gretel*

Then we went back to bed. But I didn't sleep. I lay in bed awake. I thought of help. I struggled to reach a decision. The book I had been reading was entitled *The Cave of the Robbers in the Sierra Morena, or the Angel of the Oppressed*. After my father had come home and had fallen asleep, I climbed out of bed, crept out of the room, and got dressed. Then I wrote a note: "I don't want you to work yourselves to death. I'm going to Spain. I'll get help." I placed this note on the table, put a piece of dry bread into my pocket along with some pennies from my bowling money, went down the stairs, opened the door, took a deep breath again and sobbed, but very, very softly so that nobody could hear. Then I walked without making a sound until I reached the market place where I followed the Niedergasse out of town toward Lichtenstein and Zwickern, toward Spain, country of the noble robbers, the helpers of those in distress.

> Karl May, *Mein Leben und Streben*
> (*My Life and Strivings*)

> If sailor tales to sailor tunes,
>   Storm and adventure, heat and cold,
> If schooners, islands, and maroons
>   And buccaneers and buried Gold,
> And all the old romance, retold
>   Exactly in the ancient way,
> Can please, as me they pleased of old,
>   The wiser youngsters of today:
> So be it, and fall on! If not,
>   If studious youth no longer crave,
> His ancient appetites forgot,
>   Kingston, or Ballantyne the brave,
> Or cooper of the wood and wave:
>   So be it, also! And may I
> And all my pirates have the grave
>   Where these and their creations lie!
> Robert Louis Stevenson,
> *Treasure Island*,
> *To the Hesitating Purchaser*

† From Ernst Bloch, *The Utopian Function of Art and Literature,* trans. Jack Zipes and Frank Mecklenburg (Cambridge and London: MIT Press, 1988), pp. 167–72, 182–83. Originally published 1959. © 1987 Massachusetts Institute of Technology, by permission of The MIT Press and Suhrkamp AG, Berlin.

> It is not uncommon that random wandering, random hunting
> expeditions of the imagination flush out the game which method-
> ological philosophy can use in its neatly ordered household.
>
> Lichtenberg[1]

Toward dusk may be the best time to tell stories. Indifferent prox-
imity disappears; a remote realm that appears to be better and closer
approaches. Once upon a time: this means in fairy-tale manner not
only the past but a more colorful or easier somewhere else. And those
who have become happier there are still happy today if they are not
dead. To be sure, there is suffering in fairy tales; however, it changes,
and for sure, it never returns. The maltreated, gentle Cinderella goes
to the little tree at her mother's grave: little tree, shake yourself,
shake yourself. A dress falls to her feet more splendid and marvelous than anything she has ever had. And the slippers are solid gold.
Fairy tales always end in gold. There is enough happiness there. In
particular, the little heroes and poor people are the ones who succeed here where life has become good.

The Courage of the Clever Heroes

Not all of them are so gentle that they simply wait for goodness to
come. They set out to find their happiness, the clever against the
brutes. Courage and cunning are their shield; intelligence, their
spear. Courage alone would not help the weak very much against
the mighty lords. It would not enable them to knock down towers. The
cunning of intelligence is the humane side of the weak. Despite
the fantastic side of the fairy tale, it is always cunning in the way it
overcomes difficulties. Moreover, courage and cunning in fairy tales
succeed in an entirely different way than in life, and not only that:
it is, as Lenin says, always the existing revolutionary elements that
tie the given strings of the story together here. While the peasantry
was still bound by serfdom, the poor protagonist of the fairy tale conquered the daughter of the king. While educated Christians trembled in fear of witches and devils, the soldier of the fairy tale deceived
witches and devils from beginning to end—it is only the fairy tale
that highlights the "dumb devil." The golden age is sought and mir-
rored, and from there one can see far into paradise.

But the fairy tale does not allow itself to be fooled by the present
owners of paradise. Thus, it is a rebellious, burned child and alert.
One can climb a beanstalk up into heaven and then see how angels
make gold. In the fairy tale *Godfather Death*, the Lord God himself
offers to be the godfather in a poor man's family, but the poor man

---

1. Georg Christoph Lichtenberg (1742–1799) was a German scientist and writer and is
   best known today for his investigations in the field of electricity and for the wit and
   satirical edge in his notebooks [editor's note].

responds, "I don't want you as a godfather because you give to the rich and let the poor starve." Here and everywhere, in the courage, the sobriety, and hope, there is a piece of the Enlightenment that emerged long before there was such a thing as the Enlightenment. The brave little tailor in the Grimms' fairy tale kills flies in his home and goes out into the world because he feels that his workshop is too small for his bravery. He meets a giant who takes a rock in his hand and squeezes it with such strength that water drips from it. Then he throws another rock so high into the air that one can barely see it. However, the tailor outsmarts the giant by squeezing a piece of cheese into pulp instead of a rock, and next he throws a bird so high into the air that it never returns. Finally, at the end of the fairy tale, the clever tailor overcomes all obstacles and wins the king's daughter and half the kingdom. This is the way a tailor is made into a king in the fairy tale, a king without taboos, who has gotten rid of all the hostile maliciousness of the great people. And when the world was still full of devils, there was another fairy-tale hero, the youth who goes forth to learn what fear is. He resists fear all along the way. He sets corpses on fire so that they can warm themselves up. He bowls with ghosts in a haunted castle, captures a bearded old man, who is the head of the evil spirits, and thus wins a treasure.

The devil himself is often outsmarted in the fairy tale. A poor soldier tricks him by selling his soul under the condition that the devil fill the soldier's shoe with gold. But the shoe has a hole, and the soldier puts it over a deep pit. Thus the devil must drag sack upon sack filled with gold until the first cry of dawn. Then he dashes away, the victim of a swindle. So, even shoes with holes in them can serve for the best in fairy tales if one knows how to make use of them. This is not to say that mere wishing and the simple fairy-tale-like means of achieving a goal are not mocked. But this mockery is enlightened, and it is not discouraging. In times of old, thus begins the fairy tale about the frog prince, when wishing still helped—the fairy tale does not presume to be a substitute for action. Nevertheless, the smart Hans of the fairy tale practices an art of not allowing himself to be intimidated. The power of the giant is painted as power with a hole in it through which the weak individual can crawl triumphantly.

* * *

Play and magic together have carte blanche in the fairy tale. Wish becomes a command. There is no difficulty in carrying it out. Neither is space or time divisive. In Andersen's fairy tales there is a flying trunk that lands in the country of the Turks, and there are magic boots that carry a judge back into the fifteenth century. In *1001 Nights* a magic horse flies and arrives in heaven, and it is right there that the most powerful force that fulfills wishes waits with folded arms: the genie of the lamp. It is most significant that the richest of all fairy tales, *Aladdin and the Magic Lamp*, is based upon nothing but utensils for wishing for what is not available. Smoke-works are ignited. The deceitful uncle murmurs mysterious words, and suddenly the cave opens up. There are hidden treasures which are piled up in the name of Aladdin. An underground garden appears, and the trees are covered with jewels instead of fruit. The slave of the ring and the genie of the lamp step forward—both representative of hallucinated primordial wishes for power, for power that is not limited to certain goods as in the fairy tale *The Magic Table*. Rather, the genie of the lamp brings his master everything, anything his heart desires. The genie of the lamp provides countless treasures, physical beauty, and courtly art on command, elegant speech as well as elegant wit. He builds a castle overnight, the most glorious the world has ever seen, with treasure chambers, royal stables, and an armory. The stones are made out of jasper and alabaster, the windows out of jewels. It is an easy command to carry out. And in the very next moment the lamp transports the palace from China to Tunis, then back to its old place without the carpet at the entrance to the castle, even moving at the behest of the wind. Also, the magic slate that provides the deceitful uncle with knowledge about everything that happens in the world cannot be overlooked: "But now, on a day to remember, he conceived a sand table, and he spread the figures around and studied the sequence of their movements attentively. And in the very next moment he determined the sequence of their movements, the mothers as well as the daughters."—It is the same geometrical table whose power enabled the magician in Tunis to learn about the faraway treasure in China that Aladdin obtained. Nothing but countless ways to fulfill wishes, nothing but *via regia* to attain in the fairy tale as quickly as possible what nature itself outside the fairy tale refuses to grant human beings. In general, the technological-magical digging for treasures is the fairy-tale component itself in this type of fairy tale, for the discovered treasure symbolizes above everything the miracle of the quick change, of sudden luck. Astuteness and smoke-work are necessary in the Aladdin fairy tale. Astuteness alone is sufficient in Edgar Allan Poe's *The Gold Bug*, a secularized fairy tale about treasure hunters, and also in Stevenson's *Treasure Island*. But it is still the treasure in these semi-fairy tales (which turn into adventure stories) that makes for tension and provides the turn of events. It is the very touchstone, which unlocks life and allows its splendors to be acquired. In this way the technological-magical fairy tale sets possessions as its goal only indirectly and out of need. It sets the transformation of things that are the available utility goods at any time as its goal. Instead of painting the short covers, which one has to stretch for, it portrays an old bed of nature. It intends—in order to designate the home territory of all the magic tables and also of the magic again with one fairy tale—it means to be the land of milk and honey. With milk and honey in it, it sounds moreover as if one were already hearing a social fairy tale, as if one were already hearing a state fairy tale, simpler in the goods it provides, but even more nourishing than the others.

* * *

The Wild Fairy Tale as Colportage[2]

Even in the fairy tale things do not proceed gently from the beginning. There are giants and witches in it. They block the way. They make the protagonists spin the whole night through. They lead people astray. In contrast to the much too gentle or precipitous blue sky, there is a kind of fairy tale that is very rarely considered as such. It is a wild kind of turbulent fairy tale. It is very rarely recognized not because it degenerates easily into trash, but because the ruling class does not like tattooed Hansels and Gretels. In other words, the turbulent fairy tale is the adventure story. The best way that it continues to maintain its existence today is as colportage. Its face bears the expression of a neglected crude creature, and this is the way it often appears. Nevertheless, colportage consistently reveals traits of the fairy tale, for its hero does not wait as in the magazine stories, until happiness falls into his lap. Nor does he bend down and pick it up as though it were some bundle thrown at his feet. Rather, its hero remains related to the poor swineherd of the folk tale, the daring protagonist, who sets corpses on fire and slaps the devil over the head. The hero of colportage shows a kind of courage, often like that of its readers, that have nothing to lose. And an affirmed piece of do-nothingness emanates from the runaway protagonist who does not end up dead. When he returns, he has the aroma of palms, knives, and swarming Asian cities around him. The dream of colportage is: never again to be trapped by the routine of daily life. And at the end there is: happiness, love, victory. The splendor toward which the adventure story heads is not won through a rich marriage and the like as in the magazine story but rather through an active journey to the Orient of the dream. * * *

---

2. Colportage refers to a book trade practice of the late nineteenth and early twentieth centuries, when literature was sold door-to-door through subscriptions [editor's note].

WALTER BENJAMIN

From The Storyteller: Reflections on the Works of Nikolai Leskov[†]

The term storyteller has a familiar ring to it, but the notion of the storyteller as an immediate living presence has little purchase today. There is something incongruous, almost anachronistic, about story-telling, and those who tell stories seem increasingly irrelevant to us with every passing day. To present someone like Leskov as a story-teller does not mean that we will be on any more intimate terms with him but rather that he will become an even more remote fig-ure. Viewed from a certain distance, it's possible to detect in his work the key basic features that define the storyteller. Or to put it another way, we begin to distinguish those features in the same way that a human head or the body of an animal emerges from a rock forma-tion once we situate ourselves at the proper distance from it with the right angle of vision. The distance and angle of vision enable something that we experience on what feels like a daily basis. It teaches us that the art of storytelling is drawing to a close. We encounter people who really know how to tell a story less and less frequently. And ever more often there is a sense of embarrassment when someone expresses the wish to hear a story. It's as if some kind of fundamental blessing, one that once felt like one of the most secure of our possessions, had been taken from us: the ability to share experiences.

One reason for this loss is obvious: experience has fallen in value. And it now looks as if its stock is plummeting even more. If you read the newspapers, you realize that it has reached a new low and that our understanding, not only of the world in general but also of our moral universe, has undergone changes overnight—changes that were never before thought possible. During the war years something began to stir, and it has not let up since. Wasn't it obvious by the end of the war that men returned home from the battlefields and were silent, not richer but poorer in communicable experience? What emerged in the flood of war books ten years later was anything but experience transmitted by word of mouth. There was nothing remark-able about that, of course. For never before had past experience been contradicted more thoroughly than in the contrast between earlier military strategies and a war of attrition, past economic realities and

---

[†] From Walter Benjamin, "Der Erzähler. Betrachtungen zum Werk Nikolai Lesskows," in *Ausgewählte Schriften* (Suhrkamp: Frankfurt am Main, 1977), I, pp. 385–410. Originally published 1936. Translated by Maria Tatar for this Norton Critical Edition. Leskov (1831–1895) was a Russian writer best known for his short stories.

inflation, bodily injuries and new technologies of warfare, moral understanding and political realities. A generation that had gone to school in horse-drawn streetcars now stood under the open skies in a landscape where nothing was the same but the clouds. And what remained beneath those clouds, in a force field of destructive currents and explosions: the tiny, fragile human body.

Experiences transmitted by word of mouth are the source from which all storytellers have drawn. And among those who write down stories, it is the great writers who try not to deviate from the speech of the many nameless storytellers before them. Incidentally, two groups of such storytellers surface, and they overlap in many ways. Only if you can picture both those groups will the figure of the storyteller become visible as a fully embodied presence. "When you take a trip, you return with something to talk about"—that's how a German saying goes, and people imagine the storyteller as someone who is returning from afar. But we also like to listen to those who stay at home, making an honest living and becoming familiar with local traditions and tales. If you want to envision these two groups in their archetypal manifestation, then you could imagine one as the resident tiller of the soil and the other as the sailor out in the world of commerce. Indeed, every sphere of life has, in a sense, produced its own tribe of storytellers. Each of the tribes preserves its characteristic features centuries later. * * * Of course in some ways we are just talking about basic types. The actual flourishing of storytelling in its historical breadth and depth is inconceivable without imagining the most intimate interpenetration of these two archetypes. The Middle Ages was a time when such interpenetration manifested itself through the trade structure. The resident master craftsman and the journeymen worked together in the same room, and every master had once been a journeyman before he settled down in his hometown or somewhere else. Peasants and sailors may have been experts in the art of storytelling, but the artisan class served as its training ground. It brought together the lore of faraway places— what the well-traveled man brings back home—with the lore of the past, as it reveals itself to the natives of a place. * * *

A commitment to practical knowledge is characteristic of many born storytellers. That orientation is more pronounced in a writer like [Jeremias] Gotthelf, who gave his readers advice on agricultural matters, than in Leskov. You can find it in the work of [Charles] Nodier, who was interested in the perils of gaslight, and a writer like [Johann Peter] Hebel, who slipped bits and pieces of scientific instruction for his readers into his *Schatzkästlein*, also works along these lines. These observations point to an important feature of every true story. It contains, explicitly or covertly, something that can be useful. Sometimes the value lies in a moral; at other times

practical advice is offered; and occasionally there is a proverb or
maxim. In every case, the storyteller is a man who has counsel for
his readers. If the phrase "having counsel" sounds old-fashioned, it
is because we are losing the power to communicate experience. As
a result we are stripped of the ability to give advice, not only to ourselves but also to others. After all, advice is less about answering
a question than proposing how a story that is unfolding should
continue. To get at that advice, you would first have to be able to tell
the story. (Quite apart from that, most people are receptive to counsel only to the extent that it remains relevant to their own concerns.) Counsel woven into the fabric of lived experience is wisdom.
The art of storytelling is on the wane because the epic aspect of
truth, wisdom, is dying out. That is a process that has been going
on for a long time. Nothing could be more foolish than to dismiss it
as little more than a "symptom of decay," let alone a "symptom of
modernity." It is far more like an emergent symptom of the secular,
productive forces of history, in which narrative has moved gradually out of the realm of living speech, enabling us to see renewed
beauty in what is vanishing before our eyes.

The earliest symptom of a process marked at its endpoint by the
decline of storytelling is the rise of the novel at the beginning of
modernity. What distinguishes the novel from the story (and from
the epic in the narrower sense of the term) is its deep dependence
on the book. The rise of the novel became possible only after the
invention of print. What can be handed down through oral traditions, the essence of the epic, is radically different from what constitutes the stock in trade of the novel. The novel does not derive
from oral traditions, nor does it merge with them, and that is what
makes it profoundly different from all other forms of narrative
prose—fairy tales, legends, and even the novella. And above all it is
different from storytelling in general. Storytellers take what they tell
from experience—their own or what has been passed on to them.
And they turn it into the experience of those listening to the tale.
But novelists close themselves off. The birthplace of the novel is the
solitary individual, someone no longer able to talk about the most
pressing concerns in ways that apply to everyone. The novelist is per-
plexed and unable to offer guidance. To write a novel means to
carry the incommensurable to extremes in representing human life.
The novel concedes its profound bewilderment in the face of the
fullness of life and in trying to represent it. * * *

Imagine the transformation of epic forms as a process occurring
in rhythms comparable to those that shaped the earth's surface over
a stretch of thousands of years. Scarcely any other forms of human
communication have developed more slowly and died out more
slowly. It took the novel, with its roots in classical antiquity,

hundreds of years before it encountered, in the rising bourgeoisie, the elements favoring its efflorescence. With that turn, storytelling slowly took on the aura of the archaic. It took hold of the new elements but was not really shaped by them. At the same time, we recognize how a new form of communication emerged, with the full control of a middle class that used the press as one of the most important instruments in an age of fully developed capitalism—a form that, no matter how far back its origins may lie, never influenced the form of the epic in a decisive way. But now it does exert an important influence. It turns out that it confronts storytelling as no less of a stranger than the novel, but it does so in a far more menacing way. This new form of communication, which also is creating a crisis for the novel, is information.

[Hippolyte de] Villemessant, the man who founded *Le Figaro*, famously captured the essence of information with these words: "For my readers," he used to say, "a roof that catches on fire in the Latin Quarter is more significant than a revolution in Madrid." This makes it strikingly clear that news coming from a distance has less resonance than information that provides a way of connecting with what is immediately relevant. News that came from a distance—whether from spatially remote places or temporally removed eras—possessed a kind of authority that made it valid, even when it was not subject to verification. Information, by contrast, lays claim to immediate verifiability. For one thing, it must appear "completely plausible." Often it is no more precise than the news that was passed on in earlier centuries. That news could traffic in wonders, but today it is absolutely necessary for information to sound plausible. And for precisely that reason it is incompatible with the spirit of storytelling. If the art of storytelling is fading away, the dissemination of information has played a decisive role in this state of affairs.

Every day brings news from around the world, and yet we lack noteworthy stories. This is a result of the fact that descriptions of events come to us now teeming with explanations. In other words, almost nothing that happens is shaped into a story and is instead presented as information. Half the art of telling a story is keeping the story, as you tell it, free of explanations. Leskov is a master of this art (look at plays like *The Deception* or *The White Eagle*). The most extraordinary things, marvelous things, are told with the greatest precision, yet psychological motivations are not forced on readers. It is left up to them to interpret things as they understand them, and the story acquires an amplitude that information lacks.

Leskov was schooled in the Ancients. The earliest Greek storyteller was Herodotus. In the fourteenth chapter of the third book of his *Histories*, there is a tale that is revealing. It tells the story of Psammenitus. When the Egyptian king Psammenitus was defeated and captured by the Persian King Cambyses, Cambyses was determined to humiliate his prisoner. He gave orders to position Psammenitus on the road used by the Persians for their triumphal march. And he also arranged to make sure that the prisoner would see his daughter, now a maid, walk to the well to fill a pitcher. When every single Egyptian was objecting to this spectacle and bemoaning it, Psammenitus just stood there, mute and motionless, his eyes fixed on the ground. When he saw his son, who was being led to his execution, he continued to remain unmoved. But when he next recognized one of his servants, a poor old man, in the ranks of the prisoners, he beat his fists against his forehead and displayed all the signs of deepest mourning.

This story captures the essence of true storytelling. The value of information expires the moment it is no longer new. It is alive only at that moment, and it has to submit completely to it and explain itself without losing any time. A story is completely different, for it is not self-consuming. It manages to preserve its strength and is capable of releasing it even after much time has passed. Montaigne also made reference to the Egyptian king and asked himself: "Why did he grieve only when he caught sight of the servant?" Montaigne answered, "Since his heart was already flooded with grief, it took only a small trickle for it to burst fully through the dams." That's what Montaigne tells us. You could also say, "The king was not moved by the fate of those with royal blood, for it was his own destiny." Or, "Often we are moved more by what is staged than what happens in real life. The servant was nothing more than an actor for the king." Or, "Sharp pain can be kept pent up and releases itself only when you let your guard down. The king saw the servant at that exact moment." Herodotus explains nothing in his report, which is drier than you can imagine. For that reason the story from ancient Egypt can still arouse astonishment and make us think. It resembles seeds of grain that have remained dormant for centuries in the chambers of the pyramids. Sealed in those chambers, they kept their power to take root to this day.

There is nothing that commends a story to memory more compellingly than a chaste compactness that does away with psychological analysis. The more spontaneous the process by which the storyteller lets go of psychological nuance, the greater the story's claim to a place in the minds of listeners, the more perfectly it is integrated into their own experience, and the more likely will be the wish to repeat it to someone else one day, sooner or later. The process of absorbing a story, which takes place at a subconscious level, requires a state of leisure that is becoming more and more rare today. If sleep is the height of physical relaxation, boredom is the apogee of mental relaxation. Boredom is the dream bird that hatches the egg of experience. A rustling of leaves drives it away. Its nesting places—the activities intimately associated with boredom—are already extinct in the cities and are on the decline in the country. The art of listening is on the wane, and with it communities of listeners. For storytelling is always the art of passing things along, and it is lost when the stories are no longer maintained. It has been lost because spinning and weaving no longer create circles of listeners. The more absorbed listeners are, the more deeply the story is impressed upon their minds. When the rhythms of work have been internalized, people listen to the stories in such a way that retelling them is completely spontaneous. This, then, is the web in which the storytelling instinct is situated. It is beginning to become unraveled after having been woven for thousands of years in milieus that formed the setting for practicing older forms of craftsmanship.

Storytelling, which flourished for a long time in the milieu of manual labor—agricultural, maritime, and then urban—is itself an artisanal form of communication, as it were. It is not invested in conveying the pure gist of a thing, as is the case with information or a report. It submerges the thing into the life of the storyteller in order to extract it again. Traces of the storyteller cling to the story in the way that the fingerprints of the potter cling to a clay vessel. Storytellers often begin their tales with a description of the circumstances in which they themselves learned about what follows, unless they simply pass it off as their own experience. Leskov begins his tale "Deception" with a description of a train trip on which he hears from a fellow passenger about the events that he then proceeds to narrate. In "A propos of the Kreutzer Sonata," he imagines Dostoevsky's funeral and turns it into the setting in which he meets the heroine of the story. And in "Interesting Men" he evokes a meeting with members of a reading group in which the events that he reproduces for us are told. Thus his presence is frequently felt in his narratives, if not as the person who experienced what happens in them, then as the person who is reporting them.

The craft of storytelling was understood by Leskov to be exactly that. "Writing," he declared in one of his letters, "is craftsmanship rather than art." It is no surprise that he felt a strong kinship with the crafts but faced industrial technologies as a stranger. Tolstoy, who must have sympathized with this view, puts his finger on something important about Leskov's storytelling talent, when he describes him as the first person "to emphasize the inadequacies of economic progress. . . . It is strange that everyone reads Dostoevsky. . . . But I simply cannot understand why Leskov is not read." In his artful and spirited story "The Steel Flea," which is part legend and part farce, Leskov celebrated native craftsmanship through the silversmiths of Tula. Their masterpiece, the steel flea, is shown to Peter the Great and persuades the ruler that the Russians need not feel inferior to the English.

The poetic image that captures the world of crafts and artifacts in which storytelling thrived was described nowhere more importantly than in the writings of Paul Valéry. He tells us about perfect objects in nature; flawless pearls; full-bodied, mature wines; and truly complex creatures. He describes them as the "exquisite products of a long chain of causes that resemble each other." The cumulative effect of such causes has temporal limits only when perfection has been attained. "Nature's patient way of working," Valéry continues, "was once a model for humans. Miniatures, ivory carvings crafted to the point of perfection, stones perfectly polished and engraved, lacquered objects or paintings in which thin, transparent layers are put on top of each other—all of these products of sustained effort required sacrifice and have rapidly vanished. The day and age is long gone in which time does not matter. Today people no longer work on anything that does not allow shortcuts." Today we are witnessing the evolution of the short story, which is no longer connected to oral traditions and no longer allows for the gradual accumulation of thin, transparent sheets that capture the most accurate picture of how a perfect story emerges from the layering of a variety of retellings. * * *

"And if they have not died, then they are still living today," the fairy tale tells us. The fairy tale to this day remains the first tutor of childhood because it was also the first tutor of mankind, and it lives on in storytelling. The very first true storytellers were those who told fairy tales. Whenever good advice was at a premium, the fairy tale offered it, and when need was the greatest, *its* help was right there. This need was the need created by myth. The fairy tale tells us about the earliest strategies used to shake off the nightmares that myth loaded up onto our chests. In the figure of the numbskull we see how "playing dumb" can counter the forces of myth; in the figure of the youngest brother we see how your chances get better as you distance yourself from mythical times; in the figure of the boy who leaves home to learn fear, we discover that the things we fear can be demystified; in the figure of the clever one we discover the riddles posed by myth are simple to solve, like the riddle of the sphinx; in the figure of animals that come to the rescue of fairy-tale children, we find that nature is not beholden to myth but prefers to spend time with humans. The wisest thing, as the fairy tale taught us in ancient times and continues to teach children today, is how to meet the forces of the mythical world with cunning and courage. (The fairy tale divides courage [*Mut*] into two parts so as to produce a dialectical play between cunning [*Untermut*] and high spirits [*Übermut*].) The liberating magic that the fairy tale has at its disposal does not draw nature into play in a mythical manner but shows how it partners with those who are liberated. As we mature we sense this partnership only rarely, when we are happiest; children discover it first in fairy tales and it promotes in them joy.

ROBERT DARNTON

Peasants Tell Tales: The Meaning of Mother Goose[†]

The mental world of the unenlightened during the Enlightenment seems to be irretrievably lost. It is so difficult, if not impossible, to locate the common man in the eighteenth century that it seems foolish to search for his cosmology. But before abandoning the attempt, it might be useful to suspend one's disbelief and to consider a story—a story everyone knows, though not in the following version, which is the tale more or less as it was told around firesides in peasant cottages during long winter evenings in eighteenth-century France.[1]

> Once a little girl was told by her mother to bring some bread and milk to her grandmother. As the girl was walking through the forest, a wolf came up to her and asked where she was going.
> "To grandmother's house," she replied.
> "Which path are you taking, the path of the pins or the path of the needles?"
> "The path of the needles."
> So the wolf took the path of the pins and arrived first at the house. He killed grandmother, poured her blood into a bottle, and sliced her flesh onto a platter. Then he got into her night-clothes and waited in bed.
>
> "Knock, knock."
> "Come in, my dear."
> "Hello, grandmother. I've brought you some bread and milk."
> "Have something yourself, my dear. There is meat and wine in the pantry."

[†] Robert Darnton, "Peasants Tell Tales: The Meaning of Mother Goose," in *The Great Cat Massacre and Other Episodes in French Cultural History* (New York: Basic Books, 1984), pp. 9–22. Copyright © 1984 by Basic Books, Inc. Reprinted by permission of Basic Books, a member of the Perseus Books Group. The author's footnotes have been edited for this Norton Critical Edition.

1. This text and those of the other French folktales discussed in this essay come from Paul Delarue and Marie-Louise Ténèze, *Le Conte populaire français* (Paris, 1976), 3 vols., which is the best of the French folktale collections because it provides all the recorded versions of each tale along with background information about how they were gathered from oral sources.

So the little girl ate what was offered; and as she did, a little cat said, "Slut! To eat the flesh and drink the blood of your grandmother!"

Then the wolf said, "Undress and get into bed with me."

"Where shall I put my apron?"

"Throw it on the fire; you won't need it any more."

For each garment—bodice, skirt, petticoat, and stockings—the girl asked the same question; and each time the wolf answered, "Throw it on the fire; you won't need it any more."

When the girl got in bed, she said, "Oh, grandmother! How hairy you are!"

"It's to keep me warmer, my dear."

"Oh, grandmother! What big shoulders you have!"

"It's for better carrying firewood, my dear."

"Oh, grandmother! What long nails you have!"

"It's for scratching myself better, my dear."

"Oh, grandmother! What big teeth you have!"

"It's for eating you better, my dear."

And he ate her.

What is the moral of this story? For little girls, clearly: stay away from wolves. For historians, it seems to be saying something about the mental world of the early modern peasantry. But what? How can one begin to interpret such a text? One way leads through psychoanalysis. The analysts have given folktales a thorough going-over, picking out hidden symbols, unconscious motifs, and psychic mechanisms. Consider, for example, the exegesis of "Little Red Riding Hood" by two of the best known psychoanalysts, Erich Fromm and Bruno Bettelheim.

Fromm interpreted the tale as a riddle about the collective unconscious in primitive society, and he solved it "without difficulty" by decoding its "symbolic language." The story concerns an adolescent's confrontation with adult sexuality, he explained. Its hidden meaning shows through its symbolism—but the symbols he saw in his version of the text were based on details that did not exist in the versions known to peasants in the seventeenth and eighteenth centuries. Thus he makes a great deal of the (nonexistent) red riding hood as a symbol of menstruation and of the (nonexistent) bottle carried by the girl as a symbol of virginity: hence the mother's (nonexistent) admonition not to stray from the path into wild terrain where she might break it. The wolf is the ravishing male. And the two (nonexistent) stones that are placed in the wolf's belly after the (nonexistent) hunter extricates the girl and her grandmother, stand for sterility, the punishment for breaking a sexual taboo. So, with an uncanny sensitivity to detail that did not occur in the original folktale, the psychoanalyst takes us into a mental universe that never existed, at least not before the advent of psychoanalysis.[2]

How could anyone get a text so wrong? The difficulty does not derive from professional dogmatism—for psychoanalysts need not be more rigid than poets in their manipulation of symbols—but rather from blindness to the historical dimension of folktales.

Fromm did not bother to mention his source, but apparently he took his text from the brothers Grimm. The Grimms got it, along with "Puss 'n Boots," "Bluebeard," and a few other stories, from Jeannette Hassenpflug, a neighbor and close friend of theirs in Cassel; and she learned it from her mother, who came from a French Huguenot family. The Huguenots brought their own repertory of tales into Germany when they fled from the persecution of Louis XIV. But they did not draw them directly from popular oral tradition. They read them in books written by Charles Perrault, Marie Cathérine d'Aulnoy, and others during the vogue for fairy tales in fashionable Parisian circles at the end of the seventeenth century. Perrault, the master of the genre, did indeed take his material from the oral tradition of the common people (his principal source probably was his son's nurse). But he touched it up so that it would suit the taste of the salon sophisticates, *précieuses*,[3] and courtiers to whom he directed the first printed version of Mother Goose, his *Contes de ma mère l'oye* of 1697. Thus the tales that reached the Grimms through the Hassenpflugs were neither very German nor very representative of folk tradition. Indeed, the Grimms recognized their literary and Frenchified character and therefore eliminated them from the second edition of the *Kinder- und Hausmärchen*—all but "Little Red Riding Hood." It remained in the collection, evidently, because Jeannette Hassenpflug had grafted on to it a happy ending derived from "The Wolf and the Kids" (tale type 123 according to the standard classification scheme developed by Antti Aarne and Stith Thompson), which was one of the most popular in Germany. So Little Red Riding Hood slipped into the German and later the English literary tradition with her French origins undetected. She changed character considerably as she passed from the French peasantry to Perrault's nursery, into print, across the Rhine, back into an oral tradition but this time as part of the Huguenot diaspora, and back into book form but now as a product of the Teutonic forest rather than the village hearths of the Old Regime in France.

Fromm and a host of other psychoanalytical exegetes did not worry about the transformations of the text—indeed, they did not know

2. Erich Fromm, *The Forgotten Language: An Introduction to the Understanding of Dreams, Fairy Tales and Myths* (New York, 1951), pp. 235–41, quotation from p. 240.
3. Literati [editor's note].

about them—because they got the tale they wanted. It begins with
pubertal sex (the red hood, which does not exist in the French oral
tradition) and ends with the triumph of the ego (the rescued girl,
who is usually eaten in the French tales) over the id (the wolf, who
is never killed in the traditional versions). All's well that ends well.

The ending is particularly important for Bruno Bettelheim, the
latest in the line of psychoanalysts who have had a go at "Little Red
Riding Hood." For him, the key to the story, and to all such stories,
is the affirmative message of its denouement. By ending happily, he
maintains, folktales permit children to confront their unconscious
desires and fears and to emerge unscathed, id subdued and ego triumphant. The id is the villain of "Little Red Riding Hood" in Bettelheim's version. It is the pleasure principle, which leads the girl
astray when she is too old for oral fixation (the stage represented by
"Hansel and Gretel") and too young for adult sex. The id is also the
wolf, who is also the father, who is also the hunter, who is also the
ego and, somehow, the superego as well. By directing the wolf to her
grandmother, Little Red Riding Hood manages in oedipal fashion
to do away with her mother, because mothers can also be grandmothers in the moral economy of the soul and the houses on either
side of the woods are actually the same house, as in "Hansel and
Gretel," where they are also the mother's body. This adroit mixing
of symbols gives Little Red Riding Hood an opportunity to get into
bed with her father, the wolf, thereby giving vent to her oedipal fantasies. She survives in the end because she is reborn on a higher
level of existence when her father reappears as ego-superego-hunter
and cuts her out of the belly of her father as wolf-id, so that everyone lives happily ever after.[4]

Bettelheim's generous view of symbolism makes for a less mecha-
nistic interpretation of the tale than does Fromm's notion of a secret
code, but it, too, proceeds from some unquestioned assumptions
about the text. Although he cites enough commentators on Grimm
and Perrault to indicate some awareness of folklore as an academic
discipline, Bettelheim reads "Little Red Riding Hood" and the other
tales as if they had no history. He treats them, so to speak, flattened
out, like patients on a couch, in a timeless contemporaneity. He does
not question their origins or worry over other meanings that they
might have had in other contexts because he knows how the soul
works and how it has always worked. In fact, however, folktales are
historical documents. They have evolved over many centuries and
have taken different turns in different cultural traditions. Far from

---

4. Bruno Bettelheim, *The Uses of Enchantment: The Meaning and Importance of Fairy Tales* (New York, 1977), pp. 166–83.

expressing the unchanging operations of man's inner being, they suggest that *mentalités* themselves have changed. We can appreciate the distance between our mental world and that of our ancestors if we imagine lulling a child of our own to sleep with the primitive peasant version of "Little Red Riding Hood." Perhaps, then, the moral of the story should be: beware of psychoanalysts—and be careful in your use of sources. We seem to be back at historicism.

Not quite, however, for "Little Red Riding Hood" has a terrifying irrationality that seems out of place in the Age of Reason. In fact, the peasants' version outdoes the psychoanalysts' in violence and sex. (Following the Grimms and Perrault, Fromm and Bettelheim do not mention the cannibalizing of grandmother and the strip-tease prelude to the devouring of the girl.) Evidently the peasants did not need a secret code to talk about taboos.

The other stories in the French peasant Mother Goose have the same nightmare quality. In one early version of "Sleeping Beauty" (tale type 410), for example, Prince Charming, who is already married, ravishes the princess, and she bears him several children, without waking up. The infants finally break the spell by biting her while nursing, and the tale then takes up its second theme: the attempts of the prince's mother-in-law, an ogress, to eat his illicit offspring. The original "Bluebeard" (tale type 312) is the story of a bride who cannot resist the temptation to open a forbidden door in the house of her husband, a strange man who has already gone through six wives. She enters a dark room and discovers the corpses of the previous wives, hanging on the wall. Horrified, she lets the forbidden key drop from her hand into a pool of blood on the floor. She cannot wipe it clean; so Bluebeard discovers her disobedience, when he inspects the keys. As he sharpens his knife in preparation for making her his seventh victim, she withdraws to her bedroom and puts on her wedding costume. But she delays her toilette long enough to be saved by her brothers, who gallop to the rescue after receiving a warning from her pet dove. In one early tale from the Cinderella cycle (tale type 510B), the heroine becomes a domestic servant in order to prevent her father from forcing her to marry him. In another, the wicked stepmother tries to push her in an oven but incinerates one of the mean stepsisters by mistake. In the French peasant's "Hansel and Gretel" (tale type 327), the hero tricks an ogre into slitting the throats of his own children. A husband eats a succession of brides in the wedding bed in "La Belle et le monstre" (tale type 433), one of the hundreds of tales that never made it into the printed versions of Mother Goose. In a nastier tale, "Les Trois Chiens" (tale type 315), a sister kills her brother by hiding spikes in the mattress of his wedding bed. In the nastiest of all, "Ma mère m'a tué, mon père m'a mangé" (tale type 720), a mother chops her son up into a Lyonnais-style casserole, which her daughter serves to the father. And so it goes, from rape and sodomy to incest and cannibalism. Far from veiling their message with symbols, the storytellers of eighteenth-century France portrayed a world of raw and naked brutality.

How can the historian make sense of this world? One way for him to keep his footing in the psychic undertow of early Mother Goose is to hold fast to two disciplines: anthropology and folklore. When they discuss theory, anthropologists disagree about the fundamentals of their science. But when they go into the bush, they use techniques for understanding oral traditions that can, with discretion, be applied to Western folklore. Except for some structuralists, they relate tales to the art of tale telling and to the context in which it takes place. They look for the way a raconteur adapts an inherited theme to his audience so that the specificity of time and place shows through the universality of the topos. They do not expect to find direct social comment or metaphysical allegories so much as a tone of discourse or a cultural style, which communicates a particular ethos and world view. "Scientific" folklore, as the French call it (American specialists often distinguish between folklore and "fakelore"), involves the compilation and comparison of tales according to the standardized schemata of tale types developed by Antti Aarne and Stith Thompson. It does not necessarily exclude formalistic analysis such as that of Vladimir Propp, but it stresses rigorous documentation—the occasion of the telling, the background of the teller, and the degree of contamination from written sources.[5]

French folklorists have recorded about ten thousand tales, in many different dialects and in every corner of France and of French-speaking territories. For example, while on an expedition in Berry for the Musée des arts et traditions populaires in 1945, Ariane de Félice recorded a version of "Le Petit Poucet" ("Tom Thumb" or "Thumbling," tale type 327) by a peasant woman, Euphrasie Pichon, who had been born in 1862 in the village of Eguzon (Indre). In 1879 Jean Drouillet wrote down another version as he listened to his mother Eugénie, who had learned it from her mother, Octavie Riffet, in the village of Teillay (Cher). The two versions are nearly identical and owe nothing to the first printed account of the tale, which Charles Perrault published in 1697. They and eighty other "Petits

---

5. See Aarne and Thompson, *The Types of the Folktale: A Classification and Bibliography* (2nd rev.; Helsinki, 1973); Thompson, *The Folktale* (Berkeley and Los Angeles, 1977; 1st ed. 1946); and Vladimir Propp, *Morphology of the Folktale,* trans. Laurence Scott (Austin, 1968). Aarne and Thompson used the "historical-geographical" or "Finnish" method, developed by Kaarle Krohn, to produce a world-wide survey and classification of folktales.

Poucets," which folklorists have compiled and compared, motif by motif, belong to an oral tradition that survived with remarkably little contamination from print culture until late in the nineteenth century. Most of the tales in the French repertory were recorded between 1870 and 1914 during "the Golden Age of folktale research in France," and they were recounted by peasants who had learned them as children, long before literacy had spread throughout the countryside. Thus in 1874 Nannette Levesque, an illiterate peasant woman born in 1794, dictated a version of "Little Red Riding Hood" that went back to the eighteenth century; and in 1865 Louis Grolleau, a domestic servant born in 1803, dictated a rendition of "Le Pou" (tale type 621) that he had first heard under the Empire. Like all tellers of tales, the peasant raconteurs adjusted the setting of their stories to their own milieux; but they kept the main elements intact, using repetitions, rhymes, and other mnemonic devices. Although the "performance" element, which is central to the study of contemporary folklore, does not show through the old texts, folklorists argue that the recordings of the Third Republic provide enough evidence for them to reconstruct the rough outlines of an oral tradition that existed two centuries ago.[6]

That claim may seem extravagant, but comparative studies have revealed striking similarities in different recordings of the same tale, even though they were made in remote villages, far removed from one another and from the circulation of books. In a study of "Little Red Riding Hood," for example, Paul Delarue compared thirty-five versions recorded throughout a vast zone of the *langue d'oïl*. Twenty versions correspond exactly to the primitive "Conte de la mère grand" quoted above, except for a few details (sometimes the girl is eaten, sometimes she escapes by a ruse). Two versions follow Perrault's tale (the first to mention the red hood). And the rest contain a mixture of the oral and written accounts, whose elements stand out as distinctly as the garlic and mustard in a French salad dressing.[7]

Written evidence proves that the tales existed long before anyone conceived of "folklore," a nineteenth-century neologism.[8] Medieval preachers drew on the oral tradition in order to illustrate moral arguments. Their sermons, transcribed in collections of "Exempla" from the twelfth to the fifteenth century, refer to the same stories as those

---

6. This information comes from Paul Delarue's introduction to *Le Conte populaire français*, I, 7–99, which is the best general account of folklore research in France and which also contains a thorough bibliography.
7. Delarue, "Les contes merveilleux de Perrault et la tradition populaire," *Bulletin folklorique d'Ile-de-France*, n.s. (July–Oct., 1951).
8. William Thoms launched the term "folklore" in 1846, two decades before Edward Tylor introduced a similar term, "culture," among English-speaking anthropologists. See Thoms, "Folklore" and William R. Bascom, "Folklore and Anthropology" in Dundes, *Study of Folklore*, pp. 4–6 and 25–33.

taken down in peasant cottages by folklorists in the nineteenth century. Despite the obscurity surrounding the origins of chivalric romances, *chansons de geste,* and *fabliaux,* it seems that a good deal of medieval literature drew on popular oral tradition, rather than vice versa. "Sleeping Beauty" appeared in an Arthurian romance of the fourteenth century, and "Cinderella" surfaced in Noël du Fail's *Propos rustiques* of 1547, a book that traced the tales to peasant lore and that showed how they were transmitted; for du Fail wrote the first account of an important French institution, the *veillée,* an evening fireside gathering, where men repaired tools and women sewed while listening to stories that would be recorded by folklorists three hundred years later and that were already centuries old.[9] Whether they were meant to amuse adults or to frighten children, as in the case of cautionary tales like "Little Red Riding Hood," the stories belonged to a fund of popular culture, which peasants hoarded over the centuries with remarkably little loss.

The great collections of folktales made in the late nineteenth and early twentieth centuries therefore provide a rare opportunity to make contact with the illiterate masses who have disappeared into the past without leaving a trace. To reject folktales because they cannot be dated and situated with precision like other historical documents is to turn one's back on one of the few points of entry into the mental world of peasants under the Old Regime. But to attempt to penetrate that world is to face a set of obstacles as daunting as those confronted by Jean de l'Ours (tale type 301) when he tried to rescue the three Spanish princesses from the underworld or by little Parle (tale type 328) when he set out to capture the ogre's treasure.

The greatest obstacle is the impossibility of listening in on the story tellers. No matter how accurate they may be, the recorded versions of the tales cannot convey the effects that must have brought the stories to life in the eighteenth century: the dramatic pauses, the sly glances, the use of gestures to set scenes—a Snow White at a spinning wheel, a Cinderella delousing a stepsister—and the use of sounds to punctuate actions—a knock on the door (often done by rapping on a listener's forehead) or a cudgeling or a fart. All of those devices shaped the meaning of the tales, and all of them elude the historian. He cannot be sure that the limp and lifeless text that he holds between the covers of a book provides an accurate account of the performance that took place in the eighteenth century. He cannot even be certain that the text corresponds to the unrecorded versions that existed a century earlier. Although he may turn up plenty of evidence to prove that the tale itself existed, he cannot

9. Noël du Fail, *Propos rustiques de Maistre Leon Ladulfi Champenois,* chap. 5, in *Conteurs français du XVIe siècle,* ed. Pierre Jourda (Paris, 1956), pp. 620–21.

quiet his suspicions that it could have changed a great deal before it reached the folklorists of the Third Republic.

Given those uncertainties, it seems unwise to build an interpretation on a single version of a single tale, and more hazardous still to base symbolic analysis on details—riding hoods and hunters—that may not have occurred in the peasant versions. But there are enough recordings of those versions—35 "Little Red Riding Hoods," 90 "Tom Thumbs," 105 "Cinderellas"—for one to picture the general outline of a tale as it existed in the oral tradition. One can study it on the level of structure, noting the way the narrative is framed and the motifs are combined, instead of concentrating on fine points of detail. Then one can compare it with other stories. And finally, by working through the entire body of French folktales, one can distinguish general characteristics, overarching themes, and pervasive elements of style and tone.

One can also seek aid and comfort from specialists in the study of oral literature. Milman Parry and Albert Lord have shown how folk epics as long as *The Iliad* are passed on faithfully from bard to bard among the illiterate peasants of Yugoslavia. These "singers of tales" do not possess the fabulous powers of memorization sometimes attributed to "primitive" peoples. They do not memorize very much at all. Instead, they combine stock phrases, formulas, and narrative segments in patterns improvised according to the response of their audience. Recordings of the same epic by the same singer demonstrate that each performance is unique. Yet recordings made in 1950 do not differ in essentials from those made in 1934. In each case, the singer proceeds as if he were walking down a well-known path. He may branch off here to take a shortcut or pause there to enjoy a panorama, but he always remains on familiar ground—so familiar, in fact, that he will say that he repeated every step exactly as he has done before. He does not conceive of repetition in the same way as a literate person, for he has no notion of words, lines, and verses. Texts are not rigidly fixed for him as they are for readers of the printed page. He creates his text as he goes, picking new routes through old themes. He can even work in material derived from printed sources, for the epic as a whole is so much greater than the sum of its parts that modifications of detail barely disturb the general configuration.[1]

Lord's investigation confirms conclusions that Vladimir Propp reached by a different mode of analysis, one that showed how variations of detail remain subordinate to stable structures in Russian folktales.[2] Field workers among illiterate peoples in Polynesia, Africa, and North and South America have also found that oral traditions have

1. Albert B. Lord, *The Singer of Tales* (Cambridge, Mass., 1960).
2. Propp, *Morphology of the Folktale*.

enormous staying power. Opinions divide on the separate question of whether or not oral sources can provide a reliable account of past events. Robert Lowie, who collected narratives from the Crow Indians in the early twentieth century, took up a position of extreme skepticism: "I cannot attach to oral traditions any historical value whatsoever under any conditions whatsoever."[3] By historical value, however, Lowie meant factual accuracy. (In 1910 he recorded a Crow account of a battle against the Dakota; in 1931 the same informant described the battle to him, but claimed that it had taken place against the Cheyenne.) Lowie conceded that the stories, taken as stories, remained quite consistent; they forked and branched in the standard patterns of Crow narrative. So his findings actually support the view that in traditional story telling continuities in form and style outweigh variations in detail, among North American Indians as well as Yugoslav peasants. Frank Hamilton Cushing noted a spectacular example of this tendency among the Zuni almost a century ago. In 1886 he served as interpreter to a Zuni delegation in the eastern United States. During a round robin of story telling one evening, he recounted as his contribution the tale of "The Cock and the Mouse," which he had picked up from a book of Italian folktales. About a year later, he was astonished to hear the same tale from one of the Indians back at Zuni. The Italian motifs remained recognizable enough for one to be able to classify the tale in the Aarne-Thompson scheme (it is tale type 2032). But everything else about the story—its frame, figures of speech, allusions, style, and general feel—had become intensely Zuni. Instead of Italianizing the native lore, the story had been Zunified.[4]

No doubt the transmission process affects stories differently in different cultures. Some bodies of folklore can resist "contamination" while absorbing new material more effectively than can others. But oral traditions seem to be tenacious and long-lived nearly everywhere among illiterate peoples. Nor do they collapse at their first exposure to the printed word. Despite Jack Goody's contention that a literacy line cuts through all history, dividing oral from "written" or "print" cultures, it seems that traditional tale telling can flourish long after the onset of literacy. To anthropologists and folklorists who have tracked tales through the bush, there is nothing extravagant about the idea that peasant raconteurs in late nineteenth-century France told stories to one another pretty much as their ancestors had done a century or more earlier.[5]

3. Lowie's remark is quoted in Richard Dorson, "The Debate over the Trustworthiness of Oral Traditional History," in Dorson, *Folklore: Selected Essays* (Bloomington, IN, 1972), p. 202.
4. Frank Hamilton Cushing, *Zuni Folk Tales* (New York and London, 1901), pp. 411–22.
5. Jack Goody, *The Domestication of the Savage Mind* (Cambridge, 1977). See also the studies published by Goody as *Literacy in Traditional Societies* (Cambridge, 1968).

Comforting as this expert testimony may be, it does not clear all the difficulties in the way of interpreting the French tales. The texts are accessible enough, for they lie unexploited in treasure houses like the Musée des arts et traditions populaires in Paris and in scholarly collections like *Le Conte populaire français* by Paul Delarue and Marie-Louise Tenèze. But one cannot lift them from such sources and hold them up to inspection as if they were so many photographs of the Old Regime, taken with the innocent eye of an extinct peasantry. They are stories.

As in most kinds of narration, they develop standardized plots from conventional motifs, picked up here, there, and everywhere. They have a distressing lack of specificity for anyone who wants to pin them down to precise points in time and place. Raymond Jameson has studied the case of a Chinese Cinderella from the ninth century. She gets her slippers from a magic fish instead of a fairy godmother and loses one of them at a village fête instead of a royal ball, but she bears an unmistakable resemblance to Perrault's heroine.[6] Folklorists have recognized their tales in Herodotus and Homer, on ancient Egyptian papyruses and Chaldean stone tablets; and they have recorded them all over the world, in Scandinavia and Africa, among Indians on the banks of the Bengal and Indians along the Missouri. The dispersion is so striking that some have come to believe in Ur-stories and a basic Indo-European repertory of myths, legends, and tales. This tendency feeds into the cosmic theories of Frazer and Jung and Lévi-Strauss, but it does not help anyone attempting to penetrate the peasant mentalities of early modern France.

Fortunately, a more down-to-earth tendency in folklore makes it possible to isolate the peculiar characteristics of traditional French tales. *Le Conte populaire français* arranges them according to the Aarne-Thompson classification scheme, which covers all varieties of Indo-European folktales. It therefore provides the basis for comparative study, and the comparisons suggest the way general themes took root and grew in French soil. "Tom Thumb" ("Le Petit Poucet," tale type 327), for example, has a strong French flavor, in Perrault as well as the peasant versions, if one compares it with its German cousin, "Hansel and Gretel." The Grimms' tale emphasizes the mysterious forest and the naïveté of the children in the face of inscrutable evil, and it has more fanciful and poetic touches, as in the details about the bread-and-cake house and the magic birds. The French children confront an ogre, but in a very real house. Monsieur and Madame Ogre discuss their plans for a dinner party as if they were any married couple, and they carp at each other just as Tom

6. Raymond D. Jameson, *Three Lectures on Chinese Folklore* (Peking, 1932).

Thumb's parents did. In fact, it is hard to tell the two couples apart. Both simple-minded wives throw away their family's fortunes; and their husbands berate them in the same manner, except that the ogre tells his wife that she deserves to be eaten and that he would do the job himself if she were not such an unappetizing *vieille bête* (old beast).[7] Unlike their German relatives, the French ogres appear in the role of *le bourgeois de la maison* (burgher head of household),[8] as if they were rich local landowners. They play fiddles, visit friends, snore contentedly in bed beside fat ogress wives;[9] and for all their boorishness, they never fail to be good family men and good providers. Hence the joy of the ogre in "Pitchin-Pitchot" as he bounds into the house, a sack on his back: "Catherine, put on the big kettle. I've caught Pitchin-Pitchot."[1]

Where the German tales maintain a tone of terror and fantasy, the French strike a note of humor and domesticity. Firebirds settle down into hen yards. Elves, genii, forest spirits, the whole Indo-European panoply of magical beings become reduced in France to two species, ogres and fairies. And those vestigial creatures acquire human foibles and generally let humans solve their problems by their own devices, that is, by cunning and "Cartesianism"—a term that the French apply vulgarly to their propensity for craftiness and intrigue. The Gallic touch is clear in many of the tales that Perrault did not rework for his own Gallicized Mother Goose of 1697: the *panache* of the young blacksmith in "Le Petit Forgeron" (tale type 317), for example, who kills giants on a classic *tour de France*; or the provincialism of the Breton peasant in "Jean Bête" (tale type 675), who is given anything he wishes and asks for *un bon péché de piquette et une écuelle de patates du lait* ("crude wine and a bowl of potatoes in milk"); or the professional jealousy of the master gardener, who fails to prune vines as well as his apprentice in "Jean le Teigneux" (tale type 314); or the cleverness of the devil's daughter in "La Belle Eulalie" (tale type 313), who escapes with her lover by leaving two talking pâtés in their beds. Just as one cannot attach the French tales to specific events, one should not dilute them in a timeless universal mythology. They really belong to a middle ground: *la France moderne* or the France that existed from the fifteenth through the eighteenth century.

7. This remark occurs in Perrault's version, which contains a sophisticated reworking of the dialogue in the peasant versions. See Delarue and Tenèze, *Le Conte populaire français*, I, 306–24.
8. "Jean de l'Ours," tale type 301B.
9. See "Le Conte de Parle," tale type 328 and "La Belle Eulalie," tale type 313.
1. "Pitchin-Pitchot," tale type 327C.

MAX LÜTHI

Abstract Style[†]

The clear-cut way in which the folktale achieves its depthlessness lends it a lack of realism. From the outset, the folktale does not seek empathetically to recreate the concrete world with its many dimensions. The folktale transforms the world; it puts a spell on its elements and gives them a different form, and thus it creates a world with a distinct character of its own.

Within the depthless world of the folktale, individual figures are physically set off from each other by sharp outlines and pure colors. By its nature, a flat surface calls for outlines and colors. A painter's picture needs frame and coloring, whereas a sculptor's image can dispense with both. The contours of a three-dimensional form blur in the depths of space; they fade into the indefinite. On a flat surface, however, lines are sharp and unequivocal. The exterior of a body constantly informs us of a hidden interior, whereas a flat surface is isolated in and of itself. A painting can either obscure or intensify the unrealistic character of the pure plane. It can simulate curves, three-dimensionality, and reality, and it can make the flat surface appear to have depth. But a painting can also permit the flat quality to stand by itself and can emphasize it by means of geometric lines and stark colors. The folktale follows this latter approach.

The sharp contours of the folktale are evident at once in the way that it does not describe particular objects but only names them. Action-oriented as it is, it leads its figures on from point to point without pausing to describe anything at length. The legend gazes spellbound at certain buildings, trees, caves, paths, and apparitions and constantly tries to discover new aspects of them. The stories of *The Arabian Nights* likewise tend to lose themselves in descriptions of the fabulous palaces and the towns made of stone into which the hero makes his way, and thus they attain a fullness that bewilders. Detailed descriptions do not convey distinct images, rather they make us lose all perspective. The European folktale is not addicted to description. When it has its hero set off in search of his brother and sister and come upon a town made of iron, it does not waste a single word describing the iron buildings. Looking neither left nor right, and without the slightest trace of astonishment, the hero pursues his goal:[1]

† Max Lüthi, "Abstract Style," in *The European Folktale: Form and Nature*, trans. John D. Niles (Philadelphia: Institute for the Study of Human Issues, 1982), pp. 24–36, 140–42. © 1982 by ISHI. Reprinted with permission of Ophidian Films Ltd.

1. August Leskian, *Balkanmärchen* (Jena: Diederichs, 1919), pp. 179–180 (Serbo-Croatian).

Now the new king decided to search for his brother and sister.
He wandered through many towns but found nothing. At last
he arrived at a town that was made all of iron. He entered, but
there was not a living soul there; all the houses were locked and
there was no one in the street. He found only one big house
standing open. As soon as he entered it, he saw a big dragon
roasting a lamb on a spit. He went up to it and gave it a respectful greeting. The dragon made no reply. The young king became
angry and struck the dragon a blow, and a bloody struggle broke
out between them.

Only what is essential to the plot is mentioned; nothing is stated
for its own sake, and nothing is amplified. As a rule only one attribute goes with each noun: a town made all of iron, a big house, a
big dragon, the young king, a bloody struggle. Thanks to this true
epic technique of merely naming things, everything that is named
appears as a definitively understood unit. Any attempt at detailed
description gives rise to the feeling that only a fraction of all that
could be said has in fact been told. A detailed description lures us
into the infinite and shows us the elusive depth of things. Mere naming, on the other hand, automatically transforms things into simple,
motionless images. The world is captured in the word; there is no
tentative amplification that would make us feel that something has
been left out. The brief labels isolate things by giving them sharp
outlines. Not only human beings and otherworld beings, but also all
the objects and places of the folktale are designated in this way.
The forest in which the folktale hero loses his way is always simply
named, never described. The Grimm brothers lose touch with the
style of the genuine folktale when they speak of the red eyes and
wagging head of the witch and of her long bespectacled nose (KHM
Nos. 15, 69, 193). Genuine folktales only speak of an "ugly old hag,"
an "old witch," an "evil witch," or simply an "old woman." Gerhart
Hauptmann has remarked that "Whatever one adds to the plot is
at the expense of the characters."[2] This rule applies to the folktale
as well, for the folktale consistently forgoes any individualizing
characterization. This is no loss to its construction, but gain. The
brief labels impart to all of the elements of the tale that definitive
form to which the folktale style aspires by its very nature.

Among the most frequently named things in folktales are objects
that are distinguished by sharp contours and that consist of solid
material. Rings, staffs, swords, hair, nuts, eggs, coffers, purses, and
apples pass as gifts from otherworld beings to the inhabitants of this
world. Unlike the subterranean creatures of legendry, these otherworld beings rarely live in the impenetrable thickets of the forest or

2. Gerhart Hauptmann, *Ausblicke* (Berlin: Fischer, 1924), p. 22.

in caves; the folktale gives them solid houses or castles or splendid underground lodgings. The forest witch in *Hansel and Gretel* lives in a small house that is sharply set off from its surroundings, just as both Frau Holle and the underworld devil of the Latvian folktale about Kurbads live in "a little house" in a luminous subterranean realm. The Nordic troll can be the lord of a castle;[3] even the gnome Rumpelstiltskin lives in his own little house. Again and again, the hero enters towns, castles, or rooms within whose four walls the action takes its course. "The brave youth left the chambers of white stone, walked out of the town, and went on and on, whether it was near or far, low or high—and there stood a huge barn." It is this barn that provides the setting for the following adventure.[4] How often the folktale calls up the scene in which the protagonist stays behind alone in an otherworld palace and then enters all of its rooms, one by one, even the forbidden twelfth! With what readiness it locks up the hero or the heroine in a tower, palace, trunk or chest! The human beings and the otherworld creatures of the folktale are self-contained figures with nothing indefinite about them. Even people who are sentenced to death and are torn apart by horses are not bloodily dismembered and torn to pieces, but are split neatly in two; they fall "into pieces." "At once the prince ordered his servants to tie each of the sisters to a pair of horses, one leg to each horse, and to whip the horses and drive them apart. This was done, and the sisters of the princess were thus torn into two pieces."[5] John the Bear "split the giant in two."[6] Sick princesses are cured by means of a purely mechanical treatment: they are cut into pieces and then flawlessly reassembled. Rumpelstiltskin tears himself "right in two." We see the symmetrically and sharply sundered halves, from which no blood flows and which lose none of their precision of form.

In much the same way, the folktale tends to render things and animate beings in metallic or mineral terms. Not only are towns, bridges, and shoes made of stone, iron, or glass, and houses and castles made of gold or diamonds, but forests, horses, ducks, or people can be made of gold, silver, iron, or copper, or they can suddenly turn to stone. Gems and pearls, or metal rings, keys, or bells, or golden gowns, hair, or feathers occur in almost every folktale. Golden apples are especially favored. Golden and silver pears, nuts, or flowers, tools of glass, or golden spinning wheels are some of the folktale's regular accessories. Hands, fingers, feet, or hairs are turned to silver

3. For example, Klara Strobe, ed., *Nordische Volksmärchen,* MdW (Jena: Diederichs, 1919), II, No. 24 (Norwegian).
4. August von Lewis of Menar, ed., *Russische Volksmärchen,* (Jena: Diederichs, 1927), No. 43.
5. *Balkanmärchen,* No. 17 (Bulgarian).
6. Emmanuel Cosquin, ed., *Contes populaires de Lorraine* (Paris: Vieweg, 1886), I, No. 1.

or copper. Certain folktale heroes have a golden star on their forehead or knee. The daughter of the South Slavic emperor has a star
on her forehead, a sun on her bosom, and a moon on her knee.[7] A
downpour of golden rain gilds the heroine of the tale of Frau Holle:
"Here comes our golden girl!"[8] But the antiheroine, as well, is showered with pitch or enclosed in a wooden dress that is then coated
with pitch.[9] Instead of the supple human figure, we see a rigid, black
hull. Garments made of stone, or a waistcoat[1] or trousers[2] made of
marble also occur. This predilection of the folktale for anything
metallic or mineral, for inflexible materials in general, contributes
in large measure to giving it a fixed form and well-defined shape.
This becomes especially apparent when the folktale renders living
organisms in metallic or mineral terms.

Among the metals, the folktale prefers the precious and rare: gold,
silver, copper. The flying ship is made "all of gold, the masts of silver, but the sails of silk."[3] The rare, precious object is set off against
its environment and stands alone. In addition, there is the great radi-
ance of precious metals and the stars. A golden or copper horse not
only seems unrealistic because it cannot occur in the real world, but
the sheer brilliance of its color alone strongly contrasts with any
horse in real life.

The real world shows us a richness of different hues and shadings. Blended colors are far more frequent than pure tones. By contrast, the folktale prefers clear, ultrapure colors: gold, silver, red,
white, black, and sometimes blue as well. Gold and silver have a
metallic luster, black and white are nonspecific contrasts, and red
is the least subtle of all colors and the first to attract the attention
of infants. The only blended color to appear is gray, but in the folktale gray, too, is of a metallic character. Instead of telling of a "little
gray man" (Graumännchen), the folktale sometimes speaks of a
"little iron man" (eisernes Männchen). Green, the color of living
nature, is strikingly rare. The folktale forest is a "large forest,"
sometimes a "dark forest," practically never a "green forest." The
more subtle shadings such as brown and yellowish are not found at
all. Snow White is as white as snow, as red as blood, and as black as
ebony. The sun, the moon, and the stars color and adorn the clothes
and even the bodies of princesses. The horses of folktales are black,

7. Friedrich S. Krauss, ed., Sagen und Märchen der Südslaven, II (Leipzig: Friedrich,
   1884), No. 131.
8. Johannes Bolte and Georg Polívka, Anmerkungen zu den Kinder- und Hausmärchen der
   Brüder Grimm, 5 vols. (Leipzig: Dieterich, 1913–32), I, 208.
9. See Max Lüthi, Die Gabe im Märchen und in der Sage (Bern: Francke, 1943).
1. P. Kretschmer, Neugriechische Märchen, MdW (Jena: Diederichs, 1919), No. 31
   (Cretan).
2. Balkanmärchen, No. 29 (Serbo-Croatian).
3. Russische Volksmärchen, No. 4.

white, or red;[4] there are also red sheep,[5] black men[6]—in Bulgarian folktales, as in *The Arabian Nights,* the Negro is a figure much favored[7]—and black and white wolves, billy goats, and roosters. All the same, the folktale does not overvalue colors. A rich profusion of bright colors would interfere with its strict linearity. Only a few things and persons are distinguished by a color term, and so they contrast all the more strongly with those that are colorless.

The story line of the folktale is just as sharply defined and distinct as are the outlines, substance, and color of its characters. The action of the folktale, unlike that of the legend, does not take place in a circumscribed domestic environment among an indefinite number of participants. It reaches out resolutely toward the distance and leads its few protagonists over great expanses to faraway realms—realms that stand before us as brightly illuminated and sharply outlined as does everything else. After long wanderings, a Norwegian folktale hero finally comes "in the winter to a country where all of the streets were straight and had no turnings whatsoever"[8]—a true fairy-tale landscape of wintry clarity and geometrical linearity!

Among the gifts given by otherworld helpers to folktale heroes, means of transportation are especially frequent. Fabulous horses, carriages, shoes, or overcoats carry the hero to faraway places, or a ring conveys him wherever he wishes to go. All sorts of motives are found to enable the hero or antihero to wander abroad.[9] The folktale hero is essentially a wanderer. The line of the plot unfolds before us untrammeled and clear. It is sustained by individual characters, and in the true folktale each individual character is significant to the story line. The hero is almost always alone when he sets out, even though he may be a prince or a king. He may be accompanied by a single servant, but this servant too has a function of his own,[1] and as a separate figure he is set off from his surroundings as visibly as is the hero.

4. For example, *Balkanmärchen,* No. 7 (Bulgarian).
5. A. Löwis of Menar, ed., *Finnische und estnische Volksmärchen*, MdW (Jena: Diederichs, 1922), No. 26 (Finnish).
6. *Ibid.,* No. 30 (Finnish).
7. *Balkanmärchen,* Nos. 2, 6, 12, 18 ("Everything there was black—the people, the animals, even the tsar himself").
8. *Nordische Volksmärchen,* II, No. 7 (Norwegian). A Russian folktale begins: "There once was a tsar, a mighty lord, who lived in a region as flat as a tablecloth" (*Russische Volksmärchen,* No. 43).
9. See *Gabe,* p. 95.
1. If he does not remain a truncated motif. In the Swiss folktale "Hans Tgavrêr," the princess wants to give the hero a hundred soldiers to take along on his journey. "'Certainly not, I shall go alone,' said Hans. 'No, I will not let you go like that,' she answered. So in the end he decided to take forty men along with him"—but even these he soon sends back home, and only then can his adventures begin. Leza Uffer, ed., *Rätoromanische Märchen und ihre Erzähler* (Basel: Schweizerische Gesellschaft für Volkskunde, 1945), No. 21, rpt. in Lüthi, *Europäische Volksmärchen,* p. 279, and in Uffer, *Die Märchen des Barba Plasch* (Zürich: Atlantis, 1955), p. 72.

A complete perspective is afforded by the juxtaposition and succession of narrative events rather than by their interlacement. Whatever in the real world forms an unfathomable whole or unfolds in slow, hidden development takes place in the folktale in sharply divided stages. The hero must accomplish three tasks in order to win the princess, but after that she is his once and for all: "And they lived happily ever after." "From that day forth the prince and princess lived without danger or harm."[2] Alternatively, the hero may lose his bride again, but not through her gradually turning away from him. Thanks to a certain infraction of form, usually the violation of a prohibition, she is stolen from him out of the blue, and then he takes to the road to find her again. Just as he lost her through a single mistake, he wins her back through a stroke of luck, usually at the third attempt after failing twice. No hesitation, vacillation, or half measures impede his progress or the folktale's sharp delineation of form. Right reactions or wrong reactions result in determined advances or equally determined evasions and retreats. Everything psychological is externalized onto the level of actions or objects (for example, as gifts that objectify a relationship) and thus is made distinctly and impressively manifest. Nothing remains vague or enigmatic.

Internally as well, this clear and purposeful conduct of the folktale, with its strongly colored, sharply outlined characters and its clean, ever-progressing story line, is distinguished by the most pointed effects. Its protagonists are assigned very specific tasks: they are to cure sick princesses, guard magic cows, build a golden bridge or a magnificent garden overnight, or spin a roomful of straw into gold; or they must fetch faraway magic objects, win fights against dragons and giants, defeat an enemy army, ride up a glass mountain, or ride through the air to take a golden apple from the hand of the king's daughter. Whereas the antiheroes regularly fail and often pay with their lives—for the task is usually bound up with extreme forms of reward and punishment, such as the princess and the kingdom or death—the hero succeeds in doing the impossible. He always meets precisely those otherworld beings who know or are able to do just what is necessary to accomplish the task at hand. And while, with improbable certainty, his brothers treat the otherworld beings wrongly (not always evilly!), the hero, with equal certainty and without any vacillation, treats them correctly (not always benevolently!),[3] whereupon they give him the gifts that most precisely fit the special tasks with which he is confronted. If he later must fill up one or three bowls with seeds or lentils that have been scattered,

2. *Balkanmärchen*, No. 17 (Bulgarian).
3. See *Gabe*, p. 135 (an allusion to *The Frog Prince*, KHM No. 1).

he first meets some ants who now come to his assistance, or he knows—nobody tells us why—a charm that has the power to summon pigeons, as in the Grimms' version of *Cinderella* (KHM No. 21). If he has to fetch a little ring out of the sea, the one who is indebted to him is a fish; if he has to tend colts that run away in all directions, he previously—long before he knew the difficulties that he would encounter—made friends with a fox, a wolf, and a bear whose powers are just sufficient to round up the herd.[4] If he sets out to search for a magic horse or for his lost sisters and brothers, along the way he meets a hermit or some old women who are able to give him the exact advice he needs. For all that, these advisers are by no means omniscient, but they always know whatever needs to be known at the given stage of the plot.[5]

If the hero must accomplish several tasks, the folktale frequently gives him a special helper or special charm for each. All-encompassing magic objects that can conjure up practically anything desired are rare. The hero comes in possession of a table that sets itself with food, a donkey that drops gold, or a cudgel that leaps from the sack when summoned—without exception, things endowed with a single, specific faculty. If he does happen to receive an all-encompassing magic object, he never makes full use of it.[6] The magic objects of the folktale are not meant to be used playfully, to amuse the hero or provide him with amenities or riches; rather, they are to help him get through certain very specific situations that arise in the course of the plot. Often they are made available to the hero only when he is in urgent need of them. Often he gets them long before, but even then he uses them just once or three times, at the moment when an otherwise unsolvable task calls for it. Before and after, the magic object remains unused. Sometimes the hero completely forgets what he possesses, and only in the face of the urgent task does he remember it. Once he has accomplished the task, the magic device is usually no longer mentioned; it disappears from the story. It was merely an expedient without any intrinsic value and without interest for its own sake. For the characters of the folktale not only lack a geographical and personal frame of reference; they also lack a material environment. The gifts they receive are not everyday possessions but merely flash upon the scene when the plot calls for them. Whenever the story requires, at specific turning points, they show up without fail.

In the folktale everything "clicks." The antihero falls asleep at the very moment when the crucial reconnaissance has to be made,

---

4. Zaunert, *Deutsche Märchen seit Grimm*, I, 1, rpt. in Lüthi, *Europäische Volksmärchen*, p. 301. The narrative was first printed in U. Jahn, ed., *Volksmärchen aus Pommern und Rügen*, I (Soltau: Norden, 1891).
5. See *Gabe*, pp. 61–62.
6. See *Gabe*, pp. 30–31.

whereas the hero wakes up just in time—not a moment too early nor a moment too late.[7] He arrives in the royal city on the very day on which his bride, after long refusals, is to be married to another man. Not until the flames of the pyre are licking about their sister do the twelve brothers rush up to save her, for at that very moment the seven years of enchantment have elapsed and the brothers are free.[8] Every time limit tends to be either exactly used up or exceeded by a narrow margin.[9] At the risk of having his head cut off and impaled on a stake—extreme and starkly graphic punishments are in accord with the folktale style, sharply defined and averse to all nuances—the boy who has to watch over the herd of foals and bring them back in time delays so long each night that he does not get back to the witch's courtyard until the stroke of the bell. "When the bell struck eight he was in at the gateway, and as the old woman slammed shut the portals of the gate they all but cut off his heels. 'That was just in time,' the boy breathlessly exclaimed as he entered the house. . . ."[1] Expressions such as "no sooner had he . . ." (*kaum hatte er*) or "no sooner were they . . ." (*kaum waren sie*) are idiomatic expressions that continually recur in the folktale. In French tales a favorite phrasing is, "The giant was before him in a trice" (*Le géant ne tarda pas à paraître devant lui*) or "His wife was about to . . ." (*Sa femme venait de . . .*).[2] In Rhaeto-Romanic, it is "*Bagn tgi . . .*". The marvelous runner who goes to fetch the hero the water of life falls asleep on the way back, and it is only shortly before the expiration of the allotted time that the hero's other helper, the marksman, spots the runner and awakens him, so that he arrives in the very nick of time.[3]

Not only moments of time are marked out with the utmost precision. The hero, the antihero, subordinate characters, and props also precisely accomplish or fail to accomplish the specific narrative task that is assigned to them. Objects and situations fit together to a T. "Everything fit her as if it had been tailor-made"—the marble trousers, the shirt of dew, and the shoes of pure gold, which actually were not woven or forged for the princess at all.[4] The youngest son sets out: "He wandered on and on without asking the way, until he came and stopped at the very spot where his brothers had rested years before."[5] The coffer that is destined to fall into the hands of the hero is offered

7. For example, *Balkanmärchen*, No. 23 (Serbo-Croatian).
8. Not only in Grimm but in the Yugoslavian folktale as well: *Balkanmärchen*, No. 34 (Serbo-Croatian).
9. Zaunert, *Deutsche Märchen aus dem Donaulande*, pp. 62 ff.
1. Zaunert, *Deutsche Märchen seit Grimm*, I, 1 (see note 4, p. 381).
2. See, for example, Cosquin, I, 32, 34.
3. *Russische Volksmärchen*, No. 4.
4. *Balkanmärchen*, No. 29 (Serbo-Croatian).
5. *Deutsche Märchen seit Grimm*, II, 285.

to him for 500 piasters—exactly the amount he has saved. When he later throws his wife into the river, fishermen have just cast their nets and pull the woman out of the water instead of fish. Instantly a Turk appears, the heroine tricks him out of his horse, and she rides "hour after hour, from mountain to mountain," until at nightfall she comes "unawares" to—of all places—the distant kingdom of her royal father. Her father has just died, and since he has left no legitimate heir but the lost daughter, the officers of the kingdom decide that "in this night of such severe snow and cold that anyone lying outdoors would perish, the first person to be found outside the gates of the city should be made king." The princess has just arrived there in her fisherman's clothes, and still unrecognized, she is crowned king.

There is nothing truly magical in this Albanian folktale,[6] but the abstract stylization by which the different situations dovetail is just as miraculous as any physical magic; in fact, it is far more unrealistic. Attempts at magic and a belief in magic are part of the real life of human beings. In contrast, the folktale favors abstract composition in drawing its lines.

Rounding out the abstract style[7] of the folktale are a number of other characteristics. Since most of these are familiar and have been studied for a long time, they will merely be touched on here.

The folktale works with fixed formulas. It favors the numerals one, two, three, seven, and twelve—numbers of firm definition and originally of magic significance and power. The hero or heroine either is alone or is the last member of a triad (the youngest of three children); less frequently, heroes or heroines appear as a pair, as in the tale of *The Twins or Blood-Brothers* (AT 303). This-worldly as well as otherworldly helpers and opponents appear on the scene singly (sometimes in the form of prominent leaders of a people, such as the king or prince) or in groups of three, seven, or twelve—but the latter only if their number does not at the same time serve to form episodes, for the triad rules the development of episodes. A succession of seven or twelve episodes would destroy the overall clarity of design and stability of form. The numbers seven, twelve, and one hundred are no more than stylistic formulas that embody the principle of plurality in formula-like rigidity. By contrast, pairs and triads have a structural function as well.[8] Some folktales are bipartite, with

6. *Balkanmärchen*, No. 56.
7. I am using the term after the model of Wilhelm Worringer in his 1907 Bern dissertation, *Abstraktion und Einfühlung,* published in Munich by R. Piper & Co. in 1908 and frequently reprinted thereafter, most recently in 1959. For basic remarks pertaining to this work, see *Gabe*, p. 28 n., and my article *Abstraktheit* in the *Enzyklopädie des Märchens,* I (Berlin and New York: de Gruyter, 1977), cols. 34–36.
8. See further Mackensen, p. 309. That the original magic and power of the sacred numbers still find a faint echo in the folktale is emphasized by Karl Justus Obenauer in *Das Märchen: Dichtung und Deutung* (Frankfurt: Kostermann, 1959), pp. 93–127.

the recovery of the lost spouse forming the second part. But it is above all the triad that is predominant: three tasks are accomplished in succession; three times a helper intervenes; three times an adversary appears. Since each gift that is presented to the hero is usually intended to resolve a single episode, the folktale prefers to mention three gifts, not seven, let alone twelve.

To a high degree, this preference for formulaic round numbers imparts a rigid quality to the folktale. Unlike the real world, the folktale knows nothing of numerical diversity and randomness; it aspires to abstract certainty. This aspiration is also evident in the verbatim repetition of entire sentences and long paragraphs. If the same event is repeated, it makes sense to state it in identical terms. Many storytellers avoid variation, not out of incompetence but because of stylistic demands. Strict word-for-word repetition, when it occurs, is an element of the folktale's abstract style. Such rigidity corresponds to that of the metals and minerals that abound in the folktale. Sentences repeated verbatim at certain intervals also have an articulating role. Like a rhythmically recurring ornament, they ring out in the corresponding parts of the story at certain specified points.[9] A similar result is produced by the recurrence of an individual expression within a sentence. When the word "bellissimo" is repeated four times in the course of eleven lines (*un bellissimo cavallo, un bellissimo prato, un bellissimo giardino,* and once again *un bellissimo prato*),[1] we perceive an articulating effect that would not be produced if different adjectives were employed in each instance. Thus, the folktale almost spontaneously achieves a consistency of style of the sort that modern aesthetics requires of true works of art: the special character of the overall composition is reflected in its constituent parts, right down to the individual verbal expression.

The fixed metrical and rhyming tags and the opening and closing formulas of the folktale likewise serve to stabilize its form. The clear single-strandedness (*Einsträngigkeit*) of its plot signifies an emphatic refusal to portray directly anything that is many-layered or interpenetrating. Only a single sharply defined plot line is evident. A necessary correlative of the folktale's single-stranded plot is the division of this plot into more than one episode (*Mehrgliedrigkeit*). Legends, which are nonepisodic, give us space, depth, stratification, atmosphere. The narrow line of the folktale plot is sustained by a plurality of episodes. Things that normally interpenetrate and coexist are

9. This principle is beautifully illustrated in the Lotharingian folktale of "Le Roi d'Angleterre et son filleul" (Cosquin, I, 32 ff.; German trans. in Lüthi, *Europäische Volksmärchen,* p. 150).
1. Giuseppe Pitrè, ed., *Novelle popolari Toscane,* I (Rome: Soc. Editrice del Libro Italiano, 1941), 3.

detached and isolated, and their projection onto the story line makes them successive.[2] Thus, single-strandedness and episodic structure are the foundation and the preconditions of the abstract style.

When every year the queen gives birth to a child, or even to two boys, each with golden curls and of ideal beauty, this is as much part of the abstract style of the folktale as when a gold coin or a golden ring falls out of the heroine's mouth with her every (!) word, or when the dragon must receive a human sacrifice every day or every month, or when a dwarf appears with each note of a magic flute. All of the tsar's daughter's husbands die on the very first night.[3] The folktale king is prepared to kill all of his twelve sons if he is given just one daughter; or he seeks and finds in his kingdom "eleven girls, each the perfect likeness of his daughter in countenance, figure, and size" (KHM No. 67). The sister who is to rescue her brothers keeps absolute silence unfailingly and steadfastly for seven years. Ninety-nine suitors are beheaded, but the hundredth accomplishes the task and wins the princess. A house in the forest is made entirely of gingerbread or of human bones. All this is abstract representation that is far removed from any concrete reality.

The folktale has a liking for all extremes, extreme contrasts in particular. Its characters are completely beautiful and good or completely ugly and bad; they are either poor or rich, spoiled or cast out, very industrious or completely lazy. The hero is either a king's son or a peasant's son; he is either a scurfhead or a golden boy (frequently first one and then the other, by an abrupt change); the princess marries the country bumpkin; the horse is either golden or mangy; and the gift that the hero receives either shines like gold or looks completely undistinguished. Whereas the antiheroes are magnificently provided with clothes and horses and cake, the hero must get by with crusts of bread and lame nags (or he asks for no more than these).[4]

---

2. Occasional attempts at maintaining parallel plot lines, as with the simultaneous departure of two or three brothers, disappear before the dominant preference of the folktale for plots of a single strand (*Einsträngigkeit*). A modern narrator from Lorraine enjoys to the full, with heavy-handed transitions, the unaccustomed refinement of a double-stranded plot: "Now we leave the lad in the garden and go back, we return to Rosamunde and see how things are going there." Or: "Now we leave the pilgrims again and follow the lad." See Angelika Merkelbach-Pinck, ed., *Lothringer erzählen*, I (Saarbrücken: Saarbrücker Druckerei, 1936), 226, 230. For a similar effect see Plasch Spinas, another present-day folktale narrator, in Leza Uffer, ed., *Rätoromanische Märchen*, No. 21, trans. in Lüthi, *Europäische Volksmärchen*, p. 279: "Now let us leave him to prepare the sticks while we return to the princess, because he needed about three weeks to cut sticks for all the goats." See also a modern Greek tale: "Now let us leave the princess to wail and to search for him everywhere, and let us turn to the sugar merchant and his wife" (*Neugriechische Märchen*, No. 53). Cf. Bolte-Polívka, IV: 22–24.

3. *Balkanmärchen*, No. 2 (Bulgarian). In the frame story of *The Arabian Nights*, it is king Shahriar who every night for three years takes a beautiful girl as his wife, but has her head cut off at dawn; this is at once more rational and more realistic than the unreasonable and unexplained nonviolent death of the husbands in the Bulgarian folktale.

4. For example, *Balkanmärchen*, Nos. 42 and 43 (Serbo-Croatian), *Russische Volksmärchen*, No. 41.

The contrasting figures of the folktale are coated with either pitch or gold; cruel punishments and the highest rewards are set off against one another. The hero or heroine is usually an only child or is the youngest of three; frequently he or she appears as a simpleton or ashmaid. The folktale often tells of childless couples, or then again of couples with a superabundance of children. Parents die and leave their children all alone. The hero and heroine are young, but their advisers are old men and women. Hermits, beggars, and one-eyed persons come on the scene. Shabby garments or stark nakedness appear side by side with precious furs. The hero may be as strong as a bear, but the helpless heroine is surrendered to a monster. Otherworld beings take the forms of giants or dwarves. Heinous crimes, fratricide, infanticide, and malicious slander are everyday features of the folktale, as are gruesome methods of punishment. The folktale's many prohibitions and strict conditions contribute in no small way to the elaboration of its precise style.

Miracles are the quintessence of all extremes and bring the abstract style to its most pointed expression. When the peasant woman, the maid, and the mare all eat part of the talking fish, each gives birth to a son the very next night.[5] The magic ointment immediately restores the blind man's sight and brings the dead back to life.[6] Sick people are cured by being dismembered and put back together again.[7] Abrupt metamorphoses dazzle the eye. "While he was asleep, the rose leaped down from his hat and turned into a beautiful girl who sat down at the table and ate up everything served."[8] The animal bridegroom no sooner casts off his hedgehog hide than he is revealed as a handsome young man.[9] "As the princess lay there they stuck a needle into her right ear, and immediately she turned into a bird and flew away."[1] The two states of being need not be internally related. The evil queen turns her three stepsons first into three brass candlesticks, then into three clods of earth, and finally into three wolves.[2] A fox is transformed into a beautiful shop;[3] a dragon turns into a boar, the boar into a hare, and the hare into a pigeon;[4] a witch changes into a bed or a fountain;[5] a princess turns into a lemon or a fish, then into a lump of silver, and finally into a beautiful linden tree.[6] A reed turns into a silver dress or

5. *Lettisch-litauische Volksmärchen*, No. 1 (Latvian).
6. *Balkanmärchen*, No. 36 (Serbo-Croatian); *Lettisch-litauische Volksmärchen*, No. 1.
7. *Finnische und estnische Volksmärchen*, No. 31 (Finnish).
8. *Balkanmärchen*, No. 35 (Serbo-Croatian).
9. *Ibid.*, No. 33 (Serbo-Croatian).
1. *Ibid.*, No. 17 (Serbo-Croatian).
2. *Irische Volksmärchen*, No. 21.
3. Zaunert, *Deutsche Märchen aus dem Donaulande*, p. 315; cf. *Gabe*, p. 63.
4. *Balkanmärchen*, No. 26 (Serbo-Croatian); cf. Zaunert, *Deutsche Märchen seit Grimm*, I, 133.
5. *Lettisch-litauische Volksmärchen*, No. 26 (Latvian).
6. *Nordische Volksmärchen*, II, No. 4 (Norwegian).

into a dun horse.[7] A large castle can be changed into an egg and back again at will.[8] In a Lithuanian folktale, the wolf says to the simpleton: "Slaughter me! Then my body will turn into a boat, my tongue into a rudder, and my entrails into three dresses, three pairs of shoes, and three rings." Subsequently, after the simpleton has made use of all these things, the wolf comes back to life and carries him and his princess to their destination.[9] Nothing is too drastic or too remote for the folktale. The more mechanical and extreme the metamorphosis, the more clearly and precisely it unfolds before us.

The abstract stylization of the folktale gives it luminosity and firm definition. Such stylization is not the product of incapacity or incompetence, but of a high degree of formative power. With marvelous consistency it permeates all elements of the folktale and lends them fixed contours and a sublime weightlessness. It is far removed from lifeless rigidity, for the rapid and emphatic advance of the plot is an integral part of it. The hero is a wanderer who effortlessly moves across vast expanses, often carried at the speed of the wind by flying horses, carriages, coats, or magic shoes. His progress is not arbitrary, however, for its form, direction, and laws are precisely determined. The diagrammatic style of the folktale gives it stability and shape; the epic-like forward progression of the plot gives it quickness and life. Firm form and effortless elegance combine to form a unified whole. Pure and clear, with joyous, weightless mobility, the folktale observes the most stringent laws.

SANDRA M. GILBERT AND SUSAN GUBAR

[Snow White and Her Wicked Stepmother][†]

As the legend of Lilith[1] shows, and as psychoanalysts from Freud and Jung onward have observed, myths and fairy tales often both state and enforce culture's sentences with greater accuracy than more sophisticated literary texts. If Lilith's story summarizes the genesis of the female monster in a single useful parable, the Grimm tale of "Little Snow White" dramatizes the essential but equivocal relationship between the angel-woman and the monster-woman. * * * "Little Snow White," which Walt Disney entitled "Snow White and the Seven Dwarves," should really be called Snow White and Her

---

7. *Irische Volksmärchen,* No. 20.
8. *Lettisch-litauische Volksmärchen,* No. 26.
9. *Ibid.*
† From Sandra M. Gilbert and Susan Gubar, *The Madwoman in the Attic: The Woman Writer and the Nineteenth-Century Literary Imagination* (New Haven, CT: Yale UP, 1979), pp. 36–43. Copyright © 1979. Reprinted by permission of Yale University Press.
1. Adam's first wife, before Eve was created.

Wicked Stepmother, for the central action of the tale—indeed, its only real action—arises from the relationship between these two women: the one fair, young, pale, the other just as fair, but older, fiercer; the one a daughter, the other a mother; the one sweet, ignorant, passive, the other both artful and active; the one a sort of angel, the other an undeniable witch.

Significantly, the conflict between these two women is fought out largely in the transparent enclosures into which * * * both have been locked: a magic looking glass, an enchanted and enchanting glass coffin. Here, wielding as weapons the tools patriarchy suggests that women use to kill themselves into art, the two women literally try to kill each other with art. Shadow fights shadow, image destroys image in the crystal prison. * * *

The story begins in midwinter, with a Queen sitting and sewing, framed by a window. As in so many fairy tales, she pricks her finger, bleeds, and is thereby assumed into the cycle of sexuality William Blake called the realm of "generation," giving birth "soon after" to a daughter "as white as snow, as red as blood, and as black as the wood of the window frame."[2] All the motifs introduced in this prefatory first paragraph—sewing, snow, blood, enclosure—are associated with key themes in female lives (hence in female writing). But for our purposes here the tale's opening is merely prefatory. The real story begins when the Queen, having become a mother, metamorphoses also into a witch—that is, into a wicked "step" mother: ". . . when the child was born, the Queen died," and "After a year had passed the King took to himself another wife."

When we first encounter this "new" wife, she is framed in a magic looking glass, just as her predecessor—that is, her earlier self—had been framed in a window. To be caught and trapped in a mirror rather than a window, however, is to be driven inward, obsessively studying self-images as if seeking a viable self. The first Queen seems still to have had prospects; not yet fallen into sexuality, she looked outward, if only upon the snow. The second Queen is doomed to the inward search that psychoanalysts like Bruno Bettelheim censoriously define as "narcissism,"[3] but which * * * is necessitated by a state from which all outward prospects have been removed.

That outward prospects have been removed—or lost or dissolved away—is suggested not only by the Queen's mirror obsession but by the absence of the King from the story as it is related in the Grimm version. The Queen's husband and Snow White's father (for whose

2. "Little Snow White." All references are to the text as given in *The Complete Grimm's Fairy Tales* (New York: Random House, 1972).
3. Bruno Bettelheim, *The Uses of Enchantment: The Meaning and Importance of Fairy Tales* (New York: Knopf, 1976), pp. 202–03.

attentions, according to Bettelheim, the two women are battling in a feminized Oedipal struggle) never actually appears in this story at all, a fact that emphasizes the almost stifling intensity with which the tale concentrates on the conflict in the mirror between mother and daughter, woman and woman, self and self. At the same time, though, there is clearly at least one way in which the King *is* present. His, surely, is the voice of the looking glass, the patriarchal voice of judgment that rules the Queen's—and every woman's—self-evaluation. He it is who decides, first, that his consort is "the fairest of all," and then, as she becomes maddened, rebellious, witchlike, that she must be replaced by his angelically innocent and dutiful daughter, a girl who is therefore defined as "more beautiful still" than the Queen. To the extent, then, that the King, and only the King, constituted the first Queen's prospects, he need no longer appear in the story because, having assimilated the meaning of her own sexuality (and having, thus, become the second Queen) the woman has internalized the King's rules: his voice resides now in her own mirror, her own mind.

But if Snow White is "really" the daughter of the second as well as of the first Queen (i.e., if the two Queens are identical), why does the Queen hate her so much? The traditional explanation—that the mother is as threatened by her daughter's "budding sexuality" as the daughter is by the mother's "possession" of the father—is helpful but does not seem entirely adequate, considering the depth and ferocity of the Queen's rage. It is true, of course, that in the patriarchal Kingdom of the text these women inhabit the Queen's life can be literally imperiled by her daughter's beauty, and true (as we shall see throughout this study) that, given the female vulnerability such perils imply, female bonding is extraordinarily difficult in patriarchy: women almost inevitably turn against women because the voice of the looking glass sets them against each other. But, beyond all this, it seems as if there is a sense in which the intense desperation with which the Queen enacts her rituals of self-absorption causes (or is caused by) her hatred of Snow White. Innocent, passive, and selflessly free of the mirror madness that consumes the Queen, Snow White represents the ideal of renunciation that the Queen has already renounced at the beginning of the story. Thus Snow White is destined to replace the Queen *because* the Queen hates her, rather than vice versa. The Queen's hatred of Snow White, in other words, exists before the looking glass has provided an obvious reason for hatred.

For the Queen, as we come to see more clearly in the course of the story, is a plotter, a plot-maker, a schemer, a witch, an artist, an impersonator, a woman of almost infinite creative energy, witty, wily, and self-absorbed as all artists traditionally are. On the other hand, in her absolute chastity, her frozen innocence, her sweet nullity, Snow White represents precisely the ideal of "contemplative purity" we have already discussed, an ideal that could quite literally kill the Queen. An angel in the house of myth, Snow White is not only a child but (as female angels always are) childlike, docile, submissive, the heroine of a life that *has no story*. But the Queen, adult and demonic, plainly wants a life of "significant action," by definition an "unfeminine" life of stories and storytelling. And therefore, to the extent that Snow White, as her daughter, is a part of herself, she wants to kill the Snow White *in herself*, the angel who would keep deeds and dramas out of her own house.

The first death plot the Queen invents is a naively straightforward murder story: she commands one of her huntsmen to kill Snow White. But, as Bruno Bettelheim has shown, the huntsman is really a surrogate for the King, a parental—or, more specifically, patriarchal—figure "who dominates, controls, and subdues wild ferocious beasts" and who thus "represents the subjugation of the animal, asocial, violent tendencies in man."[4] In a sense, then, the Queen has foolishly asked her patriarchal master to act for her in doing the subversive deed she wants to do in part to retain power over him and in part to steal his power from him. Obviously, he will not do this. As patriarchy's angelic daughter, Snow White is, after all, *his* child, and he must save her, not kill her. Hence he kills a wild boar in her stead, and brings its lung and liver to the Queen as proof that he has murdered the child. Thinking that she is devouring her ice-pure enemy, therefore, the Queen consumes, instead, the wild boar's organs; that is, symbolically speaking, she devours her own beastly rage, and becomes (of course) even more enraged.

When she learns that her first plot has failed, then, the Queen's storytelling becomes angrier as well as more inventive, more sophisticated, more subversive. Significantly, each of the three "tales" she tells—that is, each of the three plots she invents—depends on a poisonous or parodic use of a distinctively female device as a murder weapon, and in each case she reinforces the sardonic commentary on "femininity" that such weaponry makes by impersonating a "wise" woman, a "good" mother, or, as Ellen Moers would put it, an "educating heroine."[5] As a "kind" old pedlar woman, she offers to lace Snow White "properly" for once—then suffocates her with a very Victorian set of tight laces. As another wise old expert in female beauty, she promises to comb Snow White's hair "properly," then assaults her with a poisonous comb. Finally, as a wholesome farmer's wife, she gives Snow White a "very poisonous apple," which she has

4. Bettelheim, p. 205.
5. See Ellen Moers, *Literary Women* (New York: Doubleday, 1976), pp. 211–42.

made in "a quite secret, lonely room, where no one ever came." The girl finally falls, killed, so it seems, by the female arts of cosmetology and cookery. Paradoxically, however, even though the Queen has been using such feminine wiles as the sirens' comb and Eve's apple subversively, to destroy angelic Snow White so that she (the Queen) can assert and aggrandize herself, these arts have had on her daughter an opposite effect from those she intended. Strengthening the chaste maiden in her passivity, they have made her into precisely the eternally beautiful, inanimate *objet d'art* patriarchal aesthetics want a girl to be. From the point of view of the mad, self-assertive Queen, conventional female arts *kill*. But from the point of view of the docile and selfless princess, such arts, even while they kill, confer the only measure of power available to a woman in a patriarchal culture.

Certainly when the kindly huntsman-father saved her life by abandoning her in the forest at the edge of his kingdom, Snow White discovered her own powerlessness. Though she had been allowed to live because she was a "good" girl, she had to find her own devious way of resisting the onslaughts of the maddened Queen, both inside and outside her self. In this connection, the seven dwarves probably represent her own dwarfed powers, her stunted selfhood, for, as Bettelheim points out, they can do little to help save the girl from the Queen. At the same time, however, her life with them is an important part of her education in submissive femininity, for in serving them she learns essential lessons of service, of selflessness, of domesticity. Finally, that at this point Snow White is a housekeeping angel in a *tiny* house conveys the story's attitude toward "woman's world and woman's work": the realm of domesticity is a miniaturized kingdom in which the best of women is not only like a dwarf but like a dwarf's servant.

Does the irony and bitterness consequent upon such a perception lead to Snow White's few small acts of disobedience? Or would Snow White ultimately have rebelled anyway, precisely because she *is* the Queen's true daughter? The story does not, of course, answer such questions, but it does seem to imply them, since its turning point comes from Snow White's significant willingness to be tempted by the Queen's "gifts," despite the dwarves' admonitions. Indeed, the only hint of self-interest that Snow White displays throughout the whole story comes in her "narcissistic" desire for the stay-laces, the comb, and the apple that the disguised murderess offers. As Bettelheim remarks, this "suggests how close the stepmother's temptations are to Snow White's inner desires."[6] Indeed, it suggests that, as we have already noted, the Queen and Snow White are in some

6. Bettelheim, p. 211.

sense one: while the Queen struggles to free herself from the passive Snow White in herself, Snow White must struggle to repress the assertive Queen in herself. That both women eat from the same deadly apple in the third temptation episode merely clarifies and dramatizes this point. The Queen's lonely art has enabled her to contrive a two-faced fruit—one white and one red "cheek"—that represents her ambiguous relationship to this angelic girl who is both her daughter and her enemy, her self and her opposite. Her intention is that the girl will die of the apple's poisoned red half—red with her sexual energy, her assertive desire for deeds of blood and triumph—while she herself will be unharmed by the passivity of the white half.

But though at first this seems to have happened, the apple's effect is, finally, of course, quite different. After the Queen's artfulness has killed Snow White into art, the girl becomes if anything even more dangerous to her "step" mother's autonomy than she was before, because even more opposed to it in both mind and body. For, dead and self-less in her glass coffin, she is an object, to be displayed and desired, patriarchy's marble "opus," the decorative and decorous Galatea[7] with whom every ruler would like to grace his parlor. Thus, when the Prince first sees Snow White in her coffin, he begs the dwarves to give "it" to him as a gift, "for I cannot live without seeing Snow White. I will honor and prize her as my dearest possession." An "it," a possession, Snow White has become an idealized image of herself, and as such she has definitively proven herself to be patriarchy's ideal woman, the perfect candidate for Queen. At this point, therefore, she regurgitates the poison apple (whose madness had stuck in her throat) and rises from her coffin. The fairest in the land, she will marry the most powerful in the land; bidden to their wedding, the egotistically assertive, plotting Queen will become a former Queen, dancing herself to death in red-hot iron shoes.

What does the future hold for Snow White, however? When her Prince becomes a King and she becomes a Queen, what will her life be like? Trained to domesticity by her dwarf instructors, will she sit in the window, gazing out on the wild forest of her past, and sigh, and sew, and prick her finger, and conceive a child white as snow, red as blood, black as ebony wood? Surely, fairest of them all, Snow White has exchanged one glass coffin for another, delivered from the prison where the Queen put her only to be imprisoned in the looking glass from which the King's voice speaks daily. There is, after all, no female model for her in this tale except the "good" (dead) mother and her living avatar the "bad" mother. And if Snow White

7. An ivory statue carved by Pygmalion and brought to life by Aphrodite in response to the sculptor's longing for his creation [editor's note].

escaped her first glass coffin by her goodness, her passivity and docility, her only escape from her second glass coffin, the imprisoning mirror, must evidently be through "badness," through plots and stories, duplicitous schemes, wild dreams, fierce fictions, mad impersonations. The cycle of her fate seems inexorable. Renouncing "contemplative purity," she must now embark on that life of "significant action" which, for a woman, is defined as a witch's life because it is so monstrous, so unnatural.* * * She will become a murderess bent on the self-slaughter implicit in her murderous attempts against the life of her own child. Finally, in fiery shoes that parody the costumes of femininity as surely as the comb and stays she herself contrived, she will do a silent terrible death-dance out of the story, the looking glass, the transparent coffin of her own image. Her only deed, this death will imply, can be a deed of death, her only action the pernicious action of self-destruction.

In this connection, it seems especially significant that the Queen's dance of death is a silent one. In "The Juniper Tree" [245–52], a version of "Little Snow White" in which a *boy's* mother tries to kill him (for different reasons, of course), the dead boy is transformed not into a silent art object but into a furious golden bird who sings a song of vengeance against his murderess and finally crushes her to death with a millstone. The male child's progress toward adulthood is a growth toward both self-assertion and self-articulation, "The Juniper Tree" implies, a development of the *powers* of speech. But the girl child must learn the arts of silence either as herself a silent image invented and defined by the magic looking glass of the male-authored text, or as a silent dancer of her own woes, a dancer who enacts rather than articulates.

KAREN E. ROWE

From To Spin a Yarn: The Female Voice in Folklore and Fairy Tale[†]

I begin not, as one might expect, with a *conte de fées* or a *Märchen*[1] but instead with a story, which provides us with a more ancient paradigm for understanding the female voice in folklore and fairy tale. But to speak about voice in a tale so singularly about the voiceless is immediately to recognize that to tell a tale for women may be a

---

[†] From Karen E. Rowe, "To Spin a Yarn: The Female Voice in Folklore and Fairy Tale," in *Fairy Tales and Society: Illusion, Allusion, and Paradigm*, ed. Ruth B. Bottigheimer (Philadelphia: U of Pennsylvania P, 1986), pp. 53–73. Copyright © 1986. Reprinted by permission of the University of Pennsylvania Press.

1. French and German terms for "fairy tale," respectively [editor's note].

way of breaking enforced silences. I refer to Ovid's account in the *Metamorphoses* of Philomela and Procne, which in Western tradition can serve as a type for the narrative power of the female, capable of weaving in tapestry the brutal story of rape that leads to the enactment of a terrible revenge.[2] Since the image of Philomela as weaver and nightingale becomes the quintessential type of the woman as tale-teller, it is best to review the story, noticing Ovid's preoccupation with the varieties of utterance and silence and the analogy that can be drawn between the story of Philomela and the art of creating a tale itself. Based upon this paradigm we can begin to explore the lineage of women as tale-tellers in a history that stretches from Philomela and Scheherazade to the raconteurs of French *veillées*[3] and salons, to English peasants, governesses, and novelists, and to the German *Spinnerinnen*[4] and the Brothers Grimm. It is a complex history, which I can only highlight in this essay.

To return to Ovid. With "flame bursting out of his breast," Tereus, as Ovid recounts, in his "unbridled passion" is granted a perverse eloquence (p. 144). Although he disguises them as the pleadings of a "most devoted husband," the "crime-contriver" Tereus speaks only false reassurances of protection, honor, and kinship (p. 144). The voyage to Thrace accomplished, Tereus violently seizes Philomela and

> told her then
> What he was going to do, and straightway did it,
> Raped her, a virgin, all alone, and calling
> For her father, for her sister, but most often
> For the great gods. In vain. (p. 146)

Trembling "as a frightened lamb which a gray wolf has mangled," she vows to "proclaim" the vile ravishment, to "go where people are / Tell everybody," and "if there is any god in Heaven, [He] will hear me" (pp. 146, 147). Fearing already the potency of Philomela's voice, the cruel king Tereus

> seized her tongue
> With pincers, though it cried against the outrage,
> Babbled and made a sound something like *Father,*
> Till the sword cut it off. The mangled root
> Quivered, the severed tongue along the ground
> Lay quivering, making a little murmur,

2. Ovid, *Metamorphoses,* trans. Rolfe Humphries (Bloomington: Indiana University Press, 1963), bk. 6, pp. 143–51. All future references from book 6 will be cited parenthetically in the text by page.
3. Evening gatherings [editor's note].
4. German for "female spinners" [editor's note].

Jerking and twitching . . .
                        . . . [and] even then, Tereus
Took her, and took her again, the injured body
Still giving satisfaction to his lust. (p. 147)

What Tereus has injured, we might keep in mind, is not only the organ of speech, but the orifice of sexuality itself—and when the ravaged Philomela speaks later through another medium, it is on behalf of a body and spirit doubly mutilated. Philomela, who supposedly lacks the "power of speech / To help her tell her wrongs," discovers that

                              grief has taught her
Sharpness of wit, and cunning comes in trouble.
She had a loom to work with, and with purple
On a white background, wove her story in,
Her story in and out, and when it was finished,
Gave it to one old woman, with signs and gestures
To take it to the queen, so it was taken,
Unrolled and understood. (p. 148)

Remember too this old woman, whose servant status belies her importance as a conveyor of the tale. Having comprehended her sister's woven story, Procne enacts a dreadful punishment. She slaughters, stews, and skewers her beloved son Itys as a fitting banquet for the lustful defiler of flesh, Tereus, doomed to feast greedily "on the flesh of his own flesh" (p. 150). As we know, the gods intervene to thwart a further cycle of vengeance by transforming Tereus into a bird of prey (the hoopoe or a hawk), Philomela into the onomatopoetic image of the quivering tongue as a twittering swallow, and Procne into the nightingale. The Romans (with greater sense of poetic justice) transposed the names, making Philomela into the nightingale who sings eternally the melancholy tale of betrayal, rape, and maternal sorrow. As such, she comes down to us as the archetypal tale-teller, one who not only weaves the revelatory tapestry but also sings the song which Ovid appropriates as his myth.[5]

Ovid's account forces upon us the analogy between weaving or spinning and tale-telling. Classicist Edith Hamilton elaborates upon this connection by noting that "Philomela's case looked hopeless. She was shut up; she could not speak; in those days there was no writing. . . . However, although people then could not write, they could tell a story without speaking because they were marvelous craftsmen. . . . The women . . . could weave, into the lovely stuffs they made, forms so lifelike anyone could see what tale they

5. See also Cheryl Walker, *The Nightingale's Burden: Women Poets and American Culture Before 1900* (Bloomington: Indiana University Press, 1982), pp. 21–22.

illustrated. Philomela accordingly turned to her loom. She had a greater motive to make clear the story she wove than any artist ever had."[6] And when Procne "unrolled the web . . . with horror she read what had happened, all as plain to her as if in print." What is notable about Hamilton's account is the ease with which she elides the acts of weaving or spinning, narrating a tale in pictorial or "graphic" terms, and writing that is to be read and understood by the comprehending audience. But Hamilton's elisions find their basis in the semiotics of Greek itself, which Ann Bergren brilliantly analyzes in her study "Language and the Female in Early Greek Thought."[7] Bergren argues cogently that "the semiotic[8] activity peculiar to women throughout Greek tradition is not linguistic. Greek women do not speak, they weave. Semiotic woman is a weaver. Penelope is, of course, the paradigm," to which we might add, among others, Helen, Circe, the Fates, and Philomela. But the semiotic relationships are far more complicated. For if women weave and use the woven object, be it tapestry or robe, as a medium for narrating the truth, it must also be recalled that Greek culture inherited from Indo-European culture a tradition in which poets metaphorically defined their art as "weaving" or "sewing" words. Having appropriated the terms of what was "originally and literally woman's work par excellence," as Bergren illustrates, Greek poets "call their product, in effect, a 'metaphorical web.'" Bergren's emphasis falls upon the male appropriation of women's peculiar craft of spinning as a semiotic equivalent for the art of creating Greek poetry itself. For my purposes, the intimate connection, both literal and metaphoric, between weaving and telling a story also establishes the cultural and literary frameworks within which women transmit not only tapestries that tell stories, but also later folklore and fairy tales. In this respect, Bergren's analysis of Philomela again becomes germane, for she writes: "Philomela, according to Apollodorus (3.14.8), *huphēnasa en peplōi grammata* 'wove pictures / writing (*grammata* can mean either) in a robe' which she sent to her sister. Philomela's trick reflects the 'trickiness' of weaving, its uncanny ability to make meaning out of inarticulate matter, to make silent material speak. In this way, women's weaving is, as *grammata*

6. Edith Hamilton, *Mythology: Timeless Tales of Gods and Heroes* (New York: New American Library, 1940), pp. 270–71.
7. Ann L. T. Bergren, "Language and the Female in Early Greek Thought," *Arethusa* 16, nos. 1 and 2 (Spring and Fall 1983): 71. See also Ann L. T. Bergren, "Helen's Web: Time and Tableau in the Iliad," *Helios*, n.s. seven, no. 1 (1980): 19–34. For discussions of the shifting aesthetic theories of the relationship between art and literature, picture and poesy, see Wendy Steiner, *The Colors of Rhetoric: Problems in the Relation between Modern Literature and Painting* (Chicago: University of Chicago Press, 1982); and Richard Wendorf, ed., *Articulated Images: The Sister Arts from Hogarth to Tennyson* (Minneapolis: University of Minnesota Press, 1983).
8. Pertaining to signs [editor's note].

implies, a 'writing' or graphic art, a silent, material representation of audible, immaterial speech." Similarly, when later women become tale-tellers or *sages femmes,* their "audible" art is likewise associated with their cultural function as silent spinners or weavers, and they employ the folk or fairy tale as a "speaking" (whether oral or literary) representation of the silent matter of their lives, which is culture itself.

What then are the multiple levels through which Philomela's tale is told, that is, in which the silent tapestry is made to speak so graphically? First, we might acknowledge the actuality of Tereus' rape itself, the truth of an act which is re-presented to us in various forms. When Philomela threatens to seek an audience to whom she will tell her story, Tereus belatedly recognizes the terrible power of the woman's voice to speak, and by a possible psychological displacement, of the fear he harbors that the woman's body will reveal the foul ravishment by generating illegitimate offspring. This double recognition that both tongue and body may speak of his unspeakable act explains why Tereus must not only sever Philomela's tongue but imprison her in the woods as well, removed from society and unable to communicate her sorry fate in either way.

Second, Philomela turns in her agony to the mainstay of women's domestic life, the spinning enjoined upon women both by ancient practice and by the later biblical portrait in Proverbs (31:10–31) of the virtuous woman. She who spins is the model of the good woman and wife and, presumably, in many cultures of the subservient woman who knows her duty—that is, to remain silent and betray no secrets. Philomela, tongueless though she may be, creates a tapestry that becomes her voice. Ironically, Philomela, the innocent woman who spins, becomes the avenging woman who breaks her enforced silence by simply speaking in another mode—through a craft presumed to be harmlessly domestic, as fairy tales would also be regarded in later centuries. What is significant, however, is that Philomela's tapestry becomes the first "telling," a *grammata* (woven picture/writing) that fulfills the verbal threat previously uttered, yet so cruelly foreshortened. It is the first remove from the actual rape as an event, done this time through a medium which "writes" (*graphein*) that truth in a style governed by the conventions of pictorial narration.

Third, the tapestry, woven strand by strand, becomes itself a metaphor for Ovid's patiently detailed rendering of the myth in words. Ovid, the skilled craftsman of Roman storytelling, in a sense semiotically resembles Philomela, whose distinctive female craft is weaving. Ovid further stylizes the tale in one further remove from the act when he attaches the transformation or metamorphosis of Philomela into a swallow and Procne into a nightingale. That metamorphosis presents us with another way of envisioning the relationship of Philomela's story to Ovid's. We might conclude that Ovid himself has heard the nightingale's singing (as the emperor would later do in Hans Christian Andersen's "The Nightingale") and has articulated it for us, as part of his sequence of tales which comprise the *Metamorphoses*. Nonetheless, the event and threatened telling, the tapestry that speaks, and the eternal song of lament that retells all originate with Philomela, though we know them only through the crafted version of Ovid's poetic art.

The paradigm that I envision is, therefore, twofold. First, Philomela as a woman who weaves tales and sings songs becomes the prototype for the female storytellers of later tradition, those *sages femmes* whose role is to transmit the secret truths of culture itself. It is critical to note, as I hinted earlier, that the conveyor of the tapestry is herself an old and trusted servant woman, who takes the tapestry through which the voiceless Philomela speaks to the sister, Procne, who reads and understands the depiction. Similarly, I might suggest that in the history of folktale and fairy tale, women as storytellers have woven or spun their yarns, speaking at one level to a total culture, but at another to a sisterhood of readers who will understand the hidden language, the secret revelations of the tale. Second, Ovid, the male poet, by appropriating Philomela's story as the subject of his myth also metaphorically reinforces the connection between weaving and the art of storytelling. Through his appropriation, he lays claim to or attempts to imitate the semiotic activity of woman par excellence— weaving, by making his linguistic recounting an equivalent, or perhaps implicitly superior version of the original graphic tapestry. Like Zeus, as Ann Bergren details, who incorporates his wife, Metis, and gives birth to the virgin Athena, so too Ovid seeks to control the female power of transformative intelligence, that power which enabled Metis to shift and change shapes. Despite its primacy as a literary text, Ovid's account is nonetheless a retold version, having already been truthfully represented through the peculiarly female medium of weaving, and only imitatively represented to us through the creative, transformative power of poetic art—the weaving of a tale in a second sense. In Ovid's tale itself, Tereus more brutally attempts to usurp speech, not only by cutting out the female tongue with which Philomela threatens to "speak" of his crimes, but also by contriving a false story of her death in a duplicitous and ultimately fatal misrepresentation of reality. To appropriate the tongue/text and the fictive-making function, for both Tereus and Ovid, is fraught with triumph *and* terror, for both only approximate the truth and can do no more than render a twice-old tale.

When the French scholar Antoine Galland first translated *The Book of the Thousand Nights and a Night* from Arabic into French

(1704–17), he retitled them *Arabian Nights Entertainments,* no doubt heightening the appeal to the French court's sophisticated taste for exotic delights.[9] When we conjure up *The Arabian Nights,* we are also likely to think first of discrete tales, primarily masculine adventures ("Ali Baba and the Forty Thieves," "Aladdin; or, The Wonderful Lamp," or "Sinbad"), recalling neither the narrative framework nor the stated function which is not only to entertain but also to instruct. But who tells the tales? And for what reason? The frame story identifies Scheherazade as the tale-spinner and the purpose as a double deliverance, of virgins from slaughter and of an aggrieved king from his mania.

The frame plot of *The Arabian Nights* may thus seem straightforward. King Shahryar of India surprises his adulterous wife as she torridly copulates with a blackamoor slave. He executes his wife and swears "himself by a binding oath that whatever wife he married he would abate her maidenhead at night and slay her next morning to make sure of his honour; 'For,' said he, 'there never was nor is there one chaste woman upon the face of the earth'" (p. 14). Scheherazade, the "wise and witty" daughter of the King's Wazir, steps in to break this cycle of silent sacrifice by offering herself as a "ransom for the virgin daughters of Moslems [sic] and the cause of their deliverance" (p. 15). Her counterplot requires, however, the complicity of her sister. Admitted to the bedchamber, Dunyazad, foreshadowing each evening's formulaic plea, appeals, "Allah upon thee, O my sister, recite to us some new story, delightsome and delectable, wherewith to while away the waking hours of our latter night," so that Scheherazade in turn might "'tell thee a tale which shall be our deliverance, if so Allah please, and which shall turn the King from his blood-thirsty custom'" (p. 24). Tale after tale, Scheherazade ceases just before "the dawn of day . . . to say her permitted say," thereby cannily suspending each tale mid-way and luring the King into a three-year reprieve—or a thousand and one Arabian nights (p. 29).

Historia interrupta may be sufficient to stave off execution, but it is clearly not to be recommended as a contraceptive, for within three years' time Scheherazade has "borne the King three boy children" (p. 508). Craving release "from the doom of death, as a dole to these infants," Scheherazade elicits repentant tears from the king, who readily responds: "I had pardoned thee before the coming of these children, for that I found thee chaste, pure, ingenuous and pious!" (p. 508). Sexuality and marital fidelity are here intimately linked

9. *Tales from the Arabian Nights Selected from "The Book of the Thousand Nights and a Night,"* trans. Richard F. Burton, ed. David Shumaker (New York: Avenel Books, 1978). See David Shumaker's "Introduction" for comments on the presumed authorship that follow.

with the act of tale-telling, strikingly resembling the same motifs in
the story of Procne and Philomela. Whereas in Ovid's myth, the tapestry becomes a medium for communicating Tereus' adulterous
rape and instigating a proper vengeance, in *The Arabian Nights* the
two sisters conspire together to cure King Shahryar by telling
admonitory stories of past times and by demonstrating Scheherazade's chaste fidelity. Scheherazade's purity, signified by the legitimate product of her womb, converts the king from his "blood-thirsty
custom." But it is likewise Scheherazade's wise telling of tales that
instructs the king in precisely how to interpret his good fortune:
"'Thou marvelledst at that which befell thee on the part of women,'"
Scheherazade allows, "'and indeed I have set forth unto thee that
which happened to Caliphs and Kings and others with their
women . . . and in this is all-sufficient warning for the man of wits
and admonishment for the wise'" (pp. 508–9). Like an analyst upon
whom the patient projects his murderous jealousy, so Scheherazade's
stories function for King Shahryar, who with reasoning powers
restored and heart cleansed returns from mania to sanity.

Scheherazade's power to instruct derives from three kinds of special knowledge attributed to women: the knowledge of sexual passion, the knowledge of healing, and the wisdom to spin tales. More
a model of the intellectual and literate storyteller than, like
Philomela, of the domestic spinner and singer, Scheherazade, it is
written, "had perused the books, annals and legends of preceding
Kings, and the stories, examples and instances of by-gone men and
things; indeed it was said that she had collected a thousand books
of histories relating to antique races and departed rulers. She had
perused the works of the poets and knew them by heart; she had studied philosophy and the sciences, arts and accomplishments; and she
was pleasant and polite, wise and witty, well read and well bred"
(p. 15). The description might apply as well to those later "learned
Ladies" of the French court, Madame d'Aulnoy and Mlle. L'Héritier,
or to well-bred English governesses (Madame de Beaumont, Charlotte Brontë, Jane Eyre).[1] And one stands amazed at the immense
repertoire of Scheherazade's stories, sufficient we might imagine for
another one thousand and one nights of delectation and delight.
Scheherazade paradigmatically reinforces our concept of female storytellers as transmitters of ancient tales, told and remolded in such a
way as to meet the special needs of the listener—in this case, King
Shahryar and all men who harbor deep fears of the sexual woman

---

1. Charlotte Brontë (1816–1855), English author, who worked as a governess, as did her
   fictional character Jane Eyre. Marie-Catherine d'Aulnoy (1650–1705) and Marie-Jeanne
   L'Héritier (1664–1734), French authors who specialized in fairy tales. Jeanne-Marie
   Leprince de Beaumont (1711–1780), French author of many fairy tales, including
   "Beauty and the Beast," who worked in England as a governess [editor's note].

and the dual power of her body and voice. As readers of *The Arabian Nights,* we participate as eavesdroppers in the bedchamber, together with the King and Dunyazad, whom Scheherazade initiates into the mysterious truths of sexuality and folklore. Similar to Procne, who unrolled the tapestry and understood its *grammata,* Dunyazad comes to signify the community of all women to whom the female narrator tells tales.

The voice to tell "marvellous stories and wondrous histories," the wisdom to shape them rightly, the procreative and imaginative generativity belong to Scheherazade. But in *The Arabian Nights* we find another instance of male appropriation (p. 515). No doubt a remarkably quick student, King Shahryar retells "what he had heard from" Scheherazade during three years' time to his brother Shah Zaman, who is afflicted with the same jealous mania (p. 510). He is also miraculously redeemed and conveniently wed to Dunyazad. Having usurped the storytelling and curative power originally possessed by Scheherazade, the King further summons "chroniclers and copyists and bade them write all that had betided him with his wife, first and last; so they wrote this and named it *'The Stories of the Thousand Nights and a Night'"* (p. 515). A succeeding, equally "wise ruler," who "keen-witted and accomplished . . . loved tales and legends, especially those which chronicle the doings of Sovrans and Sultans," promptly "bade the folk copy them and dispread them over all lands and climes; wherefore their report was bruited abroad" (pp. 515–16). As the basis for a theory of the origin and dissemination of *The Arabian Nights,* this account may be as fictional as the frame story of Scheherazade; nevertheless, it usefully suggests the manner in which tales told by a woman found their way into royal circles, then were dispersed to the "folk," where presumably oral recountings insured their descent to the present day. Even the narrator hesitates to push this theory too hard, disclaiming that "this is all that hath come down to us of the origin of this book, and Allah is All-knowing" (p. 516).

Beyond this intratextual story that establishes Scheherazade as the frame tale-teller, the question of authorial identity becomes yet murkier. Scholars have suggested that Scheherazade's story appeared in the tenth-century *Hezar Afsane,* attributed to the Persian Princess Homai, daughter of Artaxerxes I, whose female authorship I would like to believe. But the alternative of a fifteenth-century Arabian collection, compiled by a professional storyteller in Cairo, sex unspecified, leaves us with no firm indication. We do know that in later centuries *The Arabian Nights* have come down to us (the folk) through French and English translations by savants, such as Galland, Henry Torrens (1838), E. W. Lane, John Payne (1882–84), and Richard Burton (1885–88), whose sixteen-volume English edition has been praised for its "exceptional accuracy, *masculine vitality,* and literary discernment" (emphasis added). Reinforcing the paradigm set by Ovid's *Metamorphoses,* Scheherazade's story and *The Arabian Nights* exemplify further the appropriation of text by a double narration in which a presumably male author or collector attributes to a female the original power of articulating silent matter. But having attributed this transformative artistic intelligence and voice to a woman, the narrator then reclaims for himself (much as Tereus and the King assert dominion over body and voice within the tales) the controlling power of retelling, of literary recasting, and of dissemination to the folk—a folk that includes the female community of tale-tellers from which the stories would seem to have originated.

Subsequent European collections of folk and fairy tales often assert a similarly double control over voice and text, whether as a mere literary convention or as a reflection of the actual informants and contexts of tale-telling. *The Book of the Seven Wise Masters,* or *Seven Sages,* probably of ninth-century Persian origin, but known in Europe, practically inverts the frame story of *The Arabian Nights Entertainments.*[2] Not a wazir's daughter, but instead a king's son, under notice of death, is saved from execution by the tales of seven philosophers, who tell stories of female deceptions, while a woman vehemently defends her sex from these slanders. Gianfrancesco Straparola (c. 1480–c. 1557), in his sixteenth-century Italian collection, *Le piacevoli Notti* or *The Delightful Nights* (1550–53), excuses the crude jests and earthy telling of tales by claiming (perhaps falsely?) to have heard them "from the lips of ten young girls." And Giambattista Basile's (1575–1632) famous *Lo Cunto de li Cunti*[3] (1634–36) or the *Pentamerone* (1674) contains a frame story attributing the fifty tales to common townswomen. Charles Perrault, borrowing perhaps from *les contes de vieilles* told by his son's nurse or repeated by his son Pierre, creates in *Histoires ou Contes du temps passé: Avec des Moralitez* (1697) the style of restrained simplicity that set the literary standard for subsequent fairy tale collections and *Kunstmärchen.*[4]

Madame d'Aulnoy (c. 1650–1705) may be the female exception that proves the rule of male appropriation, for as the author of eleven volumes she becomes notable for her elegantly ornamented fairy tales, designed to delight the adult aristocratic tastes of Louis XIV's court. As Dorothy R. Thelander establishes in "Mother Goose and Her Goslings: The France of Louis XIV as Seen through the Fairy Tale," these "fairy tales formed a distinct socioliterary genre," whose "roots lay in stories that peasant nursemaids and servants told

2. Peter Opie and Iona Opie, "Introduction," *The Classic Fairy Tales* (London: Oxford University Press, 1974), pp. 20–21.
3. *The Tale of Tales* [editor's note].
4. Literary fairy tale in German [editor's note].

children left in their charge, yet they were shaped for an adult and relatively sophisticated audience," that "shared the ideals of the Paris salons, particularly those which cultivated the refinement of language and manners associated with the précieux."[5] It is perhaps a sign of how removed Madame d'Aulnoy is from *les vieilles* as hearth-side tale-tellers that in one volume of her *contes de fées,* she imagines them to be narrated by some women during a short carriage trip. I do not intend to dispute the issues of the Ancien Régime and salon tales, or of Perrault's authorship, or of his style. My argument underscores, however, the observation of how regularly the tales are assumed and asserted to have their origins in a province definably female, and how the literary *contes de fées* become geared to an increasingly large circle of women readers—aristocratic ladies, mothers and nursemaids, governesses, young girls, and ironically the folk.

What surfaces during the period of the seventeenth century in which fairy tales become part of Western Europe's literary as well as oral tradition are "tell-tale" signs of a twofold legacy. First, we have noted already how insistently literary raconteurs, both male and female, validated the authenticity of their folk stories by claiming to have heard them from young girls, nurses, gossips, townswomen, old crones, and wise women. The female frame narrator is a particularly significant indicator, because it converts into literary convention the belief in women as truth-sayers, those gifted with memory and voice to transmit the culture's wisdom—the silent matter of life itself. Consider, for example, the term *conte de fées.* The terms *fées* and *faerie* derive originally from the Latin *Fatum,* the thing spoken, and *Fata,* the Fates who speak it. According to Andrew Lang, in his "Introduction" to *Perrault's Popular Fairy Tales* (1888), "the *Fées* answered, as in Sleeping Beauty, to Greek *Moirai* or Egyptian *Hathors.* They nursed women in labour: they foretold the fate of children."[6] And Katherine Briggs, in *An Encyclopedia of Fairies,* cites the derivation from "the Italian *fatae,* the fairy ladies who visited the household of births and pronounced on the future of the baby."[7] These Italian, French, and English derivatives from the Greek and Latin, compel us to see the origin of fairy as closely related to female acts of birthing, nursing, prophesying, and spinning—as ancient myth makes plain. Recall the three Fates: Klōthō, the spinner, spins the thread of life; Lachēsis, draws it out, thereby apportioning one's lifespan and destiny; and the dread Atropos, she who

---

5. Dorothy R. Thelander, "Mother Goose and Her Goslings: The France of Louis XIV as Seen Through the Fairy Tale," *The Journal of Modern History* 54 (1982): 467–96. ["*Précieux*": literati (editor's note).]
6. Andrew Lang, ed., *Perrault's Popular Tales* (Oxford: Clarendon Press, 1888; repr. New York: Arno, 1977).
7. Katherine Briggs, *An Encyclopedia of Fairies* (New York: Pantheon, 1976), p. xi, as quoted in Thelander, "Mother Goose," p. 487.

cannot be kept from turning the spindle, is "the blind *Fury* with th'abhorred shears," who "slits the thin-spun life."[8] *Contes de fées* are, therefore, not simply tales told about fairies; implicitly they are tales told by women, descendents of those ancestral Fates, who link once again the craft of spinning with the art of telling fated truths. In these women's hands, literally and metaphorically, rests the power of birthing, dying, and tale-spinning.

Second, it is not just the nature of the female raconteur, but also the context within which she tells tales in France, Germany, and England that reinforces associations between the literal and metaphorical spinning of yarns. Edward Shorter, among other historians of French popular culture, documents how in the *veillées,* those weekly gatherings of farm families, the women would "gather closely about the light of the nut-oil lamp," not only to "spin, knit, or darn to keep their own family's clothes in shape," but also to "tell stories and recite the old tales. Or maybe, as one disgusted observer reported of the late-nineteenth century, they just 'gossip.'"[9] The *veillée* in some parts of France became sex segregated, often a gathering exclusively of women with their marriageable daughters, in which both generations carded wool, spun, knitted, or stitched, thus enacting the age-old female rituals. As Abel Hugo, one of Shorter's nineteenth-century antiquarians, portrays it, "the women, because of the inferiority of their sex, are not admitted at all to conversation with their lords and masters. But after the men have retired, the women's reign begins. . . ."[1] Within the shared esprit of these late-evening communes, women not only practiced their domestic crafts, they also fulfilled their role as transmitters of culture through the vehicle of "old tales," inherited from oral tradition or the filtered down versions from the *Bibliothèque bleue,* those cheaply printed, blue-covered penny dreadfuls sold by traveling colporteurs.[2]

* * *

8. Bergren, "Language and the Female in Early Greek Thought," p. 87, n. 5, suggests this provocative emphasis on Atropos, who otherwise might be translated "she who does not turn." Bergren cites Thompson as the source of "she who cannot be kept from turning" the spindle itself.
9. Edward Shorter, "The 'Veillée' and the Great Transformation," in *The Wolf and the Lamb: Popular Culture in France from the Old Regime to the Twentieth Century,* ed. Jacques Beauroy, Marc Bertrand, and Edward T. Gargan (Saratoga, California: Anima Libri, 1977), pp. 127–40. The first long quotation is taken from p. 129.
1. Abel Hugo, from *La France pittoresque,* 3 vols. (Paris, 1835), 1:238, as quoted in Shorter, "The 'Veillée,'" p. 131. In *Ethnologie et langage: La parole chez les Dogon* (Paris: Gallimard, 1965), Geneviève Calame-Griaule similarly observes the "parole cachée" (concealed speech) among the Dogon women, who while spinning cotton whisper the stories of their men. It is also while mother and daughter spin that the mother teaches her daughter the necessary knowledge of marriage and sexual relations. These "confidences" are a mode dear to the Dogon women ("une parole féminine"), and as we have seen in European cultures, here too in an African tribe of the French Sudan the associations turn around the ideas of spinning yarn and of a secret, both skills and truths passed from mothers to daughters.
2. Peddlers of books [editor's note].

To have the antiquarian Grimm Brothers regarded as the fathers of modern folklore is perhaps to forget the maternal lineage, the "mothers" who in the French *veillées* and English nurseries, in court salons and the German *Spinnstube,* in Paris and on the Yorkshire moors, passed on their wisdom. The Grimm brothers, like Tereus, Ovid, King Shahryar, Basile, Perrault, and others reshaped what they could not precisely comprehend, because only for women does the thread, which spins out the lore of life itself, create a tapestry to be fully read and understood. Strand by strand weaving, like the craft practiced on Philomela's loom or in the hand-spinning of Mother Goose, is the true art of the fairy tale—and it is, I would submit, semiotically a female art. If we then recognize the continuity of this community of female storytellers, then perhaps Madame d'Aulnoy or her carriage trade ladies differ only in status and style from Basile's townswomen, the French *vieilles,* or English old wives and middle-class governesses. We may also wish to reconceptualize Madame d'Aulnoy, Mlle. L'Héritier, and Madame de Beaumont, not as pseudomasculine appropriators of a folkloric tradition, but as reappropriators of a female art of tale-telling that dates back to Philomela and Scheherazade. As such, they foreshadow, indeed perhaps foster, the eighteenth- and nineteenth-century emergence of a passion for romantic fictions, particularly among women writers and readers. Moreover, the "curious" socio-literary genres of the salon tale and Perrault's nursery tales (*contes naifs*) may be reperceived as a midstage, linking the ancient oral repertoire of folktales to the later, distinctively literary canon that embraces collections of folk and fairy tales as well as *Kunstmärchen,* moral and didactic stories, and romantic novels in which fairy tale motifs, structures, and frame narrators exert a shaping influence.

MARINA WARNER

From The Old Wives' Tale[†]

* * *

Plato in the *Gorgias* referred disparagingly to the kind of *tale*— *mythos graos,* the old wives' tale—told by nurses to amuse and frighten children. This is possibly the earliest reference to the genre. When the boys and girls of Athens were about to embark for Crete, to be sacrificed to the Minotaur, old women are described coming

† From Marina Warner, "The Old Wives' Tale," in *From the Beast to the Blonde* (New York: Farrar, Straus & Giroux, 1994), pp. 12–24. Copyright © 1994 by Marina Warner. Reprinted by permission of Farrar, Straus & Giroux, LLC, and by International Creative Management.

down to the port to tell them stories, to distract them from their grief. In *The Golden Ass*, Charite, a young bride, is captured by bandits, forcibly separated from her husband and thrown into a cave; there, a disreputable old woman, drunken and white-haired, tells her the story of Psyche's troubles before she reaches happiness and marriage with Cupid: 'The old woman sighed sympathetically. "My pretty dear," she said, ". . . let me tell you a fairy tale or two to make you feel a little better."' The picture of another's ordeals will console Charite and distract her from her own distress. William Adlington published his exuberant translation of 'sondrie pleasaunt and delectable Tales, with an excellent Narration of the Marriage of Cupide and Psiches . . .' in 1566; it is most improbable that a writer like George Peele would not have known this earliest recognizable predecessor of 'Cinderella' and 'Beauty and the Beast'.

In Latin, the phrase Apuleius uses is literally 'an old wives' tale' (*anilis fabula*); the type of comic romance to which 'Cupid and Psyche' belongs was termed 'Milesian', after Aristides of Miletus, who had compiled a collection of such stories in the second century A.D.; these were translated into Latin, but are now known only through later retellings. The connection of old women's speech and the consolatory, erotic, often fanciful fable appears deeply intertwined in language itself, and with women's speaking roles, as the etymology of 'fairy' illuminates.

The word 'fairy' in the Romance languages indicates a meaning of the wonder or fairy tale, for it goes back to a Latin feminine word, *fata*, a rare variant of *fatum* (fate) which refers to a goddess of destiny. The fairies resemble goddesses of this kind, for they too know the course of fate. *Fatum*, literally, that which is spoken, the past participle of the verb *fari*, to speak, gives French *fée*, Italian *fata*, Spanish *hada*, all meaning 'fairy', and enclosing connotations of fate; fairies share with Sibyls knowledge of the future and the past, and in the stories which feature them, both types of figures foretell events to come, and give warnings.

Isidore of Seville (*d.* 636), in the *Etymologies*, gives a famous, sceptical definition of the pagan idea of fate and the Fates: 'They say that fate is whatever the gods declare, whatever Jupiter declares. Thus they say that fate derives from *fando*, that is, from speaking. . . . The fiction is that there are three Fates, who spin a woollen thread on a distaff, on a spindle, and with their fingers, on account of the threefold nature of time: the past, which is already spun and wound onto the spindle; the present, which is drawn between the spinner's fingers; and the future, which lies in the wool twined on the distaff, and which must still be drawn out by the fingers of the spinner onto the spindle, as the present is drawn to the past.' These classical Fates metamorphose into the fairies of the stories, where they continue their fateful and prophetic roles. But fairy tales themselves also fulfil this function, quite apart from the fairies who may or may not make an appearance: 'Bluebeard' or 'Beauty and the Beast' act to caution listeners, as well as light their path to the future.

Although they do not have the same root, 'fairy' has come under strong semantic influence from 'fay' and 'fair', both of which may be derived ultimately from the Middle English *'feyen'*, Anglo-Saxon *'fegan'*, meaning to agree, to fit, to suit, to join, to unite, to bind. Thus the desirable has the power to inspire—even compel—agreement, as well as to bind. Binding is one of the properties of decrees, and of spells. Interestingly, this root also gives 'fee', as in payment, for transferrals of money too arise from agreed bonds, as a response to a desire, a need.

Although the ultimate origin, in time and place, of a fairy tale can never really be pinned down, we do sometimes know the teller of an old tale in one particular variation, we can sometimes identify the circle of listeners at a certain time and place. The collectors of the nineteenth century occasionally recorded the name of their sources when they took down the story, though they were not as interested in them as historians would be now. One salient aspect of the transmission of fairy tales has not been looked at closely: the female character of the storyteller.

Italo Calvino, in his 1956 collection of Italian *Fiabe*, or *Tales*, the Italian answer to the Grimms, drew attention to this aspect of the tradition, noticing that several of the nineteenth-century folklore anthologies he drew on and adapted cited female sources. Agatuzza Messia, the nurse of the Sicilian scholar and collector of tales Giuseppe Pitrè, became a seamstress, and, later, a quilt-maker in a section of Palermo: 'A mother, grandmother, and great-grandmother, as a little girl, she heard stories from her grandmother, whose own mother had told them having herself heard countless stories from one of her grandfathers. She had a good memory so never forgot them.' The *Kalevala*, the national poem of Finland, was collected from different oral sources and reshaped by Elias Lönnrot in the midnineteenth century in the form in which it is read today; Sibelius, who would compose many pieces inspired by the *Kalevala's* heroes and heroines, heard the epic in part direct from Larin Paraske, a woman bard, who held eleven thousand lines of such folk material in her head. Karel Čapek, the utopian Czech writer most famous for his satire *RUR* (which introduced the concept of Robots), wrote an acute essay about fairy tale in 1931, in which he decided:

> A fairy story cannot be defined by its motif and subject-matter, but by its origin and function. . . . A true folk fairy tale does not originate in being taken down by the collector of folklore but

in being told by a grandmother to her grandchildren, or by one
member of the Yoruba tribe to other members of the Yoruba
tribe, or by a professional storyteller to his audience in an Arab
coffeehouse. A real fairy tale, a fairy tale in its true function, is
a tale within a circle of listeners. . . .

He himself remembered his mother and his grandmother telling him stories—they were both millers' daughters, as if they had
stepped out of a fairy tale. The *traditio* does literally pass on, as the
word suggests, between the generations, and the predominant pattern reveals older women of a lower status handing on the material
to younger people, who include boys, sometimes, if not often, of
higher position and expectations, like future ethnographers and
writers of tales.

So although male writers and collectors have dominated the production and dissemination of popular wonder tales, they often pass
on women's stories from intimate or domestic milieux; their tale-
spinners often figure as so many Scheherazades, using narrative to
bring about a resolution of satisfaction and justice. Marguerite de
Navarre, in the *Heptaméron*, gives the stories to ten speakers, five
of whom are women: they too, like the narrator of *The Arabian
Nights*, put their own case, veiled in entertaining and occasionally
licentious fantasy. Boccaccio, and his admirer and emulator (to some
degree) Chaucer, voiced the stories of women, and some contain folk
material which makes a strong showing in later fairy stories; the
Venetian Giovan Francesco Straparola (the 'Babbler') reported the
stories told by a circle of ladies in his entertaining and sometimes
scabrous fantasies, filled with fairytale motifs and improbabilities,
called *Le piacevoli notti* (The Pleasant Nights), published in 1550;
the Neapolitan Giambattista Basile, in *Lo cunto de li cunti* (The Tale
of Tales), also known as *Il Pentamerone* (The Pentameron), published posthumously in 1634–6, featured a group of wizened and
misshapen old crones as his sources.

The women who inaugurated the fashion for the written fairy tale,
in Paris at the end of the seventeenth century, consistently claimed
they had heard the stories they were retelling from nurses and servants. Mme de Sévigné, writing to her daughter, revealingly reported
a metaphor borrowed from the kitchen to describe the new enthusiasm: '*cela s'appelle les [contes] mitonner. Elle nous mitonna donc,
et nous parla d'une île verte, où l'on élevait une princesse plus belle
que le jour*' (it's called simmering them [tales]; so she simmered for
us, and talked to us about a green isle where a princess grew up who
was more beautiful than the day).

Charles Perrault's collection of 1697 bore the alternative title
of *Contes de ma Mère l'Oye* (Mother Goose Tales); in an earlier

preface, to the tale *'Peau d'Ane'* (Donkeyskin), Perrault also placed
his work in the tradition of Milesian bawdy, like the tale of 'Cupid
and Psyche', but he added that he was passing on 'an entirely made
up story and an old wives' tale', such as had been told to children
since time immemorial by their nurses. While referring to a written
canon, he thus disengaged himself from its élite character to
invoke old women, grandmothers and governesses as his true predecessors. He was quick to add, however, that unlike the moral of
'Cupid and Psyche' (*'impénétrable'*), his own was patently clear,
which made it far superior to its classical predecessors:

> These Milesian fables are so puerile that it is doing them rather
> an honour to set up against them our own Donkeyskin tales and
> Mother Goose tales, or [they are] so filled with dirt, like *The
> Golden Ass* of Lucian or Apuleius . . . that they do not merit that
> we should pay them attention.

Perrault may have had his tongue in his cheek when he protested
that 'Donkeyskin', a tale of father-daughter incest, was morally
impeccable. But a contemporary pedant, the Abbé de Villiers, took
his argument at face value, and rounded in outrage on Perrault and
the writers of fairy tales, penning a pamphlet against the genre, 'As
a preventive measure against bad taste.' There he lumped women and
children together as the perpetrators of the new fad: 'Ignorant
and foolish, they have filled the world with so many collections, so
many little stories, and in short with these reams of fairy tales which
have been the death of us for the last year or so.' The diminutive
form of the nouns (*sornettes, bagatelles, historiettes*) recurs in the
rhetoric of detractors and supporters alike; the former branding
fairy stories as infantile, the latter praising them as childlike. This
tension between opposing perceptions of the child informs the
development of the tales and continues to do so.

Villiers sets up an imaginary debate between a fashionable Parisian and a sensible visitor from the provinces. The provincial calls
them *sottises imprimées* (follies in print) and compares them derog-
atorily to fables, scorning them as 'Tales to make you fall asleep on
your feet, that nurses have made up to entertain children'. The Parisian counters that nurses have to be highly skilled to tell them. To
which the provincial retorts that if such tales ever contained a coher-
ent moral purpose, they would not be considered in the first place
'the lot of ignorant folk and women'. The battle was joined, over the
value of fairy tales; their female origin was not really contested.

Villiers's Parisian was putting forward the views of poets and literati like Mlle Marie-Jeanne L'Héritier de Villandon (1664–1734), a
cousin and close friend of Perrault, who defended the form with
fighting spirit precisely because it conveyed the ancient, pure

wisdom of the people from the fountainhead—old women, nurses, governesses. In her preface to the story '*Marmoisan, ou l'innocente tromperie*' (Marmoisan, or the innocent trick) of 1696, she declared herself a partisan of women and their stories, remembering: 'A hundred times and more, my governess, instead of animal fables, would draw for me the moral features of this surprising story. . . . Why yes, once heard, such tales are far more striking than the exploits of a monkey and a wolf. I took an extreme pleasure in them—as does every child.'

L'Héritier could never rid her praise of its defensive tone ('the moral features'), and for good reason. The phrase 'old wives' tale' was superficially pejorative when Apuleius used it on the lips of his hoary-headed crone of a storyteller; it remained so, in the very act of authenticating the folk wisdom of the stories by stressing the wise old women who had carried on the tradition. It is still, in English, an ambiguous phrase: an old wives' tale means a piece of nonsense, a tissue of error, an ancient act of deception, of self and others, idle talk. As Marlowe writes in *Dr Faustus*, 'Tush, these are trifles and mere old wives' tales.' On a par with trifles, 'mere old wives' tales' carry connotations of error, of false counsel, ignorance, prejudice and fallacious nostrums—against heartbreak as well as headache; similarly 'fairy tale', as a derogatory term, implies fantasy, escapism, invention, the unreliable consolations of romance.

But the idealistic impulse is also driven by dreams; alternative ways of sifting right and wrong require different guides, ones perhaps discredited or neglected. Women from very different social strata have been remarkably active in the fields of folklore and children's literature since the nineteenth century. The Grimm Brothers' most inspiring and prolific sources were women, from families of friends and close relations, like the Wilds—Wilhelm married Dortchen, the youngest of four daughters of Dorothea Wild, who possessed a rich store of traditional tales, and she provided thirty-six for the collection. Dorothea, the Grimms' sister, married Ludwig Hassenpflug, and his three sisters passed on forty-one of the tales. From the Romantic literary circle of the artistic aristocratic von Haxthausens (who contributed collectively no fewer than sixty-six of the Grimms' tales) Annette von Droste-Hülshoff, the poet, and her sister Jenny were among the women who eagerly took part in telling the brothers the stories they had heard as children and more recently from their local area of Westphalia. Oscar Wilde's father, a doctor in Merrion Square, Dublin, in the mid-nineteenth century, used to ask for stories as his fee from his poorer patients: his wife Speranza Wilde then collected them. Many of these were told to him by women, and in turn influenced their son's innovatory fairy tales, like 'The Selfish Giant' and 'The Happy Prince'. At the end of the century, the omnivorous Scottish folklorist Andrew Lang relied on his wife Leonora Alleyne, as well as a team of women editors, transcribers and paraphrasers, to produce the many volumes of fairy stories and folk tales from around the world, in the immensely popular *Red, Yellow, Green, Blue, Rose Fairy Books,* which he began publishing in 1890. The writer Simone Schwarz-Bart stitched her memories of Creole stories from her Martinique childhood into her poetic, adventurous, linguistically hybrid fictions. The grandmother Reine Sans Nom (Queen-With-No-Name) in *Pluie et vent sur Télumée Miracle* (1972) embodies survival and history, and keeps the memory of slave culture, and of Africa before that. With the help of her friend, a sorceress, she passes on lore, fables, fairy tales, ghost stories to her granddaughter. As Simone Schwarz-Bart once said in an interview, 'The tale is, in large part, our capital. I was nourished on tales. It is our bible. . . . I don't have a technique, but I know. I'm familiar. I've heard. I've been nourished. . . . When an old person dies, a whole library disappears.'

It would be absurd to argue that storytelling was an exclusively female activity—it varies from country to country, from one people to another, and from place to place within the same country, among the same people—but it is worth trying to puzzle out in what different ways the patterns of fairytale romancing might be drawn when women are the tellers.

The pedagogical function of the wonder story deepens the sympathy between the social category women occupy and fairy tale. Fairy tales exchange knowledge between an older voice of experience and a younger audience, they present pictures of perils and possibilities that lie ahead, they use terror to set limits on choice and offer consolation to the wronged, they draw social outlines around boys and girls, fathers and mothers, the rich and the poor, the rulers and the ruled, they point out the evildoers and garland the virtuous, they stand up to adversity with dreams of vengeance, power and vindication.

The *veillées* were the hearthside sessions of early modern society, where early social observers, like Bonaventure des Périers and Noël du Fail in the sixteenth century, describe the telling of some of today's most familiar fables and tales, like 'Donkeyskin' and 'Cinderella'. These gatherings offered men and women an opportunity to talk—to preach—which was forbidden them in other situations, the pulpit, the forum, and frowned on and feared in the spinning rooms and by the wellside. Taking place after daylight hours, they still do not exactly anticipate the leisure uses of television or radio today—work continued, in the form of spinning, especially, and other domestic tasks: one folklore historian recalled hearing the women in her childhood tell stories to the rhythm of the stones cracking walnuts as they shelled them for bottling and pickling. As Walter Benjamin wrote in his essay on 'The Storyteller':

> [The storyteller's] nesting places—the activities that are intimately associated with boredom—are already extinct in the cities and are declining in the country as well. With this the gift for listening is lost and the community of listeners disappears. . . .

Benjamin never once imagines that his storytellers might be women, even though he identifies so clearly and so eloquently the connection between routine repetitive work and narrative—storytelling is itself 'an artisan form of communication', he writes. And later, again, it is 'rooted in the people . . . a milieu of craftsmen'. He divides storytellers into stay-at-homes and rovers—tradesmen and agriculturalists, like the tailors and the shoemakers who appear in the stories, on the one hand; on the other, the seamen who travel far afield adventuring, like the questing type of hero. He neglects the figure of the spinster, the older woman with her distaff, who may be working in town and country, in one place or on the move, at market, or on a pilgrimage to Canterbury, and who has become a generic icon of narrative from the frontispiece of fairytale collections from Charles Perrault's onwards. The Scottish poet Liz Lochhead, who has drawn on much fairytale imagery in her work, has written:

> No one could say the stories were useless
> for as the tongue clacked
> five or forty fingers stitched
> corn was grated from the husk
> patchwork was pieced
> or the darning was done . . .
>
> And at first light . . .
> the stories dissolved in the whorl of the ear
> but they
> hung themselves upside down
> in the sleeping heads of the children
> till they flew again
> into the storyteller's night.

Spinning a tale, weaving a plot: the metaphors illuminate the relation; while the structure of fairy stories, with their repetitions, reprises, elaboration and minutiae, replicates the thread and fabric of one of women's principal labours—the making of textiles from the wool or the flax to the finished bolt of cloth.

Fairy tales are stories which, in the earliest mentions of their existence, include that circle of listeners, the audience; as they point to possible destinies, possible happy outcomes, they successfully involve their hearers or readers in identifying with the protagonists, their misfortunes, their triumphs. Schematic characterization leaves a gap into which the listener may step. Who has not tried on the glass slipper? Or offered it for trying? The relation between the authentic, artisan source and the tale recorded in book form for children and adults is not simple; we are not hearing the spinsters and the knitters in the sun whom Orsino remembers chanting in *Twelfth Night*, unmediated. But the quality of the mediation is of great interest. From the mid-seventeenth century, the nurses, governesses, family domestics, working women living in or near the great house or castle in town and country existed in a different relation to the élite men and women who may have once been in their charge, as children. The future Marquise de la Tour du Pin recalled in her memoirs how her nurse was her mainstay and that, when she turned eleven and a governess was appointed instead, 'I used to escape whenever I could and try to find her [the nurse], or to meet her about the house.' Another noblewoman, Victorine de Chastenay, also wrote that her own mother alarmed her and dominated her, and that she took refuge with her nurse and her nurse's family. The rapports created in *ancien régime* childhood shape the matter of the stories, and the cultural model which places the literati's texts on the one side of a divide, and popular tales on the other, can and should be redrawn: fairy tales act as an airy suspension bridge, swinging slightly under different breezes of opinion and economy, between the learned, literary and print culture in which famous fairy tales have come down to us, and the oral, illiterate, people's culture of the *veillée*; and on this bridge the traffic moves in both directions.

Women writers like Marie-Jeanne L'Héritier and Marie-Catherine d'Aulnoy mediated anonymous narratives, the popular, vernacular culture they had inherited through fairy tale, in spite of the aristocratic frippery their stories make at a first impression. Indeed, they offer rare and rich testimony to a sophisticated chronicle of wrongs and ways to evade or right them, when they recall stories they had heard as children or picked up later and retell them in a spirit of protest, of polite or not so polite revolt. These tales are wrapped in fantasy and unreality, which no doubt helped them entertain their audiences—in the courtly salon as well as at the village hearth— but they also serve the stories' greater purpose, to reveal possibilities, to map out a different way and a new perception of love, marriage, women's skills, thus advocating a means of escaping imposed limits and prescribed destiny. The fairy tale looks at the ogre like Bluebeard or the Beast of 'Beauty and the Beast' in order to disenchant him; while romancing reality, it is a medium deeply concerned with undoing prejudice. Women of different social positions have collaborated in storytelling to achieve true recognition for their subjects: the process is still going on.

❊   ❊   ❊

JACK ZIPES

Breaking the Disney Spell[†]

It was not once upon a time, but at a certain time in history, before anyone knew what was happening, that Walt Disney cast a spell on the fairy tale, and he has held it captive ever since. He did not use a magic wand or demonic powers. On the contrary, Disney employed the most up-to-date technological means and used his own "American" grit and ingenuity to appropriate European fairy tales. His technical skills and ideological proclivities were so consummate that his signature has [obscured] the names of Charles Perrault, the Brothers Grimm, Hans Christian Andersen, and Carlo Collodi. If children or adults think of the great classical fairy tales today, be it *Snow White, Sleeping Beauty,* or *Cinderella,* they will think Walt Disney. Their first and perhaps lasting impressions of these tales and others will have emanated from a Disney film, book, or artifact. Though other filmmakers and animators produced remarkable fairy-tale films, Disney managed to gain a cultural stranglehold on the fairy tale, and this stranglehold has even tightened with the recent productions of *Beauty and the Beast* (1991) and *Aladdin* (1992). The man's spell over the fairy tale seems to live on even after his death.

But what does the Disney spell mean? Did Disney achieve a complete monopoly on the fairy tale during his lifetime? Did he imprint a particular *American* vision on the fairy tale through his animated films that dominates our perspective today? And, if he did manage to cast his mass-mediated spell on the fairy tale so that we see and read the classical tales through his lens, is that so terrible? Was Disney a nefarious wizard of some kind whose domination of the fairy tale should be lamented? Wasn't he just more inventive, more skillful, more in touch with the American spirit of the times than his competitors, who also sought to animate the classical fairy tale for the screen?

Of course, it would be a great exaggeration to maintain that Disney's spell totally divested the classical fairy tales of their meaning and invested them with his own. But it would not be an exaggeration

† Jack Zipes, "Breaking the Disney Spell," *From Mouse to Mermaid: The Politics of Film, Gender, and Culture,* ed. Elizabeth Bell, Lynda Haas, and Laura Sells (Bloomington: Indiana UP, 1995), pp. 21–42. © 1995 by Indiana University Press. Reprinted with permission of Indiana University Press.

to assert that Disney was a radical filmmaker who changed our way of viewing fairy tales, and that his revolutionary technical means capitalized on American innocence and utopianism to reinforce the social and political status quo. His radicalism was of the right and the righteous. The great "magic" of the Disney spell is that he animated the fairy tale only to transfix audiences and divert their potential utopian dreams and hopes through the false promises of the images he cast upon the screen. But before we come to a full understanding of this magical spell, we must try to understand what he did to the fairy tale that was so revolutionary and why he did it.

The Oral and Literary Fairy Tales

The evolution of the fairy tale as a literary genre is marked by dialectical appropriation that set the cultural conditions for its institutionalization and its expansion as a mass-mediated form through radio, film, and television. Fairy tales were first *told* by gifted tellers and were based on rituals intended to endow with meaning the daily lives of members of a tribe. As *oral folk tales*, they were intended to explain natural occurrences such as the change of the seasons and shifts in the weather or to celebrate the rites of harvesting, hunting, marriage, and conquest. The emphasis in most folk tales was on communal harmony. A narrator or narrators told tales to bring members of a group or tribe closer together and to provide them with a sense of mission, a *telos*. The tales themselves assumed a generic quality based on the function that they were to fulfill for the community or the incidents that they were to report, describe, and explain. Consequently, there were tales of initiation, worship, warning, and indoctrination. Whatever the type may have been, the voice of the narrator was known. The tales came directly from common experiences and beliefs. Told in person, directly, face-to-face, they were altered as the beliefs and behaviors of the members of a particular group changed.

With the rise of literacy and the invention of the printing press in the fifteenth century, the oral tradition of storytelling underwent an immense revolution. The oral tales were taken over by a different social class, and the form, themes, production, and reception of the tales were transformed. This change did not happen overnight, but it did foster discrimination among writers and their audiences almost immediately so that distinct genres were recognized and approved for certain occasions and functions within polite society or cultivated circles of readers. In the case of folk tales, they were gradually categorized as legends, myths, fables, comical anecdotes, and, of course, fairy tales. What we today consider fairy tales were actually just one type of the folk-tale tradition, namely the *Zaubermärchen* or the magic tale, which has many sub-genres. The French writers of the late seventeenth century called these tales *contes de fées* (fairy tales) to distinguish them from other kinds of *contes populaires* (popular tales), and what really distinguished a *conte de fée,* based on the oral *Zaubermärchen,* was its transformation into a literary tale that addressed the concerns, tastes, and functions of court society. The fairy tale had to fit into the French salons, parlors, and courts of the aristocracy and bourgeoisie if it was to establish itself as a genre. The writers, Mme D'Aulnoy, Charles Perrault, Mlle L'Héritier, Mlle de La Force, etc., knew and expanded upon oral and literary tales. They were not the initiators of the literary fairytale tradition in Europe (cf. Zipes 1989). Two Italian writers, Giovanni Francesco Straparola and Giambattista Basile, had already set an example for what the French were accomplishing.[1] But the French writers created an institution, that is, the genre of the literary fairy tale was institutionalized as an aesthetic and social means through which questions and issues of *civilité,* proper behavior and demeanor in all types of situations, were mapped out as narrative strategies for literary socialization, and in many cases, as symbolic gestures of subversion to question the ruling standards of taste and behavior.

While the literary fairy tale was being institutionalized at the end of the seventeenth and beginning of the eighteenth century in France, the oral tradition did not disappear, nor was it subsumed by the new literary genre. Rather, the oral tradition continued to feed the writers with material and was now also influenced by the literary tradition itself. The early chapbooks (cheap books), known as the *Bibliothèque Bleue,* that were carried by peddlers or *colporteurs* to the villages throughout France contained numerous abbreviated and truncated versions of the literary tales, and these were in turn told once again in these communities. In some cases, the literary tales presented new material that was transformed through the oral tradition and returned later to literature by a writer who remembered hearing a particular story.

By the beginning of the nineteenth century when the Brothers Grimm set about to celebrate German culture through their country's folk tales, the literary fairy tale had long since been institutionalized, and they, along with Hans Christian Andersen, Carlo Collodi, Ludwig Bechstein, and a host of Victorian writers from George MacDonald to Oscar Wilde, assumed different ideological and aesthetic positions within this institutionalization. These writers put the finishing touches on the fairy-tale genre at a time when nation-states

1. See Straparola's *Le piacevoli notti* (1550–53), translated as *The Facetious Nights* or *The Delectable Nights,* and Basile's *Lo Cunto de li Cunti* (*The Story of Stories,* 1634–36), better known as *The Pentamerone.* The reason that the Italians did not "institutionalize" the genre is that the literary culture in Italy was not prepared to introduce the tales as part of the civilizing process, nor were there groups of writers who made the fairy-tale genre part of their discourse.

were assuming their modern form and cultivating particular types of literature as commensurate expressions of national cultures.

What were the major prescriptions, expectations, and standards of the literary fairy tale by the end of the nineteenth century? Here it is important first to make some general remarks about the "violent" shift from the oral to the literary tradition and not just talk about the appropriation of the magic folk tale as a dialectical process. Appropriation does not occur without violence to the rhetorical text created in the oral tales. * * * Such violation of oral storytelling was crucial and necessary for the establishment of the bourgeoisie because it concerned the control of desire and imagination within the symbolic order of western culture.

Unlike the oral tradition, the literary tale was written down to be read in private, although, in some cases, the fairy tales were read aloud in parlors. However, the book form enabled the reader to withdraw from his or her society and to be alone with a tale. This privatization violated the communal aspects of the folk tale, but the very printing of a fairy tale was already a violation since it was based on separation of social classes. Extremely few people could read, and the fairy tale in form and content furthered notions of elitism and separation. In fact, the French fairy tales heightened the aspect of the chosen aristocratic elite who were always placed at the center of the seventeenth- and eighteenth-century narratives. They were part and parcel of the class struggles in the discourses of that period. To a certain extent, the fairy tales were the outcome of violent "civilized" struggles, material representations, which represented struggles for hegemony. As Nancy Armstrong and Leonard Tennenhouse have suggested,

> a class of people cannot produce themselves as a ruling class without setting themselves off against certain Others. Their hegemony entails possession of the key cultural terms determining what are the right and wrong ways to be a human being.[2]

No matter where the literary tale took root and established itself—France, Germany, England—it was written in a standard "high" language that the folk could not read, and it was written as a form of entertainment and education for members of the ruling classes. Indeed, only the well-to-do could purchase the books and read them. In short, by institutionalizing the literary fairy tale, writers and publishers violated the forms and concerns of non-literate, essentially peasant communities and set new standards of taste, production, and reception through the discourse of the fairy tale.

2. Nancy Armstrong and Leonard Tennenhouse, eds., *The Violence of Representation: Literature and the History of Violence* (New York: Routledge, 1989), 24.

The literary fairy tales tended to exclude the majority of people who could not read, while the folk tales were open to everyone. Indeed, the literary narratives were individualistic and unique in form and exalted the power of those chosen to rule. In contrast, the oral tales had themes and characters that were readily recognizable and reflected common wish-fulfillments. Of course, one had to know the dialect in which they were told. From a philological standpoint, the literary fairy tale elevated the oral tale through the standard practice of printing and setting grammatical rules in "high French" or "high German." The process of violation is *not* one of total negation and should not be studied as one-dimensional, for the print culture enabled the tales to be preserved and cultivated, and the texts created a new realm of pleasurable reading that allowed for greater reflection on the part of the reader than could an oral performance of a tale. At the beginning, the literary fairy tales were written and published for adults, and though they were intended to reinforce the mores and values of French *civilité,* they were so symbolic and could be read on so many different levels that they were considered somewhat dangerous: social behavior could not be totally dictated, prescribed, and controlled through the fairy tale, and there were subversive features in language and theme. This is one of the reasons that fairy tales were not particularly approved for children. In most European countries it was not until the end of the eighteenth and early part of the nineteenth century that fairy tales were published for children, and even then begrudgingly, because their "vulgar" origins in the lower classes were suspect. Of course, the fairy tales for children were sanitized and expurgated versions of the fairy tales for adults, or they were new moralistic tales that were aimed at the domestication of the imagination, as Rüdiger Steinlein has demonstrated in his significant study.[3] The form and structure of the fairy tale for children were carefully regulated in the nineteenth century so that improper thoughts and ideas would not be stimulated in the minds of the young. If one looks carefully at the major writers of fairy tales for children who became classical and popular in the nineteenth century,[4] it is clear that they themselves exercised self-censorship and restraint in conceiving and writing down tales for children.

This is not to argue that the literary fairy tale as institution became one in which the imagination was totally domesticated. On the contrary, by the end of the nineteenth century the genre served different functions. As a whole, it formed a multi-vocal network of

---

3. Cf. *Die domestizierte Phantasie: Studien zur Kinderliteratur, Kinderlektüre und Literaturpädagogik des 18. und frühen 19. Jahrhunderts* (Heidelberg: Carl Winter, 1987).

4. This list would include the Grimms, Wilhelm Hauff, Ludwig Bechstein, Hans Christian Andersen, and Madame De Ségur. In addition, numerous collections of expurgated folk tales from different countries became popular in primers by the end of the nineteenth century. Here one would have to mention the series of color fairy books edited by Andrew Lang in Great Britain.

discourses through which writers used familiar motifs, topoi, protagonists, and plots symbolically to comment on the civilizing process and socialization in their respective countries. These tales did
not represent communal values but rather the values of a particular
writer. Therefore, if the writer subscribed to the hegemonic value
system of his or her society and respected the canonical ideology of
Perrault, the Grimms, and Andersen, he/she would write a conventional tale with conservative values, whether for adults or children.
On the other hand, many writers would parody, mock, question, and
undermine the classical literary tradition and produce original and
subversive tales that were part and parcel of the institution itself.

The so-called original and subversive tales have kept the dynamic
quality of the dialectical appropriation alive, for there has always
been a danger that the written word, in contrast to the spoken word,
will fix a structure, image, metaphor, plot, and value as sacrosanct.
For instance, for some people the Grimms' fairy tales are holy, or
fairy tales are considered holy and not to be touched. How did this
notion emanate?

To a certain extent it was engendered by the Grimms and other
folklorists who believed that the fairy tales arose from the spirit of
the folk. Yet, worship of the fairy tale as holy scripture is a petrifi-
cation of the fairy tale that is connected to the establishment of
correct speech, values, and power more than anything else. This
establishment through the violation of the oral practices was the
great revolution and transformation of the fairy tale.

By the end of the nineteenth century the literary fairy tale had the
following crucial functions as institution in middle-class society:

(1) It introduced notions of elitism and separatism through a select
canon of tales geared to children who knew how to read.

(2) Though it was also told, the fact that the fairy tale was printed
and in a book with pictures gave it more legitimacy and enduring
value than an oral tale that disappeared soon after it was told.

(3) It was often read by a parent in a nursery, school, or bedroom
to soothe a child's anxieties, for the fairy tales for children were opti-
mistic and were constructed with the closure of the happy end.

(4) Although the plots varied and the themes and characters were
altered, the classical fairy tale for children and adults reinforced the
patriarchal symbolic order based on rigid notions of sexuality and
gender.

(5) In printed form the fairy tale was property and could be taken
by its owner and read by its owner at his or her leisure for escape,
consolation, or inspiration.

(6) Along with its closure and reinforcement of patriarchy, the
fairy tale also served to encourage notions of rags to riches, pulling
yourself up by your bootstraps, dreaming, miracles, etc.

(7) There was always tension between the literary and oral traditions. The oral tales have continued to threaten the more conventional and classical tales because they can question, dislodge, and deconstruct the written tales. Moreover, within the literary tradition itself, there were numerous writers such as Charles Dickens, George MacDonald, Lewis Carroll, Oscar Wilde, and Edith Nesbit who questioned the standardized model of what a fairy tale should be.

(8) It was through script by the end of the nineteenth century that there was a full-scale debate about what oral folk tales and literary fairy tales were and what their respective functions should be. By this time the fairy tale had expanded as a high art form (operas, ballets, dramas) and low art form (folk plays, vaudevilles, and parodies) as well as a form developed classically and experimentally for children and adults. The oral tales continued to be disseminated through communal gatherings of different kinds, but they were also broadcast by radio and gathered in books by folklorists. Most important in the late nineteenth century was the rise of folklore as an institution and of various schools of literary criticism that dealt with fairy tales and folk tales.

(9) Though many fairy-tale books and collections were illustrated (some lavishly) in the nineteenth century, the images were very much in conformity with the text. The illustrators were frequently anonymous and did not seem to count. Though the illustrations often enriched and deepened a tale, they were generally subservient to the text.

However, the domination of the word in the development of the fairy tale as genre was about to change. The next great revolution in the institutionalization of the genre was the film, for the images now imposed themselves on the text and formed their own text in violation of print but also with the help of the print culture. And here is where Walt Disney and other animators enter the scene.

Disney's Magical Rise

By the turn of the twentieth century there had already been a number of talented illustrators, such as Gustave Doré, George Cruikshank, Walter Crane, Charles Folkard, and Arthur Rackham, who had demonstrated great ingenuity in their interpretations of fairy tales though their images. In addition, the broadside, broadsheet, or *image d'Epinal* had spread in Europe and America during the latter part of the nineteenth century as a forerunner of the comic book, and these sheets with printed images and texts anticipated the first animated cartoons that were produced at the beginning of the twentieth century. Actually, the French filmmaker Georges Méliès began experimenting as early as 1896 with types of fantasy and fairy-tale motifs in his *féeries* or trick films.[5] He produced versions of *Cinderella*, *Bluebeard*, and *Little Red Riding Hood* among others. However, since the cinema industry itself was still in its early phase of development, it was difficult for Méliès to bring about a major change in the technological and cinematic institutionalization of the genre. As Lewis Jacobs has remarked,

> this effort of Méliès illustrated rather than re-created the fairy tale. Yet, primitive though it was, the order of the scenes did form a coherent, logical, and progressive continuity. A new way of making moving pictures had been invented. Scenes could now be staged and selected specially for the camera, and the movie maker could control both the material and its arrangement.[6]

During the early part of the twentieth century Walter Booth, Anson Dyer, Lotte Reiniger, Walter Lantz and others all used fairy tale plots in different ways in trick films and cartoons, but none of the early animators ever matched the intensity with which Disney occupied himself with the fairy tale. In fact, it is noteworthy that Disney's very first endeavors in animation (not considering the advertising commercials he made) were the fairy-tale adaptations that he produced with Ub Iwerks in Kansas City in 1922–23: *The Four Musicians of Bremen*, *Little Red Riding Hood*, *Puss in Boots*, *Jack and the Beanstalk*, *Goldie Locks and the Three Bears*, and *Cinderella*.[7] To a certain degree, Disney identified so closely with the fairy tales he appropriated that it is no wonder his name virtually became synonymous with the genre of the fairy tale itself.

However, before discussing Disney's particular relationship to the fairy-tale tradition, it is important to consider the conditions of early animation in America and role of the animator in general, for all this has a bearing on Disney's productive relationship with the fairy tale. In his important study, *Before Mickey: The Animated Film 1898–1928*, Donald Crafton remarks that

> the early animated film was the location of a process found elsewhere in cinema but nowhere else in such intense concentration: self-figuration, the tendency of the filmmaker to interject himself into his film. This can take several forms, it can be direct or indirect, and more or less camouflaged. . . . At first it was obvious and literal; at the end it was subtle and cloaked in

---

5. Lewis Jacobs, "George Méliès: Scenes," in *The Emergence of Film Art: The Evolution and Development of the Motion Picture as an Art, from 1900 to the Present*, 2d ed., ed. Lewis Jacobs (New York: Norton, 1979).
6. Jacobs, "George Méliès," 13.
7. Cf. Russell Merrit and J. B. Kaufman, *Walt in Wonderland: The Silent Films of Walt Disney*, for the most complete coverage of Disney's early development.

metaphors and symbolic imagery designed to facilitate the process and yet to keep the idea gratifying for the artist and the audience. Part of the animation game consisted of developing mythologies that gave the animator some sort of special status. Usually these were very flattering, for he was pictured as (or implied to be) a demigod, a purveyor of life itself.[8]

As Crafton convincingly shows, the early animators before Disney literally drew themselves into the pictures and often appeared as characters in the films. One of the more interesting aspects of the early animated films is a psychically loaded tension between the artist and the characters he draws, one that is ripe for a Freudian or Lacanian reading, for the artist is always threatening to take away their "lives," while they, in turn, seek to deprive him of his pen (phallus) or creative inspiration so that they can control their own lives. (Almost all the early animators were men, and their pens and camera work assume a distinctive phallic function in early animation.) The hand with pen or pencil is featured in many animated films in the process of creation, and it is then transformed in many films into the tail of a cat or dog. This tail then acts as the productive force or artist's instrument throughout the film. For instance, Disney in his Alice films often employed a cat named Julius, who would take off his tail and use it as stick, weapon, rope, hook, question mark, etc. It was the phallic means to induce action and conceive a way out of a predicament.

The celebration of the pen/phallus as ruler of the symbolic order of the film was in keeping with the way that animated films were actually produced in the studios during the 1920s. That is, most of the studios, largely located in New York, had begun to be run on the Taylor system by men who joined together under the supervision of the head of the studio to produce the cartoons. After making his first fairy-tale films in close cooperation with Ub Iwerks in Kansas City, Disney moved to Hollywood, where he developed the taylorized studio to the point of perfection. Under his direction, the films were carefully scripted to project his story or vision of how a story should be related. The storyline was carried by hundreds of repetitious images created by the artists in his studios. Their contribution was in many respects like that of the dwarfs in Snow White and the Seven Dwarfs: they were to do the spadework, while the glorified prince was to come along and carry away the prize.

It might be considered somewhat one-dimensional to examine all of Disney's films as self-figurations, or embodiments of the chief

---

8. Donald Crafton, Before Mickey: The Animated Film 1898–1928 (Cambridge: MIT Press, 1982), 11.

designer's[9] wishes and beliefs. However, to understand Disney's importance as designer and director of fairy-tale films that set a particular pattern and model as the film industry developed, it does make sense to elaborate on Crafton's notion of self-figuration, for it provides an important clue for grasping the further development of the fairy tale as animated film or film in general.

We have already seen that one of the results stemming from the shift from the oral to the literary in the institutionalization of the fairy tale was a loss of live contact with the storyteller and a sense of community or commonality. This loss was a result of the social-industrial transformations at the end of the nineteenth century with the *Gemeinschaft* (community-based society) giving way to the *Gesellschaft* (contract-based society). However, it was not a total loss, for industrialization brought about greater comfort, sophistication, and literacy in addition to new kinds of communication in public institutions. Therefore, as I have demonstrated, the literary fairy tale's ascent corresponded to violent and progressive shifts in society and celebrated individualism, subjectivity, and reflection. It featured the narrative voice of the educated author and publisher over communal voices and set new guidelines for freedom of speech and expression. In addition, proprietary rights to a particular tale were established, and the literary tale became a commodity that paradoxically spoke out in the name of the unbridled imagination. Indeed, because it was born out of alienation, the literary fairy tale fostered a search for new "magical" means to overcome the instrumentalization of the imagination.

By 1900 literature began to be superseded by the mechanical means of reproduction that, Walter Benjamin declared, were revolutionary:

> the technique of reproduction detaches the reproduced object from the domain of tradition. By making many reproductions it substitutes a plurality of copies of a unique existence. And in permitting the reproduction to meet the beholder or listener in his own particular situation, it reactivates the object reproduced. These two processes lead to a tremendous shattering of tradition which is the obverse of the contemporary crisis and renewal of mankind. Both processes are intimately connected with the contemporary mass movements. Their most powerful agent is the film. Its social significance, particularly in its most positive form, is inconceivable without its destructive, cathartic

9. I am purposely using the word designer instead of animator because Disney was always designing things, made designs, and had designs. A designer is someone who indicates with a distinctive mark, and Disney put his mark on everything in his studios. A designing person is often a crafty person who manages to put his schemes into effect by hook or by crook. Once Disney stopped animating, he became a designer.

aspect, that is, the liquidation of the traditional value of the cultural heritage.[1]

Benjamin analyzed how the revolutionary technological nature of the film could either bring about an aestheticization of politics leading to the violation of the masses through fascism, or a politicization of aesthetics that provides the necessary critical detachment for the masses to take charge of their own destiny.

In the case of the fairy-tale film at the beginning of the twentieth century, there are "revolutionary" aspects that we can note, and they prepared the way for progressive innovation that expanded the horizons of viewers and led to greater understanding of social conditions and culture. But there were also regressive uses of mechanical reproduction that brought about the cult of the personality and commodification of film narratives. For instance, the voice in fairy-tale films is at first effaced so that the image totally dominates the screen, and the words or narrative voice can only speak through the designs of the animator who, in the case of Walt Disney, has signed his name prominently on the screen. In fact, for a long time, Disney did not give credit to the artists and technicians who worked on his films. These images were intended both to smash the aura of heritage and to celebrate the ingenuity, inventiveness, and genius of the animator. In most of the early animated films, there were few original plots, and the story-lines did not count. Most important were the gags, or the technical inventions of the animators ranging from the introduction of live actors to interact with cartoon characters, to improving the movement of the characters so that they did not shimmer, to devising ludicrous and preposterous scenes for the sake of spectacle. It did not matter what story was projected just as long as the images astounded the audience, captured its imagination for a short period of time, and left the people laughing or staring in wonderment. The purpose of the early animated films was to make audiences awestruck and to celebrate the magical talents of the animator as demigod. As a result, the fairy tale as story was a vehicle for animators to express their artistic talents and develop their technology. The animators sought to impress audiences with their abilities to use pictures in such a way that they would forget the earlier fairy tales and remember the images that they, the new artists, were creating for them. Through these moving pictures, the animators appropriated literary and oral fairy tales to subsume the word, to have the final word, often through image and book, for Disney began publishing books during the 1930s to complement his films.

---

1. Walter Benjamin, "The Work of Art in the Age of Mechanical Reproduction," in *Illuminations,* trans. Harry Zohn (New York: Harcourt, Brace, and World, 1968), 223.

Of all the early animators, Disney was the one who truly revolutionalized the fairy tale as institution through the cinema. One could almost say that he was obsessed by the fairy-tale genre, or, put another way, Disney felt drawn to fairy tales because they reflected his own struggles in life. After all, Disney came from a relatively poor family, suffered from the exploitative and stern treatment of an unaffectionate father, was spurned by his early sweetheart, and became a success due to his tenacity, cunning, courage, and his ability to gather around him talented artists and managers like his brother Roy.

One of his early films, *Puss in Boots* (1922), is crucial for grasping his approach to the literary fairy tale and understanding how he used it as self-figuration that would mark the genre for years to come. Disney did not especially care whether one knew the original Perrault text of *Puss in Boots* or some other popular version. It is also unclear which text he actually knew. However, what is clear is that Disney sought to replace all versions with his animated version and that his cartoon is astonishingly autobiographical.

If we recall, Perrault wrote his tale in 1697 to reflect upon a cunning cat whose life is threatened and who manages to survive by using his brains to trick a king and an ogre. On a symbolic level, the cat represented Perrault's conception of the role of the *haute bourgeoisie* (his own class), who comprised the administrative class of Louis XIV's court and who were often the mediators between the peasantry and aristocracy. Of course, there are numerous ways to read Perrault's tale, but whatever approach one chooses, it is apparent that the major protagonist is the cat.

This is not the case in Disney's film. The hero is a young man, a commoner, who is in love with the king's daughter, and she fondly returns his affection. At the same time, the hero's black cat, a female, is having a romance with the royal white cat, who is the king's chauffeur. When the gigantic king discovers that the young man is wooing his daughter, he kicks him out of the palace, followed by Puss. At first, the hero does not want Puss's help, nor will he buy her the boots that she sees in a shop window. Then they go to the movies together and see a film with Rudolph Vaselino as a bullfighter, a reference to the famous Rudolph Valentino. This spurs the imagination of Puss. Consequently, she tells the hero that she now has an idea that will help him win the king's daughter, provided that he will buy her the boots. Of course, the hero will do anything to obtain the king's daughter, and he must disguise himself as a masked bullfighter. In the meantime Puss explains to him that she will use a hypnotic machine behind the scenes so he can defeat the bull and win the approval of the king. When the day of the bullfight arrives, the masked hero struggles but eventually manages to defeat the bull.

The king is so overwhelmed by his performance that he offers his daughter's hand in marriage, but first he wants to know who the masked champion is. When the hero reveals himself, the king is enraged, but the hero grabs the princess and leads her to the king's chauffeur. The white cat jumps in front with Puss, and they speed off with the king vainly chasing after them.

Although Puss as cunning cat is crucial in this film, Disney focuses most of his attention on the young man who wants to succeed at all costs. In contrast to the traditional fairy tale, the hero is not a peasant, nor is he dumb. Read as a "parable" of Disney's life at that moment, the hero can be seen as young Disney wanting to break into the industry of animated films (the king) with the help of Ub Iwerks (Puss). The hero upsets the king and runs off with his prize possession, the virginal princess. Thus, the king is dispossessed, and the young man outraces him with the help of his friends.

But Disney's film is also an attack on the literary tradition of the fairy tale. He robs the literary tale of its voice and changes its form and meaning. Since the cinematic medium is a popular form of expression and accessible to the public at large, Disney actually returns the fairy tale to the majority of people. The images (scenes, frames, characters, gestures, jokes) are readily comprehensible by young and old alike from different social classes. In fact, the fairy tale is practically infantilized, just as the jokes are infantile. The plot records the deepest oedipal desire of every young boy: the son humiliates and undermines the father and runs off with his most valued object of love, the daughter/wife. By simplifying this oedipal complex semiotically in black-and-white drawings and making fun of it so that it had a common appeal, Disney also touched on other themes:

(1) Democracy—the film is very *American* in its attitude toward royalty. The monarchy is debunked, and a commoner causes a kind of revolution.

(2) Technology—it is through the new technological medium of the movies that Puss's mind is stimulated. Then she uses a hypnotic machine to defeat the bull and another fairly new invention, the automobile, to escape the king.

(3) Modernity—the setting is obviously the twentieth century, and the modern minds are replacing the ancient. The revolution takes place as the king is outpaced and will be replaced by a commoner who knows how to use the latest inventions.

But who is this commoner? Was Disney making a statement on behalf of the masses? Was Disney celebrating "everyone" or "every man"? Did Disney believe in revolution and socialism? The answer to all these questions is simple: no.

Casting the Commodity Spell with Snow White

Disney's hero is the enterprising young man, the entrepreneur, who uses technology to his advantage. He does nothing to help the people or the community. In fact, he deceives the masses and the king by creating the illusion that he is stronger than the bull. He has learned, with the help of Puss, that one can achieve glory through deception. It is through the artful use of images that one can sway audiences and gain their favor. Animation is trickery—trick films—for still images are made to seem as if they move through automatization. As long as one controls the images (and machines) one can reign supreme, just as the hero is safe as long as he is disguised. The pictures conceal the controls and machinery. They deprive the audience of viewing the production and manipulation, and in the end, audiences can no longer envision a fairy tale for themselves as they can when they read it. The pictures now deprive the audience of visualizing their own characters, roles, and desires. At the same time, Disney offsets the deprivation with the pleasure of scopophilia[2] and inundates the viewer with delightful images, humorous figures, and erotic signs. In general, the animator, Disney, projects the enjoyable fairy tale of his life through his own images, and he realizes through animated stills his basic oedipal dream that he was to play out time and again in most of his fairy-tale films. It is the repetition of Disney's infantile quest—the core of American mythology—that enabled him to strike a chord in American viewers from the 1920s to the present.

However, it was not through *Puss in Boots* and his other early animated fairy tales that he was to captivate audiences and set the "classical" modern model for animated fairy-tale films. They were just the beginning. Rather, it was in *Snow White and the Seven Dwarfs* (1937) that Disney fully appropriated the literary fairy tale and made his signature into a trademark for the most acceptable type of fairy tale in the twentieth century. But before the making of *Snow White,* there were developments in his life and in the film industry that are important to mention in order to grasp why and how *Snow White* became the first definitive animated fairy-tale film—definitive in the sense that it was to define the way other animated films in the genre of the fairy tale were to be made.

After Disney had made several Laugh-O-Gram fairy-tale films, all ironic and modern interpretations of the classical versions, he moved to Hollywood in 1923 and was successful in producing fifty-six *Alice* films, which involved a young girl in different adventures with cartoon characters. By 1927 these films were no longer popular, so Disney and Iwerks soon developed Oswald the Lucky Rabbit cartoons

2. The gaining of sexual pleasure by looking at erotic images [editor's note].

that also found favor with audiences. However, in February of 1928, while Disney was in New York trying to renegotiate a contract with his distributor Charles Mintz, he learned that Mintz, who owned the copyright to Oswald, had lured some of Disney's best animators to work for another studio. Disney faced bankruptcy because he refused to capitulate to the exploitative conditions that Mintz set for the distribution and production of Disney's films.[3] This experience sobered Disney in his attitude to the cutthroat competition in the film industry, and when he returned to Hollywood, he vowed to maintain complete control over all his productions—a vow that he never broke.

In the meantime, Disney and Iwerks had to devise another character for their company if they were to survive, and they conceived the idea for films featuring a pert mouse named Mickey. By September of 1928, after making two Mickey Mouse shorts, Disney, similar to his masked champion in *Puss in Boots,* had devised a way to gain revenge on Mintz and other animation studios by producing the first animated cartoon with sound, *Steamboat Willie,* starring Mickey Mouse. From this point on, Disney became known for introducing new inventions and improving animation so that animated films became almost as realistic as films with live actors and natural settings. His next step after sound was color, and in 1932 he signed an exclusive contract with Technicolor and began producing his *Silly Symphony* cartoons in color. More important, Disney released *The Three Little Pigs* in 1933 and followed it with *The Big Bad Wolf* (1934) and *The Three Little Wolves* (1936), all of which involved fairy-tale characters and stories that touched on the lives of people during the Depression. As Bob Thomas has remarked, *"The Three Little Pigs* was acclaimed by the Nation. The wolf was on many American doorsteps, and 'Who's Afraid of the Big Bad Wolf?' became a rallying cry."[4] Not only were wolves on the doorsteps of Americans but also witches, and to a certain extent, Disney, with the help of his brother Roy and Iwerks, had been keeping "evil" connivers and competitors from the entrance to the Disney Studios throughout the 1920s. Therefore, it is not by chance that Disney's next major experiment would involve a banished princess, loved by a charming prince, who would triumph over deceit and regain the rights to her castle. *Snow White and the Seven Dwarfs* was to bring together all the personal strands of Disney's own story with the destinies of desperate Americans who sought hope and solidarity in their fight for survival during the Depression of the 1930s.

Of course, by 1934 Disney was, comparatively speaking, wealthy. He hired Don Graham, a professional artist, to train studio animators at the Disney Art School, founded in November 1932. He then

3. Leonard Mosley, *Disney's World* (New York: Stein and Day, 1985), 85–140.
4. Bob Thomas, *Disney's Art of Animation: From Mickey Mouse to Beauty and the Beast* (New York: Hyperion, 1991), 49.

embarked on ventures to stun moviegoers with his ingenuity and talents as organizer, storyteller, and filmmaker. Conceived some time in 1934, *Snow White* was to take three years to complete, and Disney did not leave one stone unturned in his preparations for the first full-length animated fairy-tale film ever made. Disney knew he was making history even before history had been made.

During the course of the next three years, Disney worked closely with all the animators and technicians assigned to the production of *Snow White*. By now, Disney had divided his studio into numerous departments, such as animation, layout, sound, music, storytelling, etc., and had placed certain animators in charge of developing the individual characters of Snow White, the prince, the dwarfs, and the queen/crone. Disney spent thousands of dollars on a multiplane camera to capture the live-action depictions that he desired, the depth of the scenes, and close-ups. In addition, he had his researchers experiment with colored gels, blurred focus, and filming through frosted glass, while he employed the latest inventions in sound and music to improve the synchronization with the characters on the screen. Throughout the entire production of this film, Disney had to be consulted and give his approval for each stage of development. After all, *Snow White* was his story that he had taken from the Grimm Brothers and changed completely to suit his tastes and beliefs. He cast a spell over this German tale and transformed it into something peculiarly American. Just what were the changes he induced?

(1) Snow White is an orphan. Neither her father nor her mother are alive, and she is at first depicted as a kind of "Cinderella," cleaning the castle as a maid in a patched dress. In the Grimms' version there is the sentimental death of her mother. Her father remains alive, and she is never forced to do the work of commoners such as wash the steps of the castle.

(2) The prince appears at the very beginning of the film on a white horse and sings a song of love and devotion to Snow White. He plays a negligible role in the Grimms' version.

(3) The queen is not only jealous that Snow White is more beautiful than she is, but she also sees the prince singing to Snow White and is envious because her stepdaughter has such a handsome suitor.

(4) Though the forest and the animals do not speak, they are anthropomorphized. In particular the animals befriend Snow White and become her protectors.

(5) The dwarfs are hardworking and rich miners. They all have names—Doc, Sleepy, Bashful, Happy, Sneezy, Grumpy, Dopey—representative of certain human characteristics and are fleshed out so that they become the star attractions of the film. Their actions are what counts in defeating evil. In the Grimms' tale, the dwarfs are anonymous and play a humble role.

(6) The queen only comes one time instead of three as in the Grimms' version, and she is killed while trying to destroy the dwarfs by rolling a huge stone down a mountain to crush them. The punishment in the Grimms' tale is more horrifying because she must dance in redhot iron shoes at Snow White's wedding.

(7) Snow White does not return to life when a dwarf stumbles while carrying the glass coffin as in the Grimms' tale. She returns to life when the prince, who has searched far and wide for her, arrives and bestows a kiss on her lips. His kiss of love is the only antidote to the queen's poison.

At first glance, it would seem that the changes that Disney made were not momentous. If we recall Sandra Gilbert and Susan Gubar's stimulating analysis in their book, *The Madwoman in the Attic* (1979), the film follows the classic "sexist" narrative about the framing of women's lives through a male discourse. Such male framing drives women to frustration and some women to the point of madness. It also pits women against women in competition for male approval (the mirror) of their beauty that is short-lived. No matter what they may do, women cannot chart their own lives without male manipulation and intervention, and in the Disney film, the prince plays even more of a framing role since he is introduced at the beginning while Snow White is singing, "I'm Wishing for the One I Love To Find Me Today." He will also appear at the end as the fulfillment of her dreams.

There is no doubt that Disney retained key ideological features of the Grimms' fairy tale that reinforce nineteenth-century patriarchal notions that Disney shared with the Grimms. In some way, they can even be considered his ancestor, for he preserves and carries on many of their benevolent attitudes toward women. For instance, in the Grimms' tale, when Snow White arrives at the cabin, she pleads with the dwarfs to allow her to remain and promises that she will wash the dishes, mend their clothes, and clean the house. In Disney's film, she arrives and notices that the house is dirty. So, she convinces the animals to help her make the cottage tidy so that the dwarfs will perhaps let her stay there. Of course, the house for the Grimms and Disney was the place where good girls remained, and one shared aspect of the fairy tale and the film is about the domestication of women.

However, Disney went much further than the Grimms to make his film more memorable than the tale, for he does not celebrate the domestication of women so much as the triumph of the banished and the underdogs. That is, he celebrates his destiny, and insofar as he had shared marginal status with many Americans, he also celebrates an American myth of Horatio Alger: it is a male myth about perseverance, hard work, dedication, loyalty, and justice.

It may seem strange to argue that Disney perpetuated a male myth through his fairy-tale films when, with the exception of *Pinocchio* (1940), they all featured young women as "heroines": *Sleeping Beauty* (1959), *Cinderella* (1950), and *The Little Mermaid* (1989). However, despite their beauty and charm, these figures are pale and pathetic compared to the more active and demonic characters in the film. The witches are not only agents of evil but represent erotic and subversive forces that are more appealing both for the artists who drew them and the audiences.[5] The young women are helpless ornaments in need of protection, and when it comes to the action of the film, they are omitted. In *Snow White and the Seven Dwarfs*, the film does not really become lively until the dwarfs enter the narrative. They are the mysterious characters who inhabit a cottage, and it is through their hard work and solidarity that they are able to maintain a world of justice and restore harmony to the world. The dwarfs can be interpreted as the humble American workers, who pull together during a depression. They keep their spirits up by singing a song "Hi ho, it's home from work we go," or "Hi ho, it's off to work we go," and their determination is the determination of every worker, who will succeed just as long as he does his share while women stay at home and keep the house clean. Of course, it is also possible to see the workers as Disney's own employees, on whom he depended for the glorious outcome of his films. In this regard, the prince can be interpreted as Disney, who directed the love story from the beginning. If we recall, it is the prince who frames the narrative. He announces his great love at the beginning of the film, and Snow White cannot be fulfilled until he arrives to kiss her. During the major action of the film, he, like Disney, is lurking in the background and waiting for the proper time to make himself known. When he does arrive, he takes all the credit as champion of the disenfranchised, and he takes Snow White to his castle while the dwarfs are left as keepers of the forest.

But what has the prince actually done to deserve all the credit? What did Disney actually do to have his name flash on top of the title as "Walt Disney's Snow White and the Seven Dwarfs" in big letters and later credit his coworkers in small letters? As we know, Disney never liked to give credit to the animators who worked with him, and they had to fight for acknowledgment.[6] Disney always made it clear that he was the boss and owned total rights to his products.

5. Solomon cites the famous quotation by Woody Allen in *Annie Hall:* "You know, even as a kid I always went for the wrong women. When my mother took me to see 'Snow White,' everyone fell in love with Snow White; I immediately fell for the Wicked Queen" [Charles Solomon, "Bad Girls Finish First in Memory of Disney Fans," *Milwaukee Journal* 17 August 1980, 28].

6. Bill Peet, for example, an "in-betweener" in the early Disney studio, worked for a year and a half on *Pinocchio* (1940). Peet relates that, after watching the film in his neighborhood theatre, "I was dumbfounded when the long list of screen credits didn't include my name" (*Bill Peet: An Autobiography* [Boston: Houghton Mifflin, 1989], 108).

He had struggled for his independence against his greedy and unjust father and against fierce and ruthless competitors in the film industry. As producer of the fairy-tale films and major owner of the Disney studios, he wanted to figure in the films and sought, as Crafton has noted, to create a more indelible means of self-figuration. In *Snow White,* he accomplished this by stamping his signature as owner on the title frame of the film and then by having himself embodied in the figure of the prince. It is the prince Disney who made inanimate figures come to life through his animated films, and it is the prince who is to be glorified in *Snow White and the Seven Dwarfs* when he resuscitates Snow White with a magic kiss. Afterward he holds Snow White in his arms, and in the final frame, he leads her off on a white horse to his golden castle on a hill. His golden castle—every woman's dream—supersedes the dark, sinister castle of the queen. The prince becomes Snow White's reward, and his power and wealth are glorified in the end.

There are obviously mixed messages or multiple messages in *Snow White and the Seven Dwarfs,* but the overriding sign, in my estimation, is the signature of Disney's self-glorification in the name of justice. Disney wants the world *cleaned up,* and the pastel colors with their sharply drawn ink lines create images of cleanliness, just as each sequence reflects a clearly conceived and preordained destiny for all the characters in the film. For Disney, the Grimms' tale is not a vehicle to explore the deeper implications of the narrative and its history.[7] Rather, it is a vehicle to display what he can do as an animator

---

7. Karen Merritt makes the interesting point that "Disney's *Snow White* is an adaptation of a 1912 children's play (Disney saw it as a silent movie during his adolescence) still much performed today, written by a male Broadway producer under a female pseudonym; this play was an adaptation of a play for immigrant children from the tenements of lower East Side New York; and that play, in turn, was a translation and adaptation of a German play for children by a prolific writer of children's comedies and fairy-tale drama. Behind these plays was the popularity of nineteenth- and early twentieth-century fairy-tale pantomimes at Christmas in England and fairy-tale plays in Germany and America. The imposition of childish behavior on the dwarfs, Snow White's resulting mothering, the age ambiguities in both Snow White and the dwarfs, the 'Cinderella' elements, and the suppression of any form of sexuality were transmitted by that theatrical tradition, which embodied a thoroughly developed philosophy of moral education in representations for children. . . . By reading Disney's *Snow White* by the light of overt didacticism of his sources, he no longer appears the moral reactionary disdained by contemporary critics. Rather, he is the entertainer who elevates the subtext of play found in his sources and dares once again to frighten children" [Karen Merritt, "The Little Girl/Little Mother Transformation: The American Evolution of 'Snow White and the Seven Dwarfs,'" in *Storytelling in Animation: The Art of the Animated Image,* ed. John Canemaker (Los Angeles: American Film Institute, 1994), 106]. Though it may be true that Disney was more influenced by an American theatrical and film tradition, the source of all these productions, one acknowledged by Disney, was the Grimms' tale. And, as I have argued, Disney was not particularly interested in experimenting with the narrative to shock children or provide a new perspective on the traditional story. For all intents and purposes his film reinforces the didactic messages of the Grimms' tale, and it is only in the technical innovations and designs that he did something startlingly new. It is not the object of critique to "disdain" or "condemn" Disney for reappropriating the Grimms' tradition to glorify the great designer, but to understand those cultural and psychological forces that led him to map out his narrative strategies in fairy-tale animation.

with the latest technological and artistic developments in the industry. The story is secondary, and if there is a major change in the plot, it centers on the power of the prince, the only one who can save Snow White, and he becomes the focal point by the end of the story.

In Disney's early work with fairy tales in Kansas City, he had a wry and irreverent attitude toward the classical narratives. There was a strong suggestion, given the manner in which he and Iwerks rewrote and filmed the tales, that they were "revolutionaries," the new boys on the block, who were about to introduce innovative methods of animation into the film industry and speak for the outcasts. However, in 1934, Disney was already the kingpin of animation, and he used all that he had learned to reinforce his power and command of fairy-tale animation. The manner in which he copied the musical plays and films of his time, and his close adaptation of fairy tales with patriarchal codes, indicate that all the technical experiments would not be used to foster social change in America but to keep power in the hands of individuals like himself, who felt empowered to design and create new worlds. As Richard Schickel has perceptively remarked, Disney

> could make something his own, all right, but that process nearly always robbed the work at hand of its uniqueness, of its soul, if you will. In its place he put jokes and songs and fright effects, but he always seemed to diminish what he touched. He came always as a conqueror, never as a servant. It is a trait, as many have observed, that many Americans share when they venture into foreign lands hoping to do good but equipped only with knowhow instead of sympathy and respect for alien traditions.[8]

Disney always wanted to do something new and unique just as long as he had absolute control. He also knew that novelty would depend on the collective skills of his employees, whom he had to keep happy or indebted to him in some way. Therefore, from 1934 onward, about the time that he conceived his first feature-length fairy-tale film, Disney became the orchestrator of a corporate network that changed the function of the fairy-tale genre in America. The power of Disney's fairy-tale films does not reside in the uniqueness or novelty of the productions, but in Disney's great talent for holding antiquated views of society *still* through animation and his use of the latest technological developments in cinema to his advantage. His adaptation of the literary fairy tale for the screen led to the following changes in the institution of the genre:

(1) Technique takes precedence over the story, and the story is used to celebrate the technician and his means.

8. Richard Schickel, *The Disney Version* (New York: Simon and Schuster, 1968), 227.

(2) The carefully arranged images narrate through seduction and imposition of the animator's hand and the camera.

(3) The images and sequences engender a sense of wholeness, seamless totality, and harmony that is orchestrated by a savior/technician on and off the screen.

(4) Though the characters are fleshed out to become more realistic, they are also one-dimensional and are to serve functions in the film. There is no character development because the characters are stereotypes, arranged according to a credo of domestication of the imagination.

(5) The domestication is related to colonization insofar as the ideas and types are portrayed as models of behavior to be emulated. Exported through the screen as models, the "American" fairy tale colonizes other national audiences. What is good for Disney is good for the world, and what is good in a Disney fairy tale is good in the rest of the world.

(6) The thematic emphasis on cleanliness, control, and organized industry reinforces the technics of the film itself: the clean frames with attention paid to every detail; the precise drawing and manipulation of the characters as real people; the careful plotting of the events that focus on salvation through the male hero.

(7) Private reading pleasure is replaced by pleasurable viewing in an impersonal cinema. Here one is brought together with other viewers not for the development of community but to be diverted in the French sense of *divertissement* and American sense of diversion.

(8) The diversion of the Disney fairy tale is geared toward nonreflective viewing. Everything is on the surface, one-dimensional, and we are to delight in one-dimensional portrayal and thinking, for it is adorable, easy, and comforting in its simplicity.

Once Disney realized how successful he was with his formula for feature-length fairy tales, he never abandoned it, and in fact, if one regards the two most recent Disney Studio productions of *Beauty and the Beast* (1991) and *Aladdin* (1992), Disney's contemporary animators have continued in his footsteps. There is nothing but the "eternal return of the same" in *Beauty and the Beast* and *Aladdin* that makes for enjoyable viewing and delight in techniques of these films as commodities, but nothing new in the exploration of narration, animation, and signification.

There is something sad in the manner in which Disney "violated" the literary genre of the fairy tale and packaged his versions in his name through the merchandising of books, toys, clothing, and records. Instead of using technology to enhance the communal aspects of narrative and bring about major changes in viewing stories to stir and animate viewers, he employed animators and technology to stop thinking about change, to return to his films, and to long nostalgically for neatly ordered patriarchal realms. Fortunately, the animation of the literary fairy tale did not stop with Disney, but that is another tale to tell, a tale about breaking Disney's magic spell.

DONALD HAASE

From Yours, Mine, or Ours? Perrault, the Brothers Grimm, and the Ownership of Fairy Tales[†]

* * *

The Revered Place of Folklore

In 1944 W. H. Auden decreed that Grimm's fairy tales are "among the few indispensable, common-property books upon which Western culture can be founded . . . [I]t is hardly too much to say that these tales rank next to the Bible in importance."[1]

Auden was in one sense right. Like the Bible, fairy tales—especially the classic tales of Charles Perrault and the Brothers Grimm—hold a revered if not sacred place in modern Western culture. Often thought to reach back like sacred works to "times past," to some ancient, pristine age in which their original tellers spoke mythic words of revelation, folk tales and fairy tales are endowed by many readers with unassailable moral and even spiritual authenticity.

Because such tales had their genesis in an oral tradition, we are tempted to imagine their original tellers as simple folk endowed with infallible wisdom and, in some cases, divine inspiration. As a consequence of that belief, tampering with the classic texts of Perrault or the Brothers Grimm is considered by some to be tantamount to sacrilege, similar to revising the text of the Holy Scriptures. As one of my undergraduate students remarked in a journal he kept while studying fairy tales in the winter term of 1990: "I am not a deeply religious person. However, I have a vague feeling that questioning the origin of fairy tales is somehow sacrilegious." Some traditionalists even go so far as to argue that the common practice of replacing *Sneewittchen,* the Grimms' original German spelling of Snow White, with the more modern orthographical form *Schneewittchen* constitutes "monument desecration."[2]

[†] From Donald Haase, "Yours, Mine, or Ours? Perrault, the Brothers Grimm, and the Ownership of Fairy Tales," in *Once Upon a Folklore: Capturing the Folklore Process with Children,* ed. Gloria T. Blatt (New York: Teachers College, Columbia U, 1993), pp. 63–75. Copyright © 1993 by Teachers College, Columbia University. All rights reserved.

1. W. H. Auden, "In Praise of the Brothers Grimm," *The New York Times Book Review* (12 Nov. 1944): 1, 28.

2. Hermann Bausinger, "Anmerkungen zu Schneewittchen," in *Und wenn sie nicht gestorben sind: Perspektiven auf das Märchen,* ed. H. Brackert (Frankfurt a.M.: Suhrkamp, 1980), 46.

When classic stories are changed unacceptably, the blame is often placed on the culture industry—publishers, advertisers, merchandisers, and even pedagogues who have capitalized on the mass appeal of the traditional tales and emptied them of their original vigor and truth. Disney's Americanized and romanticized fairy-tale movies, for example, have been severely criticized for trivializing and betraying the original themes, thus enfeebling an important cultural possession.[3] As the civilized entrepreneur and creator of the fairy tale as consumer romance,[4] Disney is the absolute antithesis of the mythic peasant or Ice Age storyteller, from whom we have supposedly inherited this allegedly sacred possession.

While this religious or quasi-religious reverence is certainly appealing and even reassuring, it is dangerously misleading. As an antidote to it, consider two of the twenty-four theses offered by the German writer Wolfdietrich Schnurre in a piece he aptly entitled "Heretical Thoughts on the Treasury of Fairy Tales." In a sardonic letter to the long deceased Brothers Grimm, Schnurre seeks to explain why he thinks fairy tales have lost their value for us. "The primary guilt for the decline of the fairy tale," he claims, "rests with those who [originally] made them. They forgot to impress on them the stamp of copyright."[5] In this case, not the culture industry, but the folk themselves are held responsible for the fairy tale's bankruptcy. Ironically, the fairy tale's status as communal property is proposed as the very cause of its neglect and demise. It is a fairy tale, Schnurre asserts, to believe "that fairy tales are the property of the *Volk*—the people. Property is cared for. The *Volk*," he asserts, "has ruined fairy tales."[6]

These statements are heretical to established views that tell us not only why folktales are still relevant but to whom they belong. However we might feel about the tales of the Brothers Grimm or Perrault, Schnurre's provocative assertions raise intriguing questions about the reception and cultural ownership of fairy tales. Who are the folk, that anonymous group we often view as the originators and owners of the fairy tale? And if the tales do not belong to the folk, then to whom do they belong? And, finally, why does the issue of ownership matter at all?

The Nationalistic View of Folklore

The concept of "the folk" is a slippery one. To some, the folk are an ethnic or national group sharing common traditions, lore, and social

3. Bruno Bettelheim, *The Uses of Enchantment: The Meaning and Importance of Fairy Tales* (New York: Knopf, 1976), 210.
4. Donald Haase, "Gold into Straw: Fairy Tale Movies for Children and the Culture Industry," *The Lion and the Unicorn* 12 (1988): 193–207.
5. Wolfdietrich Schnurre, "Ketzerisches zum Märchenschatz: 24 kurzweilige Thesen," in *Grimmige Märchen: Prosatexte von Ilse Aichinger bis Martin Walser* (Frankfurt: Fischer, 1986), 23.
6. Ibid., 23.

or cultural traits. In general parlance, "the folk" are the common folk, that is, the working or peasant classes. But as the Italian folk-lorist Giuseppe Cocchiara has suggested, the identity of the folk transcends classes and "is the expression of a certain vision of life, certain attitudes of the spirit, of thought, of culture, of custom, of civilization, which appear with their own clearly delineated charac-teristics."[7] While Cocchiara's definition avoids the class bias of ear-lier definitions, Alan Dundes excises the ethnic and national emphasis by defining the folk as *any group of people whatsoever who share at least one common factor.*"[8]

However, for the Grimms and many early folklorists, it was the so-called common people who best embodied a nation's folk life. It was their lore—including their folktales—that was to become the reservoir and model of national character. As the product of the Ger-man folk, the tales were thought to contain the scattered fragments of ancient Germanic myth, which—when collected—would pro-vide the German people with a magic mirror in which they could discern and thus reassert their national identity. In this way, the Grimms' collection of folktales was conscripted into nationalistic service and became a political weapon in the Grimms' intellectual resistance to the Napoleonic occupation of their beloved Hessian homeland.

To define the folk in nationalistic terms establishes fairy tales as national property. They are either yours, or they are mine. Following—and, it must be emphasized, grossly exaggerating—the Grimms' nationalistic understanding of fairy tales, many Germans were only too ready to exercise their right of ownership by advocat-ing the Grimms' tales as a national primer, after 1871, for the newly unified nation. In 1899, for instance, Carl Franke gave this expla-nation of the close link between the Grimms' tales and the educa-tion of a nation:

> To the spirit of German schoolchildren the tales have become what mother's milk is for their bodies—the first nourishment for the spirit and the imagination. How German [are] Snow White, Little Briar Rose, Little Red Cap, the seven dwarfs! Through such genuine German diet must the language and spirit of the child gradually become more and more German. . . .[9]

Given the Grimms' precedent and given the need of every new state to authenticate its self-image, we can understand such remarks; just

7. Giuseppi Cocchiara, *The History of Folklore in Europe,* trans. J. N. McDaniel (Philadel-phia: Institute for the Study of Human Issues, 1981), 4.
8. Alan Dundes, *The Study of Folklore* (Englewood Cliffs, N.J.: Prentice Hall, 1965), 2.
9. L. L. Snyder, "Cultural Nationalism: The Grimm Brothers' Fairy Tales," in *Roots of German Nationalism* (Bloomington: Indiana UP, 1978), 51.

as we can understand the lamentable exploitation of the Grimms' tales under National Socialism, which points up all too clearly the dangers inherent in viewing fairy tales as the property of a single group or nation. * * *

But there is another, hidden danger in this nationalistic view. Ironically, the abuse of the Grimms' tales by the culture industry of National Socialism has reinforced prejudice against the Grimms' tales. So compelling was the German identification of Germanic folktales with national identity that the Grimms' stories have very often been accepted as belonging uniquely to the Germans. But instead of identifying favorable cultural traits in the tales, some readers have discerned more ambiguous characteristics. In 1939, Vincent Brun accused the Germans of perverting the fairy tale by exploiting its rude primitive instincts to educate and not to amuse children. By the end of World War II, the German fairy tale had fallen into such disrepute that during the Allied occupation of Germany fairy tales were viewed with serious suspicion and banned from the public school curriculum. Evidently, Auden's reclamation of the Grimms' tales as common property in 1944 was not universally accepted; in 1947 T. J. Leonard let loose with his infamous attack on German fairy tales, which he unequivocally condemned as relics of Germanic barbarism, and blamed for promoting German nationalism and sadistic behavior among Germans. The reverberations of such attacks on Germanic folktales and German national character can still be felt. In 1985, Siegfried Heyer published an abridged German translation of Leonard's attack, and Jörg Becker, in response, reflected on the enduring image of the "ugly German." That the alleged connection between German national character and fairy tales should occupy scholars forty years after the war is not surprising given that Germans, as well as their former adversaries, have kept this essentially postwar issue alive.

In 1978, Louis Snyder repeated the thesis he first put forth in the 1950s that the Grimms' tales, having played a role in the development of modern German nationalism, emphasize "such social characteristics as respect for order, belief in the desirability of obedience, subservience to authority, respect for the leader and the hero, veneration of courage and the military spirit, acceptance without protest of cruelty, violence, and atrocity, fear of and hatred for the outsider, and virulent anti-Semitism."[1] Readers like Snyder clearly relinquish title to the tales and deed them back to their owners. The nationalism implicit in the message is clear: these tales are yours (German), not mine (American).

1. Ibid., 51.

Differentiating between tales belonging to different countries, and thus differentiating between the countries themselves, has become standard practice. In his study of the French folktale during the Old Regime, the historian Robert Darnton has insisted on the unique characteristics of the French folktale that distinguish it from its German counterpart. Darnton summarizes the differences in this way:

> Where the French tales tend to be realistic, earthy, bawdy, and comical, the German [tales] veer off toward the supernatural, the poetic, the exotic, and the violent. Of course, cultural differences cannot be reduced to a formula—French craftiness versus German cruelty—but the comparisons make it possible to identify the peculiar inflection that the French gave to their stories, and their way of telling stories provides clues about their way of viewing the world.[2]

Although Darnton tries to avoid stereotyping national character by adding a disclaimer and by referring instead to differing world views, in the final analysis his implicit notion of fairy tales as culturally defined property makes this difficult. However, he is at least aware of the danger of idealizing the national ethos. In pointing to the similarity between the tales of French peasants and those of Perrault, Darnton says that both groups of "tales communicated traits, values, attitudes, and a way of construing the world that was peculiarly French. To insist upon their Frenchness," he notes, "is not to fall into romantic rhapsodizing about national spirit, but rather to recognize the existence of distinct cultural styles, which set off the French . . . from other peoples identified at the time as German, Italian, and English."[3] Perhaps it is easy for Darnton to avoid rhapsodizing because he is not French. That is, the tales he discusses are "theirs," not his.

Although the French are not immune to praising the unique nature of their national fairy tales, they seem to be less dependent on the tales for the codification of their self-image than are the Germans. France lacked—indeed, did not need—strong nationalistic voices such as those of the Brothers Grimm, who set the German precedent for folktale worship. Moreover, because the French enjoyed a strong literary heritage, they were perhaps more likely to find models of the national ethos in their classical canon than in popular folk literature. After all, unlike the Grimms' tales, Perrault's stories are usually considered not so much examples of the folk culture as part of the elevated literary tradition of the Old Regime.

2. Robert Darnton, "Peasants Tell Tales: The Meaning of Mother Goose," in *The Great Cat Massacre and Other Episodes in French Cultural History* (New York: Basic Books, 1984), 50–51.
3. Darnton, *Great Cat Massacre*, 63.

Although Robert Darnton might find the French popular tale characterized by the earthy and bawdy, Paul Hazard praises Perrault's fairy tales for their expression of such typically French characteristics as logic, wit, and refined femininity.[4] Fernand Baldensperger, not without irony, has even observed that Perrault's fairies are charming Cartesian fairies.[5]

The pride the French take in their tales rarely gets more impassioned than this. Perhaps this also has something to do with the influential essay on Perrault written by Sainte-Beuve in 1851, in which he stressed not only the naivete and simplicity, but also the universal appeal of the French stories.[6]

Such a view draws on another interpretation of the folk that does not rely on national or ethnic identity and consequently proposes an alternative ownership for the fairy tale. This view of the folk is informed by a universalizing tendency that completely disregards social, historical, and cultural factors. It is the view espoused in particular by psychoanalytic, archetypal, and anthroposophical-spiritualist (Waldorf school) readers of fairy tales.[7] It is best summed up in this amazingly wrongheaded passage taken from the book *Fairy Tales and Children* by psychologist Carl-Heinz Mallet:

> Fairy Tales are popular poetry, for they originated and developed among the people [the folk]. They were born in fusty spinning rooms. Simple people told them to simple people. No one else was interested in these "old wives' tales." No superior authority, whether profane or ecclesiastic, exerted any influence. Fairy tales developed outside the great world, beyond the centers of political and cultural power. They absorbed nothing from these areas, no historical events, no political facts, no cultural trends. They remained free of the moral views, behavioral standards, and manners of the various epochs. . . . Human beings *per se* are the focal point of fairy tales, and people are pretty much alike no matter when or where they have lived.[8]

This is in striking contrast to the opinions discussed earlier in this chapter. Here the folk constitute not a national group bound together by a common culture, but an ill-defined population of idyllic innocents whose sole characteristic is simplicity. Rousseau is responsible for this model. But both this mythical peasant and the ensuing

4. Paul Hazard, *Books, Children and Men*, trans. Marguerite Mitchell (Boston: Horn Book, 1947), 121–24.
5. Cited in Hazard, *Books,* 122.
6. C.-A. Sainte-Beuve, "Charles Perrault," in *Causeries du lundi* (Paris: Garnier, 1944), V, 273.
7. Readers who follow the teachings of Rudolf Steiner, who was deeply influenced by Jungian psychology [editor's note].
8. Carl-Heinz Mallet, *Fairy Tales and Children: The Psychology of Children Revealed through Four of Grimms' Fairy Tales,* trans. J. Neugroschel (New York: Schocken, 1984), 38.

notion of a fairy tale untouched by its social or historical context are ridiculous. Yet these are the very premises upon which very influential and popular theories of the fairy tale have been built. Their unfortunate success lies in their reassuring appeal to our humanity, to the soothing promise that both human beings and values transcend time and space. In other words, as vessels of purportedly universal human truths, fairy tales belong to us all. The classic example of this view is Bruno Bettelheim, whose popular psychoanalytic interpretations of fairy tales by the Brothers Grimm and Perrault have been widely and enthusiastically embraced.

Bettelheim's Psychoanalytic Interpretations of Fairy Tales

From Bettelheim's psychoanalytic perspective, fairy tales address "essential human problems" and "have great psychological meaning."[9] Through fairy tales, Bettelheim argues, both children and adults can find their way through life's existential dilemmas. Bettelheim can come to these conclusions because he assumes that fairy tales transcend the specific time and place of their origin and give us insight into "manifold truths . . . which can guide our lives; . . . truth as valid today as it was once upon a time."[1] Thus, fairy tales, whether German or French, for example, would seem to belong to us all, not simply by virtue of our sharing a common Western culture, but because the fairy tale's transcendent nature addresses our common humanity. However, Bettelheim's point of view is problematic because what he believes to be universal truths ultimately turn out to be the values of nineteenth-century Europe.

The repressive moralizing inherent in Bettelheim's readings of fairy tales has been solidly criticized before, but I mention the issue again here because his understanding of fairy tales remains influential, especially among teachers and children's librarians who often rely on his work. * * * Jack Zipes's criticism of Bettelheim's "Use and Abuse of Folk and Fairy Tales with Children,"[2] in particular, deserves reading or rereading in light of the recent, sobering allegations by one of Bettelheim's former patients at the Orthogenic School that the author of The Uses of Enchantment was an authoritarian who physically and emotionally abused children in his care.[3] The values

9. Bettelheim, Uses, 17.
1. Ibid., 310.
2. Jack Zipes, "On the Use and Abuse of Folk and Fairy Tales with Children: Bruno Bettelheim's Moralistic Magic Wand," in Breaking the Magic Spell: Radical Theories of Folk and Fairy Tales (New York: Methuen, 1984), 160–82.
3. C. Pekow, "The Other Dr. Bettelheim: The Revered Psychologist Had a Dark, Violent Side," Washington Post (26 Aug. 1990), C1, C4; and Jack Zipes, The Brothers Grimm: From Enchanted Forests to the Modern World (New York: Routledge, 1988), 110–34.

that Bettelheim views as timeless and common to us all frequently turn out to be those of the authoritarian, patriarchal society in which he was raised.[4]

Some of Bettelheim's influence has been mitigated by recent studies that reveal the specific sociocultural roots of many tales and thus expose their historically determined values. In fact, for the last fifteen years the Grimms' tales have been the center of considerable discussion and controversy as a result of renewed interest in evidence that the Grimms did not give us authentic, unaltered folktales transcribed from the mouths of simple people, but instead drew many of their tales from highly educated informants or printed literary texts. * * * That Wilhelm Grimm had freely revised, edited, added to, and basically rewritten many of the classic tales to reflect his own aesthetic and moral values renders the universal, transcendent view of these tales untenable.

But the discrediting of theories has affected not only those who, like Bettelheim, believe in the universal nature of fairy tales. The nationalists have had to confront the discovery that many of the best known and most cherished of the Grimms' tales are not purely German. They are in many cases of mixed origin. Some of the Grimms' most significant informants have turned out to be educated bourgeois women from families of French Huguenots who had settled in Germany after the revocation of the Edict of Nantes. Of course, to say that these oral sources spoke French and were familiar with the tales of Perrault is not to say that what the Grimms have given us is a collection of French tales. They did not. But it is enough to undermine the view that makes fairy tales the possession of a single nationality.

We are left, however, with a question. If fairy tales are not the universal possession of an all-encompassing, undifferentiated humanity, and if they are not the sole property of any single national group, then to whom do fairy tales belong? This question can be best answered by turning first to the question: Why does it matter at all to whom fairy tales belong?

The Question of Ownership

The question of ownership is not an idle question. As we've seen, our specific views on the origin and nature of fairy tales necessarily imply that we have, implicitly or explicitly, a specific attitude toward their ownership. And these attitudes, in turn, have an impact on the

4. Donald Haase, "'Verzauberungen der Seele': Das Märchen und die Exilanten der NS-Zeit," in *Begegnungen mit dem "Fremden": Grenzen—Traditionen—Vergleiche: Akten des VIII. Internationalen Germanisten-Kongresses, Tokyo 1990* (Munich: iudicium, 1991), 44–50.

reception of fairy tales insofar as they determine how we both read and use fairy tales. The problem—indeed, the danger—with both the nationalistic/ethnic and universal views of fairy tales is that they prescribe forms of thought and behavior, and modes and models of humanity, that are meant to be normative. That is, they stereotype us—either as members of a nationalistic or ethnic group, or as human beings defined by a certain concept of what is or is not normal. This is why fairy tales have been so frequently utilized by *both* nationalists and universalists in the socialization of children. In both cases, fairy tales are supposed to depict or prescribe for us what is true, as well as what forms of behavior are typical, normal, and acceptable. Whether we view them as yours and mine or as ours, fairy tales—read from these perspectives—confine and limit us, narrowing our views of reality while allegedly giving us greater insight into the other, into ourselves, or into humanity. From these perspectives, fairy tales own us, we don't own them.

An important twist was added to the question of ownership with the proliferation of both printed texts and copyright law in the nineteenth century. While folktales remain in the public domain because of their anonymous origin in the oral tradition (which accounts in part for their popularity among publishers), there has been a growing tendency to stress private ownership by individuals or even corporations. This is evident in the way we speak about fairy tales. With deference to the folk's public ownership of fairy tales, the Grimms claimed only to have *collected* the stories in their famous edition. Yet we refer to them as "Grimms' fairy tales." Contemporary storytellers, who work for a fee and are cautious about allowing audio or video recordings of their performances, frequently talk of making a traditional folktale their own. Although this is in one sense an artistic claim, the vocabulary of ownership clearly implies the expectation to control and profit from the tale in question. When Disney called his animated fairy tales by his own name—*Walt Disney's Snow White and the Seven Dwarfs, Walt Disney's Sleeping Beauty,* and so on—he was not simply making an artistic statement, but also laying claim to the tales in what would become their most widely known, public versions. In 1989, when the Academy of Motion Picture Arts and Sciences used the figure of Snow White in its televised award ceremonies, the Walt Disney Company filed a lawsuit claiming "unauthorized use of its Snow White character," which the corporation felt had been treated in an unflattering manner in the comical and mildly satirical sketch.[5] When the Walt Disney Company spent $1 million for the videocassette rights to the "Rocky and

5. "Disney Company Sues over Snow White Use," *New York Times* (31 March 1989), C33; A. Harmetz, "An Apology to Disney," *New York Times* (7 April 1989), C30.

Bullwinkle" series—including the "Fractured Fairy Tales" that
sometimes parody the Disney versions and Walt Disney himself—
its corporate ownership and control of the fairy tale were extended
to even the subversive fairy tale.[6] If the Walt Disney Company cannot completely prevent unflattering parodies of its fairy-tale movies
and their creator, at least it will now be able to control and profit
from their distribution.

The Disney case demonstrates that the question of ownership is
important because it is ultimately a question of control. So who owns
fairy tales? To be blunt: I do. And you do. We can each claim fairy
tales for ourselves. Not as members of a national or ethnic folk
group—as French, German, or American. Not as nameless faces in
a sea of humanity. And not in the Disney model as legal copyright
holders. We claim fairy tales in every individual act of telling and
reading. If we avoid reading fairy tales as models of behavior and
normalcy, they can become for us revolutionary documents that
encourage the development of personal autonomy.

As some revisionist writers and storytellers have already recognized, the removal of the fairy tale from the service of nationalism
and universalism requires the subversion of traditional tales. Thus
we find contemporary literary versions of "Little Red Riding Hood,"
for instance, that offer alternative visions. In one version, by the
Merseyside Fairy Story Collective, a young girl overcomes her fear
and slays the wolf who threatens her grandmother.[7] In another, by
Angela Carter, a young woman, far from becoming the wolf's innocent victim, accepts her animal nature—her sexuality—and actually leaves her family and village to join the company of wolves.[8] In
other media, such as film, video, and music, attempts have also been
made to reclaim the fairy tale. In fact, Angela Carter's Red Riding
Hood story, "The Company of Wolves," has itself been remade as a
movie.[9] And some of the irreverent video adaptations in Shelley
Duvall's *Fairie Tale Theatre*[1] go a long way toward offsetting the sac-
charine Disney model of the Consumer Romance. Even in popular
music the Disney claim on meaning has been challenged by autho-
rized remakes of the songs from Walt Disney's fairytale movies.
Sinéad O'Connor's subtly ironic rendering of "Someday My Prince
Will Come," Betty Carter's sensual subversion of "I'm Wishing," and

6. D. A. Kaplan, "Vatch out Natasha, Moose and Squirrel Are Back," *Detroit Free Press* (7 May 1989), 3F.
7. Jack Zipes, *The Trials and Tribulations of Little Red Riding Hood: Versions of the Tale in Sociocultural Context* (South Hadley, Mass.: Bergin & Garvey, 1984), 239–46.
8. Ibid., 272–80.
9. Angela Carter and N. Jordan (Screenwriters), *The Company of Wolves*, Vestron Video, 1984–85.
1. Shelley Duvall (Producer), *Fairie Tale Theater*, Playhouse Video, 1982–85.

Tom Waits's industrialized "Heigh Ho" give us the opportunity to reinterpret Disney and "his" tales for ourselves and our time.[2]

Discovering Individual Ownership of Fairy Tales

The opportunity to reclaim fairy tales is as crucial for children as it is for adults. But the right to ownership of the tales may in some ways be more difficult for children to claim. After all, teachers, librarians, parents, and powers in the culture industry exert a certain control over the popular reception of fairy tales by determining to a great extent not only the nature of the tales that are made accessible to children, but also the context of their reception. A storyteller who buys into myths about the pristine origin of fairy tales assumes an unearned mantle of authority and shrouds the stories not only in mystery but in error. A parent under Bruno Bettelheim's spell uses time-bound tales to justify a timeless moral authority. And a teacher concerned about the so-called crisis of cultural literacy will emphasize canonized fairy-tale texts and treat them as sacred cultural artifacts. In each case, children's responses are expected to conform to the external authority of the tales they read or hear. It is no accident that parents and educators so often praise fairy tales because of their ability to enchant children. Stripped of sentimentality, enchantment—that is, being spellbound and powerless—is also a curse. We applaud the rescue of a Frog King or a Sleeping Beauty who is powerless to break the spell of a malevolent force, but when a moralistic text "enchants" and has a child in its spell, we apparently have that child exactly where we want her or him.

There are at least two ways in which children can be awakened from this form of enchantment and helped to discover their individual ownership of fairy tales. First, teachers and parents can offer children a wider variety of fairy tales than is usually proffered. Complementing the classic tales and anthologies with newer or lesser-known stories and variants places the traditional tales in a context that encourages diverse responses, questions, and significant comparisons—even among elementary school children. When I read my own daughter the Grimms' "Little Red Riding Hood" and the version of the Merseyside Fairy Story Collective, for example, she announced that she liked the second version better "because the little girl was smarter."

* * *

Beyond presenting children with a variety of fairy tales, adults can also encourage the creative reception of fairy tales. In other words,

---

2. H. Willner (producer), *Stay Awake: Various Interpretations of Music from Vintage Disney Films*, A&M, 1988.

children can make fairy tales their own by creating and re-creating their own versions. There is good evidence that given the opportunity, children will take fairy tales into their own hands in any case. In his book on the Brothers Grimm, Jack Zipes has recounted how fifth- and sixth-grade girls combined the character of Peter Pumpkin-Eater and the story of Cinderella into a new tale that explicitly reflects their developing sexuality and consciousness.[3] And Kristin Wardetzky has shown how the storytelling of children in the former East Germany does not always succumb to the dominant cultural models and re-creates the fairy tale in ways that express the children's power over the genre.[4]

At the end of his list of heresies Wolfdietrich Schnurre wonders, "Can the fairy tale be saved?" His answer: "Perhaps. If specialists expose the roots of the tales and tell them in a way that is thoroughly new and which expresses their essence."[5] Writers and professional storytellers retelling tales and making them their own can indeed renew the fairy tale. But readers, too—including children—can reread and reinterpret the tales in new ways. By experiencing a wide variety of tales, they can view the stories of the classical canon in new context. By actively selecting, discussing, enacting, illustrating, adapting, and retelling the tales they experience, both adults and children can assert their own proprietary rights to meaning. It is no heresy to re-appropriate the tales from either tradition or the culture industry. "They are not," as Auden knew, "sacred texts."[6] If the fairy tale needs saving and if we are to save it, then we need to abandon the untenable views of its ownership that put us in its power. We must take possession of it on our own terms. Saving the fairy tale in this way is nothing less than saving our very selves.

MARIA TATAR

From Sex and Violence: The Hard Core of Fairy Tales[†]

For many adults, reading through an unexpurgated edition of the Grimms' collection of tales can be an eye-opening experience. Even

3. Jack Zipes, *Don't Bet on the Prince: Contemporary Feminist Fairy Tales in North America and England* (New York: Methuen, 1986), 146.
4. Kristin Wardetzky, "The Structure and Interpretation of Fairy Tales Composed by Children," *Journal of American Folklore,* 103 (1990): 157–76.
5. Schnurre, "Ketzerisches," 25.
6. W. H. Auden, "Praise," 28.
† From Maria Tatar, "Sex and Violence: The Hard Core of Fairy Tales," in *The Hard Facts of the Grimms' Fairy Tales* (Princeton, NJ: Princeton UP, 1987), pp. 3–19. Copyright © 1987 by Princeton University Press. Reprinted by permission of Princeton University Press. Footnotes have been edited for this Norton Critical Edition.

those who know that Snow White's stepmother arranges the murder of her stepdaughter, that doves peck out the eyes of Cinderella's stepsisters, that Briar Rose's suitors bleed to death on the hedge surrounding her castle, or that a mad rage drives Rumpelstiltskin to tear himself in two will find themselves hardly prepared for the graphic descriptions of murder, mutilation, cannibalism, infanticide, and incest that fill the pages of these bedtime stories for children. In "The Juniper Tree," one of the most widely admired of the tales, a woman decapitates her stepson, chops his corpse into small pieces, and cooks him in a stew that her husband devours with obvious gusto. "Fledgling" recounts a cook's attempt to carry out a similar plan, though she is ultimately outwitted by the boy and his sister. Frau Trude, in the story of that title, turns a girl into a block of wood and throws her into a fire. "Darling Roland" features a witch who takes axe in hand to murder her stepdaughter but ends by butchering her own daughter. Another stepmother dresses her stepdaughter in a paper chemise, turns her out into the woods on a frigid winter day, and forbids her to return home until she has harvested a basket of strawberries.

Lest this litany of atrocities lead to the mistaken view that women are the sole agents of evil in German fairy tales, let us look at examples of paternal and fraternal cruelty. Who can forget the miller who makes life miserable for his daughter by boasting that she can spin straw to gold? Or the king of the same tale who is prepared to execute the girl if her father's declarations prove false? In another tale a man becomes so irritated by his son's naiveté that he first disowns him, then orders him murdered by his servants. The singing bone, in the tale of that title, is whittled from the remains of a fratricide victim; when the bone reveals the secret of the scandalous murder to the world, the surviving brother is sewn up in a sack and drowned. The father of the fairy-tale heroine known as Thousandfurs is so bent on marrying his own daughter that she is obliged to flee from her home into the woods. Another father is so firm a believer in female ultimogeniture that he prepares twelve coffins for his twelve sons in the event that his thirteenth child turns out to be a girl. One monarch after another punishes wicked females by forcing them to disrobe and to roll down hills in kegs studded with nails.

In fairy tales, nearly every character—from the most hardened criminal to the Virgin Mary—is capable of cruel behavior. In "The Robber Bridegroom," a young woman watches in horror as her betrothed and his accomplices drag a girl into their headquarters, tear off her clothes, place her on a table, hack her body to pieces, and sprinkle them with salt. Her horror deepens when one of the thieves, spotting a golden ring on the murdered girl's finger, takes an axe, chops off the finger, and sends it flying through the air into her lap. Such behavior may not be wholly out of character for brigands and highwaymen, but even the Virgin Mary appears to be more of an ogre than a saint in the Grimms' collection. When the girl known as Mary's Child disobeys an injunction against opening one of thirteen doors to the kingdom of heaven and tries to conceal her transgression, the Virgin sends her back to earth as punishment. There the girl marries a king and bears three children, each of whom is whisked off to heaven by the Virgin, who is annoyed by the young queen's persistent refusal to acknowledge her guilt. The mysterious disappearance of the children naturally arouses the suspicions of the king's councilors, who bring the queen to trial and condemn her to death for cannibalism. Only when the queen confesses her sin (just as flames leap up around the stake to which she is bound) does Mary liberate her and restore the three children to her. Compassion clearly does not number among the virtues of the Virgin Mary as she appears in fairy tales.

The Grimms only occasionally took advantage of opportunities to tone down descriptions of brutal punishments visited on villains or to eliminate pain and suffering from their tales.[1] When they did, it was often at the behest of a friend or colleague rather than of their own volition. More often, the Grimms made a point of adding or intensifying violent episodes. Cinderella's stepsisters are spared their vision in the first version of the story. Only in the second edition of the *Nursery and Household Tales* did Wilhelm Grimm embellish the story with a vivid account of the doves' revenge and with a somewhat fatuous justification for the bloody tableau at the tale's end: "So both sisters were punished with blindness to the end of their days for being so wicked and false." Rumpelstiltskin beats a hasty retreat on a flying spoon at the end of some versions of his tale, but the Grimms seem to have favored violence over whimsy. Their Rumpelstiltskin becomes ever more infuriated by the queen's discovery of his name; in the second edition of the *Nursery and Household Tales,* he is so beside himself with rage that he tears himself in two. Briar Rose sleeps for a hundred years while a hedge peacefully grows around the castle in the first recorded version of the story. In successive editions of the Grimms' collection, we not only read about the young prince who succeeds in penetrating the thorny barrier, but also learn the grisly particulars about Briar Rose's unsuccessful suitors. They fail because "the briar bushes clung together as though

---

1. Jost Hermand mistakenly claims that the Grimms deleted violent episodes from the tales ("Biedermeier Kids: Eine Mini-Polemik," *Monatshefte* 67 [1975]: 59–66). John Ellis, by contrast, finds that the Grimms actually "*increased* the level of violence and brutality when, for example, those in the tales who suffered it deserved it according to their moral outlook." See his *One Fairy Story Too Many: The Brothers Grimm and Their Tales* (Chicago: University of Chicago Press, 1983), p. 79.

they had hands so that the young princes were caught in them and died a pitiful death."

The changes made from the first to the second edition in "The Magic Table, the Gold Donkey, and the Cudgel in the Sack" show just how keen the Grimms must have been to give added prominence to violent episodes. In the first edition of the *Nursery and Household Tales*, we read about the encounter between the story's hero and an innkeeper who confiscates the property of the hero's brothers.

> The turner placed the sack under his pillow. When the innkeeper came and pulled at it, he said: "Cudgel, come out of the sack!" The cudgel jumped out of the sack and attacked the innkeeper, danced with him, and beat him so mercilessly that he was glad to promise to return the magic table and the gold donkey.[2]

The second edition not only fills in the details on the crime and its punishment, but also puts the innkeeper's humiliation on clearer display.

> At bedtime [the turner] stretched out on the bench and used his sack as a pillow for his head. When the innkeeper thought his guest was fast asleep and that no one else was in the room, he went over and began to tug and pull very carefully at the sack, hoping to get it away and to put another in its place. But the turner had been waiting for him to do exactly that. Just as the innkeeper was about to give a good hard tug, he cried out: "Cudgel, come out of the sack!" In a flash the little cudgel jumped out, went at the innkeeper, and gave him a good sound thrashing. The innkeeper began screaming pitifully, but the louder he screamed the harder the cudgel beat time on his back, until at last he fell down on the ground. Then the turner said: "Now give me the magic table and the gold donkey, or the dance will start all over again." "Oh no!" said the innkeeper. "I'll be glad to give you everything, if only you'll make that little devil crawl back into his sack." The journeyman answered: "This time I will, but watch out for further injuries." Then he said: "Cudgel, back in the sack" and left him in peace.

What the brothers found harder to tolerate than violence and what they did their best to eliminate from the collection through vigilant editing were references to what they coyly called "certain conditions and relationships." Foremost among those conditions seems to have been pregnancy. The story of Hans Dumm, who has the power (and uses it) of impregnating women simply by wishing them to be with child, was included in the first edition but failed to pass muster for

---

2. *Die Kinder- und Hausmärchen der Brüder Grimm: Vollständige Ausgabe in der Urfassung*, ed. Friedrich Panzer (Wiesbaden: Emil Vollmer, 1953), p. 155.

the second edition of the *Nursery and Household Tales*. "The Master Hunter," as told by Dorothea Viehmann, the Grimms' favorite exhibit when it came to discoursing on the excellence of folk narrators, must have struck the Grimms as unsatisfactory. Viehmann's version, which was relegated to the notes on the tales, relates that the story's hero enters a tower, discovers a naked princess asleep on her bed, and lies down next to her. After his departure, the princess discovers to her deep distress and to her father's outrage that she is pregnant. The version that actually appeared in the *Nursery and Household Tales* made do instead with a fully clothed princess and a young man who stands as a model of restraint and decorum.[3]

Pregnancy, whether the result of a frivolous wish (as in "Hans Dumm") or of an illicit sexual relationship (as in "The Master Hunter"), was a subject that made the Grimms uncomfortable. In fact, any hints of premarital sexual activity must have made Wilhelm Grimm in particular blush with embarrassment. A quick look at the "Frog King or Iron Heinrich" (the first tale in the collection and therefore the most visible) reveals the tactics he used to cover up the folkloric facts of the story. When the princess in that celebrated tale dashes the hapless frog against the wall, he "falls down into her bed and lies there as a handsome young prince, and the king's daughter lies down next to him." No printed edition of the *Nursery and Household Tales* contains this wording. Only a copy of the original drafts for the collection, sent to the Grimms' friend Clemens Brentano in 1810 and recovered many years later in a Trappist monastery, is explicit about where the frog lands and about the princess's alacrity in joining him there. In the first edition, the frog still falls on the bed. After his transformation, he becomes the "dear companion" of the princess. "She cherished him as she had promised," we are told, and *immediately* thereafter the two fall "peacefully asleep." For the second edition, Wilhelm Grimm deprived the frog king of his soft landing spot and simply observed that the transformation from frog to prince took place as soon as the frog hit the wall. In this version, the happy couple does not retire for the evening until wedding vows are exchanged, and these are exchanged only with the explicit approval of the princess's father. The Grimms' transformation of a tale replete with sexual innuendo into a prim and proper nursery story with a dutiful daughter is almost as striking as the folkloric metamorphosis of frog into prince.[4]

3. Dorothea Viehmann's tale is printed in volume 3 of Heinz Rölleke's edition of the 1856 version of the Grimms' collection: *Brüder Grimm: Kinder- und Hausmärchen* (Stuttgart: Reclam, 1980), pp. 192–93.
4. For the original manuscript version of "The Frog King or Iron Heinrich," see *Die älteste Märchensammlung der Brüder Grimm: Synopse der handschriftlichen Urfassung von 1810 und der Erstdrucke von 1812*, ed. Heinz Rölleke (Cologny-Genève: Fondation Martin Bodmer, 1975), pp. 144–46.

Another of the "conditions and relationships" that the Grimms seem to have found repugnant, or at least inappropriate as a theme in their collection, was incest and incestuous desire. In some cases, incest constituted so essential a part of a tale's logic that even Wilhelm Grimm thought twice before suppressing it; instead he resorted to weaving judgmental observations on the subject into the text. The father of Thousandfurs may persist in pressing marriage proposals on his daughter throughout all editions of the *Nursery and Household Tales,* but by the second edition he receives a stern reprimand from his court councilors. "A father cannot marry his daughter," they protest. "God forbids it. No good can come of such a sin." In later editions, we learn that the entire kingdom would be "dragged down to perdition" with the sinful king. * * *

When a tale was available in several versions, the Grimms invariably preferred one that camouflaged incestuous desires and Oedipal entanglements. The textual history of the tale known as "The Girl without Hands" illustrates the Grimms' touchy anxiety when it came to stories about fathers with designs on their daughters. That story first came to the Grimms' attention in the following form: A miller falls on hard times and strikes a bargain with the devil, promising him whatever is standing behind his mill in exchange for untold wealth. To his dismay, he returns home to learn that his daughter happened to be behind the mill at the moment the pact was sealed. She must surrender herself to the devil in three years. But the miller's pious daughter succeeds in warding off the devil, if at the price of bodily mutilation: the devil forces the father, who has not kept his end of the bargain, to chop off his daughter's hands. For no apparent reason, the girl packs her severed hands on her back and decides to seek her fortune in the world, despite her father's protestations and his promises to secure her all possible creature comforts at home. The remainder of the story recounts her further trials and tribulations after she marries a king. This is the tale as it appeared in the first edition of the Grimms' collection.

The brothers subsequently came upon a number of versions of that story, one of which they declared far superior to all the others. So impressed were they by its integrity that they could not resist substituting it for the version printed in the first edition of the *Nursery and Household Tales.* Still, the opening paragraph of the new, "superior" version did not quite suit their taste, even though it provided a clear, logical motive for the daughter's departure from home. Instead of leaving home of her own accord and for no particular reason, the girl flees a father who first demands her hand in marriage, and then has her hands and breasts chopped off for refusing him. There is no mention of devils in this version; the girl's father is the sole satanic figure. The Grimms found it easy, however, to reintroduce the devil by mutilating the folkloric text whose authenticity they so admired. The original introduction detailing the father's offenses was deleted from the tale and replaced by the less sensational account of a pact with the devil.

Even without reading Freud on the devil as a substitute for the father, it is easy to see how the devil became mixed up in this tale. Just as God, Saint Peter, and Christ came to stand in for various benefactors in folktales, so Satan in his various guises was available for the role of villain and could incarnate forbidden desire. "The Poor Man and the Rich Man," "The Devil and His Grandmother," and "The Carnation" are among the many other texts in the *Nursery and Household Tales* that mobilize divinities and devils as agents of good and evil. The Grimms seemed, in general, to have favored tales with a Christian cast of characters over their "pagan" counterparts, although there was no compelling folkloristic reason for them to do so. For "The Girl without Hands," they chose to graft the introduction from what they considered an inferior version of the tale (but one that had the advantage of demonizing Satan instead of a father) onto a "superior (and complete)" variant. Clearly the Grimms were not particularly enamored with the idea of including plots concerned with incestuous desire in a collection of tales with the title *Nursery and Household Tales*. Incest was just not one of those perfectly natural matters extolled in their preface to the tales.

Sex and violence: these are the major thematic concerns of tales in the Grimms' collection, at least in their unedited form. But more important, sex and violence in that body of stories frequently take the perverse form of incest and child abuse, for the nuclear family furnishes the fairy tale's main cast of characters just as the family constitutes its most common subject. When it came to passages colored by sexual details or to plots based on Oedipal conflicts, Wilhelm Grimm exhibited extraordinary editorial zeal. Over the years, he systematically purged the collection of references to sexuality and masked depictions of incestuous desire. But lurid portrayals of child abuse, starvation, and exposure, like fastidious descriptions of cruel punishments, on the whole escaped censorship. The facts of life seemed to have been more disturbing to the Grimms than the harsh realities of everyday life.

How is one to explain these odd editorial practices? The Grimms' enterprise, we must recall, began as a scholarly venture and a patriotic project. As early as 1811, the brothers proclaimed that their efforts as collectors were guided by scholarly principles, and they therefore implied that they were writing largely for academic colleagues. Theirs was an idealistic effort to capture German folk traditions in print before they died out and to make a modest contribution to the history of German poetry. As Jacob Grimm pointed out during his search for a publisher, the main purpose of the proposed volume was not so much to earn royalties as to salvage what was left of the priceless national resources still in the hands of the German folk. The Grimms therefore were willing to forgo royalties for the benefit of appearing in print. Still, the brothers expressed the hope that the volume in the offing would find friends everywhere—and that it would entertain them as well.

Weighed down by a ponderous introduction and by extensive annotations, the first edition of the *Nursery and Household Tales* had the look of a scholarly tome, rather than of a book for a wide audience. Sales, however, were surprisingly brisk, perhaps in part because of the book's title. Several of the Grimms' contemporaries had already registered respectable commercial successes with collections of stories for children, and the appearance of the *Nursery and Household Tales* coincided to some extent with a developing market for collections of fairy tales. By 1815 nearly all 900 copies of the first volume had been sold, and Wilhelm Grimm began talking about a second edition in light of the "heavy demand" for the collection. The Grimms had every reason to be pleased, particularly when one calculates that thirty years later (when literacy was more widespread and the demand for children's literature greater) a book such as the popular *Struwwelpeter* had a first printing of only 1,500. With their reputation for "revering trivia" and their endless struggles to get things published, they must also have been growing hungry for a measure of commercial success or at least for some indication of strong interest and support for their literary efforts. Before preparations were even set in motion for publication of the second edition of the *Nursery and Household Tales,* Wilhelm Grimm had already calculated exactly what the appropriate royalties would be for the first and second editions.

The projected royalties for the collection were by no means inconsequential. These were lean years for the Grimms, and their letters to each other are sprinkled with references to financial pressures and to indignities visited on them owing to their impecunious circumstances. From Vienna, Jacob grumbled that he was short of cash and that his clothes were shabby and his shoes worn out. In 1815, Wilhelm Grimm complained that there was not a chair in the house that could be used without imperiling the physical welfare of its occupant. Books were often borrowed and copied out by hand because they were too dear an item in a household where the number of daily meals was limited to two. Thus the 500 talers that Savigny and Wilhelm Grimm had established as appropriate royalties for the first edition of the *Nursery and Household Tales* certainly must have been a welcome prospect. And the 400 talers that Wilhelm Grimm expected to receive for the second edition would have been a substantial addition to the household budget, particularly if we bear in mind that in 1816 Jacob Grimm drew an annual salary of 600 talers as librarian in Kassel, while Wilhelm received an annual salary of 300 talers. It is thus not surprising that the royalties for the *Nursery and Household Tales* would go a long way toward paying their many debts.

* * *

The Grimms may never have made or even hoped to make a financial killing on the *Nursery and Household Tales*, but the profit motive was certainly not wholly absent from their calculations and to some extent must have guided their revisions of the first edition. Still, the potential financial benefits to be reaped from strong sales of the collection counted merely as a secondary gain. What really mattered, particularly in the years immediately following publication of the first edition, were the views of the larger literary world. Both brothers monitored reviews with special interest, and here one disappointment followed another. Jacob, on the road much of the time from 1813 to 1815 in diplomatic service, repeatedly asked his brother for news about the collection's reception. But none of the people who counted seemed to take much interest in reviewing the book, and those who actually did review it rarely had anything good to say. * * *

* * *

For many observers, the *Nursery and Household Tales* fell wide of the mark and missed its potential market because the brothers had let their scholarly ambitions undermine the production of a book for children. The Grimms' seemingly slavish fidelity to oral folk traditions—in particular to the crude language of the folk—came under especially heavy fire. August Wilhelm Schlegel and Clemens Brentano felt that a bit of artifice would have gone a long way toward improving the art of the folk and toward making the tales more appealing. "If you want to display children's clothing, you can do that quite well without bringing out an outfit that has buttons torn off it, dirt smeared on it, and the shirt hanging out of the pants," Brentano wrote to Arnim. Arnim candidly told the Grimms that they would be wise to add, in the form of a subtitle, a consumer warning to the collection. Future editions ought to state that the book was "for parents, who can select stories for retelling." Other readers were less tactful. Heinrich Voß described the collection (with the exception of a few tales) as "real junk."

* * *

* * * In successive editions of the collection, [Wilhelm Grimm] fleshed out the texts to the point where they were often double their original length, and he so polished the prose that no one could complain of its rough-hewn qualities. He also worked hard to clean up the content of the stories. Both A. L. Grimm and Friedrich Rühs singled out "Rapunzel" as a tale particularly inappropriate to include in a collection of tales that children could get their hands on. "What proper mother or nanny could tell the fairy tale about Rapunzel to an innocent daughter without blushing?" Rühs gasped. Wilhelm Grimm saw to it that the story was rewritten along lines that would meet with both critics' approval. Jacob Grimm may have responded to criticism by asserting that the collection had never been intended for young audiences, but his brother was prepared to delete or revise tales deemed unsuitable for children. He was encouraged in such efforts by his brother Ferdinand, who was all for eliminating anything that might offend the sensibilities (*Feingefühl*) of the reading public.

* * * Consider the following passage from the first edition of the *Nursery and Household Tales* (Rapunzel's daily romps up in the tower with the prince, we learn, have weighty consequences).

> At first Rapunzel was frightened, but soon she came to like the young king so much that she agreed to let him visit every day and to pull him up. The two lived joyfully for a time, and the fairy did not catch on at all until Rapunzel told her one day: "Tell me, Godmother, why my clothes are so tight and why they don't fit me any longer." "Wicked child!" cried the fairy.[5]

In the second edition of the *Nursery and Household Tales*, Wilhelm Grimm made the passage less "lewd"—and in the bargain a good deal less colorful. Here, Rapunzel's "wickedness" has a very different cause.

> At first Rapunzel was frightened, but soon she came to like the young king so much that she agreed to let him visit every day and to pull him up. The two lived joyfully for a time and loved each other dearly, like man and wife. The enchantress did not catch on at all until Rapunzel told her one day: "Tell me, Godmother, why is it that you are much harder to pull up than the young prince?" "Wicked child," cried the enchantress.

It is easy to leap to the conclusion that Teutonic prudishness or the Grimms' delicate sense of propriety motivated the kinds of changes made in "Rapunzel." That may well be the case. But it is far more logical to assume that Wilhelm Grimm took to heart the criticisms leveled against his volume and, eager to find a wider audience, set to work making the appropriate changes. His nervous sensitivity about moral objections to the tales in the collection reflects a growing desire to write for children rather than to collect for scholars.

5. *Die Kinder- und Hausmärchen der Brüder Grimm*, ed. Friedrich Panzer, p. 85.

In the years that intervened between the first two editions of the *Nursery and Household Tales,* Wilhelm Grimm charted a new course for the collection. His son was later to claim that children had taken possession of a book that was not theirs to begin with, but Wilhelm clearly helped that process along. He had evidently already done some editing behind Jacob's back but apparently not enough to satisfy his critics. The preface to the second edition emphasized the value of the tales for children, noting—almost as an afterthought—that adults could also enjoy them and even learn something from them. The brothers no longer insisted on literal fidelity to oral traditions but openly admitted that they had taken pains to delete "every phrase unsuitable for children." Furthermore, they expressed the hope that their collection could serve as a "manual of manners" (*Erziehungsbuch*).

*   *   *

LEWIS HYDE

From Slipping the Trap of Appetite[†]

The Bait Thief

The trickster myth derives creative intelligence from appetite. It begins with a being whose main concern is getting fed and it ends with the same being grown mentally swift, adept at creating and unmasking deceit, proficient at hiding his tracks and at seeing through the devices used by others to hide theirs. Trickster starts out hungry, but before long he is master of the kind of creative deception that, according to a long tradition, is a prerequisite of art. Aristotle wrote that Homer first "taught the rest of us the art of framing lies the right way."[1] Homer makes lies seem so real that they enter the world and walk among us. Odysseus walks among us to this day, and he would seem to be Homer's own self-portrait, for Odysseus, too, is a master of the art of lying, an art he got from his grandfather, Autolycus,[2] who got it in turn from *his* father, Hermes. And Hermes, in an old story we shall soon consider, invented lying when he was a hungry child with a hankering for meat.

---

† From Lewis Hyde, "Slipping the Trap of Appetite," in *Trickster Makes This World: Mischief, Myth, and Art* (New York: Farrar, Straus & Giroux, 1998), pp. 17–20, 357–58. Copyright © 1998 by Lewis Hyde. Reprinted by permission of Farrar, Straus & Giroux, LLC.
1. Aristotle, *Poetics* 1460.
2. *Odyssey* XIX:432.

But I'm making a straight line out of a narrative that twists and turns, and I'm getting ahead of myself. We must begin at the beginning, with trickster learning how to keep his stomach full.

Trickster stories, even when they clearly have much more complicated cultural meanings, preserve a set of images from the days when what mattered above all else was hunting. At one point in the old Norse tales, the mischief-maker Loki has made the other gods so angry that he has to flee and go into hiding. In the mountains, he builds himself a house with doors on all sides so he can watch the four horizons. To amuse himself by day, he changes into a salmon, swimming the mountain streams, leaping the waterfalls. Sitting by the fire one morning, trying to imagine how the others might possibly capture him, he takes linen string and twists it into a mesh in the way that fishnets have been made ever since. Just at that moment, the others approach. Loki throws the net into the fire, changes into a salmon, and swims away. But the gods find the ashes of his net and from their pattern deduce the shape of the device they need to make. In this way, Loki is finally captured.[3]

It makes a nice emblem of trickster's ambiguous talents, Loki imagining that first fishnet and then getting caught in it. Moreover, the device in question is a central trickster invention. In Native American creation stories, when Coyote teaches humans how to catch salmon, he makes the first fish weir[4] out of logs and branches. On the North Pacific coast, the trickster Raven made the first fishhook;[5] he taught the spider[6] how to make her web and human beings how to make nets. The history of trickery in Greece goes back to similar origins. "'Trick" is *dólos*[7] in Homeric Greek, and the oldest known use of the term refers to a quite specific trick: baiting a hook to catch a fish.

East and west, north and south, this is the oldest trick in the book. No trickster has ever been credited with inventing a potato peeler, a gas meter, a catechism, or a tuning fork, but trickster invents the fish trap.

Coyote was going along by a big river when he got very hungry. He built a trap of poplar poles and willow branches and set it

3. Jean I. Young, *The Prose Edda of Snorri Sturluson* (Berkeley: U California P, 1966), pp. 84–85.
4. Barry Lopez, *Giving Birth to Thunder, Sleeping with His Daughter: Coyote Builds North America* (NY: Avon Books, 1990), p. 73.
5. Mac Linscott Ricketts, "The Structure and Religious Significance of the Trickster-Transformer-Culture Hero in the Mythology of North American Indians," diss., U Chicago, 1964, p. 139.
6. Ricketts, "The Structure and Religious Significance . . . ," p. 142.
7. Norman O. Brown, *Hermes the Thief* (Madison: U Wisconsin P, 1947), pp. 21–23, and Marcel Detienne and Jean-Pierre Vernant, *Cunning Intelligence in Greek Culture and Society*, trans. Janet Lloyd (Chicago: U Chicago P, 1991), pp. 27–28. "The oldest known use" appears in one of Homer's offhand similes: "as a fisherman on a jutting rock . . . casts in his bait [*dólos*] as a snare to the little fishes, just so. . . ." (*Odyssey* XII:252).

in the water. "Salmon!" he called out. "Come into this trap."
Soon a big salmon came along and swam into the chute of the
trap and then flopped himself out on the bank where Coyote
clubbed him to death. "I will find a nice place in the shade and
broil this up," thought Coyote.[8]

Trickster commonly relies on his prey to help him spring the traps
he makes. In this fragment of a Nez Percé story from northeastern
Idaho, Coyote's salmon weir takes advantage of forces the salmon
themselves provide. Salmon in a river are swimming upstream to
spawn; sexual appetite or instinct gives them a particular trajectory
and Coyote works with it. Even with a baited hook, the victim's hunger is the *moving* part. The worm just sits there; the fish catches
himself. Likewise, in a Crow story from the Western Plains, Coyote
traps two buffalo by stampeding them into the sun so they cannot
see where they are going, then leading them over a cliff.[9] The fleetness of large herbivores is part of their natural defense against predators; Coyote (or the Native Americans who slaughtered buffalo in
this way) takes advantage of that instinctual defense by directing the
beasts into the sun and toward a cliff, so that fleetness itself back-
fires. In the invention of traps, trickster is a technician of appetite
and a technician of instinct.

And yet, as the Loki story indicates, trickster can also get snared
in his own devices. Trickster is at once culture hero and fool, clever
predator and stupid prey. Hungry, trickster sometimes devises strat-
agems to catch his meal; hungry, he sometimes loses his wits altogether. An Apache story from Texas, in which Rabbit has played a
series of tricks on Coyote, ends as follows:

Rabbit came to a field of watermelons. In the middle of the
field there was a stick figure made of gum. Rabbit hit it with
his foot and got stuck. He got his other foot stuck, then one
hand and then his other hand and finally his head. This is how
Coyote found him.

"What are you doing like this?" asked Coyote.

"The farmer who owns this melon patch was mad because
I would not eat melons with him. He stuck me on here and
said that in a while he would make me eat chicken with him. I
told him I wouldn't do it."

"You are foolish. I will take your place."

Coyote pulled Rabbit free and stuck himself up in the gum
trap. When the farmer who owned the melons came out and
saw Coyote he shot him full of holes.[1]

8. Lopez, p. 73.
9. Lopez, pp. 127–28.
1. Lopez, p. 113.

Coyote doesn't just get stuck in gum traps, either; in other stories, a range of animals—usually sly cousins such as Fox or Rabbit or Spider—make a fool of him and steal his meat.

So trickster is cunning about traps but not so cunning as to avoid them himself. To my mind, then, the myth contains a story about the incremental creation of an intelligence about hunting. Coyote can imagine the fish trap precisely because he's been a fish himself, as it were. Nothing counters cunning but more cunning. Coyote's wits are sharp precisely because he has met other wits, just as the country bumpkin may eventually become a cosmopolitan if enough confidence men appear to school him.

Some recent ideas in evolutionary theory echo these assertions. In *Evolution of the Brain and Intelligence*, Harry Jerison presents a striking chart showing the relative intelligence of meat-eaters and the herbivores they prey on.[2] Taking the ratio of brain to body size as a crude index, Jerison finds that if we compare herbivores and carnivores at any particular moment in history the predators are always slightly brainier than the prey. But the relationship is never stable; there is a slow step-by-step increase in intelligence on both sides. If we chart the brain-body ratio on a scale of 1 to 10, in the archaic age herbivores get a 2 and carnivores a 4; thirty million years later the herbivores are up to 4 but the carnivores have gone up to 6; another thirty million years and the herbivores are up to 6 but the carnivores are up to 8; finally, when the herbivores get up to 9, the carnivores are up to 10. The hunter is always slightly smarter, but the prey is always wising up. In evolutionary theory, the tension between predator and prey is one of the great engines that has driven the creation of intelligence itself, each side successively and ceaselessly responding to the other.

✳ ✳ ✳

MARIA TATAR

From Female Tricksters as Double Agents[†]

With the rise of warrior women in popular entertainments comes a degree of cultural anxiety about producing a new stereotype that, while disavowing the notion of princesses passively awaiting

2. Harry J. Jerison, *Evolution of the Brain and Intelligence* (New York: Academic Press, 1973), p. 313.
† From Maria Tatar, "Female Tricksters as Double Agents," in *The Cambridge Companion to Fairy Tales,* ed. Maria Tatar (Cambridge: Cambridge UP, 2015), pp. 39–40, 46–50, 56–59. Copyright © 2015 Cambridge University Press. Reprinted by permission of Cambridge University Press.

liberation, risks installing an even more disturbing archetype of female heroism. Hollywood may have moved from one extreme to another, first enshrining comatose heroines like Snow White and Sleeping Beauty, and now turning Red Riding Hood, Rapunzel, and Gretel into beauties with impressive arsenals at their disposal. But the folkloric legacy reminds us that there are other options and models, in particular the mythical trickster, who navigates his way (and I use the masculine pronoun with all due deliberation) to "happily ever after" by using wits and courage rather than guns and steel.

"All the regularly discussed figures are male," Lewis Hyde tells us in his magisterial study of the culture-building feats of tricksters ranging from Hermes and Loki to Coyote and Hare. Tricky women exist, he concedes, but their acts of deception and disruptive deeds fall short of the "elaborated career of deceit" that marks the lives of those cultural heroes we know by the name of Trickster.[1]

There may be a good reason for the absence of female tricksters in the mythological imagination. The male trickster-figure is never found at home, sitting by the hearth. Driven by hunger and appetite, he is always on the road, mobile and mercurial in ways unimaginable for women in most cultures. As a boundary-crosser and traveler, trickster is adept at finding ways to gratify his multiple appetites—chiefly for food and for sex, but for spiritual satisfactions as well. He is even capable of procreation, as the Winnebago trickster named Wakdjunkaga reveals, when he changes into a woman to marry the son of a chief and bear three sons. But that trickster, like Hermes (who is sometimes depicted as a hermaphrodite), remains resolutely masculine with nothing more than the capacity to become a woman.

It may well be that trickster is, by his very nature, male, a mythological construct designed to define male appetites and desires. As the product of patriarchal mythologies, trickster's powers may simply have been reserved for male agents. But it is also possible that the female trickster has carried out her own stealth operation, functioning in furtive ways and covering her tracks to ensure that her powers remain undetected. Perhaps she has survived and endured simply by becoming invisible and flying beneath the radar that we use to understand our cultural stories. And now, in cultures that grant women the kind of mobility and subversive agency unknown in earlier ages, she can join up with the more visible postmodern female counterparts that appear in cultural production today. This essay will trace the covert operations of a set of female trickster

---

1. Lewis Hyde, *Trickster Makes This World: Mischief, Myth, and Art* (New York: Farrar, Straus & Giroux, 1998), 8.

figures who may not have "fully elaborated" careers but who nonetheless remind us that there is a female counterpart to the mythical male trickster, one with its own set of defining features.

*   *   *

Trickster and Trickstar

Marilyn Jurich was the first to detect gender disturbances in the air-
waves of folkloric meditations on tricksters. She identified and
defined a female figure who operates in much the same way as the
male trickster, and used the term "trickstar" to differentiate one
from the other. If satisfying appetites, crossing boundaries, and
shape-shifting characterize the male figure, playing tricks becomes
for Jurich the hallmark of the female trickster: "Women can rescue
themselves and others *through tricks*, pursue what they need or
desire *through tricks*, transform what they find unworkable or unworthy *through tricks*."[2] Jurich's emphasis on how women "trick their
way into more desirable positions" and "use tricks to gain advantages
for their communities" can have an unsettling effect on some, for it
repeatedly emphasizes deceit and duplicity almost to the exclusion
of the nimble and creative intelligence associated with the male
trickster.

Determined to show the distaff side of a concept that has been
declared male territory, Jurich's intense focus on trickery seems at
times to impoverish the notion of female tricksters rather than
enrich it, as she searches relentlessly for examples of women's power
to dupe, hoodwink, and outmaneuver their antagonists. Using the
frame tale of the *Thousand and One Nights* as her point of departure, she suggests that Scheherazade has only one resource at her
disposal to deter the king from carrying out his murderous daily
assaults on the "treacherous" women of Baghdad. Scheherazade
knows better than to reason, beg, plead, bargain, preach, or scold.
Instead, she relies on the only strategy available to the powerless:
deceit.

What I would like to set up in contrast to Jurich's notion of a
female trickster who slavishly holds to her moniker is the notion of
female tricksters as double agents, women who operate using strategies both subversive and transformative in order to construct their
own identities but also to effect social change. Like sleuths at a
detective *agency*, they possess the ability to shape themselves even
as they serve others. At times, that form of double agency is inflected
in interesting ways. For example, Scheherazade, the first in a series

---

2. Marilyn Jurich, *Scheherazade's Sisters: Trickster Heroines and Their Stories in World
   Literature* (Westport, CT: Greenwood Press, 1998), xvii.

of female trickster figures, operates at levels both culturally productive and biologically reproductive. Both creative and procreative, she sets the stage in powerful ways for the literary progeny that spring from her story.

"I will begin with a story," Scheherazade tells her sister Dinarzad, "and it will cause the king to stop his practice, save myself, and deliver the people."[3] Scheherazade's triple project is ambitious: she is seeking the king's salvation, her own release, and the protection of other women from harm. Recall that King Shahrayar has caught a wife *in flagrante* with a "black slave," and that his brother Shahzaman has suffered a similar humiliation. Both brothers are so mortified by the betrayal of their wives that they depart together in search of someone who has been even more disgraced—only then can they continue to rule. Once they encounter a *jinni* whose wife has cuckolded him five hundred and seventy times, their dignity is restored, and they return home to behead Shahrayar's wife and the slaves.

Women's duplicity seems to know no bounds, and they are positioned as so seductive, unfaithful, and treacherous that the two brothers do not have to travel far to find women even more lascivious than their own wives. Shahrayar quickly jumps to the conclusion that all women are alike and every night, for the next three years, he swears to marry "for one night only and kill the woman the next morning, in order to save himself from the wickedness and cunning of women."[4] The folkloric repertoire features a host of female counterparts to Shahrayar and his brother. The many princesses who assign tasks to suitors also take delight in beheading or punishing bunglers and incompetents. Still the tale from the *Thousand and One Nights* remains a foundational text that, like the story of Eve's betrayal and Pandora's curiosity, reminds us of the nexus linking femininity with sexual curiosity, infidelity, and deceit.

Like the merchant's daughter in our story of "Beauty and the Beast," Scheherazade volunteers to sacrifice herself and face the monster menacing the welfare of those she loves. She plans to use her storytelling prowess to delay her execution and to cure King Shahrayar of the mania that threatens to destroy his people. On each successive night, Scheherazade tells a "strange and wonderful story," stopping midway and finishing the following night, when she begins an even "stranger and more wonderful story." Scheherazade is described as a scholarly type. "She had read the books of literature, philosophy, and medicine. She knew poetry by heart, had studied historical reports, and was acquainted with the sayings of

3. Muhsin Mahdi, ed., *The Arabian Nights*, trans. Husain Haddawy (New York: Norton, 1990), 16.
4. Ibid., 12.

men and the maxims of sages and kings. She was intelligent, knowledgeable, wise, and refined."[5]

Like Philomela in Ovid's *Metamorphoses*, Scheherazade is to double duty bound. She is no mere "clever survivor," but also an agent of change. Philomela, whose body was violated and tongue severed by Tereus, weaves the story of her rape into a tapestry not only to exact revenge but also to model ways of broadcasting what has been silenced by a culture. Both Philomela and Scheherazade begin as victims, but the arc of their stories takes them to a position enabling them to speak for themselves and to a culture.

Kay Nielsen's illustration for the frame tale to the *Arabian Nights* reminds us that Scheherazade, for all her heroic vitality, remains small and weak. Seated before the King, she is exposed literally and figuratively, the target not only of his gaze but also of his regal power. Made to appear superhuman through his oversized turban and flowing royal robes, Shahrayar may fall under the spell of Scheherazade's stories, but he remains in charge nonetheless. More like Hestia than Aphrodite or Artemis, who stand as models for twenty-first-century tricksters, Scheherazade remains a creature of hearth and home, embracing the power of domestic ritual and renewal.

Scheherazade may lack the mobility and appetites of male tricksters, but she transcends the narrow domestic space of the bedroom through her expansive narrative reach and embraces bold defiance as she sets about remaking the values of the culture she inhabits. Behind her transformative art lurks the ruse of the disempowered, and Scheherazade, despite the physical constraints placed on her, becomes a foundational double agent whose feats establish the terms of what it means to be a female trickster.

* * *

Tricksters to Double Duty Bound

I want to begin my analysis of twenty-first-century female double agents with Lisbeth Salander, the girl with the dragon tattoo. Lisbeth, as fans of Stieg Larsson's Millennium Trilogy will recognize, is a woman on a mission. Unlike Scheherazade, she does not use the civilizing power of story to change her culture (although one could argue that an author who begins his novel with statistics about the number of women in Sweden who have been threatened by a man does), but rather aims to exact revenge for injuries done to her and to a sisterhood of female victims.

5. Ibid., 13.

Lisbeth's humorlessness, her almost pathological lack of affect, makes her an unlikely candidate for the role of trickstar. But like male tricksters, Lisbeth has a bottomless appetite—for food, as well as for sexual partners, both male and female. Although she is described as an "anorexic spook" by one of the novel's villains, she gorges herself endlessly, making for herself, typically, "three big open rye-bread sandwiches with cheese, caviar, and a hard-boiled egg" or "half a dozen thick sandwiches on rye bread with cheese and liver sausage and dill pickles." Constantly brewing coffee, she shovels down Billy's Pan Pizza as if eating her last meal. Consuming "every kind of junk food," she nonetheless does not seem to have an eating disorder.[6]

Gluttony is writ large in the Millennium Trilogy, and sexual appetite as well, with Salander presented as what one critic describes as a "popular culture fantasy—adolescent-looking yet sexually experienced."[7] In fact, the depictions of Salander as both abject victim of rape and partner in consensual sado-masochistic erotic practices are so explicit as to arouse the suspicion of creating a sexual spectacle designed to play into the voyeuristic desires of readers. The violence may be appalling, but it also makes the film more appealing, as the box office numbers tell us.

That Lisbeth's physical strength, as well as her technological savvy and varied appetites, are modeled on male figures becomes evident when we learn about her superhuman strength. She is nimble and muscular enough to defeat school bullies as a child and later, as an adult, thugs twice her size in physical combat. In the second novel, we discover that Lisbeth was trained as a boxer and was once a serious competitor in male contests. Whether roaming bars or roaring off on a motorcycle, she mimics male behavior rather than shaping a unique female identity. Her appeal derives in large part from her ability to serve as an ironic double of the classic male trickster, masquerading, performing, and imitating in ways that offer both serious reenactment and gender-bending parody.

Lisbeth possesses what the author describes as "sheer magic" (31) and a "unique gift" (30). When we first "see" her, it is through the eyes of her employer, Dragan Armansky, and he describes her as one of those "flat-chested girls who might be mistaken for skinny boys at a distance" and as a "foreign creature" rather like "a painting of a nymph or a Greek amphora" (36). Like Hermes before her, she wears a cloak of "shamelessness"—Sweden's National Board of

6. Stieg Larsson, *The Girl with the Dragon Tattoo* (New York: Knopf, 2002), 346, 213, 362, 32.
7. Cecilia Ovesdotter and Anna Westerstahl Stenport, "Corporations, Crime, and Gender Construction in Stieg Larsson's *The Girl with the Dragon Tattoo*: Exploring Twenty-First Century Neoliberalism in Swedish Culture," *Scandinavian Studies*, 81 (2009): 157.

Health and Welfare declares her to be "introverted, socially inhibited, lacking empathy, ego-fixated," as well as exhibiting "psychopathic and asocial behaviour, difficulty in cooperating, and incapable of assimilating learning." Exhibiting the classic traits of Asperger's Syndrome, she is also "cunning," and her "quick and spidery" movements and "unusual intelligence" (32) align her once again with the impudent Hermes and his folkloric kin, whose clever antics disturb boundaries and challenge property rights. A master of the World Wide Web, she has, like Anansi, her own network to administer and instrumentalize.

In a study of tricksters in film, Helena Bassil-Morozow points out that hackers feed off the "mercurial qualities of the internet," breaking into networks and violating legislative and regulatory structures. Icily detached from moral imperatives, these "ubernerd villains" are represented as "invisible, unnatural, elusive, unattractive, semi-transparent from lack of fresh air and exercise, people-hating creatures."[8] Lisbeth Salander, for once, fits right in. Or does she? "Lack of emotional involvement" (32) masks Lisbeth's deep sense of a mission to avenge rapists, murderers, and other woman-hating men—and to do good. As compensation for agreeing to keep quiet about the discovery that the now dead Martin Vanger was a serial rapist and murderer, she demands donations to the National Organization for Women's Crisis Centres and Girls' Crisis Centres in Sweden (406), a bargain of convenience that could be turned against her as a crusader for social justice.

* * *

Suzanne Collins's Katniss [Everdeen in *The Hunger Games*] combines Lisbeth's survival skills with a passionate social mission, but she lacks the hipster sexual confidence and self-consciousness of her older Swedish counterpart. As many commentators have pointed out, she is modeled on Artemis, goddess of the hunt, carrying the same silver bow and arrows. Like the goddess, she too is protector of the young and volunteers to take her sister's place when her name is chosen at the Reaping. Virginal and unaware of her own sexual allure, she is that rare thing in pop culture—an intelligent, courageous heroine on a complex quest of her own. Lisbeth's near pathological lack of affect and surplus sexual energy are balanced by Katniss's compassionate intensity and sexual innocence.

Lisbeth Salander and Katniss Everdeen mark a rupture in our understanding of what it means to be a female trickster. Unlike Scheherazade, Bluebeard's wife, and even Gretel, Trickster Girls are

8. Helena Bassil-Morozow, *The Trickster in Contemporary Film* (London: Routledge, 2012), 80.

experts at getting out of the house. They send strong signals about the possibilities, and perils, of new identities in the public sphere for women. As Ricki Stefanie Tannen puts it, "The female Trickster[s], whether embodied fictionally as sleuth, cyborg, or time-traveling feminista, are messengers charged with informing the collective consciousness about how identity and subjectivity can be constructed in postmodernity."[9] The new identity of the youthful Trickster Girl is not constructed at home as a wife but rather in the public sphere, and it marks a sharp break with a Trickstar like Scheherazade, who operates exclusively in the domestic sphere, becoming wife and mother, even as she recounts adventures and adversity. Yet Trickstars and Trickster Girls seem consistently united in their double mission of remaking the world even as they survive adversity.

While the postmodern Trickster Girl shares much with Hermes, Coyote, Loki, and Anansi, she also diverges sharply from her male counterparts. In shaping a new social and cultural identity, figures like Katniss and Lisbeth disavow the role of victim, refusing to succumb to the brute force of patriarchal rule. They are both survivors, managing to cheat death (Lisbeth is buried alive and Katniss is imperiled repeatedly) and reinvent themselves with new identities. And they embark on an explicit social mission missing in the aspirations of classic male tricksters. Like Scheherazade, they assume a social mission once they refuse the status of victim, and justice becomes their consuming passion, even as they retain many of the appetites of male tricksters.

Does the arc that takes us from Scheherazade to Lisbeth mark progress? Many of the female revenge fantasies that have proliferated in popular culture have been constructions of male writers and filmmakers. Critics have been quick to point out that some of these trickster heroines are less double agents than women who mimic models of the "conventional male action hero." Part of what makes Lisbeth Salander unique is her physical appearance, both masculine, or boyish, and muscular. Her tattoos, her lovemaking (she initiates and takes control), her technological skills, her decisive actions, and even her way of looking at people deviates sharply from feminine forms of self-representation and behavior. One critic surmises that Salander embodies a "creepy man's fantasy—a smart woman with a girl's barely pubescent body"; another sees in her a fantasy about "total control."[1] Self-contained and operating comfortably as an "independent contractor," she has been conditioned by

---

9. Ricki Stefanie Tannen, *The Female Trickster: The Mask That Reveals* (London and New York: Routledge, 2007), 26.
1. Both quoted in David Geherin, *The Dragon Tattoo and Its Long Tail: The New Wave of European Crime Fiction in America* (Jefferson, NC: McFarland, 2012), 22.

her traumatic childhood as well as by her genetic makeup to act more like a man than a woman, thereby operating less as reformer than as a figure who perpetuates cultural, social, and political norms. "Larsson's work," as two critics write, "is enmeshed in the very social, gendered, and economic paradigms it appears to want to critique."[2] Ironically, the androgynous nature of Trickster Girls enables male cross-identification, thus further diluting the feminist message in the eyes of some critics.

Critics may be right to scold Stieg Larsson for embracing the pop-culture conventions of heroic individualism. The writer's work would most likely not have shot up to the top of bestseller lists had he created a heroine with impeccable feminist credentials and a pragmatic political agenda. Instead, Larsson did exactly what we expect from iconoclasts, *bricoleurs*, and myth-makers. He constructed a heroine who becomes enmeshed in cultural contradictions and thereby unsettles and disturbs us, obliging us to rethink how we have made the world. Lisbeth Salander serves as a true double agent in forging her own unique social identity and gender distinctiveness as well as seeking retribution for victims of the social structures she shows to be tainted with hypocrisy, self-serving interests, and unrestrained greed.

The Trickster Girl materializes not out of thin air but from a close look at a variety of genres and archetypal characters that cross the divide separating literature and folklore. Given the fact that the covert operations of female tricksters were carried out so long in the domestic sphere, it is not surprising to find that fairy tales rather than myths became the privileged site for capturing their activities. That the female trickster migrated into fairy tales in no way diminishes her mythic power. The time might now be right to heed the advice of Claude Lévi-Strauss and to embrace the view that all versions of a story belong to the myth and require attentive inclusion. Unbridled appetites and mercurial energy have always made tricksters easy to identify. Their double-faced nature—incarnating paradox, exploiting contradictions, and enacting dualities—can be found in nearly every cultural landscape. If the male trickster occasionally oscillates between female and male, the female trickster has developed a more fluid notion of gender identity and has embraced androgyny in her postmodern incarnations. But she has performed her most devious prank by pulling the wool over our eyes for so long, by giving herself a cloak of invisibility, even as she prowls around both at the margins and right in the center of our cultural entertainments, doing her work as double agent, to save herself and to rescue others.

2. Ibid., 160.

CRISTINA BACCHILEGA

From The Fairy-Tale Web: Intertextual and Multimedial Practices in Globalized Culture, a Geopolitics of Inequality, and (Un)Predictable Links[†]

Adapting Fairy Tales, to What Ends?

In 2005 the Bloomingdale's holiday window display in New York City featured eight popular fairy-tale scenes, ranging from "Cinderella" to "Aladdin." Highlights of what in that context was a mixed bag of traditions—narrative, festive, commercial, and touristic—remain viewable on About.com Travel to New York City Guide as a series of ten images. The "Cinderella" scene is tagged "Imagine being invited to the ball," and the "Aladdin" one "Imagine the ride of your life." In these windows, the magic helper who makes such wishes come true—respectively, the fairy godmother and the genie—has a large presence. Each chosen scene of the ensemble projects a sense of anticipation and attainable gratification. In the "Frog Prince" display, the frog is handing the young woman a translucent ball. Both characters wear crowns, signaling that their common royal status will eventually bring them together. How? No matter what the Brothers Grimm wrote, and as the very red lips of the frog in the window signal, the answer in popular cultural memory is "with a kiss."

Not only are the frog's lips larger and redder than the princess's, but also his hard and sparkling "body" is more like a gigantic conglomerate of costume jewelry than a slippery force of nature. In contrast, the fairy-tale heroine is bland, a well-dressed life-size mannequin with no expression or light of her own. The precious ball between them looks like an oversized pearl or perhaps a magic ball in which to read one's future; also strategically placed between the frog suitor and the princess but more in the background, a golden reindeer conflates the magic of fairy tales with the gift-giving rituals of the season. The scene anticipates romance and fulfillment in a preset fantasy world for both characters, and the presence of the reindeer further suggests this is a "free" exchange that is part of a gift economy. Of course, the association of fairy tales with the holiday season is hardly new, as seen in British pantomime and

† From Cristina Bacchilega, "Introduction," in *Fairy Tales Transformed? Twenty-First-Century Adaptations and the Politics of Wonder* (Detroit: Wayne State University Press, 2013), pp. 1–12, 18–22. Copyright © 2013 Wayne State University Press. Reprinted with the permission of Wayne State University Press. All parenthetical citations have been provided as footnotes.

Christmas editions of tales of magic for children. But in its fantastic showcasing of artificiality, this display is decidedly hyperreal, simulating an original that never existed and presenting it as not only desirable but also attainable. With the swipe of a credit card. In this fairy-tale scene the princess-like mannequin stands in for the consumer of a happily-ever-after fantasy that the amphibian rep for capitalism offers her.

To cash in on the genre's worldwide appeal is common in globalized consumer capitalism, where plots, metaphors, and expectations associated with fairy tales pervade popular culture, from jokes and publicity to TV shows and songs. This confirms that fairy tales continue to exercise their powers on adults as well as children. *Powers*, I stress, not power, because, historically as in the present, fairy tales come in many versions and are in turn interpreted in varied ways that speak to specific social concerns, struggles, and dreams. Even the Bloomingdale's "Frog Prince" scene tells more than the "shopping will buy you romance and happiness" story. In the online picture, we see the potential consumer reflected in the soft glow of the fake "pearl" in the window, but s/he need not be taken in by the glamour. After all, we are not passive consumers, and this is but one scene in the tale; we can imagine different choices and endings, and we do.

In Jack Zipes's words, "Fairy tales are informed by a human disposition to action—to transform the world and make it more adaptable to human needs, while we try to change and make ourselves fit for the world."[1] This statement is not, given Zipes's project in *The Irresistible Fairy Tale* (2012), to be understood as a definition that encompasses the genre of the fairy tale, but it identifies transformation as central to what most fairy tales do or anticipate. Like Zipes, I am interested in exploring how fairy tales affect the making of who we are and of the world we are in, and I agree that thinking about transformation—within the tales' storyworlds; in the genre's ongoing process of production, reception, reproduction, adaptation, and translation; in the fairy-tale's relation to other genres; and more generally as action in the social world—offers a spacious and productive way into that exploration.

Fairy tales interpellate us as consumers *and* producers of transformation. For instance, in 2009, the same year in which Tiana of *The Princess and the Frog* entered the ranks of Disney princesses, Canadian photographer Dina Goldstein put on the World Wide Web her *Fallen Princesses* series, in which she imagines fairy-tale heroines in "modern day scenarios" and replaces the "happily ever after"

---

1. Jack Zipes, *The Irresistible Fairy Tale: The Cultural and Social History of a Genre* (Princeton: Princeton UP, 2013), p. 2.

with a hyper "realistic outcome" of a different kind: "Cinderella sits in a dive bar in Vancouver's infamous Hastings Street. Snow White is trapped in a domestic nightmare, surrounded by unkempt children, with a lazy out of work prince in the background" ("About the Series" on www.fallenprincesses.com/). Just as striking as the transformative work of "critical disenchantment"—noted by Catriona McAra and David Calvin in their introduction to *Anti-Tales: The Uses of Disenchantment*[2]—that Goldstein's photographs do, is the public response that they have in turn produced, ranging from a *Marie Claire* article (published in November 2009) to innumerable blogs and fan letters. And even more striking perhaps is the online debate that Goldstein's project sparked, not only in defense of the positive role Disney magic has played in real-life individual experience but also in presenting a range of critical takes on the tales as well as on the photographs. Goldstein's photographs make visible the contradiction between what Angela Carter critically called "mythic women" and the problems we face in everyday life, including loneliness, aging, and illness, and in doing so she clearly touched a nerve with the public. But the controversy also suggests that to change women's images or more generally to disenchant the genre is not the only fairy-tale transformation in which the thousands of individuals who were touched enough to respond are invested.

"Fairy tales are ideologically variable desire machines," I wrote a few years ago in *Postmodern Fairy Tales*, and I stand by this statement, which I realize could be said of all stories really, but perhaps holds higher stakes when applied to a genre that so overtly puts a desire for transformation in motion and one that is too often reduced to the narrative articulation of purportedly universal wish fulfillment. Just as Salman Rushdie's child protagonist in *Haroun and the Sea of Stories* confronts the question "What is the use of stories that aren't even true?"[3] scholars have asked: what does the fairy tale do? Providing a neat definition of the genre within a framework that recognizes its multiple social valence is difficult, then, and necessarily self-contradictory. Fairy tales have been central to reproducing ingrained or second-nature habits, what Pierre Bourdieu calls *habitus* and Edward Said "structures of feeling"—*and* to destabilizing them. Characterized in Marina Warner's words by "pleasure in the fantastic" and "curiosity about the real,"[4] fairy tales have historically scripted a wide range of desires while maintaining a strong grip on ordinary social life. With an eye to solving problems, at

2. Catriona McAra and David Calvin, eds., *Anti-Tales: The Uses of Disenchantment* (Cambridge UK: Cambridge Scholars Publishing, 2011), pp. 1–15.
3. Salman Rushdie, *Haroun and the Sea of Stories* (London: Granta, 1990), p. 22.
4. Marina Warner, *From the Beast to the Blonde: On Fairy Tales and Their Tellers* (New York: Farrar, Straus & Giroux, 1994), p. xx.

least some versions are also produced and/or received as inspirations to undo privilege and prejudice.

To develop the idea that fairy tales "are informed by a human disposition to action,"[5] we need to ask what do they do to inspire us to seek change, in ourselves, in order to fit in the social world and/or in the social world in order for it to accommodate us. For some, fairy tales instigate compensatory escapism, while for others they offer wisdom; alternatively, fairy tales are seen to project social delusions that hold us captive under their spell; or else they promote a sense of justice by narrating the success of unpromisingly small, poor, or otherwise oppressed protagonists. Maria Tatar's recent "quilting" of published writers' and public figures' commentary on fairy tales, "passages that move us to think about the deeper meaning of fairy tales and how they have affected our lives and those of others,"[6] significantly has a patchwork effect. Our ideas about the genre's poetics depend on whether we associate the fairy tale as symbolic act with wish fulfillment, role-playing, idealization, survival, or something else; in other words, on how we use the genre. In the last two hundred years—the Grimms' *Kinder- und Hausmärchen*'s volumes were first published in 1812–15—the fairy tale has served multiple sociocultural functions.

But I believe it is also safe to say that since the popularizing of the Grimms' collection, as a genre the fairy tale's dominant or hegemonic association has been with magic and enchantment, as a result of several convergences: the segregation of fairy tales to the nursery where "magic" is normalized as the mysterious ways in which the world works to produce immediate gratification and where "enchantment" is at the service of a spellbinding discipline that has the "child exactly where we want her or him,"[7] the universalizing of "happily ever after" as the signature mark of the fairy tale, the repurposing in mass culture of fairy tales for advertising products that fulfill our every wish, and the spectacle of the fairy tale as an American capitalist utopia and as "consumer romance" in Disney's films and other fairy-tale commodities.

If generally the desired effect of this poetics of enchantment is the consumer's buying into magic, the contemporary call for disenchanting the fairy tale is directly related to a now-public dissatisfaction with its magic as trick or (ultimately disempowering) deception, a disillusionment with the reality of the social conditions that canonized tales of magic idealize. However, magic and

5. Zipes, *Irresistible Fairy Tale*, p. 2.
6. Maria Tatar, *The Grimm Reader: The Classic Tales of the Brothers Grimm* (New York: Norton, 2010), p. 305.
7. Donald Haase, "Yours, Mine, or Ours? Perrault, the Brothers Grimm, and the Ownership of Fairy Tales," *Merveilles et contes* 7 (1993).

pacifying enchantment are not the only poetics of the fairy tale, historically or in the present. As medievalist Jan Ziolkowski reminds us, "Wonder is the effect [fairy] tales seek to achieve, while magic is the means that they employ to attain this goal."[8] It is no accident that fairy tales are also known as "wonder tales." As an effect, wonder involves both awe and curiosity. In Marina Warner's eloquent words, "Wonder has no opposite; it springs already doubled in itself, compounded of dread and desire at once, attraction and recoil, producing a thrill, the shudder of pleasure and of fear. It names the marvel, the prodigy, the surprise as well as the responses they excite, of fascination and inquiry; it conveys the active motion towards experience and the passive stance of enrapturement."[9]

Fairy tales can invite us to dwell in astonishment and explore new possibilities, to engage in *wondering* and *wandering*. It is in this symbolic enactment of possibilities, "announcing what might be"—and taking us *ex-cursus*, off course, or off socially sanctioned paths to "unlock social and public possibilities," to explore alternatives we hope for—that the fairy tale's "mood is optative"[1] and wonder producing. Furthermore, wonder has been recognized as a significantly complex effect of fairy tales, but the genre's links with wonder have a complicated history, including the secularization of religious legends and miracle tales in medieval Europe; the transformation of ancient pagan tales; and, with *Arabian Nights* being the most well-known case, the appropriative translation of what Donald Haase calls other cultures' "wonder genres."

* * *

How and to what uses are fairy tales being adapted in and to the twenty-first century * * * and why should we care? For Arthur W. Frank in *Letting Stories Breathe: A Socio-Narratology* (2010), "not all stories engage all people,"[2] an important point suggesting how stories do not just connect human beings but reflect and generate differences among us; however, stories of all kinds do animate, instigate, conduct, and emplot human lives. Two of Frank's socionarratological insights about stories in general resonate with and in my project. The first is that of the making and unmaking of narrative emplotment in both fiction and life: "Stories project possible futures, and those projections affect what comes to be, although

---

8. Ziolkowski, Jan M., *Fairy Tales from before Fairy Tales: The Medieval Latin Past of Wonderful Lies* (Ann Arbor, MI: U of Michigan Press, 2006), p. 64.
9. Marina Warner, *From the Beast to the Blonde*, p. 3.
1. Ibid., p. xx.
2. Arthur W. Frank, *Letting Stories Breathe: A Socio-Narratology* (Chicago: U of Chicago P, 2010), p. 4.

this will rarely be the future projected in the story. Stories work to *emplot* lives: they offer a plot that makes some particular future not only plausible but also compelling. . . . We humans spend our lives . . . adapting stories we were once told. . . . Not least among human freedoms is the ability to tell the story differently and to begin living according to that different story."[3] The dynamics of emplotment seem to me particularly relevant to reflecting on fairy tales in social practice because this genre is so basically tied up in plot, has been hegemonically utilized to emplot or frame our lives within a heteronormative capitalist economy, and yet has such a history of and potential for adaptability as well as subversion because it operates in the optative mode.

The second of Frank's insights is a set of questions that, adapting Bakhtinian dialogism, informs his critical analysis of storytelling, which he sees as the symbiotic and dynamic work that people and stories do with, for, and on one another. Frank asks, "*what is at stake* for whom, including storyteller and protagonist in the story, listeners who are present at the storytelling, and others who may not be present but are implicated in the story? How does the story, and the particular way it is told, define or redefine those stakes, raising or lowering them? How does the story change people's sense of what is possible, what is permitted, and what is responsible or irresponsible?"[4] Readers familiar with fairy-tale studies will recognize these as the issues that Jack Zipes's critical oeuvre, from *Breaking the Magic Spell* (1979) on to *The Irresistible Fairy Tale* (2012), has taken on to trace the cultural and social history of the fairy-tale genre. * * * What are the stakes of adapting the fairy tale in the early twenty-first century? For whom? And how do today's fairy-tale adaptations affect "people's sense of what is possible," or of what transformations to anticipate/fear/desire? Because the genre's popularity is both persistent and pervasive and because questions of individual agency and social transformation are central to the tales' narrative permutations, reflecting on today's fairy-tale adaptations—both their production and reception—illuminates and affects how we construct human relations in the present and how we map out our options for the future. This broadly intellectual concern motivates my continued inquiry into the genre and its varied poetics and politics of magic, enchantment, and wonder.

* * *

* * * Fairy-tale studies emerged as a field where sociohistorical analysis has been challenging romanticized and nation-centered

3. Ibid., p. 10.
4. Ibid., pp. 74–75.

views of the genre. Noting that Angela Carter's *The Bloody Chamber* and Jack Zipes's *Breaking the Magic Spell* both came out in 1979, Stephen Benson reminds us in his introduction to *Contemporary Fiction and the Fairy Tale* of "the extraordinary synchronicity, in the final decades of the twentieth century, of [fairy-tale] fiction and fairy-tale scholarship."[5] For example, the early 1990s saw Carter's edited collections of *The Virago Book of Fairy Tales* (1990 and 1993) alongside Marina Warner's *From the Beast to the Blonde* (1994), each making a singular and lasting intervention in the ongoing feminist debate over fairy tales. One could say that if today, as Donald Haase's introduction to the 2008 *Greenwood Encyclopedia of Folktales and Fairy Tales* authoritatively attests, the international and interdisciplinary institutionalization of fairy-tale studies is a fait accompli, this has a lot to do with the extraordinary literary production by writers of "the fairy-tale generation" as well as with leftist and second-wave feminist interrogations of the value of fairy tales. Vanessa Joosen's important book, *Critical and Creative Perspectives on Fairy Tales: An Intertextual Dialogue between Fairy-Tale Scholarship and Postmodern Retellings* (2011), develops our understanding of this dialogue by centering her analysis on three key critical texts from the 1970s—Marcia K. Lieberman's "Some Day My Prince Will Come," Bruno Bettelheim's *The Uses of Enchantment*, and Sandra M. Gilbert and Susan Gubar's *The Madwoman in the Attic*—that she links thematically with an impressively "large number of retellings and illustrated versions"[6] of six well-known fairy tales. Basic to her tracing of this dynamic dialogue is Joosen's starting point that "any intertextual analysis of contemporary fairy-tale retellings has to take into account that the best-known fairy tales have been reproduced in innumerable variants and that fairy-tale material has generated countless verbal and nonverbal manifestations."[7]

* * *

As Theo Meder documented, folktale collections on the Internet have provided an impressive array of texts to researchers: "One of the earliest (1994) and still one of the finest folktale collections is the German Gutenberg Project, which as of 2006 contained some 1,600 fairy tales," and its English-language version includes not only Charles Perrault's and the Brothers Grimm's canonical texts, but also Giambattista Basile's, Marie-Catherine d'Aulnoy, and *The*

5. Stephen Benson, *Contemporary Fiction and the Fairy Tale* (Detroit: Wayne State UP, 2008), p. 5.
6. Vanessa Joosen, *Critical and Creative Perspectives on Fairy Tales: An Intertextual Dialogue between Fairy-Tale Scholarship and Postmodern Retellings* (Detroit: Wayne State UP), p. 7.
7. Ibid., p. 10.

Arabian Nights.[8] And D. L. Ashliman's extensive online research tools Folklore and Mythology: Electronic Texts, and Folklinks: Folk and Fairy Tale Sites, both of which originated in 1996, provide folktale and fairy-tale texts and links to other collections and critical resources on the Internet, some of encyclopedic nature (most prominently the *Enzyklopädie des Märchens,* the leading German-language reference on folk and fairy tales in an international research context), others devoted to specific tales (for example, Kay E. Vandergrift's Snow White site, created in 1997), still others consisting of scholarly journals (for example, *Marvels & Tales: Journal of Fairy-Tale Studies*, a print publication also available through Project MUSE and JSTOR). During the 1996–2006 period, Folklinks alone had over one million visits, while the Folklore and Mythology: Electronic Texts had more than three million visitors by June 2011. Two other well-respected fairy-tale sites, Endicott Studio and SurLaLune Fairy Tales, are also quite popular, and as such it is instructive to take a look at their profiles and trajectories.

Founded in 1987 and directed by writer-artist-scholars Terri Windling and Midori Snyder, the Endicott Studio website and its *Journal of Mythic Arts* are "dedicated to literary, visual, performance, and environmental arts rooted in myth, folklore, fairy tales, and the traditional stories of people the world over." Created in 1999 by librarian and researcher Heidi Anne Heiner, SurLaLune Fairy Tales "features 49 annotated fairy tales, including their histories, similar tales across cultures, modern interpretations and over 1,500 illustrations"; it also includes over 1,600 folktales and fairy tales from around the world in electronic books and a discussion forum. Both Endicott Studio and SurLaLune were envisioned and are run by indefatigable and creative women who have put their visionary expertise at the service of scholars, writers, teachers, students, and the public at large, and both sites have strong women-centered and feminist profiles, as seen in the essays of the *Journal of the Mythic Arts* and judging from the discussion board on SurLaLune. While "mythic projects" and healing in literary and visual arts are more of a focus in Windling's and Snyder's nonprofit project, Heiner states she "created [hers] strictly for educational and entertainment purposes." Informed by folklore and fairy-tale studies scholarship, both sites are configured to make their visitors' experience of the many wonder tales into a transformative journey, whether mythic or educational. Over time the two websites have also transformed. A small nonprofit, Endicott Studio has since 2008 reduced its activities but maintains its archives and a blog with news about

---

8. Theo Meder, "Internet," in *Greenwood Encyclopedia of Folktales and Fairy Tales,* ed. Donald Haase (Santa Barbara, CA: Greenwood, 2008), II, 490.

Endicott-Studio-associated artists' publications and awards, and currently has a presence on YouTube and Facebook. Strengthened somewhat by its association with Amazon.com, SurLaLune continues to expand its reach. The blog, which Heiner started in June 2009, is dizzyingly filled with news about fairy-tale books, films, illustrations, and more. Furthermore, Heiner has also started to publish print volumes in the SurLaLune Fairy-Tale series, including *Rapunzel and Other Maiden in the Tower Tales from Around the World* (2010), *The Frog Prince and Other Frog Tales from Around the World* (2010), *Bluebeard: Tales from Around the World* (2011), and *Cinderella: Tales from Around the World* (2012).

The fact that websites are doing more than providing a wealth of folktale and fairy-tale primary texts to those who can access the Internet is further brought home by the multiplying of online publications, like the English-language *Cabinet de Fées* and *Fairy Tale Review* (both of which have issues also available in print); discussion forums, such as SurLaLune's, which in the October 2000– June 2011 period had 3,761 average visits per day and 23,391 total posts on over six hundred different topics; blogs, including Breezes from Wonderland by Harvard-based fairy-tale scholar Maria Tatar and the one Michael Lundell has maintained since 2007, The Journal of 1001 Nights; and Facebook groups like Fairy Tale Films Research. * * *

                              *   *   *

The fairy-tale web as I conceptualize it is necessarily a twenty-first-century construct that accounts for, even depends to some extent on, the World Wide Web's impact. As such, the "fairy-tale web" seemingly builds on fashionable terminology and is an easily graspable concept, but I do not mean it at all to be coterminous with the circulation of fairy tales on the Internet. The twenty-first-century fairy-tale web I envision is more a methodological field than a state of affairs. Analytically, it has a history, or better, histories—both as metaphor and reading practice—and, I hope to show, it has critical potential. Proposing the fairy-tale web as a general site for critical inquiry into the genre's activity has a twofold purpose: to further the construction of a history and remapping of the genre that are not insulated from the power structures and struggles of capitalism, colonialism, coloniality, and disciplinarity; and to envision current fairy-tale cultural practices in an intertextual dialogue with one another that is informed not only by the interests of the entertainment or culture industry and the dynamics of globalization in a "postfeminist" climate but also by more multivocal and unpredictable uses of the genre.

The association of storytelling with the practice and metaphor of weaving, and spinning of course, has a long tradition in literature. Examples are Ovid's classic stories of Arachne's weaving contest with Athena and of Philomela's woven tapestry denouncing her rapist brother-in-law as well as Native American creation stories featuring Spider Grandmother and her singing. In language this metaphor appears in English when we "spin tales," which have "threads," and when we "weave a spell." The weaving metaphor in modern books' representation of fairy tales as children's literature is exemplified through the image of old women, iconically Mother Goose, spinning flax and tales. The metaphor shows up in narrative studies, since Roland Barthes reminded us that "etymologically, the text is a tissue, a woven fabric" and that "the plural of the Text depends, that is, not on the ambiguity of its contents but on what might be called the stereographic plurality of its weave of signifiers"[9]; and in fairy-tale studies, most prominently with Karen Rowe proposing that "strand by strand weaving, like the craft practiced on Philomela's loom or in the hand-spinning of Mother Goose, is the true art of the fairy tale" in her landmark essay "To Spin a Yarn" (1999 [1986]).[1] With varying emphases, the metaphor connects storytelling with women, intertextuality, and action or response in the face of unequal power relations of weavers, fabrication of meanings, and media or crafts. I aim to keep these links active in my exploration of the fairy-tale web, along with some ideas about what a spider's web does in nature. The spider's web catches prey, just as we get caught up in stories; it sparkles, the way fairy-tale magic or wonder does in successful performances. But it has a dilatory pattern and center because it emanates from one spinner, *unlike* the fairy-tale or any other intertextual web that depends on the activity, memories, locations, and responses of many individuals and institutions.

When it comes to storytelling in practice, we are now very familiar with the idea that all texts—oral, written, visual, and social—participate in a web of intertextual relations. While intertextuality has been central to both oral poetics and textual criticism "since the latter part of the seventeenth century, when oral tradition became a key element in marking the juncture between premodern and modern epochs in the evolution of language and culture,"[2] thinking about intertextuality as a web implies a critical conception of it that originated with Julia Kristeva and was informed by Mikhail Bakhtin's

---

9. Roland Barthes, "From Work to Text," in *Modern Literary Theory: A Reader*, ed. Philip Rice and Patricia Waugh (London: Edward Arnold, 1989), p. 168.
1. Karen Rowe, "To Spin a Yarn," reprinted in this edition. See pp. 393–405.
2. Richard Bauman, *A World of Others' Words: Cross-Cultural Perspectives on Intertextuality* (Malden, MA: Blackwell, 2004), p. 1.

multivocality. Verbal intertextuality, to gloss Kristeva, is not the dialogue of fixed meanings or texts with one another; it is an intersec-
tion of several speech acts and discourses (the writer's, the speaker's,
the addressee, earlier writers' and speakers'), whereby meanings
emerge in the process of how something is told and valued, where, to
whom, and in relation to which other utterances. "Stories echo with
other stories, with those echoes adding force to the present story.
Stories are also told to be echoed in future stories. Stories summon
up whole cultures."[3] To put it differently, * * * "each act of textual
production presupposes antecedent texts and anticipates prospective
ones,"[4] and how that works is somewhat out of the control of any one
individual or group. We cannot fully predict or control which stories
mingle with, influence, anticipate, interrupt, take over, or support
one another because every teller and recipient of a tale brings to it
her or his own texts; we also cannot fully anticipate how a story, no
matter how the teller or writer intends it, will act on its listeners/
readers/viewers. * * *

As a reading practice, the twenty-first-century fairy-tale web
reaches back in history and across space to intersect with multiple
story-weaving traditions. Several scholars have shown how French,
German, and British women's fairy tales assumed a subaltern position within literary histories of the genre that revolve around the
canonical figures of Charles Perrault, the Brothers Grimm, and
Oscar Wilde. Tracing the history of the genre has meant highlight-
ing the pioneering role of Giovan Francesco Straparola and Giambattista Basile in establishing the fairy tale as a print genre in
sixteenth-century Venice and seventeenth-century Naples, respectively, or showing how fairy tales circulated *ante nominem* in ancient
world and medieval Latin texts. Other researchers have contributed
to our understanding of how tales in the oral tradition from the nineteenth century into the present popularize, talk back at, or diverge
from the literary ones. And transnational research on *The Arabian
Nights* has reconfigured it as a "huge narrative wheel" whereby stories "flowed with the traffic across the frontier of Islam and Chris-
tendom, a frontier that was more porous, commercially and
culturally, than military and ideological history will admit."[5] Today,
the kind of multilayered and multiperspectival reading of the fairy
tale that Angela Carter's *The Bloody Chamber* inaugurated has
become part of increasingly knowing adult readers' expectations. A

---

3. Frank, *Letting Stories Breathe*, p. 37.
4. Bauman, *A World of Others' Words*, p. 4.
5. Marina Warner, *Stranger Magic: Charmed States and* The Arabian Nights (Cambridge
   MA: Harvard UP, 2012), pp. 9, 12.

greater awareness of multiple traditions and voices * * * is not limited to academic circles but also informs varied contemporary fairy-tale practices in popular culture.

However, while the twenty-first-century fairy-tale web is complex, not all its links are equal since, as mentioned earlier, maintaining a socioeconomic and cultural divide is built into a for-profit globalizing economy of cultural production. The reach of small-press authors, independent filmmakers and artists as well as the cultural capital of genre fiction—with which the fairy tale is increasingly merged—are small compared to those of the multinational corporate media circuits. This inequality, I want to underscore here, extends to the construction of the fairy-tale web's history and its geopolitics of knowledge. If "fairy tales are fiction's natural migrants,"[6] historically their traffic has been regulated by commerce, religion, and prejudice—which is not always recognized and results in an unequal flow of tales and an unequal valorization of different tellers' located knowledges. As a methodological field—whereby the web is "experienced in the activity of production,"[7] that is, of *reading*, rather than as a received or preexisting object—it matters how through the construction and reconstruction of a web of intertextuality we make multiple (hi)stories of the genre visible/narratable, or not; for instance, how we link fairy tales with folktales.

In the introduction to *The Virago Book of Fairy Tales*, Angela Carter provocatively insisted on weaving them into a "great mass of infinitely various narrative"[8]: "Ours is a highly individualized culture, with a great faith in the work of art as a unique one-off, and the artist as an original, a godlike and inspired creator of unique one-offs. But fairy tales are not like that, nor are their makers. Who first invented meatballs? In what country? Is there a definitive recipe for potato soup? Think in terms of the domestic arts. 'This is how *I* make potato soup.'"[9] But in actuality, the fairy tale comes to us today manufactured and branded differently from the folktale. As Jan M. Ziolkowski writes, "fairy tales have acquired their current niche in Western and even in world culture thanks to the imprimatur of having been subsumed in collections that are not at all anonymous or collective (as would be expected with folk literature) but that are instead attached indissolubly to particular writers."[1] The published

---

6. Andrew Teverson, "Migrant Fictions: Salman Rushdie and the Fairy Tale," in *Contemporary Fiction and the Fairy Tale*, ed. Stephen Benson (Detroit: Wayne State UP, 2008), p. 54.
7. Barthes, "From Work to Text," p. 167.
8. Angela Carter, ed., *The Virago Book of Fairy Tales* (London: Virago, 1990), p. ix.
9. Ibid., p. x.
1. Ziolkowski, *Fairy Tales from before Fairy Tales*, p. 236.

tales associated with Charles Perrault, Jacob and Wilhelm Grimm, and Hans Christian Andersen have epitomized what is commonly understood to be the fairy-tale genre and its "universal" appeal, as opposed to the outmoded and simple "folktales," which are instead associated with a specific kind of group identity (ethnic, national, gendered). As this generally accepted narrative goes, fairy tales develop out of folktales by turning a staple of narrative sustenance into a chef's signature dish, and the chef—no matter where the staple came from—could only be in the literate classes and, more specifically, the literate classes of Europe.

This popular construction of the fairy tale as a modern genre, then, reproduces what Dipesh Chakrabarty identifies as the stagist historicism of European modernity that "came to non-European peoples in the nineteenth century as somebody's way of saying 'not yet' to somebody else."[2] The genre of the "fairy tale" is still generally understood as European and North American; the Middle East constructed as the Orient has produced *The Thousand and One Nights*, wonder tales that have become identified with exotic magic and fantasy; most of the rest of the world has or had "folktales" that can become "fairy tales," but are not yet. It is from the vantage point of those who have "progressed" from listening to folktales to reading fairy tales (to children) that storytelling and story power in general are measured. Within this ethnocentric construction of magic, wonder, and enchantment, some peoples and some groups have imaginations that make art and reach for symbolic truth, and others have limited inventiveness that is hopelessly fantastic or obsolete and ultimately untrue. Furthermore, historically, the translation of oral stories from "exotic" places and cultures into European languages has meant that radically different narrative forms—including nonfiction—were reduced to and marketed as "fairy" stories. The fairy tale's cultural capital today continues to accrue interest on the commodification and appropriation of both oral and non-European storytelling traditions.

※　※　※

2. Dipesh Chakrabarty, *Provincializing Europe*, rev. ed. (Princeton, NJ: Princeton UP, 2007), p. 8.

JESSICA TIFFIN

From Magical Illusion: Fairy-Tale Film[†]

Film versions of fairy tale are inevitable, given the extreme adaptability shown by fairy-tale structures across the centuries, and its
ability to continually reinvent its voices, settings, and message as well
as its medium of expression. As with the adaptation of oral folktale
into written literature, the adaptation of written literature into film
brings with it the possibilities and the constraints of the new
medium: if writing and the printed book reinvented the oral tale,
cinema's impact on literary storytelling is perhaps even more profound. Film is a vitally different form of expression from the book,
and its creation—technical, massively expensive, requiring the input
and skills of a large and diverse body of contributors—hugely exag-
gerates the importance of technology in the transmission of cultural
artifacts. This leap in the complexity of the process is enabled by
the concomitant leap in audience: the twentieth century saw the
development of the mass market, the ability of texts to reach more
people more easily than ever before. The distance from the cozy oral
storyteller in a small circle of listeners could not be greater. With
the new costs and new audience naturally come new constraints on
the narrative, which must be adapted to its viewers on a far broader
and less personal scale to provide the necessary mass appeal which
will recoup the enormous costs of production. Film thus has a dual
nature as an exciting and powerfully visual form of artistic expression but also as a medium operating within the consumerist paradigm of modern mass culture. Both film-as-art and film-as-product
retain the potential to offer an essentially self-reflexive notion of narrative, metafiction given new expression by a new technology.

From the earliest days of cinema, in texts such as the experimental fairy-tale films of Georges Méliès, fairy-tale film has been
extremely successful. Fairy-tale motifs adapt easily to the visual, and
fairy tale's clear, simplified narratives are also far more conveniently
adaptable to the time-scale of a film than are the detailed textures
and events of a novel. This thematic simplicity also possibly explains
why fairy-tale film has become strongly associated with the particular film medium of animation, a form which similarly refuses to
reflect a realistically textured world. On the narrative level, fairy-
tale film offers an obvious articulation of the classic Hollywood

† From Jessica Tiffin, "Magical Illusion: Fairy-Tale Film," in *Marvelous Geometry: Narrative and Metafiction in Modern Fairy Tale* (Detroit, MI: Wayne State UP, 2009), pp. 179–
88. Copyright © 2009 Wayne State University Press, with the permission of Wayne
State University Press. All parenthetical citations have been provided as footnotes.

"fairy-tale" plot, which relies heavily on the comedic marriage resolution and on wish fulfillment and utopian impulses that empower the underdog. The close fit between film and fairy tale is also in some ways inevitable given folkloric narrative's long history of happy interaction with theatrical as well as literary forms. Following the adaptation of folklore into the French aristocratic pursuits of the eighteenth century, fairy-tale motifs seem to have spread rapidly to the theater, ballet, and opera. The heyday of fairy-tale ballet in the nineteenth century saw the creation of such classics as *Sleeping Beauty, Swan Lake,* and *The Nutcracker,* all with recognizable fairy-tale themes. In opera, fairy-tale awareness, although expanded into a more complex narrative, informs operas such as Mozart's *The Magic Flute*, Verdi's *Vakula the Smith*, and Puccini's *Turandot*.

As a symbolic genre, fairy tale has strong visual and dramatic potential. It is also obvious that the simple, ritualistic formulae of fairy tale would work well in ritualistic traditions, most notably ballet and opera, which are artistic productions whose meaning is expressed via a powerful system of structural codes (song, movement) rather than a process of realistic representation. Suzanne Rahn writes, "Like fairy tales, ballets are constructed as highly formalized narratives which make extensive use of repetition and tell their stories primarily through the physical actions of their characters."[1] In the twentieth century, the successful use of fairy tale in the Broadway musical follows a similar pattern; Stephen Sondheim's 1986 musical *Into the Woods*, for example, explores the dangerous gap between fairy tale and real life in a manner similar to Pratchett's *Witches Abroad*. Again, the musical is an artificial form whose encodings—the stock romantic characters, the likelihood of any character to break into song or dance at any moment—have very little to do with reality. Disney's characteristic blending of the fairy tale and the musical is a good illustration of these similarities; films such as *Beauty and the Beast* not only use the musical format but also refer constantly to the Hollywood musical.

However, theater, ballet, and other live art forms face an inherent logical problem in visually representing the marvelous, relying on stylization or at times unconvincing mechanisms to pretend to the magical; Tolkien, typically, claims that "Fantasy . . . hardly ever succeeds in Drama. . . . Fantastic forms are not to be counterfeited."[2] This is in many ways an anachronistic view in the age of CGI (computer-generated imagery), and the verisimilitude of magical spectacle in film has seen a steady increase over the last hundred

---

1. In Jack Zipes, *The Oxford Companion to Fairy Tales: The Western Fairy Tale Tradition from Medieval to Modern* (Oxford: Oxford UP, 2000), p. 34.
2. J. R. R. Tolkien, "On Fairy Stories," in *The Tolkien Reader* (New York: Ballantine, 1966), p. 49.

years, culminating in the giant leaps made by computer imagery in influential films such as Peter Jackson's three-film version of *The Lord of the Rings*. Cinema's tricky camera is thus ultimately able to overcome the difficulties of nonreal representation, harnessing fairy tale's symbolic qualities to provide a rich visual texture. The contributions of special effects and CGI have made possible visual enchantments Tolkien could not have imagined, but the film/fairy tale fit is more profound than that; even in the early days of the medium, cinema has always been the site of magic. While apparently offering the real, it is a fertile ground for trickery, in which apparently real objects may disappear, reappear, change size or orientation, change shape—in fact, the whole of the special effects man's box of tricks; David Galef's discussion of Jean Cocteau's *La Belle et la Bête* offers a detailed and interesting analysis of this kind of magical cinematic function. The authority of the camera is such that the impossible takes on the same status as the realistic, which is in any case a good working definition of magic.

On a more fundamental level, the magical paradigm of fairy tale finds echoes in the magic of the film experience even without special effects, in film's ability to create the apparent three-dimensionality of the real on a flat, unmoving screen, through the trickery of light and image. Film powerfully realizes the transcendence over reality with which magical narrative is intrinsically concerned. This is, of course, another aspect of the debate André Bazin has called "the quarrel over realism in art" that arises from ongoing technical refinement; he suggests that the eye of the camera has the power to satisfy "our obsession with realism" and "our appetite for illusion."[3] Photography and film are particularly suited to the depiction of the fantastic because they are able to produce "a hallucination that is also a fact";[4] to blur, in fact, the boundaries between fiction and mimesis, although in a way which seldom denies its own illusion to produce the frame break which would signal metafictional play.

In addition to this, the absorbing effect of the film experience— the immersion of the viewer in a constructed reality—parallels the more traditional folk storytelling experience. Jack Zipes formulates a general theory of fairy-tale film, commenting on the importance of the storyteller's ability to create a new, removed, and absorbing reality for his or her audience. He suggests, "A magic folk tale concerned not only the miraculous turn of events in the story, but also the magical play of words by the teller as performer. . . . Telling a

3. André Bazin, "What Is Cinema?" trans. Hugh Gray (Berkeley: U of California P, 1967), p. 12.
4. Ibid., p. 16.

magic folk tale was and is not unlike performing a magic trick, and depending on the art of the storyteller, listeners are placed under a spell. They are . . . transcending reality for a brief moment, to be transported to extraordinary realms of experience."[5] In this characterization, cinema, like fairy tale, is a form of illusion, its viewers willingly suspending disbelief in order to surpass reality and experience the magical. Zipes notes the association between early filmmakers and stage magic—"magic lantern shows, magician's tricks, shadow theatres, animation devices . . ."[6] The filmmaker becomes the magician, the showman with the power of technological marvels, exerting the same spell as the storyteller, but with new, spectacular special effects.

The interaction of film and fairy tale does not, however, constitute an unproblematical romance. While the magic of film may parallel some aspects of fairy tale, at the same time a visual medium can be crippling to the kind of imaginative exercise usually required of the reader by almost any magical narrative. Tolkien goes as far as to deny the validity even of illustrated literary fairy tale: "The radical distinction between all art (including drama) that offers a *visible* presentation and true literature is that it imposes one visible form. Literature works from mind to mind and is thus more progenitive."[7] In this context, film's presentation of realism is a problem as well as a strength. The recording eye of the camera intrinsically designates its objects as real, and the effect of watching a film is that of immersion in a highly detailed reality. In contrast, most forms of fantasy, fairy tale included, work on evocation, rather than being explicit; the process of imaginative interaction with the fantasy requires a tailoring of the fantasy world to the psychological reality of the individual. Film, in its extreme visuality, operates directly against this; a fairy-tale medium, in its metafictional awareness of craftedness, is specifically not realistic, and it may be jarring to have realistic representation on screen. Donald P. Haase's discussion of Neil Jordan's *The Company of Wolves* raises the same point: "The one-dimensionality, the depthlessness, and the abstract style . . . of the fairy tale do not require the auditor or reader to envision a specific reality, and thereby they encourage imaginative belief in an unreal world. In the fairy tale, then, *not seeing* is believing."[8] Yet film paradoxically offers the potential for sending strong signals through visual details of setting and costume—the presence of self-conscious

5. Jack Zipes, *Happily Ever After: Fairy Tales, Children, and the Culture Industry* (New York: Routledge, 1997), p. 63.
6. Ibid., p. 68.
7. Tolkien, "On Fairy Stories," p. 80.
8. Donald P. Haase, "Is Seeing Believing? Proverbs and the Film Adaptation of a Fairy Tale," *Proverbium* 7 (1990), p. 90.

medievalism in a fairy-tale film, together with details of fairy-tale landscapes (forests, mountains, castles) may effectively signal the unreality of long ago and far away. Thus fairy-tale films such as *The Company of Wolves* and *The Grimm Brothers' Snow White* feature particularly vast and Gothic stretches of forest, while *Ever After* makes effective use of medieval castles, sweeping landscapes, and beautiful costumes. Cocteau's unexplained surrealist images in the Beast's castle, and Jordan's dense use of apparently disconnected symbol (animals, roses, etc.) fulfill the same function. In this deliberate symbolic texturing, once again, fairy-tale film has the potential to realize visually the metafictional strategy at the heart of its structures, despite its illusory offering of realism.

Film and the Folk Voice

> A real fairy tale, a tale in its true function, is a tale within a circle of listeners.
>
> —KAREL CAPEK[9]

There are various thematic matches between film and fairy-tale narrative, but cinematic versions of fairy tale can be seen to offer their own pitfalls and drawbacks. While the power of the film medium in modern society has provided a fertile new ground for fairy-tale cultural and ideological production, the medium of film offers problems as well as possibilities for fairy tale. One of the most insidious tendencies has been that of the powerful new visual medium, rooted firmly in modern technological popular culture, to supplant all other versions, and in so doing, to deliberately claim the folk voice originally excluded by the adaptation of fairy tale into a literary form. While parallel in many ways to the process by which oral folktale became written fairy tale, the adaptation from written fairy tale into fairy-tale film is more problematical precisely because of the power of the film medium, and the striking fit between some narrative aspects of fairy tale and the narrative function of film. To unwrap the dangers of this process will require examination of the uneasy, contested spaces of folk culture, popular culture, and mass culture.

As one of the more powerful and pervasive forms of popular culture in the twentieth and twenty-first century, film offers an interesting context for the folk voice of fairy tale. Although the folktale has been replaced gradually with the literary fairy tale in the last few centuries, film versions of fairy tale tend to flirt superficially and self-consciously with the folk voice. As the most prevalent cinematic experience in Western culture, Hollywood film caters to a popular

9. In Marina Warner, *From the Beast to the Blonde: On Fairy Tales and Their Tellers* (New York: Farrar, Straus & Giroux, 1994), p. 17.

market, offering both entertainment and the opportunity to participate in a popular awareness of actors and film which centers on the
Hollywood star system. Although a form of mass culture in its reli-
ance on the budgets of wealthy studios, and the resulting need to
commodify film in order to fill cinema seats, film functions in modern Western culture as a group and social activity whose audience
participates in an essentially nonliterary popular culture. Walter
Ong argues for a modern notion of "secondary orality," a development through literacy into a kind of postliteracy under technology;
he points out that "the drive towards group sense and towards par-
ticipatory activities, towards 'happenings,' which mysteriously
emerges out of modern electronic technological cultures is strikingly
similar to certain drives in preliterate cultures."[1] The cinema experience offers far more of group participation than reading a written
text. This inheres not only in the simultaneous experience of the film
text, with shared reactions such as laughter, but also in the social
activity around a common interest in film genres or specific stars,
meeting to view a film, the discussion which often takes place either
before or afterward over drinks or a meal. The experience of a home
viewing of the video or DVD version of a film is an even more pronounced version of this communality. This is in many ways a superficial restoration of the communal folk experience of storytelling, in
some senses reversing the historical translation of the oral folk voice
into a written form experienced only by the individual, and reinstat-
ing it as shared cultural artifact. It also underlines the restitution
offered the form after its appropriation by written narrative, and
thus a social elite; Zipes comments that popular fairy-tale film "actually returns the fairy tale to the majority of people."[2]

However, while a film is certainly more communal than a single
individual reading a book, it is not a true folk culture. The group
may share the experience, but it is not *produced* from within the
group, nor does the production come from a source which has
the same status—here defined economically—as group members.
Likewise, interaction with the film narrative cannot equal the folk
experience since film is a one-way process. The film modifies the
experience of the viewer, but the film is not a genuine oral voice and
cannot in its turn be modified in response to the audience, other
than on the macrolevel represented by the research done by a studio's marketing arm before the next film is made. Walter Benjamin
suggests, in fact, that the reproduction of mass images ultimately
denies the authenticity of the artistic object, its ability to transfer

1. Walter Ong, *Rhetoric, Romance, and Technology: Studies in the Interaction of Expression and Culture* (Ithaca: Cornell UP, 1971), p. 284.
2. Jack Zipes, *Fairy Tale as Myth, Myth as Fairy Tale* (Lexington: UP of Kentucky, 1994),
   p. 83.

value, and that film "is inconceivable without its destructive, cathartic effect, that is, the liquidation of the traditional value of the cultural heritage"; the denial of tradition in this formulation speaks directly to the divide between folk and mass culture. Film may imitate folk culture, but if it functions as a true form of modern folk culture, it is within a somewhat radically restructured notion of "folk," and, indeed, of "culture."

In keeping with film's apparently transparent offer of itself as a substitute oral and folk tradition, many fairy-tale films rely heavily on an explicit evocation of the folk voice in order to frame and contextualize their narratives. In apparently receiving the story from the physical presence or voice of an onscreen narrator, the viewer is able to participate in the removal of the tale from literary capture, placing him or herself in the position of audience to an oral storyteller. The self-conscious recognition of viewer as "listener" taps into a notion of orality which is both artificial and idealized. The purpose here is only partially to participate in the metafictional play of crafted tale and its self-conscious pleasures; it is also to access the notions of communality and trust which inhere in modern notions of orality. Thus many Disney films begin with a voice-over giving the initial scenario of the tale in traditional fairy-tale form: "Once upon a time." This is usually accompanied by static images that characterize tale as artifact—*Sleeping Beauty's* medieval stills, *Beauty and the Beast's* stained-glass windows, the Grecian vases of *Hercules*. At the same time, many of Disney's films characteristically hedge their bets: the voice-over may well be associated with stills that strongly associate the tale with the written tradition, in the form of a beautifully calligraphed and illuminated book whose pages are turned as the voice-over progresses (*Sleeping Beauty, Snow White*). As well as invoking the nostalgic memory of the parent-to-child oral voice and the familiar form of the literary fairy tale, this also claims the historical status of literature—generally, in its association with literacy and education, *higher* than that of the oral tale—for the film. The use of this motif in Dreamworks' *Shrek* was notable for its acute and cynical insight into the actual status of the original tale as written narrative—Shrek's voice reads out the dragon-slaying fairy tale, after which the camera pulls back to reveal that the book is being used as toilet paper. This nods ironically to the fact that film versions of fairy tale have all but replaced the written, but the film's ideological project affirms the status of the film version in its suggestion that they *should* replace the written, which entrenches the outdated and reactionary social assumptions the film sets out to upset.

It is important to note, however, that invocation of the oral and literary are not sustained through most fairy-tale films, which quickly

give way to the immersing experience of the moving image. The
result is effectively to overwrite the literary and the oral with the
cinematic. Jack Zipes picks up on this erasure in readings of fairy-
tale film which generally rely on the characterization of modern fairy
tale within a somewhat totalitarian sense of the culture industry. He
argues that film has "silenced the personal and communal voice of
the oral magic tales and obfuscated the personal voice of literary
fairy-tale narratives"; it focuses on image rather than text, distances
its audience, and transforms traditional tales into standardized units
of mass production.[3] In this characterization, rather as the upper
classes appropriated folk narrative in the seventeenth and eighteenth
centuries, the folk voice in the twentieth and twenty-first centuries
is colonized by a ruling monolith, although one that is commercial
rather than aristocratic. Such a colonization entails, in Baudrillard's
terms, an actual *re-creation* of a spurious notion of orality; simultaneously, its commercial aspect redefines the awareness of artifact
central to metafictional storytelling as, effectively, awareness of
product. Zipes's characterization of fairy tale as "secular instructive
narratives" offering "strategies of intervention within the civilising
process"[4] becomes more sinister when, rather than reflecting the
mores and beliefs of the folk culture, fairy tales are used to reflect
the conservative and market-driven ideologies of large companies
marketing consumer culture. Such characterizations of mass cultural productions sound a note of alarm in their sense of a production elite which seeks to duplicate and usurp the popular or folk
voice. Zipes's argument implies that any claim of nostalgic orality or
literariness in fairy-tale film is entirely spurious; logically, the elements of self-conscious play that I suggest are present become in his
terms a cynical appropriation of fairy tale's metafictional project by
what are effectively market forces. He is, of course, engaging in cultural criticism firmly in the mode of the Frankfurt School, and more
specifically Adorno and Horkheimer, who suggest that modern consumer culture is a process of the deliberate discouragement of imaginative or intellectual response to the cultural products of the mass
market. Instead, the receiver of such artifacts is lulled, via strategies
such as nostalgia, familiarity, and superficial novelty, into the passive
acceptance of a standardized cultural product. This logically suggests that the essentially reciprocal functioning of a folk culture is
completely erased, as is its ability to mirror in any immediate or vital
sense the day-to-day experiences and desires of its listeners. Adorno
and Horkheimer stress the absolute lack of true participation by the
public in mass cultural production:

3. Zipes, *Happily Ever After*, p. 69.
4. Ibid., p. 65.

The attitude of the public, which ostensibly and actually favours the system of the culture industry, is a part of the system and not an excuse for it. If one branch of art follows the same formula as one with a very different medium and content . . . if a movement from a Beethoven symphony is crudely "adapted" for a film sound-track in the same way that a Tolstoy novel is garbled in a film script; then the claim that this is done to satisfy the spontaneous wishes of the public is no more than hot air. We are closer to the facts if we explain these phenomena as inherent in the technical and personnel apparatus which, down to its last cog, itself forms part of the economic mechanism of selection. . . . In our age the objective social tendency is incarnate in the hidden subjective purposes of company directors.[5]

By this definition, mass culture and folk culture are mutually exclusive; there can be no true "objective social tendency," in Adorno and Horkheimer's words, because original and spontaneous cultural impulses are modified by the purposes of mass-cultural monoliths. There can therefore be no folk voice in mass culture. This means that the pretensions to the folk voice in many fairy-tale films are, as suggested above, "hot air"—their purpose is solely to conceal their commercial manipulations.

This is perhaps too sweeping a judgment, and more recent perceptions of popular culture as a site of struggle suggest that Adorno and Horkheimer represent only one end of the popular theory spectrum. Noël Carroll offers an opposing voice which explicitly denies the truth of such claims; he maintains that numerous examples of popular art demonstrate clearly the lack of "necessary connection between accessibility and a passive audience response," and that indeed, "in some cases, the very success of the mass artwork presupposes active spectatorship."[6] This line of thought is certainly appropriate to the sf/fantasy ghetto, in which the highly specific readership may well require active participation in the text—or, indeed, to written narratives generally, as Carroll demonstrates;[7] nonetheless, it is also true, to a greater or lesser extent, of film. The self-conscious narrative play found in texts such as Disney fairy tales or Dreamworks' *Shrek* may empower a mass-market text, but it is equally able to give the artistic and intellectual pleasure of active reading to the viewer, and indeed would not be successful *without* such narrative pleasures. Theories of a mass-cultural monolith also deny the possibilities offered by the art-house end of the film

5. Theodor Adorno and Max Horkheimer, "The Culture Industry: Enlightenment as Mass Deception," in *The Cultural Studies Reader*, ed. Simon During (London: Routledge, 1993), p. 32.
6. Noël Carroll, *A Philosophy of Mass Art* (Oxford: Clarendon, 1998), pp. 38–39.
7. Ibid., pp. 40–41.

spectrum, in which films are generally made on a far lower budget, and may be more able to balance their artistic requirements against the need to recoup their costs. A good example of film's potential for self-conscious use of fairy tale is Jordan's *The Company of Wolves*, in which frame narratives and tale-within-tale represent a sustained effort to reproduce the folk voice, and thus allow ongoing metafictional awareness. This is strengthened by the film's attention to the character of the oral storytellers (unlike Disney's disembodied voices), and their association of that oral voice with the readily identifiable grandmother archetype.

However, despite innovative uses such as Jordan's of the folk voice in film, Zipes's characterization is valid in that many fairy-tale films seem to represent an appropriation as much as an exploration or celebration of folk narrative. This exemplifies the uneasy and problematical intersections between popular or folk cultures, and the mass culture of consumerism. Film narrative is dominated by Hollywood, and particularly by big-budget studio films whose economies of scale require appeal to a broad demographic; many recent fairy-tale films represent a process of identifying the kinds of narrative which are currently selling, and reproducing them as closely as possible. Disney's huge successes with fairy tale in the late 1980s and early 1990s could be seen to have prompted later films such as *Ever After* and *The Grimm Brothers' Snow White*, and ultimately *Shrek*, which has itself spawned two sequels and a host of imitators in the knowing fairy-tale parody mode, including *Hoodwinked* and *Happily N'Ever After*. At the same time, the production-by-committee effect of financial oversight on films exists in palpable tension with the impulses of particular directors or screenwriters, who may well see the artistic rather than the commercial potential in recreating a familiar folkloric text. In addition, the construction of a particular text in terms favoring commercial success does not in any way prevent counter-cultural readings of such a text, representing a very different notion of narrative pleasure from that intended by the producers. Audience-generated responses such as fan fiction demonstrate precisely the kind of active, potentially subversive receptions of mass-cultural texts described by critics such as John Fiske and Henry Jenkins. Even Disney films, perhaps the strongest example of deliberate mass-cultural packaging, are capable of being read on multiple levels which address child and adult audiences separately. Thus, like much of mass culture, fairy-tale film is a site of contestation, with the warping of metafictional play to commercial ends balanced by a wresting back of commercial requirements to artistic and individual purposes. The postmodern cultural environment of modern film also means that at times the two impulses are one: self-consciousness, irony, and the pleasures of recognition are highly saleable commodities.

* * *

HANS-JÖRG UTHER

From The Types of International Folktales[†]

In 1910, the Finnish folklorist Antti Aarne published a work called *Verzeichnis der Märchentypen* in a series dedicated to monographs in the field of folklore. The work has come to be known as the tale type index, and it provides short synopses of fairy-tale plots. That work and the six-volume *Motif-index of Folk-Literature* published by the American folklorist Stith Thompson have been valuable aids in organizing the corpus of fairy-tale texts and identifying recurring tropes or motifs. The tale-type index has come under critical fire for limiting itself to a Eurocentric corpus that fails to include, for example, Native American or African lore. The American folklorist Alan Dundes also pointed out that Stith Thompson indulged in "absurd and excessive prudery," censoring obscene tales and motifs when he translated and enlarged Aarne's work in 1928, and then published a revised edition of his work in 1961. Hans-Jörg Uther's 2004 revision offers a more capacious view of the folktale and aspires to be both international in scope and expansive in its reach. The letters and numbers in parentheses refer to motifs catalogued in Stith Thompson's motif-index.

* * *

311   *Rescue by the Sister.* Two sisters, one after the other, fall into power of a demonic suitor (cannibal, dragon, magician, devil) and are taken into his (subterranean) castle [R11.1, T721.5]. There the sisters open a forbidden room full of dead bodies, in the course of which the key (a magic egg, apple) becomes bloody, or they refuse to eat human flesh [C611, C227, C913]. The demon kills them for their disobedience [C920].

      Using a trick, the third (youngest) sister escapes from the same fate. She finds her sisters and resuscitates them by

[†] From Hans-Jörg Uther, "Revisions to the Tale-Type Index," in *The Types of International Folktales: A Classification and Bibliography. Based on the System of Antti Aarne and Stith Thompson* (Helsinki: Academia Scientiarum Fennica, 2004), pp. 191–92, 211–13, 248, 250, 252, 293–94 Reprinted by permission of the Finnish Academy of Science and Letters. Numbers in brackets refer to motifs in Stith Thompson's *Motif-Index of Folk-Literature* (1955–58).

putting their bones together [R157.1]. She hides them beneath some gold in baskets (bags) and persuades the demon to carry the baskets home without looking into them [G561]. Cf. Type 1132.

The youngest sister pretends to marry the demon and leaves a skull (straw dummy) dressed as a bride to deceive him. Unwittingly the demon carries this sister home in the third basket. Or she smears herself with honey and feathers and escapes as a "strange bird" [K525, K521.1]. Cf. Types 1383, 1681. The demon is burned in his own house or is killed in another way [Q211]. Cf. Type 312.

* * *

311B*   *The Singing Bag.* A Gypsy (old man) puts the niece of an old washer-woman (only daughter of an old couple) into a bag and carries her off. The Gypsy goes begging from door to door and exhibits his "singing bag": He gives the bag a pinch, threatens to beat it with his stick, and orders it to sing. Thereupon the girl in the bag starts singing her tale: I left my rosary on a stone by the river when I was washing. When I wanted to get it, a Gypsy put me in his bag and carried me off. (I am the only daughter of an old couple. An old man carried me off when I was gathering berries in the forest.)

One day the Gypsy arrives at the old washerwoman's house. The woman recognizes her niece, invites the Gypsy into his house, and entertains him until he gets drunk. When he is sleeping, she rescues the girl from the bag and, in her place, puts two cats (horse-dung). When the Gypsy exhibits his singing bag the next time, the cats mew. The Gypsy opens the bag and is scratched or bitten [K526].

* * *

312   *Maiden-Killer (Bluebeard)* (previously *The Giant-killer and his Dog*). An odd-looking rich man (e.g. with a blue beard [S62.1]) takes his bride to his splendid castle. She is forbidden to open a certain room, but she disobeys and finds it full of the dead bodies of her predecessors [C611]. The husband wants to kill her for her disobedience [C920], but she is able to delay the punishment (three times) [K551]. She (her sister) calls their brother (three brothers) who kills the husband (sometimes with help from a dog or other animal) and rescues his sister(s) [G551.1, G652]. Cf. Type 311.

* * *

327   **The Children and the Ogre.** This type refers to a cycle of
        related tales. It combines episodes from types 327A, 327B,
        and 327C.

                          *   *   *

327A   **Hansel and Gretel.** A (poor) father (persuaded by the step-
        mother) abandons his children (a boy and a girl) in the
        forest [S321, S143]. Twice the children find their way back
        home, following scattered pebbles [R135]. On the third
        night, birds eat the scattered peas (bread-crumbs) [R135.1].
            The children come upon a gingerbread house which
        belongs to a witch (ogress) [G401, F771.1.10, G412.1]. She
        takes them into her house. The boy is fattened [G82],
        while the girl must do housework. The witch asks the boy
        to show his finger in order to test how fat he is [G82.1], but
        he shows her a bone (stick) [G82.1.1]. When the witch
        wants to cook the boy, the sister deceives her by feigning
        ignorance and pushes her into the oven [G526, G512.3.2].
        (The witch's son finds out that his mother has been killed
        and pursues the children.)
            The children escape, carrying the witch's treasure
        with them. Birds and beasts (angels) help them across
        water. They return home. Cf. Type 327.

                          *   *   *

327B   **The Brothers and the Ogre** (previously **The Dwarf and
        the Giant**). Seven (three, twelve, thirty) brothers come to
        an ogre's house, where they are given night lodging. The
        ogre intends to cut off the brothers's heads. In order to
        recognize his own daughters, the ogre gives them night-
        caps (head-scarves). One brother (often the youngest,
        Thumbling) detects the plan, and all brothers put on the
        night-caps of the ogre's daughters (exchange their caps for
        the daughters' head-scarves, change sleeping-places with
        the daughters). In the night, the ogre cuts off his own
        daughters' heads by mistake [K1611]. The brothers escape.
        Cf. Types 327, 1119.

                          *   *   *

410   **Sleeping Beauty.** (Dornröschen, La bella addormentata.)
        (Announced by a frog [B211.7.1, B493.1]) a daughter is born
        to a royal couple. A fairy (wise woman) who has not been
        invited to the celebration (baptism) utters a curse that the
        princess (on her 15th birthday) will die of a wound from
        a spindle (needle, fiber of flax) [F361.1.1, F316, G269.4,

M341.2.13]. Another fairy changes the death sentence into a long (hundred-year) sleep [F316.1].

The king orders that every spindle (needle) in his empire be destroyed; but, because one of them has been over-looked, the prophecy is fulfilled [M370]: The girl meets an old woman who is spinning in a hidden chamber, pricks her finger with the spindle, and sinks, together with the whole court, into a magic sleep [D1364.17, D1960.3, F771.4.4, F771.4.7]. Around the castle grows a hedge of thorns [D1967.1] (the girl is enclosed in a tower).

At the end of the appointed time, a youth (prince) breaks through the hedge [N711.2] and awakens the princess with a kiss [D735, D1978.5] (he impregnates her; she gives birth to two children, one of whom sucks the fiber out of her finger and thus disenchants her).

In some variants the prince takes his wife and children to his family. During his absence the evil mother-in-law asks the cook to slaughter and roast the woman and the children. The cook disobeys, and the mother-in-law demands that the three be thrown into a tub full of poisonous toads and snakes. Unexpectedly the prince returns home, and the mother-in-law herself jumps into the tub.

* * *

425A **The Animal as Bridegroom.** (Including the previous Type 425G.) This type combines various introductory episodes with a common main part. Cf. Types 430, 432, and 441.

Introductory episodes:

(1) The youngest daughter asks her father (the king) to bring her a (musical) rose (lark, etc.) from his journey. He finds it in the garden of a beast, but in return has to promise his daughter (the first being he meets when he arrives at home) [L221, S228, S241] to the beast. The father tries in vain to send another girl instead of his daughter [S252]. Cf. Type 425C.

(2) An animal-son (snake, crayfish, also pumpkin, etc.) is born (because of the hasty wish of his parents) [C758.1]. He demands a princess for his wife and performs difficult (impossible) tasks. The princess has to marry him [T111].

(3) A girl is intended (by fate) for an animal bridegroom or agrees to marry him [B620.1, L54.1].

(4) For other reasons a girl has an animal husband and lives together with him in his castle. He becomes a beautiful man by night [D621.1, B640.1].

Main part:

When the young wife (often on the advice of her female relatives) burns the animal-skin of her bridegroom [C757.1] (looks at him during the night or burns him with candle wax [C32.1, C916.1], reveals his secret [C421], or otherwise prevents his disenchantment), he goes away [C932].

The young wife sets out for a long and difficult quest [H1385.4] (in iron shoes [Q502.2], etc.). On her way she is given directions and reveals his secret [C421], or otherwise prevents his disenchantment he goes away [C932].

The young wife sets out for a long and difficult quest [H1385.4] (in iron shoes [Q502.2], etc.). On her way she is given directions and precious gifts by the sun, moon, wind, and stars [H1232] (helpful old people or animals [H1233.1.1, H1235]. She arrives (sometimes by climbing a glass mountain [H1114]) at her bridegroom's far-away residence. She finds that her husband has another (supernatural) bride.

She takes service as maid [Q482.1] and trades her precious things (golden implements for spinning, jewels, magnificent clothes, etc.) for three nights by the side of her lost husband [D2006.1.1]. She wants to awaken his memory of her, but two times he is drugged by a soporific. He spills the soporific on the third night, stays awake, and recognizes her as his true bride [D2006.1.4]. (Death of the false bride.) Cf. Type 313.

∗　∗　∗

425B　*Son of the Witch* (previously *The Disenchanted Husband: the Witch's Tasks*). (Cupid and Psyche.) (Including the previous Types 425J, 425N, and 428.) This type combines various introductory episodes with a common main part. Cf. Type 425A.

Introductory episodes:

A young woman marries a supernatural bridegroom:

(1) She is given to her bridegroom because of a present that she has asked her father to bring back from a journey [S228].

(2) The bridegroom performs a set of difficult tasks.

(3) She pulls up an herb and discovers the bridegroom's subterranean castle (a wind carries her there).

(4) She finds him in another way.

The bridegroom is the son of a witch (ogress) or he is (during the day) an animal [D621.1].

Main part:

The young woman breaks the bridegroom's prohibition (cf. Type 425A), and he goes away [C932]. (Before he leaves, he gives her a token, e.g. ring, feather.) (In iron shoes) she sets out to find him [H1385.4, H1125].

The bride comes to the house of her bridegroom's mother, a witch, who swears by her son's name not to devour her. The witch imposes difficult tasks on the young woman, which she performs (with the help of her bridegroom): to sort a large quantity of grain [H1122], to fill mattresses with the feathers of all kinds of birds, to wash the black wool white and the white black [H1023.6, cf. Type 1183], to sweep a house but leave it unswept [H1066], etc. In some variants she enchants (three) suitors and makes them fight (part of previous Type 425N). Cf. Types 313, 875.

The young woman is sent on a dangerous journey to bring a casket from the sister of the witch. Having passed obstacles (with the advice from her bridegroom) and obtained the casket, she is forbidden to open it. (Cf. Types 408, 480.) When the bride acts against the prohibition, her husband helps her.

At the wedding of the bridegroom and the witch's daughter, the young woman has to hold ten burning candles (torches). Her bridegroom saves her from being burned.

The young woman remarries her bridegroom, or both escape by a magic (transformation) flight [D671, D672].

* * *

425C *Beauty and the Beast.* (Including the previous Type 425H.)

A merchant sets out on a journey and intends to bring back presents for his three daughters. The two elder ones demand jewels and clothes, the youngest a rose [L221]. The father is not able to find one.

He loses his way and stays overnight in a deserted castle, where he breaks off a rose. An (invisible) animal (beast) demands that the man return or send a substitute [S222]. The youngest daughter meets her father's obligation but refuses to marry the (ugly) animal, who treats her kindly.

In a magic mirror she sees her father is ill. She is allowed to visit him but (influenced by her envious sisters) overstays the allotted time [C761.2]. She returns and finds the animal near death, realizes she loves him, and caresses or kisses him. By this means she disenchants the prince from his animal shape [D735.1]. They marry.

* * *

510   **Cinderella and Peau d'Âne.** This type number refers to a cycle of related tales. See esp. Types 510A and 510B.

* * *

510A   **Cinderella.** (Cenerentola, Cendrillon, Aschenputtel.) A young woman is mistreated by her stepmother and stepsisters [S31, L55] and has to live in the ashes as a servant. When the sisters and the stepmother go to a ball (church), they give Cinderella an impossible task (e.g. sorting peas from ashes), which she accomplishes with the help of birds [B450]. She obtains beautiful clothing from a supernatural being [D1050.1, N815] or a tree that grows on the grave of her deceased mother [D815.1, D842.1, E323.2] and goes unknown to the ball. A prince falls in love with her [N711.6, N711.4], but she has to leave the ball early [C761.3]. The same thing happens on the next evening, but on the third evening, she loses one of her shoes [R221, F823.2].

    The prince will marry only the woman whom the shoe fits [H36.1]. The stepsisters cut pieces off their feet in order to make them fit into the shoe [K1911.3.3.1], but a bird calls attention to this deceit. Cinderella who had been first hidden from the prince, tries on the shoe and it fits her. The prince marries her.

* * *

720   **The Juniper Tree** (previously *My Mother Slew Me; My Father Ate Me*). A childless couple wishes for a child. A boy is born but his mother dies. The little boy is slain by his cruel stepmother who closes the lid of an apple chest on him [S121]. She cooks him and serves him to his father who eats him unwittingly [G61].

    The boy's stepsister gathers up his bones and puts them under a juniper tree [E607.1]. A bird comes forth and sings about what happened. It brings presents to the father and the sister and drops a millstone to the stepmother, killing her [Q412]. The boy is resuscitated [E30, E610.1.1, E613.0.1]. Cf. Type 780.

* * *

VLADIMIR PROPP

From Folklore and Literature[†]

* * *

Folklore is the product of a special form of verbal art. Literature is also a verbal art, and for this reason the closest connection exists between folklore and literature, between the science of folklore and literary criticism. Literature and folklore overlap partially in their poetic genres. There are genres specific to literature (for example, the novel) and to folklore (for example, the charm), but both folklore and literature can be classified by genres, and this is a fact of poetics. Hence there is a certain similarity in some of their tasks and methods.

One of the literary tasks of folklore is to single out and study the category of genre and each particular genre. Especially important and difficult is to study the inner structure of verbal products, their composition and makeup. The laws pertaining to the structure of the folktale, epic poetry, riddles, songs, charms, etc., are little known. In epic genres consider, for example, the opening of the poem, the plot, and the conclusion. It has been shown that works of folklore and literature have different morphologies and that folklore has specific structures. This difference cannot be *explained,* but it can be *discovered* by means of literary analysis. Stylistic and poetical devices belong here too. Again we will see that folklore has devices specific to it (parallelisms, repetition, etc.) and that the usual devices of poetical language (similes, metaphors, epithets) have a different content in folklore and literature. This too can be determined by literary analysis.

In brief, folklore possesses a most distinctive *poetics,* peculiar to it and different from the poetics of literary works. Study of this poetics will reveal the incomparable artistic beauty of folklore.

Thus, not only is there a close tie between folklore and literature, but folklore is a literary phenomenon. Like literature, it is a verbal art.

In its descriptive elements the study of folklore is the study of literature. The connection between these disciplines is so close that folklore and literature are often equated; methods of literature are extended to folklore, and here the matter is allowed to rest. However, as just pointed out, literary analysis can only *discover* the phenomenon and the law of folklore poetics, but it is unable to *explain*

† From Vladimir Propp, "Folklore and Literature," in *Theory and History of Folklore,* trans. Ariadna Y. Martin and Richard P. Martin, ed. Anatoly Liberman (Minneapolis: U of Minnesota P, 1984), pp. 5–9. Copyright © 1984 by the University of Minnesota Press. Reprinted by permission of University of Minnesota Press.

them. To avoid the error of equating folklore with literature, we must ascertain not only *how literature and folklore are alike,* related, and to a certain extent identical in nature, but also *how they differ.* Indeed, folklore possesses a number of features so sharply differentiating it from literature that methods of literary research are insufficient for solving all its problems.

One of the most important differences is that literary works invariably have an author. Folklore works, on the contrary, never have an author, and this is one of their specific features. The situation is quite clear: either we acknowledge the presence of *folk art* as a phenomenon in the social and cultural history of peoples or we do not acknowledge it and claim that it is a poetical or scientific fiction and that only individuals and groups can create poetry.

We believe that folk art is not a fiction, that it really exists and that the study of it is the basic objective of scientific folklore. * * * What older scholarship felt instinctively and expressed naively, awkwardly, and not so much scientifically as emotionally must now be purged of romantic errors and elevated to the height of modern scholarship, with its consistent methods and exact techniques.

Brought up in the traditions of literature, we are often unable to conceive that a poetical work can have arisen not as a literary work arises when created by an individual. It always seems to us that someone must have been the first to compose it. Yet it is possible for poetical works to arise in completely different ways, and the study of those ways is one of the most fundamental and complex problems of folklore. I cannot go into this problem here and will only mention that in its origin folklore should be likened not to literature but to language, which is invented by no one and which has neither an author nor authors. It arises everywhere and changes in a regular way, independently of people's will, once there are appropriate conditions for it in the historical development of peoples. Universal similarity does not present a problem. It is rather its absence that we would have found inexplicable. Similarity indicates a regular process; the similarity of works of folklore is a particular case of the historical law by which identical forms of production in material culture give rise to identical or similar social institutions, to similar tools, and, in ideology, to the similarity of forms and categories of thought, religion, rituals, languages, and folklore. All of these live, influence one another, change, grow, and die.

With regard to the problem of conceiving *empirically* the origin of folklore, it will suffice to note that in its beginnings folklore can be an integral part of ritual. With the degeneration or decline of a ritual, folklore becomes detached from it and continues to live an independent life. * * *

The distinction discussed here is so important that it compels us to single out folklore as a special type of verbal art and the science of folklore as a special discipline. A literary historian interested in the origin of a work looks for its author. The folklorist, with the aid of broad comparative material, discovers the conditions that brought forth a plot. But the difference between folklore and literature is not confined to this distinction; they are differentiated not only by their origin but also by their forms of existence.

It has long been known that literature is transmitted through writing and folklore by word of mouth. Until now this distinction has been considered to be purely technical. However, it captures the innermost difference between the functioning of literature and folklore. A literary work, once it has arisen, no longer changes. It exists only when two agents are present: the author (the creator of the work) and the reader. The mediating link between them is a book, manuscript, or performance. A literary work is immutable, but the reader always changes. Aristotle was read by the ancient Greeks, the Arabs, and the Humanists, and we read him too, but all read and understand him differently. True readers always read creatively. A work of literature can bring them joy, inspire them, or fill them with indignation. They may wish to interfere in the heroes' fortunes, reward or punish them, change their tragic fate to a happy one, put a triumphant villain to death. But the readers, no matter how deeply they are aroused by a work of literature, are unable and are not allowed to introduce any changes to suit their own personal tastes or the views of their age.

Folklore also presupposes two agents, but different agents, namely, the performer and the listener, opposing each other directly, or rather without a mediating link.

As a rule, the performers' works are not created by them personally but were heard earlier, so performers can in no way be compared with poets reciting their own works. Nor are they reciters of the works of others, mere declaimers reproducing someone else's work. They are figures specific to folklore, and all of them, from the primitive chorus to the folktale narrator * * *, deserve our closest attention. Performers do not repeat their texts word for word but introduce changes into them. Even if these changes are insignificant (but they can be very great), even if the changes that take place in folklore texts are sometimes as slow as geological processes, what is important is the fact of *changeability of folklore compared with the stability of literature*.

If the reader of a work of literature is a powerless censor and critic devoid of authority, anyone listening to folklore is a potential future performer, who, in turn, consciously or unconsciously, will introduce changes into the work. These changes are not made accidentally but in accordance with certain laws. Everything that is out-of-date and incongruous with new attitudes, tastes, and ideology will be discarded. These new tastes will affect not only what will be discarded but also what will be reworked and supplemented. Not a small (though not the decisive) role is played by the narrator's personality, taste, views on life, talents, and creative abilities. A work of folklore exists in constant flux, and it cannot be studied in depth if it is recorded only once. It should be recorded as many times as possible. We call each recording a variant, and these variants are something completely different from a version of a work of literature made by one and the same person.

Folklore circulates, changing all the time, and this circulation and changeability are among its specific characteristics. Literary works can also be drawn into the orbit of this circulation. For example, Mark Twain's *Prince and the Pauper* is told as a folktale. * * * What do we have in this instance: folklore or literature? The answer is fairly simple. If, for example, a story from a chapbook, a saint's life, or the like, is recited from memory with no changes from the original, or if "The Black Shawl" or an excerpt from *The Peddlers* are sung exactly as Pushkin and Nekrásov wrote them, this case differs little from a performance on the stage or anywhere else. But as soon as such songs begin to change, to be sung differently, as soon as they begin to form variants, they become folklore, and the process of their change is the folklorist's domain. To be sure, there is a difference between folklore of the first sort, which often originated in prehistoric times and has variants all over the world, and poets' verses, freely used and transmitted by word of mouth. In the first case, we have pure folklore, that is, folklore both by origin and by transmission; in the second case, folklore of literary origin, that is, folklore by transmission but literature by origin. This distinction must always be kept in mind. A song that we consider pure folklore can turn out to be literary, can have an author. * * * Such examples are numerous, and ties between literature and folklore, as well as the literary sources of folklore are among the most interesting subjects both in the history of literature and in folklore.

This case again brings us to authorship in folklore. We have taken only two extreme cases. The first is folklore that was created by no one individual and arose in prehistoric times within the framework of some ritual or in some other way and that has survived through oral transmission to the present. The second case is obviously an individual's recent work circulating as folklore. In the development of both literature and folklore, between these two extremes occur all sorts of intermediate forms, each of which is a special problem. Modern folklorists are well aware that such problems cannot be solved descriptively, synchronically, but should be studied in their development. The genetic study of folklore is just one part of *historical* study, for folklore is not only a literary but also a historical phenomenon and the science of folklore not only a literary but also a historical discipline.

VLADIMIR PROPP

From Morphology of the Folktale[†]

The Method and Material

Let us first of all attempt to formulate our task. * * * This work is dedicated to the study of *fairy* tales. The existence of fairy tales as a special class is assumed as an essential working hypothesis. By "fairy tales" are meant at present those tales classified by Aarne under numbers 300 to 749. This definition is artificial, but the occasion will subsequently arise to give a more precise determination on the basis of resultant conclusions. We are undertaking a comparison of the themes of these tales. For the sake of comparison we shall separate the component parts of fairy tales by special methods; and then, we shall make a comparison of tales according to their components. The result will be a morphology (i.e., a description of the tale according to its component parts and the relationship of these components to each other and to the whole).

What methods can achieve an accurate description of the tale? Let us compare the following events:

1. A tsar gives an eagle to a hero. The eagle carries the hero away to another kingdom.
2. An old man gives Súčenko a horse. The horse carries Súčenko away to another kingdom.
3. A sorcerer gives Iván a little boat. The boat takes Iván to another kingdom.
4. A princess gives Iván a ring. Young men appearing from out of the ring carry Iván away, into another kingdom, and so forth.

Both constants and variables are present in the preceding instances. The names of the dramatis personae change (as well as the attributes of each), but neither their actions nor functions change. From this we can draw the inference that a tale often attributes identical

---

† From Vladimir Propp, "The Method and Material," in *Morphology of the Folktale,* trans. Laurence Scott (Austin: U of Texas P, 1968), pp. 19–24. Copyright © 1968 by the University of Texas. Reprinted by permission of University of Texas Press.

actions to various personages. This makes possible the study of the tale *according to the functions of its dramatis personae.*

We shall have to determine to what extent these functions actually represent recurrent constants of the tale. The formulation of all other questions will depend upon the solution of this primary question: how many functions are known to the tale?

Investigation will reveal that the recurrence of functions is astounding. Thus Bába Jagá, Morózko, the bear, the forest spirit, and the mare's head test and reward the stepdaughter. Going further, it is possible to establish that characters of a tale, however varied they may be, often perform the same actions. The actual means of the realization of functions can vary, and as such, it is a variable. Morózko behaves differently than Bába Jagá. But the function, as such, is a constant. The question of *what* a tale's dramatis personae do is an important one for the study of the tale, but the questions of *who* does it and *how* it is done already fall within the province of accessory study. The functions of characters are those components which could replace Veselóvskij's "motifs," or Bédier's "elements." We are aware of the fact that the repetition of functions by various characters was long ago observed in myths and beliefs by historians of religion, but it was not observed by historians of the tale. * * * Just as the characteristics and functions of deities are transferred from one to another, and, finally, are even carried over to Christian saints, the functions of certain tale personages are likewise transferred to other personages. Running ahead, one may say that the number of functions is extremely small, whereas the number of personages is extremely large. This explains the two-fold quality of a tale: its amazing multiformity, picturesqueness, and color, and on the other hand, its no less striking uniformity, its repetition.

Thus the functions of the dramatis personae are basic components of the tale, and we must first of all extract them. In order to extract the functions we must define them. Definition must proceed from two points of view. First of all, definition should in no case depend on the personage who carries out the function. Definition of a function will most often be given in the form of a noun expressing an action (interdiction, interrogation, flight, etc.). Secondly, an action cannot be defined apart from its place in the course of narration. The meaning which a given function has in the course of action must be considered. For example, if Iván marries a tsar's daughter, this is something entirely different than the marriage of a father to a widow with two daughters. A second example: if, in one instance, a hero receives money from his father in the form of 100 rubles and subsequently buys a wise cat with this money, whereas in a second case, the hero is rewarded with a sum of money for an accomplished act of bravery (at which point the tale ends), we have before us two morphologically different elements—in spite of the identical action (the transference of money) in both cases. Thus, identical acts can have different meanings, and vice versa. *Function is understood as an act of a character, defined from the point of view of its significance for the course of the action.*

The observations cited may be briefly formulated in the following manner:

1. *Functions of characters serve as stable, constant elements in a tale, independent of how and by whom they are fulfilled. They constitute the fundamental components of a tale.*
2. *The number of functions known to the fairy tale is limited.*

If functions are delineated, a second question arises: in what classification and in what sequence are these functions encountered?

A word, first, about sequence. The opinion exists that this sequence is accidental. Veselóvskij writes, "The selection and *order* of tasks and encounters (examples of motifs) already presupposes a certain *freedom.*" Šklóvskij stated this idea in even sharper terms: "It is quite impossible to understand why, in the act of adoption, the *accidental* sequence [Šklóvskij's italics] of motifs must be retained. In the testimony of witnesses, it is precisely the sequence of events which is distorted most of all." This reference to the evidence of witnesses is unconvincing. If witnesses distort the sequence of events, their narration is meaningless. The sequence of events has its own laws. The short story too has similar laws, as do organic formations. Theft cannot take place before the door is forced. Insofar as the tale is concerned, it has its own entirely particular and specific laws. The sequence of elements, as we shall see later on, is strictly *uniform.* Freedom within this sequence is restricted by very narrow limits which can be exactly formulated. We thus obtain the third basic thesis of this work, subject to further development and verification:

3. *The sequence of functions is always identical.*

As for groupings, it is necessary to say first of all that by no means do all tales give evidence of all functions. But this in no way changes the law of sequence. The absence of certain functions does not change the order of the rest. We shall dwell on this phenomenon later. For the present we shall deal with groupings in the proper sense of the word. The presentation of the question itself evokes the following assumption: if functions are singled out, then it will be possible to trace those tales which present identical functions. Tales with identical functions can be considered as belonging to one type. On this foundation, an index of types can then be created, based not upon theme features, which are somewhat vague and diffuse, but upon exact structural features. Indeed, this will be possible. If we further compare structural types among themselves, we are led to the following completely unexpected phenomenon: functions cannot be distributed around mutually exclusive axes. This phenomenon, in all its concreteness, will become apparent to us in the succeeding and final chapters of this book. For the time being, it can be interpreted in the following manner: if we designate with the letter A a function encountered everywhere in first position, and similarly designate with the letter B the function which (if it is at all present) *always follows* A, then all functions known to the tale will arrange themselves within a *single* tale, and none will fall out of order, nor will any one exclude or contradict any other. This is, of course, a completely unexpected result. Naturally, we would have expected that where there is a function A, there cannot be certain functions belonging to other tales. Supposedly we would obtain several axes, but only a single axis is obtained for all fairy tales. They are of the same type, while the combinations spoken of previously are subtypes. At first glance, this conclusion may appear absurd or perhaps even wild, yet it can be verified in a most exact manner. Such a typological unity represents a very complex problem on which it will be necessary to dwell further. This phenomenon will raise a whole series of questions.

In this manner, we arrive at the fourth basic thesis of our work:

4. *All fairy tales are of one type in regard to their structure.*

We shall now set about the task of proving, developing, and elaborating these theses in detail. Here it should be recalled that the study of the tale must be carried on strictly deductively, i.e., proceeding from the material at hand to the consequences (and in effect it is so carried on in this work). But the *presentation* may have a reversed order, since it is easier to follow the development if the general bases are known to the reader beforehand.

Before starting the elaboration, however, it is necessary to decide what material can serve as the subject of this study. First glance would seem to indicate that it is necessary to cover all extant material. In fact, this is not so. Since we are studying tales according to the functions of their dramatis personae, the accumulation of material can be suspended as soon as it becomes apparent that the new tales considered present no new functions. Of course, the investigator must look through an enormous amount of reference material. But there is no need to inject the entire body of this material into the study. We have found that 100 tales constitute more than enough material. Having discovered that no new functions can be found, the morphologist can put a stop to his work, and further study will follow different directions (the formation of indices, the complete systemization, historical study). But just because material can be limited in quantity, that does not mean that it can be selected at one's own discretion. It should be dictated from without. We shall use the collection by Afanás'ev, starting the study of tales with No. 50 (according to his plan, this is the first fairy tale of the collection), and finishing it with No. 151.[1] Such a limitation of material will undoubtedly call forth many objections, but it is theoretically justified. To justify it further, it would be necessary to take into account the degree of repetition of tale phenomena. If repetition is great, then one may take a limited amount of material. If repetition is small, this is impossible. The repetition of fundamental components * * * exceeds all expectations. Consequently, it is theoretically possible to limit oneself to a small body of material. Practically, this limitation justifies itself by the fact that the inclusion of a great quantity of material would have excessively increased the size of this work. We are not interested in the quantity of material, but in the quality of its analysis. Our working material consists of 100 tales. The rest is reference material, of great interest to the investigator, but lacking a broader interest.

* * *

Propp's Thirty-One Functions

1. One of the members of a family absents himself from home (*absentation*).
2. An interdiction is addressed to the hero (*interdiction*).
3. The interdiction is violated (*violation*).
4. The villain makes an attempt at reconnaissance (*reconnaissance*).
5. The villain receives information about his victim (*delivery*).
6. The villain attempts to deceive his victim in order to take possession of him or his belongings (*trickery*).
7. The victim submits to deception and thereby unwittingly helps his enemy (*complicity*).
8. The villain causes harm or injury to a member of the family (*villainy*).
8a. One member of a family either lacks something or desires to have something (*lack*).
9. Misfortune or lack is made known; the hero is approached with a request or command; he is allowed to go or he is dispatched (*mediation, the connective incident*).

---

1. Propp bases his analyses on one hundred tales from Alexander Afanasev's *Russian Fairy Tales*, trans. Norbert Guterman (New York: Pantheon, 1945) [editor's note].

10. The seeker agrees to or decides upon counteraction (*beginning counteraction*).
11. The hero leaves home (*departure*).
12. The hero is tested, interrogated, attacked, etc., which prepares the way for his receiving either a magical agent or helper (*the first function of the donor*).
13. The hero reacts to the actions of the future donor (*the hero's reaction*).
14. The hero acquires the use of a magical agent (*provision or receipt of a magical agent*).
15. The hero is transferred, delivered, or led to the whereabouts of an object of search (*spatial transference between two kingdoms, guidance*).
16. The hero and the villain join in direct combat (*struggle*).
17. The hero is branded (*branding, marking*).
18. The villain is defeated (*victory*).
19. The initial misfortune or lack is liquidated (*liquidation*).
20. The hero returns (*return*).
21. The hero is pursued (*pursuit, chase*).
22. Rescue of the hero from pursuit (*rescue*).
23. The hero, unrecognized, arrives home or in another country (*unrecognized arrival*).
24. A false hero presents unfounded claims (*unfounded claims*).
25. A difficult task is proposed to the hero (*difficult task*).
26. The task is resolved (*solution*).
27. The hero is recognized (*recognition*).
28. The false hero or villain is exposed (*exposure*).
29. The hero is given a new appearance (*transfiguration*).
30. The villain is punished (*punishment*).
31. The hero is married and ascends the throne (*wedding*).

* * *

Propp's Dramatis Personae

1. Villain
2. Donor or provider
3. Helper
4. Princess (a sought-for person) and her father
5. Dispatcher
6. Hero
7. False Hero

MARIA TATAR

Valediction[†]

Take your hard-won diamonds
And spend them wisely
On match girls and poets,
Or scatter them in the woods
To show Thumbling a way back home.

In the night, light a candle,
The shadows will rise and stretch
And shrink back at noon to mock you
While you work the puzzle of your mind
Gazing at the skulls on Baba Yaga's fences.

All places are now your study
And the pages you turn beat time to your heart
Once you find terror and hope
Living on the same side of the street
In the neighborhood you call home.

Are you reassembled? Is the splinter out?
Which of Bluebeard's wives put you back together
And let you walk the trickster tightrope
Between appetite and hunger,
Desire and dread, gold and pitch?

"Many are the deceivers":
The briar bowers protecting beauty,
Husbands tempting you with forbidden keys,
Kings protecting daughters in locked towers,
And ogres promising you a good night's sleep.

And in rush numbskulls, fools, and ragged simpletons,
Small and meek, the runts of the family,
Ready to steal your gold, outwit your wife,
And rob you of hens and harps,
All the while claiming that they traded the cow for beans.

Now that you are acquainted with the night,
The sun, that busy old fool, has never once
Seen anything as beautiful as your knowing eyes.
Share your crusts. Magnify your apples.
Cherish the frogs and stoats, for all are enchanted.

Swarms of mice may haunt your dreams
But make them tea, give them biscuits,
Settle down in a warm corner of the house
And let the world grow calm
As you lean into stories and dream.

† Written for this Norton Critical Edition.

Selected Bibliography

ANTHOLOGIES

Abrahams, Roger D., comp. *African Folktales*. New York: Pantheon, 1983.

Afanasev, Alexander, comp. *Russian Fairy Tales*. Trans. Norbert Guterman. New York: Pantheon, 1945.

Andersen, Hans Christian. *Eighty Fairy Tales*. Trans. R. P. Keigwin. New York: Pantheon, 1976.

Arabian Nights. Trans. Richard F. Burton. Ed. David Shumaker. New York: Avenel Books, 1978.

Asbjørnsen, Peter Christian, and Jørgen Møe, comps. *Norwegian Folktales*. Trans. Pat Shaw Iversen. New York: Pantheon, 1960.

——. *Popular Tales from the Norse*. Trans. Sir George Webbe Dasent. New York: Appleton, 1859.

Auerbach, Nina, and U. C. Knoepflmacher, comps. *Forbidden Journeys: Fairy Tales and Fantasies by Victorian Women Writers*. Chicago: U of Chicago P, 1992.

Basile, Giambattista. *Giambattista Basile's The Tale of Tales, or Entertainment for Little Ones*. Trans. Nancy Canepa. Detroit: Wayne State UP, 2007.

——. *The Pentamerone of Giambattista Basile*. Trans. Benedetto Croce. Ed. N. M. Penzer. 2 vols. London: Bodley Head, 1932.

Bernheimer, Kate, ed. *Brothers and Beasts: An Anthology of Men on Fairy Tales*. Detroit: Wayne State UP, 2007.

——. *Mirror, Mirror on the Wall: Women Writers Explore Their Favorite Fairy Tales*. 2nd ed. New York: Anchor, 2002.

Bierhorst, John, ed. *Latin American Folktales: Stories from Hispanic and Indian Traditions*. New York: Pantheon, 2002.

Blecher, Lone Thygensen, and George Blecher. *Swedish Tales and Legends*. New York: Pantheon, 1993.

Briggs, Katharine M. *A Dictionary of British Folk-Tales in the English Language*. 4 vols. London: Routledge & Kegan Paul, 1970–71.

——, and Ruth L. Tongue. *Folktales of England*. Chicago: U of Chicago P, 1965.

Bushnaq, Inea, comp. *Arab Folktales*. New York: Pantheon, 1986.

Calvino, Italo, comp. *Italian Folktales*. Trans. George Martin. New York: Pantheon, 1980.

Carter, Angela. *The Bloody Chamber and Other Stories*. Harmondsworth: Penguin, 1979.

——, ed. *The Second Virago Book of Fairy Tales*. London: Virago, 1992.

——, ed. *The Virago Book of Fairy Tales*. London: Virago, 1990.

Chase, Richard, comp. *American Folk Tales and Songs*. New York: Signet, 1956.

——. *The Jack Tales*. Boston: Houghton Mifflin, 1943.

Clarkson, Atelia, and Gilbert B. Cross, comps. *World Folktales: A Scribner Resource Collection*. New York: Scribner's, 1980.

Cole, Joanna, ed. *Best-Loved Folktales of the World*. New York: Anchor, 1983.

Crossley-Holland, Kevin, comp. *Folktales of the British Isles*. New York: Pantheon, 1988.

509

Dahl, Roald. *Revolting Rhymes*. London: Jonathan Cape, 1982.

Dasent, George Webbe, comp. *East o' the Sun and West o' the Moon*. Toronto: Dover, 1970.

Datlow, Ellen, and Terri Windling, eds. *Black Thorn, White Rose*. New York: Avon, 1994.

———. *Snow White, Blood Red*. New York: William Morrow, 1993.

Dawkins, R. M., comp. *Modern Greek Folktales*. Oxford: Clarendon, 1953.

Delarue, Paul, comp. *Borzoi Book of French Folk Tales*. New York: Knopf, 1956.

Dorson, Richard M., comp. *American Negro Folktales*. New York: Fawcett, 1968.

———. *Buying the Wind: Regional Folklore of the United States*. Chicago: U of Chicago P, 1964.

———. *Folktales Told around the World*. Chicago: U of Chicago P, 1975.

Eberhard, Wolfram, comp. *Folktales of China*. Chicago: U of Chicago P, 1965.

Erdoes, Richard, and Alfonso Ortiz, comps. *American Myths and Legends*. New York: Pantheon, 1984.

Feldmann, Susan, comp. *The Storytelling Stone: Myths and Tales of the American Indians*. New York: Dell, 1965.

Grimm, Jacob, and Wilhelm Grimm. *The Complete Fairy Tales of the Brothers Grimm*. Trans. Jack Zipes. Toronto: Bantam, 1987.

Hallett, Martin, and Barbara Karasek, comps. *Folk and Fairy Tales*. 4th ed. Peterborough, ON: Broadview, 2008.

Hearn, Michael Patrick, comp. *Victorian Fairy Tale Book*. New York: Pantheon, 1988.

Jacobs, Joseph, comp. *Celtic Fairy Tales*. London: Nutt, 1892.

———. *English Fairy Tales* (1890). London: Bodley Head, 1968.

Jones, Christine A. and Jennifer Schacker, eds. *Marvelous Transformations: An Anthology of Fairy Tales and Contemporary Critical Perspectives*. Peterborough, ON: Broadview, 2012.

Lang, Andrew, comp. *The Blue Fairy Book* (1889). New York: Dover, 1974.

———. *The Green Fairy Book* (1892). New York: Dover, 1974.

———. *The Pink Fairy Book* (1897). New York: Dover, 1974.

———. *The Red Fairy Book* (1890). New York: Dover, 1974.

———. *Yellow Fairy Book* (1894). New York: Dover, 1974.

Lurie, Alison, comp. *Clever Gretchen and Other Forgotten Folktales*. New York: Crowell, 1980.

———. *The Oxford Book of Modern Fairy Tales*. Oxford: Oxford UP, 1993.

Massignon, Geneviève, comp. *Folktales of France*. Trans. Jacqueline Hyland. Chicago: U of Chicago P, 1968.

Mieder, Wolfgang, comp. *Disenchantments: An Anthology of Modern Fairy Tale Poetry*. Hanover, NH: UP of New England, 1985.

Minard, Rosemary. *Womenfolk and Fairy Tales*. Boston: Houghton Mifflin, 1975.

Montgomerie, Norah, and William Montgomerie, comps. *The Well at the World's End: Folk Tales of Scotland*. Toronto: Bodley Head, 1956.

Noy, Dov, comp. *Folktales of Israel*. Trans. Gene Baharav. Chicago: U of Chicago P, 1963.

Opie, Peter, and Iona Opie, comps. *The Classic Fairy Tales*. London: Oxford UP, 1974.

Perrault, Charles. *Perrault's Complete Fairy Tales*. Trans. A. E. Johnson et al. New York: Dodd, Mead, 1961.

Phelps, Ethel Johnston, comp. *The Maid of the North: Feminist Folk Tales from around the World*. New York: Holt, Rinehart & Winston, 1981.

———. *Tatterhood and Other Tales*. Old Westbury, NY: Feminist Press, 1978.

Philip, Neil, comp. *The Cinderella Story: The Origins and Variations of the Story Known as "Cinderella."* London: Penguin, 1989.

Pourrat, Henri, comp. *French Folktales*. Trans. Royall Tyler. New York: Pantheon, 1989.

Ramanujan, A. K., comp. *Folktales from India*. New York: Random House, 1991.
Randolph, Vance, comp. *Pissing in the Snow and Other Ozark Folktales*. Urbana: U of Illinois P, 1976.
————. *Sticks in the Knapsack and Other Ozark Folk Tales*. New York: Columbia UP, 1958.
Ranke, Kurt, comp. *Folktales of Germany*. Trans. Lotte Baumann. Chicago: U of Chicago P, 1966.
Rugoff, Milton A., comp. *A Harvest of World Folk Tales*. New York: Viking, 1949.
Schönwerth, Franz Xaver von. *The Turnip Princess and Other Newly Discovered Fairy Tales*. New York: Penguin, 2015.
Simpson, Jacqueline, comp. *Icelandic Folktales and Legends*. Berkeley: U of California P, 1972.
Straparola, Giovanni Francesco. *The Facetious Nights of Straparola*. Trans. W. G. Waters. 4 vols. London: Society of Bibliophiles, 1901.
Tatar, Maria, comp. *The Annotated Brothers Grimm*. New York: Norton, 2012.
————. *The Annotated Classic Fairy Tales*. New York: Norton, 2002.
————. *The Annotated Hans Christian Andersen*. New York: Norton, 2007.
Thompson, Stith, comp. *One Hundred Favorite Folktales*. Bloomington: Indiana UP, 1968.
————. *Tales of the North American Indians*. Bloomington: Indiana UP, 1929.
Travers, P. L., comp. *About the Sleeping Beauty*. New York: McGraw-Hill, 1975.
Walker, Barbara G. *Feminist Fairy Tales*. New York: HarperCollins, 1996.
Weinrich, Beatrice Silverman, comp. *Yiddish Folktales*. New York: Pantheon, 1988.
Williams, Jay. *The Practical Princess and Other Liberating Fairy Tales*. New York: Parents Magazine Press / London: Chatto and Windus, 1979.
Yolen, Jane. *Favorite Folktales from Around the World*. New York: Pantheon, 1986.
Zipes, Jack, comp. *Beauties, Beasts and Enchantment: Classic Fairy Tales*. New York: New American Library, 1989.
————. *Don't Bet on the Prince: Contemporary Fairy Tales in North America and England*. New York: Methuen, 1986.
————. *The Golden Age of Folk and Fairy Tales: From the Brothers Grimm to Andrew Lang*. Indianapolis/Cambridge: Hackett, 2013.
————. *The Great Fairy Tale Tradition: From Straparola and Basile to the Brothers Grimm: A Norton Critical Edition*. New York: Norton, 2000.
————. *The Outspoken Princess and the Gentle Knight: A Treasury of Modern Fairy Tales*. New York: Bantam, 1994.
————. *Spells of Enchantment: The Wondrous Fairy Tales of Western Culture*. New York: Viking, 1991.
————. *Victorian Fairy Tales. The Revolt of the Fairies and Elves*. New York: Routledge, 1987.

CRITICAL STUDIES

• indicates works included or excerpted in this Norton Critical Edition.

Aarne, Antti, and Stith Thompson. *The Types of the Folktale. A Classification and Bibliography*. Helsinki: Academia Scientiarum Fennica, 1961.
Anderson, Graham. *Fairytale in the Ancient World*. New York: Routledge, 2000.
Ashliman, D.L. *Folk and Fairy Tales: A Handbook*. Westport CT: Greenwood, 2004.
• Bacchilega, Cristina. *Fairy Tales Transformed? Twenty-First-Century Adaptations and the Politics of Wonder*. Detroit: Wayne State UP, 2013.
————. *Postmodern Fairy Tales: Gender and Narrative Strategies*. Philadelphia: U of Pennsylvania P, 1999.

Barchilon, Jacques. "Beauty and the Beast: From Myth to Fairy Tale." *Psycho-analysis and the Psychoanalytic Review* 46 (1959): 19–29.

Barchilon, Jacques, and Peter Flinders. *Charles Perrault.* Boston: Twayne, 1981.

Barzilai, Shuli. "Reading 'Snow White': The Mother's Story." *Signs* 15 (1990): 515–34.

Bascom, William. "The Four Functions of Folklore." *Journal of American Folklore* 67 (1954): 333–49.

Bauman, Richard. *Story, Performance and Event.* Cambridge: Cambridge UP, 1992.

Beckett, Sandra. *Recycling Red Riding Hood.* New York: Routledge, 2002.

———. *Red Riding Hood for All Ages: A Fairy Tale Icon in Cross-Cultural Contexts.* Detroit: Wayne State UP, 2009.

———. *Revisioning Red Riding Hood around the World.* Detroit: Wayne State UP, 2013.

Behlmer, Rudy. "They Called It 'Disney's Folly': *Snow White and the Seven Dwarfs* (1937)." *America's Favorite Movies: Behind the Scenes.* New York: Ungar, 1982.

Bell, Elizabeth, Lynda Haas, and Laura Sells, eds. *From Mouse to Mermaid: The Politics of Film, Gender, and Culture.* Bloomington: Indiana UP, 1995.

Bettelheim, Bruno. *The Uses of Enchantment: The Meaning and Importance of Fairy Tales.* New York: Knopf, 1976.

Birkhäuser-Oeri, Sibylle. *The Mother: Archetypal Image in Fairy Tales.* Trans. Michael Mitchell. Toronto: Inner City, 1988.

Blackwell, Jeannine. "The Many Names of Rumpelstiltskin: Recent Research on the Grimms' *Kinder- und Hausmärchen.*" *German Quarterly* 63 (1990): 107–12.

de Blécourt, Willem. "Fairy Grandmothers: Images of Storytelling Events in Nineteenth-Century Germany." *Relief* 4.2 (2010), 174–97.

———. *Tales of Magic, Tales in Print: On the Genealogy of Fairy Tales and the Brothers Grimm.* Manchester: Manchester UP, 2012.

• Bloch, Ernst. "Better Castles in the Sky at the Country Fair and Circus, in Fairy Tales and Colportage." In *The Utopian Function of Art and Literature.* Trans. Jack Zipes and Frank Mecklenburg. Cambridge, MA: MIT Press, 1988.

• ———. "The Fairy Tale Moves on Its Own in Time." In *The Utopian Function of Art and Literature.* Trans. Jack Zipes and Frank Mecklenburg. Cambridge, MA: MIT Press, 1988.

Bottigheimer, Ruth B. *Fairy Godfather: Straparola, Venice, and the Fairy Tale Tradition.* Philadelphia: U of Pennsylvania P, 2002.

———. "Fairy Tales and Children's Literature: A Feminist Perspective." In *Teaching Children's Literature: Issues, Pedagogy, Resources.* Ed. Glen Edward Sadler. New York: Modern Language Association of America, 1992.

———. *Fairy Tales and Society: Illusion, Allusion, and Paradigm.* Philadelphia: U of Pennsylvania P, 1986.

———. *Fairy Tales: A New History.* Albany, NY: Excelsior, 2010.

———. *Grimms' Bad Girls and Bold Boys.* New Haven, CT: Yale UP, 1987.

Briggs, Katharine. *An Encyclopedia of Fairies: Hobgoblins, Brownies, Bogies, and Other Supernatural Creatures.* New York: Pantheon, 1976.

Bronfen, Elisabeth. *Over Her Dead Body: Death, Femininity and the Aesthetic.* New York: Routledge, 1992.

Bryant, Sylvia. "Re-Constructing Oedipus through 'Beauty and the Beast.'" *Criticism* 31 (1989): 439–53.

Canepa, Nancy. *From Court to Forest: Giambattista Basile's Lo cunto de li cunti and the Birth of the Literary Fairy Tale.* Detroit: Wayne State UP, 1999.

———. *Out of the Woods: The Origins of the Literary Fairy Tale in Italy and France.* Detroit: Wayne State UP, 1997.

Canham, Stephen. "What Manner of Beast? Illustrations of 'Beauty and the Beast.'" In *Image and Maker: An Annual Dedicated to the Consideration of Book Illustration.* Ed. Harold Darling and Peter Neumeyer. La Jolla, CA: Green Tiger, 1984.

Caracciolo, Peter L., ed. *The Arabian Nights in English Literature: Studies in the Reception of the Thousand and One Nights into British Culture*. New York: St. Martin's, 1988.

Carter, Angela, ed. "About the Stories." In *Sleeping Beauty and Other Favourite Fairy Tales*. Boston: Otter, 1991.

Cashdan, Sheldon. *The Witch Must Die: How Fairy Tales Shape Our Lives*. New York: HarperCollins, 2000.

Cech, Jon. "Hans Christian Andersen's Fairy Tales and Stories: Secrets, Swans and Shadows." In *Touchstones: Reflections on the Best in Children's Literature*. Vol. 2. West Lafayette, IN: Children's Literature Association, 1983.

Chase, Richard. *The Jack Tales*. Boston: Houghton Mifflin, 1943.

Clodd, Edward. *Tom Tit Tot: An Essay on Savage Philosophy in Folk-Tale*. London: Duckworth, 1898.

Conrad, JoAnn. "Docile Bodies of (Im)material Girls: The Fairy-Tale Construction of JonBenét Ramsey and Princess Diana." *Marvels & Tales* 13 (1999): 125–69.

Cox, Marian Roalfe. *Cinderella: Three Hundred and Forty-Five Variants of Cinderella, Catskin, and Cap o' Rushes*. Intro. Andrew Lang. London: Nutt, 1893.

Crago, Hugh. "Who Does Snow White Look At?" *Signal* 45 (1984): 129–45.

• Darnton, Robert. "Peasants Tell Tales: The Meaning of Mother Goose." In *The Great Cat Massacre and Other Episodes in French Cultural History*. New York: Basic, 1984.

Davidson, Hilda Ellis, and Anna Chaudhri. *A Companion to the Fairy Tale*. Cambridge: Brewer, 2003.

Davies, Mererid Puw. *The Tale of Bluebeard in German Literature from the Eighteenth-Century to the Present*. Oxford: Oxford UP, 2001.

Dégh, Linda. *American Folklore and the Mass Media*. Bloomington: Indiana UP, 1994.

———. *Folktales and Society: Storytelling in a Hungarian Peasant Community*. Trans. Emily M. Schossberger. Bloomington: Indiana UP, 1969.

deGraff, Amy. "From Glass Slipper to Glass Ceiling: 'Cinderella' and the Endurance of a Fairy Tale." *Merveilles et Contes* 10 (1996): 69–85.

Delarue, Paul. "Les Contes merveilleux de Perrault et la tradition populaire." *Bulletin folklorique de l'Ile-de-France* (1951): 221–28, 251–60, 283–91; (1953): 511–17.

De Vos, Gail, and Anna E. Altmann. *New Tales for Old: Folktales as Literary Fictions for Young Adults*. Englewood, CO: Teacher Ideas, 1999.

Dobay Rifelj, Carol de. "Cendrillon and the Ogre: Women in Fairy Tales and Sade." *Romanic Review* 81 (1990): 11–24.

Dorson, Richard. *Folklore*. Bloomington: Indiana UP, 1972.

Dowling, Colette. *The Cinderella Complex: Women's Hidden Fear of Independence*. New York: Summit, 1981.

Duggan, Anne E. *Queer Enchantments: Gender, Sexuality, and Class in the Fairy-Tale Cinema of Jacques Demy*. Detroit: Wayne State UP, 2013.

———. *Salonnières, Fairies, and Furies: The Politics of Gender and Cultural Change in Absolutist France*. Newark, DE: Delaware UP, 2005.

Dundes, Alan. "Bruno Bettelheim's Uses of Enchantment and Abuses of Scholarship." *Journal of American Folklore* 104 (1991): 74–83.

———. *Cinderella: A Casebook*. New York: Garland, 1982; Madison: U of Wisconsin P, 1988.

———. *Little Red Riding Hood: A Casebook*. Madison: U of Wisconsin P, 1989.

———. *The Study of Folklore*. Englewood Cliffs, NJ: Prentice Hall, 1965.

Edelson, Maria. "The Language of Allegory in Oscar Wilde's Tales." In *Anglo-Irish and Irish Literature*. Ed. Birgit Bramsbäck and Martin Croghan. Stockholm: Almqvist and Wiksell and Bromsbäck, 1988.

Edwards, Carol L. "The Fairy Tale 'Snow White.'" In *Making Connections across the Curriculum: Readings for Analysis*. Ed. Kate S. Chittenden. New York: St. Martin's, 1986.

Edwards, Lee R. "The Labors of Psyche: Toward a Theory of Female Heroism." *Critical Inquiry* 6 (1979): 33–49.

Ellis, John. *One Fairy Story Too Many: The Brothers Grimm and Their Tales*. Chicago: U of Chicago P, 1982.

Estes, Clarissa Pinkola. *Women Who Run with the Wolves: Myths and Stories of the Wild Woman Archetype*. New York: Ballantine, 1992.

Farrer, Claire R., ed. *Women and Folklore: Images and Genres*. Austin: U of Texas P, 1975.

Franz, Marie-Luise von. *Archetypal Patterns in Fairy Tales*. Toronto: Inner City, 1997.

——. *Problems of the Feminine in Fairy Tales*. New York: Spring, 1972.

• Gilbert, Sandra M., and Susan Gubar. *The Madwoman in the Attic: The Woman Writer and the Nineteenth-Century Literary Imagination*. New Haven, CT: Yale UP, 1979.

Girardot, N. J. "Initiation and Meaning in the Tale of Snow White and the Seven Dwarfs." *Journal of American Folklore* 90 (1977): 274–300.

Greenhill, Pauline, and Jill Terry Rudy. *Channeling Wonder: Fairy Tales on Television*. Detroit: Wayne State UP, 2014.

Greenhill, Pauline, and Sidney Eve Matrix, eds. *Fairy Tale Films: Visions of Ambiguity*. Logan: Utah State UP, 2010.

Griswold, Jerry. *The Meanings of "Beauty and the Beast": A Handbook*. Peterborough, ON: Broadview, 2004.

Grønbech, Bo. *Hans Christian Andersen*. Boston: Twayne, 1980.

Haase, Donald, ed. *Fairy Tales and Feminism*. Detroit: Wayne State UP, 2009.

——, ed. *The Greenwood Encyclopedia of Folktales and Fairy Tales*. 3 vols. Westport, CT: Greenwood, 2008.

——. "Hypertextual Gutenberg: The Textual and Hypertextual Life of Folktales and Fairy Tales in English-Language Popular Print Editions," *Fabula* 47 (2006): 222–30.

——, ed. *The Reception of Grimms' Fairy Tales: Responses, Reactions, Revisions*. Detroit: Wayne State UP, 1993.

• ——. "Yours, Mine, or Ours? Perrault, the Brothers Grimm and the Ownership of Fairy Tales." In *Once Upon a Folktale: Capturing the Folklore Process with Children*. Ed. Gloria T. Blatt. New York: Teachers College, Columbia U, 1993.

Hallet, Martin, and Barbara Karasek. *Fairy Tales in Popular Culture*. Peterborough, ON: Broadview, 2014.

Hanks, Carole, and D. T. Hanks, Jr. "Perrault's 'Little Red Riding Hood': Victim of the Revisers." *Children's Literature* 7 (1978): 68–77.

Harries, Elizabeth Wanning. *Twice upon a Time: Women Writers and the History of the Fairy Tale*. Princeton, NJ: Princeton UP, 2001.

Hartland, E. Sidney. "The Forbidden Chamber." *Folk-Lore Journal* 3 (1885): 193–242.

Hearne, Betsy. *Beauty and the Beast: Visions and Revisions of an Old Tale*. Chicago: U of Chicago P, 1989.

Hennard Dutheil de la Rochère, Martine. *Reading, Translating, Rewriting: Angela Carter's Translational Poetics*. Detroit: Wayne State UP, 2013.

Holbek, Bengt. *The Interpretation of Fairy Tales: Danish Folklore in a European Perspective*. Helsinki: Academia Scientiarum Fennica, 1987.

Holliss, Richard, and Brian Sibley. *Walt Disney's "Snow White and the Seven Dwarfs" and the Making of the Classic Film*. New York: Simon & Schuster, 1987.

• Hyde, Lewis. *Trickster Makes This World: Mischief, Myth, and Art*. New York: Farrar, Straus & Giroux, 1997.

Johns, Andreas. *Baba Yaga: The Ambiguous Mother and Witch of the Russian Folktale*. New York: Lang, 2004.

Johnson, Faye R., and Carole M. Carroll. "'Little Red Riding Hood': Then and Now." *Studies in Popular Culture* 14 (1992): 71–84.

Jones, Steven Swann. *The Fairy Tale: The Magic Mirror of Imagination*. New York: Twayne, 1995.

————. *The New Comparative Method: Structural and Symbolic Analysis of the Allomotifs of "Snow White."* Helsinki: Academia Scientiarum Fennica, 1990.

————. "On Analyzing Fairy Tales: 'Little Red Riding Hood' Revisited." *Western Folklore* 46 (1987): 97–106.

Joosen, Vanessa, and Gillian Lathey, eds. *Critical and Creative Perspectives on Fairy Tales: An Intertextual Dialogue between Fairy-Tale Scholarship and Postmodern Retellings.* Detroit: Wayne State UP, 2011.

————. *Grimms' Tales around the Globe: The Dynamics of Their International Reception.* Detroit: Wayne State UP, 2014.

Jurich, Marilyn. *Scheherazade's Sisters: Trickster Heroines and Their Stories in World Literature.* Westport CT: Greenwood, 1998.

Kamenetsky, Christa. *The Brothers Grimm and Their Critics: Folktales and the Quest for Meaning.* Athens: Ohio UP, 1992.

Kolbenschlag, Madonna. *Kiss Sleeping Beauty Good-bye: Breaking the Spell of Feminine Myths and Models.* New York: Doubleday, 1979.

Laruccia, Victor. "Little Red Riding Hood's Metacommentary: Paradoxical Injunction, Semiotics and Behavior." *Modern Language Notes* 90 (1975): 517–34.

Lewis, Philip. *Seeing through the Mother Goose Tales: Visual Turns in the Writings of Perrault.* Stanford, CA: Stanford UP, 1996.

Lieberman, Marcia. "'Some Day My Prince Will Come': Female Acculturation through the Fairy Tale." *College English* 34 (1972): 383–95.

Lurie, Alison. *Don't Tell the Grown-ups: Subversive Children's Literature.* Boston: Little, Brown, 1990.

• Lüthi, Max. *The European Folktale: Form and Nature.* Trans. John D. Niles. Philadelphia: Institute for the Study of Human Issues, 1982.

————. *The Fairy Tale as Art Form and Portrait of Man.* Trans. Jan Erickson. Bloomington: Indiana UP, 1984.

————. *Once Upon a Time: On the Nature of Fairy Tales.* Bloomington: Indiana UP, 1970.

Mallet, Carl-Heinz. *Fairy Tales and Children: The Psychology of Children Revealed through Four of Grimms' Fairy Tales.* New York: Schocken, 1980.

Maranda, P., ed. *Soviet Structural Folkloristics.* The Hague: Mouton, 1974.

Marin, Louis. *Food for Thought.* Trans. Mette Hjort. Baltimore, MD: Johns Hopkins UP, 1989.

Martin, Ann. *Red Riding Hood and the Wolf in Bed: Modernism's Fairy Tales.* Toronto: U of Toronto P, 2006.

Marzolph, Ulrich, ed. *The Arabian Nights Reader.* Detroit: Wayne State UP, 2006.

McGlathery, James, ed. *The Brothers Grimm and Folktale.* Urbana: U of Illinois P, 1988.

McMaster, Juliet. "Bluebeard: A Tale of Matrimony." *A Room of One's Own* 2 (1976): 10–19.

Mieder, Wolfgang. "Survival Forms of 'Little Red Riding Hood' in Modern Society." *International Folklore Review* 2 (1982): 23–41.

Monaghan, David M. "The Literary Fairy-Tale: A Study of Oscar Wilde's 'The Happy Prince' and 'The Star-Child.'" *Canadian Review of Comparative Literature* 1 (1974): 156–66.

Murphy, G. Ronald, S.J. *The Owl, The Raven, and the Dove.* New York: Oxford UP, 2000.

Orenstein, Catherine. *Little Red Riding Hood Uncloaked: Sex, Morality, and the Evolution of a Fairy Tale.* New York: Basic, 2002.

Panttaja, Elisabeth. "Going Up in the World: Class in 'Cinderella.'" *Western Folklore* 52 (1993): 85–104.

Preston, Cathy Lynn. "'Cinderella' as a Dirty Joke: Gender, Multivocality, and the Polysemic Text." *Western Folklore* 53 (1994): 27–49.

• Propp, Vladimir. *Morphology of the Folktale.* Trans. Laurence Scott. Austin: U of Texas P, 1975.

• ———. *Theory and History of Folklore.* Trans. Ariadna Y. Martin and Richard P. Martin. Ed. Anatoly Liberman. U of Minnesota P, 1984.

Quintus, John Allen. "The Moral Prerogative in Oscar Wilde: A Look at the Fairy Tales." *Virginia Quarterly Review* 53 (1977): 708–17.

Röhrich, Lutz. *Folktales and Reality.* Trans. Peter Tokofsky. Bloomington: Indiana UP, 1991.

Rölleke, Heinz. *Die Märchen der Brüder Grimm: Eine Einführung.* Munich: Artemis, 1985.

———. "New Results of Research on *Grimms' Fairy Tales.*" In *The Brothers Grimm and Folktale.* Ed. James M. McGlathery. Urbana: U of Illinois P, 1991.

Rooth, Anna Birgitta. *The Cinderella Cycle.* Lund, Sweden: Gleerup, 1951.

Rose, Ellen Cronan. "Through the Looking Glass: When Women Tell Fairy Tales." In *The Voyage In: Fictions of Female Development.* Ed. Elizabeth Abel, Marianne Hirsch, and Elizabeth Langland. Hanover, NH: UP of New England, 1983.

Rowe, Karen E. "Feminism and Fairy Tales." *Women's Studies: An Interdisciplinary Journal* 6 (1979): 237–57.

• ———. "To Spin a Yarn: The Female Voice in Folklore and Fairy Tale." In *Fairy Tale and Society: Illusion, Allusion, and Paradigm.* Ed. Ruth B. Bottigheimer. Philadelphia: U of Pennsylvania P, 1986.

Sale, Roger. *Fairy Tales and After: From Snow White to E. B. White.* Cambridge: Harvard UP, 1978.

Schectman, Jacqueline. *The Stepmother in Fairy Tales: Bereavement and the Feminine Shadow.* Boston: Sigo, 1991.

Scherf, Walter. "Family Conflicts and Emancipation in Fairy Tales." *Children's Literature,* 3 (1974): 77–93.

Schickel, Richard. *The Disney Version: The Life, Times, Art and Commerce of Walt Disney.* New York: Simon & Schuster, 1968.

Schmiesing, Ann. *Disability, Deformity, and Disease in the Grimms' Fairy Tales.* Detroit: Wayne State UP, 2014.

Schwartz, Emanuel K. "A Psychoanalytic Study of the Fairy Tale." *American Journal of Psychotherapy* 10 (1956): 740–62.

Seifert, Lewis Carl. *Fairy Tales, Sexuality, and Gender in France, 1690–1715: Nostalgic Utopias.* New York: Cambridge UP, 1996.

Sendak, Maurice. "Hans Christian Andersen." In *Caldecott & Co.: Notes on Books and Pictures.* New York: Farrar, Straus & Giroux, Michael di Capua, 1988.

Shavit, Zohar. "The Concept of Childhood and Children's Folktales: Test Case—'Little Red Riding Hood.'" *Jerusalem Studies in Jewish Folklore* 4 (1983): 93–124.

Sheets, Robin Ann. "Pornography, Fairy Tales, and Feminism: Angela Carter's 'The Bloody Chamber.'" *Journal of the History of Sexuality* 1 (1991): 633–57.

Snider, Clifton. "Eros and Logos in Some Fairy Tales by Oscar Wilde: A Jungian Interpretation." *Victorian Newsletter* 84 (1993): 1–8.

Soriano, Marc. "Le petit chaperon rouge." *Nouvelle Revue Française* 16 (1968): 429–43.

Stone, Kay F. *Burning Brightly: New Light on Old Tales Today.* Peterborough, ON: Broadview, 1998.

———. "The Misuses of Enchantment: Controversies on the Significance of Fairy Tales." In *Women's Folklore, Women's Culture.* Ed. Rosan A. Jordan and Susan J. Kalcik. Philadelphia: U of Pennsylvania P, 1985.

———. "Things Walt Disney Never Told Us." *Journal of American Folklore* 88 (1975): 42–49.

Sullivan, Paula. "Fairy Tale Elements in *Jane Eyre.*" *Journal of Popular Culture* 12 (1978): 61–74.

Swahn, Jan-Öjvind. *The Tale of Cupid and Psyche (Aarne-Thompson 425 and 428).* Lund, Sweden: Gleerup, 1955.

• Tatar, Maria, ed. *The Cambridge Companion to Fairy Tales*. Cambridge: Cambridge UP, 2015.

• ———. *The Hard Facts of the Grimms' Fairy Tales*. Princeton, NJ: Princeton UP, 1987.

———. *Off with Their Heads! Fairy Tales and the Culture of Childhood*. Princeton, NJ: Princeton UP, 1992.

———. *Secrets beyond the Door: The Story of Bluebeard and His Wives*. Princeton, NJ: Princeton UP, 2006.

Teverson, Andrew. *Fairy Tale*. London: Routledge, 2013.

Thomas, Joyce. *Inside the Wolf's Belly: Aspects of the Fairy Tale*. Sheffield, UK: Sheffield Academic, 1989.

Thompson, Stith. *The Folktale*. New York: Holt, Rinehart and Winston, 1946.

———. *Motif-Index of Folk-Literature*. 6 vols., rev. and enlarged ed. Bloomington: Indiana UP, 1955–58.

• Tiffin, Jessica. *Marvelous Geometry: Genre and Metafiction in Modern Fairy Tale*. Detroit: Wayne State UP, 2009.

Tolkien, J. R. R. "On Fairy-Stories." In *The Tolkien Reader*. New York: Ballantine, 1966.

Travers, P. L. *About the Sleeping Beauty*. London: Collins, 1977.

———. "The Black Sheep." In *What the Bee Knows: Reflections on Myth, Symbol, and Story*. Wellingborough, UK: Aquarian, 1989.

Turner, Kay, and Pauline Greenhill, eds. *Transgressive Tales: Queering the Grimms*. Detroit: Wayne State UP, 2012.

• Uther, Hans-Jörg. *The Types of International Folktales: A Classification and Bibliography*. 3 vols. Helsinki: Academia Scientiarum Fennica, 2004.

Vaz da Silva, Francisco. *Metamorphosis: The Dynamics of Symbolism in European Fairy Tales*. New York: Lang, 2002.

Verdier, Yvonne. "Grands-mères, si vous saviez, . . . le Petit Chaperon Rouge dans la tradition orale." *Cahiers de Littérature Orale* 4 (1978): 17–55.

Waelti-Walters, Jennifer. *Fairy Tales and the Female Imagination*. Montreal: Eden, 1982.

• Waley, Arthur. "The Chinese Cinderella Story." *Folk-Lore* 58 (1947): 226–38.

Walker, Mary. "Wilde's Fairy Tales." *Unisa English Studies: Journal of the Department of English* 14 (1976): 30–41.

• Warner, Marina. *From the Beast to the Blonde: On Fairy Tales and Their Tellers*. New York: Farrar, Straus & Giroux, 1994.

———. *Once Upon a Time: A Short History of Fairy Tale*. Oxford: Oxford UP, 2014.

Weber, Eugen. "Fairies and Hard Facts: The Reality of Folktales." *Journal of the History of Ideas* 42 (1981): 93–113.

Weigle, Marta. *Spiders and Spinsters*. Albuquerque: U of New Mexico P, 1982.

Wilson, Sharon R. "Bluebeard's Forbidden Room: Gender Images in Margaret Atwood's Visual and Literary Art." *American Review of Canadian Studies* 16 (1986): 385–97.

———. *Margaret Atwood's Fairy-Tale Sexual Politics*. Jackson: UP of Mississippi, 1993.

Yolen, Jane. "America's Cinderella." *Children's Literature in Education* 8 (1977): 21–29.

———. *Touch Magic: Fantasy, Faerie and Folklore in the Literature of Childhood*. New York: Philomel, 1981.

Zipes, Jack. *Breaking the Magic Spell: Radical Theories of Folk and Fairy Tales*. Austin: U of Texas P, 1979.

———. *The Brothers Grimm: From Enchanted Forests to the Modern World*. New York: Routledge, Chapman & Hall, 1988.

———. *Fairy Tales and the Art of Subversion: The Classical Genre for Children and the Process of Civilization*. New York: Wildman, 1983.

• ———. *Happily Ever After: Fairy Tales, Children, and the Culture Industry*. New York: Routledge, 1997.

————. *The Irresistible Fairy Tale: The Cultural and Social History of a Genre.* Princeton, NJ: Princeton UP, 2012.

————, ed. *The Trials and Tribulations of Little Red Riding Hood.* 2nd ed. New York: Routledge, 1993.

————, Pauline Greenhill, and Kendra Magnus-Johnston, eds. *Fairy-Tale Films Beyond Disney: International Perspectives.* New York: Routledge, 2015.